ERIC
31

07/97

Copyright © Basil Blackwell Ltd 1994
Editorial organization © Bob Allen 1994

First published 1994

Blackwell Publishers
108 Cowley Road
Oxford OX4 1JF
UK

238 Main Street
Cambridge, Massachusetts 02142
USA

All rights reserved. Except for the quotation of short passages for the purposes of criticism and review, no part of this publication may be reproduced, stored in a retrieval system, or transmitted, in any form or by any means, electronic, mechanical, photocopying, recording or otherwise, without the prior permission of the publisher.

Except in the United States of America, this book is sold subject to the condition that it shall not, by way of trade or otherwise, be lent, resold, hired out, or otherwise circulated without the publisher's prior consent in any form of binding or cover other than that in which it is published and without a similar condition including this condition being imposed on the subsequent purchaser.

British Library Cataloguing in Publication Data
A CIP catalogue record for this book is available from the British Library.

Library of Congress Cataloging-in-Publication Data
The Blackwell guide to recorded country music/edited by Bob Allen.
    p. cm.—(Blackwell reference) (Blackwell guides)
    Includes bibliographical references (p.) and index.
    ISBN 0-631-19106-2
    1. Country music—Discography. 2. Country music—History and criticism. I. Allen, Bob. II. Title: Recorded country music. III. Series.
ML 156.4.C7B58 1994
016.781642 '0266–dc20   93–44462
                                                                          CIP
                                                                           MN

Typeset in Plantin and Univers on 11/12pt
by Acorn Bookwork, Salisbury, Wilts
Printed in Great Britain by T.J. Press Ltd, Padstow, Cornwall

The Blackwell Guide to
Recorded Country Music

edited by
Bob Allen

The Blackwell Guide to
Recorded Country Music

Contents

Contributors

BOB ALLEN is Editor-At-Large for *Country Music Magazine*. His articles on country music have appeared in *Esquire*, *Playboy*, *The Saturday Evening Post*, *The Washington Post*, *The Atlanta Journal*, and the Baltimore *Sun*. He is the author of the 1984 biography, *George Jones: Saga Of An American Singer*. He lives on a farm in rural Maryland with his two dogs, one cat, two pigs, and several dozen chickens.

TOM GILMORE has worked as a journalist with *The Tuam Herald* newspaper in Galway, Ireland for the past 17 years and is a regular contributor to the leading British country music magazine, *Country Music People*. He also works as a newsreader/reporter for Irish regional and national radio stations, and presents and produces the weekly "Country Roads" program on Galway Bay FM radio.

FRANK GODBEY is a bluegrass musician and an authority on the form. A record reviewer for *Bluegrass Unlimited* magazine since 1972, he has also provided liner notes for many recordings. He founded the electronic mail discussion group, "BGRASS-L," which operates over world-wide computer networks.

MARTY GODBEY, a professional writer since 1968, has published six books and hundreds of articles, many accompanied by her photographs. Her work has appeared in popular magazines and scholarly journals in the US and Europe, and on record and CD covers. She is a member of the executive board of the International Bluegrass Music Museum in Owensboro, Kentucky. With her husband, Frank, she is compiling a book of photographs of bluegrass musicians and events spanning more than 30 years.

GEOFFREY HIMES writes about country music on a regular basis for *The Washington Post* and *Country Music Magazine*. He has also written about music for *Downbeat, Request, Crawdaddy, Musician, Sing Out!*, the Baltimore *Sun,* and the Patuxent Newspapers. He lives in Baltimore with his wife Elizabeth Cusick.

PETE LOESCH is a Nashville-based attorney, record collector, and music journalist. His reviews and articles have appeared in such publications as *Music Row, The Journal Of Country Music,* and *Country Music Magazine.*

NICK TOSCHES has written for *The New Yorker, Rolling Stone,* and the *New York Times*. He is the author of *Hellfire,* the landmark biography of Jerry Lee Lewis; *Dino,* a critically acclaimed biography of Dean Martin; and the novel *Cut Numbers,* which won France's Prix Calibre 38 for the best first novel of 1990. He lives in New York City.

CHARLES WOLFE is a Professor of English at Middle Tennessee State University, and the author of some 14 books on music and folklore, including *Tennessee Strings, Kentucky Country,* and biographies of Grandpa Jones, Lefty Frizzell, Don Gibson, and (with Kip Lorvell) Leadbelly. He has annotated over 150 albums and sets, and has been nominated three times for Grammy Awards for his writing and production. A contributor to *American Grove,* he has also written numerous radio and TV scripts, and booklets for Time-Life Music, the Library of Congress, Franklin Mint, Bear Family, and others.

LAURENCE J. ZWISOHN has written numerous articles and liner notes on pop music, country music and western music as well as books on Bing Crosby and Loretta Lynn. He has produced and annotated reissue albums by artists including Fred Astaire, Al Jolson, Roy Rogers, Jim Reeves and the Sons of the Pioneers. The author of the detailed booklet accompanying the 4-CD Sons of the Pioneers boxed set issued by Bear Family Records, he has contributed essays on western films and western music to several books on this subject.

Discographical Abbreviations

Releases other than those from the United States have a notation as to the country of origin. They are as follows:

Den   Denmark

Fr   France

Ger   Germany

Jap   Japan

Neth The Netherlands

UK   United Kingdom

Introduction

As I write this, in the summer of 1993, country music is in the midst of an era of unprecedented sales and popularity. A handful of country artists, like Garth Brooks and Billy Ray Cyrus, are currently outselling even international pop and rock icons like U2, Madonna, and Michael Jackson. Million-selling albums, once unheard of in the country field, are today almost routine.

For country aficionados this turn of events affords particular satisfaction, since country music (much like the blues) has, at times, been treated as a sort of ugly, unwashed stepchild of popular American music. For decades country (again, much like the blues) occupied a relatively small and obscure niche, not only commercially but also in terms of critical acknowledgment (or the lack thereof). As a popular art form, it has consistently been under-appreciated and misunderstood.

Despite the rhetoric of politicians (like US President Richard Nixon, who, in March, 1974, in the final weeks of his term, with the Watergate scandal looming ever larger, made a last-ditch appeal to heartland America by appearing with Roy Acuff at opening ceremonies for the Grand Ole Opry's new head-quarters) and the hyperbole of record label publicists, modern country music is not a "folk" music or a music "of the people" in any pure sense of the word. Going back to the 1920s or further – back to the birth of the recording industry itself – it has been a *commercial* music. That is, music written, performed, and recorded with a specific audience in mind; music made with the conscious intention (if not always on the part of the artist, then certainly on the part of the producers and record executives) of selling records.

Thus the music, as it has evolved, has also both consciously and unconsciously reflected the changing tastes and attitudes of its audience. And, as the United States has gradually grown from a predominantly rural culture to a prevalently urban and suburban one, the music has often changed with it, and has often served as a mirror of all the sociological growing pains endured along the way.

Particularly throughout the 1960s and 1970s, the country music industry (as it exists in Nashville and, to a lesser extent, in southern California) put great emphasis on making "crossover" records – releases which were stylistically adapted to sell to the much vaster pop audience, which constitutes a potential gold mine in terms of increased record sales. For instance, Ray Price – who, ironically, was one of the true 1950s pioneers of the raucous honky-tonk style of country music – was also one of Nashville's most popular country-to-pop crossover crooners of the 1960s. Charlie Rich, Dolly Parton, and Kenny Rogers are just a few other shining examples of the many artists who have found and sustained popularity in both the country and the pop charts.

Yet for all the critical "heat" that crossover artists have sometimes taken for allegedly "diluting" or "adulterating" country music's essential grassroots rusticity, it's interesting to note that even some of country music's earliest stars were crossover artists of sorts. Even the immortal Jimmie Rodgers, generally considered to be the spiritual founding father of modern country music, angled for the crossover market of his day. As his career progressed, Rodgers abandoned the simple acoustic guitar accompaniments of his earliest recordings and instead turned to jazz, dance bands, and even Hawaiian music for accompaniment – all in order to appeal to a more demographically diverse, "uptown" audience. And – to pose further layers of irony and contradiction in the path of those who would attempt to neatly define or pigeonhole country music – the first million-selling country record, *The Prisoner's Song*, was recorded by a Texan named Vernon Dalhart. Dalhart's real name was Marion Try Slaughter, and he was, in actuality, a failed New York opera singer turned pop singer. On a similar note, it's often forgotten that many of the most memorable songs of the late, great Hank Williams, the avatar of modern country music, were introduced to a wider audience by pop idols of the fifties and sixties like Tony Bennett, Frankie Lane, Polly Bergen, and Jo Stafford. Simply put, the stylistic blurrings between country music and pop, its uptown cousin, have often been so subtle as to be indistinguishable.

Thus the difficulty for anybody who attempts to define, categorize, or stereotype country music is simply that such anomalies abound throughout its history. There are quite a few artists (Conway Twitty, Emmylou Harris etc.) who flirted with careers in rock-and-roll, pop and/or folk music before finding a niche in the country charts. There are others (Elvis Presley, the Everly Brothers, etc.) who began their careers as country artists and went on to become rock-and-roll idols. There are still other pop and rock artists (Ann Murray, John Denver, the early Eagles) whose music has often fit comfortably into the playlists of country radio stations. And all throughout the history of country music there have been artists – everyone from Jimmie Rodgers in the 1920s, to eighties and nineties innovators like Delbert McClinton, Lyle Lovett, and Wynonna Judd – who've borrowed freely from blues, pop and jazz to forge their own innovative country styles.

All of these factors, not to mention the sheer number of stylistically diverse artists presently at work in the country field, pose a tangle of confusion and misperception for the neophyte listener. *The Blackwell Guide to Recorded Country Music* has been compiled for the purpose of helping alleviate this confusion. In this guide we have broken country music down into a number of broad categories and subcategories (some of them stylistic, some of them chronological). In each category, we've listed and provided commentary on some of the best, most representative, and definitive recordings of that style or era.

For this project, a team of writers has been brought together, each of whom is widely acknowledged and extensively published in his or her respective field. Though this guide does not pose as a history or an encyclopedia of country music, it is our intention that it be useful to both new and experienced country music listeners in so far as illuminating and contextualizing country music within the broader scope of American popular music and the popular American culture (or in the instance of chapter nine, the Irish culture).

Much discussion and thought was given to the ten divisions represented by the chapters herein; a thorough attempt was made to elucidate both the chronological and stylistic evolution of the music. Some categorizations and subcategorizations (i.e. honky-tonk, rockabilly, western swing, and cowboy music) are easily defined. In more recent decades, however, as stylistic diversity and musical cross-pollenization has increased, it has proven more workable to cover the music chronologically. Always, we have attempted to show the historical sequence and the various internal and external (that is, musical and commercial) forces that played a role in shaping the music of each era.

By far, the most agonizing decision for many contributors – particularly those of us covering more recent eras – was what records to include and which to leave out. For instance, in the two chapters I myself wrote – "The 1970s" and "The 1980s and Beyond" – I could have easily listed fifty or more albums per chapter, and still would have had to leave out artists near and dear to my heart. Boiling each decade or stylistic category down to a mere 40 or fewer LPs (ten "Essential" recordings and, in most chapters, 30-odd "Basic" recordings) was, at least for some of us, a perplexing challenge.

Yet to have made the lists longer would have been to merely overwhelm the reader and, in many ways, defeat the inherent purpose of this guide. *The Blackwell Guide to Recorded Country Music* is, after all, based on the premise that a newcomer to the field, a record collector with a specialized interest seeking to broaden his or her musical knowledge, or a librarian wishing to stock a representative collection of country music, could reasonably be expected to invest in a maximum of a hundred or so records. The various contributors who wrote the ten chapters in this guide were therefore invited to select ten records which they considered *essential* to each particular category (chapter), making for a total of around 100 "Essential" recordings. Each contributor was further asked to supplement these with approximately 30 "Basic" recordings per chapter – that is, records which would provide a fuller coverage of each category, style, or era.

Contributors made every attempt to limit their "Essential" and "Basic" listings to records that are available to the reader. (If not current in either the CD or LP format, then they are, at very least, obtainable through reissue companies, specialty mail order distributors, collectors' conventions, and similar outlets.) Whenever possible (though sometimes it was not possible when writing about the earlier eras), contributors have shied away from albums that are merely extant: out of print and next to impossible to obtain (though such records, when of over-whelming importance, are occasionally mentioned in the text). With a few necessary exceptions, we've also avoided boxed sets (which have, in and of themselves, become a trend in recent years) merely on account of their cost.

Most of us who've contributed to this guide have at least some degree of mixed emotion toward the advent of the compact disc (CD) as the prevailing format for recorded music. Certainly the CD revolution has given new life to much old, exceedingly worthy and influential country music that had undeservedly lapsed out of print in the LP format. (Special credit in this department goes to superb reissue labels like Bear Family Records (Germany), Rhino Records and Rounder Records (USA), and the Country Music Foundation's splendid "Hall Of Fame" reissue series.)

Yet often, some degree of this music's original warmth and rusticity has been lost in transition to the more audially plu-perfect CD format. And – as is sometimes lamented in the text – there is still much classic early country music that is, inexplicably, not yet available on CD, or in some cases even in print at all.

Whenever albums listed in either the "Essential" or "Basic" categories are currently available in more than one format, we have listed the CD catalog number, simply because – like it or not – the CD is today's prevailing format. But we have not shied away from listing music available only on LP when we felt these particular releases were essential or basic to understanding a particular style or era of the music. In some instances contributors have selected "Best Of" or "Greatest Hits" compilations on certain artists; for others we have chosen a particular studio album, whether it be in or out of print. Though certainly – particularly in the later chapters – the question of availability was often a consideration, there are some artists who are best represented by "hits" compilations, while others are best defined or showcased by particular studio albums which are either thematic in nature or which vividly highlight that particular singer's most important stylistic and aesthetic achievements.

Although there was considerable discussion among some of the contributors, it was ultimately each individual contributor's own decision as to which recordings to include in his or her respective chapter(s). These choices were based on contributors' extensive knowledge and familiarity of the music. Each selection had to be not only stylistically vivid and original on its own; it also had to be, in some manner, representative. In a few cases, the same singer appears in more than one chapter. Sometimes this is so various stages of his or her career can be illustrated; sometimes it is due to a particular artist's overwhelming importance or creative longevity.

The basic format of *The Blackwell Guide to Recorded Country Music* is this: extended essay/critiques have been written on each of the "Essential" albums listed each chapter, and much shorter essays have been composed on the "Basic" recordings in each category. These discursive commentaries not only address the importance, representativeness, and aesthetic strengths (or weaknesses) of each album; they also contextualize the music. Often, the albums have been grouped by subthemes, and cross-references have been made between essays where appropriate.

While essential information as to each listed album – its label, catalog number, country of origin, and the name of the artists under which titles have been issued – is entered, full discographical details – recording dates, full lists of personnel, matrix and take numbers and original issue numbers – have had to be omitted. Much of this information is available in published discographies, some of which are listed with other recommended books and references in Recommended Reading, on p. 363.

As editor of this guide, I would like to especially thank the various contributors who worked long, hard, and far above and beyond the call of duty on this project, and brought great enthusiasm and considerable thought to it. My gratitude also goes out to those others – Colin Escott, Rich Kienzle, and Richard Weize in particular – whom I leaned on for advice and consultation. I hope that you, the readers, obtain as much enjoyment, satisfaction, and meaning from listening to this music as it has given us, the contributors, over the years.

BOB ALLEN

The Early Years   1

Charles Wolfe

The deep roots of country music extend far back into the nineteenth century, and long before the commercial record industry even existed. Traditional histories of country music have always stressed its folk music heritage, emphasizing especially the old British ballads that were brought over by the Scots–Irish settlers who migrated to the southern Appalachians in the late eighteenth and nineteenth centuries. Some of these ballads, such as *Barbara Allen*, certainly the most famous, had pedigrees that reached as far back as the seventeenth century. Others were being hawked on freshly printed broadside sheets the day before the emigrants boarded their ship for the New World. Some were topical songs about the latest scandal or murder; others were classic stories about love, death, and betrayal. When folksong collectors began seeking out these old songs in the mountains of Virginia and North Carolina years later the singers often referred to them as "love songs," and told collectors they had kept them alive, in part, because they were "true." Not surprisingly, such qualities are still associated with modern country music today.

Some of the old songs made it across the sea and into the hills relatively intact; others were shortened or changed to fit the new country's geography or values. A murder ballad called *The Wexford Girl* became *The Knoxville Girl*; a lengthy 35-stanza love ballad called *The Lass Of Loch Royal* survived only as a three-stanza lyric called *Who's Going To Shoe Your Pretty Little Feet*. Ghosts, quite common in the original ballads, became less popular in versions sung by hard-headed and practical Americans. Soon the settlers were creating their own ballads based on the models of the originals, and through the 1800s a native American balladry was born – a body of song that would eventually have much more impact on country music than the older British songs.

Many of the ballads were sung in the home while people did everyday chores such as carding wool or churning butter. They were almost always sung unaccompanied, and dozens of regional ballad singing styles developed. Singers in Madison County, North Carolina used a loud, boisterous, full-throat manner; eastern Kentuckians preferred a high lonesome sound that later became associated with bluegrass; singers in Arkansas liked a loose, easy-going, relaxed style that resembled the later mannerisms of Johnny Cash or Don Williams. Early fiddling contests sometimes included a competition in ballad singing; one in 1764 promised singers enough free grog to clear the windpipes. By the time of the Civil War, some singers were good enough to make money with their art; and by the end of the 1800s itinerant minstrels were wandering about the South singing on street corners and at railway stations. In some cases, these singers had printed up on small sheets of paper or postcard size cards the texts to their favorite popular songs; these "ballet cards," as they were called, were purchased by fans and taken home to be learned, much in the manner that records would later be.

The family singing tradition and the street-corner minstrels were by no means, however, the sole source for what would become country music. We now know that there were a number of professional traditions that helped create the music as well. A surprising number of songs published in nineteenth-century sheet music form made it into the repertoires of mountain singers: songs like *In The Baggage Coach Ahead*, *Wildwood Flower*, *The Little Old Log Cabin In The Lane*, *Casey Jones*, and *The Wabash Cannonball* began life as stage songs issued in ornate sheet music editions. Minstrel shows began in the 1840s and had an incredible impact on rural or mountain music.

In spite of their blackface routines and racial stereotypes, these travelling shows spread banjo and fiddle tunes, as well as comedy songs and sentimental tear-jerkers, throughout the South. Later, the vaudeville stage and its rural counterpart, the medicine show, took another generation of songs around the country and brought new performing styles to new generations. In recent years, historians have been able to trace what were once considered purely folk traditions back to nineteenth-century commercial music, and songs once thought to be "as old as the hills" have been revealed to be pop hits that sold thousands of copies, had specific composers and publishers, and were filed in the Copyright Office.

The instrumental history of the music is equally complex but harder to trace, since it left a less detailed paper trail. Fiddling was known down the entire coast of the new continent, from

Nova Scotia to Florida, and people as different as Thomas Jefferson and Davy Crockett were known as fiddlers; Jefferson even jotted down fiddle tunes in his music manuscripts. Many fiddlers at country dances, north and south, flatlands and mountains, played unaccompanied, or with an assistant to "beat the straws" as rhythm. The fiddle was the most common of all the instruments that would become associated with country music, and it is no coincidence that many of the pioneer recording artists, such as Eck Robertson and Fiddlin' John Carson, were fiddle players. For modern country fans, accustomed to hearing the fiddle accompanied by a full band or at least a guitar, the idea of one solitary fiddler playing for a dance is hard to grasp; yet the old solo fiddlers had learned how to generate their own internal rhythm, how to sing out couplets during a dance, and how to keep going on sets that lasted fifteen to twenty minutes.

The second key instrument was the banjo, which became popular in the 1840s and became a fixture on the minstrel stage a few years later. Few doubt today that the banjo was an African instrument, brought over by slaves; its ultimate origins may lie in the medieval kingdoms of sub-Sahara Africa. Though presently associated almost exclusively with bluegrass and old-time music, throughout most of the nineteenth century it was widely played by black musicians; Thomas Jefferson left one of the first references to this when he described hearing his slaves play the "banjar." Through slaves and through minstrel performers – many of whom were white men who adapted black styles – many whites in the mountains and remote South took up the banjo. The instrument was easy to make (groundhog skin made a decent head), was portable, and could be tuned up in a wonderful variety of ways.

The third instrument that formed the foundation for country music was, of course, the guitar. Modern stereotypes of folk and early country music assume the guitar was always present as the music developed; it was not. Many veteran country stars who were born before the turn of the century could remember the first guitar they ever saw or played – usually in the days just after World War I. Before then, the guitar was rare, especially in the mountains; for much of the 1800s it was considered a parlor instrument, to be played by well-bred young ladies whose delicate fingers were suited to the soft gut strings. The coming of steel strings in the early days of the century caused both white and black folk musicians to look seriously at the guitar; the new strings meant new volume, and new uses for the guitar, at dances and to accompany singing. Better quality instruments began to appear (though Sears and other mail-order stores were offering cheap guitars in their catalogues by the turn of the century) and the guitar took its place with the banjo and fiddle at dances, and as accompaniment for singers. By the time the record companies began to take early country singers into the studios in the mid-1920s, the guitar was fast becoming their instrument of choice.

Essential Recordings

(i) The Folk Roots

The big commercial record companies had discovered both jazz and blues before they realized that country music was equally salable. During the first two decades of the flat 78 rpm record industry (1900–20), most of the companies assumed their market was upper-class or upper middle-class whites who lived in the North or Mid West. Victrolas were everywhere by 1920, but they were playing the likes of Caruso, Sousa's Band, or the opera of Rosa Ponselle. It took an economic downturn in the early 1920s, coupled with the threat radio posed to the home music market, to make the companies realize they had to look elsewhere for their markets. (One company, Victor, saw its sales drop by over half in a little over a year.) Jazz and blues were two of these new markets, and by 1923 country music had emerged as a third.

The first country records were recorded almost by accident. On June 30, 1922, a pair of Texas fiddlers showed up at Victor's New York office and asked to be recorded; they had been appearing in Virginia at a Confederate veterans reunion, and had garnered a lot of publicity in the Virginia papers. Their names were Eck Robertson (the younger one) and Henry Gilliland (the older one), and to placate them the Victor engineer recorded four duets, asked Robertson to return the next day for some solos, and promptly shelved the masters. Their version of *Turkey In The Straw* was finally released the following April. Then, in the summer of 1923, OKeh Records recorded an Atlanta musician who billed himself as Fiddlin' John Carson; this was done as a favor to a local furniture store dealer who agreed to buy out the entire pressing. The company didn't even put a release number of Carson's version of an old 1870 pop song, *The Little Old Log Cabin In The Lane*. (In fact, when the OKeh producer heard Carson's voice on the disc – unlike the Texas fiddlers, Carson liked to sing with his playing, making him the first country singer – he described the singing as "pluperfect awful." To everyone's surprise, both the Carson and the Robertson–Gilliland discs sold handsomely, and within months the race was on to seek out and record more of what they then called "hill country" musicians.

Though many of the companies soon found they could garner this kind of music best by taking recording crews into the South and recording on location, they in fact captured relatively little of the older forms of the music. They recorded very few unaccompanied ballad singers, only a handful of solo fiddlers, and scant examples of the older pre-media string bands. It was not until folklorists like Robert W. Gordon and John A. Lomax began travelling the South in the 1920s and 1930s that surviving examples of this early music were captured on disc. These old, fragile acetate discs were housed in the Library of Congress's Archive of American Folk Song, and in the 1940s and 1950s a small number of them were issued on albums to the public. Though these albums represent the best examples we have of the older singing styles, virtually none of them have made it into the CD age.

In the absence of authentic field recordings of the kind of folk music that formed country's foundation, a good introduction to the sound of this music is Mike Seeger's 1991 album **Solo – Old-Time Country Music**. The son of distinguished folksong collectors, the brother of singer Pete Seeger, Mike has devoted much of his life to studying, collecting, and preserving traditional Southern music. His many albums over the last three decades – including those done with the New Lost City Ramblers, one of the best string bands to emerge from the "folk revival" in the 1960s – have been filled with his superb re-creations of traditional performances, including some learned from Library of Congress discs. This album features him playing and singing with the dulcimer (*Ground Hog*), with the quills (*Tennessee Dog*), with the jaw harp (*Sallie Gooden*, a re-creation of Eck Robertson's very first fiddle record), and the autoharp (*Tucker's Barn*). There is also an example or two of unaccompanied singing (*Poor Indian, Rockbridge Holler*), and of an old banjo tune played on a 5-string gourd "banjer" (*Roustabout*). The latter is especially interesting in that it seeks to re-create a fascinating archaic style of singing and playing that reveals the interplay between black and white banjo music. Unlike many contemporary performers, Mike Seeger respects the integrity of his sources to the point where he doesn't over-interpret the material; much of his music sounds uncannily like the originals.

African American influences on country music extend far beyond the obvious blues and spirituals. It now seems likely that, during the latter half of the nineteenth century, blacks and whites shared a common repertoire of fiddle and banjo tunes. Except in the Mississippi delta, for much of this time most black musicians preferred the fiddle and banjo to the guitar, and dozens of country veterans recall listening to black banjo players and fiddlers when they were growing up. Black string bands were the entertainment of countless rural Southern dances, from before the Civil War to the late 1930s. As the blues became popular, especially with younger black musicians, the older fiddle and banjo music drifted into obscurity and eventual extinction. Record companies seldom recorded black string bands because the records were in the 1920s issued in segregated series called "race" and "hillbilly." If an A & R man saw a group of black musicians come in for an audition, he assumed they were a blues band, and turned them down if they broke into *Grey Eagle*.

Fortunately, Library of Congress researchers had no such hang-ups, and they managed to preserve the sound of a handful of these African–American string bands. Two of them are represented in **Altamont: Black String Band Music From The Library Of Congress**. One of them was the John Lusk Band, from the Sequatchie Valley area in south-central Tennessee, the same region that produced such white fiddlers as Curly Fox, Jess Young, and Bob Douglas. Comprising a fiddle (Lusk), banjo (Murphy Gribble), and guitar (York), the band had been playing square dances – for whites and blacks – in the area since before World War I. Gribble's odd banjo style, which anticipated the later bluegrass picking of Earl Scruggs, gave the band much of its character, along with Lusk's odd dynamics on the fiddle. Captured on 12-inch discs that gave the band up to four minutes of playing time, the band charged through classic dance tunes like *Across The Sea*, *Apple Blossom*, and *Rolling River*, as well as *Altamont*, in which each member plays his individual part for the microphone. These recordings date from the 1946–9 era.

The other band is a fiddle–banjo duo comprising two Nashville street musicians, Frank Patterson and Nathan Frazier. Well past middle age when they were recorded in 1942, they were already seen as archaic by then; but their style is one of our deepest looks yet at the roots of string band music. Frazier makes high, daring, swooping runs on the banjo, and Patterson plays a style of fiddle that shows little of the smooth, "long bow" influences of modern fiddling. The researcher who discovered the pair, John Work of Fisk University in Nashville, sensed their importance and got them to a handful of folk festivals before they disappeared into obscurity. All they left us is a few recordings of *Corrine* (made more popular by western swing bands), *Old Cow Died*, *Po' Black Sheep*, and others. Detailed liner notes give what background is available on the bands.

Another key chapter on the instrumental roots is found in the remarkable collection **Tommy And Fred: Best Fiddle–**

Banjo Duets. This is the Anglo-American tradition, as it survived in the mountains of Surry County, North Carolina, and as played by two of its finest guardians, Tommy Jarrell and Fred Cockerham. Here the old-time fiddle–banjo string band style remained intact long after the guitar and string bass had smoothed it out in other areas, and in this quadrant of North Carolina and southwest Virginia, old-time music developed an intense style of its own. Both Fred and Tommy played for old-time bands in the area, and Tommy's father Ben recorded with one of the best area bands, Da Costa Woltz and his Southern Broadcasters. Both were near retirement when they recorded these cuts in the 1960s for the independent County label, but the original LPs influenced hundreds of younger musicians interested in a style that predated the turn of the century. Among the masterpieces are their version of *Yellow Rose Of Texas*, *Fortune*, and *Sally Ann*, and for many fans their recordings of these and similar tunes have become synonymous with pure old-time music. Both Fred and Tommy have died since their original LPs came out, but this CD remains a tribute to their rich heritage.

Though the record companies had been recording on location in the South since 1923, when they captured Fiddlin' John Carson on disc in Atlanta, the invention of the carbon microphone and "electrical recording process" made such location recording far more feasible. By 1927 most of the major companies were making regular trips into the South, setting up temporary studios in cities and towns from San Antonio to Richmond. These field sessions were like seining nets, capturing all sorts of grassroots music, and all sorts of musicians, from nascent professionals to embarrassed amateurs, who recorded two sides and disappeared, never to be heard from again. By now the companies had all started special numerical series for the music, calling it things like "Native American Melodies," "Old-Time Tunes," "Songs From Dixie," "Hill Country Tunes," and "Old Familiar Tunes And Novelties." During the late 1920s, the seven major companies were together releasing around fifty 78s a month, a vast body of music that reflected an amazing variety of singing styles, songs, instrumental techniques, and personalities.

In July 1927 Ralph Peer, who had actually supervised John Carson's first record back in 1923, arrived with his team of two engineers in the town of Bristol, on the Virginia–Tennessee border. Working day and night, they managed to record some 76 masters in a period of only two weeks; they attracted mountain musicians from as far away as Bluefield, West Virginia, and inadvertently documented an almost perfect cross-section of early country music – fiddle tunes, blues, gospel songs, ballads, novelty songs, folk songs, even rural play-party songs. Some of the musicians were already semi-professional, and had even recorded before: Ernest Stoneman (who would sire a generation of country stars, and would himself live to have his own syndicated TV show out of Nashville), Henry Whitter, and the Johnson Brothers. But most, lured by the newspaper accounts of the "talent hunt" going on, were basically folk musicians who were wanting to make a little money and make a record.

This session, the only one of its kind to be documented as a session, is chronicled in a 2-CD set done by the Country Music Foundation, **The Bristol Sessions**. Each one of the individual artists recorded in Bristol is represented by at least one title. They include the powerful gospel singer Alfred Karnes, who sang with a harp-guitar such items as *When They Ring Those Golden Bells*; the boisterous Holiness singers from southern Kentucky led by Ernest Phipps; and the stately Alcoa Quartet, product of the singing schools of eastern Tennessee. There were Virginia string bands, such as the Bull Mountain Moonshiners (led by Charles M. McReynolds, the grandfather of bluegrass stars Jim and Jesse) and the Shelor Family, and Tennessee bands such as the blues-heavy Tenneva Ramblers, who preserved *The Longest Train*. From West Virginia came Blind Alfred Reed, who offered a topical song about a train wreck, *The Wreck Of The Virginian*; from near Bristol came Mr and Mrs J.W. Baker, who contributed another train-wreck song, *The Newmarket Wreck*. The most dramatic contributions, though, came from two new acts that would use the Bristol sessions as a launching pad: the Carter Family, from nearby Maces Springs, and Jimmie Rodgers, who came over the mountains from Asheville. Peer heard them both within two days, and signed them both to songwriting and management contracts. The result of all this – the first session to really demonstrate the full possibilities of the new music form – was what Johnny Cash called "the single most important event in the history of country music." The 107 minutes and 35 cuts heard here give a rich picture of just where the music was on the threshold of its breakout.

Discographical Details

1   Solo – Old-Time Country Music

Mike Seeger
Rounder CD 0278

Tennessee Dog/Ground Hog/Roustabout/Sallie Gooden/The Wreck Of The Tennessee Gravy Train/Shaking The Pines In The Holler/Dog And Gun/Candy Girl/Tucker's Barn/Wind And Rain/Fare You Well, Green Fields/Poor Indian/

We're Stole And Sold From Africa/Rockbridge Holler/Quill Ditty/Rolling And
Tumbling Blue/Blue Tail Fly/Prairie Ronde Waltz

2 Altamont: Black String Band Music From The Library Of Congress

The John Lusk Band; Frazier and Patterson
Rounder CD 0238
Nathan Frazier and Frank Patterson: *Dan Tucker/Old Cow Died/Bile Them*
Cabbage Down/Po' Black Sheep/Eighth Of January/Corrine/Texas Traveller;
The John Lusk Band: *Rolling River/Old Sage Friend/Apple Blossom/Pater-*
oller'll Catch You/Across the Sea/Cincinnati/Altamont

3 Tommy And Fred: Best Fiddle–Banjo Duets

Tommy Jarrell and Fred Cockerham
County CD-2702
John Brown's Dream/Frankie Baker/When Sorrows Encompass Me 'Round/
Sugar Hill/Little Maggie/Sally Ann/Cluck, Old Hen/Bravest Cowboy/John
Hardy/Cumberland Gap/Old Bunch Of Keys/Yellow Rose Of Texas/Big-Eyed
Rabbit/Soldier's Joy/June Apple/Susanna Gal/Wreck Of The Old '97/Breaking
Up Christmas/Fortune/Fall On My Knees/Stay All Night

4 The Bristol Sessions

Various Artists
Country Music Foundation CMF-011-D (2-disc set)
Uncle Eck Dunford: *Skip To Ma Lou, My Darling*; B.F. Shelton: *O Molly*
Dear; Blind Alfred Reed: *Walking In The Way With Jesus*; Mr and Mrs J.W.
Baker: *The Newmarket Wreck*; Jimmie Rodgers: *Sleep, Baby, Sleep/The*
Soldier's Sweetheart; West Virginia Coonhunters: *Greasy String*; Ernest V.
Stoneman and his Dixie Mountaineers: *Are You Washed In The Blood/The*
Resurrection; Henry Whitter: *Henry Whitter's Fox Chase*; The Carter Family:
Bury Me Under The Weeping Willow/Little Log Cabin By The Sea/The Wan-
dering Boy/Single Girl, Married Girl/The Storms Are On The Ocean/The Poor
Orphan Child; Johnson Brothers: *The Jealous Sweetheart/A Passing Policeman*;
Alfred G. Karnes: *When They Ring Those Golden Bells/I Am Bound For The*
Promised Land/To The Work; Dad Blanchard's Moonshiners: *Sandy River*
Belle; Bull Mountain Moonshiners: *Johnny Goodwin*; Alcoa Quartet: *I'm*
Redeemed; Blue Ridge Corn Shuckers [Stoneman]: *Old-Time Corn Shuckin',*
Pts 1 and 2; Ernest Phipps and his Holiness Quartet: *I Want to Go Where*
Jesus Is; E. Stoneman, Irma Frost, and Eck Dunford: *Midnight On The*
Stormy Deep; J.P. Nestor: *Black-Eyed Susie*; E. Stoneman, Kahle Brewer,
and M. Mooney: *Tell Mother I Will Meet Her*; El Watson: *Pot Licker Blues*;
Tenneva Ramblers: *The Longest Train I Ever Saw*; Blind Alfred Reed: *The*
Wreck Of The Virginian; Shelor Family: *Billy Grimes The Rover*; Tennessee
Mountaineers: *Standing On The Promises*; E. Stoneman, Irma Frost and Eck
Dunford: *The Mountaineer's Courtship*

(ii) The First Stars

Artists like Fiddlin' John Carson, singer–harmonica player
Henry Whitter, the musical family of Cowan "Fiddlin' "

Powers, the Texas-born former light opera singer Vernon Dalhart, the Georgia banjoist Land Norris, the mountain team of Eva Davis and Samantha Bumgarner, the Roy Acuff favorite fiddler Uncle Am Stuart, and the former wandering minstrel Charley Oaks all attained popularity on records within a couple of years of John Carson's 1923 debut. Burdened with tinny acoustic recording methods and stereotyped ideas of their music, few of these early pioneers left records that have serious appeal to modern fans, and with the exception of Carson, none of them have been reissued on CD. Two other figures from this era, though, have been represented on reissue: Uncle Dave Macon and Charlie Poole.

Though Macon and Poole both had close ties to traditional music, both also had had experience with vaudeville, and had traveled widely before they began their recording careers. Macon was the older of the two, having been born in 1870 and not starting to sing full-time until he was over 50. He was a masterful banjoist, using over 20 different picking styles, ranging from clawhammer to "rapping" with complex uppicking strokes. Many of his songs were adapted from the pop hits of the vaudeville stage; others were variants of the folk tradition of the southern Tennessee mountains, where he had been born. By early 1924 Macon was recording for the Vocalion label, and appearing on the Loew's vaudeville chain as a "banjoist and comedian." He shared the stage with fiddler Uncle Jimmy Thompson for the first formal broadcast of the Grand Ole Opry in 1925, and for the first ten years was the show's biggest star. **Uncle Dave Macon: Country Music Hall Of Fame** is a set based on a 1970 LP from Decca; it features Macon in a variety of settings that date from 1926 to 1934, and that include backup by the likes of guitarist Sam McGee, fiddler Sid Harkreader, and a small string band Uncle Dave called the Fruit Jar Drinkers. Several of Macon's best known songs are here: *Late Last Night When Willie Came Home, I'm The Child To Fight*, and *When The Train Comes Along* – all often sung on the Grand Ole Opry. Macon often partook in the early country tradition of topical songs, as *Governor Al Smith* (a 1928 campaign song) and *Farm Relief* suggests his famous *From Earth To Heaven* tells the singer's own biography, and about the freight business he ran before he chucked it all to go into music. Macon continued to perform on the Opry until a few weeks before his death in 1952, and made dozens of other records, but these sides capture him at the peak of his abilities and popularity.

Charlie Poole was 22 years younger than Uncle Dave Macon, and came to fame in 1925 on the strength of the success of his Columbia records of *Can I Sleep In Your Barn Tonight, Mister*

and *Don't Let Your Deal Go Down Blues*. The latter, as well as
15 other vintage Poole favorites from 1925 to 1930, is found on
Old-Time Songs. Poole was a quick-spoken, snappy, almost
jazzy singer who came out of the rough-and-tumble cotton mill
towns in the Piedmont region of north-central North Carolina.
He was not really a rustic mountaineer, but a hard-living and
hard-drinking mill worker who took seriously the words to his
song *Coon From Tennessee*: "I'm gonna live in the highways 'til
I die." He traveled widely, picking up some of the "classic"
banjo styles that were then in vogue on the vaudeville stage by
people like Fred Van Eps. He was one of the first country
musicians to decide he could make a full-time living with his
music, and part of his legend tells of his quitting his mill job to
go north to make records. His band, the North Carolina
Ramblers, generally featured ace guitarist and singer Roy
Harvey, as well as fiddler Posey Rorrer. Compared to the wild,
driving, North Georgia bands like the Skillet Lickers, the
Ramblers had a restrained, almost polite sound. Its precision,
though, anticipated bluegrass, and made a perfect setting for
Poole's vocals. This first CD of Poole's music includes several
classics that would reverberate down through corridors of
country music. They include *White House Blues*, *Sweet Sunny
South*, *Leaving Home*, and *Take A Drink On Me*, and others
that represent the best of Poole's work. Poole himself seemed
on the verge of even greater popularity – he had even been
contacted by Hollywood – when he died suddenly after a
drinking bout in 1931.

A singer whose record sales dwarfed even Macon's and
Poole's, though, was Jimmie Rodgers. A Poole or Macon hit
would sometimes approach 100,000 copies, but some of the
Rodgers records would get to the 500,000 mark – this in an age
when hardly any country records actually sold a million. **First
Sessions** collects the first 14 of Rodgers's Victor recordings,
covering the first six months of his career. Though Rodgers's
first recording – *The Soldier's Sweetheart* and *Sleep, Baby,
Sleep* – was not exactly a smash hit, his next few included
masterworks like the first *Blue Yodel*, its original flip *Away
Out On The Mountain*, and *In The Jailhouse Now*. Even the
lesser sides from these sessions, such as the sentimental *Mother
Was A Lady*, reflect the warm, lazy style that would charm
generations of listeners. Many of these early pieces feature
Rodgers with only his guitar as accompaniment, revealing his
raw talent and uncanny control of his falsetto and yodel. Listening to all these sides brought together gives us a chance to
see Rodgers developing his art, and forging the type of singing
that would become the most influential solo style in country
music.

Success of a different sort followed the Carter Family, whose career also started in Bristol, one day before Rodgers's. Rodgers would die of tuberculosis seven years later; the Carters would found a country music dynasty, and see their children and even grandchildren continue their music. (Some fans today reflect this by referring to this group as the Original Carter Family to distinguish them from later incarnations.) Rodgers's success was more dramatic; the Carters' was more sustained. While Rodgers was making a film in Hollywood, the Carters were nailing up their own showbills to trees and fences in the rural South. Rodgers's music startled and surprised; the Carters' soothed and reassured and was as comfortable as an old shoe. Its effect was prolonged and subtle; Carter records from 1927 sound like Carter records from 1941, and neither seems dated even today. Throughout the LP era, Carter Family reissues stayed in print, and found new audiences who thought of them not as historical documents, but simply as good music.

Anchored In Love: The Carter Family Sessions, Vol. 1 helps define this mystique; like the Rodgers set, it presents the first sixteen recordings the group did for Victor. At this time, the Family consisted of A.P. Carter, his wife Sara, and his teenaged sister-in-law Maybelle. Sara's voice – the thing Ralph Peer liked about the group to begin with – stands out on most of these early sides; it is a quintessential mountain voice, pitched impossibly high, cutting through the primitive technology like a laser. It rings on *Single Girl, Married Girl, The Wandering Boy, John Hardy,* and the mythic *Wildwood Flower.* On most of the other sides, the Carter sound is a duet between Sara and A.P., with Maybelle's guitar creating the "Carter lick" that would become common throughout country music. Here too are Carter classics like *Keep On The Sunny Side* (later to be their theme song), *Little Darling, Pal Of Mine,* and the haunting *Will You Miss Me When I'm Gone.* Here is the genesis of country harmony, country guitar accompaniment, and more than a few country standards.

After the explosion of innovation and genius in the late 1920s, the 1930s seemed a period of consolidation. The influence of Jimmie Rodgers seemed to dominate the young solo singers, and even the Carter Family seemed content often to rest on its laurels and redo old favorites. **White Country Blues 1926–1938: A Lighter Shade Of Blue** is a huge collection of Columbia, OKeh, and American Record Company sides that chronicles this period. The theme of the set is the extent to which country singers absorbed or created blues – which was a considerable extent. As early as 1926 the West Virginia guitarist and singer Frank Hutchison used his knife to create a slide guitar style on popular pieces like *Cannon Ball Blues*. Tom Darby and Jimmie Tarlton, best known for their *Columbus Stockade Blues*, learned directly from black musicians in north Georgia and South Carolina, and proved their mettle with items like *Sweet Sarah Blues*. Many of the young singers from the 1930s, such as Cliff Carlisle and his brother Bill, took the Rodgers formula a step further, creating rowdy songs like *Ash Can Blues* and *Tom Cat Blues*. The Callahan Brothers, popular then on the radio, did covers of black "hokum" songs like *Somebody's Been Using That Thing*. Bill Cox, a prolific record maker from West Virginia, is heard on *Georgia Brown Blues* and *Long Chain Charlie Blues*. A rare topical blues heard here is Clayton McMichen's *Prohibition Blues*, written for Jimmie Rodgers, and even recorded by Rodgers, but never issued. A thick booklet of notes offers background on all the performers here, and testifies to the impressive strides made by this second generation of country stars.

Discographical Details

5 Uncle Dave Macon: Country Music Hall Of Fame

Uncle Dave Macon

MCA MCAD–10546

From Earth To Heaven/Farm Relief/Tom And Jerry/I'm The Child To Fight/ Go Along Mule/Governor Al Smith/Late Last Night When Willie Came Home/ Tell Her To Come Back Home/Tennessee Jubilee/The Cross-Eyed Butcher And The Cacklin' Hen/Sleepy Lou/Sourwood Mountain Medley/Uncle Dave's Travels – Pt I (Misery In Arkansas)/I'm A-Goin' Away In The Morn/Shall We Gather At The River/When The Train Comes Along

6 Old-Time Songs

Charlie Poole and the North Carolina Ramblers

County CO-CD-3501

White House Blues/Sweet Sunny South/Shootin' Creek/ He Rambled/The Letter That Never Came/Mountain Reel/You Ain't Talkin' To Me/Sweet Sixteen/ Leaving Home/Took My Gal A-Walkin'/Monkey On A String/Ramblin' Blues/ Flying Clouds/Falling By The Wayside/Don't Let Your Deal Go Down Blues/ Take A Drink On Me

7 First Sessions

Jimmie Rodgers

Rounder CD 1056

Blue Yodel/The Soldier's Sweetheart/Ben Dewberry's Final Run/Sleep, Baby, Sleep/Mother Was A Lady/Dear Old Sunny South By The Sea/Away Out On The Mountain/Treasures Untold/Blue Yodel No. 2/The Sailor's Plea/In The Jailhouse Now/Memphis Yodel/The Brakeman's Blues/Blue Yodel No. 3

8   Anchored In Love: The Carter Family, Vol. 1, 1927–1928

The Carter Family

Rounder CD 1064

Bury Me Under The Weeping Willow/Little Log Cabin By The Sea/The Poor Orphan Child/The Storms Are On The Ocean/Single Girl, Married Girl/The Wandering Boy/Meet Me By The Moonlight Alone/Little Darling Pal Of Mine/ Keep On The Sunny Side/Anchored In Love/John Hardy Was A Desperate Little Man/I Ain't Gonna Work Tomorrow/Will You Miss Me When I'm Gone/ River Of Jordan/Chewing Gum/Wildwood Flower

9   White Country Blues. 1926–1938: A Lighter Shade Of Blue

Various Artists

Columbia/Legacy C2K 47466 (2-disc set)

Frank Hutchison: *K.C. Blues/Cannon Ball Blues*; Charlie Poole with the North Carolina Ramblers: *Leaving Home/If The River Was Whiskey*; Cauley Family: *Duplin County Blues*; Tom Darby and Jimmie Tarlton: *Sweet Sarah Blues/Frankie Dean*; Riley Puckett: *A Darkey's Wail*; Clarence Greene: *Johnson City Blues*; The Carolina Buddies: *Mistreated Blues*; Tom Ashley: *Haunted Road Blues*; Roy Acuff and his Crazy Tennesseans: *Steel Guitar Blues*; Cliff Carlisle and Wilbur Ball: *Guitar Blues/I Want A Good Woman*; Cliff Carlisle: *Ash Can Blues*; Val and Pete: *Yodel Blues, Pt I and II*; Mr and Mrs Chris Bouchillon: *Adam And Eve, Part II*; W.T. Narmour and S.W. Smith: *Carroll County Blues*; Charlie Poole with the North Carolina Ramblers: *Ramblin' Blues*; Frank Hutchison: *Worried Blues/The Train That Carried The Girl From Town*; Roy Harvey and Leonard Copeland: *Lonesome Weary Blues*; W. Lee O'Daniel and his Hillbilly Boys: *Bear Cat Mama/Dirty Hangover Blues/Tuck Away My Lonesome Blues*; Blue Ridge Ramblers: *Jug Rag*; Prairie Ramblers: *Deep Elm Blues*; Clayton McMichen: *Prohibition Blues*; Larry Hensley: *Match Box Blues*; Callahan Brothers: *Somebody's Been Using That Thing*; Homer Callahan: *Rattle Snake Daddy/My Good Gal Has Thrown Me Down*; Asa Martin and his Kentucky Hillbillies: *Lonesome, Broke, and Weary*; Cliff Carlisle: *Tom Cat Blues/Chicken Roost Blues*; Bill Cox and Cliff Hobbs: *Oozlin' Daddy Blues/Kansas City Blues*; Ramblin' Red Lowery: *Ramblin' Red's Memphis Yodel No. 1*; Anglin Brothers: *Southern Whoopee Songs*; Allen Brothers: *Drunk And Nutty Blues/Chattanooga Mama*; Bill Carlisle: *String Bean Mama/Copper Head Mama*; Bill Cox: *Long Chain Charlie Blues/Georgia Brown Blues*; Al Dexter: *New Jelly Roll Blues*; the Rhythm Wreckers: *Never No Mo' Blues*

(iii) Rural Radio

Almost from the start of commercial radio, country music found itself welcome on Southern and Mid-Western stations. As early as 1922, stations in Atlanta and Dallas were inviting old-time musicians to play, and starting up "barn dance" programs to showcase their talents. By 1924 the National Barn Dance had begun in Chicago, and a year later what would become the Grand Ole Opry had started in Nashville. Musicians were paid very little on these early shows, but as radio became a successful advertising medium, this began to change.

Though the NBC network had begun in 1927, most stations in the South continued to do the majority of their programming live – especially during the day and in early morning. This created a huge demand for live talent, and made it possible for country musicians to start thinking of actually making a living with their art. National companies like Crazy Water Crystals, a laxative maker, were willing to put on salary country singers who could appeal to listening audiences. Singers also found that they could use their programs to advertise free their local appearances and schoolhouse shows in the area – another important source of revenue. The result was an increasing professionalization of the music: bands and singers who could work at their craft full time instead of just Saturday or Sunday night would obviously improve their abilities, and come up with more original songs and styles.

Radio singers soon created a style of their own. Unlike the older singers who had to make themselves heard on a medicine show platform or vaudeville stage, the new generation learned how to sing in front of a microphone, in a relatively quiet studio. Subtlety, softness, and close harmony were possible, and the so-called "brother duet" came into vogue. Though not all duet acts were really brothers, the image was there; accompanied usually by merely two guitars or a guitar and mandolin, the duet singers perfected the sentimental song, the gospel song, the intricate part-switching arrangement, and along the way changed the face of the music.

Are You From Dixie? Great Country Brother Teams Of The 1930s provides an impressive introduction to this style of singing. Almost all the top duets are heard here: the Delmore Brothers, who pioneered the style on the Grand Ole Opry in 1933, with favorites like *Blow Yo' Whistle, Freight Train* and *The Nashville Blues*; the Monroe Brothers, Bill and Charlie, who traveled all over the South featuring songs like *Roll In My Sweet Baby's Arms*; and the Blue Sky Boys, Bill and Earl Bolick, who had perhaps the closest and purest harmony of all, and who mixed old ballads like *Katie Dear* with newer songs like *I'm Just Here To Get My Baby Out Of Jail*. Drawn largely from Victor's Bluebird catalog, this CD also spotlights some of the pioneers of the brother teams: the Allen Brothers with their legendary *A New Salty Dog*, and the Shelton Brothers (heard here as the Lone Star Cowboys) with their *Deep Elm Blues* and *Just Because* – two songs that would become 1930s standards.

The voracious appetite of daily live radio consumed songs at a bewildering rate (even a 15-minute program often required half a dozen songs), and this caused some interesting changes in the country repertoire. It encouraged some performers, like the

Delmore Brothers, to write more and more original material. It encouraged others, like the Blue Sky Boys, to look at the big new commercial songbooks sent to them by companies like Chicago's M.M. Cole. Still other singers were visited by representatives of gospel publishers like Dallas's Stamps-Baxter, who were always putting out books of "radio specials." Gospel songs were always needed; listeners wrote in requesting them (the Blue Sky Boys got more requests for sacred songs than for any other kind), and many programs always ended with the cast gathering around the microphone for a gospel favorite of some sort. As a result a new genre of gospel song emerged, one that was not exactly a hymn (i.e., it was seldom sung in church services) and not exactly a singing school or quartet favorite. It was a "country gospel" song, and soon entered the country repertoire.

Something Got A Hold Of Me: A Treasury Of Sacred Music shows the extent to which this new type of music infiltrated the sound of the 1930s. Here are the original versions of standards like *What Would You Give In Exchange For Your Soul* (the Monroe Brothers), *The Tramp On The Street* (sung by its writer, Grady Cole, and his wife Hazel), *Farther Along* (Wade Mainer), *I Didn't Hear Nobody Pray*, the original version of Roy Acuff's *Wreck On The Highway*, sung here by its composers the Dixon Brothers; and the Carter Family's *I'm Working On A Building*. Most of the sides were recorded on Bluebird Victor's budget label, in the 1930s; the songs themselves reflect the morals and world view of Depression-era America, though some seem miles from today's political correctness. (Blind Alfred Reed's *There'll Be No Distinction There* sounds ahead of its time until we come to the line, "We'll all be white in that heavenly light.") Notwithstanding, it is still remarkable how many of these gospel songs remain in the country repertoire today, and how many of these performances still have the ability to move a listener.

By the late 1930s, vocal soloists were starting to come back into the spotlight. The influence of western swing and of cowboy singers like Gene Autry (see below) had been pervasive on all sorts of country radio singers; their smoother, pop-oriented, less Southern sound had won the music thousands of new fans around the country, but it had blunted the cutting edge and emotionalism that had given country singing its soul. A key figure in reversing this trend was Roy Acuff, an east Tennessee singer who joined the Grand Ole Opry in 1938 for a tenure that would last the rest of his life. Acuff sang in a high, keening voice that had direct links to the old ballad singers he had heard as a child; he sang in a loud, forceful, emotional style, often at the top of his range, usually just behind the beat, and with a "tear" in his voice that let him sell sentimental and gospel songs to the most cynical audience.

Acuff first came to fame over Knoxville radio stations in 1936 when he started singing an odd gospel song called *The Great Speckle [sic] Bird*, which he had learned from a fellow singer on the radio. The listener response was so intense that the American Record Company (Columbia-Vocalion) offered him a contract, and brought him to Chicago in 1936 to record some 20 selections, including the *Bird*. That record, as well as a substantial cross-section of Acuff's later work, is found in **The Essential Roy Acuff**, a 1992 compilation in the Columbia "Country Classics" series. Acuff's biggest hits came in the early 1940s, when he had access to the network portion of the Opry and was a regular in Hollywood films. Most of these are on this CD, including *The Precious Jewel* (1940), *Fireball Mail* (1942), *Night Train to Memphis* (1942), and *Freight Train Blues* (1947). Acuff's right-hand man through much of this time was Pete Kirby (Bashful Brother Oswald), whose screaming tenor and sophisticated dobro work augmented Acuff's own singing. Acuff continued to record until a few weeks before his death in 1992, and his later work more properly belongs in a later chapter; these early recordings, though, have direct links with the older string band and radio band tradition, and can properly be thought of as vivid adaptations of older styles.

A female counterpart to Acuff's "mountain" singing style can be found in the work of Molly O'Day, an artist whom veteran producer Art Satherly considered the greatest female country singer. Her case rests on a series of sides she did for Columbia between 1946 and 1951, all of which are collected in the 2-CD set from the distinguished German label Bear Family: **Molly O'Day And The Cumberland Mountain Folks**. In spite of the relatively late date, these sides have their roots in a much earlier era, and their ties to older country music are considerable. Born in Williamson County, Kentucky in 1923, O'Day began working on radio in 1939, and toured southeastern stations during the next ten years. She had a mature and well-honed style when she made her first Columbia sides, which included the best-known version of the gospel standard *Tramp On The Street* as well as *Six More Miles*. Her clear, powerful voice gave new meaning to the most maudlin or sentimental songs, such as *The Drunken Driver* or *I Heard My Mother Weeping*. Her association with the Acuff–Rose company led to her being one of the first to record some of Hank Williams's early songs, and her driving clawhammer banjo playing on pieces like *Poor Ellen Smith* helped maintain the links between old-time music and the 1950s. The 36 sides heard here form a remarkable legacy, and a case study in how a great singer can fuse originality and heritage. They also formed a tragically short testament; O'Day contracted tuberculosis in 1952, and she and her husband left music to become ministers.

Discographical Details

10   Are You From Dixie? Great Country Brother Teams of the 1930s

Various Artists

RCA CD 8417–2–R

The Allen Brothers: *Jake Walk Blues/Roll Down The Line/A New Salty Dog*; The Lone Star Cowboys: *Deep Elm Blues/Crawdad Song/Just Because*; The Delmore Brothers: *I've Got The Big River Blues/Blow Yo' Whistle, Freight Train/The Nashville Blues*; The Dixon Brothers: *Weave Room Blues/The Intoxicated Rat/Down With The Old Canoe*; The Monroe Brothers: *Nine-Pound Hammer Is Too Heavy/Roll In My Sweet Baby's Arms/Have A Feast Here Tonight*; The Blue Sky Boys: *I'm Just Here To Get My Baby Out Of Jail/Katie Dear/Are You From Dixie*

11   Something Got A Hold Of Me: A Treasury Of Sacred Music

Various Artists

RCA-BMG 2100–2–R

The Carter Family: *I'm Working On A Building/Something Got A Hold Of Me*; The Monroe Brothers: *On That Old Gospel Ship/What Would You Give in Exchange*/Bill Monroe and his Blue Grass Boys: *Cryin' Holy Unto The Lord*; The Blue Sky Boys: *Only One Step More/Where The Soul Of Man Never Dies*; Bill Carlisle: *The Heavenly Train*; Grady and Hazel Cole: *Tramp On The Street*; The Dixon Brothers: *I Didn't Hear Nobody Pray*; Blind Alfred Reed: *Always Lift Him And Never Knock Him Down/There'll Be No Distinction There*; Wade Mainer and the Sons of the Mountaineers: *Mansions In The Sky, Farther Along*; J.E. Mainer's Mountaineers: *Just Over In The Glory Land*; Uncle Dave Macon: *Just One Way To The Pearly Gates*

12   The Essential Roy Acuff, 1936–1949

Roy Acuff

Columbia/Legacy CK 48956

Great Speckle Bird/Steel Guitar Blues/Just To Ease My Worried Mind/ Lonesome Old River Blues/The Precious Jewel/It Won't Be Long (Till I'll Be Leaving)/Wreck On The Highway/Fireball Mail/Night Train To Memphis/The Prodigal Son/Not A Word From Home/I'll Forgive You, But I Can't Forget You/Freight Train Blues/Wabash Cannon Ball/Jole Blon/This World Can't Stand Long/Waltz Of The Wind/A Sinner's Death (I'm Dying)/Tennessee Waltz/Black Mountain Rag

13 Molly O'Day And The Cumberland Mountain Folks

Molly O'Day

Bear Family BCD 15565 (2-disc set) (Ger)

The Tramp On The Street/When God Comes And Gathers His Jewels/The Black Sheep Returned To The Fold/Put My Rubber Doll Away/The Drunken Driver/The Tear-Stained Letter/Lonely Mound of Clay/Six More Miles/ Singing Waterfall/At The First Fall Of Snow/Matthew Twenty-Four/I Don't Care If Tomorrow Never Comes/A Hero's Death/I'll Never See Sunshine Again/Too Late – Too Late/Why Do You Weep, Dear Willow/Don't Forget The Family Prayer/I Heard My Mother Weeping/Mother's Gone But Not Forgotten/The Evening Train/This Is The End/Fifteen Years Ago/Poor Ellen Smith/Coming Down From God/Teardrops Falling In The Snow/With You On My Mind/If You See My Savior/Heaven's Radio/When My Time Comes To Go/Don't Sell Daddy Any More Whiskey/Higher In My Prayers/Travelling The Highway Home/It's Different Now/When The Angels Rolled The Stone Away/It's All Coming True/When We See Our Redeemer's Face

(iv) Modern Survivals

Into the modern age, the older songs and styles have been kept alive by a wide spectrum of younger artists; in the 1940s and 1950s people like Grandpa Jones, Hank Snow, Lefty Frizzell, Bill Carlisle, James and Martha Carson, the Louvin Brothers, and others often paid tribute to the older music as they forged their own careers. During the folk revival movement in the 1960s, young fans sought out and rediscovered many veteran performers; the growing bluegrass movement fostered a new respect for the older acoustic pre-bluegrass music, and provided a festival venue for vintage styles and songs. Bands like the New Lost City Ramblers carefully copied and reproduced the sounds of the old 78s by Charlie Poole and Uncle Dave Macon. Independent record companies like Folkways, County, Rounder, and others came into being and released new albums by those, both young and old, who preferred the older music.

Rounder Old-Time Music is a CD sampler designed to introduce new listeners to the richness of the music in the company's catalog. It includes veterans who had recorded in the 1930s, like Snuffy Jenkins and Pappy Sherrill, and Bashful Brother Oswald. It includes acts best known in bluegrass circles but whose repertoire encompasses old-time music, such as Joe Val, Don Stover, the Bailey Brothers, and Ted Lundy. It includes younger revival artists such as Bob Carlin, the Highwoods String Band, and the Tompkins County Horseflies. There is the instrumental virtuosity of fiddlers Buddy Thomas and Mark O'Connor, and of guitarist Norman Blake; the classic harmony of the Louvin Brothers, and of their pupils the Whitstein Brothers; the soulful singing of Hazel Dickens and Ricky

Skaggs; and the traditional folk music of George Pegram and E.C. and Orna Ball. Overall the set offers a representative cross-section of the different musical forms that exist in modern times, and that still sail under the banner of old-time music.

By most standards, though, the best-known modern exponent of old-time music is Doc Watson, from Deep Gal, North Carolina. Discovered by folklorists in the early 1960s, Doc took his flowing guitar picking and warm singing voice onto the concert stages and astounded audiences everywhere with his ability to recast old songs in his unique style. Unlike artists such as Mike Seeger, Doc did not try to exactly emulate his sources; indeed, he won a lot of his initial fame by finger-picking fiddle tunes. He became modern old-time music's finest stylist, and found fans everywhere from bluegrass festivals to the sound stage of the Nashville Network. Starting in 1963, dozens of LPs appeared, some with his family, some with session musicians, and many with his son Merle, himself a superb instrumentalist. Merle's accidental death in October 1985 stunned Doc and his fans, but after a time of retrenchment, he was soon back in the studios.

Memories is a fair sampling of Doc's work; it begins with him playing an old banjo and singing *Rambling Hobo*, moves to a fine unaccompanied vocal in *Wake Up, Little Maggie*, and cruises through a brace of pieces that include Merle on slide guitar, banjo, and standard guitar. In between are some cuts with a crack Nashville studio band, and even a Don Gibson song (*Don't Tell Me Your Troubles*) done à la Doc. Originally released in 1975, the album lives up to its title, and treats us to a rich musical portrait of one of the genre's most unique individuals.

Discographical Details

14 Rounder Old-Time Music

Various Artists
Rounder CD 11510
Snuffy Jenkins and Pappy Sherrill: *C And NW Railroad Blues;* Norman Blake: *If I Lose, I Don't Care*; Hazel Dickens: *West Virginia, My Home*; Ricky Skaggs: *Talk About Sufferin'*; Tompkins County Horseflies: *Benton's Dream*; Highwoods String Band: *Goodbye, Miss Liza*; Don Stover: *Things In Life*: Ola Belle Reed: *You Led Me To The Wrong*; Alva Greene and Francis Gillum: *Hunky Dory*; Wade Ward: *Shady Grove*; Ted Lundy and the Southern Mountain Boys: *It Rained A Mist*; Joe Val and the New England Bluegrass Boys: *I've Been All Around This World*; James Bryan: *The First of May*; The Chicken Chokers: *Looking For Money*; Bob Carlin: *Too Young to Marry*; Bashful Brother Oswald: *That High-Born Gal of Mine*; The Whitstein Brothers: *Where The Old Red River Flows*; The Bailey Brothers: *Take Me Back To Happy Valley*; The Blue Sky Boys: *Just A Strand From A Yellow*

Curl; Buddy Thomas: *Briarpicker Brown*; The Louvin Brothers: *Let Us Travel On*; George Pegram: *Johnson's Old Grey Mule*; Clint Howard and Fred Price: *Shut Up In The Mines Of Coal Creek*; Doc Watson, Arnold Watson, and Gaither Carlton: *Reuben's Train*; Mark O'Connor: *Soppin' the Gravy*; E.C. and Orna Ball: *Fathers Have A Home Sweet Home*

15 Memories

Doc Watson
Sugar Hill SH-CD-2204
Rambling Hobo/Shady Grove/Wake Up, Little Maggie/Peartree/Keep On The Sunny Side/Double File And Salt Creek/Curly-Headed Baby/Miss The Mississippi And You/Wabash Cannonball/My Rose Of Old Kentucky/Blues Stay Away From Me/Walking Boss/Make Me A Pallet/In The Jailhouse Now/Steel Guitar Rag/Hang Your Head In Shame/You Don't Know My Mind Blues/Moody River/Don't Tell Me Your Troubles/Columbus Stockade/Mama Don't Allow No Music/Thoughts Of Never

Basic Recordings

16 Roots N' Blues: The Retrospective (1925–1950)

Various Artists
Columbia/Legacy C4K 47911 (4-disc set)
(Partial contents): Charlie Poole with the North Carolina Ramblers: *Whitehouse Blues*; Aiken County String Band: *High Sheriff*; Frank Hutchison: *The Last Scene Of The Titanic*; Vance's Tennessee Breakdowners: *Washington County Fox Chase*; Fiddlin' John Carson: *I'm Going To Take The Train To Charlotte*; Ernest V. Stoneman: *Untitled [Flop-Eared Mule]*; Austin and Lee Allen: *Chattanooga Blues*; Sherman Tedder: *Untitled*; South Georgia Highballers: *Blue Grass Twist*; Charlie Bowman and his Brothers: *Moonshiner And His Money*; Clarence Greene: *Johnson City Blues*; Daniels Deason Sacred Harp Singers: *Hallelujah*; Herschel Brown and his Happy Five: *Liberty*; The Okeh Atlanta Sacred Harp Singers: *Ortonville*; W.T. Narmour and S.W. Smith: *Sweet Milk And Peaches (Breakdown)*; Gid Tanner and the Skillet Lickers with Riley Puckett and Clayton McMichen: *Soldier's Joy*; Tom Darby and Jimmie Tarlton: *Lonesome Frisco Line*; Roy Harvey and Leonard Copeland: *Back To The Blue Ridge*; Buster Carter and Preston Young: *Darn Good Girl*; Freeny's Barn Dance Band: *Don't You Remember The Time*; Pelican Wildcats: *Walkin' Georgia Rose*; W. Lee O'Daniel and the Light Crust Doughboys: *Doughboys Theme/Ida (Sweet As Apple Cider)/Doughboys Theme Song No. 2*; Blue Ridge Ramblers: *D Blues*; The Rhythm Wreckers: *Blue Yodel No. 2 (My Lovin' Gal Lucille)*; The Anglin Brothers: *Just Inside The Pearly Gates*; Eldon Baker and his Brown County Revellers: *One-Eyed Sam*; A'ny Idy Harper and the Coon Creek Girls: *Poor Naomi Wise*; Cliff Carlisle: *Onion-Eating Mama*; Callahan Brothers: *Brown's Ferry Blues No. 2*; Sweet Violet Boys: *You Got To See Mama Every Night (Or You Can't See Mama At All)*; The Humbard Family: *I'll Fly Away*; Bob and Randall Atcher: *Papa's Going Crazy, Mama's Going Mad*; Adolf Hofner and his San Antonians: *Cotton-Eyed Joe*; Light Crust Doughboys with J.B. Binkley: *It's Funny What Love Will Make You Do*; Hank Penny and his Radio Cowboys: *Army Blues*; Bill Monroe and his Blue Grass Boys: *Goodbye Old Pal*; Gene Autry: *Dixie Cannonball*; Bailes Brothers: *You Can't Go Halfway (And Get In)*; Molly O'Day and the Cumberland Mountain Folks: *Heaven's Radio*

This remarkable anthology, put together by Larry Cohn, contains over 100 titles from the CBS vaults, ranging from blues to gospel; the listings above reflect only the country or old-time music in the collection. Full of unissued titles and obscure bands, it is nonetheless the best cross-section of pre-war country music currently available. Here are superb examples of fiddle tunes (the Skillet Lickers' *Soldier's Joy* in its first incarnation, Narmour's and Smith's bluesy *Sweet Milk And Peaches*), of old-time guitar work (Harvey's and Copeland's exciting duet *Back To The Blue Ridge*, Greene's *Johnson City Blues*), of driving string bands (the obscure Pelican Wildcats, the more popular Blue Ridge [i.e., Prairie] Ramblers), even of "Sacred Harp" and gospel (including the first recording of Brumley's classic *I'll Fly Away*). There are samples by such giants of old-time music as Darby and Tarlton, Fiddlin' John Carson, Frank Hutchison, Charlie Bowman, Ernest Stoneman, Charlie Poole, the Light Crust Doughboys, the Coon Creek Girls, and others. A huge and handsomely illustrated book explains something of the music and the artists – probably the most elaborate set of liner notes ever designed for such music by a commercial company.

17 The Singing Brakeman

Jimmie Rodgers

Bear Family BCD 15540 (6-disc set) (Ger)

The Soldier's Sweetheart/Sleep, Baby, Sleep/Ben Dewberry's Final Run/ Mother Was A Lady/Blue Yodel/Away Out On The Mountain/Dear Old Sunny South By The Sea/Treasures Untold/The Brakeman's Blues/The Sailor's Plea/In The Jailhouse Now/Blue Yodel No. 2/Memphis Yodel/Blue Yodel No. 3/My Old Pal/Mississippi Moon/My Little Old Home Down In New Orleans/ You And My Old Guitar/Daddy And Home/My Little Lady/I'm Lonely And Blue/Lullaby Yodel/Never No Mo' Blues/My Carolina Sunshine Girl/Blue Yodel No. 4/Waiting For A Train/I'm Lonely And Blue/Desert Blues/Any Old Time/Blue Yodel No. 5/High Powered Mama/I'm Sorry We Met/Everybody Does It In Hawaii/Tuck Away My Lonesome Blues/Train Whistle Blues/ Jimmie's Texas Blues/Frankie And Johnny/Frankie And Johnny/Homecall/ Homecall/Whisper Your Mother's Name/The Land Of My Boyhood Dreams/ The Land Of My Boyhood Dreams/Blue Yodel No. 6/Yodeling Cowboy/My Rough And Rowdy Ways/I've Ranged, I've Roamed, I've Traveled/I've Ranged, I've Roamed, I've Traveled/Hobo Bill's Last Ride/Mississippi River Blues/Mississippi River Blues/Nobody Knows But Me/Anniversary Blue Yodel/Anniversary Blue Yodel/She Was Happy Till She Met You/Blue Yodel No. 11/Blue Yodel No. 11/A Drunkard's Child/That's Why I'm Blue/Why Did You Give Me Your Love/Why Did You Give Me Your Love/My Blue-Eyed Jane/Why Should I Be Lonely/Moonlight And Skies/Pistol-Packin' Papa/Take Me Back Again/Those Gambler's Blues/I'm Lonesome Too/The One Rose/For The Sake of Days Gone By/Jimmie's Mean Mama Blues/The Mystery of Number Five/Blue Yodel No. 8/In The Jailhouse Now No. 2/Blue Yodel No. 9/T.B. Blues/T.B. Blues/Travelin' Blues/Travelin' Blues/Travelin' Blues/Jimmie The Kid/Jimmie The Kid/Why There's A Tear In My Eye/The Wonderful City/Let Me Be Your Sidetrack/Let Me Be Your Sidetrack/Let Me Be Your Sidetrack/Jimmie Rodgers Visits The Carter Family/The Carter Family And Jimmie Rodgers In Texas/When The Cactus Is In Bloom/Gambling Polka Dot Blues/Looking For A New Mama/Looking For A New Mama/What's It/My Good Gal's Gone/My Good Gal's Gone/Southern Cannonball/Roll Along Kentucky Moon/Roll Along Kentucky Moon/Hobo's Meditation/Hobo's Meditation/My Time Ain't Long/ Ninety-Nine Year Blues/Mississippi Moon/Mississippi Moon/Down The Old Road To Home/Blue Yodel No. 10/Home Call/Rock All My Babies To Sleep/ Whippin' That Old T.B./Whippin' That Old T.B./No Hard Times/No Hard

*Times/Long Tall Mama Blues/Peach Pickin' Time Down In Georgia/Gambling
Barroom Blues/I've Only Loved Three Women/In the Hills of Tennessee/Prairie
Lullaby/Miss The Mississippi And You/Sweet Mama, Hurry Home/Blue Yodel
No. 12/Dreaming With Tears In My Eyes/The Cowhand's Last Ride/I'm Free
From The Chain Gang Now/Dreaming With Tears In My Eyes/Yodeling My
Way Back Home/Jimmie Rodgers' Last Blue Yodel/The Yodeling Ranger/Old
Pal Of My Heart/Old Love Letters/Mississippi Delta Blues/Somewhere Below
The Mason Dixon Line/Years Ago/The Singing Brakeman (The Movie Sound-
track)/The Pullman Porters/In The Jailhouse Now No. 2/Mule Skinner Blues/
Peach Pickin' Time Down In Georgia/Mother, The Queen Of My Heart/Never
No Mo' Blues/Blue Yodel No. 1/Daddy And Home/Memphis Yodel*

One of the legendary complete editions issued by Germany's Bear Family
label, this boxed set contains every one of Jimmie Rodgers's released
recordings on six CDs. In addition, the set includes over 30 alternate or
unissued takes, as well as the eight tracks from 1955 where Hank Snow's
Rainbow Ranch Boys overdubbed modern backing to Rodgers's original
recordings. The grand total is 128 sides, beautifully remastered from (in
many cases) RCA's original acetates or factory metal parts, often with the
Cedar or No-Noise system. The result is not only the clearest Rodgers yet,
but a system that brings a startling warmth and presence to these 60-year-
old recordings.

An added bonus is a huge 12 by 12 illustrated book written by Rodgers's
biographer Nolan Porterfield. There are sumptuous photos – many never
before published or even known – as well as the most accurate discography
yet compiled. Some information – such as the original sales figures for the
Rodgers singles – had not even been uncovered at the time Porterfield
finished his book.

The music itself ranges from out-and-out blues to 1930s-style crooning,
and Rodgers's accompaniments range from Louis Armstrong to the Louisville
Jug Band, and from the Carter Family to Lani McIntyre's Hawaiians. The
chronological order allows us to follow Rodgers session by session, to see and
judge the different experiments Ralph Peer made to market country's first
really big crossover star. All the many hits are here, of course, but also the
unsuspected and little-known masterworks: *Let Me Be Your Sidetrack*, an
alternate take done with blues guitarist Clifford Gibson; *Whippin' That Old
T.B.*, done just a year before his death and featuring an unearthly blues fiddle
solo by Clayton McMichen; even *In The Hills Of Tennessee*, done with a
small (still anonymous) studio orchestra, which might have pointed the way
Rodgers would have moved had he lived.

This is an expensive import, difficult to obtain, but worth seeking out; and
it is a crucial cornerstone to country music as we know it.

18 No Hard Times, 1932

Jimmie Rodgers
Rounder CD 1062

*Blue Yodel No. 10/Whippin' That Old T.B./Whippin' That Old T.B./Rock All
Our Babies To Sleep/Home Call/Mother, The Queen Of My Heart/No Hard
Times/No Hard Times/Peach Pickin' Time Down In Georgia/Long Tall Mama
Blues/Gambling Bar Room Blues/I've Only Loved Three Women/In The Hills of
Tennessee/Prairie Lullaby/Miss The Mississippi And You/Sweet Mama, Hurry
Home*

Here is the mature Jimmie Rodgers, a little more than a year away from his
own death from TB, struggling to keep his own record sales up in the face of

the hard times he was singing about. There are still some classics here – *Peach Pickin' Time Down In Georgia, Miss The Mississippi And You, Mother, The Queen Of My Heart*, and *Home Call*. But there are also some of his most biting blues – *Whippin' That Old T.B.* and his version of *St James Infirmary* which he called *Gambling Bar Room Blues*. Some late experiments with a small studio orchestra and hot guitarist Slim Bryant (*In The Hills Of Tennessee, Prairie Lullaby*) round out the set. The superior liner notes are by Rodgers expert Nolan Porterfield.

19   My Clinch Mountain Home: The Carter Family Vol. 2, 1928–1929

The Carter Family

Rounder CD 1065

I Have No One To Love Me/Forsaken Love/Sweet Fern/My Clinch Mountain Home/ God Gave Noah The Rainbow Sign/I'm Thinking Tonight Of My Blue Eyes/Little Moses/Lulu Walls/The Grave On The Green Hillside/Don't Forget This Song/The Foggy Mountain Top/Bring Back My Blue-Eyed Boy/Diamonds In The Rough/Engine 143/The Homestead On The Farm/The Cyclone Of Ryecove

The second volume in Rounder's series of the complete Carter Family sides for RCA Victor, this set includes some of the trio's best-selling early sides: *Forsaken Love, I Have No One To Love Me, My Clinch Mountain Home, The Foggy Mountain Top*, and the railroad ballad *Engine 143* – the song Sara Carter was supposedly singing when A.P. first met her. The bulk of this album is the session at Camden, New Jersey in February 1929 – a session which saw the family emphasize sentimental and folk songs rather than gospel ones. By now A.P.'s own songwriting was flowering – he wrote the title lament for Clinch Mountain while he was working in Indiana – and the trio was really developing the 3-part harmony that would become its trademark. Full annotations give the histories of most of the songs, based on old Carter interviews and fresh research.

20   Ragged But Right: Great Country String Bands Of The 1930s

Various Artists

RCA CD 8416–2–R

Riley Puckett and Ted Hawkins [of the Skillet Lickers]: *Ragged But Right*; Gid Tanner and the Skillet Lickers: *Ida Red/Soldier's Joy/On Tanner's Farm*; Riley Puckett and Ted Hawkins: *Hawkins' Rag/Tokio Rag*; The Prairie Ramblers: *Go Easy Blues/Blue River/Kentucky Blues/Shady Grove, My Darling/Tex's Dance*; Patsy Montana: *Montana Plains*; J.E. Mainer's Mountaineers: *Maple On The Hill/Seven And A Half/Johnson's Old Grey Mule*; Wade Mainer and Zeke Morris: *Short Life And It's Trouble*; Wade Mainer, Zeke Morris, and Steve Ledford: *Riding On That Train 45*; Wade Mainer and the Sons of the Mountaineers: *Mitchell Blues*

Most of the string bands of the 1930s lacked the drive and panache of the great outfits of the 1920s; radio, songbooks, and showbiz domesticated them. The hottest and the wildest of the old bands, The Skillet Lickers, did one last session for Bluebird in 1934, but some of their key personnel had gone, and the result was an appealing, if archaic, sound. On this set we hear favorites like the mandolin masterpiece *Hawkins Rag*, as well as Gid Tanner's fiddling on *Soldier's Joy*. Far more driving are the young Prairie Ramblers, charging through *Shady Grove* and fiddler Tex Achison's *Tex's Dance*. This was a year before the band hooked up with Gene Autry and became a domesticated radio band; here they are still a lean and hungry band from western Kentucky. The Mainer Brothers, Wade and J.E., became the most-recorded band of the time, and several of their groups are heard here, doing favorites like *Maple On The Hill*, *Johnson's Old Grey Mule*, and *Riding On That Train 45*.

21 A Few Old Memories

Hazel Dickens
Rounder CD 11529
A Few Old Memories/Beyond The River Bend/Busted/Old And In The Way/ It's Hard To Tell The Singer From The Song/Don't Bother To Cry/Hills Of Home/Pretty Bird/Only The Lonely/Coal Tattoo/Little Lenaldo/Old Calloused Hands/Scares From An Old Love/You'll Get No More Of Me/Mama's Hands/ Working Girl Blues/West Virginia, My Home/Play Us A Waltz

The daughter of a coal miner who grew up in the poverty-stricken mining camps of West Virginia, Hazel Dickens first came to fame as half of the duo of Hazel and Alice; in the 1960s they became one of the most influential women's acts in traditional music, inspiring, among others, Naomi and Wynonna Judd. Since the early 1980s, Hazel has been on her own and her six albums – from which this anthology is drawn – have won her the reputation as the best woman singer in old-time music. Her "hard country" voice is especially effective on original songs like *Working Girl Blues* and *You'll Get No More Of Me* – new songs in classic modes.

22 Clinch Mountain Treasures

The Carter Family
County/Sony Music Special Products CCS-CD-112 A 22449
Little Poplar Log House On The Hill/The Dying Mother/Buddies In The Saddle/Heaven's Radio/Beautiful Home/There'll Be No Distinction There/Give Him One More As He Goes/Lonesome For You, Darling/Blackie's Gunman/ You've Got To Righten That Wrong/Meeting In The Air/My Home Among The Hills/Black Jack David/Look Away From The Cross/We Shall Rise/I Found You Among The Roses/Bear Creek Blues/I'll Never Forsake You/Beautiful Isle O'er The Sea/It's A Long, Long Road To Travel Alone

Here is the mature Carter Family at the peak of their skills, as heard in a complete 1940 recording session done in Chicago for the old American Recording Company. In the months before this session, the Family had been broadcasting over the notorious "border" station XERA, and they had built up a fund of new and interesting songs. Some of these, such as *There'll Be No Distinction There*, *Bear Creek Blues*, *We Shall Rise*, *Meeting In The Air*, and the gangster ballad *Blackie's Gunman*, were to become some of their most popular and long-lasting pieces. A.P. himself is especially heard to good advantage, thanks to several solos and an improved recording technology. Singer Bill Clifton's warm and personal liner notes round out the set.

23   The Chuck Wagon Gang: Columbia Historic Edition

The Chuck Wagon Gang

Columbia FC 40152 (LP)

We Are Climbing/The Church In The Wildwood/After The Sunrise/As The Life Of A Flower/The Engineer's Child/He Set Me Free/Whisper My Name In Prayer/Don't You Weep For Me/O Why Not Tonight/A Beautiful Life/Get A Touch Of Heaven In Your Soul/When I Thank Him For What He Has Done/Help Me, Lord, To Stand/Texas Star/I Want To See My Jesus/A Soul Winner For Jesus

For three decades the most popular and influential country gospel group on radio was the "other Carter family," Texas's Chuck Wagon Gang, founded by D.P. "Dad" Carter. These vintage recordings, which date from 1936 to 1960, form a cross-section of their best work, and include *He Set Me Free*, the model for Hank Williams's *I Saw The Light*, as well as their best-selling *Church In The Wildwood* and the seminal *After The Sunrise*. Numerous major singers, including Hank Williams, Willie Nelson, and Johnny Cash, have recalled listening to the Chucks on radio during their youth, and getting their first notions of country harmony from the group's simple but powerful arrangements. Not on CD, but worth seeking out on vinyl.

24   Blue Sky Boys On Radio – Vol. 1

The Blue Sky Boys

Copper Creek CCCD-0120

Opening And Theme/The Blood Of Jesus/Just A Strand From A Yellow Curl/ Comedy/Will You Meet Me Over Yonder/Katy Hill/Will My Mother Know Me There/Take Me Back To Renfro Valley/Advertisement/Comedy/The Holiness Mother/Eighth Of January/When I Reach That City On The Hill/ Trail To Mexico/Comedy/Someone's Last Day/Ida Red/That Beautiful Home/ The Longest Train I Ever Saw/Advertisement/Comedy/What Would You Give In Exchange For Your Soul/Old Joe Clark/Row Us Over The Tide/Why Should It End This Way/Comedy/Gathering Buds/Lost Train Blues/Closing And Theme

Too few of the haunting Victor sides by the Blue Sky Boys are available today, but this generous sampling of their vintage radio transcriptions helps fill the void. The shows date from 1946 and 1947, when the Bolick Brothers were at the peak of their abilities. Here are versions of several of the duo's best-known songs, such as *What Would You Give In Exchange For Your Soul, Row Us Over The Tide, Someone's Last Day*, and *Gathering Buds*. In addition, though, there are samples of the comedy featuring Uncle Josh, earnest commercials (some touting the virtues of the Jeep as a civilian vehicle), fiddle breakdowns by Curly Parker, who for some time was a regular member of the act. (On more than a few cuts, he does lead vocals, making the Blue Sky Boys a trio.) Here is how the best known of the brother duet acts really sounded to thousands of faithful listeners in homes across the South. The sound is amazingly good, and comes with detailed song notes and recollections by Bill Bolick himself. A second volume, Cooper Creek CCCD-0121, offers another sampling from the same transcriptions.

25 16 Greatest Hits

Grandpa Jones

Hollywood (Starday) HCD-224

*Mountain Dew/Fifteen Cents Is All I Got/Eight More Miles To Louisville/
Uncle Eff's Got The Coon/East-Bound Freight Train/She's The Steppin' Out
Kind/I'm My Own Grandpa/Old Rattler's Treed Again/Old Rattler/Are You
From Dixie/There's A Hole In The Ground/Grandpa's Boogie/My Old Red
River Home/It's Raining Here This Morning/Here, Rattler, Here/Jonah And
The Whale*

These are some of the original King sides that won Grandpa Jones his
national reputation in the 1940s. Many reflect an exuberant mixture of
modern and old-time – lap steel guitars sometimes jostle with Grandpa's
frailing banjo and wife Ramona's mandolin – and the best of them show why
King was the most important independent label in country history. You can
hear Merle Travis playing electric lead on cuts like *Eight More Miles To
Louisville*, and Cowboy Copas backing Grandpa's vocal on *Old Rattler*. The
sound here is not great, the liner notes are non-existent, and the programming is so sloppy that *Old Rattler* is inadvertently included twice – but the
set is still worth having.

26 Songs That Tell A Story

The Louvin Brothers

Rounder CD 1030

*Theme/Kneel At The Cross/I Have Found the Way/Weapon Of Prayer/I'll
Never Go Back/What A Friend We Have In Mother/Theme/Jesus Is Whisper-
ing Now/The Family That Prays/Robe Of White/Let Us Travel On/Sinner,
You'd Better Get Ready/Shut In At Christmas/Shut In Prayer*

Before Ira and Charlie Louvin found success in Nashville using modern
country back-up and having hits like *When I Stop Dreaming*, they served a
lengthy apprenticeship at smaller radio stations around the South. Much of
the time they featured gospel or sentimental songs, delivered with their
powerful harmony and simple guitar–mandolin accompaniment. Much of this
early music is lost for ever, but in 1952 the brothers transcribed a series of
radio shows called *Songs That Tell A Story*, designed for syndication. The
plan failed, but several of the shows were preserved by Charlie, and two of
them are presented here. Replete with Ira's emcee work, an earnest announcer named Tyce Teraway, and a battery of early classics like *The Weapon Of
Prayer*, the album shows just how deep the roots of Louvin music run.

27 Treasures Untold

Doc Watson and Family

Vanguard VCD 77001

*Lights In The Valley/Beaumont Rag/I Heard My Mother Weeping/Billy In The
Low Ground/Omie Wise/Reuben's Train/Hicks' Farewell/Ramblin' Hobo/White
House Blues/Jimmy Sutton And The Old Buck Ram/I Want to Love Him More/
Grandfather's Clock/Chinese Breakdown/Handsome Molly/Beaumont Rag* (with
Clarence White)/*Farewell Blues* (with Clarence White)/*Lonesome Road Blues*
(with Clarence White)/*Footprints In The Snow* (with Clarence White)

Drawn from unreleased concert tapes of the 1964 Newport Folk Festivals, these performances feature Doc with his 15-year-old son Merle, his mother, his brother Arnold, his father-in-law Gaither Carlton (on fiddle), and his wife Rosa Lee. They form a natural sequel to Doc's first album, **The Watson Family**, and present a cross-section of old ballads (*Omie Wise*), fiddle tunes (*Beaumont Rag*), old gospel songs (*Lights In The Valley, Hicks' Farewell*), and old banjo tunes (*Reuben's Train*). Here is Doc's music in its original, natural setting, augmented by four guitar duets with young bluegrass star Clarence White.

28   The Blue Sky Boys In Concert, 1964

The Blue Sky Boys
Rounder CD 11536
Are You From Dixie/Quit That Ticklin' Me/I'm Just Here To Get My Baby Out Of Jail/Worried Man Blues/After The Ball/Behind These Prison Walls Of Love/The Last Letter/The Fox/The Sweetest Gift/Only One Step More/Uncle Josh Comedy Skit/Don't Trade/Kentucky/If I Could Hear My Mother Pray Again/Sweetheart Mountain Rose/It Was Midnight On The Stormy Deep/ Beautiful/In The Hills Of Roane County/I'm Saved/Whispering Hope/The Butcher's Boy/Are You From Dixie

After being retired for years, the Blue Sky Boys (Bill and Earl Bolick) did a "reunion" concert in 1964 before a folk music audience at the University of Illinois. It was the first time the brothers had performed for a Northern, non-country audience, and both took the concert very seriously, designing it to be a microcosm of their rich career. Many of their big hits are here – *The Sweetest Gift, Kentucky, Hills Of Roane County* – but also unusual tunes they thought would appeal to their new audience, such as *The Fox*. The brothers were still in fine form, and the CD makes a good introduction to their work.

29   Step By Step: Lesley Riddle Meets The Carter Family: Blues, Country And Sacred Songs

Lesley Riddle
Rounder CD 0299
Little School Girl/Frisco Blues/Broke And Weary Blues/Hilltop Blues/Mother-less Children/Titanic/I'm Out On The Ocean A-Sailing/I'm Working On A Building/I Know What It Means To be Lonesome/Red River Blues/One Kind Favor/If You See My Savior/The Cannon Ball/Step By Step

Lesley Riddle, from Kingsport, Tennessee, was a gifted African American guitarist and singer who has been best known for his relationship to the original Carter Family. He often stayed and traveled with the Family during their formative years; he influenced both Sara's and Maybelle's guitar styles, taught songs to all the Carters, and helped A.P. collect songs. Unfortunately, he never recorded commercially in his prime, but folk music historian Mike Seeger managed to make field recordings of Riddle between 1965 and 1978. Such tapes comprise this CD, and show that Riddle was still an impressive musician, as well as a vital link between black and white folk music.

30 Sara And Maybelle Carter

Sara and Maybelle Carter
Bear Family BCD 15471 (Ger)
Maybelle and Sara Carter: *Higher Ground/Lonesome Pine Special/The Hand That Rocked The Cradle/Goin' Home/The Ship That Never Returned/Three Little Strangers/Sun Of The Soul/Weary Prodigal Son/While The Band Is Playing Dixie/Farther On/No More Goodbyes/Happiest Days Of All*; Maybelle Carter: *Charlie Brooks/I Told Them What You're Fighting For/We All Miss You, Joe/San Antonio Rose/Mama's Irish Jig/Black Mountain Rag/Let's Be Lovers Again/Give Me Your Love And I'll Give Mine/A Letter From Home/There's A Mother Always Waiting/Tom Cat's Kitten/Kitty Puss*

In 1966, Maybelle Carter's son-in-law Johnny Cash noticed that Sara and Maybelle were in the habit of exchanging tapes and that the two of them were still in fine voice, some 25 years after they had last recorded together. He persuaded his label, Columbia, to record them in a "comeback" album that was called **An Historic Reunion**. With Sara's son Joe filling in for A.P., the pair did a fresh slate of great songs, and produced a swansong appropriate to the Carter legacy. This CD, richly annotated with song histories and photos, supplements the original LP with the contents of a Columbia solo album by Maybelle, **A Living Legend** (1966).

31 Grandpa Jones Live

Grandpa Jones
Sony Music Special Products AK 52416
Fix Me A Pallet/Dooley/The Air, The Sunshine, And The Rain/Castles In The Air/Old Rattler's Pup/My Bonnie Lies Over The Ocean/Rocky Top/I Don't Love Nobody/John Henry/The Last Old Shovel/Southern Bound/Fifteen Cents Is All I Got

Grandpa Jones always felt that his best recording work was done for Fred Foster's Monument label in the 1960s, but very little of that has been reissued on CD. A notable exception is this live album – Grandpa's only one – done in 1969 in Cincinnati with his regular road band and his wife Ramona. The repertoire is a little unusual – none of Pa's signature songs are here – but is is a rare chance to see how one of the giants of traditional country music handles a live show.

32 The Championship Years

Mark O'Connor
Country Music Foundation CMF-015-D
Grey Eagle/Clarinet Polka/Dusty Miller/I Don't Love Nobody/Wednesday Night Waltz/Herman's Rag/Sally Goodwin/Sally Johnson/Yellow Rose Waltz/Tom And Jerry/Billy In The Lowground/Herman's Rag II/Allentown Polka/Brilliancy/Black And White Rag/Tom And Jerry II/Clarinet Polka II/Dill Pickle Rag I/Leather Britches/Don't Let The Deal Go Down/Golden Eagle Hornpipe/I Don't Love Nobody II/Brilliancy II/Tug Boat/Grey Eagle III/Beaumont Rag/Hell Among The Yearlings/Bill Cheatum/Sally Goodwin II/Herman's Rag III/Choctaw/Westphalia Waltz/Black And White Rag II/Herman's Hornpipe/Dill Pickle Rag II/Sally Ann/Clarinet Polka III/Arkansas Traveller/Jesse Polka

One of the most respected and busiest Nashville session fiddlers of the late 1980s, Mark O'Connor won his initial fame as a teenager who dominated the fiddle contest circuit in the years from 1975 to 1984. His interest in old-time fiddling and its repertoire waned somewhat in later years, but fans kept asking him to record some of his "contest favorites." To answer this, he compiled this collection of live contest performances from his earlier years at the National Old Time Fiddler's Contest at Weiser, Idaho. O'Connor was only 13 when he recorded the first seven tunes heard here, and was 20 when he did the last eight in 1985. Different versions of some tunes let us trace how the fiddler's own style was developing, and the overall package is a great introduction to the world of contest fiddling and how this particular facet of old-time music is still preserved today.

33 Cadillac Rag

John Hartford and Mark Howard: The Hartford String Band
Small Dog A-Barkin' SD-191CD
All American Rodeo Reel/Cadillac Rag/Time To Get Together/Old John Hartford's Walkaround/Alaskan Hornpipe/Stones River/Nickajacks Lament/Rose Of Gilroy/Boy Unloading Crossties/Fritz Waltz

Though best known to mainstream country fans for his bluegrass work and for his classic *Gentle On My Mind*, John Hartford has for years had a passion for early string band and fiddle music. His own extensive research into the printed fiddle tune book tradition is the inspiration for this set of original instrumentals. Hartford himself does the banjo parts, with friends like John Yudkin, Buddy Spicher, and Ted Masden helping out on fiddle. The result is a slickly produced, occasionally overdubbed, and thoroughly engrossing project to inject new life in a century-old musical style.

34 Rambler

The Red Clay Ramblers
Sugar Hill SH-CD-3798
Cotton-Eyed Joe/Cajun Billy/Black Smoke Train/Saro Janes/Annie Oakley/ Queen of Skye/Ninety And Nine/Mile Long Medley/Darlin' Say – Pony Cart/ Hiawatha's Lullabye/What Does the Deep Sea Say/Ryan's – Jordan Reel/ Barbeque/One Rose – Hot Buttered Rum/Polkas

One of the few old time "revivalist" bands that survived into the 1990s, and arguably the best, the Red Clay Ramblers show here just how well they combine originality and tradition. The songs come from sources as diverse as Uncle Dave Macon, the Carter Family, 1920s Tin Pan Alley, nineteenth-century fiddle tune books, polkas, Irish fiddle tunes, and old gospel song books. Band founder Tommy Thompson's banjo and vocals, as well as those of Jack Herrick, continue to spark the group and carry their music to new generations.

35 Songs Of The Civil War

Various Artists
Columbia CK 48607
Jay Unger: *Ashokan Farewell*; Sweet Honey in the Rock: *No More Auction Block For Me*; Ronnie Gilbert: *Lincoln And Liberty*; United States Military Academy Band: *Dixie*; Kathy Mattea: *The Southern Soldier Boy*; John

Hartford: *Aura Lee*; Waylon Jennings: *Rebel Soldier*; Ritchie Havens: *Follow The Drinking Gourd*; Judy Collins: *Battle Hymn Of The Republic*; United States Military Academy Band: *When Johnny Comes Marching Home*; Kate and Anna McGarrigle: *Was My Brother In The Battle*; Hoyt Axton: *The Yellow Rose Of Texas*; Sweet Honey in the Rock: *Run, Mourner, Run*; Richie Havens: *Give Us A Flag*; John Hartford: *The Secesh (Shiloh)*; Kathy Mattea: *Somebody's Darling*; Waylon Jennings: *An Old Unreconstructed*; Kathy Mattea: *Vacant Chair*; Kate and Anna McGarrigle with Rufus Wainwright: *Better Times Are Coming*; John Hartford: *Lorena*; Jay Unger and Molly Mason with Fiddle Fever: *Marching Through Georgia*; Kate and Anna McGarrigle and Families: *Hard Times Come Again No More*; Hoyt Axton: *Oh I'm A Good Old Rebel*; Ronnie Gilbert: *When Johnny Comes Marching Home*; Staff Sgt Steve Luck: *Taps*

The music of the Civil War era included a number of popular and traditional songs that had an effect on country music's development. This chapter of country's prehistory has been partially documented in this appealing re-creation produced in part by Ken Burns, who was responsible for the famed PBS television series on the War. Waylon Jennings, John Hartford, Kathy Mattea, Hoyt Axton, along with folksingers Judy Collins, Ronnie Gilbert (formerly of the Weavers), and Richie Havens, are among the singers offering readings of some two dozen 1860s hits. While there has been an attempt to stick to an authentic "acoustic" style – at least there are no steel guitars or electric basses – the performances are in some cases heavily stylized and modern-sounding. The result is a collection that is interesting, if not especially historically enlightening.

36 Dancing Home

Stephen Wade

Flying Fish FF 70543

Lost Gander/John Greer's Two-Step/Money Musk And White Cockade/ Snowdrop/Davy Davy/Pig Ankle Rag/Georgia Buck And Cluckin' Hen/ Shooting Creek/Rye Straw/Buckdancer's Choice And Needlecase/Old Joe/ Mulberry Gap/Baptist Shout/Drunken Waggoner/Rockhouse Joe/Pateroller/ Reuben Was An All-Around Man/Spanish Fandango

A native of Chicago, and a pupil of veteran old-time masters Fleming Brown and Doc Hopkins, Stephen Wade made his reputation not on the bluegrass or festival stage, but as the writer and star of a wildly successful one-man theatrical show called "Banjo Dancing." In his spare time, Wade traveled around the South interviewing and studying with the last generation of banjo players who had learned their craft before the advent of radio and records. In this album, Wade presents sparkling interpretations of tunes he learned from people like Sam and Kirk McGee (early Opry stars), Frank Profitt, Frank Jenkins (an early Galax area recording star), Fleming Brown, and ballad singer Dee Hicks. Fully annotated and lovingly recorded, this album is a superb introduction to pre-bluegrass banjo styles.

37 In The Land Of Melody

Wade and Julia Mainer

June Appal JA 0065D

Ramshackle Shack/Be Kind To A Man When He's Down/Bring Back My Mountain Boy To Me/ Hobo's Waltz/ Royal Telephone/Charles Lawson/Trick-

ling Water/The Land I Love (Away Down Yonder)/Down By The Railroad Tracks/Sugar In The Gourd/Down At The End Of Memory Land/How Sweet To Walk/You Will Never Miss Your Mother Until She's Gone/Cider Mill/The Girl I Left In Sunny Tennessee/Peg And Awl/Jonah/When It's Time For The Whippoorwill To Sing/I Can't Sit Down

North Carolina banjoist and singer Wade Mainer was, along with his brother J.E., one of the most prolific recording acts of the 1930s. About 1953, though, he retired from music and went to work for General Motors in Michigan, feeling his older mountain style of music was obsolete. In the 1970s he retired from GM, and began to gradually re-enter the music scene, working with his wife Julia, who had been a radio singer when they first met back in the 1930s. This CD is their first digital recording, and is an engrossing mixture of old novelty songs, instrumentals, sentimental favorites like *Be Kind To A Man When He's Down*, and original pieces like *How Sweet To Walk*. The Mainers resist the temptation to do remakes of Wade's greatest hits, and prove themselves to still be dynamic artists. A thick booklet of annotations serves as a capstone to the project.

38 Shady Grove: Traditional Appalachian Banjo Player

Morgan Sexton
June Appal JA 0066D
Cumberland Gap/Little Birdie/Lonesome Scene Of Winter/Jenny Get Around/ Little Bessie/John Henry/Old East Virginia/Goin' Down In Town/London City Where I Did Dwell/Old Grey Beard/Pretty Little Miss In The Garden/I Want Some Liquor/Making Moonshine (story)/ Little Brown Jug/Rocky Island/Sugar Baby/Froggy Went A-Courtin'/It's A Beautiful Doll/Little Frankie/The Last Of Callahan/Omie Wise/Mexico/Old Aunt Jenny/Little Sparrow/Hook And Line/Shady Grove

One of the best current selections of basic, authentic mountain music, played by 77-year-old Morgan Sexton, described as "one of the best-kept secrets in the music business." In his stately, archaic style borne of his family tradition in southeastern Kentucky, Morgan sings 26 ballads and songs that date from the age before Appalachian music had been exposed to radio, records, and vaudeville. Like most traditional musicians, Morgan spent most of his life working: timbering, coal mining, farming. The repertoire heard here, drawn from an early LP called **Rock Dust** and from newer recordings, is not all that rare, but the singer's style is powerful and effective, and represents one of our deepest looks yet at country music's roots. His nephew Lee Sexton accompanies him occasionally on fiddle. A thick booklet of liner notes gives full song texts and biographical information on the singer. Morgan Sexton died in 1992, a year after being awarded a prestigious National Endowment Fellowship for his work in preserving the old music.

39 Fresh Old-Time String Band Music

Mike Seeger, with Various Artists
Rounder CD 0262
Boatman/Mabel/Black Jack Davey/Billy in Waynesboro/Poor Black Sheep/East Tennessee Blues And Goin' Crazy/Ten Broeck And Mollie/Cotton-Eyed Joe/ Pork Fat Makes My Chicken Tan/Wagnerd/Wedding Waltz

An anthology of new recordings designed, in the words of project leader Seeger, to explore "alternative ways that [old-time string band music] might have been played or ways that it still might be developed without losing its country feel or spontaneity." The result was a new collection of fresh and unusual arrangements of traditional Southern songs played by unusual instruments like a gut-string nineteenth-century banjo, a tin whistle, a cello, a "mando quartet," a fretless banjo, and others. Participants include the cream of modern old-time musicians: Norman and Nancy Blake, James Bryan, Alan Jabbour, Kirk Sutphin, as well as two creative young bands, the Agents of Terra, and the Horseflies.

40   The Norman And Nancy Blake Compact Disc

Norman and Nancy Blake

Rounder CD 0211

Hello Stranger/New Bicycle Hornpipe/Marquis Of Huntley/Florida Rag/Jordan Am A Hard Road To Travel/Belize/Elzic's Farewell/Lighthouse On The Shore/ Grand Junction/Butterfly Weed/President Garfield's Hornpipe/In Russia (We Have Parking Lots, Too)/Wroxall/If I Lose, I Don't Care/The Chrysanthemum/Lima Road Jig/Boston Boy And Last Night's Joy/My Love Is Like A Red, Red Rose/Peacock's Feather/Wildwood Flower/Tennessee Mountain Fox Chase

The music of Norman and Nancy Blake has always been hard to classify; for a time he was a versatile session musician for Johnny Cash, and later did some influential bluegrass albums with Tony Rice. In more recent years he has applied his unique guitar style and earnest vocalizing to a series of recordings in which he celebrates old-time music and creates new original pieces in that style. His wife Nancy is best known for her cello and mandolin work and original tunes like *Belize* and *New Bicycle Hornpipe*. This CD is drawn from two earlier LPs, Norman's **Lighthouse On The Shore** and Nancy's **Grand Junction**, and also features the fiddle of James Bryan, arguably the best young traditional fiddler working today. It is a fine introduction to the distinctive Blake style of acoustic music; it reinvents Uncle Dave Macon, the Carters, and a host of lesser lights.

41   Old-Time Duets

The Whitstein Brothers

Rounder CD 0264

Mansion On The Hill/We Parted By The Riverside/There's An Open Door Waiting/Sinner, You'd Better Get Ready/We Met In The Saddle/I'm Troubled/ That Silver-Haired Daddy Of Mine/Seven Year Blues/Weary Lonesome Blues/ Somewhere In Tennessee/Maple On The Hill/If I Could Hear My Mother Pray Again/Pitfall/Beautiful Lost River Valley

Charles and Robert Whitstein, from central Louisiana, became the best-known exemplars of the classic duet tradition in the 1980s and 1990s. Though the brothers had been active in country music for a couple of decades (and though Charles has worked with Charlie Louvin, doing Ira's part), it took a series of Rounder albums in the eighties to establish their credentials as the natural heirs to the Louvins' music. In this album, they pay tribute to these roots; armed with just a mandolin and guitar (the classic style), they revive songs originally done by the Louvins (*Seven Year Blues*), the Delmores (*Weary Lonesome Blues*), and the Blue Sky Boys (*I'm Troubled*). The result is a heartfelt and moving acknowledgement of the staying power of classic country harmony.

42   Grandfather's Greatest Hits

David Holt

High Windy HW 1251

John Henry (with Duane Eddy)/*Fire On The Mountain*/*Wabash Cannonball*/ *Little Log Cabin In The Lane* (with Doc Watson)/*Pretty Polly* (with Mark O'Connor)/*Corrina*/*Bound to Ride*/*Cripple Creek*/*Old-Time Medley* (with Mark O'Connor)/*Wreck Of The Old '97*/*Wildwood Flower*/*Dixie*

Known for his work on the Nashville Network's "Fire on the Mountain" and "American Music Shop" television shows, David Holt emerged in the 1980s as one of the most personable young performers in the old-time vein. His dedication to veteran traditional performers has given him strong links with the past, and his considerable talents as a singer and banjoist have made him one of the best interpreters of 1920s and 1930s music. This album, comprised of most of the most popular old-time country hits, showcases Holt in company with the likes of Doc Watson, Mark O'Connor, and Jerry Douglas, as well as Chet Atkins and Duane Eddy. The mixture garnered Holt a Grammy nomination for Best Traditional Album.

43   My Carolina Home

Laura Boosinger

Upstream UP 888

When The Roses Bloom In Dixieland/*Sweet Sunny South*/*Grandfather's Clock*/*I Will Arise*/*Under The Weeping Willow Tree*/*What'll We Do With The Baby-O*/*Free Little Bird*/*Over the Mountain*/*Wondrous Love*/*Pretty Little Miss Out In the Garden*/*Are You Tired Of Me, My Darlin'*/*My Carolina Home – Carolina Moon*

Widely known for her concerts and workshops, North Carolina singer and instrumentalist Laura Boosinger has emerged in the 1990s as one of the best interpreters of folk and early country music. She often worked (and still works) with the Nashville Network TV star David Holt and veteran string bandleader Luke Smathers, and her high, clear voice has been described as quintessential mountain singing by bluegrass star Red Rector. This debut CD features backing by Holt, as well as Raymond McLain and others; the repertoire is drawn from the Carter Family, Uncle Dave Macon, Bascom Lamar Lunsford, Cousin Emmy, and others. Highlights include what is the definitive modern reading of *When The Roses Bloom In Dixieland*.

44   My Dear Old Southern Home

Doc Watson

Sugar Hill SH-CD-3795

My Dear Old Southern Home/*The Ship That Never Returned*/*Your Long Journey*/*My Friend Jim*/*No Telephone In Heaven*/*Dream Of The Miner's Child*/*Wreck Of The Number Nine*/*Grandfather's Clock*/*Don't Say Goodbye If You Love Me*/*Sleep, Baby, Sleep*/*Signal Light*/*That Silver-Haired Daddy Of Mine*/*Life Is Like A River*

This 1992 album spotlights Doc's warm, lazy vocal style, and features a baker's dozen of the kind of old-time country songs he grew up with. Sources include the obvious – Jimmie Rodgers, the Carter Family – but also sources like Blind Andy Jenkins (*Dream Of The Miner's Child*), Carson J. Robison

(*Wreck Of The Number Nine*), the Delmore Brothers (*My Friend Jim*), Grayson and Whitter (*Signal Light*), and Bonnie Dodd (*Don't Say Goodbye If You Love Me*). Accompanied by regular companion Jack Lawrence, as well as crack Nashville men like Jerry Douglas, Sam Bush, Stuart Duncan, and Nashville Bluegrass Band member Alan O'Bryant, Doc does these old chestnuts proud.

Honky-Tonk

Nick Tosches

H*onky-tonk*: a strange phrase, an etymological riddle that seems to have originated in the Red River region of northern Texas and southern Oklahoma. The earliest-known instance of it is traced to the town of Ardmore, the seat of Carter County, Oklahoma, about 20 miles north of the Red River and about a hundred miles north of Fort Worth. On Saturday, February 24, 1891, Ardmore's little newspaper, *The Daily Ardmorite*, reported on its front page that "the honk-a-tonk last night was well attended by ball-heads, bachelors and leading citizens." The strange phrase eventually spread to become a living part of the American language. By 1916, it had entered the parlance of Tin Pan Alley songwriters; by 1927, the poet Carl Sandburg used it. In 33 years, the odd phrase had traveled from obscure, little Ardmore to Tin Pan Alley and Pulitzer Prize territory in the big city.

The phrase entered country music in 1936, with Al Dexter's Vocalion recording of *Honky Tonk Blues*. Ironically, Dexter (1902–84) later claimed that he had never heard the term until that year.

"One day I went to see Paris," he told me, referring to his friend and fellow songwriter James B. Paris. "He said, 'I thought of a title last night that'll set the woods on fire.' I asked him what it was, and he said, *Honky Tonk Blues*. I asked him where he got that idea. I never heard the word, so I said, 'What is a honky-tonk?' So he said, 'These beer joints up and down the road where the girls jump in cars and so on.' I said, 'I never thought about it like that.' He said, 'Use your thinker-upper and let's write a song like that.' "

Without ever referring to it as such, Dexter himself had owned and operated a Texas honky-tonk, the Round-up Club, since the early 1930s. He had always called it a tavern. As for Paris's brainstorm, it came a year after Pat Shelton copyrighted

Honky Tonk Blues, seven years after Hunkie Smith came up with *Hunkie Tunkie Blues*. But those were not country songs. In any case, it was Al Dexter's *Honky Tonk Blues* that marked the true beginning of country music's honky-tonk fever. Considering Dexter's historical importance, and the fact that he subsequently had the best-selling country hit of the 1940s (*Pistol-Packin' Mama*), it is vexing that he is so poorly represented amid the reissues of today.

The first country honky-tonk songs, like the earlier pop and jazz songs that appropriated the phrase, were upbeat and trifling. But it was not long before the term came to describe a whole new strain of music. From a mere lyrical catch-phrase, "honky-tonk" came to denote a spirit of the times, a state of mind, and the music that reflected that spirit and state. Eventually, honky-tonk would recast the nature of country music itself.

The upbeat, trifling aspect of honky-tonk, exemplified by songs that, like Dexter's, were whimsical celebrations of drinking, dancing, and good-time payday nights, intensified into a quality of deeper and wilder abandon. And, with that increasing sense of abandon, there came a darker side of guilt and remorse, world-weariness and despair. That is what honky-tonk came to be: a genre of country – and, at first, distinctly Texan – music that both celebrated the wild side of life and lamented its wages; howls of abandon and laments of anguish sharing a sound that grew ever bolder, louder, more electric, and urbane.

The years of World War II were the years of its growth and development. And while honky-tonk essentially would remain a music of sin and guilt, a sort of danceable neon psychomachia of inner demons and open revelry, it also reflected the vaster wartime mood of conflicting fears and hopes, fatalism and estrangement, of days of prosperity that were days without a future as well; and its sound reflected the new hard-edged tensions of the increasing drift during those years from rural to urban, from agrarian to industrial life in the South.

Essential Recordings

(i) Born To Lose

The amplified steel guitar, which came to define the honky-tonk sound, had been introduced two years before Dexter's *Honky Tonk Blues*. Bob Dunn, country music's first electric steel guitarist, had joined Milton Brown and his Musical Brownies, the Fort Worth-based western swing band, late in 1934, soon after Rickenbacker began experimenting with electromagnetic guitar pickups. From January, 1935, when he made his first recordings with the group, through March, 1936, the month preceding Milton Brown's untimely death, Dunn's inventive brilliance had made the Brownies the most musically fascinating of the western swing bands and a distinct antecedent of honky-tonk things to come.

On the Brownies' last 50 Decca recordings, made that March, in New Orleans, the band was joined by a second fiddler, a 20-year-old Texan named Cliff Bruner. After Brown's death, Bruner, based in Houston, formed his own band, Cliff Bruner's Texas Wanderers, whose music was broadcast from the Rice Hotel by KTRH. Lusty, capricious, raucous, and reflecting the sophisticated influence of western swing, Bruner's music embodied the evolving style and sensibilities of honky-tonk.

In February, 1937, in San Antonio, Bruner's band, which included pianist Papa Calhoun of the Brownies, made the first of many recordings, for Decca. The evolution of Bruner's wonderful music over the years 1937–41 is documented in **Cliff Bruner's Texas Wanderers**. The group featured electric instruments: the amplified mandola of Leo Raley, the amplified steel guitar of J.D. Standlee. By 1938, Calhoun had been replaced by 29-year-old Moon Mullican, from Corrigan, Texas, north of Beaumont. A songwriter and singer as well as a pianist, Mullican was the author of *Can't Nobody Truck Like Me*, one of the songs that Bruner's Texas Wanderers had recorded at their first session. As Bruner told me, "Moon developed his own, he used to call it 'three-finger' style. And he didn't play very good when I hired him, but he developed into a fine piano man, terrific showman."

On September 13, 1938, Bob Dunn, replacing Standlee, traveled with Bruner, Mullican, and the others to San Antonio for the group's third session. At that session, the band recorded the first great honky-tonk classic, *It Makes No Difference Now*.

The song was written by 23-year-old Floyd Tillman. Born in Oklahoma, raised in Texas, Tillman played guitar and sang with Leon Selph's Blue Ridge Playboys, another seminal Houston band, whose membership had also included Moon Mullican. Soon after Bruner's Texas Wanderers recorded his song, Tillman sold it outright, for $300, to the singer Jimmie Davis, who recorded it that November. (Davis, born in Jackson Parish, Louisiana, in 1902, had been recording since 1929. A purveyor of lewd songs and an accomplished blue-yodeler in the Jimmie Rodgers vein, Davis, since 1934, had shown a growing affinity to the gathering spirit of honky-tonk.) As sung by Bruner's guitarist, Dickie McBride, *It Makes No Difference Now* was a stark, simple masterpiece, a song of surrender to somber, baneful fate. On March 25, 1939, when *Billboard* published its first list of best-selling hillbilly records, *It Makes No Difference Now* by Cliff Bruner's Texas Wanderers held the number 1 position. It was an immense hit. Jimmie Davis's cover version also became a bestseller. Eventually, Bing Crosby recorded the song, and there was even a Cajun version, *Ça Tait Pas Difference Asteur*, by the Sons of Acadians. Above all, it marked the dawn of honky-tonk's golden age. That Bruner's recording of *It Makes No Difference Now* is not available on any modern collection says much about the dire state of historical country music reissues compared to those of blues, jazz, and rock-and-roll.

Houston was the music's breeding-ground. Bruner's group (which, by the summer of 1939, often went by the more prosaic name of Cliff Bruner and his Boys) was by far the most successful of the Houston bands. But the others, such as the Blue Ridge Playboys, were no less intriguing; and, throughout the late 1930s and early 1940s, there was continuous interplay and synergy among them. The activities of a single day, September 5, 1939, at the Decca recording studio at the Rice Hotel in Houston, give an idea of the intensity of this musical interaction:

Earlier in the year, Floyd Tillman had recorded as a member of Leon Selph's Blue Ridge Playboys. Following the success of his song *It Makes No Difference Now*, Tillman had left the Blue Ridge Playboys and begun recording under his own name. At his first session, on August 29, he had been backed by members of Cliff Bruner's band, including Bruner, Mullican, and Bob Dunn. Now, on September 5, just a few days later, both Mullican and Dunn, while remaining with Bruner, recorded as members of Selph's Blue Ridge Playboys. On that same day, Dunn and Mullican also recorded under the name of Dunn's own spin-off group, Bob Dunn's Vagabonds, which was basically Bruner's band without Bruner and the guitarist–singer Dickie McBride. On that same day again, Dickie McBride also recorded under his own name, accompanied by Cliff Bruner's Texas Wanderers.

Recordings Tillman made with the Blue Ridge Playboys, Cliff Bruner, Bob Dunn, and Moon Mullican can be heard on the Country Music "Hall Of Fame" collection **Floyd Tillman**. Unfortunately, MCA, which owns many of the greatest honky-tonk recordings, has not undertaken even the most cursory reissue of the works of Cliff Bruner and others. A reissue of the September 5, 1939, sessions alone would be welcome.

Throughout 1939–41, Bruner, Dunn, Mullican, and other Wanderers also recorded with Buddy Jones (1906–56), a Shreveport, Louisiana, police officer who was certainly one of

honky-tonk's most captivating characters. Again, MCA itself
has neglected to reissue any of its wealth of Jones recordings;
but we do have the obscure **Louisiana's Honky Tonk Man:
Buddy Jones**.

It was as a singing partner of Jimmie Davis, a fellow emana-
tion of the wondrous Louisiana political machine, that Jones
made his first Decca recordings, in 1935. Eighteen months
later, he began recording under his own name, with his brother
Buster on steel guitar and Cliff Bruner's bass player, Hezzie
Bryant. Beginning in 1939, Dunn accompanied him more often
than Buster. The titles of Jones's songs are indicative of the
sort of honky-tonk he pioneered: *Butcher Man Blues* (1937),
Streamlined Mama (1937), *Evil Stingaree* (1937), *She's Sellin'
What She Used To Give Away* (1938), *Easy-Rollin' Sue* (1938),
and *Rockin' Rollin' Mama* (1939). There had always been
risqué songs in country music. In his blues-inflected Victor
recordings of the early 1930s, Jimmie Davis, following the lead
of Jimmie Rodgers's few recordings in this vein, had been, like
Cliff Carlisle and others, a notable precursor of Jones in this
respect. In fact, after leaving Victor for Decca, in 1934, Davis
had distinguished himself as a consummate honky-tonk singer
with a decidedly lascivious bent. His *Jellyroll Blues* (1934),
High-Geared Mama (1936; with yodeling by Jones), *High-
Geared Daddy* (1937), and *Honky Tonk Blues* (1937) were
representative of the music Davis made before forsaking honky-
tonk for more mundane and gentler fare, and eventually riding
the song *You Are My Sunshine* to gubernatorial victory in
Louisiana. Jones's salacious songs, however, were imbued with
the full spirit of honky-tonk, raunchy and nasty as a back-alley
rollick. According to Bruner, Jones in reality was a "very clean-
cut" and quiet man who neither drank nor smoked.

In addition to Floyd Tillman and Moon Mullican, the Blue
Ridge Playboys of 1934 had featured the 22-year-old steel
guitarist Ted Daffan. Born in Beauregarde Parish, Louisiana,
raised in Houston, Daffan, a disciple of Bob Dunn, had
performed on KTRH with a steel guitar group called the Blue
Hawaiians, in 1933. Two years later, after leaving the Blue
Ridge Playboys, he joined another Houston band, the Bar-X
Cowboys. By then, he was playing a Volutone-model amplified
steel guitar, which he used when he first recorded with the Bar-
X Cowboys, for Bluebird, in February, 1940. By his own reck-
oning, Daffan's artistry fell far short of Dunn's. "I admired his
steel-playing terrifically, but I could never duplicate it," he told
me. "He had a very individualist style, and I never even tried.
I stuck mostly to straight lead. He played a very sophisticated
jazz steel." Indeed, it was as a songwriter rather than as a
musician that Daffan made his mark. Like his fellow Blue

Ridge Playboys alumnus Floyd Tillman, Daffan wrote a song that proved successful for Bruner's band: *Truck Driver's Blues*, recorded by Bruner in August, 1939 (and included on the Texas Wanderers album).

The song was a big enough hit to attract the attention of producer Art Satherly of Columbia and OKeh Records. Forming his own five-piece group, Ted Daffan's Texans, he began recording for Satherly in April, 1940. The following year, he wrote *Born to Lose*, the song that would prove to be his fame and fortune. Perhaps the darkest song of a dark genre, the source of its inspiration was something Daffan would never reveal. "That one has to remain my secret," he told me. He did explain, however, why the song bore the pseudonym of Frankie Brown:

> Brown was my mother's maiden name. The reason for that, I did 24 sides in January of '42 for Columbia. We knew my band was breaking up and we would be going in the service, and Columbia wanted a huge number of sides. I wrote 24 songs and recorded 'em. Mr. Satherly said, "Ted, we wouldn't take 24 sides at one time from Irving Berlin. How about puttin' a pen-name on some of 'em?" So we did half of 'em under a pen name, and the first two out were both million sellers, *No Letter Today* and *Born To Lose*. So we threw the pen-name away on the rest of 'em.

Due to the wartime requisitioning of Columbia's resources and facilities, both recordings, coupled as one OKeh release, were not issued until the spring of 1943. Both became immense hits, but it was *Born To Lose*, as sung by Daffan's vocalist Leon Seago, that captured America, expressing both the essence of the honky-tonk credo and, as the new year came, the darkening mood of the country's most ominous wartime hours. **Born To Lose** contains the best of Daffan's work, 1942–8.

The only hit of 1943–4 that outsold *Born To Lose* was another Okeh release, *Pistol-Packin' Mama*, written and recorded by Al Dexter and his Troopers. Dexter's song, the commercial apotheosis of honky-tonk's lighter side, became the first country hit to be performed on "Your Hit Parade," the weekly presentation of America's most popular songs. (When the show's troupe performed Dexter's song, the word "beer" was censored from the lyrics.) In addition to being an immense country hit, the song, in the summer of 1943, crossed over to become a number 1 hit on the *Billboard* pop charts, and that fall, crossed over to the "Harlem Hit Parade," *Billboard*'s early black-music chart.

In 1945, Ted Daffan brought dark and light together in *Headin' Down The Wrong Highway*, a striking foreshadowing of the ambivalent and ambiguous nature of the post-war honky-tonk spirit: a song of wretchedness and alcoholic despair that was altogether swinging, altogether danceable.

Floyd Tillman's first hit, *They Took The Stars Out Of Heaven* (included on the "Hall Of Fame" collection), was also a victim of wartime postponement, recorded in 1941 but unreleased until 1943. When it eventually did appear on the charts, in January, 1944, it rose to number one. With the success of Daffan, Dexter, and Tillman, honky-tonk in the post-war years became the domain of singers rather than bands. The hard, electrified Texas sound pioneered by Bruner, Dunn, and the others could still be heard, but now the singer stepped to center-stage. Daffan used vocalists other than himself, and Dexter at best was a lackluster singer. Likely that is why they faded fast from glory. Tillman, however, had an odd but interesting voice, and he continued to produce hits after leaving Decca for Columbia: *Drivin' Nails In My Coffin* (1946), an upbeat song about alcoholic suicide that had been written and first recorded by Jerry Irby, another former Texas Wanderer; *I Love You So Much It Hurts* (1948); and his classic cheating-song, *Slippin' Around* (1949).

Discographical Details

45 Cliff Bruner's Texas Wanderers

Cliff Bruner's Texas Wanderers
Texas Rose TXR-2710 (LP)
I Saw Your Face On The Moon/Truck Driver's Blues/I'll Keep On Loving You/Tequila Rag/Bringin' Home The Bacon/Don't Make Me Blue/I'm Tired Of You/Draft Board Blues/One Sweet Letter From You/New Falling Rain Blues/Beaumont Rag/I'll Try Not To Cry/Sittin' On The Moon/Truckin' On Down/Milk Cow Blues/Peggy Lou

46 Floyd Tillman: Country Music Hall Of Fame

Floyd Tillman
MCA MCAD-10189
A Precious Memory/Why Do I Love You/I'm Always Dreaming Of You/Don't Be Blue/Maybe I'll Get By Without You/I'd Settle Down For You/I'll Come Back To You/Daisy May/It's Been A Long Long Time/I've Learned My Lesson Now/Rio Grande/They Took The Stars Out of Heaven/Why Do You Treat Me This Way/There's No Use To Try It Anymore/Dreams Won't Let Me Forget You/Each Night At Nine

47 Louisiana's Honky Tonk Man: Buddy Jones

Buddy Jones
Texas Rose TXR-2711 (LP)
Don't Ever Leave Me Alone/Shreveport County Jail Blues/I'll Get Mine Bye And Bye No. 2/Settle Down Blues/She's A Hum-Dum Dinger/Ease My

Troubled Mind/Oklahoma City Blues/Ragged But Right/I'm Going To Get Me A Honky Tonky Baby/Butcher Man Blues/She's Sellin' What She Used To Give Away/Dear Old Sunny South By The Sea/Red River Blues/Carry The Good Work On/Mean Old Sixty-Five Blues/You've Got Just What It Takes

48 Born To Lose

Ted Daffan and his Texans

Cowgirlboy LP 5051 (Ger) (LP)

Born To Lose/No Letter Today/Shut That Gate/Broken Vows/Look Who's Talkin'/Bluest Blues/Poor Little Bar Fly/Go On, Go On/Trouble Keeps Hangin' Round My Door/Beyond The Shadow Of A Doubt/You Better Change Your Ways/Baby, You Can't Get Me Down/Two Of A Kind/Just Born That Way/Time Won't Heal My Broken Heart/You're Breaking My Heart

(ii) Drivin' Nails In My Coffin

By 1950, Tillman's star too was on the descent. It was another honky-tonk singer, one whose success predated his, who enjoyed the longest career of them all.

Ernest Tubb was born on a farm near Crisp, Texas, about 40 miles south of Dallas, on February 9, 1914. When he was 12, his parents separated, and, in the years that followed, work took precedence over schooling. Later in life, it was not uncommon for him to read a dozen or more books a month, but, back then, it was all labor: "I had a lot of jobs and I hated them all." After traveling from relative to relative to live, he ended up on a road crew near Benjamin, in 1933. After that, there was W.P.A. construction work around San Antonio, and then jobs with several beer-distributors in San Angelo and Corpus Christi. He was still working for the outfit in Corpus Christi – Southern Brewing, owned by Howard Hughes – when it went out of business, in 1939. By then, he had a wife named Lois Elaine, a son named Justin (a second son, Rodger Dale, had been killed the year before in a car wreck, at the age of seven weeks), and – though few outside and not many more within Texas seemed to know it – he had a recording career as well.

His idol had always been Jimmie Rodgers, who had died in the spring of 1933, when Tubb was 19. By 1935, in addition to his W.P.A. work, Tubb had a 15-minute show at KONO, a small radio station in San Antonio. Realizing that Rodgers had been a citizen of San Antonio at the time of his death, he opened the city directory and found the telephone number of Rodgers's widow, Carrie. He called, was invited to visit, and, two months later, received a call in return.

Carrie Rodgers arranged Tubb's first recording session, with her late husband's company, Victor, at the Texas Hotel in San Antonio, in October, 1936. Tubb recorded two maudlin tributes to Rodgers, written by Carrie's sister, Elsie McWilliams, and four songs written and sung by Tubb in the manner of his idol. For a while, Tubb dwelled in the shadow of Jimmie Rodgers. Carrie had loaned him Rodgers's custom-made Martin guitar, and the labels of those first records bore, beneath Tubb's name, the legend "Singing and yodeling with accomp. played on Jimmie Rodgers' own guitar." For his first photo session, he wore one of his dead idol's tuxedos. The pants did not fit, and later Mrs Rodgers bought him a new pair. The whole matter had about it the scent of the macabre: the widow trying to breathe life into the ghost of her husband, and the ghost's protégé seeking to inhale that spectral life.

But the ghost music did not sell. Victor lost interest, and it took Carrie and Tubb three years to get another deal. He began recording, for Decca, at the Rice Hotel in Houston, in April, 1940, sharing the day with one of the Texas Wanderers' sessions. His first Decca release did what his Victor records had not done – it sold. Something had happened: Tubb had begun to discover his own voice. Instead of continuing to emulate the style of his idol, he had begun to express, in his own natural way, the sensibilities he had absorbed from Rodgers. At the same time, he had become aware of the new barroom music called honky-tonk that was thriving around him. He was on his way to empowering country music and recasting honky-tonk with his own newfound voice.

Decca released his *Walking The Floor Over You* in the summer of 1941. With its sparse backing of electric lead guitar, bass, and Tubb's own rhythm guitar, it was the anthem that every honky-tonk had unknowingly been waiting for. It crossed to the pop market, and eventually sold more than a million copies. Though he wrote and recorded a song that fall called *I Ain't Goin' Honky Tonkin' No More*, Tubb continued to be the apotheosis of honky-tonk throughout the decade. The best of his work – such as *Wasting My Life Away* (1941), *Tomorrow Never Comes* (1944), *Drivin' Nails In My Coffin* (1946), his version of Rodgers's *Waiting For A Train* (1947), *Warm Red Wine* (1949), and others, commercial hits and misses alike – became the classic, nickel-a-play corpus of honky-tonk.

Tubb continued to produce hits through the 1950s and, decreasingly, into the 1960s. His marriage fell apart at the height of his glory; he married again, in 1949. His emphysema worsened, and he quit smoking. Then everything worsened, and he quit drinking. But still he stood there and grinned and sang his songs, as noble and endearing a figure in his later years as country music has ever been fortunate enough to claim as its own. In 1975, after 35 years with Decca (by then it was MCA), he was cast aside. He made a few records for small Nashville labels. His last session was held in August, 1982. Johnny

Walker of Atlas Artists, Tubb's booking agency, recalled that, like his idol, Jimmie Rodgers, Tubb sang his final song lying, sick and in pain, on a cot. He died two years later, on September 6, 1984. Today, **Ernest Tubb** offers the finest single-disc overview of a long and unflagging career.

Discographical Details

49 Ernest Tubb: Country Music Hall Of Fame

Ernest Tubb
MCA MCAD-10086
Walking The Floor Over You/Our Baby's Book/You Nearly Lose Your Mind/ Tomorrow Never Comes/Soldier's Last Letter/It's Been So Long, Darling/ Seaman's Blues/Forever Is Ending Today/Have You Ever Been Lonely (Have You Ever Been Blue)/Letters Have No Arms/Throw Your Love My Way/ Fortunes In Memories/Love Lifted Me/Two Glasses, Joe/Thanks A Lot/Waltz Across Texas

(iii) Honky Tonkin'

Though honky-tonk might seem to have been exclusively the dominion of Texans, Hank Williams, who was perhaps the greatest, certainly the most legendary, honky-tonk singer, was from Alabama. He was born there, near the railroad town of Georgiana, on September 17, 1923. Farther north, in Montgomery, he began performing at radio station WSFA, in 1936, when he was barely 13. He was still working there ten years later, in the fall of 1946, when he journeyed to Nashville and met Fred Rose. It was Rose, a Tin Pan Alley veteran and publishing partner of Roy Acuff, who set up Williams's first session, in December of that year, at WSM Studio D in Nashville. Rose sold the recordings to Sterling, the new subsidiary of Al Middleman's year-old Juke Box Record Company, located in New York. The Sterling records were good, but they did not sell. The last of them, *Honky Tonkin'*, recorded in February, 1947, proclaimed Williams's allegiance to the sound that was in the air.

In the early spring of 1947, Williams signed with the newly formed MGM label. His first MGM release, *Move It On Over*, was issued in May, and by midsummer, it was high on the charts. It was a raucous, raw-swinging piece of backwoods jitterbug jive, a record whose spirit, lyrics, sultry rhythms, and electric-guitar break presaged the importance of honky-tonk as one of the main tributaries of rock-and-roll.

Hank's music – Hank himself, really – was a mixture of whiskey, lamb's blood, and cemetery dirt. Self-doomed and self-tormenting, Williams wrote and sang of a world where love danced endlessly with loss, sin with salvation, laughter with despair. It was for him quite natural to drift, as he did during a session in April, 1947, from *Move It On Over* to *I Saw The Light* to *Six More Miles (To The Graveyard)*.

From the perfect simplicity of *Cold, Cold Heart* and *You Win Again* to the subtle imagery of *I'm So Lonesome I Could Cry* to the sublime surliness of *Mind Your Own Business*, Williams gave country music its most enduring songs. Through those songs, he also brought a new and greater depth, a sort of fatal poetic sense, to honky-tonk. That depth and poetry can be experienced in **40 Greatest Hits**.

Hank's *Honky Tonk Blues*, recorded in September, 1951, was both a summation of all that had come before him and a celebration of the moment. His fame and fortune seemed to be limitless; but so did the intensity of his self-killing ways. By the fall of 1952, at the height of his success, he was in the worst shape of his life, living in physical and emotional wretchedness at his mother's boardinghouse in Montgomery. He pined for his faithless wife, Miss Audrey; drank, took chloral hydrate, drank, fell and cracked his skull, drank some more, and wrote *I'll Never Get Out Of This World Alive*. In October, without truly divorcing his wife, Audrey, he married Miss Billie Jones of Bossier City, Louisiana, on the stage of the New Orleans Municipal Auditorium. Tickets were priced from $1 to $2.80, and an estimated 14,000 people paid to attend. Little more than ten weeks later, in the first hours of the new year, 1953 – *I'll Never Get Out Of This World Alive* was on the charts – Williams was dead in the backseat of a chauffeured Cadillac en route to an engagement in Canton, Ohio. He was 29 years old.

Discographical Details

50   40 Greatest Hits

Hank Williams

Polydor 821 233–2 (2-disc set)

Move It On Over/A Mansion On The Hill/Lovesick Blues/Wedding Bells/Mind Your Own Business/You're Gonna Change (Or I'm Gonna Leave)/Lost Highway/My Bucket's Got A Hole In It/I'm So Lonesome I Could Cry/I Just Don't Like This Kind of Living/Long Gone Lonesome Blues/My Son Calls Another Man Daddy/Why Don't You Love Me/Why Should We Try Anymore/They'll Never Take Her Love From Me/Moanin' The Blues/Nobody's Lonesome For Me/Cold, Cold Heart/Dear John/Howlin' At The Moon/I Can't Help It (If I'm Still In Love With You)/Hey, Good Lookin'/Crazy Heart/(I Heard That) Lonesome Whistle/Baby, We're Really In Love/Ramblin' Man/Honky Tonk Blues/I'm Sorry For You, My Friend/Half As Much/Jambalaya/Window Shopping/Settin' The Woods On Fire/You Win Again/I'll Never Get Out Of This World Alive/Kaw-Liga/Your Cheatin' Heart/Take These Chains From My Heart/I Won't Be Home No More/Weary Blues From Waitin'/I Saw The Light

(iv) The Wild Side Of Life

The Tennessee-born crooner Eddy Arnold was the most prolific and successful country music recording artist of the decade 1945–55. His RCA-Victor hits, a blend of canned Opry-style rusticity and mainstream pop, were the antithesis of honky-tonk. But though he dominated the charts, those years belonged to honky-tonk, which produced the best and most exciting of the decade's hits. Towering above all those who outlived Williams was Lefty Frizzell.

Born William Orville Frizzell, on March 31, 1928, in Corsicana, Texas, south of Dallas, Lefty came to the attention of Columbia Records in 1950. From late that year through the close of the next, he had an astounding run of five number 1 hits: *If You've Got The Money I've Got The Time*, which was knocked out of the number 1 position by Hank Williams's *Moanin' The Blues*, in December, 1950; *I Love You A Thousand Ways*, which in turn replaced *Moanin' The Blues*, in January, 1951; *I Want To Be With You Always*, which remained on the charts for 21 weeks; *Always Late (With Your Kisses)*, which replaced Hank's *Hey, Good Lookin'* at number 1, in September, 1951, and held the position for three months; and *Give Me More, More, More (Of Your Kisses)* (1952). A boozer and a brawler, Frizzell, like Tubb and Williams, was a honky-tonk singer. But his voice was as pure and pretty and melodic as theirs were raw. Frizzell continued to have the occasional hit – *The Long Black Veil*, in 1959; *Saginaw, Michigan*, in 1964 – but after 1952, his popularity entered into a period of slow, and inexplicable, decline. He was 47 when he died, of a stroke, on July 19, 1975, in Nashville. Today, Frizzell's finest work is available on **The Best Of Lefty Frizzell**.

Besides Tubb and Frizzell, there were others: Hank Thompson (born in Waco, Texas, in 1925), Webb Pierce (born in West Monroe, Louisiana, in 1921; died in Nashville, in 1991), and Ray Price (born in Perryville, Texas, in 1926). Thompson's *The Wild Side Of Life* (1952; originally done by Jimmy Heap and the Melody Masters, for Imperial), Pierce's *Back Street Affair* (1952) and *There Stands The Glass* (1953), Price's *Release Me* (1954; also originally recorded by Jimmy Heap) were among the most haunting of honky-tonk's poison-love songs. The new louder, lusher, and more powerful sound of the Bigsby electric pedal-steel guitar on Pierce's records did as much to define the evolving sound of country music as Bob Dunn's work had done twenty years before. A fine sampling of Pierce's output is available on **Webb Pierce: In The Jailhouse Now**.

By the late 1950s, Ray Price had adopted a more mainstream,

pop-tempered sound, and Tubb, Thompson, and Pierce, like Frizzell before them, were all fading from glory. But the man who would bring honky-tonk, alive and kicking, into the decades beyond, was already making his mark.

Discographical Details

51   The Best Of Lefty Frizzell

Lefty Frizzell

Rhino R2 71005

If You've Got The Money I've Got The Time/Love You A Thousand Ways/ Look What Thoughts Will Do/I Want To Be With You Always/Always Late (With Your Kisses)/Mom And Dad's Waltz/Travellin' Blues/Give Me More, More, More (Of Your Kisses)/How Long Will It Take (To Stop Loving You)/ Don't Stay Away (Till Love Grows Cold)/Forever/I'm An Old, Old Man (Tryin' To Live While I Can)/Run 'Em Off/The Long Black Veil/Saginaw, Michigan/She's Gone, Gone, Gone

52   Webb Pierce: In The Jailhouse Now

Webb Pierce

Intersound CDA 5012

Back Street Affair/Cryin' Over You/I Ain't Never/I'm Tired/In The Jailhouse Now/It's Been So Long/I Don't Care/Slowly/There Stands The Glass/Tupelo County Jail/Cowtown/Yes, I Know Why

(v) Another Place, Another Time

The Best Of George Jones chronicles the career of the man who is arguably the greatest country singer alive. His was, and is, a voice capable of imbuing the commonplace sorrows and joys of the human universe with poignance and puissance, of crystallizing the simplicities of the mundane and the time-worn into subtle, complex new glintings, of discovering in and mining from the plain phrases, tired metaphors, and graceless rhyme of song a hidden, underlying honesty and depth. These are gifts that have been shared by Jimmie Rodgers, Hank Williams, Jerry Lee Lewis, and, to lesser profundity, a few other legendary country singers. But while Jones and his idol Hank Williams have both affected generations with a plaintive veracity of voice that has set them apart, Jones, unlike Williams, has further been gifted with a voice of remarkable range, natural elegance, and lucent tone. Gliding to high tenor, plunging to deep bass, the magisterial melisma of his onward-coursing baritone sends off white-hot sparks and glissades of blue, investing his poison-love songs with a tragic *commedia-è-finita* gravity, inflaming his celebrations of honky-tonk abandon with the heat of careening, heartfelt delight, and turning songs such as *Warm Red Wine* into harrowing wails from the abyss.

Jones was born in Saratoga, Texas, on September 12, 1931. In 1938, when his drunken father brought home a radio, Jones was mesmerized by the high, piney nasal style of Roy Acuff's singing on the Saturday-night Opry broadcasts. In 1942, when his family moved to a government-subsidized housing project in the port town of Beaumont, north of Houston, he became aware of that new sort of country music that was quite different from the quaint stuff that still represented the "Opry" sound. Then, in April, 1947, he heard Hank Williams's voice for the first time. The record – he would never forget it – was *I Don't Care (If Tomorrow Never Comes)*. By the year of Williams's death, Jones, fascinated now as well by the sound of Lefty Frizzell, had become a part of the honky-tonk milieu of Beaumont and Houston, performing on occasion with old-timers such as Cliff Bruner and Moon Mullican. In November, 1953, when he returned from service in the marines, Jones found his way to a new record company that had started up in Beaumont during his absence. Its founders, Jack Starnes, a former manager of Lefty Frizzell, and Pappy Daily, the operator of a Houston-based jukebox-and-vending-machine outfit, had named their little company after an elision of their combined surnames: Starday. Though it produced few hits, Starday became a hotbed of progressive honky-tonk and rock-abilly.

Jones made his first recordings in January, 1954. Several months later, in the spring of 1955, he recorded his first hit, an up-tempo, goddamn-her-eyes honky-tonk ditty called *Why, Baby, Why*. The record brought him to national prominence and served as his entrée to "The Louisiana Hayride," the influential Shreveport radio show on which Hank Williams had made his big-time debut and which now featured Elvis Presley.

In early 1960, Jones wrote a song called *The Window Up Above*. Of all the songs he has written, it would remain his favorite. "I wrote it in about 20 minutes," he said. "Sometimes it's hard to even figure where the ideas come from." The idea, of a man's delusion of happy home-life shattered by a single, providential glimpse of infidelity, was invested in the song with the uncanny, dreamlike quality of wellbeing subsumed by dread. Though, as George said, it sometimes might be difficult to figure out where ideas come from, *The Window Up Above* seemed to issue directly from a lifelong insecurity and ambivalence, a deep-rooted, heartfelt fear of what lurked beneath the dream of hearth and home and happiness. The song remained on the country charts for more than eight months, and George even had the tailor Nudie Cohen make him a stage-suit based on it, a chartreuse affair replete with faces peering forlornly from sequin-stitched windowframes.

The Window Up Above marked what many purists felt to be an egregious development in George's music itself: the use of background voices to sweeten the effect of his own hard-edged honky-tonk delivery. Through the sixties and into the seventies, background voices and orchestral string sections were to become an increasing presence in country music. Jones's voice, however, with its noble gravity, its capacity to wring from every word its full color and power, and its instinctive poet's sense of rhythm, usually was able to transcend the stultifying effects of the so-called "countrypolitan" trend. Considering that Jones, for much of his career, has been a complaisant victim of minimal or bad production, insipid arrangements, and frequently pedestrian or mawkish material, the surpassing power of that voice as documented in such less-than-optimal recordings is all the more remarkable.

Looking back, Jones would regard the early sixties as his finest period. "We did a lot of the pure country then," he said. This was the time of his reconstituted-rockabilly hit *The Race Is On* (1964) and of less-known but magnificent honky-tonk performances such as *Warm Red Wine* (1962) and *Open Pit Mine* (1962), a chilling little tale of adultery and remorseless murder.

In the fall of 1971, two years after marrying his third wife, Tammy Wynette, Jones signed with Epic Records and began work with Tammy's producer, Billy Sherrill. Sherrill's production was skilled and sophisticated. Though the lush orchestral arrangements and saccharine background voices that were Sherrill's trademark were regarded by many as further softening and diminishing the natural grandeur of Jones's voice, there can be little doubt that his production helped keep the singer commercially alive at a time when country music was increasingly beset, and the old guard increasingly endangered, by the winds of a new era. Jones himself was ambivalent about the sound of his recordings. "I went along with the record company against my better judgment," he told me in the days when he was working with Sherrill:

> I didn't want to do it, but I let them put strings on my sessions just out of curiosity, more or less, just to see what they might do. But we've talked about it, and we're gonna get back to a more hardcore sound. If the song's there, that's all I need. That's all anybody needs. I like a good, solid honky-tonk song.

But he did not begin to fully return in his recordings to that "more hardcore sound" for years to come; and in 1993, he repeated to me his intention of long ago: "I'm trying to get back to the pure country." It struck me then that "pure country" might be the unattainable goal that kept him moving onward.

Jones's life has been as turbulent as his career has been wondrous. Bob Allen's biography, *George Jones: the saga of an American singer*, recounts a life very nearly destroyed by alcoholism, drug addiction, madness, and violence – a honky-tonk saga of nearly operatic sweep. Above all, however, Jones's story has been one of survival. In Birmingham, in March, 1984, while Allen's book was at press, Jones performed the first stone-cold-sober show of his career; and he has not taken a drink in the years since then.

In those years, country music has become the domain of a new generation of rock-nurtured singers. Garth Brooks, presently the most successful of country artists, has also become an international pop star, achieving higher album sales than Michael Jackson and other pop stars. Country music itself, which today constitutes a bigger share of the Arbitron radio ratings than Top 40 pop fare and has its equivalent of MTV in CMT (the Country Music Television network), bears little resemblance to the music of George Jones, whose traditionally rooted, hardcore honky-tonk sound is now an anomaly in Nashville.

While most country singers his age have fallen on hard times, Jones, in December, 1990, signed a lucrative new deal with MCA, and since then has increasingly enjoyed the stature and respect due him as an American master. For Garth Brooks, "George Jones is king." In fact, nearly all of today's country music youngbloods have named Jones as their idol, echoing the sentiment of Waylon Jennings that, "If we could all sound like we wanted to, we'd all sound like George Jones." Jones has been more fortunate than Jennings, a country music veteran whose own recording career has been brought to an end by the present inimical state of the industry. As to the adulation he commands among the new generation, Jones is nonplused. "That's the hard part to understand," he said. Maybe "they all pretty much like country music to start with, they just didn't get into it themselves."

The truth, to Jones, is simple:

> Country music is something you love. It's a music you *love*. I don't know, for some reason, being a star or anything like that never did really enter my mind. If they hadn't paid me for singing, I would've still done it, long as I could've got enough to eat somewhere. It don't matter to me that much. I like to sing with my heart. I like to sing soul country songs. And that's the way it'll always be with me.

In *Hellfire*, my biography of Jerry Lee Lewis, I used as an epigraph a statement of Jerry Lee's that I felt not only summed up his own attitude toward his music but also placed that music, and the subject of the book, in the proper context of an almost mythic realm of haunted darkness and Pentecostal light: "I'm draggin' the audience to hell with me."

Jerry Lee Lewis's life is the stuff of legends. And his music is cut from that same magical fustian. He himself will tell you that there have only been four stylists in the history of American music: Al Jolson, Jimmie Rodgers, Hank Williams, and him. This megalomania is made all the more disarming by its essential veracity: he was a true original from the very beginning, back in the 1950s, when he was rock and roll's original, Louisiana-born prince of darkness. Even then, the vortex of his music transcended strict classification. Turning over his 1956 *Great Balls of Fire*, one found his rendering of Hank Williams's *You Win Again*. When he fell in infamy, in 1958, at the age of 22, he was sure that he would rise anew. And by the time he fulfilled his prophecy, ten years later, the honky-tonk element of his music had become its lifeblood.

Killer: The Mercury Years, Vol. 1, 1963–1968 captures the power and force of that honky-tonk comeback. *Another Place, Another Time*, the vehicle of that comeback, recorded in January, 1968, is a beautiful performance of loneliness and muted anguish. Like many of the other renditions here, it is one of the classic honky-tonk performances of the 1960s; and his versions of *The Wild Side Of Life* and *Walking The Floor Over You* illuminate the unique powers with which he breathed new life into an old form. As brilliant a country singer as he was a rock-and-roll singer, Lewis has left in his wake one of the finest and most endlessly engrossing bodies of music that America has ever produced.

Discographical Details

53 The Best Of George Jones (1955–1967)

George Jones
Rhino R2 70531
Why, Baby, Why/What Am I Worth/Just One More/Don't Stop The Music/ Color Of The Blues/White Lightning/The Window Up Above/Tender Years/ Aching, Breaking Heart/She Thinks I Still Care/A Girl I Used To Know/We Must Have Been Out Of Our Minds/You Comb Her Hair/The Race Is On/I've Got Five Dollars And It's Saturday Night/Love Bug/I'm A People/Walk Through This World With Me

54   Killer: The Mercury Years, Vol. 1, 1963–1968

Jerry Lee Lewis

Mercury 836 935–2

Corrine, Corrina/The Hole He Said He'd Dig For Me/She Was My Baby (He Was My Friend)/Got You On My Mind/Mathilda/Memphis Beat/Don't Let Go/Skid Row/I Believe In You/Baby, Hold Me Close/Funny How Time Slips Away/This Must Be The Place/Who Will The Next Fool Be/Rockin' Jerry Lee/ Dream Baby/Louisiana Man/Today I Started Loving You Again/I'm On Fire/ The Wild Side Of Life/Walking The Floor Over You/Another Place, Another Time/Break My Mind/Swinging Doors/What's Made Milwaukee Famous

Basic Recordings

Born To Lose

55   Pioneer Western Swing Band: 1935–1936

Milton Brown and his Musical Brownies

MCA 1509 (LP)

The Sheik of Araby/Yes Suh/Fan It/Chinese Honeymoon/Somebody's Been Usin' That Thing/Goofus/Down By The O-H-I-O/I've Got The Blues For Mamy/Hesitation Blues/When I Take My Sugar To Tea/Black And White Rag/Easy Ridin' Papa

An interesting set featuring the amplified steel guitar wizard Bob Dunn, as well as Dunn's earliest interplay with Cliff Bruner, one of the key figures of early honky-tonk. (Dunn's most astounding flight of virtuosity, on the Brownies' 1935 *Cheesy Breeze*, is included on Rhino CD 70718, **Legends Of The Guitar.**)

56   Cliff Bruner/The Rice Brothers Gang

Cliff Bruner and the Rice Brothers Gang

MCA VIM-4016 (Jap) (LP)

Cliff Bruner: *Bringin' Home The Bacon/Corrine, Corrina/Under The Silvery Moon/Old-Fashioned Love/Beaumont Rag/San Antonio Rose/I'll Forgive You*; Rice Brothers Gang: *King Cotton Stomp/Sugar Blues/On The Sunny Side Of The Street/When I'm Walking With My Sweetness/Alabama Jubilee/You Are My Sunshine/Is It True What They Say About Dixie*

A fine compilation of Bruner's music, complemented by a sampling of the Rice Brothers' Gang. Featuring the amplified guitar and singing of Hoke Rice, the Gang was a minor honky-tonk band (1938–41) that recorded the first version of *You Are My Sunshine*, later credited to and associated with Jimmie Davis. (Their 1939 version credits authorship to brother Paul Rice.)

57   Jimmie Davis: Country Music Hall Of Fame

Jimmie Davis

MCA MCAD-10087

Nobody's Darling But Mine/Jellyroll Blues/It Makes No Difference Now/You Are My Sunshine/I Just Dropped In To Say Goodbye/I Hung My Head And Cried/In The Pines/Mama's Getting Hot And Papa's Getting Cold/There's A

New Moon Over My Shoulder/Come On Over To My House (Ain't Nobody Home But Me)/I Wish I Had Never Seen Sunshine/Sweethearts Or Strangers/ Grievin' My Heart Out For You/Bed Bug Blues/When You're Not Forgotten By The Girl You Can't Forget/Supper Time

During his early Decca years, Davis worked at times in a solid honky-tonk vein. Here, in and out of that vein, he is at the height of his powers, in between the salacious novelties of his earlier, Victor recordings and the increasingly religious music of his later years with Decca.

58   Moon Mullican Sings His All-Time Greatest Hits

Moon Mullican

King KCD-555

I'll Sail My Ship Alone/Honolulu Rock-a Roll-a/The Leaves Mustn't Fall/ Mona Lisa/Sugar Beet/New Jole Blon/Sweeter Than The Flowers/Pipeliner's Blues/I Was Sorta Wondering/Cherokee Boogie/You Don't Have To Be A Baby To Cry/Foggy River

A compact-disc reissue of Mullican's first, 1958 album, featuring recordings from the previous decade, when Mullican, with several national country hits to his credit, was still a force in the Houston area, performing with fellow honky-tonk veterans such as Cliff Bruner and youngbloods such as George Jones.

59   Floyd Tillman: Columbia Historic Edition

Floyd Tillmann

Columbia FC-39996 (LP)

There's Blood In The Moon Tonight/Westphalia Waltz/Drivin' Nails In My Coffin/Each Night At Nine/Got Out And Find Somebody New/I Almost Lost My Mind/I Love You So Much It Hurts/I'm Checkin' Out On You/Sentenced To A Life (Without You)/Slippin' Around/Stars Fell Out Of Heaven

A collection of hits and representative recordings from the late 1940s, this contains some of Tillman's best and most successful work.

60   Classic Country Music II

Various Artists

Smithsonian Collection RD 042-2

Al Dexter: *Pistol-Packin' Mama*; Elton Britt: *The Cattle Call*; Eddy Arnold: *The Cattle Call/I Really Don't Want To Know*; Roy Acuff: *Wabash Cannon Ball*; The Blue Sky Boys: *Kentucky*; Moon Mullican: *New Pretty Blonde*; Maddox Brothers and Rose: *Philadelphia Lawyer*; Merle Travis: *I Am A Pilgrim*; Bill Monroe: *It's Mighty Dark To Travel*; Flatt and Scruggs: *Randy Lynn Rag*; Floyd Tillman: *Slippin' Around*; Molly O'Day: *The Tramp On The Street*; Hank Snow: *I'm Moving On*; Jimmy Dickens: *Take An Old Cold Tater*; Pee Wee King: *Tennessee Waltz*; Red Foley: *Peace In The Valley*; Hank Williams: *Lovesick Blues Your Cheating Heart*; Lefty Frizzell: *I Love You A Thousand Ways*; Hank Thompson: *The Wild Side Of Life*; Kitty Wells: *It Wasn't God Who Made Honky Tonk Angels*; Webb Pierce: *Slowly*; Chet Atkins: *Country Gentleman*; Tennessee Ernie Ford: *Sixteen Tons*; Elvis Presley: *Blue Moon Of Kentucky*; Everly Brothers: *Bye Bye Love*

Not strictly a honky-tonk anthology, but it does include the biggest honky-tonk hit of them all, Al Dexter's *Pistol-Packin' Mama*, and is a finer set than any of the others that offer it. Other relevant artists here include Moon Mullican, Floyd Tillman, Hank Williams, Lefty Frizzell, Hank Thompson, and Webb Pierce, as well as Kitty Wells, whose *It Wasn't God Who Made Honky Tonk Angels* was the rebuttal to *The Wild Side Of Life*. Both Dexter's *Pistol-Packin' Mama* and Ted Daffan's *Born To Lose* (along with Gene Autry's version of *It Makes No Difference Now*) are included on another anthology, **Columbia Country Classics: The Golden Age** (Columbia CK 46029), but that collection as a whole is less commendable.

Drivin' Nails In My Coffin

61   Honky Tonk Classics

Ernest Tubb

Rounder Special Series 14 (LP)

Filipino Baby/That Wild And Wicked Look In Your Eyes/Letters Have No Arms/You Don't Have To Be A Baby To Cry/I Need Attention Bad/Jealous Loving Heart/Blue-Eyed Elaine/I Ain't Going Honky Tonkin' Anymore/Try Me One More Time/You Nearly Lose Your Mind/Answer To Walking The Floor Over You/There's Gonna Be Some Changes Made Around Here

A worthy set of some of Tubb's most interesting work, 1940–54, this includes his earliest Decca recording, *Blue-Eyed Elaine*.

62   Ernest Tubb: Let's Say Goodbye Like We Said Hello

Ernest Tubb

Bear Family BCD 15498 (5-disc set) (Ger)

An impressive collection of 115 recordings: the entirety of Tubb's extant recorded work covering the years 1947–53. An accompanying booklet offers a biographical study, by Ronnie Pugh, and a discography, by Richard Weize. Though not for the casual listener or anyone just beginning to form a country music library, this Tubb set, like Bear Family's Frizzell, Pierce, and Faron Young sets (and others outside the scope of this chapter), is a triumph of historical reissuing.

Honky Tonkin'

63   Hank Williams: I Ain't Got Nothin' But Time (Vol. 1)

Hank Williams

Polydor 825 548-2

Calling You/Never Again/Wealth Won't Save Your Soul/When God Comes And Gathers His Jewels/I Don't Care (If Tomorrow Never Comes)/My Love For You (Has Turned To Hate)/Pan American/Honky Tonkin'/Move It On Over/I Saw The Light/(Last Night) I Heard You Crying In Your Sleep/Six More Miles (To The Graveyard)/Cool Water/Swing Wide Your Gate Of Love/ Roly Poly/Tennessee Border/Old Country Church/Alone And Forsaken/Rock My Cradle (Once Again)/Battle Of Armageddon/I Ain't Got Nothin' But Time

This volume comprises the earliest recordings, December, 1946, through April, 1947. Like each that follows in this important series, it presents a comprehensive, chronological chapter of the recording career of Hank Williams, the most legendary figure in country music history. With Colin Escott's biography of Williams (*Little, Brown*) and the **Rare Demos** collection, this series (conceived and compiled by Escott) renders Williams – and deservedly so – the most thoroughly documented of country singers. (This documentation will be complete with the long-awaited – and, alas, not immediately foreseeable – publication of the bio-discographical logbook of Williams by Bob Pinson of the Country Music Foundation.) The other volumes in this Polydor series, all equally worthy, are: **2** (1947–8), **Lovesick Blues** (825 551–2); **3** (1948–9), **Lost Highway** (825 554–2); **4** (1949), **I'm So Lonesome I Could Cry** (825 557–2); **5** (1949–50), **Long Gone Lonesome Blues** (831 633–2); **6** (1950–1), **Hey, Good Lookin'** (831 634–2); **7** (1951–2), **Let's Turn Back The Years** (8313 749–2); **8** (1952), **I Won't Be Home No More** (833 752–2).

64   Rare Demos: First To Last

Hank Williams
Country Music Foundation CMF-067-D
Won't You Sometimes Think Of Me/Why Should I Cry/Calling You/You Broke Your Own Heart/Pan American/Mother Is Gone/I Watched My Dream World Crumble Like Clay/In My Dreams You Still Belong To Me/Wealth Won't Save Your Soul/I Told A Lie To My Heart/Singing Waterfall/I'm Goin' Home/Jambalaya/Heaven Holds All My Treasures/You Better Keep It On Your Mind/Lost On The River/Your Cheatin' Heart/A House Of Gold/Honky Tonk Blues/Help Me Understand/'Neath A Cold Gray Tomb of Stone/There's Nothing As Sweet As My Baby/Fool About You/The Log Train

These raw, solo recordings by Williams of his compositions, honky-tonk and otherwise, offer a rare glimpse into the creative processes of country music's master songwriter.

65   There's Nothing As Sweet As My Baby

Hank Williams
Mount Olive MO 1153 (Den) (LP)
*Lovesick Blues (Theme)/There's Nothing As Sweet As My Baby/Blue Eyes Crying In The Rain/California Zephyr/Where He Leads Me I Will Follow/Interview/Lovesick Blues (Theme)/Low And Lonely/Lonely Tombs/Cherokee Boogie/I Can't Help It (If I'm Still In Love With You)/*Audrey Williams: *Blue Love In My Heart/Lovesick Blues (Theme) and spoken sign-off*

An extraordinary documentary album, taken from rare 1951 radio transcriptions, this includes a freewheeling version of Moon Mullican's 1950 *Cherokee Boogie* and a brief interview with Williams done backstage at The Grand Ole Opry by a Columbus, Georgia, broadcaster called Cousin Benny. Also of interest is **Hank Williams: Health And Happiness Shows** (Mercury 314 517 862–2), a collection of transcriptions from 1949.

The Wild Side Of Life

66   Lefty Frizzell: Life's Like Poetry

Lefty Frizzell
Bear Family BCD 15550 (12-disc set) (Ger)
A sumptuous 12-CD set that offers a complete chronicle of Frizzell's 24-year recording career. The lavishly illustrated 152-page booklet that accompanies

the set contains a thorough biographical study, by Charles Wolfe, and a complete discography, by Richard Weize.

67 Webb Pierce: The Wondering Boy, 1951–1958

Webb Pierce

Bear Family BCD 15522 (4-disc set) (Ger)

These 100-odd recordings present a complete picture of the most successful of the honky-tonk singers of the 1950s. Pierce's music is much better, and more important, than its current lack of vogue might lead one to believe. He was, in his glory years, a fine singer, responsible for many of the hardest-cutting and daring recordings of honky-tonk's golden age. An enclosed 36-page booklet, by Otto Kitsinger, includes full discographical details.

68 Hayride Boogie, 1950–1951

Webb Pierce

Krazy Kat KK 7456 (UK) (LP)

California Blues/Shuffle On Down/I Need You Like A Hole In The Head/I'm Watching The Stars/Steeling The Mood/Have You Ever Had The Feeling/Drifting Texas Sand/I Got Religion On A Saturday Night/In The Jailhouse/The Last Waltz/I Saw Your Face In The Moon/I'm Sitting On Top Of The World/Freight Train Blues/Poor Boy Rag/You Scared The Love Right Out Of Me/Hayride Boogie

A collection of fine early recordings by Pierce, made for the Pacemaker label in Shreveport.

69 All-Time Greatest Hits

Hank Thompson

Capitol Collector's Series CDP-7 92124 2

Humpty Dumpty Heart/Whoa, Sailor/The Wild Side Of Life/Waiting In The Lobby Of Your Heart/Rub-A-Dub-Dub/Yesterday's Girl/Wake Up, Irene/Breakin' The Rules/Honky Tonk Girl/We've Gone Too Far/The New Green Light/Breakin' In Another Heart/Rockin' In The Congo/Squaws Along The Yukon/A Six Pack To Go/She's Just A Whole Lot Like You/Oklahoma Hills/Hangover Tavern

Inhaling western swing and honky-tonk, exhaling his highly individual blend of both, Hank Thompson was an heir of a Texas musical style that had its roots in the hillbilly jazz of Milton Brown and Cliff Bruner. Thompson represented 1950s honky-tonk at is most musically erudite. A similar anthology, but with fewer selections, is available as **All-Time Greatest Hits** (Curb D2-77329).

70 Hank Thompson And His Brazos Valley Boys

Hank Thompson and his Brazos Valley Boys

Country Routes RFD 9003 (Fr) (LP)

Square Dab From The Country/Darling, What More Can I Do/Shotgun Boogie/Brand On My Heart/Judy/Be My Life's Companion/I Gotta Have My Baby Back/Heart Full Of Love/I Can't Help It (If I'm Still In Love With You)/

Easy To Please/Would You Care/Sixty Minute Man/Could You Take Me Back Again/Lost Highway/River Road Two-Step/I'm Lost Without You

These are rare live performances taken from 1952 radio shows. Thompson at the time was 26 years old, had been making records since 1946, and had recently, in December, 1951, recorded *The Wild Side Of Life*.

71   American Originals

Ray Price

Columbia CK 45068

Under Your Spell Again/San Antonio Rose/Faded Love/Crazy Arms/Talk To Your Heart/Crazy/Night Life/For The Good Times/Funny How Time Slips Away/Release Me

There have been two Ray Prices: the smooth, urbane country-pop singer of the 1960s and beyond, and the honky-tonk leader of the Cherokee Cowboys, in the 1950s. More often than not, this set shows him close to his roots.

72   Jimmy Heap: Release Me

Jimmy Heap

Bear Family BCD 15617 (Ger)

Release Me/Love In The Valley/Just To Be With You/(I Wanna Go Where You Go) Then I'll Be Happy/Heartbreaker/You're In Love With You/Just For Tonight/Girl With A Past/Lifetime Of Shame/You Don't Kiss Me 'Cause You Love Me/The One That I Won/Ethyl In My Gas Tank (No Gal In My Arms/ My First Love Affair/Love Can Move Mountains/Conscience, I'm Guilty/This Song Is Just For You/You Oughta Know/I Told You So/Butternut/Long John/ Mingling/Heap Of Boogie/You're Nothin' But A Nothin'/That's All I Want' From You/I'll Follow The Crowd/It Takes A Heap Of Lovin'/Cry, Cry, Darling/You Didn't Have Time/Let's Do It Just Once/This Night Won't Last Forever

Heap (1922–77), whose band did *The Wild Side Of Life* before Hank Thompson and *Release Me* before Ray Price, was one of the unsung heroes of Texas honky-tonk in the late 1940s, when his Melody Masters recorded for Lasso Records of Austin, and when, in the 1950s, he moved from Imperial to Capitol. This collection of Capitol recordings, 1952–6, offers a taste of the sort of music that thrived in the sawdust-and-jukebox joints but never quite made it on a wider scale. (*Release Me*, in 1954, was Heap's only national hit.)

73   When They Let The Hammer Down

Delmore Brothers and Wayne Raney

Bear Family BFX 15167 (Ger) (LP)

Red Ball To Natchez/Jack And Jill Boogie/Lost John Boogie/Catfish Baby/ Mobile Boogie/Beale Street Boogie/Peach Tree Street Boogie/Boogie Woogie Baby/Hillbilly Boogie/Freight Train Boogie/Down Home Boogie/Stop That Boogie/Del Rio Boogie/Pan American Boogie/Real Hot Boogie/Used Car Boogie

The Delmore Brothers pioneered a new sort of music, hillbilly boogie, from a marriage of honky-tonk, old-timey dance songs, and boogie-woogie. Like honky-tonk as a whole, their sound in particular was one of the commanding influences on early rockabilly. These recordings, from the years 1946–9, illustrate why.

74 All-Time Greatest Hits

Faron Young
Curb D2–77334
Hello Walls/Live Fast, Love Hard, Die Young/Sweet Dreams/Goin' Steady/ Country Girl/Alone With You/I Miss You Already (And You're Not Even Gone)/Riverboat/The Comeback/Your Old Used To Be

Young, from honky-tonk's second city of Shreveport, was 23 when he added a new, rebel-without-a-cause dimension to honky-tonk with *Live Fast, Love Hard, Die Young* (1955). Like George Jones, he was one of the most popular singers of the late 1950s. No one sounded surlier, even when peddling love. Also recommended: the 5-CD set **Faron Young: The Capitol Years** (Bear Family BCD 15483).

75 Johnny Horton: The Early Years

Johnny Horton
Bear Family BFX 15289 (7–LP set) (Ger)
Born in Tyler, Texas, Horton (1929–60) was barely 22 when he began performing on Shreveport's "Louisiana Hayride" and recording for the Cormac and Abbott labels, in 1951. Bursting to national celebrity, in 1956, with *Honky Tonk Man*, Horton was a honky-tonk singer with an exuberant, youthful, and oddly wholesome voice. He married Hank Williams's ex-wife Billie Jean, rendering her a widow once again when he died in a car wreck, at the age of 31. **Johnny Horton: Rockin' Rollin'**, a more modest Horton collection, on CD, is also available from Bear Family (BCD 15543), but its scope is limited to the later, Columbia years, 1956–60.

76 Columbia Country Classics: Honky Tonk Heroes (Vol. 2)

Various Artists
Columbia CK 46030
Bob Wills: *Brain Cloudy Blues*; Floyd Tillman: *Slippin' Around/This Cold War With You/I Love You So Much It Hurts*; Stuart Hamblen: *(Remember Me) I'm The One Who Loves You*; George Morgan: *Room Full Of Roses*; Carl Smith: *I Overlooked An Orchid/Let Old Mother Nature Have Her Way/Hey, Joe*; Jimmy Dickens: *Country Boy/A-Sleepin' At The Foot Of The Bed*; Lefty Frizzell: *If You've Got The Money, I've Got The Time/I Love You A Thousand Ways/Always Late (With Your Kisses)*; Marty Robbins: *I Couldn't Keep From Crying/Knee Deep In The Blues*; Johnny Horton: *Honky Tonk Man*; Ray Price: *Crazy Arms/Invitation To The Blues/Heartaches By The Number/Heart Over Mind*; Charlie Walker: *Pick Me Up On Your Way Down/ Who Will Buy The Wine*; Stonewall Jackson: *Why I'm Walkin'*; Carl Butler: *Honky Tonkitis/Don't Let Me Cross Over*

This is good anthology that, through selections by various Columbia singers, illustrates the continuity of honky-tonk from the 1940s to the 1960s.

Another Place, Another Time

77   Stars Of Texas Honky Tonk

Various Artists

Ace Limited Edition LTD 603 (UK) (LP)

Bill Nettles: *Wine-O-Boogie/Gumbo-Mumbo*; R.D. Hendon and his Western Jamboree Cowboys: *Lonely Nights/Return My Broken Heart/My Old Guitar*; Luke Gordon: *Doin' What's Right*; Louisiana Lannis: *Muscadine Eyes*; Bill Mack: *Guess I'll Keep On Dreaming*; Glenn Barber: *Ain't It Funny*; Lucky Wray: *It's Music She Says*; Leo Ogletree: *Crooked Dice*; Tibby Edwards: *Fool That I Was/I Don't Want To Say I Love You*; Benny Barnes: *No Fault Of Mine*; Sonny Burns: *It's Easier Said Than Done*; Mel Price: *Gonna See My Baby*; Luke Gordon: *Let This Kiss Bid You Goodbye*; James O'Gwynn: *I Cry*

This superb album, drawn from Starday recordings, 1954–6, presents a variety of intriguing honky-tonk singers who never quite made it commercially: Bill Nettles (1907–67), who had been recording since 1937 and whose only hit, *Hadacol Boogie*, had come in 1949; the Houston bandleader R.D. Hendon; Bill Mack, who moved from honky-tonk to rockabilly; Benny Barnes, the Beaumont singer who was likened by many to George Jones, both in terms of his local popularity and the power of his voice; Sonny Burns, who subsequently recorded several Starday duets with Jones.

78   Boppin' Hillbilly, Vol. 22

Various Artists

White Label WLP 2822 (Neth) (LP)

Cliff Bruner: *Ouch*; Dickie McBride: *I Don't Get No Lovin'*; Don Holt: *My Baby Still Loves Me*; Cliff Gross: *Hog Pen Hop*; Jesse James: *Joaquin Special*; Jerry Irby: *Buy Me A Bottle Of Beer*; Glen Barber: *Styles And Ways Of The World*; Ruddy Gaddis: *Girl From Mars*; Woody Carter: *Runnin' Around*; Art Gunn: *Chicksaw Chick/Pickin' and Singin'*; Dusty Rivers: *Peanut Pie*; Bashful Vic Thomas: *You're Gonna Change (Or I'm Gonna Leave)*; Harmon Tucker: *You Can't Win*; Virgel Bozman: *Troubles, Troubles*; Otis Glover: *I Lost My Heart*; Paul Blunt: *Walking Up Stairs*; Rip Ramsey: *Wanderers Swing*

Another interesting anthology bringing to light a variety of obscure Texas honky-tonk recordings from the 1950s, this album is especially noteworthy in that it presents recordings made c. 1950 (for Ayo, a little-known Houston company) by two honky-tonk pioneers of the late 1930s, Cliff Bruner and Dickie McBride, as well as an early 4 Star recording by Jerry Irby.

79   I'm A Honky Tonk Daddy

Various Artists

Flyright CD 44 (UK)

Lou Millet: *When I'm Out Honky Tonkin' With You/If You Didn't, Don't, 'Cause it Ain't*; Jim and Johnny: *I Can't Go On*; Lefty Frizzell: *Send Her Here To Be Mine/Lost Love Blues/That's Me Without You*; Benny Frugé: *Bayou Boogie*; Tommy Hill: *The Life That I'm Living*; Tommy and Kenny Hill: *I Must Leave You*; Joey Gills: *Baby, Leave Your Troubles At Home*; Smokey Stover: *Go On And Leave My Baby Alone*; Wink Lewis: *I'm A Honky Tonk Daddy*; Mack Hamilton: *Will You Will Or Will You Won't*; Jimmie Lee Durden: *Old Mr Moon/Should I Should Or Should I Shouldn't*;

Lynn Howard: *I'm a Cry, Cry Baby*; Bill Hutto: *She's My Five Foot Five/If You Think You Got Troubles*; Al Montgomery: *It Wasn't God Who Made Honky Tonk Angels*; Feature House Band: *Open Strings*

This is another fine collection of relevant 1950s obscurities, drawn from the Louisiana-based Feature label.

80 Cat'n Around

Various Artists

Krazy Kat KK CD 07 (UK)

Harry Choates: *Cat'n Around/Harry's Blues*; Ray Welch: *Louisiana Blues*; Ramblin' Tommy Scott: *Tennessee/When A Man Gets The Blues*; Vance Bros: *Can't Get You Out Of My Dreams/Draftboard Blues*; Art Gunn: *Cornbread Boogie*; Woody Carter: *Sittin' On The Doorstep/Who's Gonna Chop My Baby's Firewood*; LaVerl Carrico: *My Life's Story*; Dolores: *Pickin'*; Bill Grady: *I'll Always Get Along*; Morris Mills: *Steppin' On Feet For Fun*; Curley Rash: *Was It Just A Year Ago*; Clint Small: *Texas Rag/Someone Cares;* Yodelling Bob Stotts: *I Guess I Learn A Lot Every Day;* Barney Vardeman: *Let's Call It Quits*; Sonny Hall: *Just A Little Bit More*; Art Gunn: *Boogie Woogie Blues*; Bob Greene: *Somebody Stole My Rag Mop*; Bar-X Cowboys; *Fairweather Friend*; Bill Grady: *Ramblin' Man*; Curley Rash: *Humble Road Boogie*

A superb anthology, this represents the honky-tonk and country-boogie music of the Macy's label, one of Houston's most intriguing companies (1949–51). The set includes excellent notes by Phillip J. Tricker of *The Hillbilly Researcher*.

81 Live At Dancetown USA

George Jones

Ace CDCHM 158 (UK)

Jones Boys: *Untitled Instrumental*; Don Adams: *One More Time*; George Jones: *White Lightning/Something I've Dreamed/Aching, Breaking Heart*; George Jones and Don Adams: *We Must Have Been Out Of Our Minds*; George Jones: *Window Up Above/Bony Moronie/She Thinks I Still Care/Rio City Chimes/Accidentally On Purpose/Who Shot Sam/*Jones Boys: *Intermission Riff/Untitled Instrumental*; Don Adams: *Please Talk To My Heart/Sing A Sad Song*; Buddy Emmons: *Panhandle Rag*; Don Adams: *Act Naturally*; George Jones: *Ragged But Right/Poor Man's Riches/Tender Years/Where Does A Little Tear Come From/Jole Blon/Big Harlan Taylor/She's Lonesome Again/The Race Is On*

Recorded in June, 1965, at a dancehall in Houston, this live performance captures the essence of honky-tonk at its most raucous and sublime; a rare and fascinating piece of history that conveys some sense of the music's natural environment.

82 Don't Stop The Music

George Jones

Ace CDCH 912 (UK)

Into My Arms Again/Who Shot Sam/You Gotta Be My Baby/Mr Fool/Time Lock/Candy Hearts/What'cha Gonna Do/Vitamins L-O-V-E/Don't Stop The

Music/Accidentally On Purpose/All I Want To Do/Giveaway Girl/Cup Of Loneliness/A Wanderin' Soul/My Sweet Imogene/The Likes Of You/What Am I Worth/Boogie Woogie Mexican Boy/I'm With The Wrong One/With Half A Heart/Ship Of Love/The Honky Tonk Downstairs

Culled from the Starday and Mercury years 1955–61, this collection gives a good sense of Jones's style subtly evolving, away from the heavy influence of Hank Williams towards his own maturing individuality. It is regrettable that, amid the surfeit of Jones CD reissues (some of them quite technically deplorable), there is nothing to fairly represent his United Artists years, 1962–4, which is Jones's own favorite period. Though long unavailable, the 1971 2-LP **George Jones Superpak** (United Artists UXS-85) is the only compilation to fill this gap.

83   Anniversary

George Jones

Epic EGK 38323

We Can Make It/Loving You Could Never Be Better/A Picture Of Me (Without You)/What My Woman Can't Do/Nothing Ever Hurt Me (Half As Bad As Losing You)/Once You've Had The Best/Her Name Is . . ./Old King Kong/Bartender's Blues/I'll Just Take It Out In Love/Someday My Day Will Come/The Grand Tour/The Door/These Days (I Barely Get By)/Memories Of Us/The Battle/He Stopped Loving Her Today/I'm Not Ready Yet/If Drinkin' Don't Kill Me (Her Memory Will)/Good Ones And Bad Ones/Still Doin' Time/Same Ole Me

In retrospect, Jones's Epic recordings stand up remarkably well; and these really are the cream of a plentiful crop. His is a voice that has grown more powerful with the passing years. One would also be well advised to be aware of his current work with MCA.

84   Wynn Stewart: Wishful Thinking

Wynn Stewart

Bear Family BFD 15261 (2-LP set) (Ger)

Wishful Thinking/Heartaches For A Dime/Open Up My Heart/Three Cheers For The Losers/Rain, Rain/I Sold The Farm/Slightly Used/Falling For You/I'd Rather Have America/Yankee, Go Home/Come On/Uncle Tom Got Caught/ Never Out Of My Heart/Long Black Limousine/School Bus Love Affair/She Just Tears Me Up/Big, Big Love/Donna On My Mind/How The Other Half Lives/With This Ring/Another Day, Another Dollar/Wrong Company/Wall To Wall Heartaches/I'm Not The Man I Used To Be/Couples Only/Loversville/ Don't Look Back/I Don't Feel at Home/I Done Done It/Above And Beyond/ Come On/Wishful Thinking/Big City/If You See My Baby/Playboy/Girl in White/One More Memory/Searching For Another You/One Way To Go/ Hungry Heart

Stewart (1935–85) moved with his family from the Mid West to California, in 1949. A founder of West Coast honky-tonk, and a mentor of Merle Haggard, he made his first recordings at the age of 16, and first appeared on the national charts, with *Waltz Of The Angels*, in 1956. These recordings, originally made for the Challenge label, predate his success and reveal him to be a honky-tonk singer with a singular, if under-appreciated, full-throated style.

85 More Of The Best Of Merle Haggard

Merle Haggard

Rhino R2 70917

Sing A Sad Song/Branded Man/Mama Tried/Silver Wings/White Line Fever/
Someday We'll Look Back/It's Not Love (But It's Not Bad)/Everybody's Had
The Blues/If We Make It Through December/It's All In The Movies/If We're
Not Back In Love By Monday/Ramblin' Fever/I'm Always On A Mountain
When I Fall/It's Been A Great Afternoon/Red Bandana/My Own Kind Of
Hat/I Think I'll Just Stay Here And Drink/Rainbow Stew

Born in Bakersfield, in 1937, Haggard began recording in 1962, about two
years after he was released from San Quentin. By the mid-sixties, he had
established himself, like George Jones, as one of the reigning voices of honky-
tonk. Melancholy, brooding, rambunctious in turns, his music, into the
1970s, provided an antidote to the increasingly bland creepings of the
"countrypolitan" sound that eventually subsumed the hard-core honky-tonk
tradition. These performances, from 1962 to 1981, offer a good introduction
to one of the last authentic honky-tonk innovators.

86 Killer: The Mercury Years, Vol. 2, 1969–1972

Jerry Lee Lewis

Mercury 836 938–2

Jambalaya/Home Away From Home/I Can't Stop Loving You/Oh Lonesome
Me/You've Still Got A Place In My Heart/Why Don't You Love Me (Like
You Used to Do)/Reuben James/Since I Met You Baby/You Went Out of Your
Way (To Walk On Me)/Handwriting On The Wall/You Don't Miss Your
Water/On The Jericho Road/I'll Fly Away/Flip, Flop And Fly/Blue Suede
Shoes/Stagger Lee/Today I Started Loving You Again/Shoeshine Man/I'm In
The Gloryland Way/When He Walks On You (Like You Walked On Me)/
Workin' Man Blues/I Get The Blues When It Rains/Please Don't Talk About
Me When I'm Gone/Another Hand Shakin' Goodbye/Me And Bobby McGee

This collection is every bit as wonderful as the essential first volume
(Mercury 836 935–2: see "Essential Recordings," this chapter). Often, the
older this music gets, the more astounding it seems. The third and final
volume in this series (Mercury 836 941–2), covering the years 1973–7, is also
highly recommended. (Anyone not sated by these three albums is referred to
Bear Family's 3-box, 33-LP set, **The Killer** [BFX 15210, 15228, 15229].) By
the close of the Mercury years, Lewis at 42, sounded somewhat tired, as if he
had not drawn a salutary breath since 1956. But a weary Lewis is still a force
to be reckoned with; and, in this age of malls, muzak, and milk-skinned
honky-tonk poseurs, his howlings, diminished but still with us, are like rare
fire in the desert.

Regional Musics: Cajun, 3 Western Swing, and the Bakersfield Sound

Geoffrey Himes

Amerian music has gathered much of its vitality from its willingness to mix genres: blues and swing combined to make rhythm and blues; hillbilly and R & B combined to make rock-and-roll; honky-tonk and rock-and-roll combined to make country-rock; and so on.

Paradoxically, American music has also drawn strength from regional musics that had little opportunity to mix with other styles. Isolated by geography and economics, these little pockets of musical activity were protected from the homogenizing tendencies of pop culture. Left on their own, the Cajuns and Creoles of Louisiana, the farmworkers and defense workers of California, and the ranchers and oil workers of Texas developed unique sounds that proved invaluable when the time for mixing came around. You can't mix musical styles if distinctly different genres don't exist, and you can't develop distinctive forms unless independent regional musics are allowed to flourish on their own.

Of course, before the widespread advent of the radio and phonograph record, almost all American music was regional music. Country music itself began as a regional music of the southern Appalachian mountains and only spread throughout the rest of the South and eventually the West when the radio and phonograph came along to carry the message. Because southern Appalachian music was still so close to its British/ Celtic origins, it struck a fundamental chord with the Anglo-Saxon farmers, who dominated the white population in the South, and either absorbed or overwhelmed the competing regional musics.

Several pockets of regional music, however, were strong enough to meet the spread of country head-on and insist on being equal partners with the trans-regional music. This chapter will focus on the three most important of those regional musics within the country sphere: Cajun, western swing and the Bakersfield sound.

These three regional styles shared four crucial characteristics. First, they all flourished west of the Mississippi River in isolated geographic pockets. The French Louisianians of Acadiana were cut off by rivers and swamps as well as language; the farmers and oil workers of Texas and Oklahoma were cut off by wide open spaces, and the farmworkers of the San Joaquin Valley were cut off by mountains on either side. And even at the end of the twentieth century, the Western US remains a less organized, less controlled place than the East, and Westerners are more likely to do things their own way.

Second, Cajun, western swing and the Bakersfield sound were all created by displaced migrants trying desperately to hang on to a piece of the culture they had left behind. The Cajuns were forced out of Acadia (aka Nova Scotia) by the British and settled in the swamps of Louisiana; the Texans and Oklahomans were restless spirits from the Eastern US who settled the then-open frontier at the turn of the century, and the Great Depression pushed many of those same Louisianians, Texans and Okies off their farms and out to California's San Joaquin Valley. Each of these groups held on tightly to the music they brought with them, but that music was inevitably changed by new circumstances into something unprecedented. The new music resembled neither the sounds they left behind nor the sounds they first found in their new homes.

Third, all three musics maintained a central role for the fiddle, long after the instrument had been shunted to the side-lines in mainstream country music. The fiddle's importance was directly related to the fourth and most important characteristic: Cajun, western swing and the Bakersfield sound were all created for and sustained by the dancehall.

In places like Lawtell, Louisiana, Waco, Texas, and Bakersfield, California, many of the locals didn't spend their Saturday nights with the radio or TV or even at the movies. Instead, they headed for the local dancehall, a sprawling, rickety wooden building – often an old dairy barn or an old house with countless additions. The air soon clouded with cigarette smoke and the wood slat floor quickly grew slick with sloshed beer. At one end of the room – on a small riser if they were lucky, often on the dance floor itself – was the band that alternated brisk two-steps with slower waltzes. Except for the few guitar nerds who crowded around the band and the small kids who dozed off on the pile of coats in the corner, everyone came to dance.

The demands of the dancehall had a major influence on the music in these areas. The musicians had to play with emphatic rhythms and lots of energy to keep the dancers happy. This by itself distinguished Western bands from their Eastern counterparts who relied more on sit-down shows. In search of high-energy, rhythmic music, Western bands often turned to local African American sources, and this further strengthened their distinct regional identities.

In most areas of the country, regional differences were steamrollered by the homogenizing influence of the Grand Ole Opry and like-minded radio stations and booking agencies, who promoted a national country music sound. In these isolated pockets of Louisiana, Texas, Oklahoma and California, however, country musicians could make a good enough living from the local dance halls that they could safely ignore national trends. The women – who were usually in charge of local dance styles – were less concerned about the new star on the Opry and more concerned with what dance steps they could try out with their neighborhood friends.

These factors conspired to produce regional country musics of astonishing vitality and endurance in southern Louisiana, northeast Texas, eastern Oklahoma and central California. Cajun, western swing and the Bakersfield sound remain strong influences today because they are similar enough to country music to invite borrowing and yet different enough to make the borrowing worthwhile.

Essential Recordings

(i) Cajun

In 1604 (three years before the colonization of Jamestown in Virginia), a wooden boat full of French Catholics fleeing religious persecution crossed the Atlantic and finally reached the easternmost shores of North America. They settled in Canada's maritime provinces, and they called their new land Acadia. The colony, separated geographically and culturally from the eventual colony of New France in what is now Quebec, thrived until the British started making increasingly aggressive claims to the land. In the 1713 Treaty of Utrecht, England was awarded Acadia and promptly renamed it Nova Scotia. In 1753, the English demanded that the French residents either make an unconditional oath of allegiance to the British Crown or face confiscation of property and deportation.

In 1755, 16,000 Acadians reluctantly took the latter course, and found themselves bouncing atop the ocean in wooden boats, much like their ancestors. Many of these refugees eventually landed in Louisiana, which was a French colony. By 1763, however, the Spanish had gained control of the territory, but the Spanish rulers offered the homeless Acadians land grants if they would settle the wilderness west and south of the Mississippi River. So it was that the Acadians finally settled along the bayous and prairies of southern Louisiana, where the local patois referred to them as Cajuns.

The Cajuns shared their new home with dwindling numbers of American Indians and growing numbers of Creoles, the latter being former African slaves who had either purchased their freedom or escaped to it. Just as importantly, there were few Anglo-Americans in the area, and a Cajun culture was created at first without much influence from the dominant US culture. Cajun or Creole, the South Louisianians fished shrimp and oysters from the Gulf of Mexico and redfish and alligators from its feeder bayous or grew rice, cotton, beans and cattle in the prairie just to the north. It was hard work – 12 hours a day, six days a week – and when Saturday night rolled around, the locals headed to the nearest house party or dance hall to unwind.

The French who had first settled Acadia were from the western, Celtic part of France, and the music they brought across the ocean was very similar to the jigs and reels of Irish and Scotch fiddle tunes. But when that style interacted with the African, Caribbean and proto-blues influences of the Creole culture, something entirely new was born.

The fiddle was the perfect frontier instrument, for it was cheap and portable. Its high pitch made its melody line easy to hear above a rhythm guitar, and a second fiddle could play a droning harmony to the first. The Creoles taught the Cajun fiddlers how to find those half-step "blue" notes and a distinctive music was born. In the mid- and late 1800s, German and Czech settlers brought the button accordion, which was equally cheap and portable. By the 1920s, the squeezebox had caught on big in the Cajun community and its exceptional loudness made the dance rhythms of Cajun music all the more emphatic even if the single-scale nature of the diatonic accordion cut back on the harmonic possibilities of the music and forced the fiddle to play within the box's limitations.

With the success of Vernon Dalhart and the Carter Family in the 1920s, record companies sent field-recording units out into the hinterlands looking for hillbilly performers who might sell some 78s. A Columbia unit stumbled into southern Louisiana in 1928 and discovered a brand of hillbilly music so strange that it was sung in French and played on German accordions. George Burr, a jeweler from Rayne, promised to buy 250 copies of a record by a local accordionist named Joe Falcon if Columbia would only record it. When Falcon with his accordion, and his striking, raven-haired wife, Cleoma, with her guitar, showed up at the New Orleans hotel on April 27, 1928, the Columbia engineers in their stiff collars were dubious.

"That's not enough to make a record," the engineers told the Falcons. Only when Burr doubled his initial order to 500 copies did the record company men agree to a run-through. The song was an old one, *Allons A Lafayette*, but the 28-year-old accordionist and his 23-year-old wife leaned into their instruments so hard that even today the music seems to jump off the grooves and pull you out on the dance floor. Even the engineers had to admit, "Lord, but that's more music out of two instruments than we ever heard in our lives."

Thus was the recorded history of Cajun music begun, and there's no better way to understand that history than to see the 1989 film, "J'ai Ete au Bal" (now available on video) or to listen to its wonderful soundtrack. Expertly blending interviews – from Marc Savoy's corny jokes to a tour of D.L. Menard's chair-making factory – with archival photographs, vintage recordings and contemporary performances, the movie gives a splendid overview of Cajun music and its African American alter egos, Creole and zydeco music.

The film – directed by Les Blank, Chris Strachwitz and Maureen Gosling – is full of wonderful anecdotes like the one about the Falcons' first recording session. In one scene, Edwin Duhon of the Hackberry Ramblers explains why a Cajun dance is called a "fais do do." Every dancehall had a "cry room" where the infants and small children were put to sleep. When a baby started crying, a young mother would hurriedly breastfeed it and encourage it to "go to sleep" ("fais do do") so she could get back to dancing with her husband before another woman did.

The soundtrack, which offers extra songs and unedited performances but none of the interviews, is even longer than the whole movie. With 46 numbers adding up to 130 minutes, the 2-CD package covers a lot of ground, from the Falcons' original version of *Allons A Lafayette* to Wayne Toups and the ZydeCajuns' modern swamp-rock version of the same song.

The accordion was still an innovation when Falcon's first single became a hit in South Louisiana (the idea of a woman dance musician was even more radical), but it soon took over the field. Beausoleil's Michael Doucet argues strongly in the movie that the recordings made by the unlikely duo of Dennis McGee, a white fiddler, and Amede Ardoin, a black accordionist, best define the common ground from which both Cajun and Creole/zydeco sprang.

The two young sharecroppers (pictured in Lynda Barry's folkloric cover for the soundtrack) were first teamed by their employer Oscar Commeaux in 1921, and the combination of McGee's Celtic fiddle melodies and Ardoin's African rhythms on the box and blue-note harmonies in his voice created an unprecedented sound; Louisiana musicians would be borrowing from the duo's few recordings for 60 years to come.

One of those recordings is on the "J'ai Ete au Bal" soundtrack; *Madame Atchen* sounds eerily ancient, as if its keening, moaning harmonies were just one short step away from the Acadian exile boats and the African slave ships. And yet the 1929 recording also sounds compellingly modern, as McGee and Ardoin find a way to vary the melody endlessly and still stay right inside the rhythm. The song seems to spin around and around on its own momentum and then suddenly leap up on every fourth bar like a dancer. It's a thrilling performance. McGee is also heard playing solo fiddle on three other selections, and Ardoin's cousin Boisec Ardoin is heard on another number.

The advent of recording was accompanied by the invasion of the radio, part of the "Americanization" of Cajun country. Oil was discovered there, and populist governor Huey Long started building bridges across the rivers and bayous of this watery area in the 1930s. Before long, South Louisiana wasn't quite so isolated anymore; and at this point the self-contained pond of Cajun music started interacting with the national currents of country music. The local dancers entranced by the western swing sounds coming from across the border with Texas were soon demanding that the local Louisiana bands serve up something similar.

The band that made the most of this opportunity was the Hackberry Ramblers. Luderin Darbone was a fiddler who loved the hillbilly music of Bob Wills and Jimmie Rodgers; across the street from him lived Edwin Duhon, a guitarist/accordionist who loved Cajun music. They both loved the black jazz band that played at the local dancehall; putting it all together, they soon had an immense repertoire. Darbone convinced his new partner that the accordion would make them sound old-fashioned, that an all-string band would appeal to the younger fans of Bob Wills's radio show.

When they formed a trio with singer/guitarist Lennis Sonnier and called themselves the Hackberry Ramblers, however, they soon found that their acoustic string instruments couldn't match the volume of an accordion band (which is why the box had become so popular in Louisiana's crowded, noisy dancehalls). So Luderin ordered a $60 sound system out of a catalogue from Chicago and suddenly, the Hackberry Ramblers were louder than any accordion band or any other band in French Louisiana, and the crowds started flocking to their shows.

The Hackberry Ramblers weren't just loud; they were very good. At times, they sounded like a Texas swing band with a French singer; at other times they sounded like an expanded, sleeker version of the early Cajun fiddle duos led by McGee and Leo Soileau. On the "J'ai Ete au Bal" soundtrack, you can hear the late-1980s version of the Hackberries doing *Une Piastre Ici*.

The Hackberry Ramblers' success at hillbilly-influenced Cajun encouraged other Louisiana musicians to go the same route. Though Darbone's band was the best, the Cajun country movement soon included Leo Soileau and the Four Aces, Happy Fats and the Rayne-Bo Ramblers, Hector Duhon and the Dixie Ramblers, J.B. Fuselier and his Merrymakers, Chuck Guillory and Papa Cairo. Though the Hackberry Ramblers were the first Cajun string band to have a hit with *Jole Blon* in 1936, it was the similar 1946 version by fiddler Harry Choates (who had played for Soileau, Cairo, and Happy Fats) that caught the fancy of returning GIs and became a reputed million seller. Choates's version is on the soundtrack.

In the late 1940s, however, the appeal of the string band faded and the accordion made a big comeback, thanks in large part to a dazzling, impassioned accordion player named Iry LeJeune. The movie opens with LeJeune's version of *J'ai Ete Au Bal*, and in his fast, driving rhythms and reckless vocal, you can hear the changed atmosphere of the post-war era as surely as you could in the music of Big Joe Turner or Hank Williams. LeJeune's success led the way for a new wave of accordionists, including Aldus Roger, Lawrence Walker, Octa Clark, Austin Pitre and especially Nathan Abshire, who had a big hit in 1949 with *Pine Grove Blues* and who is represented in the film by some rare 1969 footage.

None of them could compare, though, with LeJeune, perhaps the most exciting musician South Louisiana ever produced. Born in 1928 outside Church Point with no better than 20 percent vision, even with thick glasses LeJeune couldn't see well enough to do regular farm work. Instead, he spent hours listening to his uncle's old 78s by accordion pioneers Amede Ardoin, Amede Breaux and Uncle Angelas LeJeune himself. Before long the younger LeJeune was hitch-hiking with his own squeezebox in a pillowcase to whatever house party or barroom might pay him a few bucks. He made his first recording in 1948 for Houston's Opera Records ("Hits of the Hillbillies"), and *Evangeline Special* was a revolutionary record.

The accordion, jumping back and forth between a low phrase and a high one and alternating eighth-notes and triplets, gets a rhythm going that's more aggressive and relentless than anything in Cajun up to that point. LeJeune gives a high, wordless cry that seems to combine an anguished wail with a defiant shout; then he addresses an ex-girlfriend in French, singing of how she hurt him by standing him up the other night. You can hear the pained, helpless "cry" in his voice in that first verse, but by the third verse he's telling her not to bother coming back because she had her chance and blew it. He gives a few more high cries and concludes the song with the box huffing and puffing harder than ever.

Cajun veterans have often spoken of how LeJeune's emotionally transparent tenor captures the hurt and frustration of the prairie farmers, but his ability to transform that pain into the assertive, proud sound of his ferocious accordion rhythms and triumphant cries is what makes LeJeune so special. Even a pretty, slower song like *Love Bridge Waltz*, which backed his *Evangeline Special* 78 and which was adapted from one of his uncle's tunes, is played with impatient rhythms. It was clear that LeJeune, like the recently returned World War II veterans, wasn't going to stoically accept his fate as an impoverished farm worker, as earlier generations of Cajuns had.

The accordion, however, was still considered the sound of primitive hicks, and a radio station manager in Lake Charles told disc jockey Eddie Shuler to keep LeJeune's "ungodly music" off the air. Instead Shuler founded Folk-Star Records (which later became Goldband) and released LeJeune's *Lacassine Special* (years later recorded by Emmylou Harris) in 1949. This time the fast and furious accordion phrases take the shape of repeating melodic riffs, and his vocals take on the quality of the high, desperate cries of his earlier record.

Shuler went on to record 23 numbers in all by LeJeune between 1949 and 1955. Many of them were borrowed directly from Amede Ardoin, Dennis McGee, or LeJeune's Uncle Angelas. Both *Grand Bosco* and its later remake under the title *It Happened To Me* are French-language reworkings of Jimmie Rodgers's *I Was A Stranger*, and these tunes make it obvious that LeJeune is mixing Cajun and blues in much the same way Rodgers and Hank Williams were mixing hillbilly and blues. LeJeune has Rodgers's rhythmic verve and Williams's willingness to confess his pain without accepting it.

All of LeJeune's recordings for Opera, Folk-Star and Goldband have been collected on two anthologies. The US version, **The Legendary Iry LeJeune**, on Goldband includes the distracting electric bass overdubbed onto the original tapes in the mid-1960s. The UK version, **Iry LeJeune – Cajun's Greatest: The Definitive Collection**, on Ace features the original 78s without the dubbed bass. Because his eyesight was so poor, LeJeune relied on his fellow musicians for transportation to jobs. When he rode home with fiddler J.B. Fuselier after a gig on October 8, 1955, they had a flat tire. While they were changing it, they were blindsided by another car that instantly killed LeJeune and seriously injured Fuselier. LeJeune was just

35. As a brilliant young musician who died too young, LeJeune has the same mythic place in Cajun music that Robert Johnson has in the blues and Williams has in honky-tonk.

Like a lot of regional musics, Cajun was hit hard by the rock-and-roll revolution which swept through the land in the mid-1950s. Some younger Cajuns – including Warren Storm, Tommy McLain and Clint West – eventually joined the rock-and-roll movement in a subgenre that was eventually dubbed swamp-pop, and Johnnie Allan represents them on the "J'ai Ete au Bal" soundtrack with *Do You Love Me So*. Others moved more toward country, and Jimmy C. Newman, and Doug and Rusty Kershaw even had national hits out of Nashville. The best of the country-Cajun singers, though, was D.L. Menard, represented on the soundtrack by two compositions that became Cajun standards, *The Back Door* and *Under A Green Oak Tree*.

Doris Leon Menard was born outside Erath in 1932 and heard very little music at all until the family moved into town when he was 16. He heard his Uncle Paul's Cajun band and was so inspired that he ordered an $11 guitar from Montgomery Ward, but the first song he learned to play was Hank Williams's *Mansion On The Hill*, and the first song he sang in public was Lefty Frizzell's *If You Got The Money, I Got The Time*. The teenage musician didn't see much difference between the Cajun musicians like Lawrence Walker or Aldus Roger and honky-tonkers like Williams or Frizzell. They all played simple melodies with steady two-beat or three-beat rhythms. The Louisianians sang in French and played triplets against a 2/4 rhythm on the fiddle or accordion, but they sang about problems with women, bosses and bottles with the same twangy lament as the Anglos.

In 1951, Williams was playing at the Teche Club near the Bayou Teche, and the 19-year-old Menard got there early, hoping to meet his idol. The teenager had already been playing with accordionist Elias Badeaux and his Louisiana Aces for two years, and would stay with them for another 20. He met Williams, who asked when Menard planned to start recording. "Hank," Menard replied, "I'm not gonna record; it's just French music." Williams set him straight, "All music's good if it's yours."

The meaning of that sentence stayed with Menard through the years, and in 1962, when he was pumping gas at his day job in Erath, he got the idea for a song. It was loosely based on Williams's own *Honky Tonk Blues* and told the story of a man who stayed out all night with his girl friend and then had to sneak in through the back door of his parents' house. Between customers at the service station, Menard scribbled down the lyrics in French. When the Louisiana Aces went back in to the studio, Menard begged them to record his new song, *La Porte D'En Arrière* (*The Back Door*), and after much argument they finally relented, figuring it would be relegated to the B side of the single. Instead it became one of the most famous Cajun songs ever released.

The record was released under Badeaux's name and his accordion reinforced the song's stomping rhythm, but it was Menard's show all the way. He sets the beat with his acoustic guitar and tells the tale, "Moi et la belle on avait ete-z-au bal/ On a passe dans tous les honky tonks" ("Me and my gal went to the dance/We visited all the honky tonks"), in a striking nasal voice that hints at both the thrills and loneliness of the independent, dissolute life. The original single is included on **D.L. Menard Sings "The Back Door" And His Other Cajun Hits**, a fine collection of the dozen best songs he recorded for Swallow between 1961 and 1976.

He never again matched the impact of *La Porte D'En Arrière*, but he kept writing and singing fine honky-tonk songs with French lyrics that earned him the well-deserved nickname of "The Cajun Hank Williams." *She Didn't Know I Was Married*, recorded in 1963, is a traditional Cajun waltz, but it features a prominent pedal steel part and the guilty confession of a married man who wooed a young girl and broke her heart. On the flip side was a bouncy Cajun two-step that celebrated the joys of the *Bachelor's Life*.

Rebecca Ann, recorded in 1964, is a hillbilly waltz that, with the hard-won authority of lost innocence, warns a young girl to stay in school and not marry an older divorced man. On the flip side was a swampier Cajun waltz, *I Can Live A Better Life*. The lyrics describe a typically distinctive Menard scenario, of a young wife who has taken up with another man and suggests that she and her husband live as a brother and sister. When Menard cries out, "Je peux vivre un tas mieux que ca" ("I can live a lot better than that"), he speaks not just for the husband but for all the Cajuns who knew there was a better life out there than subsistence farming.

Despite the success of swamp-pop and country-Cajun, the traditional, undiluted Cajun music was in serious decline, relegated for the most part to weddings, family reunions and old people's bars. In the rush to assimilation, many Louisianians were eager to slough off the Cajun association that their non-French neighbors looked down upon – and that included the chanky-chank music that went with it. When talent scouts for the Newport Folk Festival came to South Louisiana looking for Cajun musicians, an editorial in one local paper suggested that the whole state would be embarrassed if it were represented by Cajun musicians at a major folk festival.

Dewey Balfa went anyway. The son of a sharecropper who sold insurance and drove a school bus on weekdays, Balfa had been playing fiddle on weekends with his older brother Will, also a fiddler, and their younger brother Rodney, a guitarist, since 1948. They had recorded a 78 for Khoury Records and had backed up Nathan Abshire, but they had never played for more than 200 people and had never played outside South Louisiana. When folklorist Ralph Rinzler asked Dewey to play guitar with fiddler Louis LeJeune and accordionist Gladius Thibodeaux at the 1964 Newport Folk Festival, Dewey had no idea what a festival was or what all this talk about workshops and concerts meant. But he drove up to Rhode Island and had one of those experiences that changes a person's life.

Sharing the stage that weekend with Joan Baez, Bob Dylan and Peter, Paul and Mary, the three Cajun musicians were greeted by a standing ovation from the 17,000 people in the audience. They were astounded. After years of playing for small clumps of chattering drinkers in stuffy barrooms and deflecting insults about their old-fashioned, backwards chanky-chank music, they were suddenly being cheered by thousands for the exact same music. Dewey returned to Louisiana determined, as he says in the "J'ai Ete au Bal" film, to "bring the echo of that standing ovation home."

Dewey was a "cultural guided missile," in Michael Doucet's words, and became a tireless advocate for Cajun music and, by extension, all of French Louisiana culture. He wanted traditional Cajun music played in concert halls and schools where people could hear what an exquisite music it really was. He wanted Cajun French taught in classes so a younger generation could understand the songs and stories of the culture. He pestered Swallow Records' Floyd Soileau to record the Balfa Brothers playing traditional acoustic music in French. He begged Rinzler to bring the whole Balfa Brothers Band to Newport so he could present his family's unique musical tradition to the festival.

It all paid off. The Balfa Brothers performed at the 1967 Newport Folk Festival to thunderous acclaim and were soon playing at folk festivals all over North America and Europe. CODOFIL, the Council for the Development of French in Louisiana, was formed in 1968, and Dewey convinced them to sponsor the first Tribute to Cajun Music Festival in 1974. And Swallow Records released **The Balfa Brothers Play Traditional Cajun Music** in 1965. It remains one of the most beautiful albums of Cajun music ever recorded.

Dewey played the melodic leads on his fiddle, and Will played the droning "baritone" harmony on his. Rodney played the driving rhythm on acoustic guitar and sang the vocals (harmonized by Dewey); another brother Harry played second guitar; yet another brother Burke played the triangle and a family friend named Hadley Fontenot played the button accordion. They played with the telepathic rapport only available to family bands; the twin fiddles took the lead and lent a lyricism rarely heard in any music. A follow-up album was released in 1974, with Marc Savoy replacing Fontenot on accordion and Rodney's son Tony replacing Burke on triangle and percussion. All 24 songs have now been gathered onto a single CD, **The Balfa Brothers Play Traditional Cajun Music, Vols 1 and 2.**

The CD begins with *'Tit Galop Pour Mamou,* the traditional source of *Diggy, Diggy Lo,* and the Balfas take the song at a brisk pace, with the triangle and guitar pushing the beat along. The fiddles help establish the rhythm at first, but after Rodney's first vocal, Dewey jumps up above the rhythm to play a high-tenor variation on the tune. His coda solo is even better, as he jumps in and out of the repeating riff to reinvent the melody as a carefree romp and thus capture the feeling of release that Cajun music at its best provides.

La Valse Du Bamboucheur (The Drunkard's Sorrow Waltz) is a splendid example of how Will's droning fiddle harmonies creates an undercurrent of unappeasable sadness in certain songs. *Les Flammes D'Enfer (The Flames Of Hell)* showcases how the Balfas could saw away at bluegrass tempos and still maintain their distinctive swamp rhythms. *Valse De Balfa* is an old waltz tune that the brothers' father and grandfather used to play around the farmhouse in Grand Louis. The sons remembered the tune but not the words, so Will made up some new lyrics and Rodney sings them to the eerily captivating drone melody.

The album's most haunting selection, though, is *La Danse De Mardi Gras.* On Mardi Gras morning in French Louisiana, the men in each town dress up in tall, conical, cloth-draped hats, wire-screen masks and circus-like costumes and ride their horses out to the local farms to collect birds, meat and vegetables for the big gumbo at the dance that evening. This song not only describes the Mardi Gras "courir" with its lyrics but evokes the ritual's ambience with clip-clop, horse-hoof rhythms and a minor-key melody as strange and other-worldly as the riders in their masks. With Dewey playing little embellishments above the droning melody figure and the relentless rhythms, the effect is hypnotic.

Fate was not kind to Dewey Balfa. His son died in 1971; his wife died in 1980, and his brothers Will and Rodney died in an auto accident in 1979. Each time, though, he bounced back to pick up the fiddle and play traditional Cajun music with his faith in the music's artistic value and uplifting properties intact. He passed along that faith, as well as his high musical standards, to his daughter, nephews, Michael Doucet, Steve Riley, Tracy Schwarz and many others. When Dewey finally died himself in 1992, his legacy was in safe hands.

When Michael Doucet grew up outside Lafayette in the 1950s and 1960s, Cajun music was just something he heard at family reunions and weddings. Though you could still get whipped at school for speaking French, it was the language everyone spoke around the house and everyone still danced to the old fiddle-and-accordion songs. Doucet's uncle T-Will Knight was a fiddler and several aunts sang, but the music seemed so common and old-fashioned that he just took it for granted.

Even in the early 1970s, as the Balfa Brothers' Cajun renewal movement was in full swing and Doucet was playing guitar in a bar band called the Bayou Drifters, the music seemed more like a hobby than a profession. It wasn't until 1974, as he was graduating from Louisiana State University and preparing to go off to graduate school in English literature, that the breakthrough came.

France was undergoing its own folk revival, and Cajun was popular there as the newest creative form of French folk music. A Frenchman heard Doucet's band in a bar and asked them if they'd like to play a festival in France. So the band went off to Europe for two weeks and ended up staying six months. It was a life-changing experience. After years of hearing Cajun culture put down in Louisiana as backwards, Doucet suddenly found himself facing standing ovations for the same music. The music hadn't changed, but its meaning for Doucet had.

He committed himself to learning traditional Cajun fiddle and won a National Endowment for the Arts apprenticeship grant to do just that. It took a good bit of searching, but Doucet finally tracked down the older, mostly retired, fiddle masters – Dennis McGee, Hector Duhon, Varise Connor, Canray Fontenot and the Balfa Brothers – and soaked up their tunes as well as their technique. In 1975, Doucet formed a Cajun-jazz-rock band called Coteau (which included his cousin Zachary Richard) but as his fiddle lessons progressed, he opted instead for a more traditional, more acoustic format that he dubbed Beausoleil (after Joseph Broussard dit Beausoleil, a resistance leader during the forced exile of the French Acadians).

From the beginning Beausoleil included Doucet's kid brother David on acoustic guitar and local pals Tommy Comeaux on mandolin, (and later electric bass) and Billy Ware on triangle (and later rubboard and congas). They learned and eventually excelled at the traditional Cajun repertoire, but two crucial factors distinguished these young musicians from their predecessors like Iry LeJeune, Dennis McGee and the Balfa Brothers: the members of Beausoleil had been to college and they had grown up listening to the Beatles, Bob Dylan, Willie Nelson and Miles Davis.

This meant several things. First, Doucet and his fellow travelers saw no reason they shouldn't draw on South Louisiana's African American traditions of Creole and zydeco music as readily as they drew on Cajun. Second, they were willing to follow the rhythmic and harmonic possibilities of the music wherever they might lead. Third, each musician was encouraged to expand the possibilities of his instrument, so David Doucet added bluegrass flat-picking to the traditional rhythmic role of the Cajun guitar; drummer Tommy Alesi added New Orleans R & B and zydeco licks to the steady chanky-chank of Cajun, and Al Tharp made the banjo fit in the Cajun context. And fourth, Michael Doucet and the others were aggressive about writing new songs in French and within the tradition but with original twists of their own. The result was the one Cajun group that could do it all: old or new, black or white, solo or ensemble.

Beausoleil started recording in 1980, and by 1993 they had released 11 studio albums, one live album and two anthologies as well as countless solo albums by various members plus contributions to a number of multi-artist collections. The one best album, though, is **Bayou Deluxe: The Best Of Michael Doucet And Beausoleil**, which draws 17 tracks from 10 of the other albums (plus one newly re-recorded tune) to tell the story of this remarkable band. Beausoleil has never forgotten that they are primarily a dance band, and this album is arranged not chronologically but with the rhythms of a dance hall set – kinetic two-steps alternating with stately waltzes, traditional Cajun for the old folks alternating with raucous zydeco/ Caribbeana for the young folks.

The album opens with *Le Jig Francais*, which is not actually a jig but a traditional Cajun two-step originally written by Wallace "Cheese" Reed and rewritten by Doucet for Beausoleil's best traditional Cajun album, **Parlez-Nous A Boire**, of 1984. The tune became a staple of the band's live shows and grew increasingly loose and energetic as the group learned how to muscle up the old rhythms and extend the old fiddle breaks into new harmonic territory. Those changes are reflected in the 1993 recording of the song, which boasts a rocking beat and fiddle, guitar and accordion solos that turn the melody inside out.

Even more raucous and exhilarating is *Zydeco Gris-Gris*,

which opens with Doucet screaming like a monkey and proceeds to turn an old Amede Ardoin tune into a fast dance number worthy of Clifton Chenier, with an electric guitar solo by John Hiatt's Louisiana sidekick, Sonny Landreth. An admiring Richard Thompson adds electric guitar to the droning, mesmerizing *Sur Le Pont De Lyon*, and Cajun-country star Jo-el Sonnier adds accordion to *Travailler, C'Est Trop Dur*. The band even tackles the old Delta blues tune, *Baby, Please Don't Go*, and gives it a swampy jump without lessening its desperate moan.

The band nods to its influences with versions of Dennis McGee's *Donnez Moi Pauline* and Lawrence Walker's *Les Bons Temps Rouler Waltz*, and with affectionate revisions of the Balfa Brothers versions of *La Chanson De Mardi Gras* and *Les Flammes D'Enfer*. The sweetness of Michael Doucet's patient fiddle lines over his brother's steady guitar rhythms is never more apparent than on the old-style, acoustic numbers like *Madame Sosthene* and *Je M'Endors*. On every song, you hear a band that believes completely in the Cajun tradition and believes just as strongly that the tradition is still being invented by musicians like themselves.

The last song on the "J'ai Ete au Bal" soundtrack is the Beausoleil version of the title song. Playing with such unity that it seems each member is breathing in and out on the same beat, Doucet's band blurs the line between solos and ensemble work by keeping the soloists in the rhythmic pocket and by encouraging the comping players to vary their lines. With every musician in Beausoleil combining the lyricism of the Balfas with the fiery drive of Iry LeJeune, the future of Cajun music seems just as impressive at its past.

Discographical Details

87 J'Ai Ete Au Bal (I Went To The Dance). Vols 1 and 2

Various Artists

Arhoolie CD 331/2 (2-disc set)

Volume 1: Walter Mouton and the Scott Playboys: *J'Ai Ete Au Bal*; Walter Mouton and the Scott Playboys: *Convict Waltz*; Queen Ida and the Bon Ton Zydeco Band: *Ful Il Sa*; Lionel LeLeux: *J'Ai Ete Au Bal*; Lionel Leleux and Michael Doucet: *Lake Arthur Stomp*; Michael Doucet: *Acadian Waltz*; Michael Doucet: *Reel Cajun*; Canray Fontenot: *Lorita*; Canray Fontenot: *Bernadette*; Dennis McGee: *Happy One-Step*; Dennis McGee: *O, Malheureuse*; Amede Ardoin and Dennis McGee: *Madame Atchen*; Boisec Ardoin and Sons: *Lake Charles Two-Step*; Nathan Abshire: *Domino Two-Step*; Nathan Abshire: *Jolie Petite Blonde*; Marc Savoy: *Melville Two-Step*; Marc and Ann Savoy: *I Made A Big Mistake*; Joe Falcon and Cleoma Breaux: *Allons A Lafayette*; Odile Falcon: *La Reine De La Salle*; Solange Falcon: *Ninety-Nine Year Waltz*; Luderin Darbone and the Hackberry

Ramblers: *Une Piastre Ici*; Leo Soileau and his Four Aces: *Hackberry Hop*; Chuck Guillory with Preston Manuel and the Rhythm Boys: *Grand Texas*; Harry Choates: *Jole Blonde*; Iry LeJeune: *J'Ai Ete Au Bal*; Iry LeJeune: *La Valse De Grands Chemins*
Volume 2: Joseph Jones: *Blues De Prison*; Jimmy Peters and the Ring Dance Singers: *Zydeco Sont Pas Sales*; Sidney Babineaux: *Zydeco Sont Pas Sales*; Clifton Chenier: *Louisiana Blues*; Clifton Chenier: *Zydeco Sont Pas Sales*; D.L. Menard and the Louisiana Aces: *The Back Door*; D.L. Menard with the California Cajuns: *Under A Green Oak Tree*; Belton Richard: *Another Lonely Night*; Johnny Allen: *Do You Love Me So*; Dewey Balfa: *Port Arthur Blues*; The Balfa Brothers Band: *Acadian Two-Step*; The Balfa Brothers Band: *La Valse Criminelle*; Rodney Balfa: *Jongle A Moi*; Michael Doucet and Beausoleil: *Quoi Faire*; Paul Daigle: *Rayne One-Step*; Paul Daigle and Cajun Gold: *I Told Lies*; John Delafose and the Eunice Playboys: *Joe Pitre A Deux Femmes*; Boozoo Chavis: *Johnny Ain't No Goat*; Clifton Chenier and the Red Hot Louisiana Band: *I'm A Hog For You*; Rockin' Sidney: *My Toot Toot*; Wayne Toups and ZydeCajun: *Allons A Lafayette*; Michael Doucet and Beausoleil: *J'Ai Ete Au Bal*

88 Iry LeJeune – Cajun's Greatest: The Definitive Collection

Iry LeJeune
Ace CDCHD 428 (UK)
Grand Nuit Especial/Grande Bosco/Duraldo Waltz/I Went To the Dance/La Valse De Bayou Chene/I Made A Big Mistake/Come And Get Me/Donnes Moi Mon Chapeau/Waltz Of The Mulberry Limb/Church Point Breakdown/La Valse Du Grande Chemin/Jolie Catin/La Fitte La Vove/Bayou Pon Pon Special/La Valse De Cajun/Don't Get Married/Convict Waltz/It Happened To Me/Parting Waltz/Evangeline Special/Love Bridge Waltz/Teche Special/Calcasieu Waltz/Te Mone/Lacassine Special

89 D.L. Menard Sings "The Back Door" And His Other Cajun Hits

D.L. Menard
Swallow LP-6038 (LP)
The Back Door/I Can't Forget You/She Didn't Know I Was Married/Bachelor's Life/Valse De Jolly Rogers/Miller's Cave/The Water Pump/It's Too Late You're Divorced/Riches Of A Musician/The Veil And The Crown/I Can Live A Better Life/Rebecca Ann

90 The Balfa Brothers Play Traditional Cajun Music, Vols 1 and 2

The Balfa Brothers
Swallow SW-CD-6011
'Tit Galop Pour Mamou/Je Suis Orphelin/T'En A Eu Mais T'En N'Aras Plus/ Two-Step De L'Anse A Paille/La Danse De Mardi Gras/Je Me Suis Marillie/ Enterre-Moi Pas/Chere Joues Roses/Chere Bassette/J'Ai Passé Devant Ta Porte/Les Flammes D'Enfer/Madeleine/La Valse Du Bamboucheur/Lacassine Special/My True Love/La Valse De Grand Bois/Family Waltz/Newport Waltz/ Indian On A Stomp/T'Es Petite Et T'Es Mignonne/Two-Step A Hadley/Valse De Balfa/Parlez Nous A Boire/Les Blues Du Cadien

91   Bayou Deluxe: The Best Of Michael Doucet And Beausoleil

Michael Doucet and Beausoleil

Rhino R2 71169

Le Jig Francais/Tasso/McGee's Reel/Madame Sosthene/Zydeco Gris-Gris/Blues A Bebe/Je M'Endors/Dimanche Après-Midi/Vieux Crowley/La Chanson De Mardi Gras/Travailler, C'est Trop Dur/J'Ai Ete Au Zydeco/Chez Seychelles/ Baby, Please Don't Go/Les Bons Temps Rouler Waltz/Awesome Ossun Two-Step/Donnez-Moi Pauline/Les Flammes D'Enfer/Sur Le Pont De Lyon

(ii) Western Swing

When he was just eight years old, in 1913, Bob Wills and his family made a 500-mile trek from their farm near Limestone County in East Texas to Hall County in West Texas. The family piled into two covered wagons and young Jim Rob, as he was called then, tagged along on his donkey. The trip took several months, for the family stopped at every cotton farm along the way that was hiring pickers. At these farms, the family shared rickety shacks with blacks and other Anglos, and after 12 or 14 hours a day of plucking the white cotton balls from the reluctant plants, the workers would gather in front of the shacks for some music and dancing.

The fiddle and guitar – the two instruments best suited for the itinerant life – dominated the proceedings. While the Anglos played the Celtic and British fiddle tunes and ballads they had brought with them from the East, the blacks played blues and ragtime not too far removed from the African music of their grandparents. Giddy children and drunken adults would "jig-dance" to either brand of music. Wills's father was usually the best fiddler at every camp they visited, and the young boy, who danced at every chance, soaked it all up like a sponge. Even during the daylight hours, the blacks would sing blues and work songs between the rows of cotton, helping to pass the long hours.

In 1929, 16 years later, a 24-year-old Wills was still kicking around Texas, trying to find a way to make a living. He had tried working as a barber, a preacher, farm worker, shoe shiner, carpenter and a salesman, but nothing took. He was three years married, but his restless spirit could not settle down. The one thing he kept coming back to, though, was the music he heard in those cotton camps. He picked up some good change playing fiddle at the occasional weekend dance, and it gradually dawned on him that the one thing he was good at was combining his daddy's frontier fiddle music with the blues he loved so much.

He marched into a Fort Worth radio station in 1929 and persuaded the manager to give the trio he'd formed a regular slot.

The show generated lots of mail, but not much money, so Wills joined a travelling minstrel show, where his genuine feel and affection for African American music made his blackface routine all the more effective. Around the same time, Wills and Herman Arnspiger, a guitarist from the minstrel show, landed a paying radio job in Fort Worth. With the publicity they generated from their 6.30 a.m. broadcast, the duo – dubbed the Wills Fiddle Band – was hired to play lots of house dances in the evenings.

Most of the people at these dances were, like Wills himself, recent arrivals in the city from the countryside. They hungered for a music whose form – a fiddle band playing fiddle tunes – was reassuringly familiar, but whose content – the skipping syncopation of the dawning jazz age – appealed to their mobile, newly urban circumstances. With his childhood experiences and his genuine enthusiasm for both strands of music, Wills was uniquely qualified to satisfy the dancers' craving.

As his popularity increased, Wills moved to bigger radio stations. His group became the Aladdin Laddies when sponsored by Aladdin Lamps and the Light Crust Doughboys when sponsored by Burrus Mills. They moved from Fort Worth to Waco, then Oklahoma City and finally, in 1934, to Tulsa where they officially became the Texas Playboys. Wills kept adding musicians as he could afford it, and the 1934 septet featured two fiddles, two guitars, bass, piano, and banjo. When dancers spotted the Texas Playboys at one end of Cain's dancehall outside Tulsa, what they saw was a traditional country string band.

What they heard, however, was a new kind of jazz band. The rhythms had a Dixieland syncopation, and as Wills later told his biographer Charles Townsend, "I slurred my fiddle in order to play the blues." For newly urbanized ex-farmers who craved both the nostalgic familiarity of rural string bands and the excitement of a jumping, city music, Wills's Texas Playboys were the perfect blend. And this collision of Euro-American and Afro-American strands created a brilliant new form of music, as it always does.

In 1934 and 1935, Wills redefined the possibilities of country-music instrumentation and arrangements. The steel guitar was beginning to come into vogue, and Wills bought an amplified model for Leon McAuliffe in 1935: suddenly the instrument's sliding, weeping lines could be heard in a noisy dancehall. That same year, he hired a second violinist, Jesse Ashlock, away from Milton Brown, the terrific singer who had left Wills's band in 1932 to form his own successful band. Ashlock, whose hero was Joe Venuti, would play the jazz breaks, while Wills would play the frontier fiddle breakdowns.

In the summer of 1935, Wills added a piano player, Al Stricklin, a Fort Worth jazz player whose hero was Earl "Fatha" Hines. Wills instructed Stricklin not to play melody in the country fashion but rhythm and harmony in the jazz style.

Wills loved the pioneering swing bands led by Fletcher Henderson and longed to imitate their horn arrangements. He often encouraged his fiddlers and guitarists to imitate horn lines, and when trumpeter Everett Stover and saxophonist Zeb McNally began to sit in with the band in 1934, Wills liked the sound so much that he soon had them playing on the radio broadcasts and out-of-town tours, too. All these additional instruments required a more forceful rhythm section, and Wills broke with tradition again when he hired Tulsa Dixieland drummer Smokey Dacus.

Dacus's job was to accent the two and four beats that were the key to Wills's swinging dance rhythms. The snare drum wasn't getting the job done, so Dacus took to walloping the big case that he carried his drums in, and its booming tone put the dancers in motion. The Texas Playboys called it the "suitcase rhythm," and it became a foundation for the western swing sound.

The emphasis was not on playing the right notes but on playing the right "feel" as a blues or jazz musician might. This "feel" was symptomized by Wills's famous shout of "a-ha!", whenever he recognized the "feel" he wanted. The cry was much more than a show-biz gimmick; it was the leader's way of alerting the band that they were on the right track and should keep going in that direction. To keep the music spontaneous and his players on their toes, Wills never allotted solo slots in advance. He'd wait until he was in the middle of a tune and had the "feel" for who should come next. Then he'd cry out in his yodel-like voice, "Take it away, Leon!" or "Ah, Jesse!" and the musician would jump right in. And woe to anyone who wasn't ready.

Wills had recorded two songs for Brunswick Records in 1929 which were never released, but he was ready when a second chance came around in 1935. He had finally assembled what some consider his greatest band: vocalist Tommy Duncan, banjoist Johnnie Lee Wills, bassist Son Lansford, trumpeter Everett Stover, saxophonist Zeb McNally, guitarist Herman Arnspiger, trombonist Art Haines, fiddler Jesse Ashlock, steel guitarist Leon McAuliffe, guitarist Sleepy Johnson, drummer Smokey Dacus, pianist Al Stricklin, and Wills himself.

They started with the old black string band song, *Osage Stomp*, on September 21, 1935, in a makeshift Dallas studio. According to Wills's biographer, Charles Townsend, when Wills started encouraging the musicians with his usual shouts,

Brunswick producer Arthur Satherley, an Englishman who loved "pure" American folk music, objected that all the hollering was covering up the music. "Is that right?" Wills replied, before telling the band, "Pack up; we're going home." Satherley tried to reassure the bandleader but was told, "You want Bob Wills, you get Bob Wills and Bob Wills hollers any time he feels like it and says what he wants to say." Satherley relented in the face of this fiercely determined hillbilly, and the band recorded 20 songs over the next five days.

Maiden's Prayer, one of the instrumentals from that initial session, kicks off **Anthology (1935–1973)**, the best available overview of Bob Wills and his Texas Playboys. The pretty country melody, carried by the two fiddles and steel guitar, flows smoothly against the choppy Dixieland rhythm played by the rest of the band. It sold well enough for the band to be invited to Chicago in 1936 for another session. By this time Satherley had been converted to the cause (Wills began to call him "Uncle Art"), and he encouraged the band's exuberance. This resulted in the big hit instrumental, *Steel Guitar Rag*, which heavily featured McAuliffe. Stricklin and the horns get their chances, too, to strut their stuff on this more modern swing tune, and Dacus is everywhere at once, pushing the musicians with forceful drum accents.

In the late-1930s, Wills added still more horns (saxophonists Joe Ferguson, Don Harlan, Louis Tierney, Tiny Mott and Wayne Johnson, and trumpeter Tubby Lewis) and a jazz-schooled guitarist named Eldon Shamblin was added to write arrangements. By 1940, Wills had assembled his greatest band ever and was ready to record his biggest hits. Wills's composition, *Time Changes Everything*, is an old-fashioned Appalachian-style lament, but Duncan's Bing Crosby-like crooning and the solos by Ashlock and McAuliffe make it paradoxically modern. From the same session came *Corrine, Corrina*, an old 12-bar blues given a joyful lilt by the band's effortless swing.

The biggest hit of all was recorded the next day, April 16, 1940. During a brief sojourn in New Mexico in 1927, where he had played with a Mexican band, Wills had written a fiddle tune called *Spanish Two-Step*. Recorded in 1938 as a slightly altered instrumental called *San Antonio Rose*, it became a modest hit. Irving Berlin's organization wanted to publish the song, provided it was given lyrics.

After several tries, Wills and Stover came up with some particularly evocative words, and the Texas Playboys recorded the tune again as *New San Antonio Rose*. It opens with all eight horns playing the lovely melody in a way that combines Benny Goodman with a mariachi band, while the rhythm section chops out a Dixieland beat. Duncan's baritone vocal provides the buttery smoothness appropriate for this vision of disappointed love underneath the moonlit West Texas sky, but it was Wills's impromptu parenthetical cries that gave the recording its contagious giddiness. The record went to number 11 on the Billboard charts, and Bing Crosby's cover version went to number 7 a few months later.

In the early 1940s, the band recorded *Take Me Back To Tulsa*, one of the catchiest, liveliest songs it ever did; Cindy Walker's *Cherokee Maiden* (which Merle Haggard remade into a number 1 country hit in 1976); and *Stay A Little Longer* (which became a staple of Willie Nelson's live show in the 1970s and 1980s). World War II had broken up the band by 1943, however, and Wills and Duncan (who left but rejoined in 1943) were the only members of the great 1940 band still around for 1945's *Texas Playboy Rag*. After a brief, unsuccessful spell in the army himself, Wills reorganized the Texas Playboys and relocated to California, where many of their old Texas and Oklahoma fans had relocated anyway to work in the defense plants. It was during these years that Wills sowed the seeds for the California country movement and the Bakersfield sound that was its choicest fruit.

In 1946, Wills started recording "transcriptions" for the Tiffany Music Corporation of Oakland, California. These were intended to be sold as syndicated radio programs to stations throughout the Southwest. That didn't work out, but the recordings capture the band in a looser, more playful mood than on its studio recordings. Six of those transcriptions (available in their entirety from Kaleidoscope Records, now owned by Rhino Records) are featured on **Anthology**, and they are among the highlights of the set. The horns have been reduced to a single trumpet, and the new stars are Lester "Junior" Barnard, who plays the newly introduced solid-body electric guitars with the hot, bluesy instincts of a Charlie Christian or T-Bone Walker, and Tiny Moore, who plays a jazzy electric mandolin. Shamblin and Duncan are back in the band, and steel guitarist Herb Remington and pianist Millard Kelso are able replacements for McAuliffe and Stricklin.

In 1947, Wills ended 12 years with Columbia Records and signed with MGM. He found another scintillating fiddler in a Texas youngster named Johnny Gimble and started to use his youngest brother, Billy Jack Wills, as a singer after Duncan left again. The big hit of this period was *Faded Love*, based on an old fiddle tune played by Bob's father John Wills, with new lyrics by Billy Jack. Despite a saccharine vocal-harmony arrangement, the song boasted a striking fiddle solo by Gimble and an irresistible melody. The song became a Top 10 country hit not only for Wills in 1950 but also for Patsy Cline in 1963 and the duo of Willie Nelson and Ray Price in 1980.

By 1955, Wills's best days were behind him. Crowds were down; the band got smaller; his longtime drinking problems got worse, and he suffered heart attacks in 1962 and 1964. He made some mediocre records for Decca, Liberty and Kapp, both before and after he finally broke up the band in 1964. In 1969, he suffered a debilitating stroke. Merle Haggard reunited many of the original Texas Playboys for his 1970 album, **A Tribute To The Best Damn Fiddle Player In The World**, and organized a reunion album for the band itself. The first session for that album took place on December 3, 1973, with a wheelchair-bound Wills crying "a-ha!" and cueing the solos as he had in the past. That evening he suffered another massive stroke, and though he lingered on till his death in 1975, he never regained consciousness. **Anthology** ends, fittingly enough, with Wills himself delivering the sing-song answer to the musical question, "What makes Bob holler," from that final session.

There were many other western swing acts in the thirties, forties and fifties, as Wills's innovations spread like wildfire across the dance halls, radio stations and recording studios of the Southwest, but few of these bands escaped Wills's long shadow. The best ones seemed to be led by Wills's former sidekicks (Milton Brown, Leon McAuliffe, Jesse Ashlock) or by Wills's own brothers (Johnnie Lee Wills and Billy Jack Wills). Even those that had no direct connection to Wills borrowed liberally from his sound and repertoire. Some of these other bands were very good – most notably Milton Brown and his Musical Brownies (Bruner was a former member of Brown's Brownies), Roy Newman and his Boys, Cliff Bruner's Texas Wanderers and Jimmie Revard and his Oklahoma Playboys – but they were eclipsed by Wills, and today their recordings are very hard to find.

Western swing continued to exert a great influence over country music even after its heyday, and you can hear the tradition thriving in mainstream acts like Haggard, Nelson, Hank Thompson, George Strait, Red Steagall, Alvin Crow and Junior Brown. The genre got a second life, however, from a most unlikely source. In the 1970s and 1980s, a bunch of hippies fell in love with Bob Wills and created a western swing revival through groups like Commander Cody and his Lost Planet Airmen, Dan Hicks and his Hot Licks, Cowboy Jazz and especially Asleep at the Wheel.

Ray Benson, Reuben Gosfield and Danny Levin discovered western swing in the unlikely environs of suburban Philadelphia. They played in school bands and rock-and-roll bands together in high school, but more importantly they egged each other on to discover the most obscure American roots music recordings they could find. Gosfield would dig up some Delta blues by Charley Patton; Levin would counter with Appalachian ballads by Dock Boggs, and Benson would weigh in with Dixieland sides by King Oliver.

When they discovered the western swing of Bob Wills, however, it seemed like the perfect music for them, because it incorporated everything else: blues, Appalachian fiddle tunes, Dixieland, big-band swing, boogie-woogie and honky-tonk. If they explained to people that they were playing western swing, there was almost nothing they couldn't play. Gosfield put aside his slide guitar and bought a pedal steel; Ray bought a cowboy hat, and they were in business.

They first started using the name Asleep at the Wheel in 1970 in Columbia, Maryland, where Reuben was going to college. They picked up a songwriter/drummer named Leroy Preston and a female singer named Chris O'Connell and moved out to Paw Paw, West Virginia, where they lived on a farm for free, practiced as hard as they could and played down at the local Sportsman's Club. The locals were puzzled by the sight of these long-haired and bearded Easterners, but they had to admit the newcomers could play a mean two-step.

When they were ready, in 1971, the band moved out to the Bay Area, where they were soon befriended by Commander Cody and his Lost Planet Airmen, a similar group of college dropouts also using western swing as well as honky-tonk and rockabilly, as a vehicle for their eclectic tastes. The Wheels, though, were more interested in the authentic western swing of Bob Wills and Milton Brown, and they sharpened their skills in that area while Commander Cody favored hillbilly novelty numbers. Levin had declined to make the trip westward, but the band picked up a regular bassist in Gene Dobkin and a brilliant pianist named Jim Haber.

Most of the country-rock bands in those days played the country ingredients in their music with a patronizing wink, as if to say, "We know this music is corny, but it's so corny it's fun." Asleep at the Wheel never winked. Their affection for the music was unquestionably sincere, and that's why it sounded so true when they played it. They realized that the western swing and boogie-woogie aspects of country music were weirder and hipper than 95 percent of rock-and-roll and gave them all the latitude they needed. Gosfield and Haber changed their stage names to Lucky Oceans and Floyd Domino, and the whole band bought embroidered cowboy outfits.

They even got Bob Wills's final producer, Tommy Allsup, to produce the first Asleep at the Wheel album, **Comin' Right**

At Ya, in 1973. Fiddlers Andy Stein (of the Lost Planet Airmen) and Buddy Spicher (Gimble's Nashville buddy) also joined the sessions. The album included songs written by Wills, Hank Williams and Moon Mullican plus originals in the same style.

When the band brought the finished tape to United Artists Records in LA, however, the company didn't know what to do with it. They said it was too country and sent it to their Nashville office. The Nashville officials said it was certainly country music, but it was 20 years out of date. It was a story Asleep at the Wheel would hear again and again: too country for pop radio and simultaneously too old-fashioned and too weird for country radio.

The band persevered, though, and moved to Austin, Texas, so they could be closer to the heart of western swing. In 1974 the group added bassist Tony Garnier and fiddler Richard Casanova for one album with Epic, **Asleep At The Wheel**. The following year Danny Levin returned for the next album with Capitol, **Texas Gold**. Produced again by Allsup, this album added a new drummer, Scott Hennige, to free Preston to concentrate on singing and songwriting, and a full-time saxophonist, Ed Vizard. This was the great Asleep at the Wheel lineup, and **Texas Gold** is the best introduction to the band.

The album opens with *The Letter That Johnny Walker Read*, the song that finally broke Asleep at the Wheel on commercial country radio. Co-written by Preston, Benson and Commander Cody, the song boasts the kind of pretty melody, "tears-in-the-beer" story and title pun that country fans feel comfortable with. It has a good dose of Asleep at the Wheel strangeness, though. Not only do Floyd Domino, Lucky Oceans and Johnny Gimble slip in quicksilver swing licks at every opening, but the song makes a sudden shift from fiddle-laced honky-tonk to horn-spiked mariachi every time it goes from the verse to chorus.

Tonight The Bartender Is On The Wrong Side Of The Bar is typical of the many competent but less-than-special mainstream country songs that Preston wrote for Asleep at the Wheel. Far more original were his compositions, *Runnin' After Fools*, which successfully combines a Texas swing 2/4 beat against New Orleans triplets, and *Bump Bounce Boogie*, another hit single for Asleep at the Wheel. On the latter song, Chris O'Connell does her best Connee Boswell imitation with a sassy swing vocal over a rollicking boogie-woogie beat, and the massed horns and fiddles supply the echoing harmonies for the missing Boswell Sisters.

The best vocal of O'Connell's whole career can be heard, though, on the remake of *Nothin' Takes The Place Of You*. On nearly every album, Asleep at the Wheel included a Louisiana tune, and this 1967 soul ballad by Toussaint McCall was the inspired choice for this collection. The weeping fills from Gimble's fiddle and Oceans's pedal steel help turn it into a honky-tonk lament, and O'Connell's best Patsy Cline impersonation puts it over the top.

The old Bob Wills instrumental, *Fat Boy Rag*, begins with hot solos on electric mandolin and fiddle by Gimble, but he's followed by solos from Domino, Levin, Benson, and Oceans. Best of all is the authoritative way the rhythm section of pianist Domino, rhythm guitarist Preston, bassist Garnier and drummer Hennige swing this big band, which on this cut features all nine regular members of the band plus four extra guests.

Of all the good players in the band, though, the best was Domino, and he got one of his best showcases ever on *Roll 'Em Floyd*, a medley of the legendary jump-blues collaborations between singer Big Joe Turner and pianist Pete Johnson. With Benson playing the Turner role and a three-man horn section punching out the riff, Domino fools around with the rhythms – sometimes playing with it, sometimes implying it, sometimes doubling or tripling it. When Benson crows with joy in mid-song that they're "swinging the blues," he was never more right.

Asleep at the Wheel followed up **Texas Gold** in 1976 with **Wheelin' And Dealin'**, which was nearly as good. The latter album – nearly a Texas Playboys reunion with the presence of Gimble, Tiny Moore and Eldon Shamblin – featured some of the band's most popular songs: the locomotive remake of Nat King Cole's *Route 66*, the tribute to their adopted state, *Miles And Miles Of Texas* and the lively party yell, *Shout Wa Hey*. That was followed in 1977 by **The Wheel**, an album of all-original material, and in 1978 by the excellent **Collision Course**, which included the Grammy Award-winning version of Count Basie's *One O'Clock Jump*, and saw the roster reach the high-water mark of 12 musicians.

After that the great Asleep at the Wheel line-up began to dissolve. Oceans moved to Australia; Domino joined Waylon Jennings's band and today records frequently with George Strait; Preston moved to Nashville to become a songwriter; O'Connell and Levin drifted away. By the early eighties, Benson was the only original member still in the band. More than 80 musicians had passed through the ranks of Asleep at the Wheel by the early nineties – some of them more than once – and like his heroes Wills and Basie, Benson always hired good players. Benson made sure the sound was consistent and the musical standards high, and Asleep at the Wheel has kept authentic western swing alive for a new generation.

Discographical Details

92 Anthology: (1935–1973)

Bob Wills and his Texas Playboys

Rhino R2 70744

*Maiden's Prayer/Steel Guitar Rag/Right Or Wrong/Time Changes Everything/
Corrine, Corrina/Big Beaver/New San Antonio Rose/Take Me Back To Tulsa/
Cherokee Maiden/Home In San Antone/Miss Molly/My Confession/Texas
Playboy Rag/Roly-Poly/Stay A Little Longer/Basin Street Blues/My Window
Faces South/Fat Boy Rag/Three Guitar Special/Deep Water/Bubbles In My
Beer/Blues For Dixie/South/Cotton Patch Blues/Boot Heel Drag/Faded Love/St
Louis Blues/Cadillac In Model "A"/Heart To Heart Talk/The Jobob Rag/Blue
Bonnet Lane/What Makes Bob Holler*

93 Texas Gold

Asleep at the Wheel

Capitol ST-11441

*The Letter That Johnny Walker Read/Fat Boy Rag/Runnin' After Fools/Let
Me Go Home, Whiskey/Nothin' Takes The Place Of You/Roll 'Em Floyd/
Tonight The Bartender Is On The Wrong Side Of The Bar/Bump Bounce
Boogie/Where No One Stands Alone/Trouble in Mind*

(iii) The Bakersfield Sound

It was more than dust storms that drove tens of thousands of
poor farmers off their land during America's Great Depression.
Low prices and unyielding mortgage-holders did more than the
wind to force families from their small farms. Of course, the
bankers had an ulterior motive in claiming lots of small plots
that could be consolidated into large holdings better suited to
tractor farming. No matter what the cause, though, thousands
of rural families in a belt from Texas and Oklahoma through
Alabama and Tennessee found themselves homeless. They did
what thousands of Americans had done before them; they
headed west.

In 1933, this fate befell sharecropper Charlie Maddox and
his wife and five kids in Boaz, Alabama. The family started
hitch-hiking west and quickly learned how to jump a freight
train and avoid the railyard bulls. They landed in California's
San Joaquin Valley, a seeming Eden of green fruit trees as far
as the eye could see. The first impression was deceiving, for the
only work available to the Maddoxes was picking the fruit off
those trees at 50 cents a day. After four years of this, Fred
Maddox, then 17, sat down in a cotton field near Fresno one
day and announced he was tired of farm work. He said they
should go into the music business.

This was quite a notion, for the family had never played
music except for each other and their friends around the

campfire in whatever labor camp they were staying at that week. Fred was not to be deterred, however, and he dragged the family down to Modesto, where he convinced a local furniture store to sponsor them on local station KTRB. The sponsor demanded a girl singer, so 12-year-old Rose Maddox was pressed into service even though she only knew three songs. Against all odds, the inexperienced musicians were a hit, and by 1939, they were broadcasting twice a day on a network that reached from Arizona to Washington State. Their career was interrupted when Fred and Cal were drafted for World War II, but they picked up where they left off in 1945, and they started recording for 4 Star Records in 1946.

Listening to those early recordings today on the Arhoolie compilation, **America's Most Colorful Hillbilly Band: Their Original Recordings 1946–1951**, it's easy to understand why "The Maddox Brothers and Rose," as they were billed, were so popular. In those early singles, you can also hear the origins of the Bakersfield sound later refined by Buck Owens and Merle Haggard.

The Maddox family brought with them the southern Appalachian instrumentation and music of their roots in Boaz. Fred played upright bass; Cliff played mandolin; Don played fiddle; Cal played acoustic guitar and harmonica, and Rose sang. Their repertoire was full of Appalachian ballads, fiddle tunes and gospel hymns that could have been sung by the Carter Family. The recently arrived "Dust Bowl refugees" from back East obviously felt a connection to their old homes through the Maddox Brothers' hillbilly music.

As time went on, though, the Maddoxes sounded less and less like the Carters and more and more like an unprecedented brand of California country music. The Maddox family drew their songs from everywhere: from the cowboy movies of Gene Autry and Roy Rogers, from the new bluegrass 78s of Bill Monroe, from the even newer honky-tonk sounds of Hank Williams and Hank Thompson, from the country-music boogie-woogie craze, from the western swing of Bob Wills, even from the blues of Jimmie Rodgers and their Uncle Foncy.

Three factors transformed all these sources into a distinctive California sound: the driving rhythms of Fred's proto-rockabilly slap bass and Cliff's choppy mandolin chords; the unbridled comic showmanship that replaced the past sentimentality of country music with a healthy irreverence; and Rose's willingness to sing about such controversial topics as infidelity, seduction and divorce without cloaking them in sanctimoniousness.

Paradoxically, these revolutionary developments appealed to

the same migrant workers who longed nostalgically for the old songs. These workers found the transient, uncertain nature of their new lives echoed in the Maddoxes' quickened rhythms and frank talk. Nor did it hurt that the Maddoxes' firm backbeat and raucous approach were perfect for the nightly release from hard work in the dance halls of the San Joaquin Valley. The rhythms grew even more forceful when the family band hired Bud Duncan on steel guitar and a series of electric guitarists (Jimmy Winkle, Roy Nichols, Gene Breeden, etc.)

When the Maddoxes first got started on the radio, they would capitalize on their small fame by playing for tips at rodeos, local bars and even street corners. Working the same circuit at the time were a pair of genuine Okies named Jack and Woody Guthrie. Rose learned one of Woody's early songs, *Reno Blues*, and it became the Maddoxes' biggest hit when it was later recorded and released as *Philadelphia Lawyer*.

The recording opens with the bluegrass sound of Cliff's mandolin, then slides into the honky-tonk sound of Duncan's steel guitar. Guthrie's lyrics, based on a newspaper clipping, tell the story of a rich, slick Eastern attorney who woos a pretty young girl in Reno and offers to get her an easy divorce from her cowboy husband. The song begins in the style of a traditional country lament where a rural innocent is mistreated by a city slicker. Guthrie was no fatalist, however, and he turns the tables on the lawyer in the inspired final verse. In similar fashion, Rose begins the narrative in the somber sing-song style of cowboy crooners, but by the end of the song the whole band is subverting the song's melodrama with Rose's exaggerated vibrato, Fred's fake weeping and gunshot sound effects.

Here was a new kind of country music that wasn't content to merely commiserate over its audience's troubles, but offered an ultimate triumph over them. You could hear it in songs like *I Wish I Was A Single Girl Again* and *(Pay Me) Alimony*, where Rose isn't willing to mope and weep over a bad marriage or a divorce but demands her rights instead. Their version of *Honky Tonkin'* (recorded before Hank Williams could do his own version) is so loose and joyful with its snorting, whistling, giggling vocals and stomping beat that it makes nightclubs sound like the promised land rather than the dens of iniquity they had always been described as in country songs.

Roy Nichols's free-wheeling guitar leads on songs like the rocking version of the Delmore Brothers' *Step It Up And Go* defy all limitations. Most convincing of all are the raucous boogie-woogie numbers like *Mean And Wicked Boogie* and *Water Baby Boogie* which are played as fast and hard as any of the rockabilly numbers to come. In those carefree romps, spiked by Cal's Bob Wills-like falsetto cries of joy, you can hear the irrepressible optimism that has marked California music from the Sons of the Pioneers to the Beach Boys.

Henry, the youngest brother, took over mandolin when Cliff died in 1949, and the Maddoxes left 4 Star Records to sign with Columbia in 1951. In fact, they signed three different contracts: one for the Maddox Brothers and Rose, one for Rose as a solo artist and one for the duo of Rose and her sister-in-law Loretta, known as Rose and 'Retta. They recorded some fine records and some big hits for Columbia, but they gave up some of the uninhibited spontaneity of the 4 Star days. The family band broke up in 1956 in the face of the rock-and-roll onslaught, but Rose continued as a professional singer on into the 1990s.

The California country sound that the Maddoxes pioneered lived on after them, however, as other newcomers to the San Joaquin Valley refined their approach. Wynn Stewart, born in Missouri, moved to Bakersfield in 1949. Terry Preston, also born in Missouri, moved to Bakersfield in 1949 and became Ferlin Husky. Leonard Sipes, born in Oklahoma City, moved to Bakersfield in 1952 and became Tommy Collins. Stewart, Husky and Collins focused on the honky-tonk strain in the Maddoxes' music and gave it an upbeat California kick. Husky was the first one to have hits; the Terry Preston–Jean Shepard duet, *Dear John Letter*, topped the country charts in 1953, and *Hank's Song* (a tribute to Williams) was a hit under the Ferlin Husky name the same year.

Husky convinced the new Hollywood label, Capitol Records, that there was a lot more country talent in the Valley. Capitol eventually signed the cream of Bakersfield: Husky, Collins, Stewart, Buck Owens, and Merle Haggard. At Collins's second recording session in 1953, they needed a lead guitarist for the novelty song, *You Better Not Do That*, and they called in an unrecorded 24-year-old named Buck Owens, who was leading the house band at the Blackboard in Bakersfield. Owens had replaced his old hollow-body Gibson electric with a solid-body Fender Telecaster, and the new guitar helped Owens get a tougher, raunchier sound that sent Collins's song to number 2 on the country charts.

It would be four more years before Owens recorded for Capitol under his own name – four years that included some poor-selling singles on Pep, a short tour as Collins's guitarist, and lots of shows at the Blackboard with such local pals as Stewart and Harlan Howard. During those years, Owens found that the rousing vocals and bristling guitars of the early rockabilly singles, which contrasted so sharply with the Eastern honky-tonk stylists, fit right in with the Bakersfield brand of honky-tonk. Combining that with the irreverent playfulness of the Maddoxes, Owens created a hopped-up Bakersfield sound that kept them dancing at the Blackboard and appealed to the mobile, seeking-a-better-life Californians in his audience.

Owens himself had come to Bakersfield from Phoenix in 1951, looking for better opportunities as a musician. It wasn't until 1958 that he convinced Capitol to let him record his songs the way he heard them – with fiddle, pedal steel and electric guitar – but once he did there was no stopping him. *Second Fiddle* was the first top 30 hit, and *Under Your Spell Again* was the first to crack the top 10. Owens found his musical alter ego in Don Rich, who played the kind of swing fiddle that looked to country's dancehall past, and yet made it fit perfectly with Owens's rockabilly Telecaster licks.

The early singles included *Under the Influence of Love*, *Excuse Me (I Think I've Got A Heartache)* and *Foolin' Around*, all co-written by Owens and his Bakersfield buddy, Harlan Howard. Howard went on to become one of Nashville's top tunesmiths, but he got his start in California with Owens. During this same period, Owens recorded two duets with the still-better-known Rose Maddox and enjoyed a double-sided hit with *Loose Talk* and *Mental Cruelty*.

The breakthrough song, though, came in 1963, with *Act Naturally*, which was not only Owens' first number 1 hit but also the song that solidified the sound he had been looking for. Instead of the easy-going honky-tonk shuffles that Owens had been recording, *Act Naturally* is set in the 2/4 dance beat that Bob Wills popularized, but with some crucial differences. Wills had pioneered the use of drums in country music, but he kept them low and boomy like a slap bass. Owens, by contrast emphasizes the snare drum and high hat, which are sharp and bright – like the solid-body guitar, now played by Rich. The guitar leads are unmistakably electric and assertive, and that confidence extends to Owens's vocals which more often than not are contagiously joyful.

Love's Gonna Live Here Again, the follow-up to *Act Naturally*, also went to number 1 and stayed there 16 weeks. This Owens composition is the exact opposite of the usual honky-tonk self-pity about a busted marriage. Here is an up-tempo, upbeat insistence that problems can be overcome and happiness can flourish, an argument driven home by Rich's jaunty guitar solo and Mel King's ticking drum beat.

The drums are even more prominent on *My Heart Skips A Beat* (1964), which features a tom-tom roll into and out of the bouncy chorus and adds a slight syncopation to the 2/4 beat. The flip side of the single was *Together Again*, Owens's greatest ballad. Written as a honky-tonk sigh of relief over a romantic reconciliation, it boasts a gorgeous melody delivered with equal expressiveness and legato fluidity by Owens's voice and Tom Brumley's pedal steel guitar. One week, *My Heart Skips A Beat* was number 1 and its flip side, *Together Again* was number 2. The next week they traded places and the following week they reversed positions again.

By the summer of 1964, Owens had in place his greatest band: Rich on lead guitar, Brumley on steel, Doyle Holly on guitar and bass and Willie Cantu on drums. The Buckaroos, as they were dubbed by Owens's short-time bassist Merle Haggard, played all of Owens's concert and studio dates through 1967 and were one of best bands in country music history. They proved you could make records with the bright, clean sound and driving energy of rock-and-roll and still sound unmistakably country by keeping the parts simple. Within that simplicity, though, was an astonishingly disciplined sense of time and an ability to speak volumes in a 2-bar fill.

Owens referred to it as the "freight train" sound, and it rolled over the competition on the country charts as he racked up an astonishing string of number 1 country hits between 1964 and 1969: *I Don't Care (Just As Long As You Love Me)*, *I've Got A Tiger By The Tail*, *Before You Go*, *Only You (Can Break My Heart)*, the instrumental *Buckaroo*, *Waitin' In Your Welfare Line*, *Think Of Me*, *Sam's Place*, *Your Tender Loving Care*, *How Long Will My Baby Be Gone*, *Who's Gonna Mow Your Grass*, *Johnny B. Goode*, and *Tall Dark Stranger*. Most of them were minor variations on the models of *My Heart Skips A Beat* and *Together Again*, but like Hank Williams's and Chuck Berry's songs, the formula never grew tiresome, for the songs were filled with so much melody and exuberance.

The hits slowed down in the early 1970s and pretty much stopped after that. Even as his commercial profile fell, however, Owens's artistic reputation rose. The Beatles had recorded *Act Naturally* at the height of Owens's popularity because Ringo Starr was a big Owens fan, and many other rock-and-rollers acknowledged that they felt the same. Feelings were even more intense in Nashville as a younger generation of country singers hailed Owens as a major influence. Emmylou Harris recorded *Play Together Again, Again* as a duet with Owens in 1979, and when Owens and Dwight Yoakam recorded a new duet version of *Streets Of Bakersfield*, a 1973 album cut for Owens, it went to number 1.

All the Buck Owens songs mentioned in this chapter can be found on Rhino Records' 3-CD compilation, **The Buck Owens Collection (1959–1990)**. We don't generally recommend boxed sets in this book, but there aren't a lot of good in-print alternatives in Owens's case, and this compilation is so well done that almost nothing of importance has been left out. And no understanding of the "western" in country and western is possible without a healthy sampling of Owens's contagiously merry music.

Merle Haggard barely mentions Buck Owens in his auto-biography, *Sing Me Back Home*, but Owens played a major role in Haggard's life. Not only did Haggard get one of his first professional breaks playing bass in Owens's band, but he fought Owens over the publishing rights to his early songs and was for a time married to Owens's ex-wife Bonnie. More importantly, Haggard took Owens's Bakersfield sound and made it more subtle, more swinging and more serious. In the process, Haggard became one of the greatest artists in the history of country music.

Haggard's parents had moved to the San Joaquin Valley from Checotah, Oklahoma (just south of Muskogee), in 1934, just three years before Merle was born. His father died in 1946, and soon after, Merle began a pattern of running away from home in freight trains and "borrowed" cars, and stealing to keep the adventures going. He made stabs at real jobs – packing potatoes, picking cotton and rousting oil rigs – but the wander-lust always got the best of him. He was in and out of juvenile reform schools and then adult prisons for years until he drew some serious time for a robbery gone wrong and spent 1958–60 at San Quentin Prison.

Throughout it all, however, Haggard had clung to his love of country music and his biggest heroes: Jimmie Rodgers, Bob Wills, Lefty Frizzell and Hank Williams. For a kid without much education, much luck or any prospects, country music was just about the only thing he felt good about. It was the one thing he could do well, and it was the single creative channel available to him for expressing his turbulent feelings. It would be a foolish romanticism to claim that Haggard's hard life and prison time made him a great artist. It's more plausible to suggest that Haggard was a great artist searching for the right medium, and for an undereducated Okie and felon from Bakersfield, country music was the only medium that made sense.

The hard times did affect Haggard's approach to the music. While the Maddox Brothers and Rose and Owens brought a carefree, joyful feel to the Bakersfield sound, Haggard lent a more tragic cast to his songs. The music still had that dis-tinctively resilient bounce and assertive Telecaster sound, but Haggard wrote eloquently about men caught between their desires for the ideal home and family and their compulsive rambling, drinking, arguing and law-breaking. The powerful drama of Haggard's best songs springs from his refusal to praise one side of this male dichotomy and damn the other; instead he allows both sides to coexist in brilliant, fascinating tension.

When Haggard was paroled, he formed the High Pocket Band that played up on "Beer Can Hill" in Bakersfield. After short stints as a bassist for Wynn Stewart and Owens, Haggard started cutting singles for Tally Records, a local label. Haggard's *Sing A Sad Song* broke into the Top 20 for Tally, and the singer was finally signed to Capitol in 1965. He hit the Top 10 that same year with *(All My Friends Are Gonna Be) Strangers*; the Top 5 with *Swinging Doors* and *The Bottle Let Me Down* in 1966, and finally number 1 with *I'm A Lonesome Fugitive* at the end of that year.

He followed that with a string of masterful number 1 hits: *Branded Man, Sing Me Back Home, Mama Tried, Hungry Eyes,* and *Daddy Frank (The Guitar Man)*. Unfortunately, Haggard was best known for the cartoonish novelty number, *Okie From Muskogee*, a song that deserted the careful balance of his best songs to applaud the straight-arrow citizen he longed to be and to condemn the unruly nonconformist he actually was. As if to make up for his pandering hit, Haggard recorded a series of brilliant album tributes to Jimmie Rodgers (**Same Train, Different Time**, in 1969), Bob Wills (**A Tribute To The Best Damn Fiddle Player In The World**, in 1970), Dixieland (**I Love Dixie Blues**, 1974), and Hank Williams and Lefty Frizzell (**The Way It Was In '51**).

In 1977, Haggard switched from Capitol to MCA, and in 1981, from MCA to Epic. Regardless of the label or the era, Haggard kept releasing singles and albums of remarkably consistent quality. Many of them are listed in this book, and they all deserve to be. Perhaps the best way to understand Haggard's contribution to the Bakersfield sound, however, is to listen to his last MCA album, recorded in 1981: **Rainbow Stew: Live At Anaheim Stadium**. It finds the singer in his natural element – playing a live concert for his fellow Californians with his great road band, the Strangers.

Far more than any of his other albums, **Rainbow Stew** displays Haggard's and the Strangers' gift for virtuosic "country-jazz" (Haggard's term). Like the Texas Playboys, the Strangers play sophisticated swing rhythms and jazz harmonies on traditional country instruments. In fact, three of the Strangers on **Rainbow Stew** are ex-Texas Playboys: fiddler–mandolinist Tiny Moore, guitarist Eldon Shamblin and fiddler Gordon Terry. Haggard is also one of the few country artists since Wills to use horns, and Don Markham plays trumpet and sax both with a little twist that seems to give his big-band lines a rural twang.

The longtime stalwarts of the band, guitarist Roy Nichols (who got his start with the Maddox Brothers and who was hired away from Wynn Stewart by Haggard) and pedal steel guitarist Norm Hamlet, have played with Hag so long that they know just how to amplify the feeling in his vocals with a quick echoing burst of notes. Haggard is no slouch himself, and his electric guitar solos have the gritty toughness of Don Rich's. And for the *Fiddle Breakdown* on **Rainbow Stew**, Haggard displays his great swing feel by joining Terry and Moore for a bout of high-spirited triple fiddling.

The album begins with three of Haggard's best drowning-your-sorrows-in-alcohol songs: *Misery And Gin*, *I Think I'll Just Stay Here And Drink* and *Back To The Barrooms Again*. The theme of a man on a barstool downing shots to ease his broken heart is as common as steel guitars in country music, but Haggard gives the well-worn formula new life by refusing to stoop to self-pity. His warm, robust voice retains its dignity even as he describes his deplorable circumstances, suggesting that his plight stems not from weakness but from the very real quandary of a man who loves his freedom no more and no less than he loves his woman. Haggard has a way of holding out certain notes (underlined by Hamlet's sustained steel notes) that evokes that dilemma. At the end of *I Think I'll Just Stay Here And Drink*, that tension breaks loose in the let-it-all-go solos by Haggard and Nichols on guitar and Mark Yeary on piano.

A medley of two songs about his early rambling days – *The Running Kind* and *I'm A Lonesome Fugitive* – get a lively bounce from the Strangers that reinforces the theme of constant motion. In fact, the rhythm is so lively that the PA announcer breaks into the medley to warn, "Attention, for your own safety, please don't dance on the stadium's second level." When Haggard purrs, "Every front door found me hopin'/I would find the back door open," the mix of sadness and fond memories in his voice betrays his mixed feelings. He continues that rambling theme with a song by his hero Jimmie Rodgers, the original freight-train hobo, and a new composition, *Rainbow Stew*, which is Haggard's best evocation of Rodgers's spirit.

The album ends with *Sing Me Back Home*, the true story of a death-row inmate at San Quentin who asked Haggard to sing him one last number. It's about the healing power of music – and as much about the music that saved Haggard's life as about the song that comforted that inmate. In his big vocal that holds nothing back, he captures the awe of a dancehall hillbilly music that has allowed him to be both the comforter and the comforted.

Discographical Details

94 America's Most Colorful Hillbilly Band: Their Original Recordings, 1946–1951

The Maddox Brothers and Rose

Arhoolie CD 391

George's Playhouse Boogie/Midnight Train/Shimmy Shakin' Daddy/Careless Driver/Move It On Over/Whoa, Sailor/Milk Cow Blues/Mean And Wicked Boogie/Brown Eyes/Honky Tonkin'/Time Nor Tide/Philadelphia Lawyer/Sally, Let Your Bangs Hang Down/When I Lay My Burden Down/Hangover Blues/ Water Baby Boogie/Dark As The Dungeon/Mule Train/Oklahoma Sweetheart/ Sally Ann/Faded Love/New Step It Up And Go/(Pay Me) Alimony/I Wish I Was A Single Girl Again/Your Love Light Never Shone/Meanest Man In Town/I Want To Live And Love

95 The Buck Owens Collection: 1959–1990

Buck Owens

Rhino R2 71016 (3-disc set)

Second Fiddle/Under Your Spell Again/Above And Beyond/Excuse Me (I Think I've Got A Heartache)/Foolin' Around/Loose Talk/Mental Cruelty/ Under The Influence Of Love/Nobody's Fool But Yours/Save The Last Dance For Me/Kickin' Our Hearts Around/You're For Me/Act Naturally/Love's Gonna Live Here/My Heart Skips A Beat/Together Again/Close Up The Honky Tonks/Hello Trouble/A-11/I Don't Care (Just As Long As You Love Me)/Buck's Polka/I've Got A Tiger By The Tail/Cryin' Time/Memphis/Before You Go/Only You (Can Break My Heart)/Gonna Have Love/Buckaroo/ Waitin' In Your Welfare Line/Dust On Mother's Bible/Think Of Me/Open Up Your Heart/Sam's Place/Your Tender Loving Care/It Takes People Like You (To Make People Like Me)/How Long Will My Baby Be Gone/Sweet Rosie Jones/Let The World Keep On A Turnin'/I've Got You On My Mind Again/ Who's Gonna Mow Your Grass/Johnny B. Goode/Tall Dark Stranger/Big In Vegas/We're Gonna Get Together/The Kansas City Song/The Great White Horse/I Wouldn't Live In New York City (If They Gave Me The Whole Dang Town)/Bridge Over Troubled Water/Ruby (Are You Mad)/Rollin' In My Sweet Baby's Arms/I'll Still Be Waiting For You/Made In Japan/You Ain't Gonna Have Ol' Buck To Kick Around No More/Ain't It Amazing, Gracie/ Streets Of Bakersfield/Big Game Hunter/On The Cover Of The Music City News/(It's A) Monsters' Holiday/Play Together Again Again/Streets Of Bakersfield/Hot Dog/Act Naturally

96 Rainbow Stew: Live At Anaheim Stadium

Merle Haggard

MCA MCAD-31101

Misery And Gin/I Think I'll Just Stay Here And Drink/Back To the Barrooms Again/Our Paths May Never Cross/The Running Kind/I'm A Lonesome Fugitive/Rainbow Stew/Blue Yodel No. 9/Dealing With The Devil/Fiddle Breakdown/Sing Me Back Home

Basic Recordings

(i) Cajun

97 Le Gran Mamou: A Cajun Music Anthology – The Historic Victor–Bluebird Sessions, 1928–1941

Various Artists

Country Music Foundation CMF-013-D

Leo Soileau and Mayuse Lafleur: *Basile*; Columbus Fruge: *Saut' Crapaud*; Delin T. Guillory and Lewis Lafleur: *Quelqu'Un Est Jaloux*; Amede Ardoin and Dennis McGee: *Les Blues De Voyage*; Falcon Trio: *Mon Vieux D'Autrefois*; Bixy Guidry and Percy Babineaux: *Je Vais Jouer Celea Pour toi*; Berthmost Montet and Joswell Dupuis: *L'Abandoner*; Soileau Couzens: *Trois Jours Apres Ma Mort*; Oscar Doucet and Alius Soileau: *O! Bébe!*; Joe Credeur and Albert Babineaux: *Ma Cherie*; Falcon Trio: *La Valse J'Aime*; Leo Soileau and Moise Robin: *Grosse Mama*; Arteleus Mistric: *Belle Of Point Clair*; Nathan Abshire and the Rayne-Bo Ramblers: *One-Step De Lacassine*; The Hackberry Ramblers: *Jolie Blonde*; Joe's Acadians: *Il Y A Pas La Clair De Lune*; The Four Aces: *Lake Charles Waltz*; Rayne-Bo Ramblers: *Valse De Marais Bulleur*; Thibodeaux Boys: *La Two-Step A Erby*; Leo Soileau and his Three Aces: *Le Gran Mamou*; Lawrence Walker: *Alberta*; The Hackberry Ramblers: *Je Va T'Aimer Quand-Meme*; J.B. Fuselier and his Merrymakers: *Viens Donc Me Rejoindre*; Dixie Ramblers: *Barroom Blues*; Happy Fats and his Rayne-Bo Ramblers: *La Veuve De La Coulee*

The Victor Company followed Columbia into Louisiana just three months after Joe Falcon's first Cajun recording in 1928, and captured the first-ever Cajun fiddle recording with *Basile*, by Leo Soileau, with accordionist Mayuse Lafleur. That began a long and brilliant series of Cajun recordings on Victor and its subsidiary Bluebird label through 1941. This volume is the first and best of a series assembled by the Country Music Foundation to document those rare and invaluable 78s. The subsequent volumes (so far) are **Raise Your Window**, a similar overview, and **Gran Prairie**, a collection of late 1930s Cajun string bands. **Le Gran Mamou** begins with the "high and lonesome" sound of the early Cajun fiddle-and-accordion duos and trios and climaxes with the more polished string bands. Soileau and Falcon are both featured prominently, but the highlight is Hector Duhon's chilling revision of *St James Infirmary* as *Barroom Blues*.

98 His Original Recordings, 1928–1938

Amede Ardoin

Old Timey 124 (LP)

La Valse A Abe/Two-Step D'Eunice/Madame Etienne/Quoi Faire/Two-Step De Maman/Tante Aline/La Valse A Austin Ardoin/La Valse De Mon Vieux Village/Le Midland Two-Step/Valse Brunette/Two-Step D'Ossun/Valse De La Pointe d'Eglise/Two-Step De Jennings/Les Blues De La Prison

The first half of these 14 songs are the legendary duets between Ardoin, the black sharecropper with the desperate blues voice and hypnotic accordion style, and Dennis McGee, the white sharecropper with the slippery fiddle embellishments. Despite the sometimes scratchy sound, the music lives up to the legend as the two men work inspired harmonic variations on the tunes and make every song compelling. The second half is just Ardoin with his voice and box.

99   Early Recordings, 1935–1948

The Hackberry Ramblers

Old Timey 127 (LP)

Jole Blonde/Mementau Stomp/J'Ai Passé Devonde Ta Porte/J'Ai Pas Bien Fey/ J'Ai Pres Parley/Rice City Stomp/On Top Of The World/Jolie Fille/Oh, Josephine, Ma Josephine/'Neath The Weeping Willow/Dan Le Grand Bois/Faux Pas Tu Bray Cherie/Fais Pas Ca/One-Step De L'Amour/Hippitiyo/Tu Vas Pluerie/ Lake Charles Hop

Louisiana's finest hillbilly string band was composed of Cajuns who often sung in French and usually lent a swampy syncopation to their rhythms. On the other hand, this album could also fit comfortably under the western swing section of this chapter, for these Bob Wills fans swung crisply. Luderin Darbone's fiddle solos weren't afraid to take a jazzy detour, and Lennis Sonnier's vocals made the broad emotional gestures of country music, even when they were in French. This album includes the first big hit version of *Jole Blon*.

100   Fiddle King Of Cajun Swing

Harry Choates

Arhoolie CD 380

Allons A Lafayette/Basile Waltz/Cajun Hop/Port Arthur Waltz/Harry Choates Special/It Won't Be Long/Wrong Keyhole/Draggin The Bow/Te Petite/Rubber Dolly/Louisiana/Poor Hobo/Devil In The Bayou/Rye Whiskey/Fais Do Do Stomp/Lawtell Waltz/Bayou Pon Pon/Chere Meon/Harry Choates Blues/Mari Jole Blon/Honky Tonking Days/Grand Mamou/Je Pase Durvan Ta Port/Hackberry Hop

Choates tilted even further in the direction of Texas swing than the Hackberry Ramblers; the Louisiana fiddler even adopted Wills's patented "a-ha!" cry. Moreover, Choates made most of his recordings and live appearances along Texas's Gulf Coast. Nonetheless, he often sang traditional Cajun tunes in French and used Cajun fiddle phrasing over his bands' swing arrangements. This anthology, strangely enough, doesn't include his big hit, *Jole Blon* (which is on the "J'ai Ete au Bal" soundtrack), but does include 26 other recordings he made for Houston's Gold Star Records between 1946 and 1950.

101   A Legend At Last

Lawrence Walker

Swallow LP-6051 (LP)

Les Bon Temps Rouler/Osson Two-Step/Les Deux Pour La Meme/Johnny Can't Dance/Creole Waltz/Wandering Aces Special/Walker Special/Midnight Waltz/ La Valse Qui Me Fais Du Mal/Keep Your Hands Off Of It/Country Waltz/ Waltz Of Sorrow

When the Cajun accordion made its big comeback after World War II, Lawrence Walker was one of the main beneficiaries, along with Iry LeJeune and Nathan Abshire. Born in 1907 near Duson, Walker had a fluid style on the squeezebox and a knack for writing simple but irresistibly catchy tunes. This album collects his best singles from the forties, fifties and sixties for Khoury and Swallow.

102 A Cajun Legend

Aldus Roger

La Louisianne LLCD-1007

Lafayette Two-Step/Steppin' Past/Les Flammes D'Enfer/Fi-Fi Poncho/Over The Waves/Jambalaya/Johnny Can't Dance/Lafayette Playboy Waltz/Hicks Wagon Wheel/Love-Sick Waltz/Zydeco Sont Pas Sale/Une Autre Chance/Diga Ding Ding Dong/Louisiana Waltz/Mamou Two-Step/The Last Waltz/Wafus Two-Step/KLFY Waltz/Perrodin Two-Step/Jolie Blonde/Petite Au La Grosse/ Creole Stomp.

Aldus Roger was the king of the Cajun dancehalls in the 1950s and 1960s, an otherwise low point for the music. Not only was Roger a virtuoso accordionist, but he also filled his Lafayette Playboys with top-notch talent like fiddler Doc Guidry and pedal steel guitarist Phillip Alleman. Both contribute to this fine mid-1960s album project of Cajun and his signature tune, *Johnny Can't Dance.*

103 Swamp Gold, Vol. 1

Various Artists

Jin JIN-CD 106

Rod Bernard: *This Should Go On Forever*; Jivin' Gene: *Breaking Up Is Hard To Do*; Cookie and the Cupcakes: *Mathilda*; Johnnie Allan: *Lonely Days And Lonely Nights*; Randy and the Rockets: *Let's Do The Cajun Twist*; Clint West: *Our Love*; Lee Martin: *Born To Be A Loser*; Phil Bo: *Don't Take It So Hard*; Rufus Jagneaux: *Opelousas Sostan*; Tommy McLain: *Sweet Dreams*; Lil' Bob and the Lollipops: *I Got Loaded*; Dale and Grace: *I'm Leaving It All Up To You*; Rockin' Sidney: *Shirley Jean*; Rod Bernard: *Diggy Liggy Lo*; Irma Thomas: *It's Raining*; Warren Storm: *Prisoner's Song*

In the late 1950s and early 1960s, a number of French Louisianians came up with an inspired mix of Cajun, New Orleans R & B, Memphis rockabilly, and Nashville country to create a genre that came to be known as swamp-pop. Marked by Fats Domino-like piano triplets and Roy Orbison-like teen-opera singing, these singles nonetheless retained the distinctive rhythmic underpinning of South Louisiana dancehalls. Of the above songs, those by Bernard, Jivin' Gene, Cookie and the Cupcakes, McLain, Storm, and Dale and Grace made the national pop charts. *I Got Loaded* is the original version of the Los Lobos song.

04 A Cajun Legend . . . The Best Of Nathan Abshire

Nathan Abshire

Swallow SW-CD-6061

Pine Grove Blues/A Musician's Life/Sur Le Courtableu/Belisaire Waltz/Fi-Fi Poncho/Service Blues/French Blues/Valse De Bayou Teche/Choupique Two-Step/Valse De Holly Beach/J'Etais Au Bal/Kaplan Waltz/Lemonade Song/I Don't Hurt Anymore/Shamrock/Tracks Of My Buggy/Dying In Misery/Games People Play/Tramp Sur La Rue/Partie A Grand Basile

Nathan Abshire was born in 1913, became Amede Ardoin's protégé on accordion as a teenager and recorded with the Rayne-Bo Ramblers in the late 1930s. He then left music for several years until he was invited to join the Pine Grove Boys in 1948. The band cut a series of local hits for OT, Lyric and Khoury Records, which are collected on the fine Arhoolie CD, **French Blues**. In the early 1970s, Abshire started cutting singles for Swallow with the help of the Balfa Brothers, and those recordings, collected on this CD, are the finest work he ever did. The combination of Abshire's bluesy accordion and vocals with Dewey Balfa's sweet fiddle sounded like the Ardoin/McGee duets brought into the modern era with a sympathetic rhythm section.

105 La Vieille Musique Acadienne

Sady Courville and Dennis McGee

Swallow LP-6030 (LP)

Kathleen's Waltz/Fruge's Reel/The Waltz Of Love/Courville Breakdown/Valse Du Coteau Magnolia/Valse Du Vacher/Deviller Two-Step/Rosa, Tomorrow Is Not Sunday/The Waltz That Finished In The Corner Of The House/Tante Aleene's Waltz/Napoleon's Waltz/Papa's Waltz

Though it was recorded in 1977, this is one of the best examples of the rich fiddle tradition that flourished in Cajun music in the early part of this century before the diatonic accordion contracted the harmonic possibilities of the music. Dennis McGee was 84 at the time of this recording, and his brother-in-law Sady Courville was 72; the duo re-created the twin-fiddle pieces they used to play in the early 1920s. Until their early 78s for Vocalion are reissued, this is the best example of their ancient, Celtic-derived, blues-inflected, rhythmic music.

106 Cajun Saturday Night

D.L. Menard

Rounder CD-0198

Cajun Saturday Night/Why Should We Try Anymore/This Little Girl/Wedding Bells/The Judge Did Not Believe My Story/Green Oak Tree/Letters Have No Arms/House Of Gold/The Bachelor's Life/Banks Of The Old Pontchartrain/My Son Calls Another Man Daddy/Long Gone Lonesome Blues

If you want to hear the "Cajun Hank Williams" singing in English with his Cajun/honky-tonk fusion tilted in the honky-tonk direction, this is the album. On this 1984 recording, an admiring Ricky Skaggs, Jerry Douglas, Don Helms and Buck White back up Menard as he remakes some of his Cajun hits, introduces the catchy title tune, and sings five of Hank's songs.

107 The Best Of Doug And Rusty Kershaw

Doug and Rusty Kershaw

Curb/Cema D21K-77456

Louisiana Man/Kaw Liga/Diggy, Diggy Lo/(Our Own) Jole Blon/Cajun Joe (The Bully Of The Bayou)/The Love I Want/Oh Love/Why Don't You Love Me/Hey, Mae/Your Crazy, Crazy Heart/Sweet Thing (Tell Me That You Love Me)/I Like You Like This

Doug and Rusty Kershaw were only 18 and 16 when they were signed by Hickory Records in Nashville in 1955, but the brothers from the Louisiana oil town of Jennings had already cut several Cajun singles for the local label Feature. Combining their Everly Brothers-style close vocal harmonies with Doug's energetic swamp fiddling, the duo had country hits with Cajun-flavored songs like *Louisiana Man* and *Diggy, Diggy Lo*. Rusty went back home in 1963 to become an electrician, and Doug went on to play Cajun-hippie country-rock, but these early duo singles for Hickory were his best work.

08   Louisiana Saturday Night

Jimmy C. Newman

Charly 71 (LP)

Sugar Bee/Jambalaya/Alligator Man/Louisiana Saturday Night/Hippy-Ti-Yo/ Jole Blon/Thibodeaux And His Cajun Band/Boo-Dan/Corinne, Corinna/Allons A Lafayette/Big Bayou/Sweet Susanna/Big Texas/Cajun Man Can/Colinda/ Big Mamou/Daydreamin'/Lache Pas La Patate/Basile Waltz/Grand Chenier/ Diggy, Diggy Lo/Happy Cajun/More Happy Cajun

Newman, a relative of Dennis McGee's, grew up in Mamou where he fell in love with the music of cowboy singers like Gene Autry and Roy Rogers. So it was natural that he was hired by Cajun fiddler Chuck Guillory to sing the English-language hillbilly songs the crowds demanded. From there it was a natural progression to Nashville, where Newman enjoyed mainstream country hits in the late 1950s and early 1960s with *A Fallen Star*, *Alligator Man*, *Louisiana Saturday Night* and *Bayou Talk*. Later in his career, he returned to his Cajun roots and recorded (or re-recorded) the appealing blend of country-pop and Cajun featured on this collection.

09   Parlez-Nous A Boire And More

Beausoleil

Arhoolie CD 322

Le Jig Francais/Voyage Au Mariage/Courtableu/La Rue Canal/Paquet d'Epingles/Valse De Grand Meche/Mercredi Soir Passe/Sue/Reels Cadien/Chanson D'Acadie/Pierrot Grouillette Et Mamselle Josette/Ma Douce Amie/Parlez-Nous A Boire/Your Mama Threw Me Out/Robin's Two-Step/Acadian Blues/Midland Two-Step/Le Bozo Two-Step

This all-acoustic, practically bass-less album, recorded in 1981, represents Beausoleil at its most traditional. Drawing from the repertoire of their Cajun heroes like the Balfas, Nathan Abshire, Wallace Reed, Moise Robin, and Octa Clark, the Doucet brothers and the brilliant accordionist Errol Verret (who soon left the band because he hated touring) blended so well that they seemed to breathe together, and yet they made the rhythms so flexible that they refute every charge of monotony ever leveled at Cajun music. Another plus is that there's no overlap between this album and **Bayou Deluxe**.

10   Home Music With Spirits

The Savoy–Doucet Cajun Band

Arhoolie CD 389

Bosco Stomp/Aux Natchitoches/Quelle Etoile/La Valse J'Aime/One-Step De Chameau/Baby And The Gambler And The Happy One-Step/Reno Waltz/ Lacassine Special/Mon Chere Bebe Creole/Johnny Can't Dance/Lawtell Waltz/ Evangeline Special/'Tit Galope Pour La Pointe Aux Pins/'Tits Yeux Noirs/Port Arthur Blues/Une Vieille Valse/Chere Bassette/Melville Two-Step/Jolie Blonde

The title of this compilation from three earlier albums is important, for the husband-and-wife team of Marc and Ann Savoy are committed to the plea-

sures of "home music," Cajun tunes that are played on the front-porch or in
the back kitchen for the pleasure of kin and neighbors rather than strangers in
bars. Most of these tunes feature only the trio of Ann on acoustic guitar,
Marc on button accordion and their longtime pal Michael Doucet on fiddle.
The rhythms are still there, but the emphasis is on the harmonies and the
feeling of friendly warmth. Ann is the most important female figure in Cajun
music since Cleoma Falcon.

111 Trace Of Time

Steve Riley and the Mamou Playboys
Rounder CD 6053

*Bayou Noir/Back Of Town Two-Step/Mon Vieux Wagon/Old Home Waltz/
Church Point Breakdown/Parlez-Nous A Boire/Lovers' Waltz/Sur Le Courta-
bleau/La Valse Du Regret/La Pointe-Au-Pic/The Corner Post/Zarico Est Pas
Sale*

Riley played button accordion in Dewey Balfa's last band, and his 1993
album as a leader finds him playing with Balfa's fiddle students David Greely
and Peter Schwarz, and with Balfa's daughter Christine on triangle. Recorded
soon after Dewey's death, this album is suffused with affection for the man
and the tradition he represented, but is also marked by the high standards of
musicianship that Dewey always demanded. Produced by Beausoleil's Al
Tharp, Riley's third album marks him as the best of the young Cajun bandleaders in the post-Doucet generation.

(ii) Western Swing

112 The Golden Era

Bob Wills and his Texas Playboys
Columbia C2 40149 (LP)

*I've Got The Wonder Where She Went (Blues)/Harmony/Four Or Five Times/
Good Old Oklahoma/Weary Of The Same Ol' Stuff/Sugar Blues/Blue River/
Steel Guitar Stomp/Bring It On Down To My House/Gambling Polka Dot
Blues/Beaumont Rag/Rosetta/Get Along Home, Cindy/Drunkard's Blues/Way
Down Upon The Swanee River/There's No Disappointment In Heaven/Keep
Knockin' (But You Can't Come In)/Ida Red/Blue Bonnet Rag/Got A Letter
From My Kid Today/Whoa, Babe/William Tell/You Don't Love Me (But I'll
Always Care)/Dreamy Eyes Waltz/New San Antonio Rose/The Girl I Left
Behind/Liebestraum/When It's Honeysuckle Time In The Valley/Hang Your
Head In Shame/I'm Gonna Be Boss From Now On/Stay A Little Longer/New
Spanish Two-Step*

Anyone who wants to hear more by Wills's great 1936–45 bands on Columbia
should track down this 1987 anthology, which repeats only two songs from
the Rhino collection (and different takes at that). By contrast, 13 of the 20
songs on the widely available **The Essential Bob Wills** from the same era
are also on the Rhino collection. Taken from the original 78s, **The Golden
Era** has some minor scratchiness, but it contains some of the bluesiest and
jazziest playing ever cut by great musicians like Jesse Ashlock, Leon McAuliffe, Al Stricklin, and Eldon Shamblin.

13 Fiddle

Bob Wills

Country Music Foundation P-20156 (LP)

Smith's Reel/Waltz in D/Crippled Turkey/Spanish Two-Step/Tulsa Waltz/ Maiden's Prayer/Silver Bells/Oklahoma Rag/Carolina In The Morning/San Antonio Rose/Don't Let The Deal Go Down/Bluin' The Blues/Twinkle, Twinkle, Little Star/Prosperity Special/That Brownskin Gal/I Don't Lov'a Nobody/Lone Star Rag/Bob Wills Special/Bob Wills Stomp/Liberty

Wills's roots in frontier fiddle music often get lost in the big-band jazz sound of his classic cuts with the Texas Playboys, but this album focuses on the cowboy violin. It begins with four unaccompanied fiddle/guitar duets that Wills recorded in 1935 – the best recorded evidence of where the music came from – and continues with 16 more tunes that feature the fiddle in a prominent role with the big band. Not only is Wills himself spotlighted; so are his fellow fiddlers: Clifton "Sleepy" Johnson, Louis Tierney, Art Haines, Joe Holley, and especially the brilliant Jesse Ashlock.

14 OKeh Western Swing

Various Artists

Epic EG 37324 (LP)

Al Bernard, accompanied by the Goofus Five: *Hesitation Blues*; Emmett Miller and his Georgia Crackers: *Lovesick Blues*; Roy Newman and his Boys: *Sadie Green*; Blue Ridge Playboys: *Give Me My Money*; Range Riders: *Range Riders Stomp*; W. Lee O'Daniel and his Hillbilly Boys: *There'll Be Some Changes Made*; Crystal Springs Ramblers: *Fort Worth Stomp*; Bob Wills and his Texas Playboys: *Get With It/Who Walks In When I Walk Out/Too Busy/ Playboy Stomp/Ozzlin' Daddy Blues/Pray For The Lights To Go Out/The Girl I Left Behind Me*; Saddle Tramps: *Hot As I Am*; Sons of the Pioneers: *One More River To Cross*; Light Crust Doughboys: *Knocky, Knocky*; Hi Neighbor Boys: *Zeke Terney's Stomp*; Hank Penny and his Radio Cowboys: *Chill Tonic*; Swift Jewel Cowboys: *When I Put On My Long White Robe*; Sweet Violet Boys: *I Love My Fruit*; Ocie Stockard and his Wanderers: *Bass Man Jive*; Hi-Flyers: *Reno Street Blues*; Sons of the West: *Panhandle Shuffle*; Adolf Hofner and his Orchestra: *Gulf Coast Special*; Slim Harbert and his Boys: *Brown Bottle Blues*; Spade Cooley and his Orchestra: *Three-Way Boogie*; Leon McAuliffe and his Western Swing Band: *Take It Away, Leon*

A sense of the breadth and depth of the western swing movement are provided by this anthology and **Texas Sand**, the one below. Western swing was the most popular music from Louisiana to California from 1935 to 1945, and nearly every local kid who wanted to play music tried to imitate Bob Wills. This set includes those who recorded for Wills's label, OKeh Records. Wills himself is represented by seven obscure selections from his golden 1935–41 era. The set begins, however, with two minstrel show stars, Al Bernard and Emmett Miller, who had a great influence on Wills and his peers. It includes Roy Newman, one of the earliest western swing leaders, and the Blue Ridge Playboys, who included Moon Mullican and Floyd Tillman. Hank Penny and his Radio Cowboys, one of the few western swing bands east of the Mississippi, feature a young Boudleaux Bryant on fiddle, and future Texas Playboy Noel Boggs on guitar. Also represented are Adolf Hofner, who emphasized the Czech polka element in western swing, and Spade Cooley, the Lawrence Welk of western swing.

115 Texas Sand: Anthology Of Western Swing

Various Artists

Rambler 101 (LP)

Tune Wranglers: *Texas Sand*; Roy Newman and his Boys: *Everybody's Trying To Be My Baby*; Milton Brown and his Brownies: *Ida! Sweet As Apple Cider*; Cliff Bruner: *That's What I Like About The South*; Prairie Ramblers: *Deep Elm Blues*; Jimmie Revard and his Oklahoma Playboys: *Let Me Live And Love You*; Johnny Tyler and his Riders of the Rio Grande: *I Never See My Baby Along*; Curly Williams and his Georgia Peach Pickers: *Southern Belle (From Nashville Tennessee)*; Tune Wranglers: *Lonesome Blues*; Jimmie Revard and his Oklahoma Playboys: *Old Waterfall*; Roy Newman and his Boys: *Texas Stomp*; The Sunshine Boys: *No Good For Nothin' Blues*; Jesse Ashlock: *Betty Ann*; "T" Texas Tyler and his Oklahoma Melody Boys: *Tex Tyler Ride*

In the late 1970s and early 1980s, Rambler Records assembled some of the best western swing reissues ever released. The company is defunct and the albums are hard to find, but this anthology and the Milton Brown album below are symptomatic of the treasures this company unearthed. This album includes "T" Texas Tyler moaning about those "honky tonk women" and Roy Newman's original version of *Everybody's Trying To Be My Baby*, later claimed by Carl Perkins for his rockabilly classic. The great Texas pianist Moon Mullican can be heard with the Sunshine Boys on one cut and with the influential fiddler Cliff Bruner on another; Bruner is also heard with Brown's superlative final band. Jesse Ashlock, Wills's best fiddler ever, leads his own band through the lively version of *Betty Ann*.

116 Country And Western Dance-O-Rama

Milton Brown and his Musical Brownies

Western WS 1001 (originally Decca DL 5561) (LP)

St Louis Blues/Sweet Jennie Lee/Texas Hambone Blues/Brownie Special/Right Or Wrong/Washington And Lee Swing/Beautiful Texas/Little Betty Brown

Both issues of this 10-inch, eight-song album are out of print, but no collection of western swing is complete without this dazzling collection from Wills's original partner. Brown's relaxed, fluid tenor made him the best male singer in western swing, and he was backed by a great band that included steel guitarist Bob Dunn, guitarist Durwood Brown, pianist Fred Calhoun, banjoist Ocie Stockard, and fiddlers Cecil Brower and Cliff Bruner. Together they went even deeper into Dixieland, blues, and swing than Wills before Brown died in a 1936 auto accident.

117 Leon McAuliffe And His Western Swing Band

Leon McAuliffe

Columbia FC 38908 (LP)

Panhandle Rag/The Three Bears/You Left Me Cryin'/Mr Steel Guitar/Take It Away, Leon/T-U-L-S-A Straight Ahead/The Steel Guitar Polka/I've Never Lived In Tennessee/Blue Man's Blues/Bonaparte's Retreat

McAuliffe sang and played steel guitar with the Light Crust Doughboys, Milton Brown and Wills's Texas Playboys before becoming a civilian naval flight instructor during World War II. After the war, the man who had popularized the instrument with Wills's hit single, *Steel Guitar Rag*, organized his own "Western Swing Band" and was first signed by Majestic Records, then Columbia, in 1948 right after the label lost Wills. McAuliffe had a Top 10 hit with *Panhandle Rag*, a reworking of his earlier hit, and made some fine records with the help of top-notch fiddlers Cecil Brower (another Milton Brown alumnus) and Jimmy Hall.

118 Tulsa Swing

Johnnie Lee Wills

Rounder 1027 (LP)

In The Mood/Ridin' Down The Canyon/Cowboy's Dream/Southland Swing/ Don't Let Your Deal Go Down/Keep A Light In The Window Tonight/Never Alone/Four Or Five Times/Leather Britches/Sally Goodin/Buffalo Gals/Silver Dew On The Bluegrass Tonight/Smoke On The Water/Boogie Woogie Highball/ Love You So Much/Black-Eyed Susan Brown/Farther Along/Smith's Reel

In 1940, when Bob Wills had more offers for gigs than he could fill and more musicians who wanted to play with him than he could afford to hire, he asked his younger brother Johnnie Lee to form a second band. And when Bob reorganized his band after World War II and relocated to California, he asked Johnnie Lee to take charge of things in the Tulsa Oklahoma area. Johnnie Lee Wills and his Boys often shared musicians with the Texas Playboys and created some classic music during western swing's heyday. This album is drawn from live radio transcriptions Johnnie Lee Wills and his Boys recorded in 1950–1 with a band that included singer Leon Huff, fiddler Curley Lewis and clarinetist Don Harlan.

119 A Tribute To The Best Damn Fiddle Player In The World (Or, My Salute To Bob Wills)

Merle Haggard and the Strangers

Capitol ST-638 (LP)

Brown-Skinned Gal/Right Or Wrong/Brain Cloudy Blues/Stay A Little Longer/Misery/Time Changes Everything/San Antonio Rose/I Knew The Moment I Lost You/Roly Poly/Old-Fashioned Love/Corrine, Corrina/Take Me Back To Tulsa

As a kid in California, Haggard would ride his bicycle to Bakersfield whenever Wills came to town and would listen through the window because he couldn't afford a ticket. In 1970, when Haggard had enough clout in the music business to do what he wanted, he recorded this tribute to Wills with his own swing specialists in the Strangers and with these ex-Texas Playboys: Johnnie Lee Wills, Joe Holley, Eldon Shamblin, Johnny Gimble, Tiny Moore, Alex Brashear, Gordon Terry, and George French. It's no insult to Tommy Duncan or anyone else to point out that Haggard is the best singer to ever tackle these numbers, and in shifting the emphasis from picking to singing, he redefines the songs and creates a classic western swing album.

20 Johnny Gimble's Texas Dance Party

Johnny Gimble

Columbia/Lone Star KC 34284 (LP)

Lone Star Rag/I'll Keep On Loving You/La Zinda Waltz/Texas Fiddle Man/ Texas Skip/Under The "X" In Texas/Blues For Joe Tee/Bosque Bandit/Slow 'N' Easy/End Of The Line

The title is a good description of this album, recorded live at the Chapparal dancehall in Austin in 1975. Gimble gathered up some of his old western swing cronies – like pianist Curly Hollingsworth and steel guitarist Maurice Anderson – to pay tribute to the old bandleaders and their tunes. Gimble fills the Wills role ably – setting the tempos, singing the vocals, fiddling the melody, cueing the solos, and generally encouraging musicians and dancers alike to let go and enjoy themselves. They obviously did.

121   Asleep At The Wheel

Asleep at the Wheel

Epic KE 33097

Choo Choo Ch'Boogie/You And Me Instead/Jumpin' At The Woodside/Last Letter/Don't Ask Me Why (I'm Going To Texas)/The Kind of Love I Can't Forget/I'm Gonna Be A Wheel Someday/Our Names Aren't Mentioned (Together Anymore)/Miss Molly/Bloodshot Eyes/Dead Man

Asleep at the Wheel's second album boasts the strongest material of any of their albums. Louis Jordan's *Choo Choo Ch'Boogie*, Bob Wills's *Miss Molly*, Count Basie's *Jumpin' At The Woodside* and Fats Domino's *I'm Gonna Be A Wheel Someday* provide as good a summary of mid-century American music as one could hope for. Floyd Domino rocks the piano on the Basie tune, and Benson is at his Louis Armstrong best singing a comic number like *Bloodshot Eyes*, originally written by Western Swing bandleader Hank Penny and then made famous by jump-blues singer Wynonie Harris. *Don't Ask Me Why* and *Dead Man* are two of Preston's best compositions, and *The Kind of Love I Can't Forget* is an obscure Jesse Ashlock fiddle tune.

122   We've Got A Live One Here!

Commander Cody and his Lost Planet Airmen

Warner Bros 2LS 2939 (LP)

One of Those Nights/Semi Truck/Smoke! Smoke! Smoke!/Big Mammau/San Antonio Rose/Eighteen Wheels/Mama Hated Diesels/Lookin' At The World Through A Windshield/My Window Faces South/Milkcow Blues/It Should've Been Me/Back To Tennessee/Seeds And Stems/Rock That Boogie/Riot In Cell Block No. 9/Don't Let Go/Too Much Fun/Hot Rod Lincoln/Lost In The Ozone

This live album from a 1976 English tour provides the best summary of a band that brought a hippie looseness and irreverence to western swing and rockabilly. Founded in Michigan in 1968 by pianist George "Commander Cody" Frayne, singer Billy C. Farlow, and guitarist Bill Kirchen, the band migrated to the Bay Area in 1969 and dazzled the locals with a sure-handed command of America's musical roots. They enjoyed a fluke Top 10 pop single with their spirited remake of the country novelty tune, *Hot Rod Lincoln*, and their set was peppered with old chestnuts by Bob Wills and Merle Travis as well as their own imitations of vintage honky-tonk comedy songs.

123   That's What We Like About The West

Cowboy Jazz

Rounder 0149

Baby, Don't Call/Cow-Cow Boogie/Sugar Moon/Don't Be Blue/Sophisticated Mind/That's What I Like About The West/Too Much Fun/Stickin' To My Honey/Hey, Good Lookin'/Country Blue/Nagasaki

This Maryland sextet managed to blend the 3-part female vocal harmonies of the Andrews Sisters and Boswell Sisters with the rocking swing of Asleep at the Wheel and Commander Cody on this delightful 1981 release – a mix of country standards, jazz standards and originals. Deanna Bogart, Kate Bennett and Denise Carlson handled the tightly arranged vocals, while Carlson's fiddle and Barry Sless's steel guitar engaged one another in exhilarating instrumental duels.

24 Chill Of An Early Fall

George Strait
MCA MCAD–10204
The Chill of an Early Fall/I've Convinced Everybody But Me/If I Know Me/ You Know Me Better Than That/Anything You Can Spare/Home in San Antone/Lovesick Blues/Milk Cow Blues/Her Only Bad Habit Is Me/Is It Already Time

Though Strait is best known for his hit singles, which tend to be honky-tonk ballads, his albums and live shows are always full of hot western swing. The son of a South Texas rancher, Strait is a real cowboy and a legitimate heir to the Texas dancehall tradition. This album affords the best view of that side of Strait's music. There are three mainstream Nashville ballads, sung with Strait's usual good taste, but the other seven tracks are pure swing. Whether it's the all-star studio band (featuring the ubiquitous Johnny Gimble, Floyd Domino, and steel guitarist Paul Franklin) or Strait's touring Ace in the Hole Band (featuring the great fiddler Gene Elders and quick-fingered guitarist Benny McArthur), the results are delightful.

(iii) The Bakersfield Sound

25 Dust Bowl Ballads

Woody Guthrie
Rounder 1040
The Great Dust Storm (Dust Storm Disaster)/I Ain't Got No Home/Talking Dust Bowl Blues/Vigilante Man/Dust Can't Kill Me/Dust Pneumonia Blues/ Pretty Boy Floyd/Blowin' Down The Road (I Ain't Going To Be Treated This Way)/Tom Joad – Part 1/Tom Joad – Part 2/Dust Bowl Refugee/Do Re Mi/ Dust Bowl Blues/Dusty Old Dust (So Long, It's Been Good To Know You)

Woody Guthrie was one of the actual Okies who fled the Dust Bowl for California in the 1930s. Before he became a political activist and a favorite of the urban left, Guthrie was a country singer who played at the migrant-worker camps, barrooms and rodeos of California. He made up his own words to familiar country and cowboy songs, and he had a country radio show with a woman dubbed Lefty Lou. You can't understand the Bakersfield story without this album of Guthrie's story-songs about the great migration that made Bakersfield possible. Nor can you understand the music that followed without hearing where it started – in simple voice-and-guitar performances like these which were typical of the migrant-worker camps.

126   The Maddox Brothers and Rose: Columbia Historic Edition

The Maddox Brothers and Rose

Columbia, FC 39997 (LP)

I've Got Four Big Brothers (To Look After Me)/Dig A Hole/A Rusty Old Halo/Ugly And Slouchy/I'm Cocquita Of Laredo/Green Grow The Lilacs/ Bringing In The Sheaves/Old Black Choo Choo/Tall Men/The Death Of Rock-And-Roll/The Hiccough Song/Will There Be Any Stars In My Crown/Love Is Strange

The recordings by the Maddox Brothers and Rose for Columbia Records between 1951 and 1957 were more conventional than their sides for 4 Star in the late 1940s but often quite appealing just the same. This album collects 13 of their best Columbia sides and proves that Rose was never less than a striking singer and that her brothers never lost their zest for jumping hillbilly rhythms. From charming novelty numbers like *The Hiccough Song* to a pretty ballad like *Will There Be Any Stars In My Crown*, from the Mexican impersonation of *I'm Cocquita Of Laredo* to the left-field assaults on rock-and-roll tunes like *I've Got A Woman (The Death Of Rock-And-Roll)* and *Love Is Strange*, this group was never less than spirited and one-of-a-kind.

127   Hillbilly Music . . . Thank God! (Vol. 1)

Various Artists

Bug/Capitol CDP–7 91346 2

Hank Thompson and his Brazos Valley Boys: *How Cold-Hearted Can You Get*; Jimmy Bryant with Speedy West: *Stratosphere Boogie*; Merle Travis: *Nine Pound Hammer/Merle's Boogie-Woogie*; The Louvin Brothers: *You're Learning*; Jean Shepard and Speedy West: *Twice The Lovin' (In Half The Time)*; Faron Young: *Live Fast, Love Hard, Die Young*; The Farmer Boys: *Yearning, Burning Hearts*; Tennessee Ernie Ford and Ella Mae Morse, with Cliffie Stone's Orchestra: *Hog-Tied Over You*; Skeets McDonald: *You Oughta See Grandma Rock*; "Big Bill" Lister: *There's A Tear In My Beer*; The Milo Twins: *Johnson To Jones*; Foy Willing and his Riders of the Purple Sage: *Texas Blues*; Tex Ritter: *Fort Worth Jail*; Jimmy Lee: *I'm Diggin' A Hole To Bury My Heart*; Gene O'Quin: *It's No Use Talkin', Baby (I'm Through)*; The Farmer Boys: *Flash, Crash and Thunder*; Jean Shepard: *Two Whoops And A Holler*; The Louvin Brothers: *I Wish It Had Been A Dream/The Great Atomic Power*; Red Simpson: *Roll, Truck, Roll*; Rose Maddox: *Take Me Back Again*; Buck Owens and Rose Maddox: *Mental Cruelty*; Buck Owens: *You're For Me*

As a new company based in nearby Hollywood, Capitol Records had both the flexibility and proximity to capitalize on the nearby Bakersfield sound. This 24-track, single-CD anthology of Capitol's early country releases compiled by Marshall Crenshaw isn't limited to California, but the West Coasters dominate the proceedings. Most of the sessions were cut in LA with Bakersfield stalwarts like Buck Owens, Joe Maphis, Ralph Mooney and Jelly Sanders. Bakersfield songwriters Owens, Harlan Howard, and Tommy Collins have their songs sung by fellow Californians the Farmer Boys, Skeets McDonald, Red Simpson, and Rose Maddox. Hot guitarists Jimmy Bryant and Speedy West show off their red-hot picking, while Merle Travis and Tex Ritter, out in Hollywood, demonstrate their own brand of "western" music.

128   Buck Owens Sings Harlan Howard

Buck Owens

Capitol T1482 (LP)

Foolin' Around/Heartaches For A Dime/Heartaches By The Number/Let's Agree To Disagree/Keeper Of The Key/I Don't Believe I'll Fall In Love Today/Pick Me Up On Your Way Down/Lyin' Again/The One You Slip Around With/Think It Over/Keys In The Mailbox

Harlan Howard has been one of Nashville's greatest songwriters over the past three decades, but he got his start in Bakersfield as Buck Owens's partner in Blue Rock Music. Howard has a knack for finding fresh ways to approach the experience of a broken heart; his clever wordplay and bright, catchy melodies fit together so naturally it's impossible to find the seams. Howard has seldom enjoyed a vocal interpreter as appealing as Owens, and this collection is brimming with the optimism of two young men just beginning their careers. Only one of these songs, the bubbly hit *Foolin' Around*, is also on **The Buck Owens Collection**.

129   The Epic Collection (Recorded Live)

Merle Haggard

Epic 39159

Honky Tonk Night Time Man/Old Man From The Mountain/Holding Things Together/Sing A Sad Song/Every Fool Has A Rainbow/Blue Yodel No. 2/ Trouble In Mind/Things Aren't Funny Anymore/(My Friends Are Gonna Be) Strangers/I Always Get Lucky With You/Workin' Man Blues

Released just two years after **Rainbow Stew**, this live set contains entirely different material and boasts the warmer, more subtle feel of the smaller venue. The songs include two of Haggard's earliest singles (*Sing A Sad Song* and *My Friends Are Gonna Be) Strangers*, two jazzy blues numbers (*Blue Yodel No. 2* and *Trouble In Mind*) and several fairly new Haggard compositions. The Strangers have rarely played with such grace, and Haggard has seldom sung so easily and seductively.

30   5:01 Blues

Merle Haggard

Epic EK 44283

Broken Friend/Losin' In Las Vegas/5:01 Blues/Someday We'll Know/Wouldn't That Be Something/Sea Of Heartbreak/A Better Love Next Time/If You Want To Be My Woman/A Thousand Lies Ago/Somewhere Down The Line

This overlooked gem from 1989 is the best evidence available of the way Haggard has refined his art late in his career. Like his pal Willie Nelson, Haggard has adopted the honeyed tone and quicksilver phrasing of timeless pop-jazz vocalists like Ray Charles and Frank Sinatra. The Strangers have never sounded so much like a 1940s swing band, and Haggard's original songs take a philosophical long view on heartbreak. In his hushed, intimate vocals, you can hear all the distance between now and a romance that started *A Thousand Lies Ago*.

131   Just Lookin' For A Hit

Dwight Yoakam

Reprise 9 25989–1

Long White Cadillac/Little Ways/Honky Tonk Man/I Got You/Little Sister/I Sang Dixie/Guitars, Cadillacs/Sin City/Please, Please, Baby/Streets Of Bakersfield

Yoakam grew up in Kentucky, but when he found Nashville unsympathetic to his passion for hardcore country, he moved to California. There he cut an EP called **Guitars, Cadillacs, Etc., Etc.** in the style of the classic Bakersfield sound. That connection was formally blessed when Yoakam recorded a duet with Owens on *Streets Of Bakersfield* with Owens's Tom Brumley playing steel. This 1989 greatest-hits collection also includes versions of Elvis Presley's *Little Sister* and Johnny Horton's *Honky Tonk Man* as well as *Long White Cadillac*, a blistering tribute to Hank Williams by Dave Alvin of the LA rockabilly band, the Blasters. Yoakam proves that California country is still alive and growing into the future.

Western Music: the Songs of the Cowboy

4

Laurence J. Zwisohn

Western music, the songs of the cowboy. For many years this distinct form of music has seemingly been an orphan. It isn't pop music and it certainly isn't rhythm and blues, or jazz. It is closest to country music and so, often incorrectly, has been grouped with this genre. Since the late 1940s, the phrase "country and western" has housed this wonderful, purely American form of music. In recent years the jargon has been condensed to "country-western". Yet little in the way of western music is heard in today's country music. Even though many mainstream country music entertainers have dressed in western attire, dating back to Jimmie Rodgers in the late 1930s, few, if any, of these performers' repertoires have included cowboy songs.

Meanwhile, though, western performers have continued to sing the songs of the cowboy, both the traditional songs and more recently written songs of the American West. Western music usually tells a story; the better ones actually paint a picture, of the adventure, struggle, joy and sorrow that made up the rugged life in the West: songs that told of the trails the cowboy rode (like *The Old Chisholm Trail*, with its countless verses), tragic songs (such as *When The Work's All Done This Fall*), songs of love and happiness (like *The Yellow Rose Of Texas*), songs like *Tumbling Tumbleweeds* and *Blue Prairie*, which describe the beauty and mystery of the West.

Cowboy songs come out of that period in history when the American frontier moved ever further westward until it reached the Pacific Ocean, with the settling of California, Oregon, and Washington. As settlers, ranchers, miners, and the railroad moved west they brought their music with them. Wagon trains often took months traveling from St Joseph, Missouri to the far reaches of Wyoming, the Dakotas, Idaho, California and Oregon. The only means of entertainment the settlers had was

that which they provided for themselves. Singing helped pass
the long day's journey. Families helped keep their young
children occupied by singing songs to each other or having the
entire family join in singing a *roundelay* (a group sing-along).
In the evening after supper, families would often gather around
the campfires. Someone would bring out a fiddle or banjo and
the ensuing music and songs helped ease the tensions or
boredom of traveling over the seemingly never-ending plains.
On occasion these gatherings turned into dances which always
helped lift everyone's spirits before the next day's journey
began.

For those who had settled down on a ranch or homestead,
music was often the only break from the hard work of building
a new future. Homes and ranches were usually miles apart and
neighbors rarely got together. Family singing helped ease the
loneliness while occasional get-togethers of neighbors auto-
matically called for singing, playing musical instruments and
dancing. The songs they sang were a combination of traditional
songs originating in the countries the settlers or their parents
had migrated from, along with songs that were popular at the
moment. The more creative members of these gatherings would
perform songs they had made up, often about the experiences
they were encountering in their new surroundings.

Few contributed more to the music of the American West
than did the cowboy. Hard, tedious and lonely, the cowboy's
life was demanding and didn't pay well either. Ranches were
usually a long way from town, which meant visits there were
infrequent. Nights in the bunkhouse were spent repairing
saddles and guns, gambling, telling tall tales with an occasional
song to help break the monotony. A few cowboys had small
musical instruments, such as a guitar, banjo, harmonica, fiddle
or concertina. When the cowboy was out on the range he often
sang to himself to help pass the day. Riding the night guard
was a tiresome job. Through the long night the cowboy had to
keep himself awake and alert, watching the cattle and helping to
keep them calm. Cattle could become jumpy quite easily and
stampedes had to be prevented. The cowboy often sang softly
to help keep himself awake or to help calm the herd. They sang
everything from bawdy songs to church hymns. Some cowboys
made up songs about life on the range: tales of the trails they
had ridden, outlaws they had heard tell of, towns they had
visited, women they had known and tragedies they had witnessed.

Most of these songs were known to few and were quickly
forgotten, but some of them became popular and have come
down to us through the years. Cowboys would move on to
work at other ranches and would bring these songs with them.

Some of these songs became popular only in the areas in which they had originated, while others became a part of the lore of the west. Songs like *Red River Valley*, *The Old Chisholm Trail*, *The Streets Of Laredo*, *The Yellow Rose Of Texas*, and *Home On The Range* have since become a part of America's musical history. Many of the songs the cowboys created had lyrics about life on the range but had melodies that came from songs they had known all their lives. *The Cowboy's Dream* is sung to the tune of the Scottish song *My Bonnie Lies Over The Ocean*, *Whoopee Ti-Yi-Yo's* melody is the Irish ballad *Rocking The Cradle*, while *Bury Me Not On The Lone Prairie* has a melody taken from the old English song *The Ocean Burial*.

The West was fairly well settled by the end of the nineteenth century. The telegraph and the railroad had connected even the farthest reaches of the country with the rest of the United States. The early years of the twentieth century saw the phonograph become a part of many family parlors, and movies were beginning to grow dramatically in popularity and influence. Cowboy songs gradually slipped into the past as new styles and tastes developed. Fortunately many of the songs the cowboys had originally sung were collected and published in a number of songbooks and folios. The two most important of these were *Songs Of The Cowboy* by N. Howard Thorp, which was published in 1908, followed two years later by John A. Lomax's *Cowboy Songs And Other Frontier Ballads*.

Still, western music remained fairly dormant until the 1920s. By that time record companies were expanding their catalogs to include all varieties of music. The larger record companies sent representatives out with field equipment to record local musicians who sang and played hillbilly music, blues, gospel, jazz and any number of other styles of music. Since the major record labels were based in New York City, the majority of these field trips were made to the southeastern part of the United States. Only several years later did the record companies begin venturing out West to record. In the meantime several singers of cowboy music had traveled East in hopes of landing recording contracts. Carl T. Sprague, Harry "Mac" McClintock, Goebel Reeves (the Texas Drifter) and Jules Verne Allen were among the earliest to record cowboy songs. Records such as *When The Work's All Done This Fall* by Carl T. Sprague, recorded in 1925, and *The Old Chisholm Trail* which Harry "Mac" McClintock recorded two years later helped lead a rebirth in the popularity of western music.

Many localities had bands whose members dressed as cowboys and played western music. One of the earliest was Otto Gray and his Oklahoma Cowboys, which was formed in

1924. Louise Massey and the Westerners were featured on radio's National Barn Dance which was based in Chicago. (The Barn Dance preceded even Nashville's Grand Ole Opry onto the radio airwaves.) In southern California Len Nash and his Country Boys, Sheriff Loyal Underwood's Arizona Wranglers and Jack LeFevre and his Texas Outlaws were playing and singing cowboy songs. The Beverly Hillbillies were formed in 1928 and became very popular with their repertoire of cowboy songs, mountain ballads and hillbilly music. Stuart Hamblen's Lucky Stars were another popular group in the area which featured cowboy songs in their performances.

With the coming of sound in the 1927 film "The Jazz Singer," Al Jolson's utterance of "You ain't heard nothin' yet" proved to be right on the mark. Western films had been a staple of the motion picture industry right from the very beginning; the first American film to have wide distribution was "The Great Train Robbery" in 1903. In a short span of time, westerns were being made by the hundreds. Bronco Billy Anderson, the first western film star, made almost 400 one- and two-reel westerns in an eight-year period. Tom Mix, Hoot Gibson, William S. Hart, Harry Carey, Ken Maynard and Buck Jones soon became heroes of the western screen. The coming of sound enabled western music to be used in films. At first, songs were used only occasionally in scenes around a campfire or at a town dance. But before long, the role of cowboy songs in cinema began to expand. Ken Maynard and Bob Steele sang in a few of their own films. In 1935 a new form of western came into existence when Gene Autry starred in his first film "Tumbling Tumbleweeds." Within a couple of years Gene Autry was the top western star at the box office and film studios were competing with each other to find the next singing cowboy star. The sustained popularity of westerns, along with the increased use of cowboy songs in these films, led to a boom in the popularity of western music.

Shortly before the dawn of the golden era of the singing cowboy, the most influential ensemble in western music was created. The Sons of the Pioneers were formed as a result of Roy Rogers's love of vocal harmony and his unwillingness to give up after a number of earlier western groups he had worked with had failed. Rogers had joined the hillbilly musical group the Rocky Mountaineers late in 1931. Before too long he had talked the group into adding another singer with whom he could sing harmony. The man Roy hired was Bob Nolan, who would go on to become the finest songwriter in the history of western music. When Bob Nolan decided the Rocky Mountaineers weren't going anywhere he left the group, and Tim Spencer was brought in to take his place.

Over the next few years, Rogers and Spencer were in and out of a number of different groups, many of which folded soon after they were formed. In September 1933 the two of them returned from a disastrous tour of the southwestern United States with a group called the O-Bar-O Cowboys; the group members straggled back into Los Angeles and went their separate ways. Rogers was able to land a job with an outfit called Jack and his Texas Outlaws, who were performing on Radio KFWB in Hollywood. Still, he was restless; he wanted a group specializing in close harmony. Rogers talked Tim Spencer into quitting his job at a supermarket warehouse, and together they went out to talk with Bob Nolan, who was working as a caddy at a Los Angeles golf course. Despite the fact that this was the bottom of the Great Depression, when jobs were scarce and money was hard to find, these three decided to give Western Music another try. They roomed together in a boarding house in Hollywood and rehearsed for hours on end, sometimes until their voices gave out. As they honed their distinctive style of close harmony, they decided that their repertoire should be built around cowboy songs. Although other groups in the Los Angeles area featured some western music Roy, Bob, and Tim – who had by then decided to call themselves the Pioneer Trio – decided to concentrate on cowboy music (though they would never limit themselves completely to that genre). Rogers's group was able to secure an audition at KFWB. They were hired, and before long, their quality and popularity led to their own program, along with staff jobs at the station where they were featured on several daily programs. The Sons of the Pioneers (as they became known after the addition of two fine instrumentalists to the group) eventually became the most influential western ensemble the music has ever known. Their harmonies influenced countless other groups and their songs became the very foundation of non-traditional western music.

The decades of the 1910s and 1920s found Tin Pan Alley songwriters turning out a steady stream of songs about the American South. *Rock-a-Bye Your Baby With A Dixie Melody*, *Swanee*, *Carolina In The Morning*, *Alabamy Bound* and *Mississippi Mud*, to list but a few, paid tribute to a part of America that many of these New York City songwriters had never even visited. The decade of the 1930s saw a sudden revival of interest in cowboy songs. Once again, Tin Pan Alley songwriters were in the forefront with songs like *The Last Roundup*, *Empty Saddles*, *Take Me Back To My Boots And Saddle*, *Silver On The Sage*, *The Hills Of Old Wyomin'*, *Wagon Wheels*, *I'm An Old Cowhand*, and on into the 1940s with *Don't Fence Me In*, *Along The Navajo Trail* and *Jingle, Jangle, Jingle*. Just as few of the Tin Pan Alley songwriters had ever visited the South, even fewer (if any) had ever riden the Western range. Thus, the cowboy songs these songwriters composed tended to be romanticized visions of the West. The rigors, travail and peril the real cowboy had faced were rarely mentioned. Instead, the Tin Pan Alley lyrics tended to be sentimental odes to the cowboy and his horse. Still, many of these songs became major hits and ultimately helped sustain the popularity of western music. The songs Sons of the Pioneers Bob Nolan and Tim Spencer were writing were not exactly extensions of traditional cowboy songs. Instead they told of the beauty of the West and the adventure of the days when the real cowboys rode the range. Two of Bob Nolan's songs also became major pop hits during this period. In 1934 *Tumbling Tumbleweeds* became one of the year's most popular songs, was performed by numerous big bands and pop singers, and has been recorded by countless artists in almost every style of music over the years. *Cool Water*, written by Nolan in 1936, became even more popular a few years later. Meanwhile, Cowboy singer Gene Autry was selling lots of records, and the leading popular singers and orchestras were recording many western songs. Bing Crosby was particularly comfortable with cowboy songs, beginning with his 1933 hit recording of *Home On The Range*, and continuing throughout the next decade with *I'm An Old Cowhand*, *There's A Goldmine In The Sky*, *Tumbling Tumbleweeds*, *Mexicali Rose*, *Sioux City Sue*, and *San Antonio Rose*, among the many other western songs he recorded.

Movies were also continuing to spread the popularity of western music thanks to such singing cowboy film stars as Gene Autry, Roy Rogers, Tex Ritter, Jimmy Wakely, Eddie Dean, and others. Western groups like the Riders of the Purple Sage, the Ranch Boys, the Cass County Boys, the Plainsmen and many others patterned themselves after the Sons of the Pioneers, though none achieved the same degree of success. The noted director John Ford began using western music in a number of his films. Western movie classics such as "Stagecoach" and "She Wore A Yellow Ribbon", starring John Wayne, and "My Darling Clementine," with Henry Fonda, had stamped John Ford as the finest director of westerns; by the late 1940s he was featuring the Sons of the Pioneers in films such as "Rio Grande," starring John Wayne, "Wagon Master," and later, in the classic western "The Searchers," which also starred John Wayne. After early screenings of the Gary Cooper and Grace Kelly film "High Noon" fared poorly, Tex Ritter was brought in to sing the film's theme song as a narrative at various points throughout the movie. The film, a landmark of the cinema, went on to become a box-office success and heralded a period of a few years when western theme songs were widely recorded by many singers.

Yet, ironically, the end of western music's golden era was already close at hand. The introduction of television into American homes began in the late 1940s, but didn't take firm root until the early 1950s. The "B" western (lower budget films that were usually turned out in a series, all starring a particular western hero) had been a staple of the motion picture industry for over 30 years. With the arrival of television many of these old films were sold for airing by TV stations throughout the country. Now kids didn't have to wait for the Saturday matinee to see an exciting western. Instead they merely came home from school and turned on the television set. Thus, the "B" western soon faded into oblivion.

A few of its top stars – Roy Rogers and Gene Autry – switched over to television with their own half-hour programs. This shorter format meant that music was featured much less than in the "B" westerns. Those big-budget Hollywood westerns that were still being made offered little in the way of cowboy songs, and the end result was a dramatic decline in the popularity of western music. Performers such as Tex Ritter, Rex Allen, and the Sons of the Pioneers still kept busy with personal appearances. This, along with the continuing popularity of Roy Rogers, Dale Evans, and Gene Autry kept western music going, but the overall popularity of that music was on the wane. Although country and western music was growing in popularity, the fact was that, despite the genre's misleading name, it was really only country music that was being played on radio, and it was only country artists who were selling records.

In the years since, there have been occasional spurts of popularity for western music. In 1959 Marty Robbins recorded the album **Gunfighter Ballads And Trail Songs**. The song *El Paso* was released as a single and became a surprise number one hit on the pop and country charts despite the fact that it was over four minutes long. That album and the later western albums Robbins recorded sold well but didn't lead to a sustained reemergence of popularity for western music. There have been a handful of other western hits in the intervening years, including *Don't Go Near The Indians* by Rex Allen, *Hoppy, Gene And Me* by Roy Rogers and *Riders In The Sky* by Johnny Cash. In 1990 Michael Martin Murphey released the album **Cowboy Songs** which brought renewed attention to western music and even encouraged his record company to create a subsidiary label for western music. To date the label's success has been limited.

Still, western music lives on. It is a style of music that is purely American. It traces a romantic and exciting era in the settlement of the United States. Today, cowboys and the American West are worldwide symbols: songs from the days of the old West such as *Home On The Range, The Yellow Rose Of Texas, When The Work's All Done This Fall, I Ride An Old Paint, The Old Chisholm Trail,* and *Red River Valley* have achieved the same widespread popularity as the later *Tumbling Tumbleweeds, Riders In The Sky, High Noon, El Paso,* and *Cool Water.* Just as the western film will always be popular (even if there haven't been as many made as in years past), so too will western music retain its lasting appeal. It is unique and holds a warm spot in the hearts of countless people. The American cowboy's influence will never die and neither will his music.

Essential Recordings

(i) Sons of the Pioneers

Building a library of essential recordings of western music means keeping one basic thought in mind – the Sons of the Pioneers. Rarely has any field of music been so thoroughly dominated by one artist or group. Clearly there was western music before the Sons of the Pioneers, but no artist has so thoroughly defined or refined this genre of music. In 1933 Roy Rogers, Bob Nolan, and Tim Spencer set out to create a quality harmony group built upon the music of the cowboy. They had no idea that their group, with considerable personnel changes over the years, would still be in existence as the twenty-first century approached. The sound they created reflected the cowboy in his virility and masculinity, yet they were also fully capable of singing tender and sentimental songs.

Founding Member Bob Nolan had begun writing songs during his high school years. Born in New Brunswick, Canada and spending part of his youth in Boston, his move to Tucson, Arizona at the age of 14 had a powerful impact on him. He was overwhelmed by the beauty and majesty of the desert. As the years passed, Bob wrote songs that captured the wonders of nature and the adventure of the old West.

Tim Spencer grew up in Missouri, New Mexico and Oklahoma. He didn't begin writing songs until after the Sons of the Pioneers were formed. His first tunes were old-fashioned and sentimental, but before long Bob Nolan's influence had rubbed off on him and Tim began writing classic western songs. The songs Bob Nolan and Tim Spencer wrote have become basic to the repertoire of almost every performer or group that sings cowboy songs, and the true foundation of western music.

The Sons of the Pioneers' first recordings were made in August 1934 for the newly formed Decca Records. In 1937 they recorded for the American Record Company (which later became Columbia Records). In 1945 the Pioneers began recording for RCA Victor. It is these recordings, from the period most western music aficionados believe to be their peak years, that are their finest, and also their most successful. Any collection of western music must include several Sons of the Pioneers albums at a minimum.

The distinctive harmonies and creative vocal arrangements that are hallmarks of the Sons of the Pioneers were at their zenith during the decade of the 1940s. The Pioneers' move to RCA Victor resulted in better production, more varied instrumental arrangements and more frequent recording sessions than in prior years. Their most important commercial recordings were made in the period from 1945 through 1947. Although they had recorded *Cool Water* and *Tumbling Tumbleweeds* in earlier years for Decca, their RCA Victor recordings of these Pioneer signature songs remain the finest performances of these western classics. Bob Nolan's *Cool Water* captures the beauty of the desert, as well as the peril it presented to anyone trying to cross it. His *Tumbling Tumbleweeds*, the Pioneers' theme song almost from their start, describes the cowboy's love of the land, desolate though it might be. Tim Spencer's *Blue Prairie* is a haunting song of the mystical nature of that place called the West. In a more romantic style he describes the beauty and history of *The Everlasting Hills of Oklahoma*.

The cowboy could be sentimental, as evidenced by Bob Nolan's *Let's Pretend* and *Let Me Share Your Name*. There is humor in *Cowboy Country*, reverence in *Lead Me Gently Home, Father*, poetry in *Trees* and wistfulness in *Will There Be Sagebrush In Heaven*. **Tumbling Tumbleweeds** offers a solid introduction to the classic songs and recordings of the Sons of the Pioneers (compiled and annotated by the author of this chapter).

Discographical Details

32   Tumbling Tumbleweeds – The RCA Victor Years Vol. 1

Sons of the Pioneers
RCA 9744–2–R

Tumbling Tumbleweeds/Chant Of The Wanderer/No One To Cry To/Cowboy Camp Meeting/Trees/The Timber Trail/Let's Pretend/The Everlasting Hills Of Oklahoma/Cool Water/Teardrops In My Heart/Pecos Bill (with Roy Rogers)/ *Blue Prairie/Let Me Share Your Name/Will There Be Sagebrush In Heaven/Lead Me Gently Home, Father/Cowboy Country/A Penny For Your Thoughts/Blue Shadows On The Trail* (with Roy Rogers)/*The Last Roundup/My Best To You*

(ii) Gene Autry

Gene Autry's first starring film, "Tumbling Tumbleweeds," revolutionized westerns and led to a rebirth in the popularity of western music. Born in Tioga, Texas and raised in Oklahoma, Autry was a railroad telegrapher who usually kept a guitar nearby to help while away the long hours on the night shift. An oft-told story recounts how one evening in 1927 Autry was playing his guitar and singing when a man stopped by to send a telegram. The customer, who turned out to be the beloved humorist Will Rogers, listened to Autry sing and then suggested he consider going to New York to try to get a recording contract. The idea appealed to Autry all the more, since Will Rogers was not one to make such suggestions idly. Still, it was another year before Autry went east.

Autry was inexperienced and met with little success on his first trip to New York. However, a record company executive did give him some good advice. He suggested Autry return home and get some experience singing on radio before giving New York another try. Two years later, with such experience under his belt, Autry again ventured east. This time his luck was better and he began recording for a number of record companies under a variety of different names (a practice that was common at the time). Many of Autry's early recordings were of songs recorded by Jimmie Rodgers, considered the father of country music, or songs in the Rodgers style. It would be some time before Gene Autry's own style of singing began to emerge on records. The turning point came when he joined the National Barn Dance radio program in Chicago. He quickly developed a strong following there, and his recordings became more reflective of his natural style of singing. Cowboy songs eventually became a major part of Autry's repertoire, although it was a sentimental song he recorded in 1931, *That Silver-Haired Daddy Of Mine*, that really put him on the map.

In 1934, he was offered a small role in the Ken Maynard western film "In Old Santa Fe." His film debut was so successful that he was soon starring in the science fiction/western serial "Mystery Mountain." This was followed by the September 1935 release of his film "Tumbling Tumbleweeds." From 1935 until 1953 Autry starred in over 90 western films. Radio, records, television and personal appearances made him one of the biggest stars in show business. Astute investments resulted in a later business career that has been no less successful.

In the years before Autry recorded the perennial Christmas song *Rudolph The Red-Nosed Reindeer* he was the biggest-selling singing cowboy on records. His Christmas recordings only added to his fame. With the exception of *The Yellow Rose*

Of Texas, Red River Valley, and a few other songs, Autry actually recorded few traditional cowboy songs. Instead, he recorded many of the best contemporary cowboy songs of his era. Ray Whitley's *Back In The Saddle Again* became his theme song and one of the best loved of all modern cowboy songs. His nasal style and his feeling for country music resulted in vast popularity with rural audiences; but his comfortable way with a song made him popular throughout the world. Whether it was cowboy songs like *The Last Roundup* or *Take Me Back To My Boots And Saddle*, country songs like *You Are My Sunshine* or *It Makes No Difference Now*, or pop songs like *Blueberry Hill* or *Amapola*, Autry handled them all in a relaxed, confident manner. **The Essential Gene Autry** presents a worthy sampling of some of his most popular recordings.

Discographical Details

33   The Essential Gene Autry 1933–1946

Gene Autry

Columbia/Legacy CK 48957

The Yellow Rose Of Texas/The Last Roundup/Tumbling Tumbleweeds/Mexicali Rose/Take Me Back To My Boots And Saddle/Back In The Saddle Again/El Rancho Grande/Blueberry Hill/The Call Of The Canyon/You Are My Sunshine/It Makes No Difference Now/Amapola/Maria Elena/Deep In The Heart of Texas/I'm Thinking Tonight Of My Blue Eyes/Jingle, Jangle, Jingle/Ole Faithful/Red River Valley

(iii) Roy Rogers

Roy Rogers's preeminence in western music was assured when he organized the Sons of the Pioneers. It was his idea and his perseverance that resulted in the group's success. His selection of Bob Nolan and Tim Spencer as band mates laid the foundation for the most influential force in western music.

Rogers was a member of the Pioneers for five years before he ventured out on his own. Republic Pictures signed him as an actor after Gene Autry made repeated threats to walk out because he was dissatisfied with his film contract. When Autry actually did leave Republic Rogers suddenly found himself starring in "Under Western Stars," which had been scheduled as the next Gene Autry film. Rogers was an immediate success, reaching number 3 at the western box office after only his first year in films. In 1943, with Autry in the Army Air Force, Roy led at the box office and remained at number 1 throughout 1954. The "King of the Cowboys" (the title he earned as the top western star) then turned to television, with equal success.

Over the years, Roy Rogers's continuing popularity in all areas of entertainment has made him one of America's most loved figures. The screen hero has become a larger-than-life hero to several generations.

Roll On, Texas Moon brings together the best of Rogers's 1940s western recordings for RCA Victor. Included are songs from nine of his films, highlighted by fine performances of *San Fernando Valley*, *On The Old Spanish Trail*, *Rock Me To Sleep In My Saddle* and *The Yellow Rose Of Texas*.

Discographical Details

134 Roll On, Texas Moon

Roy Rogers

Bear Family BDP 15203 (Ger) (LP)
The Yellow Rose of Texas/Don't Fence Me In/A Gay Ranchero/Roll On, Texas Moon/I Met A Miss In Texas/On The Old Spanish Trail/May The Good Lord Take A Likin' To Ya (with Dale Evans)/*San Fernando Valley/I'm A Rollin'/ Little Hula Honey/California Rose/Home In Oklahoma/Rock Me To Sleep In My Saddle/Old-Fashioned Cowboy/There's A Cloud In My Valley Of Sunshine/Along The Navajo Trail*

(iv) Tex Ritter

Few people had better credentials or have contributed more to western music than Tex Ritter. Born in Murvaul, Texas (not far from country singer Jim Reeves's birthplace), Ritter developed a love of western songs during his youth. Deciding to become a lawyer, he entered the University of Texas, at Austin. Along with his law classes, he joined the glee club and choral society. This not only gave him an opportunity to learn to sing properly, it also resulted in a lifelong friendship with the choral director J. Frank Dobie. Dobie was a noted author and historian of western music. Additionally, Oscar J. Fox, a noted western music composer and historian, spent time at the university and Tex benefited from his knowledge, as well.

After his senior year at the university, Tex decided to journey to New York in search of musical opportunities. During the next eight years, he did considerable work on radio, and also made some Broadway stage appearances (including a role in "Green Grow The Lilacs," which was later turned into the Rodgers & Hammerstein musical "Oklahoma)." It was also during these years that Tex made his earliest recordings. Gene Autry's great success in films led other studios to seek out potential singing cowboys. The first real competition for Autry came when the small Grand National Pictures signed Ritter. "Song Of The Gringo," his first film, was released late in 1936. He would star in more than 50 westerns over the next nine years.

Ritter's recording career was somewhat slower in developing. He had recorded a few songs for the American Record Company during his years in New York. Between 1935 and 1939 Ritter recorded for Decca but with little succes. Then, in 1942, Capitol Records was formed. Johnny Mercer, one of the label's founders and the writer of countless pop standards, including *Blues In The Night, Moon River, Come Rain Or Come Shine*, and *Days Of Wine And Roses*, produced Ritter's first recordings for the label. Better songs, better production, and successful promotion soon resulted in Ritter's becoming one of Capitol's best-selling artists. He remained with them for 31 years, until his death in January 1974.

None of the cinema singing cowboys had a better feel for traditional cowboy songs than Tex Ritter. He grew up loving them, and he studied them in college, yet he sang them from the heart. Whether the songs were of sadness, like *Streets Of Laredo*, or *Bury Me Not On The Lone Prairie*, or rollicking songs, like *Rye Whiskey*, Ritter knew how to interpret them. One of his earliest and best albums was **Blood On The Saddle**. He knew these songs intimately and delivered one of the finest of all western albums with this recording.

Discographical Details

35   Blood On The Saddle

Tex Ritter

Capitol T/ST 1292 (LP)

Blood On The Saddle/Barbara Allen/Samuel Hall/Bury Me Not On The Lone Prairie/Little Joe The Wrangler/When The Work's All Done This Fall/The Face On The Barroom Floor/Boll Weevil/Billy The Kid/Streets Of Laredo/Sam Bass/Rye Whiskey

(v) Rex Allen

The era of the singing cowboy was coming to an end when a man who possessed one of the genre's finest voices first appeared on screen. Rex Allen was born on a ranch in Willcox, Arizona and was imbued with a love of the West and a flair for singing cowboy songs. After high school Allen moved to Phoenix, Arizona and landed a job singing on the radio on Saturday mornings. The rest of his week was spent working in the plastering business. Phoenix's hot weather took its toll on Allen, so he began moving around the country. Eventually he found himself in Trenton, New Jersey, far from the ranches and desert of his native Arizona. Radio work in Trenton led to an opportunity to audition for the National Barn Dance in Chicago. The Barn Dance had nurtured the early radio career of Gene Autry, and would soon do the same for Rex Allen.

Allen's years with the National Barn Dance won him strong regional popularity and led to his first recordings for newly-formed Mercury Records. Both Autry and Rogers felt Allen had what it took to become a singing cowboy film star. Rogers recommended him to the head of Republic Pictures who eventually had Allen come to Hollywood for a screen test. Not too long after that Allen's first film, "The Arizona Cowboy," was released. Allen became an immediate success and was soon number 3 at the western box office.

Unfortunately, though, the days of the series western were already numbered. Between 1950 and 1954, Allen starred in 19 westerns before Republic ceased production. Still, his fine voice and winning personality allowed for a long personal appearance career in rodeos, fairs and other venues. His later years have been occupied with doing narration work for Walt Disney nature films as well as a lucrative career doing voice-overs in television and radio commercials.

Recorded in 1972 and released on the small JMI label under the title **Bony-Kneed, Hairy-Legged Cowboy Songs** this fine album vanished quickly, owing to poor distribution. Fortunately, Bear Family Records took the album, added six additional country songs Rex recorded during the original sessions, retitled it **Voice Of The West**, and put this gem back in circulation. This is simply the finest album of Allen's career. From his beautiful reading of the nineteenth-century cowboy song *When The Work's All Done This Fall*, to tongue-in-cheek musical tall tales like *The Cowboy Fireman* and *Tyin' Knots In The Devil's Tail*, this album is filled with wonderful moments.

Discographical Details

136   Voice Of The West

Rex Allen
Bear Family BCD 15284 AH (Ger)
Moonshine Steer/Tyin' Knots In The Devil's Tail/Windy Bill/Little Joe The Wrangler/When The Work's All Done This Fall/Droop Ears/Streets Of Laredo (I'm A Young Cowboy)/The Fireman Cowboy/Braggin' Drunk From Wilcox/ Fiddle Medley/Gone Girl/Catfish John/You Never Did Give Up On Me/Just Call Me Lonesome/Today I Started Loving Her Again/Reflex Reaction

(vi) Jimmy Wakely

Jimmy Wakely was born just over the Oklahoma state line in Arkansas. When he was three his family moved back across the line to Oklahoma. This meant that Jimmy was raised in the heart of the Dust Bowl during the years of the Great Depression when Oklahoma's soil was being blown away, destroying many farms, ranches and lives in the process. Music, which had been a Wakely family pastime, would prove to be Jimmy Wakely's salvation. Moving to Oklahoma City, he found work on radio with a country band. Before long, he'd formed a vocal trio that included Johnny Bond, who would go on to become a successful solo singer and one of country music's finest songwriters. When Gene Autry came through Oklahoma City on a tour the trio asked him to appear on their radio program. From this meeting a lifetime friendship between Wakely, Bond and Autry developed. Autry had the trio come out to Hollywood where they began appearing on his Melody Ranch radio program.

The trio also found work in western films, and in 1944 Jimmy Wakely began starring in his own series of singing cowboy films. The demise of the "B" western didn't slow Wakely who became one of the most popular recording artists of the early 1950s. Among the many hits he had on the pop and country charts during that decade were *One Has My Name*, and his duet version of *Slipping Around* with Margaret Whiting. Until his death in 1982, Wakely continued to record, make personal appearances and operate Shasta Records, his own successful mail-order record company.

Bing Crosby, the consummate crooner of the 1930s and 1940s, had recorded a goodly number of cowboy songs that were well suited to his mellow pop style. Jimmy Wakely's **Santa Fe Trail** album is cut from that same stylistic mold. The songs, primarily written by Tin Pan Alley writers, fit his relaxed vocal style perfectly. The album stirs memories of the Saturday matinee westerns where Wakely would often take a break from the action and hold forth with an unhurried vocal performance of a contemporary cowboy song. As this album shows, few of the cowboys sang more smoothly than Jimmy Wakely.

Discographical Details

37 Santa Fe Trail

Jimmy Wakely
Decca DL 8409 (LP)
Along The Santa Fe Trail/Take Me Back To My Boots And Saddle/There's A Gold Mine In The Sky/Red River Valley/Blue Shadows On The Trail/Call Of The Canyon/We'll Rest At The End Of The Trail/It's A Lonely Trail/Sierra Nevada/It's Lonely On The Trail Tonight/Carry Me Back To The Lone Prairie/True Love (Is A Sacred Thing)

(vii) Marty Robbins

Marty Robbins was born in Glendale, Arizona in 1925, and like so many of his generation, grew up watching western films. His favorite cowboy was Gene Autry and his favorite group was the Sons of the Pioneers. Years later he would write a song titled *Gene Autry, My Hero*. The Sons of the Pioneers' influence on Robbins would be even greater. He began recording for Columbia Records in 1951. From then, until his death in 1982, he was rarely without a hit: *A White Sport Coat, Don't Worry, Devil Woman*, and *My Woman, My Woman, My Wife* were but a few of his hits which he also wrote, and countless other chart-toppers, including *Singing The Blues, Ruby Ann* and *I'll Walk Alone*, kept his records selling steadily, over the years. In 1959 Robbins got the opportunity he had been waiting for when he recorded the album **Gunfighter Ballads And Trail Songs**, an entire LP of western songs. Although country music was his career mainstay, cowboy music was the music closest to his heart.

The single *El Paso* was released from this album, and despite being over four minutes in length, became a runaway hit on both the pop and country charts. While country music would dominate the remainder of Robbins's career, he would always return periodically to the songs of the cowboy. Thus, almost singlehandedly, he kept western music alive during the 1960s.

Robbins's talents as a songwriter were virtually limitless. He could write a pop song like *A White Sport Coat*, a country song like *Devil Woman*, or a cowboy song like *El Paso*. His *You Gave Me A Mountain* became a hit for pop singer Frankie Laine, and later a mainstay in Elvis Presley's concert repertoire. The cowboy songs Marty wrote, like those of Bob Nolan, could be about adventure (*El Paso* or *Running Gun*), or spiritual in nature (*The Master's Call*.) He was at home with the traditional cowboy songs like *Billy The Kid* and *Utah Carol* or pop-flavored cowboy tunes like *A Hundred And Sixty Acres*. The commercial success of **Gunfighter Ballads and Trail Songs** allowed Marty to become even more creative and adventurous in his later albums of western music.

Discographical Details

138 Gunfighter Ballads And Trail Songs

Marty Robbins
Columbia CK 116
Big Iron/Cool Water/Billy The Kid/A Hundred And Sixty Acres/They're Hanging Me Tonight/Strawberry Roan/El Paso/In The Valley/The Master's Call/Running Gun/Down In The Little Green Valley/Utah Carol

(viii) Michael Martin Murphey

Michael Martin Murphey was born in Dallas, Texas and grew up listening to cowboy songs as a child. However, like many of his generation, as he grew older, rock-and-roll became his favorite music. During the late 1960s Murphey was a member of the rock-and-roll group, the Lewis and Clarke Expedition, but by the mid 1970s he had made the switch to country music. Ironically, his first major record was *Wildfire*, a song about a girl and her horse which became a major pop hit in 1975. A number of country hits followed including *What's Forever For*, *Still Taking Chances* and *A Long Line Of Love*.

As the 1990s dawned, Murphey was living on a ranch in New Mexico and had become fascinated with cowboy songs once again. The result was his 1990 album **Cowboy Songs** which generated excellent reviews, solid sales, and refocused attention on western music. So successful was the album that Warner Bros Records, the label for which he'd begun recording in 1986, formed the Warner Western label and began signing other western recording artists. Like Marty Robbins 30 years earlier, Michael Martin Murphey singlehandedly led a revival of the songs of the cowboy.

Leaning heavily on traditional western music **Cowboy Songs** offers an outstanding overview of the songs of the cowboy: songs of the trails they rode, the liquor they drank, the girls they knew, the land they loved and their abiding curiosity about the hereafter. Rounding out the album are two of the best-known contemporary western songs: *Tumbling Tumbleweeds*, the Sons of the Pioneers theme song, and *Happy Trails*, which was written by Roy Rogers's wife, Dale Evans, and is the couple's theme song. Just as *Happy Trails* has become a part of Americana, so too have most of the cowboy numbers in **Cowboy Songs**. This is another "must" recording for anyone interested in western music.

Discographical Details

39 Cowboy Songs

Michael Martin Murphey

Warner Bros 26308–2

Cowboy Logic/I Ride An Old Paint/Whoopee-Ti-Yi-Yo/Tumbling Tumbleweeds/Tying Knots In The Devil's Tail/The Old Chisholm Trail/Home On The Range/What Am I Doing Here/Wild Ripplin' Waters/The Yellow Rose Of Texas/Spanish Is The Lovin' Tongue/Cowboy Pride/Red River Valley/Let The Cowboy Dance/Jack Of Diamonds (Rye Whiskey)/Texas Rangers/When The Work's All Done This Fall/The Streets Of Laredo/O Bury Me Not On The Lone Prairie/Where Do The Cowboys Go When They Die/Reincarnation/Goodbye Old Paint/Happy Trails

(ix) Cowboy Songs: an Historical Overview

While pop music, jazz, blues and country music have seen some fine reissues of essential historic recordings, western music has seen virtually no such reissues in recent years. In 1966 RCA Victor released **Authentic Cowboys And Their Western Folksongs** (see "Basic Recordings" section, this chapter). That long-out-of-print album was the only effort any of the major American record companies had made at reissuing the earliest recordings of cowboy music. In 1983 New World Records made an attempt at remedying this situation. **Back In The Saddle Again** traces the history of recorded cowboy music by way of over two dozen selections, ranging from Carl T. Sprague's 1925 recording of the classic cowboy song *When The Work's All Done This Fall*, to the Riders in the Sky 1980 recording of *Cowboy Song*. The album offers an excellent overview of the evolution of cowboy songs, from the traditional *The Old Chisholm Trail* to contemporary western selections like *Rusty Spurs*.

Because of the popularity of the cinematic singing cowboy, the decade of the 1930s saw more cowboy music recorded than any decade before or since. **Legendary Songs Of The Old West** brings together a wide array of this era's cowboy songs from the Columbia Records vaults. Ken Maynard, the first cowboy hero to sing on the screen, delivers *Home On The Range* in a voice that makes clear why he did *not* become a singing cowboy. Tex Ritter's earliest recordings are featured and prove just how fine a cowboy singer he was from the very start. Roy Rogers's rendition of *I've Sold My Saddle For An Old Guitar* not only shows what a wonderful voice he had, but presents a long-overlooked gem. Early recordings by Gene Autry and the Sons of the Pioneers, along with a variety of other artists, make this one of the best packages of cowboy music ever released. The material leans towards the non-traditional western song, but presents a clear reflection of western music's most popular era.

Discographical Details

140   Back In The Saddle Again

Various Artists
New World NWD 314/315–2 (LP)

Harry "Mac" McClintock: *The Old Chisholm Trail*; Harry Jackson: *The Pot Wrassler*; Van Holyoak: *The Gol-Durned Wheel*; Carl T. Sprague: *When The Work's All Done This Fall*; John G. Prude: *Streets Of Laredo*; Marc Williams: *Sioux Indians*; Jules Verne Allen: *The Dying Cowboy*; Powder River Jack and Kitty Lee: *Tyin' Knots In The Devil's Tail*; Arizona Wranglers: *Strawberry*

Roan; Ken Maynard: *Lone Star Trail*; Glen Rice and his Beverly Hillbillies: *Ridge Runnin' Roan*; John White: *Whoopee-Ti-Yi-Yo*; Jimmie Rodgers: *Cowhand's Last Ride*; Wilf Carter: *Little Old Log Shack I Always Call Home*; Tex Ritter: *A-Ridin' Old Paint*; Patsy Montana: *I Want to Be A Cowboy's Sweetheart*; Tex Owens: *Cattle Call*; Sons of the Pioneers: *One More Ride*; Texas Ruby: *Dim Narrow Trail*; Girls of the Golden West: *I Want To Be A Real Cowboy Girl*; Gene Autry: *Back In The Saddle Again*; Rex Allen: *My Dear Old Arizona Home*; Bob Wills: *Cowboy Stomp*; Slim Critchlow: *D-Bar-2 Horse Wrangler*; Sam Agins: *City Boarders*; Glenn Ohrlin: *The Cowboy*; Chris LeDoux: *Rusty Spurs*; Riders in the Sky: *Cowboy Song*

41   Legendary Songs Of The Old West

Various Artists

Columbia Special Products P4–15542 (LP)

Gene Autry: *Back In The Saddle Again/Red River Valley/The Yellow Rose Of Texas/Way Out West In Texas/The Last Roundup/Ole Faithful/Tumbling Tumbleweeds*; Sons of the Pioneers: *Song Of The Bandit/Open Range Ahead/Billie the Kid/Hold That Critter Down*; Bob Wills: *My Little Cherokee Maiden/Little Liza Jane/Rockin' Alone (In An Old Rockin' Chair)*; Prairie Ramblers: *Lucy Long/Ghost in the Graveyard*; Roy Rogers: *I've Sold My Saddle For An Old Guitar/Cowboy Night Herd Song/When The Black Sheep Gets The Blues/Hadie Brown/Listen To The Rhythm Of The Range/Hi Yo Silver*; Rocky Mountain Rangers: *Seven Years With The Wrong Man/Seven Years With The Wrong Woman*; Bonnie Blue Eyes: *Seven Beers With The Wrong Man*; Tex Ritter: *Rye Whiskey, Rye Whiskey/Everyday In The Saddle/Goodbye Old Paint/A-Ridin' Old Paint*; Bob Atcher and Bonnie Blue Eyes: *You Are My Sunshine*; Sons of the West *My Prairie Queen*; Patsy Montana: *I Want To Be a Cowboy's Sweetheart/I Only Want A Buddy, Not A Sweetheart/I'm An Old Cowhand*; Ken Maynard: *Home On The Range*; Light Crust Doughboys: *Oh! Susannah*; Bob Atcher: *Cool Water*; Louise Massey: *I'm Thinking Tonight Of My Blue Eyes/Ragtime Cowboy Joe*; Smiley Burnette: *Minnie The Moocher At The Morgue*

Basic Recordings

42   Sons Of The Pioneers: Country Music Hall Of Fame

Sons of the Pioneers

MCA MCAD–10090

Way Out There/Tumbling Tumbleweeds/There's A Roundup In The Sky/When Our Old Age Pension Check Comes To Our Door/Echoes From The Hills/The Hills Of Old Wyomin'/Ride Ranger Ride/One More Ride/Rye Whiskey/Cool Water/When The Moon Comes Over Sun Valley/Private Buckaroo/I Hang My Head And Cry/Let Me Keep My Memories/Sierra Nevada/Somebody Bigger Than You And I

Beginning with the Sons of the Pioneers' very first recording, *Way Out There* – which features their famous three-part harmony yodeling – this album provides an overview of the group's earliest work. Also included are cuts from the early 1940s, and two from 1954. This is the best representation of how the legendary group sounded in their early days.

143 Sons Of The Pioneers: Columbia Historic Edition

Sons of the Pioneers

Columbia CK 37439

Song Of The Bandit/At The Rainbow's End/Hold That Critter Down/When The Golden Train Comes Down/Cajon Stomp/You Must Come In At The Door/ The Devil's Great Grandson/Cowboy Night Herd Song/Send Him Home To Me/The Touch Of God's Hand

In late 1937 the Sons of the Pioneers recorded 32 songs in four sessions for the American Record Company. Although Roy Rogers had just left the group after signing with Republic Pictures, he returned to record these sides with the Pioneers. By this time, the group's sound was growing smoother and more polished, and Bob Nolan was writing some of his best songs. *Song Of The Bandit* and *At The Rainbow's End* particularly showcase these developments, while Roy's solo on *Cowboy Night Herd Song* foretell his success as a singing cowboy star.

144 Trail Dust

Sons of the Pioneers

RCA Victor LPM/LSP 2737 (LP)

Trail Herdin' Cowboy/Over The Santa Fe Trail/(Down The) Trail To San Antone/Autumn On The Trail/The Oregon Trail/There's A Long, Long Trail/ Trail Dust/The Utah Trail/By A Campfire On The Trail/Trail Dreamin'/We'll Rest At The End Of The Trail/Silent Trails

During the 1960s, the Sons of the Pioneers were the only western singers still recording for a major label. Throughout the sixties they recorded a number of fine albums. Twelve songs of the trail are featured on this 1963 album. Highlights are Bob Nolan's carefree *Trail Dreamin'* and *Trail Herdin' Cowboy*, along with Tim Spencer's metaphoric *Over The Santa Fe Trail*, and his pensive *Silent Trails*.

145 Legends Of The West

Sons of the Pioneers

RCA Victor LPM/LSP 3551 (LP)

Buffalo/Destiny/The Strawberry Roan/The Shifting Whispering Sands/Little Joe The Wrangler/O Bury Me Not On The Lone Prairie/Ringo/Me And My Burro/Outlaws/Billy The Kid/Green Ice And Mountain Men/Jesse James

Two years after their **Trail Dust** album the Sons of the Pioneers recorded **Legends of the West**, an album of traditional cowboy songs and newer songs written in that style. The Pioneers' matchless, evocative harmonies give testimony to the adventure and excitement of these songs.

146 The Gene Autry Collection

Gene Autry

Murray Hill M61072 (4–LP set)

That Silver-Haired Daddy Of Mine/The Life Of Jimmie Rodgers/The Death Of Jimmie Rodgers/Blue Yodel No. 5/Rhythm Of The Range/Nobody's Darling But

Mine/You're The Only Star In My Blue Heaven/Rainbow Valley/Mexicali Rose/The One Rose/When It's Springtime In The Rockies/Take Me Back To My Boots And Saddle/There's A Gold Mine In The Sky/Sail Along Silvery Moon/Back In The Saddle Again/South Of The Border/The Singing Hills/El Rancho Grande/Blueberry Hill/Be Honest With Me/You Are My Sunshine/It Makes No Difference Now/Maria Elena/Sweethearts Or Strangers/Dixie Cannonball/I'm Thinking Tonight Of My Blue Eyes/Jingle, Jangle, Jingle/At Mail Call Today/Gallivantin' Galveston Gal/Oklahoma Hills/Memories Of That Silver-Haired Daddy Of Mine/End Of My Roundup Days/My Star Of The Sky/My Rose Of The Prairie/Down A Mountain Trail/Don't Take Out Your Spite On Me/I Don't Belong In Your World/Panhandle Pete/Riders In The Sky/Diesel Smoke, Dangerous Curves

Gene Autry really put the singing cowboy on the map. Over the years he recorded a great number of cowboy songs, along with some of the best pop and country songs of his era. This boxed set presents 40 of his Columbia recordings spanning the years 1931 through 1952. A number of previously unissued recordings are also included. This is the largest single package of Autry's recordings released, as of this writing. It presents an excellent survey of his non-Christmas recording career, as well as a worthy sampling of his western recordings.

47   16 Great Songs Of The Old West

Roy Rogers and Dale Evans

Golden A198: 7 (LP)

Roy Rogers: *I Ride An Old Paint/Whoopee-Ti-Yi-Yo/The Old Chisholm Trail/Colorado Trail/The Railroad Corral/The Streets Of Laredo/The Night Herding Song/Doney Gal/Goodbye Old Paint/Bury Me Out On The Lone Prairie*; Dale Evans: *Home On The Range/Tumbling Tumbleweeds/Red River Valley*; Roy Rogers and Dale Evans: *Song Wagon/Cool Water/The Cowman's Prayer*

The only album of traditional cowboy songs sung by Roy Rogers is this album, recorded for the children's label, Golden Records, in the mid 1950s. Not only is the album a child's primer of the songs of the cowboy, it is fine listening for adults as well. Backed by a vocal chorus and sparse instrumentation, Rogers obviously enjoyed getting to sing many of the songs he'd sung as a member of the Sons of the Pioneers. Dale Evans solos on a few songs and joins her husband on several others.

48   Roy Rogers: Columbia Historic Edition

Roy Rogers

Columbia, FC 38907 (LP)

Ridin' Ropin'/That Pioneer Mother Of Mine/She's All Wet Now/A Lonely Ranger Am I/The Mail Must Go Through/Headin' for Texas And Home/Old Pioneer/When I Camped Under The Stars/Dust/My Little Lady (Hadie Brown)

A fine sampling of Rogers's first solo recordings recorded in the late 1930s. Most of these songs come from his early films. Three in particular stand out: *Dust* was featured in Roy's first film, "Under Western Stars," and presents a dramatic description of the grim Dust Bowl tragedy that drove farmers off their land during the years of the Great Depression. Also from that film, but on a much brighter note, is Tim Spencer's melodic *When I Camped Under The Stars*. Tim also wrote *That Pioneer Mother Of Mine*, which Roy sings with deep feeling.

149 Pecos Bill

Roy Rogers and the Sons of the Pioneers
RCA Camden CAL 1054 (LP)
Blue Shadows On The Trail/Pecos Bill/Story Of Pecos Bill

Cowboys were notorious for telling tall tales, but none did it better than cowboys from Texas. **Pecos Bill** tells the story of the cowboy who roped a raging cyclone, dug the Rio Grande, wrestled a grizzly bear, was raised by wolves, and was done for by the love of a woman. The Pecos Bill segment of Walt Disney's "Melody Time" featured Roy Rogers and the Sons of the Pioneers singing and narrating the story of the rootin' tootin'-est cowboy to ever come out of Texas. The musical highlight is Rogers's and the Pioneers' beautiful performance of *Blue Shadows On The Trail*.

150 High Noon

Tex Ritter
Bear Family BCD 15634 AH (Ger)
High Noon/Blood On The Saddle/Jingle, Jangle, Jingle/Boogie Woogie Cowboy/ He's A Cowboy Auctioneer/Rye Whiskey/The Texas Rangers/The Chisholm Trail/Billy The Kid/Cattle Call/The San Antone Story/The Marshall's Daughter/Wichita/Prairie Home/Gunsmoke/Remember The Alamo/The Last Frontier/The Searchers/Buffalo Dream/The Bandit/Brave Man/Trooper Hook/ The Wayward Wind/When It's Springtime In The Rockies/The Night Herding Song

Gathering together most of Ritter's non-album recordings of cowboy songs, **High Noon** is a fitting tribute to this beloved man. Few performers brought such dignity and feeling to western music. This album combines traditional western songs with Tin Pan Alley cowboy songs and western film theme songs. Thus the cowboy songs come from three different directions, all handled masterfully by Ritter.

151 Tex Ritter's Wild West

Tex Ritter
Capitol ST 2974 (LP)
Texas/Dusty Skies/Bad Brahma Bull/The Blizzard/Conversation With A Gun/ High Noon/The Wayward Wind/The Long Tall Shadow/The Everlasting Hills Of Oklahoma/The Governor And The Kid/Stranger On Boot Hill/Me And Tennessee

Even after moving to Nashville and becoming president of the Country Music Association, Tex Ritter continued to record western songs. **Tex Ritter's Wild West** features contemporary songs of the west. Along with two narrations (*Conversation With A Gun* and *The Governor And The Kid*) – at which Tex had no equal – highlights include *The Wayward Wind*, *The Blizzard*, and Cindy Walker's delightful *Texas*.

52 Under Western Skies

Rex Allen

Decca DL 8402 (LP)

The Trail Of The Lonesome Pine/Nothin' To Do/The Last Roundup/The Last Frontier/Rocky Mountain Lullaby/Ole Faithful/Twilight On The Trail/The Railroad Corral/I'm A Young Cowboy (The Streets Of Laredo)/At The Rainbow's End/Sky Boss/Too-Lee-Roll-Um

Backed by a full orchestra and chorus conducted by the noted composer Victor Young, Rex Allen is in fine fettle on this solid collection of Tin Pan Alley cowboy songs, with a few traditional numbers thrown in for good measure. Rex's version of *The Streets Of Laredo* (titled *I'm A Young Cowboy* on this album) is a *tour de force*, and shows why his voice is the envy of so many aspiring western singers.

53 Mister Cowboy

Rex Allen

Decca DL 8776/78776 (LP)

Cindy/Sweet Betsy From Pike/Sleep, Little Moses/The Cowboy's Dream/Alla En El Rancho Grande/Softly And Tenderly/Lonesome Valley/Hoosen Johnny/Curtains Of Night/Rarin' To Go/Old Joe Clark/On Top Of Old Smokey/Feeling Bad/Prayer Of The Frontier Doctor

Eschewing the large orchestra, Allen sings a noteworthy selection of traditional cowboy songs, nineteenth-century popular songs and hymns here. Whether the backing is a full orchestra or just a few basic instruments, Allen's voice is always at home with the songs of the cowboy.

54 More Gunfighter Ballads And Trail Songs

Marty Robbins

Columbia CL 1481/CS 8272 (LP)

San Angelo/Prairie Fire/Streets Of Laredo/Song Of The Bandit/I've Got No Use For The Women/Five Brothers/Little Joe The Wrangler/Ride, Cowboy, Ride/This Peaceful Sod/She Was Young And She Was Pretty/My Love

Marty Robbins's followup to his **Gunfighter Ballads And Trail Songs** didn't produce any hit singles, but succeeded artistically and commercially. Robbins continued writing songs of western adventure like *San Angelo*, and also reprised some of his favorite traditional cowboy songs, as well as *Song Of The Bandit*, one of Bob Nolan's most creative songs. Country music accounted for the majority of Robbins's recorded repertoire, but he never let western music get too far from his grasp.

55 The Drifter

Marty Robbins

Columbia CL 2527/CS 9327 (LP)

Meet Me Tonight In Laredo/The Wind Goes/Cry Stampede/Feleena/Never Tie Me Down/Cottonwood Tree/Oh, Virginia/Mr Shorty/Take Me Back To The Prairie

This is the least known of Marty Robbins's western albums. Although it produced a moderate hit single in *Mr Shorty*, the album was too adventurous for non-western Robbins devotees. Still, the LP displays Robbins's love of the west and his ability to tell adventurous stories in song. Building on the popularity of *El Paso*, Robbins's composition *Feelena (Of El Paso)*, at over eight minutes, is almost twice as long. Marty had a shortlived syndicated television series titled "The Drifter," which was the inspiration for this album.

156   All Around Cowboy

Marty Robbins

Columbia JC 36085 (LP)

All Around Cowboy/The Dreamer/Pride And The Badge/Restless Cattle/When I'm Gone/Buenos Dias Argentina/Lonely Old Bunkhouse/San Angelo/Tumbling Tumbleweeds/The Ballad Of A Small Man

Robbins's final album of cowboy songs, **All Around Cowboy**, was released in 1979. Country music had changed since Robbins had first come on the scene; though he wasn't completely happy with all the material he was recording, when it came time to make an album of cowboy songs his old enthusiasm returned. This was the music that was closest to his heart and the music which he had helped keep alive when few others of national prominence were recording the music of the West. On this, his final western album, Robbins paid tribute to one of his heroes when he recorded Bob Nolan's *Tumbling Tumbleweeds*. Robbins died in December, 1982.

157   Cattle Call/Thereby Hangs A Tale

Eddy Arnold

Bear Family BCD 15441 AH (Ger)

The Streets Of Laredo/Cool Water/Cattle Call/Leanin' On The Old Top Rail/ Ole Faithful/A Cowboy's Dream/The Wayward Wind/Tumbling Tumbleweeds/ Cowpoke/Where The Mountains Meet The Sky/Sierra Sue/Carry Me Back To The Lone Prairie/(Jim) I Wore A Tie Today/Tom Dooley/Nellie Sits A-Waitin'/Tennessee Stud/The Battle Of Little Big Horn/The Wreck Of The Old '97/The Red-Headed Stranger/Johny Reb, That's Me/Riders In The Sky/Boot Hill/Ballad Of Davy Crockett/Partners/Jesse James

Although Eddy Arnold was known as the "Tennessee Plowboy" early in his singing career, it was the cowboy song *Cattle Call* which became his theme song. Country music isn't western music, but Arnold finds success with both styles in this album. Highlights of the **Cattle Call** half of the CD are his stereo recording of the title song and his fine performance on Stan Jones's *Cowpoke*. The other half of the CD, **Thereby Hangs A Tale** features a selection of folk and western songs. A particular highlight is his hit version of *Tennessee Stud*.

158   The Wild, Wicked But Wonderful West

Johnny Bond

Starday SLP 147 (LP)

The Bully/At Dawn I Die/Empty Saddles/The Long Tall Shadow/High Noon/ The Deadwood Stage/Dusty Skies/The Pass/The Fool's Paradise/Carry Me Back To The Lone Prairie/Sadie Was A Lady/Conversation With A Gun/ Wanderers Of The Wasteland

Oklahoma-born Johnny Bond started out in Jimmy Wakely's vocal trio, singing songs he'd heard the Sons of the Pioneers perform. Before long Bond was writing fine western songs like *Cimarron (Roll On)*, and country songs like *Tomorrow Never Comes* and *Your Old Love Letters*. A successful career in country music produced hit records like *Ten Little Bottles* and *Hot Rod Lincoln*. Still, cowboy songs remained close to his heart. **The Wild, Wicked But Wonderful West** gave Johnny an opportunity to sing of the humor, adventure, and sorrow that were so much a part of the old West.

59   Johnny Cash Sings The Ballads Of The True West

Johnny Cash

Columbia C2L 38/C2S 838 (LP)

Hiawatha's Vision/The Road To Kaintuck/The Shifting Whispering Sands/The Ballad of Boot Hill/I Ride An Old Paint/Hardin Wouldn't Run/Mister Garfield/The Streets Of Laredo/Johnny Reb/A Letter From Home/Bury Me Not On The Lone Prairie/Mean As Hell/Sam Hall/Twenty-Five Minutes To Go/The Blizzard/Sweet Betsy From Pike/Green Grow The Lilacs/Stampede/Reflections

Dyess, Arkansas, isn't exactly the West; still Johnny Cash grew up there listening to country music and seeing an occasional cowboy movie. As a recording artist Cash has always tried to expand his horizons, although country music has always remained his music of choice. Cash has recorded two western albums to date. **Bitter Tears** is filled with thought-provoking songs of the American Indian, which tell how poorly the native Americans have been treated over the years. **Ballads Of The True West** is primarily cowboy songs – both traditional and of more recent vintage, written in the folk music vein. From the maudlin *Streets Of Laredo* to the comical *25 Minutes To Go*, this album is filled with fascinating music.

60   Dean Of The West

Eddie Dean

WFC 61576 (LP)

Hills Of Old Wyoming/Wagon Wheels/Courtin' Time/Tumbleweed Trail/Black Hills/Driftin' River/Ain't No Gal/Stars Over Texas/Way Back In Oklahoma/Banks Of The Sunny San Juan

After appearing in supporting roles in a number of western films, Eddie Dean began starring in his own series of singing cowboy films in 1944. He possessed a strong, Broadway-type of voice, and his songs were the real highlights of these less than outstanding westerns. When his film career waned, Dean found success as a songwriter with *One Has My Name (The Other Has My Heart)* and *I Dreamed Of A Hillbilly Heaven*. **Dean Of The West** features ten songs from his films, including fine versions of *The Hills Of Old Wyoming* and *Banks Of The Sunny San Juan*.

61   This Was The West

Stan Jones

Disneyland WDL 3033 (LP)

Sacajawea/Ol' Kit Carson/Jim Marshall's Nugget/Wagons West/Pony Express/Cowpoke/Buffalo/Indian Spirit Chant/Yellow Stripes/The Lilies Grow High/Coffin In The Cabin/Saddle Up/Stars Of The West/Songs Of The Dance Hall Girls/Rollin' Dust

Stan Jones was a ranger in the National Park Service when he began writing western songs. One of the first of his songs, *(Ghost) Riders In The Sky,* became a major hit and opened the door for him to write for films, as well as for the Sons of the Pioneers. Stan made few recordings but **This Was The West** features 15 of his songs through which he tells the story of the Old West. This is a little-known but most unusual recording. Uncredited vocal accompaniment on the album is by the Sons of the Pioneers.

162   The Cowboy Way

Riders in the Sky

MCA MCAD-31244

Back In The Saddle Again/That's How The Yodel Was Born/Carry Me Back To The Lone Prairie/When Payday Rolls Around/Concerto For Violin And Longhorns/Riders In The Sky/Texas Plains/Reincarnation/Lonely Utah Stars/ Mr Sincere/Salting Of The Slug/My Oklahoma/Ridin' Down The Canyon/Miss Molly/Happy Trails

The Sons of the Pioneers have influenced countless vocal groups since their inception in 1933. One of the many affected by their music is Doug Green, who has listened to their records since childhood. Green is one of the leading contemporary authorities on country *and* western music, and had written prolifically on both genres before he decided to form a western singing group of his own. Calling themselves the Riders in the Sky Green's group took their inspiration from the Sons of the Pioneers. However, the Riders have placed a much heavier emphasis on comedy in their songs and stage performances. A number of albums, television, and radio series, and a busy schedule of personal appearances have spelled success for the Riders in the Sky. **The Cowboy Way** offers a splendid opportunity to hear them at work.

163   Chuck Wagon Days

Tex Ritter

Capitol ST 213 (LP)

Git Along, Little Dogies/A-Ridin' Old Paint/Red River Valley/Rounded Up In Glory/Every Day In The Saddle/The Old Chisholm Trail/The Border Affair/ Home On The Range/A Cowboy's Prayer/Chuckwagon Son Of A Gun

Ritter's final visit to the songs of the Old West came with this 1969 album. Leaning on traditional cowboy songs, Ritter clearly showed that his heart was still tied to the songs he'd learned in his youth. Highlights are his spirited version of *The Old Chisholm Trail,* and the cowboy hymn, *Rounded Up In Glory.* A fine coda to one of the true sons of the West.

164   Cowboy Christmas

Michael Martin Murphey

Warner Bros 9–26647–2

I Heard The Bells On Christmas Day/Jolly Old St Nicholas/The Creak Of The Leather/Christmas On The Line/Sleigh Ride/Jingle Bells/The Christmas Trail/ Merry Texas Christmas, You All/Ridin' Home On Christmas Eve/Corn, Water And Wood/The Cowboy Christmas Ball/Polka Medley/Christmas Cowboy Style/ The Santa Claus Schottische/Two-Step 'Round The Christmas Tree/Two-Step Medley/Log Cabin Home In The Sky/Waltz Medley/Pearls In The Snow/ Goodnight, Ladies/Auld Lang Syne

The cowboy loved Christmas as much as anyone, and Michael Martin Murphey's **Cowboy Christmas** captures the feel of Christmas in the West. For someone who came late to recording western music, Murphey has managed to set a very high standard.

65   Authentic Cowboys And Their Western Folksongs

Various Artists
RCA Victor LPV 522 (LP)
Harry McClintock: *The Old Chisholm Trail/Sam Bass*; Powder River Jack and Kitty Lee: *Powder Buck/Tyin' A Knot In The Devil's Tail*; Carl T. Sprague: *Following The Cow Tail/When The Work's All Done This Fall/The Mormon Cowboy/Utah Carroll*; Jules Allen: *Zebra Dun, The Cowboy's Dream*; J.D. Farley: *Bill Was A Texas Lad*; Eck Robertson: *There's A Brown-Skin Girl Down The Road Somewhere*; Mildred and Dorothy Good (Girls of the Golden West): *Bucking Broncho (My Love Is A Rider)*; Cartwright Brothers: *Texas Rangers*; Jack Webb: *The Night Guard*; Billie Maxwell: *Haunted Hunter*

As has been said, one of the most overlooked areas of music when it comes to reissues is western music. This 1966 RCA Victor album presents an excellent sampling of early Victor cowboy recordings. RCA recorded more early cowboy music than any other label. One hopes they will soon see fit to dip into their vaults again and give us another package of such vintage recordings on CD.

66   My Rifle, My Pony And Me

Various Artists
Bear Family BCD 15625 AH (Ger)
Dean Martin and Rick Nelson: *My Rifle, My Pony And Me*; James Stewart: *The Legend of Shenandoah*; Sons of the Pioneers: *Montana/The Searchers/Wagons West/Song Of The Wagonmaster*; Merle Kilgore: *Nevada Smith*; Marty Robbins: *Ballad Of The Alamo/The Hanging Tree*; Johnny Western: *Ballad Of Paladin*; Johnny Cash: *The Sons Of Katie Elder/The Rebel – Johnny Yuma*; Frankie Laine: *Rawhide/Gunfight At The O.K. Corral*; Fess Parker: *Ballad Of Davy Crockett*; Dean Martin: *Rio Bravo*; Tab Hunter: *I'm A Runaway*; Lorne Greene: *Bonanza*; Johnny Horton: *North To Alaska*; Tex Ritter: *High Noon*; Kirk Douglas: *And The Moon Grew Brighter*; Roy Rogers and the Sons of the Pioneers: *Pecos Bill*; Roy Rogers: *The Yellow Rose Of Texas/Roll On, Texas Moon/Don't Fence Me In*; Dickson Hall: *Cowboy*

Film music has a following all its own; western theme songs have been popular since the earliest days of the singing cowboys in the 1930s. **My Rifle, My Pony And Me** brings together a potpourri of western themes from film and television. These are as diverse as Jimmy Stewart's narration of *The Legend Of Shenandoah*, Kirk Douglas's (attempt at) singing *And The Moon Grew Brighter*, to much stronger selections by Tex Ritter and Roy Rogers. Some of these tracks bear listening to again and again, while others wear themselves out with one play. Still, a most interesting western album, all in all.

167   Songs Of The West

Various Artists

Rhino R2 71263 (4-CD set)

Cowboy Classics: Gene Autry: *Back In The Saddle Again/Cowboy Blues*; Sons of the Pioneers: *Tumbling Tumbleweeds/Cool Water*; Tex Owens: *Cattle Call*; Tex Ritter: *Take Me Back To My Boots And Saddle/The Wayward Wind*; Walter Brennan: *Gunfight At The O.K. Corral*; Marty Robbins: *Big Iron/The Strawberry Roan*; Ian Tyson: *Leavin' Cheyenne*; Patsy Montana: *I Want To Be A Cowboy's Sweetheart*; Foy Willing and the Riders of the Purple Sage: *Ragtime Cowboy Joe*; Riders in the Sky: *Ride, Cowboy, Ride/The Line Rider*; Frankie Laine: *Mule Train*; Rex Allen: *The Last Roundup*; Roy Rogers and Dale Evans: *Happy Trails*

Silver Screen Cowboys: Roy Rogers: *Rock Me To Sleep In My Saddle/California Rose*; Tex Ritter: *Singin' In The Saddle/When It's Lamplighting Time In The Valley/Jingle, Jangle, Jingle*; Sons of the Pioneers: *I'm An Old Cowhand/A Melody From The Sky*; Gene Autry: *That Silver-Haired Daddy Of Mine/Sioux City Sue/Ridin' Down The Canyon*; Bob Wills: *New San Antonio Rose*; Jimmy Wakely: *One Has My Name/I Love You So Much It Hurts*; Foy Willing and the Riders of the Purple Sage: *Twilight On The Trail*; Walter Brennan: *Old Rivers*; Rex Allen: *Don't Go Near The Indians*; Slim Pickens: *Desperados Waiting For A Train*; Rex Allen, Jr, Roy Rogers, and Rex Allen, Sr: *Last Of The Silver Screen Cowboys*

Gene Autry and Roy Rogers: Gene Autry: *The Yellow Rose Of Texas/Under Fiesta Stars/Home On The Range/Ages And Ages Ago/Teardrops On My Pillow,/Tweedle-O-Twill/Be Honest With Me/Buttons And Bows/Dixie Cannonball*; Roy Rogers: *That Pioneer Mother Of Mine/Dust/When I Camped Under The Stars/Lovenworth/Hoppy Gene And Me*; Roy Rogers and Sons of the Pioneers: *Roving Cowboy/Echoes From The Hills/Blue Bonnet Girl/Cowboy Night Herd Song*

Movie and Television Themes: Al Caiola: *The Magnificent Seven/Bonanza*; Tex Ritter: *High Noon*; Hugo Montenegro: *The Good, The Bad And The Ugly*; Gene Autry: *South Of The Border*; Frankie Laine: *Rawhide*; Roy Rogers: *On The Old Spanish Trail/Don't Fence Me In*; Marty Robbins: *Ballad Of The Alamo*; Johnny Cash: *The Rebel – Johnny Yuma*; Johnny Western: *The Ballad Of Paladin*; Hugh O'Brien: *Legend Of Wyatt Earp*; Bill Hayes: *The Ballad Of Davy Crockett*; Soundtrack: *Gunsmoke/The Lone Ranger/Wagon Train/Maverick/The Rifleman*

Finally, a comprehensive package of western music that should be readily available, unlike long-out-of-print packages, or the few still in print but with limited distribution. This survey of western music concentrates on the singing cowboys and the music from famous western films and television programs. An excellent accompanying booklet adds to the enjoyment of this compilation.

Bluegrass 5

Frank and Marty Godbey

The term "bluegrass," although not in common use until the 1960s, refers to an acoustic string-band style of country music first made popular by Bill Monroe and his Blue Grass Boys in the 1940s. A more sophisticated outgrowth of the commercial country string bands of early radio days, its influences include black blues, country church singing, and jazz, coupled with the close vocal harmonies of professional "brother duets."

Bluegrass is an ensemble music, generally played by five or six people, using guitar, 5-string banjo, mandolin, fiddle, and bass, although dobro (a raised-string resonator guitar noted with a steel bar) and multiple fiddles are sometimes included, and an electric bass guitar occasionally replaces the acoustic bass. The delimiting characteristic of bluegrass, however, is not instrumentation but "timing," in which the downbeat of guitar and bass is balanced by the offbeat mandolin "chop" and the driving roll of three-finger-style banjo.

Lead singing in bluegrass is often "high lonesome," but varies according to the range of the singer; two or three voices combine in bluegrass harmony, usually on choruses, but frequently throughout an entire song. In bluegrass quartets, primarily of a religious nature, a vocal bass line is added.

Topics of bluegrass songs may be nostalgic (home and mother, idyllic life), personalized statements (love lost, love found, regret for past actions), sentimentality (death of child, sweetheart, or other loved one, broken heart), or re-working of "murder ballads" and traditional songs. In recent years, more modern subjects (alienation of rural person in the city, ecology, economy, war, women's issues) are touched upon, and a surprising number of songs are written from a humorous or light-hearted vantage-point.

Throughout its history, Christian religious material has formed an important part of bluegrass music; nearly every performance includes two or three "gospel" songs, many of which are based upon the New Testament. Some combine religion with old-fashioned values and childhood memories. Whatever the theme, bluegrass songs emphasize individualism and independence, a kind of self-reliance that is evident in the "bluest" of bluegrass. There is no self-pity.

The bluegrass professionals of recent years, strong-minded, proud people determined to play "their" music, have deliberately chosen to perform music that is out of the mainstream, knowing fame and financial rewards will be far less than if they had chosen a style of music with frequent airplay and abundant backing, and their music reflects that strength of character.

Essential Recordings

(i) Roots

Bill Monroe, credited with being "father" of bluegrass, first recorded duets in 1936 with his brother Charlie as the Monroe Brothers. He formed his own band (named for his home state of Kentucky, "The Bluegrass State" in 1939, and toured, primarily in the southeastern United States, as Bill Monroe and his Blue Grass Boys. Although similar in many ways to other string bands of the era, the Blue Grass Boys prided themselves on higher-pitched (B-flat, B-natural, E) singing and faster tempos, with instruments tuned a half step above standard pitch for a brighter, louder sound. They were not only musicians, but entertainers, making up a complete show that included comedians, dancers, and baseball teams.

Monroe became a member of the Grand Ole Opry in 1939, and his introduction of young North Carolina banjo player Earl Scruggs on the air in 1945 is generally accepted as the beginning of bluegrass music.

(ii) Genesis

Prior to Earl Scruggs, the banjo in Monroe's band had been chiefly a rhythm instrument, evolving from brush-style to a two-finger "picked" style over the years. Scruggs's three-finger (thumb, index, middle) style, derived from several Carolina-based musicians; but with his far more versatile and complex style, he changed forever the perception of the banjo. It became a lead instrument as important as Monroe's mandolin or the fiddle; and Scruggs's style of playing, imitated or adapted by other musicians, remains one of the defining sounds of bluegrass.

By January, 1946, the Blue Grass Boys consisted of Monroe, mandolin; Earl Scruggs, banjo; Lester Flatt, guitar; Robert

Russell "Chubby" Wise, fiddle; and Howard "Cedric Rain-water" Watts, bass. The energy and excitement of the two years they were together may be experienced on **The Essential Bill Monroe And His Blue Grass Boys 1945–1949** (sessions 2, 3, 4, and 5). (Unfortunately, where alternate takes are included, the original release has been omitted.)

Discographical Details

68 **The Essential Bill Monroe And His Blue Grass Boys 1945–1949**

Bill Monroe and his Blue Grass Boys
Columbia Country Classics C2K 52478 (2-disc set)
Session 2: *Heavy Traffic Ahead/Why Did You Wander/Blue Moon Of Kentucky/Toy Heart/Summertime Is Past And Gone/Mansions For Me/ Mother's Only Sleeping/Blue Yodel No. 4*
Session 3: *Will You Be Loving Another Man/How Will I Explain About You/ Shining Path/Wicked Path Of Sin*
Session 4: *I'm Going Back To Old Kentucky/It's Mighty Dark To Travel/I Hear A Sweet Voice Calling/Little Cabin Home On The Hill/My Rose Of Old Kentucky/Blue Grass Breakdown/Sweetheart, You Done Me Wrong/The Old Cross Road*
Session 5: *That Home Above/Remember The Cross/Little Community Church/ Along About Daybreak/When You Are Lonely/Molly And Tenbrooks*

Excerpts from these four sessions appeared on **The Original Bluegrass Band: Bill Monroe With Lester Flatt And Earl Scruggs**, Rounder Records Special Series 06 (LP). It is out of print, but still possibly available.

(iii) Establishing a Style

Though accomplished over a period of months, the metamorphasis of Monroe's band from a flashy string band into the "original bluegrass band" revealed new-found subtlety and an imposing sense of dynamics. The difference was immediately apparent; fans multiplied, and young musicians who heard the Blue Grass Boys on Opry radio broadcasts began to incorporate elements of the new sound in their own music.

In Virginia, Carter Stanley, a veteran string-band performer, teamed up with his brother Ralph, West Virginia mandolin player Darrell "Pee Wee" Lambert, and fiddler Leslie Keith. The Stanley Brothers and the Clinch Mountain Boys began performing daily on Bristol's WCYB in early 1947, and their personal appearances were very successful in the region.

Ralph, at that time a two-finger-style banjo player, sang baritone in the trios; Pee Wee sang tenor and played mandolin, both in a style intentionally duplicating Monroe's; and Carter's guitar style was based upon that of Lester Flatt.

The Stanley Brothers recorded six sides for the Rich-R-Tone

label in late 1947. By March 1, 1949, when they began recording for Columbia, Ralph had learned a three-finger banjo style similar to Scruggs's; former Blue Grass Boy Art Wooten had passed through the band, contributing additional Monroe influence; and the usual lead–baritone–tenor trio was frequently altered to one in which Pee Wee sang a high baritone part above the tenor.

Although obviously inspired by Monroe's music, the Stanleys had input from family and other sources, and Carter had begun to write the haunting, mountain-flavored songs that contributed so much to the Stanley sound.

The 22 sides recorded for Columbia show the development of that style, reissued on **The Stanley Brothers And The Clinch Mountain Boys 1949–1952.**

Several other bands in the southeast were influenced by Monroe's group during this period. Existing string bands and brother duets modified their sound to approximate that of the Blue Grass Boys, and new bands were created in the hope of achieving similar success.

Jim and Jesse McReynolds, in southwestern Virginia, had a radio show on WNVA in 1947, and, as "the McReynolds Brothers and the Cumberland Mountain Boys," performed frequently in the area. Later, moving from one station to another, Jesse developed his distinctive "cross-picking" style on the mandolin, patterned after Scruggs's banjo technique, but using a flat pick rather than finger picks.

Their duets, with Jesse's mellow lead topped by Jim's perfectly matched tenor, could be adapted to many styles of music; while working out of Middletown, Ohio's WPFB, they teamed with Larry Roll to record ten gospel songs for Kentucky Records in 1951 as "the Virginia Trio."

In 1949, the Lonesome Pine Fiddlers, a long-established West Virginia string band, added Scruggs-style banjo picker Larry Richardson, and Bobby Osborne, a remarkably clear, powerful tenor singer, on guitar, to become more in line with the newer sound.

These were among the first, but in a short span of time, Carl Sauceman in South Carolina, the Bailey Brothers (the Happy Valley Boys) in Knoxville, Tennessee, and the Blue River Boys in North Carolina all emerged, the beginning of an identifiable genre.

In early 1948, Flatt and Scruggs, with bassist Howard "Cedric Rainwater" Watts, left Monroe, and started their own band, the Foggy Mountain Boys. They were joined by fiddler Jim Shumate, and in May, adding guitarist Malcolm "Mac" Wiseman to sing tenor, moved to WCYB in Bristol, where the Stanley Brothers had their show.

Flatt and Scruggs's recordings during this formative period (1948–50) clearly show their intent to create their own sound, yet also reflect the work they had done with Monroe; records made with him were popular on radio, and material from those recordings formed part of their public appearance repertoire.

Instrumentally, their first four recordings, made for Mercury in the fall of 1948, were quite different from those made with Monroe: there was no mandolin, and Scruggs's banjo, alternating only with the fiddle, was more prominent; Wiseman's second guitar (played with a flat pick; Flatt used a thumb pick) provided additional rhythm; and on gospel songs, Scruggs's lead guitar (played three-finger style) was an entirely new sound.

By their second session in the spring of 1949, Wiseman and Shumate had left the band, replaced by John Ray "Curly" Seckler, whose "shout" singing style and uncomplicated mandolin were quite unlike Monroe, and fiddler Art Wooten, who had worked with both Monroe and the Stanleys.

Although other personnel changes took place, their 28 sides for Mercury, recorded in seven sessions, define the early Flatt and Scruggs sound, and may be found on **Flatt And Scruggs 1948–1959**, Disc 1.

This collection introduces the fine collaborative songs for which Flatt and Scruggs would be known, and includes material they had performed with Monroe (*Pike County Breakdown*), and songs by other bands who were performing at the time (*Pain In My Heart*, by Bobby Osborne and Larry Richardson; *Roll In My Sweet Baby's Arms*, by Charlie Monroe; *Doin' My Time*, by Jimmie Skinner). These, with the Monroe "covers" by the Stanleys, initiated the interchange of material among practicing bands; later, this would become the core of the bluegrass corpus.

In 1948, Monroe, wounded by the defection of three-fifths of his band, immediately set about replacing them. He and fiddler Benny Martin were joined by Don Reno, another North Carolina banjo player whose early influences had been similar to Scruggs's, Jackie Phelps, guitar player and lead singer, and bassist Joel Price.

These able musicians and those who followed continued to be an important part of Monroe's band, but he would never again give his musicians the opportunity to leave in a body, taking with them "his" sound.

Monroe's legendary dislike of Flatt and Scruggs and the Stanleys stemmed from what he perceived as their "competition" in a limited market; it would be years before he saw himself as the founder of a style, and those who pursued a similar sound as his disciples, rather than rivals.

Phelps was replaced with Jim Eanes and later Mac Wiseman, both of whom had worked with Flatt and Scruggs, making it clear that Blue Grass Boys' personnel could change without greatly altering Monroe's sound (see **Essential Bill Monroe And His Blue Grass Boys**, session 6); Foggy Mountain Boys, too, could come and go with only minor influence on Flatt and Scruggs.

During this early period, the interchange of musicians between these bands and others became frequent, engendering the "cross-pollination" that created a genre.

Discographical Details

169   The Stanley Brothers And The Clinch Mountain Boys 1949–1952

The Stanley Brothers and the Clinch Mountain Boys
Bear Family Records BCD 15564 (Ger)
A Vision Of Mother/The White Dove/Gathering Flowers For The Master's Bouquet/The Angels Are Singing/It's Never Too Late/Have You Someone (In Heaven Awaiting)/Little Glass Of Wine/Let Me Be Your Friend/We'll Be Sweethearts In Heaven/I Love No One But You/Too Late To Cry/The Old Home/The Drunkard's Hell/The Fields Have Turned Brown/Hey! Hey! Hey!/ The Lonesome River/I'm A Man Of Constant Sorrow/Pretty Polly/A Life Of Sorrow/Sweetest Love/The Wandering Boy/Let's Part The Best Of Friends/The Fields Have Turned Brown (alternate)*/Little Glass Of Wine* (alternate)

170   Flatt And Scruggs 1948–1959

Lester Flatt and Earl Scruggs
Bear Family BCD 15472 (4-disc set) (Ger)
Disc 1: *God Loves His Children/I'm Going To Make Heaven My Home/We'll Meet Again, Sweetheart/My Cabin In Caroline/Baby Blue Eyes/Bouquet In Heaven/Down the Road/Why Don't You Tell Me So/I'll Never Shed Another Tear/No Mother Or Dad/Foggy Mountain Breakdown/I'll Be Going To Heaven Sometime/So Happy I'll Be/My Little Girl in Tennessee/I'll Never Love Another/Doin' My Time/Pike County Breakdown/Cora Is Gone/Preachin', Prayin', Singin'/Pain In My Heart/Roll In My Sweet Baby's Arms/Back To The Cross/Farewell Blues/Old Salty Dog Blues/Take Me In A Lifeboat/Will The Roses Bloom (Where She Lies Sleeping)/I'll Just Pretend*

This material is separately available on the following CDs: **The Complete Mercury Sessions** (Polygram 314 512 644–2), or **Mercury Sessions, Vol. 1** (Rounder RDRS 18) and **Mercury Sessions, Vol. 2** (Rounder RDRS 19).

171   The Essential Bill Monroe And His Blue Grass Boys 1945–1949

Bill Monroe and his Blue Grass Boys
Columbia Country Classics C2K 52478 (2-disc set)
Session 6: *Can't You Hear Me Callin'/Travelin' This Lonesome Road/Blue Grass Stomp/The Girl In The Blue Velvet Band*

(iv) Expanding the Style

When they signed with Capitol Records in 1952, Jim and Jesse McReynolds changed the name of their band to "Jim and Jesse and the Virginia Boys." At that time, additional members consisted of Curly Seckler (who had worked with Flatt and Scruggs) and three-finger-style banjo player Hoke Jenkins, a nephew (and student) of "Snuffy" Jenkins, an early influence on both Earl Scruggs and Don Reno.

The 20 sides cut from then until 1955 (interrupted for two years by Jesse's military service) featured the gentle, romantic songs for which Jim and Jesse are noted, many of which they wrote themselves. They changed labels in 1958, and recorded 14 more sides for Starday, with banjo player Bobby Thompson and fiddler Vassar Clements.

Jim and Jesse's 24 sides for Epic, beginning in 1960, **Bluegrass Special/Bluegrass Classics**, reissued on Columbia, are considered by many to be their finest work. Their entire output for Epic and Columbia is now available as **Bluegrass And More** (Bear Family BCD 15716).

Young Kentucky banjo player Sonny Osborne, brother of singer Bobby Osborne, had spent his 14th summer as the youngest musician to work and record with Bill Monroe. He returned to Dayton, Ohio, where his parents then lived, and in the fall of 1952, while Bobby was in the Marines, Sonny recorded for the Gateway and Kentucky labels. These recordings, and others made when Bobby, by then an accomplished mandolinist, returned, were basically covers, but showcased the brothers' talent so well they remained in print for years, issued and reissued on several labels.

In 1954, Bob and Sonny teamed up with Tennessean Jimmy Martin, a singer/guitarist who had worked briefly with Bobby in the early 1950s, and had spent most of the previous four years with Monroe. The shortlived but influential association of Martin and the Osbornes included a year's work in Detroit and a recording session for RCA.

After their split, Martin retained the name "Sunny Mountain Boys," and, by 1956, featured another young banjo player from Kentucky, J.D. Crowe, who had profited from his dedicated study of Flatt and Scruggs during their stint in Lexington.

The Osbornes returned to Dayton and joined fellow Kentuckian, singer/guitar player Harley "Red" Allen. They played in the area and on the WWVA Jamboree in Wheeling, West Virginia, recording for MGM in 1956. By 1958, they had developed their famous "high lead" trio, with Bobby's amazing tenor voice singing the melody above the baritone, and a "low tenor" a full octave lower than usual.

The Osbornes continued to rely on this structure, emphasizing Bobby's voice; and their subsequent bands, with more than a half-dozen "third part" singers, are virtually indistinguishable. Sonny, as he matured, expanded the Scruggs style, integrating his own ideas, to create a recognizable, individualized sound.

The MGM Days Of The Osborne Brothers includes 60 sides recorded between 1956 and 1963. In this period, they evolved from a derivative bluegrass band to innovative stylists who blended bluegrass with country music (sometimes with heavy electric backup instrumentation), and the intricate harmony and slow, breathtaking endings that foreshadowed their strong appeal to country audiences in the mid-1960s.

Many other musicians, as they left the better-known bands, began their own; often the new bands combined people with experience in several bands, strengthening the various influences into a recognizable – although still untitled – form. Banjo player Don Reno had auditioned successfully with Monroe before Scruggs, but had already enlisted in the service. He returned to follow Scruggs as a Blue Grass Boy, and stayed about a year before working with guitarist/singer Arthur Lee "Red" Smiley in several bands.

In 1951, they formed their own band, in which Reno's clear tenor contrasted with Smiley's warm, rich lead, and Reno's complex jazz-influenced banjo and flat-picked lead guitar – the first recorded in bluegrass – floated over the solid underpinning of Smiley's authoritative rhythm guitar. Moreover, in an effort to create a distinctive identity, they incorporated dance-band rhythms and uninhibited comedy routines that made the Tennessee Cutups what has been termed "the greatest show band ever assembled in the field of bluegrass."

The enormous body of work they recorded between 1952 and 1964, when Smiley's always precarious health decreed retirement, includes some of the finest bluegrass songs ever written, most of them penned by Reno. The 1993 boxed set **Don Reno And Red Smiley And The Tennessee Cutups 1951–1959** contains, in chronological sequence, their entire recorded output for King Records during that period, as well as four titles for the Federal label they did in 1951 as side-men for Tommy Magness, a fiddler for Bill Monroe. The "Classic" Reno and Smiley band, featuring fiddler Mack MaGaha and bassist John Palmer (and often an extremely young Ronnie Reno on mandolin) performs on many of these selections, but other well-known bluegrass personalities served as Tennessee Cutups at various times, including Red Rector, Smiley Hobbs and Benny Williams.

Jimmy Martin, a forceful lead singer, had worked with

Monroe, the Lonesome Pine Fiddlers, and the Osbornes before starting his own band in 1955. By 1956 he had a contract with Decca, and in the next ten years, Jimmy Martin and a series of fine musicians, working as the Sunny Mountain Boys, made an impact on the bluegrass audience.

The combination featuring mandolinist Paul Williams's softer sound (he used a round-hole mandolin, as opposed to the F-hole mandolin usual in bluegrass), J.D. Crowe's impeccable timing and flawless backup banjo, and Martin's rhythm guitar – hailed as "the best in bluegrass" – was outstanding. Vocals focused on Martin's raw, energetic lead, and tight close harmony.

As personnel changed through the years, Martin has insisted that bands maintain the high standards set forth by this definitive group, as heard on most cuts on **You Don't Know My Mind**. Through his band have passed some of the most capable and influential musicians in bluegrass, and many (Crowe, Bill Emerson, Doyle Lawson, Alan Munde, and Earl Taylor, among others) have gone on to form long-lasting and respected bands of their own.

Flatt and Scruggs had moved to the Columbia label in November, 1951, and this, with their discovery in 1953 by Martha White Mills, would escalate their career far beyond the expectations of any bluegrass band – and most country bands. Under this corporate sponsorship, Flatt and Scruggs had sequential radio and television shows in various locations in the period before syndication, and were finally accepted (despite Opry politics) on the Grand Ole Opry. Columbia, by adding studio musicians to their recording sessions, kept the band more in line with mainstream country trends and audiences. The dual sponsorship provided more exposure than any other bluegrass band, and performances generated by the exposure garnered a host of new fans.

The Flatt and Scruggs sound, always reliant on Lester's warm voice, Earl's magical banjo, and a succession of excellent fiddle players, underwent a drastic change in 1955, when it was augmented by the acoustic resonator guitar of Burkett "Uncle Josh" Graves. Alternating breaks and split-breaks with other lead instruments, his versatile "hound dog" provided both a slicker, jazzier – even sexier – appeal, and a connection (via Roy Acuff's band) with traditional country music.

Josh teamed with bassist English P. "Cousin Jake" Tullock to enliven performances with riotous old-fashioned comedy and novelty tunes, in addition to his musical proficiency and well-choreographed (the band worked with two microphones, and dodged in and out for breaks) showmanship.

Flatt and Scruggs's work for Columbia during this period is

collected on the remaining discs of **Flatt And Scruggs 1948–1959** and on several individual CDs.

When the band no longer carried a singer/mandolin player, Jake took over the vocal "high part," frequently singing high baritone. Fiddler Paul Warren sang the bass line on secular material, as well as gospel quartets, and with Earl's (and often Josh's) baritone, created the "gang singing" sound criticized by bluegrass purists.

The term "bluegrass" was not used by Flatt and Scruggs, of course; they thought of themselves as country musicians, although Nashville had grown increasingly resistant to traditional forms of music, deeming them quaint and old-fashioned – especially after being confronted with the rock-and-roll phenomenon of the late 1950s.

As a result, many traditional bands lost their record contracts, or their records were infrequently released and poorly promoted. Flatt and Scruggs, by contrast, were more successful than ever. Following appearances at the Newport Folk Festival and on college campuses, they found themselves riding the folk music boom while maintaining their country audiences; it was good for business, but the band suffered artistically, and Lester and Earl went their separate ways in 1969.

Monroe, during the 1950s, continued to play his music counter to the Nashville trend toward electrified instruments and a "softer" sound. He remained stubbornly acoustic, holding to the old song topics and his strongly emotional style of singing.

As transplanted rural people drew away from their roots, and the "star" and "hit record" system was emphasized, the divergence of Monroe's path from the "less country-sounding" country performers grew more noticeable. Ironically, the cruelest blow occurred when Monroe's *Blue Moon Of Kentucky* was recorded by a young Mississippian with a revolutionary sound: Elvis Presley.

In a frantic scramble for survival, the Nashville Music industry rejected both traditional country music and rock-and-roll; this attitude, nearly the death of country music, created the "hungry years," for bluegrass. No longer promoted or acceptable to many country audiences, no longer given airplay on many country stations, bluegrass musicians were driven to smaller and smaller markets, driving hours to play to small crowds in schoolhouses or seedy taverns.

Hardship only intensified Monroe's determination to stick with his concept. Fortunately, as folk music became an alternative to rock and roll, he attracted the attention of city people outside the mainstream country-music audience.

Following an influential article by Ralph Rinzler in *Sing Out* magazine in 1963, and under Rinzler's subsequent management, Monroe began playing folk music festivals, coffeehouses, and other such venues. About this time he hired Bostonian Bill (Brad) Keith, whose "fiddle style" banjo playing extended Scruggs's technique with "chromatic" licks, so every note of the melody was played. Keith, the first of many city-bred Blue Grass Boys, had an impact on banjo players analogous to that of Earl Scruggs 20 years earlier – a generation of "pickers" have since imitated and built on his style.

The work of Monroe throughout the 1960s, through hard times and good ones, brought diverse musicians to work with him. City boys, country boys, professionals and college boys working for the summer, they shared respect for Monroe and a love of the music they performed. **Bill Monroe 1959–1969** is at once a portrait of a strong and versatile musician, and a presentation of bluegrass musicians of that era, many of whom are prominent today.

No longer perceived as strictly "Southern" or "rural," bluegrass attracted a younger, college-educated audience. Bill Monroe, elevated to "father" of bluegrass by Rinzler, became a cult hero, a role he had the temperament and presence to fulfill perfectly.

Folk festivals were the inspiration for the first bluegrass festival, held in Virginia in 1965. Its success spawned others, and today there are more than 500 held each summer. Part picnic, part family reunion, part continuous jam session, these celebrations of bluegrass music provided a lifeline, then a livelihood, for musicians, and a chance for fans to enjoy music too seldom heard on radio and TV.

Among the first Eastern, city bluegrass bands was the Country Gentlemen, who played the Washington, DC area after 1957. With the rich, deep voice of guitarist Charlie Waller and the bell-like tenor of John Duffey at its core, the band utilized several of the area's best musicians on banjo and bass before coalescing into the "classic" Country Gentlemen in about 1960. Virginia "Travis-style" banjo player/baritone Eddie Adcock and Tom Gray, whose "walking" bass was equally innovative, rounded out what would be called "the first progressive bluegrass band."

Recording for Folkways, which had primarily urban distribution, the Country Gentlemen had enormous influence, as they combined folk music, bluegrass, and country into their own distinctive sound. Their material, drawn from obscure country records, old folk songs, and the writing of members and friends, was also unlike that of any other band. With their "hip" comedy and likeable stage persona, they were eagerly accepted on the college and coffeehouse circuit, were stars at early festivals, and were imitated by young bands all over the country.

As original members left, they were replaced by other fine musicians, and the band, under the leadership of founder Charlie Waller, is still popular after more than 30 years of performance. The work of the "classic" group, however, is still greatly appreciated; it is well represented on the 1961 recording, **Folk Songs And Bluegrass**, reissued on CD in 1991.

In addition to providing musicians and "listening clubs," the DC area was responsible for bringing together the widely separated bluegrass community; a number of dedicated enthusiasts began a newsletter in 1966 that would grow to become the voice of bluegrass. *Bluegrass Unlimited*, the first source of information for the bluegrass fan, has, for 28 years, reviewed recordings and performances, provided articles about musicians, and – most important – a listing of shows and clubs that feature bluegrass music.

With this guidance, fans began traveling, first to nearby cities, then farther afield. When festivals proliferated, the magazine gave dates, locations, and performers, and for the first time, bluegrass people became acquainted with their counterparts in other sections of the country. This, in turn, led to the success of festivals, the survival of performers, and a devoted band of activists who have helped bluegrass to become more accepted.

The most recent effect of this cohesion was the formation of the International Bluegrass Music Association in 1985, and the establishment of a bluegrass "home" in Owensboro, Kentucky, just 30 miles from the birthplace of Bill Monroe. Executive offices operate year-round, and a trade show and convention is held each September, followed by a three-day "FanFest" at which donated performances contribute to a trust fund for bluegrass musicians.

Next to the trade association offices is the International Bluegrass Music Museum, where artifacts related to bluegrass may be seen, a Hall of Honor recognizes the achievements of bluegrass pioneers, and a growing library and archives will soon be available for research.

Discographical Details

172 Bluegrass Special/Bluegrass Classics

Jim and Jesse and the Virginia Boys
Columbia Special Products BN 26031/26074 (2-LP set)
Sweet Little Miss Blue Eyes/Somebody Loves You, Darling/She Left Me Standing On The Mountain/Don't Say Goodbye If You Love Me/I Wish You Knew/When It's Time For The Whippoorwill To Sing/Grave In The Valley/

Blue Bonnet Lane/Are You Missing Me/Congratulations, Anyway!/Pickin' And A-Grinnin'/Stoney Creek/Las Cassas, Tennessee/Drifting And Dreaming Of You/The Grass Is Greener (In The Mountains)/What About You/I Wonder Where You Are Tonight/Why Not Confess/Nine-Pound Hammer/The Violet And A Rose/Take My Ring From Your Finger/The Little Paper Boy/When My Blue Moon Turns To Gold Again/Just When I Needed You

73 The MGM Days Of The Osborne Brothers

The Osborne Brothers
Polydor POCP-1048/50 (3-disc set) (Jap)
Who Done It/Ruby, Are You Mad/My Aching Heart/Teardrops In My Eyes/ Wild Mountain Honey/Down In The Willow Garden/Ho, Honey, Ho/Della Mae/She's No Angel/(Is This) My Destiny/Once More/Two Lonely Hearts/Lost Highway/Love Pains/It Hurts To Know/If You Don't Somebody Else Will/Give This Message To Your Heart/You'll Never Know/I Love You Only/It's Just The Idea/Lonely, Lonely Me/Sweethearts Again/Blame Me/There's A Woman Behind Every Man/Fair And Tender Ladies/Each Season Changes You/The Black Sheep Returned To The Fold/At The First Fall Of Snow/Poor Old Cora/ Five Days Of Heaven/It Ain't Gonna Rain No Mo'/The Banjo Boys/Old Joe Clark/Old Hickory/Big Ben/Billy In The Low Ground/John Henry Blues/Banjo Boy Chimes/Walking Cane/Red Wing/Seeing Nellie Home/Jessie [sic] James/ Cumberland Gap/Lost Indian/Send Me The Pillow That You Dream On/ Worried Man Blues/May You Never Be Alone/New Partner Waltz/How's The World Treating You/Night Train To Memphis/Mule Skinner Blues/White Lightning/Bluegrass Music's Really Gone To Town/Lovey Told Me Goodbye/ Ballad Of Jed Clampett/Memories Never Die/Mule Train/Ruby, Are You Mad/ Sour Wood Mountain/Sweet Thing

74 Don Reno And Red Smiley And The Tennessee Cutups 1951–1959

Don Reno and Red Smiley and The Tennessee Cutups
King KBSCD-7001 (4-disc set)
When I Safely Reach That Other Shore/Little Country Preacher/Wings Of Faith/Jesus Will Save Your Soul/The Lord's Last Supper/I'm Using My Bible For A Roadmap/I Want To Live Like Christ My Savior/Let In The Guiding Light/There's A Highway To Heaven/Some Beautiful Day/Jesus Is Standing At My Right Hand/Hear Jerusalem Mourn/A Pretty Wreath for Mother's Grave/ A Rose On God's Shore/There's Another Baby Waiting For Me Down The Line/Maybe You Will Change Your Mind/I'm Gone, Long Gone/Drifting With The Tide/Tennessee Cut-Up Breakdown/Crazy Finger Blues/Tennessee Break-down/He's Coming Back To Earth Again/I Can Hear The Angels Singing/My Mother's Bible/Please Don't Feel Sorry for Me/I Could Cry/Springtime In Dear Old Dixie/Choking the Strings/Mountain Church/Love Call Waltz/I'm The Talk Of The Town/Always Be Kind To Your Mother/Since I've Used My Bible For A Road Map/I'm Building A Mansion In Heaven/My Shepherd Is God/Tree Of Life/Emotions/Your Tears Are Just Interest On The Loan/All I Have Is Just A Memory/Someone Will Love Me In Heaven/Limehouse Blues/ Dixie Breakdown/Barefoot Nellie/Cruel Love/I'm The Biggest Liar In Town/ It's Grand To Have Someone To Love You/Let's Live For Tonight/Old Home Place/Trail Of Sorrow/Charlotte Breakdown/How I Miss My Darling Mother/ Family Altar/Jesus Is Waiting/I'm So Happy/Hen Scratchin' Stomp/Double Banjo Blues/Reno Ride/Banjo Riff/Banjo Signal/Mack's Hoedown/Jesus Answers My Prayers/Get Behind Me, Satan/Home, Sweet Home/Green

Mountain Hop/If It Takes Me A Lifetime/Country Boy Rock 'N' Roll/I Know You're Married/No Longer A Sweetheart Of Mine/Forgotten Men/Never Get To Hold You In My Arms Anymore/Kneel Down/Cumberland Gap/Remington Ride/Beer Barrell Polka/Richmond Ruckus/When You And I Were Young, Maggie/Unwanted Love/Better Luck Next Time/Wall Around Your Heart/ Another Day/Banjo Signal/Country Line Special/Get Ready/Keep Me Humble/ Brighter Mansion Over There/He Will Forgive You/Missile Ride/Buggy Ride/I Want To Know/The New Jerusalem/He's Not Ashamed Of You/God's Record Book Of Life/Pray/Passing Of Time/I'll Trade My Cross For A Crown/Sailing Home/Pretending/I Wouldn't Change You If I Could/Little Rock Getaway/ Sockeye/Under Your Spell Again/Money, Marbles And Chalk/Dark As A Dungeon/Freight Train Boogie/Gathering Flowers From The Hillside/East Bound Freight Train/Charlie Brooks And Nellie Adair/Lonesome Wind Blues/ Mountain Rosa Lee/She Has Forgotten/Don't Let Your Sweet Love Die/Eight More Miles To Louisville/I'm Blue And Lonesome

175 You Don't Know My Mind

Jimmy Martin

Rounder CD SS21

You Don't Know My Mind/Ocean of Diamonds/Hit Parade Of Love/Stepping Stones/Crowe On The Banjo/Don't Give Your Heart To A Rambler/What Would You Give In Exchange/Sophronie/Homesick/Red River Valley/Sunny Side Of The Mountain/Rock Hearts/Hold Whatcha Got/Prayer Bell [sic] Of Heaven

176 Flatt And Scruggs 1948–1959

Lester Flatt and Earl Scruggs

Bear Family BCD 15472 (4-disc set) (Ger)

Disc 2: *Come Back, Darling/I'm Head Over Heels In Love/I'm Waiting To Hear You Call Me Darling/The Old Home Town/I'll Stay Around/We Can't Be Darlings Anymore/Jimmie Brown, The Newsboy/Somehow Tonight/Don't Get Above My [sic] Raising/I'm Working On A Road/He Took Your Place/I've Lost You/'Tis Sweet To Be Remembered/I'm Gonna Settle Down/Earl's Breakdown/I'm Lonesome And Blue/Over The Hills To The Poorhouse/My Darling's Last Goodbye/Get In Line Brother/Brother, I'm Getting Ready To Go/Why Did You Wander/Flint Hill Special/Thinking About You/If I Should Wander Back Tonight/Dim Lights, Thick Smoke/Dear Old Dixie*
Disc 3: *Reunion In Heaven/Pray For The Boys/I'll Go Stepping Too/I'd Rather Be Alone/Foggy Mountain Chimes/Someone Took My Place With You/ Mother Prays Loud In Her Sleep/That Old Book Of Mine/Your Love Is Like A Flower/Be Ready For Tomorrow May Never Come/Till The End Of The World Rolls Around/You're Not A Drop In The Bucket/Don't This Road Look Rough And Rocky/Foggy Mountain Special/You Can Feel It In Your Soul/ Old-Fashioned Preacher/Before I Met You/I'm Gonna Sleep With One Eye Open/Randy Lynn Rag/On My Mind/Blue Ridge Cabin Home/Some Old Day/ It Won't Be Long/No Mother In This World/Gone Home/Bubbling In My Soul/Joy Bells/What's Good For You*
Disc 4: *No Doubt About it/Who Will Sing for Me/Give Mother My Crown/ Six White Horses/Shuckin' The Corn/I'll Take The Blame/Don't Let Your Deal Go Down/A Hundred Years From Now/Give Me The Flowers While I'm Living/Is There Room For Me/I'll Never Shed Another Tear/I Won't Be Hanging Around/I Don't Care Anymore/Big Black Train/Mama's And Daddy's Little Girl/Crying Alone/A Million Years In Glory/Heaven/Building On Sand/*

Jesus, Savior, Pilot Me/Crying My Heart Out Over You/Ground Speed/Who Knows Right from Wrong/Iron Curtain/Cabin on the Hill/Someone You Have Forgotten/Foggy Mountain Rock/You Put Me On My Feet

This material is separately available on the following CDs: **The Golden Era** (Rounder RDRS 5); **Don't Get Above Your Raisin'** (Rounder RDRS 8); **Blue Ridge Cabin Home** (County CC 102); **Flatt And Scruggs: Columbia Historic Edition** (Columbia CK 37469).

77 Blue Grass 1950–1958

Bill Monroe

Bear Family BCD 15423 (4-disc set) (Ger)

Blue Grass Ramble/New Muleskinner Blues/My Little Georgia Rose/Memories Of You/I'm On My Way To The Old Home/Alabama Waltz/I'm Blue, I'm Lonesome/I'll Meet You In Church Sunday Morning/Boat Of Love/The Old Fiddler/Uncle Pen/When The Golden Leaves Begin To Fall/Lord Protect My Soul/River of Death/Letter From My Darling/On The Old Kentucky Shore/Raw Hide/Poison Love/Kentucky Waltz/Prisoner's Song/Swing Low, Sweet Chariot/Angels Rock Me To Sleep/Brakeman's Blues/Travelin' Blues/When The Cactus Is In Bloom/Sailor's Plea/My Carolina Sunshine Girl/Ben Dewberry's Final Run/Peach Pickin' Time In Georgia/Those Gambler's Blues/Sugar Coated Love/You're Drifting Away/Cabin Of Love/Get Down On Your Knees And Pray/Christmas Time's A-Coming/The First Whippoorwill/In The Pines/Footprints In the Snow/Walking In Jerusalem/Memories Of Mother And Dad/The Little Girl And The Dreadful Snake/Country Waltz/Don't Put It Off 'Til Tomorrow/My Dying Bed/A Mighty Pretty Waltz/Pike County Breakdown/Wishing Waltz/I Hope You Have Learned/Get Up, John/Sitting Alone In The Moonlight/Plant Some Flowers By My Grave/Changing Partners/Y'All Come/On And On/I Believed In You, Darling/New John Henry Blues/White House Blues/Happy On My Way/I'm Working On A Building/A Voice From On High/He Will Set Your Fields On Fire/Close By/My Little Georgia Rose/Put My Little Shoes Away/Blue Moon Of Kentucky/Wheel Hoss/Cheyenne/You'll Find Her Name Written There/Roanoke/Wait A Little Longer, Please Jesus/Let The Light Shine Down On Me/Used To Be/Tall Timber/Brown County Breakdown/A Fallen Star/Four Walls/A Good Woman's Love/Cry, Cry, Darlin'/I'm Sittin' On Top Of The World/Out In The Cold World/Roane County Prison/Goodbye Old Pal/In Despair/Molly And Tenbrooks/Come Back To Me In My Dreams/Sally-Jo/Brand New Shoes/A Lonesome Road To Travel/I Saw The Light/Lord, Build Me A Cabin In Glory/Lord, Lead Me On/Precious Jewel/I'll Meet You In The Morning/Life's Railway To Heaven/I've Found A Hiding Place/Jesus, Hold My Hand/I Am A Pilgrim/Wayfaring Stranger/A Beautiful Life/House Of Gold/Panhandle Country/Scotland/Gotta Travel On/No One But My Darlin'/Big Mon/Monroe's Hornpipe

78 Folk Songs And Bluegrass

The Country Gentlemen

Smithsonian Folkways CD SF 40022

Train 45/Little Bessie/The Fields Have Turned Brown/They're At Rest Together/Strutting On The Strings/Remembrance Of You/Red Rocking Chair/Will The Circle Be Unbroken/Handsome Molly/Victim To The Tomb/Behind These Prison Walls Of Love/Wear A Red Rose/I'm Coming Back (But I Don't Know When)/Southbound/Come All Ye Tender-Hearted/Standing In The Need Of Prayer

Basic Recordings

179 Red Allen And The Kentuckians

Red Allen and the Kentuckians

County 710 (LP)

We Live In Two Different Worlds/There Must Be A Better Way To Live/ Maiden's Prayer/Send Me Your Address In Heaven/Milk Cow Blues/Love Gone Cold/Lonesome And Blue/Have You Come To Say Goodbye/Bluegrass Blues/If That's The Way You Feel/I Wonder Where You Are Tonight/No Mother Or Dad

If bluegrass music has an underground cult hero, it is Red Allen, whose clear, emotion-packed voice and metronomic rhythm guitar hypnotized listeners. In a career that lasted from the 1950s, until health problems took him off the road in the 1980s, Red influenced hundreds with his uncompromising, hard driving style of bluegrass. Young musicians who would later achieve recognition – David Grisman, Pete Kuykendall (now publisher of *Bluegrass Unlimited* magazine, Richard Greene, and Bill Keith – passed through Red's band, sharing the spotlight with such veterans as Frank Wakefield, Porter Church, and Bill Emerson.

Although noted for his ground-breaking MGM recordings with the Osborne Brothers in the late 1950s, the bulk of Allen's output appeared on such small or special interest labels as Folkways, County and King-Bluegrass. His recording with Wakefield (Folkways FA-2408) contains vocal and instrumental innovations merged with passionate delivery, and is highly recommended; this 1966 County release, however, captures the essence of his lean arrangements and approach to band organization. It has not been reissued on compact disc, but the LP is one to keep on your want-list.

180 ASH&W

ASH&W

Rebel CD-1686

Turn Your Love Down/The Likes Of You/(Now And Then There's) A Fool Such As I/When You And I Were Young, Maggie/The Wrong Road/Lovesick and Sorrow/You Done Me Wrong/I'm Going Back Home (Cabin Song No. 47)/ Train On The Island/Old-Fashioned Preacher

This self-titled CD by the North Carolina band, "ASH&W" (an acronym of the initials of band members' last names) has become a favorite among lovers of the classic style of bluegrass as developed by the great bands of the 1950s. Characterized by tight ensemble playing and singing, the music of ASH&W clearly reflects the debt to the music's founding fathers still being paid by young musicians. This 1990 release reveals some new aspect of ASH&W talents on each replaying.

181 Master Fiddler

Kenny Baker

County CD-2705

Floparino/First Day In Town/Denver Belle/Sugar Tree Stomp/Cricket On The Hearth/Tune For Andy/Washington County/Festival Waltz/Grassy Fiddle Blues/Smoky Mountain Rag/Brandywine/Dry And Dusty/Make A Little Boat/

Gold Rush/Roxanne Waltz/Lost Indian/Cross-Eyed Fiddler/Sweet Bunch Of Daisies/Indian Killed A Woodcock/Daley's Reel

Kenny Baker is, indeed, a "master fiddler". In several different stints with the Blue Grass Boys, spanning four decades, he contributed significantly to the evolution of Bill Monroe's music. He appears on many of Monroe's classic, definitive recordings, and in his own right has influenced an entire generation of young fiddle players with his smooth, liquid technique. His highly melodic playing has a lyrical quality that sets it apart from the bluesy styles often thought of as bluegrass fiddling, making his work readily identifiable.

In addition to his work with "the father of bluegrass," Baker released a series of LPs for County Records that focused more closely on his fiddling and gave him exposure far greater than that of a side-man in someone else's band. This 1993 CD is compiled from the best tracks released between 1968 and 1983.

82 The Bluegrass Album, Vol. 2

Tony Rice, J.D. Crowe, Doyle Lawson, Bobby Hicks, Todd Phillips
Rounder CD 0164
Your Love Is Like A Flower/We May Meet Again Someday/Take Me In The Lifeboat/Sittin' Alone In The Moonlight/Back To The Cross/Just When I Needed You/One Tear/Ocean of Diamonds/Is It Too Late Now/So Happy I'll Be/Don't This Road Look Rough And Rocky/I'll Never Shed Another Tear

Beginning in 1981, guitarist Tony Rice launched the production of a series of albums that would give him and his co-performers a respite from their various divergent forms of music and take them back to their roots. Recruiting J.D. Crowe to play banjo, Doyle Lawson on mandolin, Bobby Hicks on fiddle, and Todd Phillips on bass, the goal was to play the full-tilt, straight-ahead traditional bluegrass music they (except Phillips) had played since childhood.

Any volume in the series will provide an entertaining glimpse of this aggregation; Volume 2 is listed because of its broad range of material and particularly exuberant performances. In 1993 all five in the series were available on CD.

83 Bill Clifton: The Early Years 1957–1958

Bill Clifton
Rounder CD 1021
The Girl I Left In Sunny Tennessee/Dixie Darlin'/You Don't Think About Me When I'm Gone/I'll Be There, Mary Dear/Paddy On The Turnpike/I'll Wander Back Someday/Darlin' Corey/When You Kneel At Mother's Grave/Blue Ridge Mountain Blues/Are You Alone/Springhill Disaster/I'm Living The Right Life Now/Lonely Heart Blues/Cedar Grove/You Go To Your Church/Walking In My Sleep/Pal Of Yesterday/Just Another Broken Heart/Little White-Washed Chimney

When the music was still in its infancy, young people outside the usual rural audience began discovering the sounds of Bill Monroe, Flatt and Scruggs, and the Stanley Brothers. Bill Clifton was among the first non-rural followers to plunge wholeheartedly into the idiom, combining it with his interest in folk and early commercial country music. Characterized by Clifton's mellow baritone, these performances have a soft, almost antique sound, but with a drive and intensity imposed by high tenor harmony and bluegrass instrumentation. Occasional use of the autoharp and clawhammer banjo add a bit of the flavor of the Carter Family and the other older forms Clifton studied. Originally appearing on the Starday label, these performances are heard for the first time on CD in this 1992 reissue.

184   Welcome To Virginia

The Bluegrass Cardinals

Rounder 0097 (LP)

Roll on Muddy River/She Keeps Hangin' On/Journey To My Savior's Side/ Lorene/We Know The Man/Cora's Gone/Ridin' On The L & N/Blue-Eyed Boston Boy/Plant Some Flowers/Darcey Farrow/Jesus, Lead Me Evermore/Mississippi River Man

Founded in the early 1970s in California by transplanted Kentuckian Don Parmley, the Bluegrass Cardinals became fixtures on the bluegrass circuit after their relocation to Virginia in 1976. This LP, released early the next year, showcases the strong harmony singing and tasteful instrumental backup that was, and remains, a major part of their appeal.

The Cardinals' core trio in the beginning was Parmley and his son David, singing the two low parts, with Randy Graham's powerful tenor or high lead at the top. This LP captures them on their career ascent and contains several excellent selections, including a remarkable full-length trio on *Blue-Eyed Boston Boy*. Their only release for Rounder, it is unfortunately not scheduled for CD reissue, but is well worth seeking out.

The Cardinals also had strong performances on other labels; many CMH cuts appear on sampler CDs issued in the 1990s. Their more recent efforts are on their own BGC label.

185   Hello Operator . . . This Is Country Gazette

The Country Gazette

Flying Fish FF-112

Saro Jane/Virginia Boys/Love Lost And Found/Don't Let Nobody Tie You Down/Sweet Allis Chalmers/You Can't Get The Hell Out Of Texas/Charlotte Breakdown/The Great Joe Bob/Still Feeling Blue/Uncle Clooney Played The Banjo/Molly And Tenbrooks/Kentucky Waltz/Blue Light/Tallahassee/Highland Dream/Last Thing On My Mind/Hello Operator/Great American Banjo Tune/ Nothing Left But The Blues/Cabin On A Mountain/Done Gone

An outgrowth of the fertile southern California musical melting pot, Country Gazette's roots lie as much in the folk-rock band, the Flying Burrito Brothers, as they do in bluegrass. Their traditional ties are by no means shallow, however; of the original members, Byron Berline fiddled with Bill Monroe; Alan Munde played banjo in Jimmy Martin's Sunny Mountain Boys; and bassist Roger Bush was a member of the Kentucky Colonels with legendary guitarist Clarence White.

This retrospective covers the band's tenure on Flying Fish from 1976 through the 1980s, and includes contemporary performances by Munde (the only continuing original member), Roland White on mandolin, and many other fine musicians who passed through the band.

186 25 Years

The Country Gentlemen
Rebel CD-2201
Matterhorn/I Am Weary, Let Me Rest/Two Little Boys/This World's No Place To Live/Girl From The North Country/Five Hundred Miles/Aunt Dinah's Quilting Party/Copper Kettle/Helen/Little Bessie/Many A Mile/Come All Ye Tender-Hearted/Teach Your Children/Where I'm Bound/Redwood Hill/Letter To Tom/Less Of Me/Devil's Little Angel/The Likes Of You/This Morning At Nine/Dixieland For Me/The Fields Have Turned Brown/Doin' My Time/Steel Guitar Rag/Over The Hills To The Poor House/Come And Sit By The River

Formed in 1957, the Country Gentlemen were among the earliest bands to introduce urban sensitivities into what had previously been primarily a rural form. By the 1960s they were performing songs by Bob Dylan as often as those of Carter Stanley. In 1993 the band continues with its original guitarist and lead singer, Charlie Waller, along a path that has remained open to many influences and ideas. In celebration of the Country Gentlemen's 25th year, Rebel Records released this retrospective in 1980. It covers highlights of their career with that label, an association that began in the mid-1960s, and features selections from the band's various configurations, including performances by what many consider the classic group: John Duffey, Charlie Waller, Eddie Adcock, and Tom Gray. Tight vocals and innovative instrumental ideas always characterize the music of the Country Gentlemen, and the choice of this one over any of dozens of equally fine releases is made solely on the basis of the variety and perspective it offers.

87 There Is A Time

The Dillards
Vanguard CD 131
Banjo In The Hollow/Dooley/Polly Vaughn/The Old Home Place/Somebody Touched Me/Hamilton County Breakdown/Walkin' Down The Line/Never See My Home Again/Paddy On The Turnpike/Old Blue/Liberty/There Is A Time/The Whole World Round/Sally Johnson/Yesterday/Ebo Walker/Rainmaker/Copperfields/Old Man At The Mill/Lemon Chimes/I'll Fly Away/Nobody Knows/Listen To The Sound/Reason To Believe/Hey, Boys/I've Just Seen A Face/Don't You Cry/She Sang Hymns Out Of Tune

In the 1960s, many gained their first exposure to bluegrass music from appearances of the Dillards on the Andy Griffith television program, on which they portrayed members of a backwoods family whose only talents seemed to be playing music and getting into comical scrapes. Beneath that façade were four skilled musicians who took the sounds of their Ozark backgrounds and molded a career that touched folk, bluegrass and popular music fields.

Their initial release, aimed at the folk music boom of the 1960s, had limited influence in the country music market, which was still the host, albeit reluctantly, to most bluegrass. After three acoustic albums for Elektra the band turned toward an emerging sound that combined bluegrass, folk, rock, and country music into what was later dubbed "folk-rock." Their final two albums for Elektra pushed further in that direction, and were of limited interest to bluegrass fans.

There Is A Time covers the Dillards' career with Elektra from 1963 through 1968 with examples from all five LPs. Included are many of their most exciting bluegrass titles, as well as the beginning of their expansion into more commercial styles.

188   Foggy Mountain Banjo

Lester Flatt and Earl Scruggs

Sony Special Products A-23392

Ground Speed/Home, Sweet Home/Sally Ann/Little Darlin' Pal Of Mine/ Reuben/Cripple Creek/Lonesome Road Blues/John Henry/Fire Ball Mail/Sally Goodwin/Bugle Call Rag/Cumberland Gap

Although Earl Scruggs's banjo playing is one of the elements that created bluegrass music from earlier string band styles, there was no major compilation focussing especially on his gift until 1961, when **Foggy Mountain Banjo** was originally released. Scruggs's influence was pervasive from the start, but here on one disc is a master's course in the touch, tone, and timing at which he excelled. He provides, with Paul Warren on fiddle and Josh Graves on dobro, the essence of subtle musicianship and delicate instrumental interplay. There are no vocals on this recording, relegating Flatt to the background, but his presence is felt through his steady rhythm guitar playing.

189   Home Is Where The Heart Is

David Grisman

Rounder CD 0251/0252

True Life Blues/Down In The Willow Garden/My Long Journey Home/Little Willie/Highway Of Sorrow/Sophronie/My Aching Heart/Close By/Feast Here Tonight/Leavin' Home/Little Cabin Home On The Hill/I'm Coming Back, But I Don't Know When/Salty Dawg Blues/If I Lose/Sad And Lonesome Day/My Little Georgia Rose/Foggy Mountain Top/I'm My Own Grandpa/Pretty Polly/ Home Is Where The Heart Is/Nine-Pound Hammer/Memories Of Mother And Dad/Teardrops In My Eyes/House Of Gold

This CD represents a trip back in time for mandolinist David Grisman; the creator of "dawg" music and founder of the quartets and quintets that bear his name, was, during his formative years, a serious bluegrass musician, concentrating his energies toward learning the music of Bill Monroe. For this 1988 release, Grisman wanted to feature, and pay tribute to, as many of his early heros and influences as possible. The result is a spirited assortment of traditional bluegrass, showcasing, in a variety of settings, Grisman with his favorite musicians.

190   Home To Me

High Country

Swallow LP-2004 (LP)

Blues For Your Own/Battle Mountain/Love Is A Summer Rose/Home To Me/ Nearer, My God, To Thee/Hard Times/Can't You Hear Me Calling/Say You Only Will Be Mine/Who's That Knocking At My Door/Big Hendy Grove/ Footprints In The Snow/Heaven Here On Earth/Stay Away From Me/A Lonesome Highway

The San Francisco Bay area has been receptive to both traditional and contemporary bluegrass music; High Country falls into the former category, primarily influenced by the first-generation bluegrass pioneers. The band has been in continuous existence since the 1960s when they recorded for the Warner Brothers subsidiary, Raccoon Records; their current releases are on the Turquoise label. This 1984 LP appeared on a small label based in Louisiana and is no longer in print, but it features the band in one of its tighter configurations, characterized by crisp musicianship, many strong original songs and excellent singing.

91 Bluegrass

Hot Rize

Flying Fish CD FF 206

Blue Night/Empty Pocket Blues/Nellie Kane/High On A Mountain/Ain't I Been Good To You/Powwow The Indian Boy/Prayer Bells Of Heaven/This Here Bottle/Ninety-Nine Years (And One Dark Day)/Old Dan Tucker/ Country Boy Rock 'N' Roll/Standing In The Need Of Prayer/Durham's Reel/ Midnight On The Highway

Throughout the 1980s Hot Rize skillfully walked the line between modern and traditional bluegrass music with straightforward treatments of contemporary songs and deft arrangements of older material. Soulful singing by mandolinist/fiddler Tim O'Brien brought the approval of fans from both ends of the bluegrass spectrum, and thoughtful accompaniment by all band members ensured continued success on the bluegrass circuit. After great success as Hot Rize and their musical alter egos, 1950s-style country band Red Knuckles and the Trailblazers, the group decided to disband rather than continue with replacement personnel when O'Brien left to launch a solo career in country music.

This, their initial release in 1979, contains energetic and enthusiastic performances of 14 selections and effectively demonstrates the appeal and talents of Hot Rize.

92 At The Old Schoolhouse

The Johnson Mountain Boys

Rounder CD 0260

Black Mt. Blues/Let The Whole World Talk/Long Journey Home/Bluest Man In Town/John Henry, The Steel Driving Man/Weathered Gray Stone/ Unwanted Love/Ricestrow [sic]/Waltz Across Texas/Five Speed/Dream Of A Miner's Child/Georgia Stomp/Sweetest Gift/I've Found A Hiding Place/With Body And Soul/Orange Blossom Special/Get Down On Your Knees And Pray/ Going To Georgia/Now Just Suppose/Don't You Call My Name/Do You Call That Religion/Daniel Prayed/Wake Up, Susan

The 1970s were curious times for bluegrass; new ideas and influences led to departures from tradition as bands enlarged their definitions of what was suitable. In the midst of this expansion the Johnson Mountain Boys appeared, playing music that was a throwback to the styles of the mid-1950s. More akin to the Stanley Brothers than to hot musicians nearer their own ages, the "JMB" quickly built a following among fans who welcomed this resurgence of old-fashioned music, unabashed sentimentality and vigorous performance. This live recording, intended as a farewell (the band had planned to dissolve) is full of the energy and spirit that won nearly universal approval.

193 Appalachian Swing

The Kentucky Colonels

Rounder CDSS 31

*Clinch Mountain Backstep/Nine Pound Hammer/Listen To The Mocking Bird/
Wild Bill Jones/Billy In The Low Ground/Lee Highway/I Am A Pilgrim/
Prisoner's Song/Sally Goodin/Faded Love/John Henry/Flat Fork*

After the definitions were laid down by the "original bluegrass band," few
have had as much impact on a single instrument as the late Clarence White.
Almost singlehandedly, he took the guitar from its basic role as a rhythm
instrument to new solo heights. Combining ideas from such earlier guitarists
as Don Reno, George Shuffler (a frequent Stanley Brothers side-man) and
Doc Watson, White added rhythmic and melodic components that stirred the
imagination of bluegrass fans and fellow musicians as soon as they were heard
on the 1964 release, **Appalachian Swing**.
    Originally released on World Pacific, this CD reissue became available in
late 1993.

194 Every Time You Say Goodbye

Alison Krauss

Rounder CD 0285

*Every Time You Say Goodbye/Another Night/Last Love Letter/Cluck, Old
Hen/Who Can Blame You/It Won't Work This Time/Heartstrings/I Don't
Know Why/Cloudy Days/New Fool/Shield Of Faith/Lose Again/Another Day,
Another Dollar/Jesus, Help Me Stand*

Bluegrass music has attracted a continuing flow of young performers, but
none in the 1990s has had the impact of Alison Krauss. As an appealingly
talented teenager, she emerged to capture the attention of bluegrass fans with
her smooth, intense fiddling and singing. Her dedication to expanding the
style while preserving its traditions leads to recordings that contain a mix of
acoustic selections carefully chosen to appeal to varied tastes. Side by side
with "softer" performances, Krauss includes hard-edged pieces from some of
bluegrass music's more obscure sources – listen, for example, to the Stanley
Brothers' *Another Night* or Aubrey Holt's *It Won't Work This Time*.
    Although clearly the star, Alison Krauss is always mindful of the impor-
tance of her band and the ensemble nature of her music. Recently, at age 22,
she became the newest and youngest member of the Grand Ole Opry.

195 I'll Wander Back Someday

Doyle Lawson and Quicksilver

Sugar Hill SH-CD-3769

*A White Rose/Trust Each Other/One Way Train/Dreaming/I'll Wander Back
Someday/Let Us Travel On/Out On The Ocean/Too Late/That's How I Can
Count On You/Devil's Little Angel/Our Last Goodbye/What A Wonderful
Savior He Is*

Doyle Lawson received his musical schooling standing next to many of the
finest musicians in bluegrass, beginning with Jimmy Martin, and including
J.D. Crowe, Red Allen, and Charlie Waller. Drawing ideas from early
country music, Southern Gospel quartet singing and popular music, as well
as bluegrass, Lawson's own band took shape in late 1979, after he left the

Country Gentlemen. He released his first LP for Sugar Hill in 1980. Though known for intricate *a cappella* gospel singing and innovative arrangements of new material, Lawson's bands are always capable of delivering straight blue-grass with economy and vitality, as evidenced by this 1989 release.

96 Windy Mountain

The Lonesome Pine Fiddlers
Bear Family BCD-501 (Ger)

Pain In My Heart/Lonesome, Sad And Blue/Don't Forget Me/Will I Meet Mother In Heaven/You Broke Your Promise/I'm Left All Alone/Nobody Cares (Not Even You)/Twenty-One Years/My Brown-Eyed Darling/You Left Me To Cry/That's Why You Left Me So Blue/I'll Never Make You Blue/ Honky Tonk Blues/You're So Good/I'll Never Change My Mind/Dirty Dishes Blues/Lonesome Pine Breakdown/Five String Drag/Don't Forget Me/Baby, You're Cheatin'/I'm Feeling For You (But I Can't Reach You)/Some Kinda Sorry/Windy Mountain/No Curb Service/A New Set Of Blues/There's Just One You

Like Bill Monroe's Blue Grass Boys, the Lonesome Pine Fiddlers date from the 1930s when they were a string band. Inspired by the popularity of Monroe's sound, the group added a three-finger-style banjo player and a high tenor singer, and embarked on a radio and recording career that took them from the small Cozy label to the studios of RCA Victor and Starday Records.

The band provided early exposure for several significant figures in the history of bluegrass: Bobby Osborne of the Osborne Brothers; longtime Blue Grass Boy, Charlie Cline; Ralph Stanley side-man Curly Ray Cline; Paul Williams, an important contributor to the sound and style of Jimmy Martin; and Melvin and Ray Goins.

Their songs vary from catchy (*No Curb Service, Honky Tonk Blues*) to straightforward and intense (*Windy Mountain, My Brown-Eyed Darling*), with emphasis on close harmony singing and instrumental accompaniment that is crisp, uncluttered, and to the point.

Collected on this 1992 CD is their entire output for Cozy and RCA.

97 The Deal

The Lost and Found
Rebel CD-1658

Your Love Is Dying/Sweet Rosie By The River/Rain/Dream Softly, My Love/ Southern Train/Southbound/I Don't Know Why I Love You/Virginia, That's My Home/If I Had My Life To Live Over/Anita/Why Do You Weep, Dear Willow/Don't Let Your Deal Go Down

Apart from being good singers and musicians, the strength of the Lost and Found lies in their understanding of the way bluegrass music is related to country music, in both current and historical terms. Where much of today's bluegrass features a hard-driving, high-energy attack, the Lost and Found follow a more moderate path. While they are certainly capable of intensity, their music frequently relies on gentle subtlety to convey its message, and their performances emphasize entertainment values over musical pyro-technics. This 1987 release contains sentimental songs and ballads, sung with feeling and emotion that draw the listener into the story.

198 Don't Stop The Music

The Del McCoury Band

Rounder CD 0245

Trainwreck Of Emotion/Lights On The Hill/You'll Find Her Name Written There/Highway Of Pain/I'll Put Someone In Your Place/Blue Is The Way That I Feel/Knee Deep In The Blues/Sea Of Sorrow/Blues On My Mind/I Feel the Blues Moving In/Don't Our Love Look Natural/How Lonely Can You Get/ Crazy Heart

Del McCoury is a bluegrass veteran whose experience includes apprenticeship in Bill Monroe's Blue Grass Boys as well as fronting his own bands since the 1960s. His performances are taut with emotion, yet stoic in that they do not wallow in self-pity despite the preponderance of "blues" numbers in his repertoire. A highly regarded vocalist and rhythm guitarist, Del is joined on this 1990 release by sons Ronnie and Robbie, who effectively show the results of their father's tutelage. Outstanding performances by the McCourys and supporting musicians make this an excellent example of the "high-lonesome" variety of bluegrass.

199 The Boys Are Back In Town

The Nashville Bluegrass Band

Sugar Hill SH-CD-3778

Get A Transfer/Long Time Gone/Big River/Hard Times/Connie And Buster/ Don't Let Our Love Die/I'm Rollin' Through This Unfriendly World/Rock Bottom Blues/Diamonds And Pearls/The Ghost Of Eli Renfro/Weary Blues From Waitin'/Big Cow In Carlisle/Dark As The Night, Blue As The Day/The Boys Are Back In Town

The Nashville Bluegrass Band was formed in the 1980s in response to a job offer with no one to play it. Banjo player Alan O'Bryant recruited a band from among the community of musicians in Nashville, Tennessee, and the "NBB" was born.

Relying on a signature sound built around the duet singing of O'Bryant with Pat Enright, the NBB also incorporates trios and intricately arranged Gospel quartets into their performances.

Though known and respected for the power and emotion in their vocal work, the musicianship of the NBB is also highly regarded, especially that of fiddle virtuoso Stuart Duncan.

While all NBB's recordings are effective, this CD is characterized by superb choice of material, varying from the raucous title track to impassioned readings of *Long Time Gone* and Stephen Foster's *Hard Times*.

200 When The Storm Is Over/Fly Through The Country

New Grass Revival

Flying Fish CD 32

Four Days Of Rain/White Freightliner Blues/Sail To Australia/When The Storm Is Over/And He Says "I Love You"/Vamp In The Middle/Like A Child In The Rain/Tennessee Wagoner/Colly Davis/Crooked Smile/Skippin' In The Mississippi Dew/Good Woman's Love/Glory/All Night Train/Fly Through The Country/This Heart Of Mine /The Dancer/When She Made Laughter Easy/ Doin' My Time/These Days

The New Grass Revival evolved when four members of the Bluegrass Alliance, desiring a less constrained musical atmosphere, defected in 1972 to start their own band. Sparked by the genius of fiddler/mandolinist Sam Bush, the band quickly gained a following, especially among younger listeners. Though their roots included deep connections to traditional music, the New Grass Revival's primary thrust was into uncharted areas where rock-and-roll aesthetics met acoustic instrumentation, and the musical rules of bluegrass did not necessarily apply. It was brave new music, highly improvisational yet encompassing a structure of its own, and continued through various personnel changes until they disbanded in the early 1990s. This CD is a compilation of two LPs released in the 1970s.

01 The New South

The New South
Rounder CD 0044

Old Home Place/Some Old Day/Rock Salt And Nails/Sally Goodin/Ten Degrees/Nashville Blues/You Are What I Am/Summer Wages/I'm Walkin'/ Home Sweet Home Revisited/Cryin' Holy

J.D. Crowe is noted for his precise, Scruggs-derived yet individualistic banjo playing, and was, in the late 1950s and early 1960s, a major factor in defining the sound of Jimmy Martin's Sunny Mountain Boys. His own bands have been extremely influential; the lead guitar work and singing of Tony Rice, in particular, combined with Crowe's banjo, have spawned numerous derivative bands; and New South alumni have formed such groups as Boone Creek, Doyle Lawson and Quicksilver, and the Tony Rice Unit. Some, Ricky Skaggs and the late Keith Whitley, went on to fame in the country music world.

Released in 1975, this CD features some of Crowe's best musicians. In performance it both clings to and departs from tradition, with material that dates from the earliest days of bluegrass music side by side with songs drawn from rock-and-roll and new compositions by some of country music's (then) new young song writers.

02 The Bluegrass Collection

The Osborne Brothers
CMH 9011 (USA)

Kentucky Waltz/Pain In My Heart/Blue Ridge Cabin Home/When You Are Lonely/Some Old Day/I Hear A Sweet Voice Calling/My Cabin In Caroline/ (It's A Long Long Way) To The Top Of The World/Sunny Side Of The Mountain/Head Over Heels/Don't That Road Look Rough And Rocky/I'm Going Back To Old Kentucky/Your Love Is Like A Flower/Sweethearts Again/ Little Cabin Home On The Hill/No Mother Or Dad/Toy Heart/Rank Strangers/A Vision Of Mother/Lonesome Day/My Rose Of Old Kentucky/This Heart Of Mine (Can Never Say Goodbye)/Thinking About You/White Dove

Owing in part to the phenomenal chart success of *Rocky Top* in 1968, the Osborne Brothers' career in country music took a remarkable turn, for a bluegrass band. They began appearing on package shows with major country music stars, many with Merle Haggard, and their recordings received air play at a time when bluegrass on commercial radio was a rarity.

During this period, the early to mid-1970s, their recordings tended toward a "Nashville sound" with their unique trio and standard bluegrass instrumentation augmented by drums, electric guitar, and steel guitar. While these additions proved profitable for them, they were not well received in the bluegrass community, which considered electrification counter to the definitions of the style.

A mid-1970s move to CMH Records saw the Osbornes return to more traditional music, and resulted in several releases that were enthusiastically received by the growing bluegrass audience. Of these, **The Bluegrass Collection** stands out as an example of their gifted musicianship, while it pays tribute to the songs and bands that influenced their own early development.

203 Once More, Vols 1 and 2

The Osborne Brothers

Sugar Hill SH-CD-2203

The Cuckoo Bird/Beneath Still Waters/Arkansas/Pain In My Heart/Blue Moon Of Kentucky/Once More/Listening To The Rain/High On A Hilltop/Each Season Changes You/Kentucky/Nobody's Darling But Mine/Bluegrass Express/ One Tear/Windy City/Two Lonely Hearts/I'll Be Alright [sic] Tomorrow/ Making Plans/Lonesome Feeling/Big Spike Hammer/My Favorite Memory/ Unfaithful One/Me And My Old Banjo/One Kiss Away From Loneliness/ Fastest Grass Alive

In the early 1980s, after several successful sets for CMH, the Osborne Brothers began a series of albums for Sugar Hill Records. Of these, two LPs (combined into this single CD release in 1991) stand out. Re-recorded here are many titles from their MGM and Decca/MCA sessions which are out of print. Some of these, particularly the ones done originally for Decca featuring country-style instrumentation, appear here for the first time with bluegrass accompaniment unobscured by studio musicians.

204 The First Whippoorwill

Peter Rowan

Sugar Hill SH-CD-3749

The First Whippoorwill/I'm On My Way Back To The Old Home/I'm Just A Used To Be/I Believed In You Darling/Sweetheart, You Done Me Wrong/ When The Golden Leaves Begin to Fall/I Was Left On The Street/Goodbye Old Pal/When You Are Lonely/Sitting Alone In The Moonlight/Boat Of Love/It's Mighty Dark To Travel

Peter Rowan's musical credentials include a significant stay with one of Bill Monroe's most influential bands – the 1965–7 version – which brought him together with fiddler Richard Greene and banjoist Lamar Grier. Later Rowan and Greene would collaborate in bands as varied as Sea Train, playing experimental rock-and-roll, and Muleskinner, with David Grisman and Clarence White, where the focus was bluegrass. Rowan's music always represents a personal view of life, and can take widely divergent forms, but he is ever mindful of roots and influences. His 1993 release, **Awake Me In The New World**, has received high praise for its vision, but for pure bluegrass performances, Rowan's 1986 tribute to his mentor, Bill Monroe, is the recording of choice.

205 Tony Rice

Tony Rice

Rounder CD 0085

Banks Of The Ohio/Rattlesnake/Mr Engineer/Plastic Banana/Don't Give Your

Heart To A Rambler/Farewell Blues/Way Downtown/Stoney Creek/Hills Of Roane County/Eighth Of January/Big Mon/Temperance Reel

Tony Rice's rise to prominence as a guitarist and singer began as a member of the Bluegrass Alliance, and came to full flower after he joined banjo player J.D. Crowe's band, The New South, early in 1972. His recordings attracted national attention, and by the end of the 1970s it was apparent that Rice had inherited the late Clarence White's leadership role in the world of bluegrass and related acoustic guitar playing. Known for solid rhythm and inventive lead playing, Rice's work on this 1977 release includes examples of his ties to traditional music as well as his more adventurous inclinations. Rice can also be heard on mid-1970s recordings by the David Grisman Quartet, 1980s sessions with the Bluegrass Album Band, and currently as leader of the Tony Rice Unit.

06   Act 1

The Seldom Scene
Rebel CD-1511
Raised By The Railroad Line/Darling Corey/Want Of A Woman/Sweet Baby James/Joshua/Will There Be Any Stars In My Crown/City Of New Orleans/ With Body And Soul/Summertime Is Past And Gone/Five-Hundred Miles/Cannonball/What Am I Doing Hanging 'Round

Formed in 1971 by a surgeon, a cartographer, a mathematician, a commercial artist and a professional eccentric, the Seldom Scene was originally designed to provide a part-time outlet for the considerable musical talents of this unlikely group. They had not counted on success, but recognition and acclaim came in response to their skillful blend of traditional and modern themes and stylings. There have been a few changes in personnel since the band began, but the 1993 version still contains four of the original members.

Almost any recording by the band will provide an interesting program, but their initial 1972 release, reissued on compact disc in 1993, is notable for its energy and enthusiasm, characteristics often associated with beginnings.

07   Classic Bluegrass

Larry Sparks and the Lonesome Ramblers
Rebel CD-1107
Tennessee 1949/Kentucky Girl/John Deere Tractor/Love Of The Mountains/A Face In The Crowd/Just Lovin' You/Six More Miles/Cannonball Blues/Smoky Mountain Memories/Roving Gambler/You Could Have Called/Don't Neglect The Rose/Great High Mountain/Blue Love/Too Late to Walk The Floor/Waltz Of The Wind/Girl At The Crossroads Bar/Blue Virginia Blues

As a teenager in the mid-1960s, Larry Sparks was an occasional member of the Stanley Brothers band, the Clinch Mountain Boys; after the death of Carter Stanley in 1966, Sparks filled the rhythm guitarist/lead singer role in Ralph Stanley's new band for nearly three years.

A typical Lonesome Ramblers line-up features Larry's blues-influenced vocals and intense, driving, guitar work at the forefront, supported by bluegrass instrumentation and vocals.

The selections on this CD are from Sparks's work in the 1970s and 1980s and include many of his finest performances. His heart-wrenching delivery of

John Deere Tractor, You Could Have Called, and *A Face In The Crowd* fixed
Larry Sparks's reputation as one of the most powerful singers in bluegrass.

208   The Early Starday–King Years 1958–1961

The Stanley Brothers

King KBS CD-7000 (4-disc set)

*Holiday Pickin'/Gonna Paint The Town/That Happy Night/Christmas Is Near/
Love Me, Darling, Just Tonight/She's More To Be Pitied/Heaven Seemed So
Near/Your Selfish Heart/How Mountain Girls Can Love/The Memory Of Your
Smile/Mastertone March/Clinch Mountain Backstep/Midnight Ramble/Train
45/Think Of What You've Done/Keep A Memory/Old Daniel Prayed/He Said
If I Be Lifted Up/This Wicked Path of Sin/I'll Meet You In Church, Sunday
Morning/Are You Afraid To Die/The White Dove/How Can We Thank Him
For What He Has Done/Mother's Footsteps Guide Me On/That Home Far
Away/My Lord's Gonna Set Me Free/The Angel Of Death/Wings Of Angels/
Suwannee River Hoedown/Choo Choo Comin'/Carolina Mountain Home/Trust
Each Other/Beneath The Maple/Highway Of Regret/A Little At A Time/
Another Night/Ridin' That Midnight Train/Mountain Dew/Sunny Side Of The
Mountain/Tragic Romance/Shenandoah Waltz/Next Sunday, Darling, Is My
Birthday/Sweet Thing/Sweeter Than The Flowers/It's Raining Here This
Morning/Shackles And Chains/Weeping Willow/Old Rattler/I'm A Man Of
Constant Sorrow/My Main Trial Is Yet To Come/Mother Left Me Her Bible/
Jacob's Vision/I'll Not Be A Stranger/From The Manger To The Cross/Four
Books In The Bible/Purple Robe/When Jesus Beckons Me Home/Jordan/Pass
Me Not/Lonely Tombs/Over In The Glory Land/How Far To Little Rock/A
Few More Seasons/Where We'll Never Die/In Heaven We'll Never Grow Old/
Mother No Longer Awaits Me At Home/If I Lose/Little Maggie/God Gave You
to Me/Don't Go Out Tonight/The Darkest Hour Is Just Before Dawn/Rank
Stranger/Let The Church Roll On/Rock Of Ages/I Saw The Light/What A
Friend/Gathering Flowers For The Master's Bouquet/I'm Ready To Go/Let Me
Love You One More Time/Little Bennie/Old Love Letters/Daybreak In Dixie
(undubbed)/Daybreak in Dixie (overdubbed)/Wildwood Flower/Let Me Rest/
Are You Tired Of Me, Darling/Finger Poppin' Time (undubbed)/Finger
Poppin' Time (overdubbed)/Rank Stranger (previously unissued)/Come All Ye
Tender-Hearted/The Window Up Above/Lover's Quarrel/The Story Of The
Lawson Family/Hey, Hey, Hey/The Wild Side Of Life/Jenny Lynn/What
About You/Little Willie/Big Tilda/Wild Bill Jones/You're Still To Blame/I'll
Take The Blame/I'll Just Go Away/Steel Guitar Rag (previously unissued)/I'd
Worship You/Just Dreamin'/The Drunken Driver/Handsome Molly*

The 109 selections in this boxed set were cut between 1958 and 1961, a time
of transition and label-hopping for the Stanley Brothers during which they
recorded for Starday and King Records, and had releases available simultaneously from both companies.

The earlier selections feature instrumentation consistent with most bluegrass bands of the period, but as they became more involved with King
Records their sound was altered, placing less emphasis on fiddle and
mandolin, and featuring more lead guitar, which they had used on a few
tunes recorded for Mercury in 1955 and 1956.

Some of the Stanley Brothers' most enduring titles come from this period,
including *Think Of What You've Done, Clinch Mountain Backstep, Rank
Stranger,* and *Riding That Midnight Train,* and are characterized by the
trademark duets and trios, highly rated for their raw mountain mournfulness
and unselfconscious sentimentality.

209 Howdy, Neighbor, Howdy

The Traditional Grass

Rebel CD-1698

Howdy, Neighbor, Howdy/Lover's Quarrel/You'll Never Be The Same/My Memories Aren't Precious Anymore/Pretending I Don't Care/Six White Horses/ Let Me Walk, Lord, By Your Side/The Blues Are Still The Blues/Pretending/ Katie Kline/The Shuffle Of My Feet/Dixie Breakdown/Your Selfish Heart/ Lord, Lead Me On Home

In this aggregation, formed in 1983, youthful enthusiasm teamed with experience (fiddler Paul Mullins played with the Stanleys in 1958, and has been an important part of numerous fine bands since) to create a band with the heart and traditions that formed the great bands of the 1950s. Keeping the styles and material of that era uppermost in their minds, the Traditional Grass have added their own songs and talents to become one of the top bands of the 1990s, and have contributed to a rising interest in more traditional bluegrass. Their work is not to be missed.

210 Classic Bluegrass

Mac Wiseman

Rebel CD-1106

Little Home In Tennessee/Letter Edged In Black/Girl Of My Dreams/Fire In My Heart/Shackles And Chains/Hills Of Roane County/You Can't Judge A Book By Its Cover/Mary Of The Wild Moor/Four Walls Around Me/Reveille Time In Heaven/Fireball Mail/Crazy Blues/Knoxville Girl/I Haven't Got The Right To Love You/Going To See My Baby/Little White Church/Footprints In The Snow/Georgia Waltz/Don't Let Your Sweet Love Die/When The Roses Bloom Again/Black Sheep/Let Me Borrow Your Heart

Mac Wiseman's place in the history of bluegrass music is secure. A member of the original version of Flatt's and Scruggs's Foggy Mountain Boys and, later, Bill Monroe's Blue Grass Boys, he made limited but significant recordings with each. For several years Wiseman was an executive with Dot Records as well as a recording artist, and much of his output for that label has recently become available on CD. For a better picture of Mac Wiseman as a bluegrass balladeer, listeners might prefer this 1976 session, which contains excellent reworkings of many of his earlier recordings as well as material he had not previously recorded.

211 Mighty Lonesome

Lonesome Standard Time

Sugar Hill SH-CD-3816

The Bigger The Fool/I'm Lonesome And Blue/Sugar In The Gourd/Lonesome For You/I'm Lonesome Without You/Heaven's Green Fields/Kentucky Thunder/ My Hands Are Tied/Bandit/Whistlestop Willie/The Sweetest Love/The Tracks We Leave

Though successfully working within the Nashville country music establishment as highly regarded session player and songwriter respectively, bluegrass is the music of choice for Lonesome Standard Time founders, fiddler Glen Duncan and guitarist Larry Cordle.

They honor their earliest influences – Bill Monroe, the Stanley Brothers, and Flatt and Scruggs – by capturing, without imitating, the flavor and spirit of those definitive sounds, and with evocative original compositions by Cordle, they enlarge and enhance the bluegrass repertoire. The music of "LST" is very much 1990s bluegrass, but with a decided traditional bias.

This 1993 release features outstanding harmony singing by Duncan, Cordle, and Billy Rose, and impeccable instrumental support by Butch Baldassari on mandolin and Larry Perkins on banjo.

212 Blue Heartache

Stoney Lonesome

Red House Records RHR CD-51

Mason Harris/Goin' Away/I'd Rather Be Alone/Blue Heartache/Flame In My Heart/The Train Carrying Jimmie Rodgers Home/Long Time Gone/Same Old Moon/I'm Lonely Tonight/Cochichando (Whispering)/One More Town/Count Your Blessings

Stoney Lonesome achieved wide exposure in the 1980s through frequent appearances on National Public Radio's "Prairie Home Companion." These performances did much to improve public perception of bluegrass music, showing it in an intelligent setting and on an equal footing with other music forms.

Women have been in bluegrass almost from the beginning, but only within the last decade have they gained commanding roles in the music. Guitarist Kate MacKenzie, singing with deep feeling and controlled passion, is especially effective on the George Jones song, *Flame In My Heart*. Her own *Same Old Moon* reveals her to be a creditable composer as well as a deft singer of gentler ballads.

Youth and enthusiasm enhance Stoney Lonesome's appeal, but it is their broad-ranging skills and the depth of their interpretations that make this CD desirable.

213 Classic Bluegrass

Ralph Stanley and the Clinch Mountain Boys

Rebel CD-1109

Love Me, Darling, Just Tonight/Could You Love Me One More Time/Flood of '57/The Fields Have Turned Brown/A Little Boy Called Joe/Loving You Too Well/Train 45/Poor Rambler/Old Richmond Prison/No School Bus In Heaven/John Henry/Little Maggie/Your Worries And Troubles Are Mine/Rank Stranger/Lonesome And Blue/Poison Love/Little Glass Of Wine/On And On/I'm Lonesome Without You/Gonna Paint The Town

Following the death of his brother, Carter, in 1966, banjo player Ralph Stanley was faced with the difficult choice of whether to retire or to continue playing music during a period when bluegrass faced a doubtful future. Summer festivals had not yet become established, and the market for bluegrass performers was uncertain at best, but Ralph chose to re-form his Clinch Mountain Boys, returning to the road and the recording studio with mounting success. Motivated by the demands of fans, Stanley's post-1966 output has been prolific; consequently his recordings have varied considerably, but within even the coarsest product some jewel makes purchase obligatory. Here the jewels have been assembled into a single, elegant release that gives you the "best" of Ralph Stanley.

The 1950s and 1960s: Hillbilly, Rockabilly, and Early Country-Pop

6

Bob Allen and Pete Loesch

C ountry music in the 1950s and 1960s has been chronicled elsewhere in this guide – specifically in the chapters on honky-tonk, bluegrass, and western swing and western music. Yet a significant number of vastly influential artists from this era – the preponderance of whom recorded in Nashville – do not fit snugly into any of the above-mentioned categories. Thus this chapter is, to some extent, a catch-all for these artists.

Nashville, since 1925, has been home to the Grand Ole Opry, the longest continuous-running live musical radio show in the world, and for decades a career springboard for dozens of country's most popular artists. And by the early 1950s, the city, largely because of the Opry's presence, was also beginning to come into its own as a recording capital. Previously, country music was, often as not, recorded in various regional locales – Texas, rural Tennessee – or in Northern recording centers like Chicago, New York, or Los Angeles. But with Nashville's emergence as a recording capital, country music began to develop a stronger sense of itself – both as a viable commercial art form and as an industry quite separate from the pop music scene in New York and elsewhere.

Yet at the outset of the fifties, country music was still very much a rural cult music in terms of its (to use a dreaded phrase favored by number-crunching record executives everywhere) "demographic appeal." Even in the late fifties, sales of 25,000 on a country hit were deemed respectable. Yet at the same time, pop artists like Patti Page and Rosemary Clooney were having million-sellers with country songs (written by Hank Williams, Pee Wee King, and the like) recorded in a pop style. Thus the sound of ringing cash registers and the allure of the more lucrative pop-crossover market became the inspiration for the "Nashville sound:" an industry-driven musical dialectic that coalesced in the late fifties and early sixties. The Nashville sound – which to some extent began as an abreaction to rockabilly, which sapped mainstream country sales, has – through both action and abreaction, shaped the course of country music ever since.

As William Ivey, director of the Country Music Foundation, observed in *The Encyclopedia of Folk, Country and Western Music*:

> The entire decade of the 1960s had been given over to integrating country music into the larger pop music mainstream. Record producers like Chet Atkins and Owen Bradley had consciously utilized pop music techniques of instrumentation and recording to develop a sound acceptable to both pop and country audiences. It was in the 1960s that the use of string sections, brass, and background choruses on country records resulted in "The Nashville Sound," which brought fame to that southern recording center . . . [But, as a result of it] many pundits predicted that country music would not survive.

The "Nashville sound," which has been much maligned in recent years, did what it was intended to do in terms of increasing Nashville's – and country music's – "market share," even if it watered down the music's traditional rusticity and aggressive instrumentation in the process. This growth was evidenced by the number of fulltime country radio stations in the US, which burgeoned from 81 in 1961, to 606 in 1969. By 1989, the number had leaped to 1434.

Yet for all the resentment it engendered among more tradition-minded country artists, the Nashville sound proved a worthy stylistic vehicle for talented artists like Patsy Cline and Eddy Arnold, whose influence is still widely felt today.

But earlier in the mid-1950s, in Memphis, 200 miles west of Nashville, and elsewhere throughout the South, another very exciting and very different musical hybrid was alchemizing out of the seemingly disparate forces of country music, bluegrass, hillbilly-boogie, and old-time blues. This was music that had little or nothing to do with mainstream Nashville, yet which would indelibly change the face of country and pop music alike and soon give rise to the birth of rock-and-roll. This strange, wild new music was called rockabilly, and its most fervent acolytes were young Elvis Presley, Jerry Lee Lewis, Johnny Cash, and Carl Perkins.

Essential Recordings

(i) Rockabilly: Sam Phillips and the Million Dollar Quartet

In an era when country music is suffused with rock overtones, and country artists over the age of 40 are routinely sentenced to life imprisonment at Branson, Missouri, the world's largest country music theme park, it may be difficult to comprehend the anxiety with which the Nashville establishment viewed the Memphis rockabilly movement spearheaded by Sam C. Phillips in the mid-1950s. At the dawn of that decade, Phillips – a northwest Alabama native who had migrated to Memphis in pursuit of a radio career – would not have appeared likely to disturb the peace in the Music City. Though having opened his Memphis Recording Service at 706 Union, he was then engaged primarily in leasing masters by blues artists like Howlin' Wolf and B.B. King to independent record companies in Chicago and Los Angeles. Later, in 1952, Phillips launched his own Sun label; yet the bulk of its initial product was also devoted to blues men having such colorful names as Doctor Ross, Billy "The Kid" Emerson, and Hot Shot Love.

But Sam Phillips had a musical vision shaped by his upbringing on a Southern plantation. Enamored of the unbridled spirit of black gospel and rhythm and blues, he wondered at the commercial potential of a white singer who could genuinely assimilate those exciting idioms and rouse younger audiences from the sterile tranquillity of country and pop. When that singer arrived in the person of Elvis Presley, country music – as well as popular culture – was forever changed.

Following Presley's stirring debut on Sun in 1954, Phillips concentrated on the kinetic, predominantly white Southern fusion of country and blues that became known as rockabilly. Foremost among the label's other practitioners in that relatively shortlived (albeit lastingly influential) genre were Carl Perkins (who was serving up his version of rockabilly in local roadhouses while Elvis Presley was still in high school), Jerry Lee Lewis, and Johnny Cash. On December 4, 1956, about one year after financial constraints impelled Phillips to assign Presley's recording contract to RCA Victor, "The King" returned to the Sun Studio at 706 Union and encountered the rest of this aptly-dubbed "Million Dollar Quartet" (Presley, Perkins, Cash, and Lewis). The ensuing jam session – like virtually all of Sun's recorded output – has come to be chronicled as painstakingly and avidly as the American Civil War.

To be sure, Sun's mid-South location was conducive to attracting artists who had absorbed the area's rich musical traditions. Undeniably, however, it was Sam Phillips's remarkable ability to recognize and nurture talent that was most responsible for the label's run of success through the 1950s. In this regard, Phillips's keen appreciation of simplicity, spontaneity, and feeling cannot be over-emphasized. As the producer of Sun's landmark recordings, his only significant concession to technical gimmickry was the famed "slap-back" echo which enhanced the impact of combos wedged in the tiny studio.

By the early sixties, an assortment of innocuous teen idols and dance crazes had been fabricated; and Sun's fortunes waned. As his main discoveries (including Roy Orbison and Charlie Rich) defected to major labels, Sam Phillips gradually lost interest in the company. Finally, in 1969, it was sold to Nashville impresario Shelby Singleton – who promptly embarked on an abominable series of fake stereo reissues which litter the landscape to this day. Happily, the extraordinary artists comprising the Million Dollar Quartet have since been treated with elaborate boxed sets, incorporating everything from song fragments to studio chatter. More importantly, for the purposes of this book, there also exist attractive individual volumes representing the singers' celebrated Sun recordings.

Elvis Presley: The Complete Sun Sessions CD, a slightly abridged version of a 2-record album released in 1987, includes 16 finished masters, eight outtakes, and four alternative takes. Together, these tracks fascinatingly trace the evolution of a sound conceived in July, 1954. Presley, whose family had settled in Memphis from Tupelo, Mississippi, was then a 19-year-old truck driver employed by the Crown Electric Company. Having impressed Sam Phillips as a capable vocalist through a personal, or "custom" disc he had previously recorded at the Sun studio, Presley was summoned to return there for an audition. Also present at the session were electric guitarist Scotty Moore and upright bassist Bill Black – local country musicians with whom the singer had lately practiced at Phillips' suggestion.

At the outset, negotiating such pop ballads as *Harbor Lights,* and Leon Payne's country hit, *I Love You Because*, Presley's efforts lacked distinction. Suddenly, during a break, his theretofore restrained tenor connected with a Mississippi memory: Arthur "Big Boy" Crudup's *That's All Right (Mama).* With Scotty and Bill convincingly backing his prominent acoustic strumming, Presley tackled the frisky blues number with astonishing gusto. By the time the transformation of bluegrass patriarch Bill Monroe's *Blue Moon Of Kentucky* into an equally charged flip side was complete, Sam Phillips had clearly found the musical integration he coveted. Indeed, after a slower outtake of the tune, the producer is heard to exclaim, "That's fine, man! Hell, that's different! That's a pop song now, nearly 'bout!"

Of the eight other tracks actually issued on Sun, rockabilly aficionados understandably prize the exuberant rhythm-and-blues interpretations exemplified by *Good Rockin' Tonight*. Plainly, these are not slavish imitations. By freely adjusting lyrics and tempos, Presley imprints on *Mystery Train* (originally recorded for Sun by Little Junior's Blue Flames in 1953) and *Baby, Let's Play House* a personal stamp fully as real as the one bearing his name on US Mail. In the latter selection, recorded in early 1955, Presley delivers a potent combination of hiccups, stutters, and swagger. Meanwhile, driven by Bill Black's propulsive plucking, Scotty Moore heightens the tension with noticeably more searing guitar licks. Thus were the rockabilly rules laid down.

The remaining cuts, ranging from pop standards (*Blue Moon*) to country laments (*I'm Left, You're Right, She's Gone*), demonstrate the kind of versatility that always buttressed Presley's appeal. The alternate takes also offer revealing glimpses of a developing style. *I Love You Because*, for example, features the sort of spoken interlude that would be employed to great effect in *Are You Lonesome Tonight*.

At this stage of Presley's career, when his record sales were confined mainly to the South, the "Hillbilly Cat" was perceived and marketed as a country and western act. In fact, near the end of his brief tenure on Sun, he was voted the "Most Promising New C & W Artist" at the annual country Disc Jockeys' Convention in Nashville. Notwithstanding the overwhelming acclaim Presley would achieve on RCA, critics commonly maintain that he never recaptured all of the raw inspiration and vigor of his Sun recordings. Arguably, that assessment is colored by an overreaction to the more sophisticated technology and production values that would inevitably come into play. Nonetheless, some 40 years after they were made, these recordings remain as much a vital listening experience as an historical document.

When Presley departed from the Sun stable in November, 1955, Sam Phillips pinned his hopes for widespread acceptance of rockabilly largely on Carl Perkins. The impoverished son of a rural west Tennessee tenant farmer, Perkins had gravitated to the Memphis scene after hearing Presley's *That's All Right* on the radio. The new hybrid sound resembled that which Carl and brothers Jay (rhythm guitar) and Clayton (bass), augmented by drummer W.S. "Fluke" Holland, had been purveying as the Perkins Brothers Band in clubs around Jackson, about 80 miles northeast, before Presley even began recording.

Perkins's first two records, released in 1955, coupled traditional fiddle/steel weepers with guitar-based hillbilly boogies. Although vestiges of full-fledged rockabilly surfaced in *Gone, Gone, Gone,* these sides – proficient as they were – hardly presaged what was to come in December of that year. With the Tupelo, Mississippi flash gone, Perkins was encouraged by Phillips to – in rockabilly jargon – *get real gone.* He responded with a rockabilly anthem. In *Blue Suede Shoes,* the blues juice which black sharecroppers had implanted in his blood united with the lingering specter of Hank Williams. The results were unprecedented: Perkins's composition ascended to the top of the pop, country, and rhythm-and-blues charts; and it outsold Presley's competing version. Sun Records was, as Sam Phillips put it, "in the black."

Tragically, Carl Perkins's momentum was abruptly halted by an auto accident (on the way to national television appearances) in which he and brother Jay were seriously injured. Inasmuch as *Blue Suede Shoes* proved to be Perkins's only substantial hit, **Carl Perkins: Original Sun Greatest Hits** is something of a misnomer. (Indeed, five of the 16 tracks were never commercially released as singles.) But these songs, spanning his 3-year stint on the label, affirm that Perkins posed a "triple threat" on the order of black rock-and-roller Chuck Berry.

As evidenced by *Matchbox* (a reworking of Blind Lemon Jefferson's venerable *Match Box Blues*), Perkins's naturally slurred hillbilly vocals were ideally suited to the loose-jointed feel of rockabilly. Occasionally, without the affectation characteristic of singers less committed to the style, Perkins celebrates the newfound joy of *Boppin' The Blues* by erupting into a yelp or shout. As the writer of most of this material, he graphically captured the youthful passion for "cat clothes" and good times to create a definitive rockabilly vocabulary and repertoire. In all his performances, Perkins's homegrown lead guitar solos and fills crackle with a spitfire intensity well beyond the pale of an instructional manual.

For all his ability, however, it cannot reasonably be supposed that only misfortune – and a drinking problem exacerbated by his brother Jay's death from cancer in 1958 – prevented Carl Perkins from attaining superstardom. Though a fine performer, he admittedly possessed neither the looks nor moves which induced so many teenaged girls to want to accept Presley's invitation to "play house." Moreover, whereas the citified Presley could cite Dean Martin and Pat Boone as personal favorites, Perkins remained unmistakably "country" in orientation, vocal inflection, and mode of expression. As the mainstream inexorably swung in the direction of more refined crooners, Carl wound up as "Dixie Fried" as the incorrigible subject of his own unabashedly redneck masterpiece – a prisoner, in a sense, of the hardscrabble honky-tonks and road-houses from which he sprang.

Until late 1956, guitars had always been the centerpieces of the Sun rockabilly rebellion. And then, with a talent as massive as his eventual debt to the Internal Revenue Service, came Jerry Lee Lewis and his Pumping Piano.

At the tender age of 21, Lewis arrived in Memphis from his hometown of Ferriday, Louisiana through a rather circuitous route. By that time, Jerry Lee had played professionally in Natchez, Mississippi; had been rejected by various Nashville record companies; and – in a vain attempt to walk the funda-mentalist line espoused by cousin Jimmy Lee Swaggart – had been dismissed from a Bible school in Waxahachie, Texas for boogie-ing up the hymn *My God Is Real*.

In typically brash fashion, Jerry Lee demanded an audition at Sun. As it happened, Sam Phillips was out of town; so the task devolved upon his associate Jack Clement. Perceiving potential in Lewis's unique approach to country songs, Clement arranged for a session with guitarist Roland Janes and drummer Jimmy Van Eaton – though not before counseling Lewis to adopt the red-hot Memphis beat.

That, as is now universally known, turned out to be no problem. After taking up piano in his childhood, Jerry Lee had been lured by the rollicking rhythm and blues played at a black roadhouse outside of Ferriday. Lewis had also soaked up the spiritual fervor – if not the message – of *When The Saints Go Marching In* and the like.

On **Jerry Lee Lewis: Original Sun Greatest Hits**, we really experience the genius of two men: Jerry Lee Lewis, and Sam Phillips, who let him *be* Jerry Lee Lewis. Setting the rhythmic pace with his powerful left hand, "The Killer" un-leashes a dazzling array of triplets, trills, and glissandos. Beneath these accomplished flourishes, however, lies an innate sense of timing which enables the pianist to build or lower the energy level at just the right moment. An equally masterful vocalist, Lewis seems to know precisely when to insert colorful commentary or leap into the upper register to maximize the excitement. Phillips, for his part, has the good sense not to overload the studio. So expansive is the coverage of Lewis's piano-pounding that only Janes's pungent guitar and Van Eaton's amazingly complementary drumming are required for accompaniment. Further, like a baseball manager who gives a speedy baserunner the "green light" to steal a base at any time, Phillips apprehended that lightning could strike whenever Jerry Lee entered the room. As a result, we are able to hear such unpolished gems as the lascivious *Big-Legged Woman* (which – despite the singer's concluding proclamation that "It's a hit!" – stood no more chance of airplay than a Marxist editorial).

The disc is highlighted, of course, by the incendiary recordings that fueled Jerry Lee Lewis's meteoric rise in 1957–8: *Whole Lotta Shakin' Goin' On*, *Great Balls Of Fire*, *Breathless*, and *High School Confidential*. Other efforts in this vein – notably the self-laudatory *Lewis Boogie* (a rare original composition) and the transcendent *Ubangi Stomp* (previously recorded by labelmate Warren Smith) – pack scarcely less wallop. But, alas, news of the artist's marriage to his 13-year-old cousin inflicted even more professional damage than had Carl Perkins's wayward Chrysler. Owing greatly to the consequent moral outrage, Lewis would revisit the Top 40 only once more (via a thumping version of Ray Charles's *What'd I Say*) before leaving Sun in 1963. It was not until five years later that Jerry Lee – who, in a memorable religious colloquy with Sam Phillips, declared that "I've got the Devil in me" – would find earthly salvation through more subdued country recordings (in the manner of *Crazy Arms*, his first Sun release) for Mercury's Smash subsidiary in Nashville. He had come full circle.

The fact that Johnny Cash had disappeared before the impromptu Million Dollar Quartet session began in earnest is not without symbolic significance. For Cash, then in his second year at Sun Records, was obviously less afflicted by the rock-and-roll fever sweeping the nation. Yet his recent election to the Rock and Roll Hall of Fame confirms the "Man in Black's" lofty stature among rock as well as country followers.

Johnny Cash's more purely country style may be attributable to the absence of blacks in the rural Arkansas farmland where he was born (in 1932) and raised. During his four years in the Air Force, Cash cultivated an early interest in music by joining a group and starting to write songs. Following his discharge in 1954, he got a job in Memphis as an appliance salesman. That door-to-door exercise in futility apparently provided all the encouragement Cash needed to pursue his musical aspirations. Through a brother, he was introduced to Marshall Grant and Luther Perkins – the future "Tennessee Two" on whom Cash would rely for instrumental support in his Sun recordings. A representative sample of that enduring body of work is available in **Johnny Cash: The Sun Years** (1955–8).

Even by traditional country standards, the sound of Johnny Cash was exceedingly austere. Almost invariably, its foundation lay in an insistent "boom-chicka-boom" pattern constructed of his acoustic rhythm guitar (with a piece of paper woven between the neck and strings to create a percussive effect), Grant's straightforward bass, and Perkins's methodical single-string backing on electric guitar. True to form, Sam Phillips resisted ornamentation of this unimposing three-piece framework. To his discerning ear, it served to spotlight the commanding aura and tone of Cash's untrained baritone/bass. That Phillips was correct in this regard is demonstrated not only by such compelling narratives as *Folsom Prison Blues* and *Rock Island Line*, but also by such rockabilly-flavored tracks as *Get Rhythm* (which reveals a creeping blues influence).

Toward the end of 1957, in an apparent attempt to recapture the pop market invaded by Cash's haunting *I Walk The Line* the year before, new recording supervisor Jack Clement ushered in additional instruments and – in a serious breach of rockabilly decorum – background vocals. These touches paid commercial dividends in Cash's recordings of Clement's *Ballad Of A Teenage Queen* and *Guess Things Happen That Way*. While even the incongruous *Teenage Queen* retains considerable charm, the overall results were less artistically satisfying than those achieved in Phillips's sparser productions.

Upon the expiration of his contract with Sun in 1958, Johnny Cash commenced a 28-year affiliation with Columbia Records. (More on Cash's later years in the "Basic" listings of this chapter.) During that period he continued to explore the trains, rivers, prisons, and other thematic inspirations for his Sun material. Indeed, much of that material would be re-recorded and help to establish him as the personification of country music around the world. Yet, significantly, Johnny Cash's later work – like that of Elvis Presley, Carl Perkins, and Jerry Lee Lewis – would always be measured against his seminal records bearing the bright Sun logo.

Discographical Details

4 Elvis Presley: The Complete Sun Sessions CD

Elvis Presley
RCA 6414–2–R
That's All Right/Blue Moon Of Kentucky/Good Rockin' Tonight/I Don't Care If The Sun Don't Shine/Milk Cow Blues Boogie/You're A Heartbreaker/Baby, Let's Play House/I'm Left, You're Right, She's Gone/Mystery Train/I Forgot To Remember To Forget/I Love You Because/Blue Moon/Tomorrow Night/I'll Never Let You Go (Little Darlin')/Just Because/Trying To Get To You
Outtakes: *Harbor Lights/I Love You Because/That's All Right/Blue Moon Of Kentucky/I Don't Care If The Sun Don't Shine/I'm Left, You're Right, She's Gone (My Baby's Gone)/I'll Never Let You Go (Little Darlin')/When It Rains, It Really Pours*
Alternate takes: *I Love You Because/I'm Left, You're Right, She's Gone (My Baby's Gone)*

215   Carl Perkins: Original Sun Greatest Hits

Carl Perkins

Rhino R2 75890 (USA)

*Blue Suede Shoes/Honey, Don't/Boppin' The Blues/Everybody's Trying To Be
My Baby/Movie Magg/Sure To Fall/All Mama's Children/Put Your Cat
Clothes On/Matchbox/Your True Love/Lend Me Your Comb/Dixie Fried/You
Can Do No Wrong/Glad All Over/Perkins' Wiggle/Gone, Gone, Gone*

216   Jerry Lee Lewis: Original Sun Greatest Hits

Jerry Lee Lewis

Rhino R2 70255 (USA)

*Whole Lotta Shakin' Goin' On/Great Balls Of Fire/Breathless/High School
Confidential/What'd I Say/Drinkin' Wine Spo-Dee-O-Dee/Matchbox/Jamba-
laya/When The Saints Go Marchin' In/Lewis Boogie/It'll Be Me/All Night
Long/Big Blon' Baby/Crazy Arms/Ubangi Stomp/Big-Legged Woman/Put Me
Down/Wild One*

217   Johnny Cash: The Sun Years

Johnny Cash

Rhino R2 70950 (USA)

*Folsom Prison Blues/Hey, Porter/I Walk The Line/Get Rhythm/Guess Things
Happen That Way/Rock Island Line/Home Of The Blues/Big River/Come In,
Stranger/Train Of Love/There You Go/Ballad Of A Teenage Queen/So
Doggone Lonesome/The Ways Of A Woman In Love/Luther Played The Boogie/
Mean-Eyed Cat/Next In Line/Give My Love To Rose*

(ii) The Women of the 1950s and 1960s

Often referred to as "the Queen of Country Music," in recognition of her status as country's first *bona fide* female star and
her long reign in the charts (from 1952, well into the 1970s),
Kitty Wells was the first artist to give legitimacy to the
woman's perspective in country.

It's telling that Wells (real name Muriel Ellen Deason, born
in Nashville, Tennessee, 1919) actually began her recording
career as a shy back-up singer in a group fronted by her
husband, Johnnie Wright (who, along with Jack Anglin, would
later enjoy fleeting chart success as the popular duo, Johnnie
and Jack – see "Basic Recordings" in this chapter). For that
matter, Wells seemed perfectly content working in Wright's
shadow, and it was only at his behest that she later ventured
tentatively into the solo spotlight.

Wells first tested the waters on her own in 1949 and the very
early fifties, recording for RCA. She had no great expectations,
and when these sides went unnoticed, she quietly went back to
raising her and Wright's three children and singing with her
husband Johnnie (and sometimes Jack, as well) on Sundays.

Years later, guitarist/producer Chet Atkins, who produced Wells's RCA sessions, speculated as to why things did not click for Wells her first time around, with RCA: "You know record companies; they'll record a mule braying if they think it will sell," Atkins observed. "It wasn't because they had any prejudice against women [that they didn't record or promote many of them]. They just didn't think they could make any money off them. No one ever had in the past, and in those days women were confined by conformity."

Indeed, America was deep in the throes of ultra-conformity, McCarthy-style political repression, and artistic somnambulism as it entered the post-war era of the fifties. This was an age when the entire nation – or nearly the entire nation – held almost unswaying faith in the rightness of industrial progress, nuclear power, the nuclear family, and "The American Way." The credo of the age was that it was a man's world and the woman's place was in the home.

Yet beneath the placid, ultra-conformist surface of things, the fifties was an age of rampant social turbulence, and hypocrisy: a time when traditional assumptions about women's proscribed social roles were subtly beginning to change – mainly through women themselves. During World War II, millions of American women had joined the work force as part of the war effort while their husbands were overseas; thus they'd had a taste of economic independence and the freedom that comes with it. Consequently, many discovered restlessness and discontentment when they went back to the domestic dreariness of housewifery in a male-dominated post-war world. And by the mid-1950s, US divorce and alcoholism rates were burgeoning past all historic precedents. Quite naturally, this discontentment, disillusionment, and malaise bubbled out in the music of the day (particularly 1950s honky-tonk music, which was more or less spawned by rural America's rampant post-war culture shock and insecurity).

Ironically, Kitty Wells, a seemingly content church-going Southern home-maker and faithful wife was, if anything, the antithesis of the "liberated" 1950s woman. In fact, it was once again only because of her husband's insistence that she make another run at recording that she returned to the studio, this time recording for Decca Records.

Thus it was that the reticent, prim, and proper Wells almost unwittingly contributed a woman's voice to the male-dominated 1950s honky-tonk/country movement with songs that candidly addressed timely themes like infidelity (*I Hear The Jukebox Playing*), divorce (*Will Your Lawyer Talk To God*), single parenthood (*Mommy For A Day*), and bitter romantic disillusionment (*Icicles Hanging From Your Heart*). These topics, at least up until then, had been almost exclusively the domain of male singers.

The social constraints of the era being what they were, Wells's message was made all the more palatable and persuasive by her low-key, thoroughly down-home and unpresumptuous vocal style. When she sang, she intimated heartbreak and resignation, rather than anger or rebellion. She even conveyed a sense of innocence, tainted but not quite lost. All in all, she would serve as a contrast to the styles of those who would soon follow along the trail she blazed: the urbane brassiness of Patsy Cline, the boisterous, good-natured sass of Loretta Lynn.

Kitty Wells first connected with national radio audiences in a big way when *It Wasn't God That Made Honky Tonk Angels* (written by country promoter/songwriter J.D. Miller) became a number 1 hit in 1952. *Angels* was an "answer" song to Hank Thompson's *The Wild Side Of Life*. It not only shared the same melody (which resulted in the inevitable copyright infringement suit), but also spoke up in defense of the fallen woman who'd been maligned and chastised in Thompson's popular honky-tonk anthem of romantic betrayal.

Yet even when Wells – always the shrinking violet – recorded *It Wasn't God Who Made Honky Tonk Angels* – in May, 1952 at the old Castle Studio in Nashville's Tulane Hotel – she had no high hopes for it. She'd enjoyed Thompson's *The Wild Side Of Life*, and it had never occurred to her that it might need an "answer." Mainly, she was just figuring on recording a few sides for Decca, then once again going back to her quiet domestic life. "I said, 'Well, it probably won't make a hit, but we will at least get a session fee ($125 union scale) out of it,' " she later recalled.

Much to Wells's surprise, *It Wasn't God Who Made Honky Tonk Angels* topped the country charts. It eventually sold a million copies, and launched one of the most celebrated careers in post-war country music.

Kitty Wells: Country Music Hall Of Fame is – like most all the historic collections in MCA's "Hall Of Fame" series (compiled in conjunction with the Country Music Foundation) – a well-balanced, scrupulously annotated single-CD collection of Wells's vintage recordings. (Bear Family Records' far more prodigious, ambitious – and expensive – 95-song **Kitty Wells: The Golden Years (1949–1957)** (BFX 15239) gathers all Wells's early work in one hefty boxed set.)

The 16 selections on **Kitty Wells: Country Music Hall Of Fame** span nearly a decade and a half of her recording career – from her 1952 debut hit, *It Wasn't God Who Made Honky Tonk Angels*, to *A Woman Half My Age*, a bitter lament she recorded 13 years later. These 16 songs also chronicle her slow stylistic drift from prototypical honky-tonk queen to relatively staid practitioner of Nashville-sound balladry.

The lush background vocals of the famed Jordanaires can even be heard on two cuts from the very late 1950s and early 1960s – *Amigo's Guitar* and *Password*. These tracks present quite a contrast to the instrumental austerity of *It Wasn't God Who Made Honky Tonk Angels*, which was produced by Owen Bradley. (Bradley, in later years, would also produce Patsy Cline, Loretta Lynn, and even 1980s Patsy Cline disciple, k. d. lang.) *Angels*, one of quite a few "answer" songs that Wells recorded, features the sparse honky-tonk instrumentation played by a core of musicians who often backed up Wells and Wright on the road. Most notable of these is Shot Jackson on steel guitar.

Included in this collection, along with songs by many of the leading country writers of the fifties and sixties (Harlan Howard, Buck Owens, John D. Loudermilk, and Boudleaux and Felice Bryant) are Wells's versions of two of the most enduring standards in country music: Eddie Miller's *Release Me*, and Don Gibson's *I Can't Stop Loving You*, which hit the Top 10 for Wells in 1958.

Wells's success may not have opened a floodgate, but it clearly did open the door for another woman whose pervasive influence is still felt today: Patsy Cline, who died in a plane crash at age 30, in 1963, just as she was beginning to blossom into a national country, and pop, star.

The power of Cline's music, since her untimely death three decades ago, instead of diminishing, has grown by leaps and bounds. Today, the legacy of this "country girl with a pop voice" has become a yardstick by which the talents of all women who've come since are sooner or later measured. It's further testimony to Cline's enduring appeal that her records still sell hundreds of thousands of units a year – far more than they did in her too-brief lifetime. At a recent count, nearly 40 different compilations of her music were available on CD.

Cline, simply put, possessed a voice so amazingly vibrant, sensual, and melismatic – an alluring mix of disarming boldness dulcet nuance, and sultry innocence – that she was able to unselfconsciously bridge the narrow stylistic parameters that segregated 1950s country from mainstream pop. It is a tribute to the loftiness of her talent that she was also able to similarly transcend the constraints routinely placed on female country singers of her era in a male-dominated industry. (For all the enduring power of her recordings, Cline, at the time, had little or no say in choosing or arranging her own material.) Cline not only prevailed but flourished amidst the slick, corporate-conscious, producer-dominated era of the "Nashville sound," which, in attempting to refine many country artists for the pop audience, ended up stuffing them into ill-fitting stylistic boxes.

As Paul Kingsbury of the Country Music Foundation observed in his salient liner notes to **The Patsy Cline Collection** (MCAD 4–10421), a magnificent, all-inclusive – albeit costly – 104-track survey of Cline's recording career (1954–63):

> Patsy Cline came along in an opportune time in the history of country music. Kitty Wells, the first great woman country star, blazed a trail for her in the early 1950s, demonstrating once and for all that women could sell country records. Patsy would also cross over to the pop charts, thanks to Hank Williams, who paved the way with his songs. Thus, the public accepted Patsy as country *and* pop in the way that few performers since have been accepted.

Cline (real name: Virginia Patterson Hensley) was born in 1932 in Winchester, a small city in northern Virginia's Shenandoah Valley. Oddly enough, she attributed her larger-than-life vocal prowess to a near-fatal illness she suffered early in life. "In childhood, I developed a serious throat infection and my heart stopped beating," she told a Washington, DC, newspaper reporter years ago. "I was placed in an oxygen tent and the doctors brought me back to life. I recovered from the illness with a voice that boomed forth like Kate Smith's."

From a very early age, Cline never missed an opportunity to sing, or perform (as a tap dancer). She possessed as much chutzpah and self-confidence as she did talent; and while still in her early teens, she talked her way into an audition for a local country radio show and ended up as a regular performer on the program.

When her father, an itinerant blacksmith and mechanic, deserted his wife and three children, the burden of helping her mother support the family devolved to Patsy, the oldest child. She quit school and balanced a day job in a Winchester drug store with singing pop songs by night in a supper club in nearby Front Royal, Virginia.

When Grand Ole Opry star Wally Fowler made an appearance in the Winchester area, the young and unusually aggressive Cline bluffed her way into an audition with him. Fowler was impressed enough to give her a regular slot on his touring show and also took her along when he returned to Nashville.

Though Cline managed to sing on WSM-Radio in Nashville, her initial attempts to break into the Grand Ole Opry and land a recording contract went for naught. She returned to Winchester, disappointed, but undaunted.

Back home, she persisted with her singing – in local clubs

and talent shows and on radio. Some of her earliest surviving recordings are, in fact, radio transcriptions from around this time. These include competent but essentially derivative covers of Webb Pierce's *I'm Walkin' The Dog* and Kitty Wells's *It Wasn't God Who Made Honky Tonk Angels*. These transcriptions (included in **The Patsy Cline Collection**) not only show her nascent roots in 1950s honky-tonk (which she would drift away from as her recording career unfolded); they also demonstrate the stark contrast between her smooth yet uninhibited style and her predecessor Kitty Wells's subdued, maundering vocalizations.

By the mid-1950s, Cline's persistence in pursuing her dreams of a big-time recording career at last paid dividends. She landed a contract with 4 Star Records, and, in 1961, with Decca (now MCA), and – no less important – a spot on "Arthur Godfrey's Talent Scouts," a nationally televised musical variety show. She performed *Walkin' After Midnight* on Godfrey's show, an obscure song that had been passed over by numerous artists before it was brought to her. She buried Godfrey's "applause meter," received a standing ovation from the sound crew, and became an instant favorite with the TV-gazing millions. *Walkin' After Midnight* soon became a hit in both the country and pop charts, and a new crossover star was born.

1962 proved a banner year for Cline, in terms of chart success. *Crazy* (a Willie Nelson composition, which she also turned into a pop-country standard) hit the Top 10, and *I Fall To Pieces* – another definitive Cline recording – became her first number 1 record. In 1963, *Sweet Dreams* – yet another lovely song that has since become a Cline hallmark – reached number 5 in the charts, just weeks after her untimely death.

The selections on **12 Greatest Hits** (one of dozens of reissues and compilations of Cline's work that MCA currently has on the market, and perhaps the best single-CD collection available) displays the full range of power, emotion, and nuance that make her early 1960s recordings such milestones in country music history. This set includes a half-dozen of her most famous recordings, as well as some lesser known, but no less worthy selections.

Discographical Details

Kitty Wells: Country Music Hall Of Fame

Kitty Wells
MCA MCAD-10081
*It Wasn't God Who Made Honky Tonk Angels/I Heard The Jukebox Playing/
Icicles Hanging From Your Heart/My Cold, Cold Heart Is Melted Now/I Gave
My Wedding Dress Away/Release Me/Making Believe/I'd Rather Stay Home/*

Searching (For Someone Like You)/I Can't Stop Loving You/Mommy For A Day/Amigo's Guitar/Heartbreak, USA/Will Your Lawyer Talk To God/ Password/A Woman Half My Age

219   12 Greatest Hits

Patsy Cline
MCA MCAD-12
Walkin' After Midnight/Sweet Dreams (Of You)/Crazy/I Fall To Pieces/So Wrong/Strange/Back In Baby's Arms/She's Got You/Faded Love/Why Can't He Be You/You're Stronger Than Me/Leavin' On Your Mind

(iii) Kings of 1950s and 1960s Country

Known throughout his long career as "the Singing Ranger," Hank Snow was the first Canadian-born singer to become a major star in the US charts. Snow, as a youngster, cut his musical teeth listening to his mother's Vernon Dalhart and Jimmie Rodgers's records, and began his own career as a Rodgers disciple of sorts. Yet American-made western movies also had an indelible impact on Snow. "America . . . always I just loved the sound," the singer once recalled. "I would go to any movie when I lived in Canada if it showed anything of America. Texas was always big on my mind. I wrote a lot of songs about Texas, you know. I'd read about those places, seen them in the movies."

Snow was born Clarence Eugene Snow in the village of Brooklyn, in Nova Scotia, in 1914. His parents divorced when he was eight, and that effectively spelled an end to his child-hood innocence. ("I never had a childhood," he once lamented.) When Snow's mother remarried he found himself at the mercy of a step-father who physically abused him and tried to crush his nascent musical ambitions. "I was treated by him, mildly speaking, like a dog," Snow told country music historian Charles K. Wolfe in an early 1990s interview. "I took many beatings from him and still carry scars across my back from his ham-like hands."

To escape from this familial tyranny, Snow ran off and became a cabin boy on a fishing schooner that trawled for squid and scallops in the North Atlantic, off the Grand Banks of New Foundland. To while away the off-hours, he began singing and playing guitar and harmonica to entertain the ship's crew. Much to his surprise, his efforts were enthusiastically received. Later, back ashore, he worked as a dockside stevedore and a door-to-door salesman who rewarded his paying customers by serenading them with a song.

Modeling himself heavily on the "blue yodeling" style of Jimmie Rodgers, Snow kicked around the US and Canada for quite a few years with only fair-to-middlin' success. (He sang and played everywhere from Halifax to Hollywood, where he made an unsuccessful stab at breaking into western movies.)

It was with the help of Texas honky-tonk troubadour Ernest Tubb, (another devout Jimmie Rodgers disciple) that Snow finally managed to catch the ear of the management of Nashville's Grand Ole Opry (where, on his debut appearance, he was introduced by none other than Hank Williams). But, as he later explained to Charles Wolfe, the Opry looked like just one more dead-end street when he first stepped out on its hallowed stage in the very early 1950s. "I don't mind telling you I bombed," he recalled. "The people just sat there while I sang. And sat. No applause, no nothing, almost. Just sat."

Snow, despite this inauspicious start, would go on to become one of the most enduring and revered figures on the Opry. (As of this writing he's still performing there.) He'd also begun recording for RCA Victor in Canada as early as 1936; and, by 1949, he'd made his first recordings in the US (in Chicago, and later, Nashville). His first significant showing in the American country charts came in 1949 with a sentimental ode to matrimony called *Marriage Vow*. In mid-1950, Snow had his first number 1 with the self-penned *I'm Movin' On*, a rambling "train" song, propelled by a rowdy, insistent beat that has become a country standard as well as Snow's "signature song." (*I'm Movin' On* has been covered over the years by dozens of artists, even the early Rolling Stones, and the song still earns Snow standing ovations on the Grand Ole Opry after all these years.)

The 20-song **Hank Snow: I'm Movin' On And Other Great Country Hits** gathers many of Snow's crowning chart successes from the 1950s, along with a handful of lesser-known cuts – like *Silver Bell*, an instrumental done with guitarist Chet Atkins; *When Jimmie Rodgers Said Goodbye*, Snow's salute to his musical idol; and *Down The Trail Of Achin' Hearts*, a soulful, old-timey duet with Anita Carter of the revered Carter Family. *Rhumba Boogie* (one of many "country-boogies" inspired by the "jitterbug" dance craze of Snow's era) is a lively, syncopated tribute to American dance music and its many regional variations. *The Wreck Of The Old '97* (an old public domain song originally recorded by Snow's childhood hero Vernon Dalhart in 1924) demonstrates (as does *Movin' On*) how effectively Snow (like Jimmie Rodgers before him and Johnny Cash in years to come) captured America's enduring fascination with the lore of the steel rails, as well as the nation's eagerness to find endless metaphors for its own turbulent history in sagas of long-ago railroad disasters.

On many of the recordings in this passably well-rounded

sampling of Snow's vast body of work (he's recorded more than 840-odd sides in his long career) Snow's droll vocal bravado is augmented by his talented backup hand, the Rainbow Ranch Boys.

Eddy Arnold was one of the true kings of the early country crooners and one of the forerunners of the country-pop fusion that would coalesce as the 1950s and 1960s Nashville sound. Arnold's rural roots were as genuine as those of the most down-home honky-tonk singer. (He was born in 1918 on a hardscrabble West Tennessee farm that was lost to foreclosure after his father's death in 1929, on the eve of the Great Depression.) Yet, as a youngster, he was as unabashedly influenced by pop-crooning icon Bing Crosby as he was by singing cowboy Gene Autry (who was himself a Crosby aficionado)

By 1935, when he was 17, Arnold was already performing with local country bands around the West Tennessee city of Jackson. Eventually his easy, mellow vocal style landed him a job as lead singer and front man with 1940s bandleader and noted country tunesmith Pee Wee King (of *Tennessee Waltz* fame). Within a few years, Arnold also signed with RCA Records and became a popular performer on Nashville's Grand Ole Opry, which was something akin to the Promised Land for every aspiring country star of the 1940s and 1950s. (The Opry's powerful clear-channel AM signal on Radio-WSM beamed all throughout the south, and into parts of Canada, thereby affording vast exposure to those lucky enough to be heard on it.)

Arnold's mellow, refined, and subdued singing style made him a stark contrast to dedicatedly twangy, home-fried Opry stars of the day like Ernest Tubb and Roy Acuff. His fame burgeoned (with career record sales in excess of 80 million, he remains one of country music's all-time biggest sellers). In fact, by the late 1940s, he'd established such a large and devoted following that he ventured to do what few artists before him had dared: with an eye toward the pop market, he resigned from the Opry to graze in more wide-open musical pastures.

By the mid-1960s, after watching artists like former Texas honky-tonker Ray Price find renewed popularity as easy-listening, Nashville sound crooners, Arnold himself plunged back into the country-pop fray and stylistically took the trend a step further. Specializing in romantic ballads marked by lush string and choral arrangements and even full-orchestra accompaniments, Arnold – more than any other single artist – put country music in a tuxedo, stylistically speaking. His sophisticated warbling (which often seemed to owe vastly more to Perry Como and Dean Martin than to Hank Williams or Webb Pierce) spoke of affluence, maturity, and romantic *ennui* amidst material affluence. (If a man like Roy Acuff sang to the poor white dirt farmer, then Arnold particularly as time went by sang more to the farmer's son, who'd gotten himself a good education, landed a well-paying "sit down" job in the city, and moved into a plush ranch house in a new subdivision near the old family farm.) In the 1960s Arnold's style also appealed mightily to older borderline country-pop fans who felt alienated by a national music scene then dominated by the youthful, priapic, high-decibel threat of invading British rockers like the Beatles and the Rolling Stones. Arnold enjoyed massive success with songs like *Make The World Go Away*, *You Don't Know Me*, *What's He Doin' In My World*, and *Misty Blue*, which, aside from the fact that they were hits in the country charts were (as often as not) indistinguishable from pop music.

Aside from a few periodic slumps when the inevitable swinging pendulum of public taste put his crooning out of favor, Arnold remained a dominant force in the country charts during the 1950s and 1960s, and has continued recording even into the early 1990s.

The debate will forever rage as to when America heard the *real* Eddy Arnold; hardcore country believers much prefer his earthier recordings of the 1940s and the early 1950s. Yet the success he achieved in the 1960s with much glossier and more uptown material made him one of the true giants of the Nashville sound, as well as one of the most commercially successful and enduringly popular Nashville artists of all time.

One would not expect to attain anonymity in country music circles if he had: (1) married June Carter of the legendary Carter Family and sired a frisky daughter, Carlene, who has since become a country star in her own right; (2) been a member of the Grand Ole Opry before it degenerated into commercial insignificance; (3) appeared regularly on television and in two movies; and (4) sold some 15 million country records in a career spanning three decades.

However, abetted by an entertainment industry whose grasp of history seldom extends beyond last week's number 1 party, Carl Smith has seemingly accomplished this feat since retiring to his ranch in Williamson County, Tennessee, less than 20 years ago. That Smith is largely forgotten is all the more remarkable inasmuch as a number of the songs he popularized during his 1950s heyday have been successfully revived by such artists as Mickey Gilley (*I Overlooked An Orchid*) and Gail Davies (*It's A Lovely, Lovely World*).

Born March 15, 1927 in Maynardville, Tennessee, Carl Smith served his musical apprenticeship on the same Knoxville radio circuit which spawned such luminaries as Chet Atkins, and Johnnie and Jack. In early 1950, a field representative for a prominent Nashville music publisher directed samples of Smith's work to the attention of WSM and Columbia Records in Nashville. Following a showdown in which each of these heavyweights waited for the other to make a move, Smith procured a recording contract as well as a slot on the Grand Ole Opry.

The Essential Carl Smith focuses on the singer's peak period from 1950 until 1956, when he forsook Nashville for the greater exposure which motion pictures and television shows afforded. In retrospect, Smith can be seen as a key transitional figure: his sliding drawl and traditional accompaniment reflect the profound honky-tonk influence of Ernest Tubb and Hank Williams; but also readily discernible in his style is a degree of refinement and sophistication, foreshadowing the Nashville sound that would be manufactured by Music Row producers and executives as an antidote to the untamed fury of rock-and-roll.

Though Johnny Sibert's sinewy steel guitar is featured throughout these tracks, they are noticeably lacking in fiddles. In fact, two other players in Carl's "Tunesmiths" band – bassist Junior Huskey and, later, drummer Buddy Harman – would become pillars of the Nashville sound as studio musicians.

Represented in this collection is a veritable all-star cast of songwriters. Undeniably, Carl Smith's musical legacy stands on a bedrock of forlorn love ballads like the Louvin Brothers' *Are You Teasin' Me* and Eddie Miller's *There She Goes*. Yet, with seeming effortlessness, his supple voice also conveys all the spirit and verve of Ernest Tubb's *(When You Feel Like You're In Love) Don't Just Stand There* (Smith's first number 1 hit, released in 1951), Freddie Hart's *Loose Talk*, and Boudleaux Bryant's *Hey Joe!* (Indeed, *Go, Boy, Go* – recorded shortly before Elvis Presley's debut on Sun – approaches the formidable punch of primal rockabilly.) In *Trademark*, an early Porter Wagoner composition, Smith even weaves a bluesy spell reinforced by Grady Martin's electric guitar lines.

It is fitting that this 20-song set concludes with Leon Payne's timeless *You Are The One*, which was also included in Smith's daughter Carlene's fine 1991 "comeback" album, **I Fell In Love**. For, in view of his graceful withdrawal from the microphone, it is on the supremely talented (and ever-quotable) Carlene that hopes for future appreciation of her father's vital but sadly overlooked contributions to country music may rest.

Few artists of his era – or any era – could so effortlessly, yet convincingly cover such a broad stylistic range as Marty Robbins. Though Robbins's musical heyday was in the 1950s and 1960s, he remained a vital recording artist almost up to the time of his death, in 1982. Through the years, Robbins enjoyed success (as both a singer and songwriter) with everything from winsome teenage country-pop ballads (*A White Sport Coat (And A Pink Carnation)*, *Singin' The Blues*), to cowboy/gunfighter ballads (*Big Iron* and *El Paso* – the first country song to win a Grammy Award). He made occasional forays into honky-tonk (His *Smokin' Cigarettes And Drinkin' Coffee Blues* was a hit for Lefty Frizzell in 1958 and a hit for Robbins himself in 1963.) And he even ventured into pop-jazz (*September In The Rain*), Hawaiian music (*The Hawaiian Wedding Song, Beyond The Reef*), and rockabilly. (His 1954 cover of Arthur Crudup's *That's All Right (Mama)* was a country hit after Elvis Presley had already scored in the charts with it just a few months earlier.)

Marty Robbins was born in 1925 in the desert near Glendale, Arizona, one of eight children. When his father, an itinerant worker of Polish extraction, went too long between jobs, the family sometimes ended up living in a tent. "We were about as poor as you could get," he recalled later in life. "I know what it's like to be laughed at because your shoes don't have soles on them."

Robbins's mother was of mixed European, Mexican, and Paiute Indian extraction; and one of the few bright spots in his otherwise grim childhood was the influence of his maternal grandfather, a former Texas Ranger and medicine show performer named Texas Bob Heckle. It was Heckle who instilled an abiding love of the Old West and its music in his wayward grandson.

Though he idolized Heckle, Robbins harbored no such fond memories of his father, who separated from his mother when he was 12. ("He had a bad temper, he'd whip me for nothin . . . I'm not sure whatever became of him.") From an early age, Robbins was left to fend for himself. He picked cotton, dug irrigation ditches for ten cents an hour, herded goats in the Arizona's Bradshaw Mountains, and was repeatedly kicked out of school for brawling, truancy and petty thievery. As a youth, he logged more than 70 bouts as an amateur boxer, but admitted that he did most of his fighting outside the ring. After he beat another boy badly enough to require hospitalization, and after falling under the local sheriff's department's scrutiny as a suspect in a series of unsolved petty crimes, Robbins fled Glendale to avoid arrest.

He ended up serving three years with the US Navy in the South Pacific during World War II, and it was there that he learned to play guitar. Yet back in Arizona, after the war, he was plagued by aimlessness, and a marked aversion to the 40-hour work week. "I tried everything," he later recalled. "I worked on a water-rigging team, I delivered ice, I drove a brick truck. At one point, I had eight jobs in six months and quit them all."

His musical career, for all its eventual greatness, started

inauspiciously. "I heard this guy singing on the radio (on KTYL in Phoenix) and it dawned on me that, hell, I could do better than that." After an audition – in which he sang *Strawberry Roan*, an old cowboy folk song – the station manager fired the other singer and hired Robbins. Soon he was cutting his musical teeth playing Phoenix's rough and tumble beer joints and roadhouses.

The stylistic range that would distinguish Robbins as a recording artist surfaced early, though at first it merely signaled more a lack of musical direction than sheer versatility: "[Back then] I did everything," he recalled. "Perry Como songs, western songs, Ernest Tubb songs, Roy Acuff, Eddy Arnold. Everybody's songs."

In 1951, Grand Ole Opry star Little Jimmy Dickens came through Phoenix and heard Robbins sing when he dropped by Radio KPHO, where Robbins was then performing. Dickens was impressed enough to arrange an audition for Robbins with his label, Columbia. The audition resulted in a recording session for Robbins; but when a producer involved in the session tried to coerce Robbins into signing over to him half the writing credits (and royalties) on his original songs (an extortion tactic used on young recording artists even today), Robbins nearly walked out, until the producer relented. "At the time, it just didn't mean anything to me to record. I wasn't concerned."

The Essential Marty Robbins: 1951–1982 is an exemplary and excellently annotated 50-song, 2-CD summary of Robbins's long-running career, which flourished right up until his death, which came at age 57, after a 13-year history of congenital heart problems. This outstanding collection gathers not only Robbins's most significant and representative chart-toppers, but also quite a few lesser known album cuts that draw out his lifelong flair for innovation and his restless and inspired musical explorations.

For a far more lavish sampling of the ever-prolific Robbins's early recordings, there is also Bear Family's 5-CD **Marty Robbins: Country, 1951–58** (BCD 15570 EH).

Discographical Details

220   I'm Movin' On And Other Great Country Hits

Hank Snow

RCA 9968–2-R

I'm Movin' On/Marriage Vow/The Rhumba Boogie/With This Ring I Thee Wed/Down The Trail Of Achin' Hearts/The Golden Rocket/Stolen Moments/ Unwanted Sign Upon Your Heart/Wreck Of The Old '97/Silver Bell/I Don't Hurt Anymore/Music-Makin' Mama From Memphis/My Mother/Would You Mind/When Jimmie Rodgers Said Goodbye/The Gold Rush Is Over/The Gal Who Invented Kissin'/Let Me Go, Lover/Spanish Fire Ball/One More Ride

21   Eddy Arnold: A Legendary Performer

Eddy Arnold
RCA CPL2-4885 (2-LP set)
Anytime/How's The World Treating You/Molly Darling/That's How Much I Love You/Mommy, Please Stay Home With Me/Did it Rain/I'll Hold You In My Heart (Till I Can Hold You In My Arms)/Just Call Me Lonesome/I Really Don't Want To Know/The Kentuckian Song/(Jim) I Wore A Tie Today/Cattle Call/The Lovebug Itch/Tennessee Stud/You Don't Know Me/ That Do Make It Nice/I'm A Good Boy/Though Your Sins Be As Scarlet/Just Out Of Reach/After Loving You/Make The World Go Away/The Last Word In Lonesome Is Me/In The Misty Moonlight/My Sweet Lord

22   The Essential Carl Smith, 1950–1956

Carl Smith
Columbia/Legacy CD 47996
Guilty Conscience/I Just Dropped In To Say Goodbye/I Overlooked An Orchid/ If Teardrops Were Pennies/Let's Live A Little/(When You Feel Like You're In Love) Don't Just Stand There/Let Old Mother Nature Have Her Way/It's A Lovely, Lovely World/Are You Teasing Me/This Orchid Means Goodbye/Hey, Joe!/Trademark/Just Wait Till I Get You Alone/Dog-Gone It Baby, I'm In Love/Back Up, Buddy/Go, Boy, Go/Loose Talk/Kisses Don't Lie/There She Goes/You Are The One

23   The Essential Marty Robbins: 1951–82

Marty Robbins
Columbia C2K 48537 (2-disc set)
Tomorrow You'll Be Gone/I'll Go On Alone/I Couldn't Keep From Crying/Pain And Misery/That's All Right/Maybellene/Tennessee Toddy/I Can't Quit/ Singing The Blues/Knee Deep In The Blues/Mister Teardrop/The Story Of My Life/A White Sport Coat (And A Pink Carnation)/She Was Only Seventeen (He Was One Year More)/Just Married/Ain't I The Lucky One/Kaw-Liga/ The Hanging Tree/El Paso/Big Iron/Song Of The Bandit/Cool Water/A Little Sentimental/September In The Rain/All The Way/Unchained Melody/Don't Worry/Devil Woman/Ruby Ann/Smokin' Cigarettes And Drinkin' Coffee Blues/ I'm Gonna Be A Cowboy/(Ghost) Riders In The Sky/San Angelo/Man Walks Among Us/Beautiful Dreamer/Beyond The Reef/The Hawaiian Wedding Song/ Yours (Quiereme Mucho)/Tonight Carmen/Ribbon Of Darkness/Feleena (From El Paso)/Hello Heartache/Begging To You/I Walk Alone/You Gave Me A Mountain/My Woman, My Woman, My Wife/Among My Souvenirs/Return To Me/Some Memories Just Won't Die/El Paso City

Basic Recordings

Rockabilly

24   Rockin' In The Country

Wanda Jackson
Rhino R2 70990
Let's Have A Party/Honey Bop/Baby Loves Him/Hot Dog! That Made Him Mad/Mean Mean Man/Cool Love/Riot In Cell Block No. 9/Fujiyama Mama/

Savin' My Love/Why I'm Walkin'/Right Or Wrong/Tears Will Be The Chaser For Your Wine/In The Middle Of A Heartache/Fancy Satin Pillows/My Big Iron Skillet/The Box It Came In/A Girl Don't Have To Drink To Have Fun/ Making Believe

Oklahoma teenager Wanda Jackson had experienced only modest success in the country field when she was encouraged by Elvis Presley to enter the rockabilly fray. Aided by such stellar musicians as Joe Maphis and Buck Owens, she proceeded to rock Hollywood's Capitol Tower with some of the genre's raspiest, sassiest sides. Alas, *Let's Have A Party* (originally performed by Elvis) marked Wanda's lone rockabilly hit; so she repaired to Nashville in 1961 and regularly visited the country charts over the next decade with tamer fare – notably *In The Middle Of A Heartache*, and her own *Right Or Wrong*.

225   The Best Of Conway Twitty – Vol. 1: The Rockin' Years

Conway Twitty
Mercury 849 574–2

I Need Your Lovin'/Maybe Baby/Shake It Up/Born To Sing The Blues/It's Only Make Believe/Halfway To Heaven/Lonely Blue Boy/Is A Blue Bird Blue/ Long Black Train/Got My Mojo Workin'/I Vibrate/Platinum High School/ Danny Boy/Mona Lisa/C'Est Si Bon/Comfy N' Cozy/What A Dream/What Am I Living For/It's Too Late/Looking Back

Before amassing his unequaled string of number 1 country hits, Conway Twitty (born Harold Jenkins in Friar's Point, Mississippi) enjoyed several years of rock-and-roll prosperity, beginning in 1958.

In this compilation, which includes four recordings for Mercury as well as most of Twitty's MGM successes, we hear the earliest applications of his theatrical growls and moans to big-beat ballads like his classic *It's Only Make Believe* and *Lonely Blue Boy*. As *Long Black Train* demonstrates, Twitty could also rock convincingly. Unfortunately, though, the impact of some of these tracks is diminished by strings and choruses – frequent intruders in second-generation rockabilly recordings.

226   Get Hot Or Go Home: Vintage RCA Rockabilly, '56–59

Various Artists
CMF-014-L

Joe Clay: *Duck Tail/Sixteen Chicks/Doggone It/Goodbye, Goodbye/Slipping Out And Sneaking In/Get On The Right Track/You Look That Good To Me/ Cracker Jack/Did You Mean Jelly Bean (What You Said Cabbage Head)*; Ric Cartey; *Ooh-Eee/Heart Throb/I Wancha To Know/Let Me Tell You About Love/Born To Love One Woman/Mellow Down Easy/My Babe*; Homer and Jethro: *Two Tone Shoes*; Pee Wee King: *Catty Town*; David Houston: *Sugar Sweet*; Tommy Blake and The Rhythm Rebels: *Honky Tonk Mind (Woman I Need)/All Night Long*; Martha Carson: *Now Stop*; Janis Martin: *Love Me To Pieces/Two Long Years/All Right, Baby*; Dave Rich: *Chicken House*; The Sprouts: *Teen Billy Baby*; Milton Allen: *Don't Bug Me, Baby*; Morgan Twins: *Let's Get Goin'*; Jimmy Dell: *Rainbow Doll*; Gordon Terry: *It Ain't Right*; Roy Orbison: *Almost Eighteen*; Hoyt Johnson: *Little Boy Blue*

Like other major labels, RCA Victor endeavoured to catch the rockabilly wave both by signing new acts and revving up country warhorses into rockabilly singers. As this carefully researched anthology reveals, Joe Clay and

Janis Martin stood out among RCA's recruits. Not all of the other artists sampled found their rockabilly "cat clothes" to be a good fit; but after acquiring the services of Elvis Presley, "the Nipper" (RCA) could obviously afford an occasional blunder.

Stars of the Grand Ole Opry and Other Country Innovators

27   Red Foley: Country Music Hall Of Fame

Red Foley
MCA MCAD-10084
Hang Your Head In Shame/Old Shep/Tennessee Saturday Night/Tennessee Border/Careless Kisses/Just A Closer Walk With Thee/Chattanoogie Shoeshine Boy/When God Dips His Love In My Heart/Don't Be Ashamed Of Your Age/ Peace In The Valley/Alabama Jubilee/Midnight/One By One/Deep Blues/As Far As I'm Concerned/Sugarfoot Rag

Red Foley's humble rural Kentucky origins (he was born in Blue Lick, in 1910) attested to his authentic country roots. Yet the classical voice training he received at Kentucky's Georgetown College would always set him a little apart from more rustic stars of his times; and he had some of his hits with straight pop tunes. His warm baritone, and his fondness for sentimental songs, made him eminently popular with Grand Ole Opry audiences of the 1940s and 1950s. His 1949 rendition of the oft-recorded *Chattanoogie Shoeshine Boy*, included here, was a million-seller.

28   "Little" Jimmy Dickens: Columbia Historical Edition

Little Jimmy Dickens
Columbia FC 38905 (LP)
Take An Old Cold Tater/I'll Be Back A-Sunday/I'm Little, But I'm Loud/The Last Time/I May Be Silly (But Ain't It Fun)/Out Behind The Barn/Slow Suicide/I Wish You Didn't Love Me So Much/The Tramp On The Street/John Henry/Salty Boogie

Dickens, a long-time member of the Grand Ole Opry, is best remembered for his novelty songs and was overshadowed by more versatile contemporaries like Roy Acuff and Hank Snow. But, as this volume (which features Dickens's novelty side, as well as a more serious side – highlighted by his version of an obscure Hank Williams song and several previously unissued late 1940s and early 1950s tracks) demonstrates, he was an important – if eccentric – talent in his heyday.

29   The Best Of Porter Wagoner

Porter Wagoner
RCA CS 61089-4 (cassette)
Green, Green Grass Of Home/Misery Loves Company/Dooley/Uncle Pen/Company's Comin'/I Thought I Heard You Call My Name/Skid Row Joe

It's hard to figure why a label would even bother to release such a meager (7-cut) "hits" package on an artist as talented and representative of his times as longtime Grand Ole Opry star Porter Wagoner (whose biggest claim in the minds of less historically informed country fans is as Dolly Parton's former duet partner).

It's even more deplorable that some of his most classic – and popular – recordings are not included here. Yet, as half-baked a representation as this is, it's just about the only thing currently on CD representing Wagoner's impressive contributions.

230 Johnny Cash: Columbia Records, 1958–86

Johnny Cash

Columbia CGK 40637

Sunday Mornin' Coming Down/A Boy Named Sue/Without Love/Don't Take Your Guns To Town/Five Feet High And Rising/Folsom Prison Blues/Highway Patrolman/I Still Miss Someone/The Legend of John Henry's Hammer/Man In Black/The Ballad Of Ira Hayes/The Baron/Oh What A Dream/One Piece At A Time/Ghost Riders In The Sky/Ring Of Fire/San Quentin/Seasons Of My Heart

Cash's towering presence and far-reaching musical vision (which often encompassed the social protest of modern folk music) reigned so supreme over the 1950s and 1960s that one is tempted to include him *twice* in this chapter's "Essential" entries. He began as a rockabilly pioneer in the mid-1950s (see "Essential" listings, this chapter) and remained a formidable presence in country music for the next three decades.

This Columbia compilation does a good job of culling through Cash's vast repertoire and chronicling some – though certainly not all – of the high points.

For those wishing to delve deeper into Cash's incredibly rich catalogue there is also the 3-CD **The Essential Johnny Cash, 1955–1983** (Columbia C3K 47991) and the noteworthy 4-CD German boxed-set reissue, **Come Along And Ride This Train** (Bear Family BCD 15563).

231 Johnny Cash At Folsom Prison And San Quentin

Johnny Cash

Columbia CGK 33639

Folsom Prison Blues/Dark As A Dungeon/I Still Miss Someone/Cocaine Blues/ Twenty-Five Minutes To Go/Orange Blossom Special/The Long Black Veil/A Picture Of Mother/The Wall/Dirty Old Egg-Sucking Dog/Flushed From The Bathroom Of Your Heart/Jackson (with June Carter)/*Give My Love To Rose* (with June Carter)/*I Got Stripes/Green, Green Grass Of Home/Greystone Chapel/Wanted Man/Wreck Of The Old '97/I Walk The Line/Darlin' Companion/Starkville City Jail/San Quentin/A Boy Named Sue/(There'll Be) Peace In The Valley/Folsom Prison Blues*

These two prison LPs (released here on one CD) capture the raw, aggressive vitality of Cash's live sound, and also showcase the remarkably wide stylistic range (folk songs, novelty tunes, mainstream country, etc.) that Cash covered in his prime.

232 American Originals: Stonewall Jackson

Stonewall Jackson

Columbia CK-45070

Wound Time Can't Erase/Life To Go/Waterloo/Me And You And A Dog Named Boo/Life Of A Poor Boy/Mary, Don't You Weep/Leona/Blues Plus Booze (Means I Lose)/Don't Be Angry/Smoke Along The Track

Grand Ole Opry stalwart Stonewall Jackson (it's his real name; he was named after the legendary Confederate general) had consistent chart success throughout the late 1950s and 1960s with his rough-hewn style, which ranged from rustic balladry to quasi-honky-tonk fervor. This collection features some of the North Carolina-born singer's early hits, along with a handful of his more recent and slightly more obscure recordings.

33 Johnny Horton's Greatest Hits

Johnny Horton

Columbia CK 40665

When It's Springtime In Alaska (It's Forty Below)/Whispering Pines/Commanche/Jim Bridger/All For The Love Of A Girl/Sink The Bismark/Honky Tonk Man/I'm Ready If You're Willing/Johnny Freedom/Johnny Reb/Mansion You Stole/The Battle Of New Orleans/North To Alaska

Fairly early in his career, Johnny Horton made a mark as a Texas honky-tonker. Yet before his untimely death in an auto accident in 1960, he made an even bigger name for himself with a string of hit "saga songs" that focused on sure-fire themes like patriotism and America's mythical great outdoors. A couple of these songs ended up as Hollywood movie themes, as well. This collection gathers Horton's classic sagas, as well as a couple of his earlier honky-tonk cuts.

34 Modern Sounds In Country And Western Music

Ray Charles

Rhino R2 70099

That Lucky Old Sun/Worried Mind/You Are My Sunshine/You Don't Know Me/You Win Again/Careless Love/Just A Little Lovin'/Bye Bye Love/Born To Lose/Half As Much/Here We Go Again/Hey, Good Lookin'/I Can't Stop Loving You/I Love You So Much It Hurts/It Makes No Difference Now

Pop/R & B/soul king Ray Charles is not often thought of as a country artist, but this CD reissue of his classic 1962 LP proves that he was not only heavily influenced by the genre, but, in turn, made a major impact on it himself. Included here are Charles's renditions of tunes by noteworthy country writers like Hank Williams, Don Gibson, Eddy Arnold, Boudleaux Bryant, and Floyd Tillman.

35 Same Train, A Different Time: Merle Haggard Sings The Great Songs Of Jimmie Rodgers

Merle Haggard

Capitol SWBB-223 (LP)

California Blues/Hobo's Meditation/Waitin' For A Train/Mother, The Queen Of My Heart/My Carolina Sunshine Girl/Train Whistle Blues/Why Should I Be Lonely/Jimmie's Texas Blues/Blue Yodel No. 6/Mule Skinner Blues/Blue Yodel No. 8/Peach Pickin' Time Down In Georgia/Down The Old Road To Home/Travelin' Blues/Miss The Mississippi And You/Frankie And Johnny/No Hard Times/Hobo Bill's Last Ride/My Old Pal/Nobody Knows Me But Me/Jimmie Rodgers' Last Blue Yodel (Women Make A Fool Out Of Me)

This marvelous tribute to one of country music's founding fathers, from an artist who has been no less influential in his own time, somehow made the circle complete and re-awakened a generation to the magic of Rodgers's music while also underscoring Haggard's own rich sense of history. This is one of several important "tribute" LPs that Haggard made during his early years.

236　I've Found Someone Of My Own

Cal Smith

Decca 75369 (LP)

I've Found Someone Of My Own/A Handful Of Stars/Song Sung Blue/Sweet Things I Remember About You/The Lord Knows I'm Drinking/I Love You More Today/For My Baby/Empty Arms/(Sittin' On) The Dock Of The Bay/ That's What It's Like To Be Lonesome/Ballad Of Forty Dollars

One of the truly great but nearly forgotten singers of the 1960s and early 1970s. His career may have been relatively short and his trips into the charts relatively few and sporadic; yet as a vocalist he ranks with the likes of George Jones and Vern Gosdin.

Great Singer–Songwriters of the 1950s and 1960s

237　All-Time Greatest Hits

Don Gibson

RCA 2295–2-R

Selections: *Oh Lonesome Me/Sweet Dreams/Look Who's Blue/Give Myself A Party/Watch Where You're Going/Funny, Familiar, Forgotten Feelings/Just One Time/Blue, Blue Day/Heartbreak Avenue/Far, Far Away/(Yes) I'm Hurting/I Can't Stop Loving You/Lonesome Number One/Don't Tell Me Your Troubles/Sweet, Sweet Girl/(I'd Be) A Legend in My Time/Bad, Bad Day/My Hands Are Tied/Sea Of Heartbreak/Who Cares (For Me)*

In terms of his facility as both singer and popular composer, Don Gibson ranks alongside greats like Marty Robbins and Conway Twitty. His original songs, some of the best of which are gathered here, have been recorded by dozens of country stars of more recent generations and it's a mere quirk of fate that he did not himself achieve greater stardom.

238　The Best Of Roger Miller, Vol. 2: King Of The Road

Roger Miller

Mercury 314 512 646–2

Poor Little John/Billy Bayou/Big Harlan Taylor/Home/Dang Me/Chug-A-Lug/ King Of The Road/(And You Had A) Doo-Wacka-Do/You Can't Roller Skate In A Buffalo Herd/Reincarnation/Engine Engine/Kansas City Star/It Happened Just That Way/My Uncle Used To Love Me But She Died/England Swings/ Little Green Apples/Me And Bobby McGee/Where Have All The Average People Gone/(The Day I Jumped) From Uncle Harvey's Plane/Hoppy's Gone

Roger Miller, an immensely talented Nashville songwriter who became a pop sensation with his hoked-up novelty tunes, could also be a terribly serious writer. (Aside from his numerous Grammy Awards, he is probably the only country artist to win Broadway's coveted Tony Award – for his original musical score for the hit Broadway play, "Big River.")

This CD collects some of the more enduring and disingenuously clever novelty hits that made Miller a household name in the 1960s.

239 The Bill Anderson Story

Bill Anderson

Decca DXSB 7198/MCA 2–4001 (LP)

Bright Lights And Country Music/No One's Gonna Hurt You Anymore/I Get The Fever/Mama Sang A Song/I Love You Drops/The Tip Of My Fingers/Po' Folks/City Lights/Get While The Gettin's Good/Eight Times Ten/That's What It's Like To Be Lonesome/For Loving You (with Jan Howard)/*Still/Easy Come, Easy Go/Once A Day/I Can Do Nothing Alone/Cincinnati, Ohio/Golden Guitar/Wild Weekend/Think I'll Go Somewhere And Cry Myself To Sleep/Ninety-Nine/Papa/Happiness/Five Little Fingers*

"Whispering" Bill Anderson was a great country songwriter (his original songs were popularized by Jim Reeves, Ray Price, Connie Smith, and others) who metamorphosed into a mediocre but oddly charming singer who had impressive chart success. Often, his singing is little more than a muted, euphonious monotone, yet somehow he gets the job done, and was often the best "interpreter" of his own fine original songs.

240 Jack Scott's Greatest Hits

Jack Scott

Curb CRBD 10635

My True Love/Goodbye Baby/Leroy/With Your Love/The Way I Walk/There Comes A Time/Midgie/Apple Blossom Time/Burning Bridges/What in The World's Come Over You/Running Scared

Although this fine Canadian-born rockabilly and country singer recorded two million-sellers (*My True Love* of 1958, and *What In The World's Come Over You* of 1960), he is today seldom remembered. Nonetheless, his vocal performances hold up under the test of time remarkably well.

Great Duos

41 The Best Of The Early Louvin Brothers

The Louvin Brothers

Rebel REB-852 (LP)

I Don't Believe You've Met My Baby/Hoping That You're Hoping/Pitfall/You're Running Wild/Memories And Tears/When I Stop Dreaming/Don't Laugh/Childish Love/Plenty Of Everything But You/Cash On The Barrelhead/I Wish You Knew/My Baby's Cone

The roots of this extraordinary Alabama-born brother-duet team were in gospel and bluegrass, but they also had a string of country hits up until the mid-1960s, when they disbanded to pursue separate solo careers. Tragically, Ira Louvin, shortly thereafter, died in a 1965 auto accident on his way home from a personal appearance. This collection highlights their irresistible harmony style.

242 All The Best Of Johnnie And Jack

Johnnie and Jack
RCA VPM 6022 (2-LP set)
*Cryin' Heart Blues/Poison Love/Hummingbird/When My Blue Moon Turns
To Gold Again/Stop The World And Let Me Off/Slow Poison/Let Your
Conscience Be Your Guide/Ashes Of Love/You Tried To Ruin My Name/
Don't Let The Stars Get In Your Eyes/What About You/I'm Gonna Love
You One More Time/Oh Baby Mine (I Get So Lonely)/South In New
Orleans/I Can't Tell My Heart That/We Live In Two Different Worlds/
Banana Boat Song/I Want To Be Loved/Three Ways Of Knowing/Sincerely/
The Smile On My Lips/Lonely Island Pearl/Cheated Out Of Love/Called
From Potter's Field*

Johnnie Wright (the husband of 1950s country queen Kitty Wells) and Jack
Anglin were heavily influence by earlier "brother" acts like the Monroe
Brothers (Bill and Charlie), and the Delmore Brothers. However, by the early
1950s they'd developed a unique sound of their own.

Johnnie and Jack's relatively meager showing in the country charts
throughout the 1950s and early 1960s is an unfair measure of their
enduring influence. Their association was cut short in 1963, owing to Jack
Anglin's untimely death. As he was hurrying home from getting his hair
cut to attend the funeral of 1960s country diva Patsy Cline (who'd died in
a plane crash just a day or two earlier) he was himself killed in an auto
accident.

A comprehensive survey of Johnnie and Jack's entire career is collected in
the 6-CD German Bear Family reissue, **Johnnie And Jack And The
Tennessee Mountain Boys** (Bear Family LCD 15553 R).

243 Cadence Classics – Their 20 Greatest Hits

The Everly Brothers
Rhino R2 05258 (USA)
*Bye Bye Love/I Wonder If I Care As Much/Wake Up, Little Susie/This Little
Girl Of Mine/Brand New Heartache/Hey, Doll, Baby/All I Have To Do Is
Dream/Claudette/Bird Dog/Devoted To You/Problems/Love Of My Life/I'm
Here To Get My Baby Out Of Jail/Take A Message To Mary/Poor Jenny/
(Till) I Kissed You/Let It Be Me/Since You Broke My Heart/Like Strangers/
When Will I Be Loved*

Having virtually grown up performing on their father Ike's radio shows in
the Mid West, the Everly Brothers relied on solid country credentials to
launch their distinguished career in Nashville. From 1957 to 1960, on
Archie Bleyer's pop-oriented Cadence label, Don's and Phil's impeccable
harmonies and churning rhythm guitars consistently lifted songwriter
husband-and-wife team, Boudleaux and Felice Bryant's songs of teen
anguish to lofty positions in the "Hot 100" charts.

In addition, this collection features exemplary original material (*I Wonder
If I Care As Much, When Will I Be Loved*) and *I'm Here To Get My Baby
Out Of Jail* – a beautiful manifestation of the folk/country roots which per-
meated this duo's much-admired work.

Country Guitar Innovators and Early Country-Boogie

244 The Best Of Merle Travis

Merle Travis

Rhino R2 70993

Selections: *Sweet Temptation/Trouble, Trouble/I Am A Pilgrim/Dark As A Dungeon/Divorce Me C.O.D./Cincinnati Lou/No Vacancy/Three Times Seven/ Lawdy, What A Gal/Fat Gal/I Like My Chicken Fryin' Size/Re-enlistment Blues/When My Baby Double Talks To Me/Kinfolks In Carolina/Cannon Ball Rag/Sixteen Tons/So Round, So Firm, So Fully Packed/Steel Guitar Rag*

Not only was Kentucky-born Merle Travis an immensely innovative guitarist (Chet Atkins, and lelgendary Sun Records/Elvis Presley sideman Scotty Moore, are just two of many guitarist who fell heavily under the influence of his unique finger-picking style); he was also an amazingly dexterous, witty, and sometimes caustic songwriter. Many of his classic compositions – like *Sixteen Tons*, which was popularized by Tennessee Ernie Ford, and *Dark As A Dungeon* – were written on the spur of the moment. (When inspiration hit him like lightning, he could write a song while painting a fence or sitting on his motorcycle under a street light.) A surprising number of his songs were hits (either for Travis or more established artists like Ford, Tex Williams, or other stars of the day). This collection skims the cream of Travis's recordings, from the 1950s into the late 1960s.

245 Gallopin' Guitar (The Early Years: 1945–1954)

Chet Atkins

Bear Family BCD 15714 (4–disc set) (Ger)

Guitar Blues/Brown Eyes Cryin' In The Rain/Ain'tcha Tired Of Makin' Me Blue/I'm Gonna Get Tight/Canned Heat/Standing Room Only/Don't Hand Me That Line/Bug Dance/(I Know My Baby Loves Me) In Her Own Peculiar Way/The Nashville Jump/My Guitar Is My Sweetheart/I'm Pickin' The Blues/ Gone, Gone, Gone/Barnyard Shuffle/Save Your Money/(I May Be Colorblind But) I Know When I'm Blue/I've Been Working On The Guitar/Dizzy Strings/ Money, Marbles And Chalk/Wednesday Night Waltz/Guitar Waltz/Telling My Troubles To My Old Guitar/Dance Of The Goldenrod/Galloping Guitar/Barber Shop Rag/Centipede Boogie/Under The Hickory Nut Tree/I Was Bitten By The Same Bug Twice/One More Chance/The Old Buck Dance/Boogie Man Boogie/ Main Street Breakdown/Confusin'/Music In My Heart/Indian Love Call/Birth Of The Blues/Mountain Melody/You're Always Brand New/My Crazy Heart/ Hybrid Corn/Jitterbug Waltz/One Man Boogie/Crazy Rhythm/Crazy Rhythm/ Rustic Dance/Rainbow/In The Mood/Spanish Fandango/Midnight/Goodbye Blues/Your Mean Little Heart/Sweet Bunch Of Daisies/Blue Gypsy/The Third Man Theme/One Man Boogie/St Louis Blues/Nobody's Sweetheart/Lover, Come Back To Me/Stephen Foster Medley/Hangover Blues/Imagination/Black Mountain Rag/Guitar Polka (vocal: Rosalie Allen)/*Dream Train* (vocal: Rosalie Allen)/*Meet Mr Callaghan/China Town, My China Town/High Rockin' Swing/Pig Leaf Rag/Oh By Jingo!/Hello Ma Baby/The Bells Of St Mary's/Country Gentleman/Memphis Blues/Alice Blue Gown/12th Street Rag/ Peeping Tom/Three O'clock In The Morning/Georgia Camp Meeting/City Slicker/Dill Pickles Rag/Rubber Doll Rag/Beautiful Ohio/Kentucky Derby/ Wildwood Flower/Guitars On Parade/Simple Simon/Rubber Doll Rag/Get Up And Go* (vocal: Chet Atkins)/*Pagan Love Song/Beautiful Ohio/Downhill Drag/*

Avalon/Sunrise Serenade/San Antonio Rose/Set A Spell (vocal: Red Kirk)/
Mister Misery (duet vocal)/*Get Up And Go* (vocal: Red Kirk)/*South/Alabama
Jubilee/Corrine, Corrina/Indiana (Back Home In Indiana)/Red Wing/Frankie
And Johnnie/A Gay Ranchero/Ballin' The Jack/Honey Suckle Rose/Darktown
Strutters Ball* (with Hank Snow)/*The Old Spinning Wheel* (with Hank Snow)/
Silver Bells (with Hank Snow)/*Under The Double Eagle* (with Hank Snow)/
*The Birth Of The Blues/Have You Ever Been Lonely/Caravan/Old Man River/
Mister Sandman/New Spanish Two-Step*

For nearly five decades, Chet Atkins has – much like Merle Travis – been
acknowledged as one of the most innovative guitar stylists in popular
American music. (During the 1960s and 1970s, as a staff producer and record
executive with RCA/Nashville, he also signed, produced and developed many
of the artists who would become the cornerstones of 1960s and 1970s country
music; and he is generally considered one of the pioneers of the "Nashville
sound.")

Though Atkins has recorded countless guitar albums throughout the years,
these 111 vintage recordings from the 1940s and 1950s are as good a representation as is currently available of the fine music on which his current
reputation was built.

246 16 Tons Of Boogie: The Best Of Tennessee Ernie Ford

Tennessee Ernie Ford

Rhino R2 70975

*Sixteen Tons/Shotgun Boogie/Mr And Mississippi/Catfish Boogie/Tailor-Made
Woman/Smokey Mountain Boogie/Anticipation Blues/Stack-O-Lee/Mule Train/
I'm Hog-Tied Over You/Blackberry Boogie/Hey, Mr Cotton Picker/I'll Never
Be Free/Rock City Boogie/Tennessee Border/Kissin' Bug Boogie/Oceans Of
Tears/I Don't Know*

Tennessee Ernie Ford is perhaps best remembered as an early TV star, and
for his million-selling 1955 hit version of Merle Travis's *Sixteen Tons*. With
"country-boogie" hits (*Blackberry Boogie, Shotgun Boogie*, etc.) Ford also
presaged the rockabilly movement. This fine collection gathers many of
Ford's stylistically quintessential recordings.

Early Country-Pop/Nashville Sound Crooners and Crossover Balladeers

247 Welcome To My World: The Essential Jim Reeves Collection

Jim Reeves

RCA 66125–2 (2-disc set)

*My Heart's Like A Welcome Mat/Mexican Joe/My Rambling Heart/The Padre
Of Old San Antone/Where Does A Broken Heart Go/Yonder Comes A Sucker/
According To My Heart/Four Walls/Blue Boy/Billy Bayou/Am I Losing You/
Home/Partners/Need Me/I Know One/He'll Have To Go/In A Mansion Stands
My Love/I Missed Me/A Railroad Bum/Welcome To My World/I'm Gonna
Change Everything/Little Ole Dime/Love Is No Excuse/Rosa Rio/I Won't
Forget You/Maureen/Is It Really Over/Missing You/Oh, How I Miss You
Tonight/Have You Ever Been Lonely*

Like quite a few of his peers, Texas-born Jim Reeves began his recording career in a honky-tonk groove in the 1950s, but eventually found greater success in a much smoother, "Nashville sound" ballad-singing mode, much like Eddy Arnold or George Morgan. This beautifully annotated collection offers a definitive survey of a bright career which was cut short in 1964 when Reeves died in the crash of a single-engine plane he was piloting.

248   All-Time Greatest Hits

Roy Orbison

CBS AGK 45116

Blue Angel/Blue Bayou/Uptown/Working For The Man/Candy Man/Crying/ Dream Baby/The Crowd/Shahadaroba/Falling/I'm Hurtin'/In Dreams/It's Over/Leah/Love Hurts/Mean Woman Blues/Oh, Pretty Woman/Only The Lonely/Pretty Paper/Running Scared

The late Roy Orbison is most often remembered as a rock icon of sorts – which he became in his later years. His legend stems from his string of compelling 1960s pop/rock Top 40 standards which showcased his astounding 3-octave vocal range.

Orbison actually started out as a fringe player in the Sun Records/Memphis rockabilly movement. Later, in the 1960s, when he did hit the pop Top 40 charts in a big way, he did it from Nashville, working by and large with Nashville songwriters, producers, and "A-team" Nashville studio musicians.

249   George Morgan: American Originals

George Morgan

Columbia CK 45076

Little Dutch Girl/Please Don't Let Me Love You/Candy Kisses/Room Full Of Roses/In Your Eyes/Cry Baby Heart/I'm In Love Again/You're The Only Good Thing (That's Happened To Me/Just Out Of Reach

Another longtime Grand Ole Opry favorite and talented utility player in the "Nashville Sound" movement. Best known for his country standard, *Candy Kisses*, Morgan's career was cut short by a fatal heart attack; he died, at age 50, in 1975.

50   Sonny James: Collector's Series

Sonny James

Capitol CDP 7 91630 2

Young Love/First Date, First Kiss, First Love/The Minute You're Gone/Balti-more/Ask Marie/You're The Only World I Know/True Love's A Blessing/Take Good Care Of Her/Room In Your Heart/Need You/I'll Never Find Another You/Heaven Says Hello/Only The Lonely/Since I Met You, Baby/It's Just A Matter Of Time/My Love/Empty Arms/Bright Lights, Big City/Only Love Can Break A Heart/That's Why I Love You Like I Do

This smooth, capable singer earned extraordinary chart success with his ease at gliding over stylistic boundaries which tended to trip up lesser singers. For years, James specialized in "covering" non-country songs for the country market and he enjoyed numerous country hits with songs first popularized by rock, rhythm and blues, and pop artists like Ivory Joe Hunter, Jimmy Reed, Teresa Brewer, and Petula Clark.

Though perhaps not the most original artist of his generation, James's talent, charm, and long-running popularity speak for themselves. His facility for "retro-fitting" non-country songs for the country market also reveals a lot about the stylistic tensions that were on the loose in country music during the 1960s.

251   David Houston: American Originals

David Houston
Columbia CK 45074
Already It's Heaven/Where Love Used To Live/Almost Persuaded/My Elusive Dreams/I Do My Swinging At Home/Have A Little Faith/Baby, Baby (I Know You're A Lady)/My Woman's Good To Me/With One Exception/Mountain Of Love

A talented, if minor, player in the 1960s, Houston is best remembered for his fine vocal performance on the country classic *Almost Persuaded*, which won him two Grammy Awards in 1967. Some of Houston's best chart moments are gathered here.

252   The Best Of Glen Campbell

Glen Campbell
Liberty C2–46483
Sunflower/Try A Little Kindness/Wichita Lineman/Where's The Playground, Susie/By The Time I Get To Phoenix/Country Boy (You Got Your Feet In LA)/Hey, Little One/All I Have To Do Is Dream/Dream Baby (How Long Must I Dream)/Dreams Of The Every-Day Housewife/Galveston/Gentle On My Mind/It's Only Make Believe/Rhinestone Cowboy/Southern Nights

This influential Arkansas-born country-pop singer had most of his successes in the pop charts in the 1960s and early 1970s, but he always seemed to have at least one foot in the country field. He started as a session player and road musician who backed everyone from Elvis Presley to Frank Sinatra, and even did a brief stint with the hit harmony rock group, the Beach Boys. He also hosted a popular 1960s TV show that proved an important showcase for many Nashville artists.

Though it was a pop hit, his *Rhinestone Cowboy* seemed to symbolize all the uptown glitter and Hollywood connections which, by the time Campbell hit the big time, were seeping into mainstream country music. This compilation collects many of Campbell's biggest chart hits.

More Women of the 1950s and 1960s

253   The Best Of Connie Smith

Connie Smith
RCA CS 61087–4 (cassette)
Ain't Had No Lovin'/Then And Only Then/Hurtin's All Over/If I Talk To Him/I'll Come Running/Darling, Are You Ever Coming Home/I Saw A Man/ Once A Day

This is another one of the sort of inexcusably meager compilations that RCA has often specialized in. These seven tracks offer only a fleeting glimpse of one of the most underrated women singers of 1960s country. It is – begrudgingly – mentioned here, simply because it's the only thing on this fine vocalist currently in print.

254 The Brenda Lee Story: Her Greatest Hits

Brenda Lee
MCA MCAD-4012
Sweet Nothin's/Thanks A Lot/That's All You Gotta Do/Too Many Rivers/We Three/You Always Hurt The One You Love/Break It To Me Gently/You Can Depend On Me/I'm Sorry/Coming On Strong/All Alone Am I/Dum O Dum/ Emotions/Fool No. 1/Anybody But Me/I Want To Be Wanted/As Usual/Jambalaya (On The Bayou)/Johnny One Time/Just Out Of Reach (Of My Open Arms)/Losing You/My Whole World Is Falling Down

During her heyday, when she reigned in the pop Top 40 charts, Brenda Lee eschewed the notion that she was a country singer. Yet, like the Everly Brothers and Roy Orbison she was both a 1960s teen "bobbysox" idol *and* a quintessential product of Nashville's studio/publishing/songwriting system. Her tough, sassy rockers, and her poignant laments of teenage love gone bad were actually adored by both pop and country listeners.

255 The Best Of Skeeter Davis

Skeeter Davis
RCA LPM 3374 (LP)
The End Of The World/(I Can't Help You) I'm Falling Too/I'm Saving My Love/I Will/Something Precious/Now I Lay Me Down To Weep/Gonna Get Along Without You Now/He Says The Same Things To Me/I Can't Stay Mad At You/I Forgot More Than You'll Ever Know/My Last Date (With You)/ Am I That Easy To Forget

This outstanding Kentucky-born singer and longtime Grand Ole Opry member had fleeting success on the 1960s pop charts (with *The End Of The World*), but even a quick listen to this worthy collection makes it clear that she's not only a country girl, through and through, but one of the very best singers to grace Nashville with her presence in the 1950s and 1960s. Given her talent, it's amazing that no one has yet re-released her hits of yesteryear in CD form.

56 Billboard Top Country Hits: 1959–1968

Various Artists
Rhino R2 70680–70689 (10-disc series of single CD issues)

This series of ten 10-track reissue CDs compiles the ten top country chart records for each year, from 1959 through 1968, thus offering a year-by-year chronological survey of the "hottest" country sounds of the 1960s.

The 1970s   7

Bob Allen

The 1970s were uneasy times for country music: times of
booms and busts, of flashing brilliance and stultifying med-
iocrity. As with any era, the music's evolution (or, in the case
of Nashville in the early 1970s, its *revolution*) was never as
linear as it might appear in retrospect. Rather, like the currents,
cross-currents, and eddies of a wide, twisting river, the decade
was marked by any number of countervailing aesthetic and
commercial movements, counter-movements, and sub-move-
ments – some of them industry-driven fads, some of them
fueled by the genuine grassroots creativity of the musicians
themselves.

One of the most dramatic of these early 1970s grassroots
uprisings was the so-called "Outlaw" movement, spearheaded
by iconoclastic Texas musicians, Willie Nelson and Waylon
Jennings, and to a lesser extent by others like songwriter–singer
Kris Kristofferson, and Hank Williams, Junior, son of the
country legend Hank Williams, Senior. (The Outlaw moniker
itself was actually a record company marketing ploy of sorts –
one which intentionally conjured up romantic images of the
Old West and suggested a latterday cowboy ethic of rugged
individualism.) But despite the record company hype, the
Outlaws' music was, by and large, a grassroots phenomonon. It
marked a return to the rawer and more rugged musical sensibilities of earlier eras (honky-tonk, rockabilly, etc.), coupled
with a swaggering, gypsyish rock-and-roll attitude, lyric frank-
ness and sensuality, and a sort of cowboyish, post-hippyish
counter-cultural image. The Outlaw ethos was captured in
spades by chart-topping Jennings/Nelson anthems like *Mamas,
Don't Let Your Babies Grow Up To Be Cowboys*, *Good-Hearted
Woman*, and *Luchenbach, Texas*. These songs expressed not
only Nelson's and Jennings's own fascination with the images
of the Old West (neither man had ever been a real "cowboy"

by any stretch of the imagination); they also spoke of the quest for an unreconstructed vision of personal freedom that applied not only to the way they lived, but the way they made music. All of this, of course, appealed heartily to the anti-establishment sentiments of American youth of the post-Woodstock, post-Vietnam generation.

The Outlaw movement paralleled, fed off, and was, in many ways, inseparable from, the Southern rock movement of the early 1970s, personified by nationally popular bands like the Allman Brothers, Marshall Tucker, ZZ Top, Lynyrd Skynyrd, and Nashville's own Charlie Daniels (a former Music Row session man who achieved multi-platinum success with his hard-rocking, irreverent brand of Southern music.)

Yet, during the early and middle 1970s, when the Outlaws were coming into their own (by the late 1970s Jennings's and Nelson's record sales had dwarfed those of any previous country artist), any number of other more old-line country acts and country-to-pop crossover and "Nashville sound" artists continued to flourish. The "Nashville sound" – soft-edged, pop-inflected country music with its twang and rusticity modified or eradicated by lush strings and smooth background vocals which replaced the weeping steel guitars, churning guitars, and sawing fiddles of honky-tonk and hard country – was still going strong. One of its most talented and popular practitioners was Charlie Rich, a white blues/jazz singer from Arkansas who (under the guidance of producer Billy Sherrill) modified his eclectic style into a "Lite Country" mode, and had enormous success with a couple of across-the-board pop hits, *Behind Closed Doors* and *The Most Beautiful Girl*, in 1973. Later in the decade, country-pop crooners like Kenny Rogers and Barbara Mandrell would follow somewhat similar courses. For much of the 1970s, Glen Campbell, a West Coast artist, was burning up the pop charts with his own highly accessible country-pop sound personified by hits like *Rhinestone Cowboy*, *Wichita Lineman*, *By The Time I Get To Phoenix*, and *Gentle On My Mind*.

Chart-wise, an even more unusual thing was happening, which also illustrates the degree to which mainstream country music was still floundering for a sense of itself. In a "reverse crossover" phenomenon of sorts, the records of easy listening-style pop artists like John Denver, Ann Murray, and Australian Olivia Newton-John (all of whom had already achieved immense success in the pop charts) began dominating the country charts – in the process, displacing the records of more *bona fide* country acts in *Billboard*'s country "Hot 100." When, in 1974 and 1975, the Country Music Association (CMA), the Nashville music industry's leading trade organization, bestowed its highest annual achievement awards on John Denver (who received country music's top laurel, the "Entertainer Of The Year" award, in 1975) and Newton-John (who was the CMA's "Female Vocalist Of The Year" in 1974), there was outrage among country music's more purist and conservative elements. Later in the decade, as a protest against this musical watering-down effort, a shortlived organization called the Association Of Country Entertainers (ACE) was formed as an alternative to the Country Music Association. "Keep the *country* in country music," was their battle cry.

It really took the Outlaws to break through Nashville's country-pop gridlock. What artists like Jennings, Nelson, and Hank Williams, Jr were really fighting for, was something that most rock artists had long been taking for granted: artistic autonomy. That is, the right to produce their own records, to write (or at least *choose*) their own material, to pick their own studio personnel, and to basically chart their own musical courses. (Ironically, these were the sort of decisions which, in country music, had traditionally been reserved for the producer, rather than the artist.) In short, they were fighting for the right to make the kind of music they heard in their own imaginations, as opposed to the purblind musical agenda foisted on them by some second-rate record company-appointed producer. All through the 1970s, despite the various extremes personified by the Outlaws, the pop-to-country crossover speci-alists, and country-to-pop crossover stars, there was still lots going on in the middle ground. Any number of tried and true country artists who'd come of age in the 1950s and 1960s con-tinued to flourish. Revered singers like Johnny Cash, Merle Haggard, George Jones, Tammy Wynette, Loretta Lynn, Conway Twitty, and Charley Pride (one of country music's few black superstars) were simply too straight or conservative to fit the outlaw mode and simply too country to attempt to cross-over.

Also a handful of immensely talented newcomers – like Smoky Mountain-born songstress Dolly Parton, former folk singer/country-rocker Emmylou Harris, and Florida neo-honky-tonker Gary Stewart – managed to establish themselves during the decade, enriching country's mainstream with their vastly diverse talents. (Though admittedly the trickle of new talent that found its way into the charts during the 1970s seems minor when compared to the virtual flood of the 1980s and early 1990s.) Waylon Jennings's and Willie Nelson's Texas connections would also spark a shortlived boom in which many Lone Star State musicians would enjoy a brief but shining moment in the charts as they rode on the coattails of the Outlaw movement.

The 1970s was indeed a strange era for country music – disastrous in some respects, glorious in others, and marked by the sort of creative tension and stylistic diversity that ultimately seems to impel the music toward still greater change and innovation.

Essential Recordings

(i) The Outlaws

Willie Hugh Nelson, one of the most popular and influential artists of the 1970s and early 1980s, was born in Abbot, Texas, in 1933. Nelson made his musical debut around age ten, playing guitar in polka bands that were then popular in the German–American settlements of central Texas. By the early 1960s, Nelson was in Nashville, toiling as a songwriter and recording artist. Soon, he was earning a healthy six-figure income turning out stunningly original country classics like *Night Life*, *Funny How Time Slips Away*, and *Family Bible* that would eventually recorded by dozens of artists – everyone from Patsy Cline and Doris Day to Frank Sinatra and Elvis Presley.

Throughout the 1960s Nelson also recorded some memorable records of his own. Yet RCA/Nashville, which had him under contract for much of the decade, seemed at a loss as to how to properly produce and market his unconventionally gravelly, vocal style, which was made even more distinctive by his jazz-like phrasing – that is, singing either slightly ahead of or behind the beat. (Nelson later explained that he learned this listening to Frank Sinatra records.) Nelson's songs, which were often deep and introspective in subject matter and complex in chord structure, were also deemed to be slightly out of synch with the times. "The (Nashville) executive producers and the record company producers had a very small opinion of the intelligence of people who listened to country music," Nelson recalled disparagingly of his early years of frustration in Music City. "They felt (the public) was not capable of hearing words that had more than three syllables, or songs that had more than three chords . . . As soon as I hit town I realized I was in the wrong place." (**Willie Nelson: All-Time Greatest Hits, Vol. 1** (RCA 8556-2-R) is a fascinating 20-song CD compilation of Nelson's somewhat lesser-known early releases.)

By 1970, Nelson had already been performing extensively in his native Texas for many years, and had built a strong cult following there. So he decided to move his base of operations back to Texas (where he has resided ever since). There, he began redirecting his musical energies and was eventually discovered by a younger, somewhat counter-cultural audience – the same folks who were already flocking to stadium rock concerts by the likes of the Allman Brothers and ZZ Top.

By the early 1970s, free at last of the narrow constraints of the Nashville studio system, Nelson really began to come into his own as a recording artist, and proceeded to make some of the best and most vital recordings of his long recording career (which, as of this writing, has spanned nearly three and a half decades). Signed by legendary producer/executive Jerry Wexler to Atlantic Records, Nelson made a pair of memorable LPs for that label in the early 1970s: **Shotgun Willie** and **Phases And Stages**, both of which did reasonably well until Atlantic dismantled its country division.

By 1975, Nelson had signed a new distribution deal with Columbia/Nashville which enabled him to record for his own Lone Star label with complete artistic autonomy. **Red-Headed Stranger** (1975), Nelson's first Columbia LP, proved to be the cornerstone of the immense popularity he has since earned. Though Nelson's many hardcore aficionados will debate endlessly as to which of the many albums he's recorded since the early 1960s is his best, **Red-Headed Stranger** seems to make everybody's short-list.

Thematically, **Red-Headed Stranger** is a dark, semi-mystical concoction of romance, autobiography, and stark cowboy mythology. Its themes of betrayal, retribution, despair, and redemption are universal. All told, it's a brilliantly conceived, wholly original work unlike anything that preceded it – one which rubbed thoroughly against the grain of the prevailing conventions of early 1970s mainstream country music.

Nelson used his own accomplished road band (later called the Family Band) as his sole accompanists on **Red-Headed Stranger**. He produced and recorded the LP in a day and a half, on a shoestring budget of $20,000 in a small studio in Garland, Texas, that was normally used for radio commercials and jingles. Earlier, Nelson had sketched out the conceptual story line for **Red-Headed Stranger** with his then-wife Connie during an all-night drive from Colorado to Texas. The songs are a seamlessly interlaced collection of Nelson originals, older country standards along with several traditional (public domain) selections, all of which are woven together in an almost flawless conceptual tapestry. Most of the austere arrangements are built around Nelson's battered acoustic guitar and meditative vocal performances.

The mood of **Red-Headed Stranger**, as Nelson relates this fabulistic tale of a man's symbolic journey through heartbreak, rage, insanity, homicide, resignation, and finally personal salvation, is traditional, timeless, and cinematic in its sweep. (Some years later, Nelson would make a feature film based on the LP's storyline.)

Red-Headed Stranger became Nelson's first million-selling LP and launched him on the road to stardom. *Blue Eyes Cryin' In The Rain*, a haunting old country ballad (written by Fred Rose in 1945), was released as a single, became the first Number 1 hit of Nelson's career, and earned him a Grammy Award in 1975 for his vocal performance.

Critical acclaim for **Red-Headed Stranger** was resounding and also played a big part in getting the Nelson juggernaut rolling. "Willie Nelson has recently recorded an album so remarkable that it calls for a redefinition of the term 'country music,' " esteemed popular-music journalist Chet Flippo wrote in *Texas Monthly*. "The difference between Nelson's **Red-Headed Stranger** and any other current C & W album is astounding . . . The world that Nelson has created is so seductive that you want to linger indefinitely."

Waylon Jennings was born in 1937, in the small West Texas community of Littlefield, just below the Texas Panhandle. As a teenager, Jennings met, befriended, and came heavily under the musical influence of soon-to-be rock legend Buddy Holly, who hailed from nearby Lubbock, Texas. Jennings eventually became the bass player in Holly's band, the Crickets, and played with Holly right up until the singer's death in a plane crash in early 1959. Holly, before his death, also produced Jennings's very first independent record releases.

By the mid-1960s, Jennings had relocated to Nashville and had begun recording for RCA. Some of his earliest releases for the label were produced by legendary guitarist Chet Atkins, who then headed RCA's Nashville operations. It was during these years that he became fast friends with fellow Texan Willie Nelson.

Jennings's prolific 1960s RCA recordings (many of which are still in print) reveal an artist very much in search of himself. Though a country artist first and foremost, Jennings was nonetheless heavily anchored in the prevailing rock and pop trends of his youth. Not surprisingly, considering his vocal versatility, RCA initially attempted to market him as a "folk-country" artist; and during the last half of the 1960s, this diverse stylist drew his material from sources as unlikely as the Beatles (*Norwegian Wood*) and Simon and Garfunkle (*Bridge Over Troubled Waters*). He even won a Grammy Award for his countrified version of the bloated pop standard, *McCarthur Park*.

Yet the 1960s were years of frustration for Jennings – years of illness, indebtedness, personal strife, and barely enough chart success to keep him going. Though he seemed at a loss to find his own musical self-definition, the various RCA staff producers assigned to produce his records weren't much help either. "They wouldn't let me pick my own songs. They didn't even want me to use my own band in the studio," Jennings has since recalled with some bitterness. "It seemed like when it came to making my records, they asked everybody's advice but mine. I'd cut a basic track and by the time they were through (overdubbing) stuff to it, I wouldn't even recognize it."

By the late 1960s, though, Jennings had succeeded in wresting a degree of artistic autonomy from the label, and began making the kinds of records he'd long wanted to make. He emerged with a much more hard-edged sound that emphasized his own booming, gruff vocals and his bold, electrified "chicken-pickin' " Telecaster guitar signature – a sound that often borrowed freely from both the spirit of 1970s rock as well as Texas honky-tonk (Over the years, his abiding fondness of rock-and-roll has inspired him to record songs by the Rolling Stones, Fleetwood Mac, Neil Young, and the like; he had a particularly big country hit with a version of Young's grassroots-rock anthem, *Are You Ready For The Country*.)

By the early 1970s, Jennings was already making some of his all-time best and most definitive albums: **Ladies Love Outlaws** (1972), **Lonesome, On'ry And Mean** (1973), **Honky Tonk Heroes** (1973), **Dreamin' My Dreams** (1975) and **Are You Ready For The Country** (1976).

Jennings fanatics will argue incessantly as to which of these is his best. **Dreamin' My Dreams** (produced by the legendary Jack Clement) is perhaps his most soulful, and is exceedingly recommended. But it is the more earthy **Honky Tonk Heroes** that most captures the gritty, free-wheeling spirit and imagery of the Outlaw movement. It also showcases another seminal figure from early 1970s *Outlawry*: Texas songwriter Billy Joe Shaver (see "Basic Recordings," 1970s), who wrote or co-wrote all but one of the ten songs on **Honky Tonk Heroes**, including the title tune.

Whereas later Jennings albums would bear his rock influences more heavily, **Honky Tonk Heroes** (as its title implies) is anchored more steadfastly in Jennings's Texas honky-tonk roots. The accompaniment on most of these songs is raw and basic: electric guitars, steel guitar, etc.

Jennings's distinctive vocal style – a gruff, booming baritone that manages to sound both achingly soulful and tougher than leather all at the same time – goes hand-in-glove with Shaver's philosophical grassroots anthems of hard times and lovable losers (*Old Five And Dimers Like Me*, *Honky Tonk Heroes*), and the never-ending search for personal freedom (such as *Low Down Freedom*, *Ain't No God in Mexico*).

Many top-flight Nashville session players can be heard on **Honky Tonk Heroes**, including Randy Scruggs, Billy Reynolds, Joe Allen, Henry Strzlecki, and Reggie Young. Yet on a number of cuts (perhaps as a willful exercise of his newfound creative autonomy) Jennings also utilized his own eminently talented road band, the Waylors. Jennings also produced the bulk of these tracks himself, with occasional assistance from various co-producers, including Tompall Glaser, a producer/publisher/artist who carried much behind-the-scenes weight in the early Outlaw movement.

With Shaver's songs and Glaser's shrewd counsel, Jennings, on **Honky Tonk Heroes**, found the "voice" and the sense of direction that had eluded him throughout the 1960s. This LP – much like Willie Nelson's **Red-Headed Stranger** – would become a cornerstone in one of the most commercially successful careers of the 1970s and early 1980s. And when Nelson, Jennings, and Tompall Glaser teamed up in 1976 on an adroitly packaged, bestselling hodge-podge of an LP called **Wanted: The Outlaws** (which became the first Nashville-produced LP to sell a million copies), the Outlaw movement, with Jennings and Nelson at the forefront, grew from cult following to rage of the age.

For those wishing to delve further into Jennings's extensive catalogue, **Greatest Hits, Vol. 1**, (RCA CD-8506–2–R), is a sterling collection of many of Jennings's biggest chart records from the 1970s. **Waylon Jennings: The Early Years** (RCA 9561–2–R) is a noteworthy 12-cut sampling of Jennings's earlier and more obscure RCA recordings. Nearly all of Jennings's 1960s RCA LPs have also been re-released on the German Bear Family label.

Discographical Details

7 Red-Headed Stranger

Willie Nelson

Columbia CK 33482

Time Of The Preacher/I Couldn't Believe It Was True/Time Of The Preacher Theme/Medley: Blue Rock, Montana/Red-Headed Stranger/Blue Eyes Cryin' In The Rain/Red-Headed Stranger/Time Of The Preacher Theme/Just As I Am/Denver/O'er The Waves/Down Yonder/Can I Sleep In Your Arms/ Remember Me (When The Candelights Are Gleaming)/Hands On The Wheel/ Bandera

258 Honky Tonk Heroes

Waylon Jennings
Mobile Fidelity MFCD-10–00779
RCA APLI-0240 (LP)
Honky Tonk Heroes/Old Five And Dimers (Like Me)/Willy, The Wandering Gypsy And Me/Low Down Freedom/Omaha/You Ask Me To/Ride Me Down Easy/Ain't No God In Mexico/Black Rose/We Had It All

(ii) In the Hank and Lefty Tradition . . .

No survey of modern country music could possibly be complete without the inclusion of George Jones. (See also "Essential Recordings" listings in the Honky-Tonk chapter.) He is perhaps the single most influential living singer in country music, and possibly the most talented vocalist in country music history. He is to his respective field (hard country/honky-tonk) what Ray Charles and Frank Sinatra are to theirs; he has set the standards by which nearly all others are inevitably measured. Jones's supple, painfully expressive baritone with its remarkable range, dexterity, and pathos is unmatched. And, to one degree or another, he has influenced nearly every country singer who's since come down the pike.

Jones was born in Saratoga, Texas in 1931 and came of age playing the honky-tonks, barn dances and radio shows of the greater Beaumont/Houston region of southeast Texas. When he began his recording career in the mid-1950s (he had his first Top 10 record with a self-written song called *Why, Baby, Why* in 1955), he was still heavily under the influence of his own musical heroes of a previous generation: Hank Williams, Lefty Frizzell, and Roy Acuff.

Jones's longevity (as of this writing he is in his early sixties and is still going strong as a recording artist) is somewhat surprising (perhaps even to him), since – like many of the early blues masters – he has tended to "live out" many of his songs about lost love, whiskey and hard living.

When Jones recorded his classic 1976 **Alone Again** LP, he already had two decades of hits behind him. Yet, in the mid-1970s he found himself very much swimming against the current with his unreconstructed brand of hard country/honky-tonk music. Jones was definitely not an Outlaw (though he had loose associations with many of the Outlaws and found a legion of new fans among the Outlaws' youthful following). And his style was the very antithesis of the "countrypolitan" crossover music of, say, Charlie Rich. **Alone Again** was indeed a stark contrast to prevailing trends, and marked Jones's return to his honky-tonk roots. Gone were the glossy string arrangements and background vocals heard on many of Jones's earlier (1960s and early 1970s) Musicor and Columbia recordings, including the popular duets he'd recorded with his ex-wife, singer Tammy Wynette. **Alone Again**, by contrast, is raw, unrestrained, and thoroughly countrified with basic guitar/steel guitar/fiddle arrangements.

Though not "thematic" by any stretch of the imagination, **Alone Again** is nonetheless powerful in its bleak, confessional nakedness. It was recorded during a pathetically low point in Jones's life and career. A few years earlier he and Tammy Wynette had divorced after a tempestuous and occasionally violent six-year marriage. Jones was, by all accounts, still very much in love with his ex-wife and was tortured by the marriage's failure and his own inability to control his drinking. By 1976, he was beginning a long, slow slide into a quagmire of legal problems, alcohol and cocaine abuse, and personal turmoil that would lead to several arrests and institutionalizations – all of which only served to enhance his legend as the king of honky-tonk heartache.

A Drunk Can't Be A Man (written by Jones and his longtime friend and co-writer Earl "Peanut" Montgomery) speaks directly of Jones's bitter remorse over the damage he's inflicted upon his life with his raging, uncontrollable excesses. (Note the lyrics' macabre "Jekyll and Hyde" references.) *Stand On My Own Two Knees* (written by R. Bowling and Jerry Crutchfield) is the statement of a man who has been debilitated not by the bottle but by the humiliation and hurt of a twisted love affair. The casual self-pity of *Ain't Nobody Gonna Miss Me* (also written by Jones and Montgomery) resonates along similar lines. *Diary Of My Mind* (J. Starks and S.M. Starks) is the painful admission of a man so devastated by lost love that he can only keep his sanity by retreating into his memories and fantasies. The utter naturalness and conviction with which Jones sings these songs makes it clear that they cut close to the bone.

Alone Again is not all unrelenting *Sturm und Drang* and dreariness, though. There are a couple of heartfelt love songs. (*You're The Best Living* and *She Needs Me*.) And there's also *Her Name Is . . .*, a catchy novelty song (Jones has had a weakness for novelties his entire career) that did well in the charts. In this song (written by Bobby Braddock, who's written his share of Jones's hits), Jones teases and tantalizes listeners by offering up sly hints about a secret lover whose identity he never quite reveals. (His fans, of course, just assumed it was Tammy he was singing about.) Clever instrumental licks – supplied by a Clavinet, an electronic keyboard instrument with a bright percussive attack similar to a harpsichord (played here by veteran session man Hargus "Pig" Robbins) and run through phase-shifter – fill in the blanks where the mystery lover's name should be.

Not only was **Alone Again** George Jones's most inspired LP of the 1970s; it also reasserted his talent and influence at a time when, owing to personal problems and prevailing tastes in the music industry, many in Nashville were ready to write him off as just another Texas/honky-tonk burn-out case left over from the sixties.

To call George Jones and Tammy Wynette the Sonny and Cher of seventies country music is to trivialize their vast appeal and influence as a duet team. Yet it does convey the immense media fascination that their stormy, ill-fated celebrity marriage (and subsequently divorce) and high-profile rags-to-riches lifestyle inspired; it also suggests the uneasy balance between artistry and bathos that typified many of their duets.

By the time they married in 1969, Jones and Wynette were both already stars. But united, their popularity quickly outgrew the sum of its two separate parts. When she and Jones began recording together, Wynette, a Mississippi-born, Alabama-raised sharecropper's daughter from Red Bay, Alabama, and a former hairdresser, waitress, and barmaid, was riding the crest of the immense success that followed her 1968 international hit, *Stand By Your Man*. This latter song was a strident anthem to the unliberated working class woman. Her other early hits – *D-I-V-O-R-C-E*, *Your Good Girl's Gonna Go Bad*, *Take Me To Your World* – were obliquely described by one tongue-in-cheek reviewer as "music to wash dishes by."

Jones, for his part (by dint of his numerous 1950s and early 1960s Texas honky-tonk hits and his mid- and late 1960s hard country balladry for the Musicor label) already enjoyed a stalwart reputation as a Texas "heart song" hero turned latter-day hard country crooner.

United in matrimony and in song, Jones and Wynette began recording and touring extensively together and became a fixture on Nashville's Grand Ole Opry. They became known to their multitude of fans and to the tabloid press as "Mr and Mrs Country Music."

Producer Billy Sherrill's role in igniting the Jones/Wynette musical alchemy cannot be understated. He'd "discovered" Wynette one day in the mid-1960s when she walked into his Music Row office unannounced after being brushed off by every other label in Nashville. Sherrill also almost singlehandedly created Wynette's bottle-blonde persona as the downtrodden sixties working-class housewives' hero and even dreamed up her stage name. ("You look like a Tammy to me," he supposedly told the callow young singer, whose given name is Virginia Wynette Pugh.) Additionally, he not only produced, but also co-wrote many of the songs – *Stand By Your Man, Your Good Girl's Gonna Go Bad, I Don't Wanna Play House,* and *Take Me To Your World* – which helped Wynette shape her unique musical persona.

As soon as Jones got contractually free from the Musicor label and signed his own 10-year solo deal with Columbia, Tammy's label, Sherrill wasted little time in putting them together in the recording studio and putting his sharp imagination to work both finding and/or writing songs that shrewdly mirrored the soap opera-ish vicissitudes of their marital ups and downs. (Even after they divorced in the mid-1970s and Wynette remarried, she and Jones continued to sporadically tour and record as a duet team.)

It's not surprising that many of the earlier songs heard on their 1977 **Greatest Hits** LP – *Take Me, The Ceremony,* and *Let's Build A World Together* – express a newfound sense of hopefulness and optimism. In later years, as Jones's alcoholism and increasingly erratic behavior, and Wynette's depression and hypochondria took an ever-greater toll on their fishbowl marriage and finally led to their separation, duets like *Golden Ring, We're Gonna Hold On,* and *Southern California* echoed the doubt, bitterness, and desperation that had crept into their lives.

Sherrill, the most successful and controversial producer of the 1970s and early 1980s (he also produced Charlie *Behind Closed Doors* Rich, Johnny Paycheck, and David Allan Coe, Tanya Tucker, and a host of other leading artists) pushed the heavily orchestrated, elaborately produced "Nashville sound," with its heavyhanded string and choral arrangements to such excessive new heights that the very style became known as the "Sherrillization" of country music. Yet, for all the criticism it evoked among country's more conservative elements, "Sherrillization" (as evidenced by multi-million-selling hits like *Stand By Your Man,* and *Behind Closed Doors*) met with immense commercial success as Sherrill reached for a wider audience and quickly found it. (Ironically, Sherrill could also produce good hard country records when he chose to, including some of Jones's most memorable hard country recordings from this era, like *Alone Again.*

Some testaments to Sherrill's lavish production style (it seemed to be his trademark to use a musical double exclamation point in the form of melodramatic full-octave string glissandos and weeping, wailing steel guitar passages, where another producer might be content with a mere period) stand the test of time better than others – as evidenced by the selections on this **Greatest Hits** package. Yet Sherrill had an uncanny knack for blending Jones's rich, thoroughly rural baritone and Wynette's slightly more "uptown," sometimes subtle, sometimes shrill singing style into a compelling mix.

Admittedly, some of the selections here, like *God's Gonna Get'cha For That* (an ode to small-town religious hypocrisy) and *The Ceremony*, seem a bit mawkish, soggy, and languid by latterday standards. Yet other selections, like *Golden Ring*, a powerful story-song about a piece of precious metal that outlives more than one of the shortlived romances it was bought to commemorate, are compelling. Wynette's and Jones's hauntingly restrained vocal performance and the stark, straight-forward acoustic guitar/steel guitar arrangements on *Golden Ring* bring out all the song's dark irony and drama, and epitomize one of the finest three minutes in 1970s country music.

Born in Oildale, California, a tiny suburb of Bakersfield, in 1937, Merle Haggard is the son of "Okies:" Depression-era Oklahoma Dust Bowl refugees who fled to California after being driven from their native state by incessant drought and economic hard times. Haggard himself was born into relative comfort. (His parents had, by the time of his birth, both found steady employment.) Even so, he quickly set about inventing hard times of his own. And his early hardscrabble experiences – along with the humble but proud rural heritage of his Oklahoma forefathers and the grim, daunting Depression-era world of "Hoover Camps" and migrant workers that they encountered in California in the 1930s – have often echoed through his music.

Haggard did a stretch at California's San Quentin State Penitentiary for charges ranging from car theft to burglary. (Ironically, he was in the audience when country superstar Johnny Cash came there in the 1960s to record his famous **Live At San Quentin** LP.) Once out of prison, Haggard turned his restless energy to music. After a brief apprenticeship as a guitarist in Buck Owens's backup band, the Buckaroos, he embarked upon an illustrious solo career of his own. In the years since, he has amassed a stunning body of work that has often caused his name to be whispered in the same breath with those of Hank Williams, Lefty Frizzell, Jimmie Rodgers, and other formative figures of country music.

Haggard's influence and accomplishments during the late 1960s and 1970s were immense (see also Honky-Tonk chapter). He made his mark not just as a singer–songwriter nonpareil, but also as a bandleader. (His band, the Strangers, was, for years, the most accomplished country/western swing band in the field, and Haggard is the only country star ever to be featured on the cover of the prestigious American jazz magazine, *Downbeat*.) Over the years, Haggard also distinguished himself as a musical ethnographer of sorts; during the 1970s, he recorded stirring LP tributes to his own musical heroes – Bob Wills, Jimmie Rodgers, Lefty Frizzell – which did much to keep the influence of these men alive in a new decade.

And just as the above-mentioned greats inspired Haggard, he has, in turn, been a musical role model for younger generations of country singers who've since come along. In fact, the argument can easily be made that Haggard is the most all-around talented and important country artist of the last half-century (neck and neck with other greats like Willie Nelson and Johnny Cash) – or at least since the death of Hank Williams. His influence has even surpassed that of a great artist like the late Lefty Frizzell (upon whose vocal style Haggard modeled his own). As esteemed American music critic Nat Hentoff noted of Haggard in the *Village Voice* in 1980: "There's nobody playing country music now who knows as much as Haggard. He's a practicing expert on Jimmie Rodgers, Bob Wills's western swing, Lefty Frizzell, and Hank Williams. And Haggard himself is (one of) the only singer–musician–writers left whose own work makes him fit right into that company of lasting originals." Added Jim Miller in *Rolling Stone* magazine in 1975: "[Haggard] is the greatest country artist of our time."

Throughout the mid- and late 1960s, the 1970s, and the early 1980s, Haggard was a dominant force on the country scene. Recording and working out of southern California, he (like Buck Owens before him) personified West Coast country and offered a fresh alternative to Nashville music – just as Buck Owens did before him. Haggard's extraordinary repertoire from these years (which is amply represented in Capitol's 2-LP **Songs I'll Always Sing**) ranged from classic, straight-ahead country tear-jerkers and drinking songs (*Swingin' Doors, The Bottle Let Me Down, Today I Started Loving You Again, I'm Turning Off A Memory*, to unforgettable prison songs (*Lonesome Fugitive, Mama Tried, Branded Man, Sing Me Back Home*, and trenchant working class social commentaries (*Okie From Muskogee, The Fightin' Side Of Me*, and *Workin' Man's Blues*).

By the turn of the decade, however, Haggard, by then in his early forties, going through a divorce and world-weary after nearly a decade and a half of touring, went through a painful period that he referred to as "male menopause." His music, which had often been autobiographical, now turned even more subjective, introspective, and soul-searching. He often explored the darker side of fame and vividly charted his own struggle with the personal demons of restlessness, loneliness, and isolation.

Serving 190 Proof (1979) is generally considered to be Haggard's best work ever. Before and after, he made records that featured more self-consciously sophisticated and arresting instrumental arrangements; and he would write many more songs that vividly captured his stark world view and troubled spirit. But on **Serving 190 Proof** (the LP title itself attests to the unflinching, unsentimental, and confessional nature of the tracks therein) Haggard distilled his interpersonal frustrations and pain into music that is not only devastatingly honest, but which represents popular art at its best and most revealing.

In *Footlights*, the opening cut, Haggard agonizes as he tries to summon the strength to set aside his loneliness and exhaustion and hit the stage and do it all over again. In the process, he pulls back the curtains on his own fame and stardom to reveal the dark shadows that lurk within – shadows of self-doubt, sadness, loss, and dislocation. On *Lonely Too Early*, the song's swingy, jazzy, horn arrangement gives an almost wistful inevitability to the reality of waking up alone and lonesome in a big hotel room. In *Heaven Was A Drink Of Wine* (written by Sanger D. Shafer, and one of the few non-Haggard originals on here), a man devastated by heartbreak visits a "psychoed-out psychiatrist." He confesses the root of his problems to the good doctor ("When she left me I went to hell/And Heaven was a drink of wine") and concludes that he's maybe even too far gone to be helped by modern psychiatry.

Yet as moody and soul-searching as the music on **Serving 190 Proof** often is, Haggard's resolute vocal performances and the impeccable but unobtrusive arrangements always salvage him from the mire of outright self-pity. On *Driftwood*, a lovely ballad, he blames his failed marriage on his own innate restlessness, yet seems sadly resigned to the inevitable consequences of the kind of man he is and the life he leads. Similarly, on *I Can't Get Away* (where he laments, "I keep runnin' from life/Always runnin' from life . . .") he seems to grimly acknowledge that there really is no easy escape from his demons – not even drink or self-pity – and that the only solution is to enjoy whatever fleeting moments of solace or serenity he can find. On *I Must Have Done Something Bad* (written by Red Lane, who also co-wrote a couple other of these selections with Haggard), he seems to touch on the notion of original sin as he searches his own past for some explanation for the excessive pain and guilt he's forced to endure as an adult.

My Own Kind Of Hat, on the other hand, is one of the more upbeat songs here. Written by Haggard, it's a jaunty, lyrically dazzling statement of resolve: a declaration of personal freedom that quietly flies in the face of conformity and compromise. It speaks of Haggard's need to follow his own peculiar path through life, come what may.

Almost as a respite from these ruminations on mid-life identity crises, the final two cuts of **Serving 190 Proof** deal with more uplifting subjects. On *Sing A Family Song*, Haggard relives precious childhood memories. On *Roses In The Winter* he sings longingly of an everlasting love that – unlike the kind of ephemeral love he mourns in the aforementioned songs – withstands all the obstacles of time and uncertainty.

Serving 190 Proof is, by all measures, a powerful work. Though Haggard has continued recording (with varying degrees of inspiration) in the years since, he has seldom come close to surpassing the devastating intensity and candor of this near-perfect marriage of public art and personal suffering.

Discographical Details

259 Alone Again

George Jones
Epic KE 34290 (LP)
A Drunk Can't Be A Man/Ain't Nobody Gonna Miss Me/Stand On Your Own Two Knees/You're The Best Living/Over Something Good/Her Name Is . . ./ I'm All She's Got/She Needs Me/Right Now I'd Come Back And Melt In Her Arms/Diary Of My Mind

260 Greatest Hits

George Jones and Tammy Wynette
Epic EK 34716
Golden Ring/We're Gonna Hold On/We Loved It Away/Take Me/Near You/ Southern California/God's Gonna Get'cha (For That)/(We're Not) The Jet Set/Let's Build A World Together/The Ceremony

261 Serving 190 Proof

Merle Haggard
MCA-3809 (LP)
Footlights/Got Lonely Too Early This Morning/Heaven Was A Drink Of Wine/ Driftwood/I Can't Get Away/Red Bandana/My Own Kind Of Hat/I Must Have Done Something Bad/I Didn't Mean To Love You/Sing A Family Song/ Roses In The Winter

(iii) Singer–Songwriters

Tom T. Hall, along with Kris Kristofferson (see "Essential Recordings" entry below) was one of the most vivid, insightful, and accomplished masters of the country story-song to emerge in the late 1960s and early 1970s. With his good-naturedly jaundiced perception of the human condition – fueled by his wry wit, journalistic eye for detail, sharp intellect – and his bluegrass-grounded musical sensibilities, Hall, in his heyday, was sort of country music's answer to Raymond Carver, John Updike, and other celebrated American masters of the short story. (It's not surprising that, over the years, Hall has numbered American literary figures like William Styron and Kurt Vonnegut among his friends.)

Like many country stars of his day (and unlike many of the 1980s and 1990s, who quite often tend to be products of middle-class suburbia), Hall has drawn from his humble eastern Kentucky origins for his most vivid musical inspiration. He was born in Olive Hill, Kentucky, in 1939 (in a log cabin, at that!) He was the sixth of Virgil L. Hall's eight children. After Hall's mother died and his father was disabled in a hunting accident, Hall was compelled to quit school and work in an overall factory to help the family make ends meet. Later, he formed a bluegrass band, the Kentucky Travelers, and worked as a deejay for Radio Station WMOR in Morehead, Kentucky for several years, until he joined the US Army.

Hall's tour of duty with the army took him to Germany, where he first began writing songs. Back in Kentucky several years later, he bought and ran a grocery store for a time, worked again as a country deejay, and put another band together. Later he attended college in Roanoke, Virginia, on the GI Bill, and studied writing. Around this time, a friend of Hall's took some his original songs to Nashville where they ended up being recorded and popularized by hit artists of the day like Jimmy C. Newman and Dave Dudley. This initial taste of success inspired Hall to move to Nashville in 1964; by the early 1970s, he'd not only emerged as one of Music City's most celebrated songwriters, but also as a popular recording artist. (It was cowboy singer Tex Ritter who dubbed Hall "the Story Teller," a nickname that has stuck through the years.)

Hall's insight as a social commentator and observer of everyday life came into particular focus on his 1971 LP, **In Search Of A Song**. In preparation for this album, Hall, with notebook and tape recorder in hand, made an automobile pilgrimage back to his eastern Kentucky roots in search of his past, in search of a song, in search of himself. He returned to Nashville with this extraordinary collection of story-songs and brilliant character sketches which stand among of the best he's written in his long career. As Hall noted in his book, *The Storyteller's Nashville* (Doubleday & Co., 1979):

> In searching for songs, I had found something that I was not aware of seeking – me . . . I told the untellable and dragged

the past into the present, word by word. I was, at the same time, proud and ashamed . . . While it might be embarrassing to admit the source of our inspiration, most songwriters have lived, either in fantasy or reality, the source of their songs. It seems that nothing else works . . . I had escaped my environment, and yet I longed for the simplicity and the independence that was demonstrated by the people that I had left behind. I had to learn that we never escape who we are.

Clayton Delaney, the lead-off song on the LP (and also one of the biggest hit singles of Hall's career) is a wistful, irony-tinged reminiscence about one of Hall's childhood heroes and his tragic early death through tuberculosis. (The boy's real name was Floyd Carter.) Despite its sorrowful theme and sense of childhood loss, the song has a lilting, almost uplifting bluegrass flavor and tempo. It's accentuated by producer Jerry Kennedy's dobro slides, which vividly punctuate Hall's almost offhanded, conversational delivery of the song. The hidden charm and power of this and so many of Hall's recordings lies in the way he conveys the casual intimacy and unguarded candor of some late-night conversation overheard in some dimly-lit small-town barroom. The bold flourishes of trumpet in the chorus also give *Clayton Delaney* an enticing, nostalgic, 1930s ragtime feel.

Who's Gonna Feed Them Hogs, another eastern Kentucky character vignette, is about a man who makes a miraculous recovery from grave illness through his obsession and determination to get back to his farm and take care of his 400 pigs. ("His way was hogs and his nature was tough," Hall tells us in the lyrics.) Hall's homespun delivery is deftly punctuated by Charlie McCoy's muffled, low-register harmonica flourishes. *Tulsa Telephone Book* is a lighthearted, rather silly, love song with a typical Hall twist: a homesick man, desperately infatuated with a stranger who drifted into and back out of his life, rifles through the local phone directory in his vain search for her – though he doesn't even know her last name. ("I was in Tulsa and had nothin' goin'/She lived in Tulsa and had nothin' on . . ." Hall wryly explains in the lyrics.)

Much grimmer and pathos-ridden is *It Sure Can Get Cold In Des Moines*. This song, which is as succinctly written and rife with dark, unstated portent as any award-winning Raymond Carver short story, is the unsettling recollection of a lonely, ordinary-seeming evening spent in a strange city on a cold, cold night. But beneath the surface, as the lyrics make continuing reference to the falling temperature outside ("The desk clerk said it was fourteen below/I just said, man, that's cold, man, that's cold"), and Hall observes a woman with a suitcase, alone at a barroom table, crying her eyes out for no apparent reason, the song conveys a chill and desolation of a different kind – one which seems to reflect on the inherent coldness and uncertainty of life itself.

Trip To Hyden, a no less powerful song, is about Hall's mid-winter journey to a grim eastern Kentucky coal-mining town which had recently been the scene of a grisly mining disaster that claimed several hundred lives and made national headlines. Where a less accomplished writer might have honed in on the particulars of the mine accident itself, Hall, through a series of loosely connected images ("temporary-lookin' houses with their lean and bashful kids . . .") and small-town character cameos, paints an offhanded portrait of the hard-bitten stoicism of an economically depressed community where death, disaster, loss, and hard times are merely part of the quotidian tapestry of life.

Little Lady Preacher is a more lighthearted but no less insightful slice of small-town life, and a sardonic commentary on religious hypocrisy and the weakness of the human flesh. It's told through the first-person recollections of a young Christian fundamentalist church-goer who secretly lusts after a comely lady preacher who "would punctuate the prophesies with movements of her hips." *A Million Miles To The City* is a simple song about the painful innocence and yearning of country children who dream about life in a far-away world they've never seen. *Second-Handed Flowers* is a poignant recollection of a last visit to a dying friend.

Hall wrote all the songs on **In Search Of A Song**. Taken as a whole, they represent one of the highest artistic water marks in the long, distinguished career of this man who – despite the fact that he's got enough gravel in his voice to fill a dump truck – has been hailed as "the Dean of Nashville songwriters" and "the Poet Laureate of country music."

Tom T. Hall's Greatest Hits (Mercury 824 143–2) is also a worthy collection of some of Hall's best early work. The German Bear Family reissue label has also re-released four of Hall's classic early LPs – **Ballad Of Forty Dollars, Homecoming, 100 Children**, and **I Witness Life** – on two double-album CDs (BCD 15658 and BCD 15631).

Kris Kristofferson was another undisputed king of the early 1970s songwriters-turned-recording artists. He is one of a scant handful of writers (Tom T. Hall, Harlan Howard, Mickey Newbury, and Billy Joe Shaver being others) who had a far-reaching influence in widening the parameters of country songs in terms of both sophistication of language and subject matter.

Kristofferson's best original songs – such as *Help Me Make It Through The Night*, *Sunday Morning Coming Down*, *Me 'N' Bobby McGee*, *Loving Her Was Easier Than Anything I'll Ever Do Again*, *For The Good Times* – are marked by both a sophisticated sense of rhyme and metaphor (borrowed from both the Romantic poets and the 1960s New York folk poet/singers) and a sexual candor which had seldom been heard previously in country music (It's significant that Kristofferson, a former Rhodes Scholar and Oxford University attendee, abandoned a career as an Army officer and passed up an offer to teach English at Westpoint, the US Army officers' academy, coming instead to Nashville to write songs.) Like Bob Dylan and other leading 1960s folkies, Kristofferson wrote songs that frequently dealt with the issue of personal freedom in an increasingly complex and regimented world – as in the famous line from *Me 'N' Bobby McGee*: "Freedom's just another word for nothin' left to lose . . ."

Kristofferson spent more than a half a decade living a marginal existence in Nashville, janitoring and emptying ashtrays in the Columbia recording studios and tending bar in Music Row taverns, before his songs began attracting attention. As heard on **The Songs Of Kris Kristofferson**, a fine collection of his best and earliest compositions, Kristofferson is a gruff, awkward vocalist who sometimes tends to nonchalantly mumble and drawl his lyrics rather than actually sing them. Yet, as these tracks attest, he – much like his friend Bob Dylan – is also living proof that one's vocal limitations can sometimes be made to work in one's favor – if one's original songs have a poignant enough message.

All the same, Texas-born Kristofferson's voice has always been a little too rough-hewn for country radio (though he's been a very popular live performer over the years). Hence few of his own versions of the songs heard herein were chart hits. Yet his own renditions of his classic compositions are, in many cases, considerably more intimate and moving than the versions recorded by various leading country, bluegrass, and rock artists with more accessible vocal styles – everyone from Johnny Cash, Jerry Lee Lewis, Waylon Jennings, Bobby Bare, Ronnie Milsap, Ray Price, Hank Williams, Jr, and Willie Nelson (who, at one point, recorded an entire album of Kristofferson's songs), to the late Janis Joplin.

By the mid-1970s, as Kristofferson's fame increased and he departed Nashville for southern California and Hollywood film stardom, his creative muse began to wane. He has never come near to equaling the crystalline lyric beauty and the poetic clarity of these songs from his early career.

Discographical Details

262   In Search Of A Song

Tom T. Hall

Mercury SR 61350 (LP)

The Year That Clayton Delaney Died/Who's Gonna Feed Them Hogs/Trip To Hyden/Tulsa Telephone Book/It Sure Can Get Cold In Des Moines/The Little Lady Preacher/LA Blues/Kentucky, February 27, 1971/A Million Miles To The City/Second-Handed Flowers/Ramona's Revenge

263   The Songs Of Kris Kristofferson

Kris Kristofferson

Monument AK-44352

The Silver-Tongued Devil/Loving Her Was Easier (Than Anything I'll Ever Do Again)/Me And Bobby McGee/Help Me Make It Through The Night/For The Good Times/Sunday Mornin' Comin' Down/You Show Me Yours (And I'll Show You Mine)/The Pilgrim: Chapter 33 (Hang In, Hopper)/Stranger/I Got A Life Of My Own/Why Me/Who's To Bless And Who's To Blame

(iv) Women of the 1970s

The immense influence of Loretta Lynn has, like that of any number of other artists listed here, more or less straddled the 1960s and 1970s. Lynn was, in fact, arguably the single most influential woman in country music for that period of time between the death of her friend and mentor, Patsy Cline, and the rise of Dolly Parton in the early 1970s.

Lynn's quintessential rags-to-riches story has been chronicled in countless magazine articles, as well as in an autobiography, *Coal Miner's Daughter*, and an Academy Award-winning feature film of the same title. (A 1973 Gallup Poll named her one of the 20 most admired women in the world.) Her spunky original songs and often hilarious musical candor have done much to redefine and enlarge upon the role of women in country music.

Lynn (real name: Loretta Webb) was born in 1935 in Butcher Holler, a remote rural coal-mining settlement in eastern Kentucky (an area of the US that has produced a disproportionately high number of bluegrass and country music's leading talents). She was the second of eight children born into the semi-impoverished world of Ted Webb, a smalltime farmer and coal miner. Lynn herself was married at age 13, and had four children by the time she was 18 – an unlikely start for a future country superstar!

Moving to Washington State with her husband, Oliver V. ("Moonie") Lynn, Loretta began her career in the late 1950s singing in local clubs and honky-tonks. Her proverbial big break came when she won a talent contest sponsored by Buck

Owens and was given an opportunity to appear on his television show. When *I'm A Honky Tonk Girl*, an original song she recorded in Los Angeles, was released as her first single and made a showing in the charts, she and Moonie headed for Nashville. By the end of 1960, she'd made her first of many appearances on the Grand Ole Opry. In Nashville, Lynn also became a friend and protégé of the late Patsy Cline – then in her musical heyday as a country and pop crossover star, and, ironically, the last years of her life (Cline died in 1963). Cline, along with Kitty Wells, a celebrated honky-tonk queen of the 1950s, have been Lynn's two most abiding influences.

As evidenced by these tracks, Lynn's own music has, throughout the years, actually hewed closer to the determinedly homespun tradition of Kitty Wells than the pop-flavored stylings of Cline. As her boldly twangy down-home vocals attest, there has never been much "crossover" in Lynn. (Ironically, her younger sister, Crystal Gayle, became one of the most successful country pop-crossover mavens of the 1970s and early 1980s with a smooth, sultry vocal style which was almost the antithesis of her older sister Loretta's soulful hard country sound.)

The 16 selections on **Loretta Lynn: Country Music Hall Of Fame** (1991) are actually drawn as heavily from the 1960s as from the 1970s – from 1964 to 1976, to be exact. Nonetheless, the album is included here simply because it's by far the strongest and single most comprehensive single-CD anthology ever assembled from Lynn's prodigious body of work. These classic performances highlight (as well if not better than any other hits collection) the rustic charm, frank outspokenness, and sparkling wit and defiance that vivify Lynn's inspired musical tributes to her rural heritage and honky-tonk musical roots. Many of these songs are actually "protest" songs of sorts, in that they candidly echo the anger, concerns, preoccupations, and dreams of millions of women of Lynn's generation. With empathy, sincerity, and humor, Lynn indeed gave a new voice of assertiveness and empowerment to rural American women and helped change the way they perceived themselves within the context of marital relationships. With unforgettable songs like *The Pill*, *One's On The Way*, *Don't Come Home A-Drinkin' (With Lovin' On Your Mind)*, and *Your Squaw Is On The Warpath*, Lynn also often took an aggressively pro-woman stance on such then-taboo subjects as birth control and alcoholic spousal abuse – subjects which, up until her time, women country singers only touched with kidgloves, if at all. It took Loretta Lynn to take the gloves off.

The proudly autobiographical *Coal Miner's Daughter* (recorded in 1969) is the most famous song on here, and has,

over the years, become Lynn's signature song. *You're Lookin'
At Country*, a somewhat less universally known but hardly less
memorable selection, is a similar salute to her humble
Kentucky origins and thoroughly rural temperament.

I'm A Honky Tonk Girl (the version heard here is a 1968
remake of the quasi-hit which launched her career in 1960) is
one of many songs where Lynn typically turns the tables on an
old formula. In most country songs of her era, it was the
woman's lot to sit at home, and passively suffer the consequences of her unfaithful husband's beer-swilling, skirt-
chasing ways. But here, it's the woman herself who's out in a
bar drowning her sorrows in a swirling sea of booze and loud
music. *Your Squaw Is On The Warpath* (one of eight songs that
Lynn wrote in this collection) has a tongue-in-cheek arrangement that utilizes *Drums Along The Mohawk*-style tom-toms
and growling male vocal harmonies to playfully emulate an
Indian war-chant. In the song, Lynn impudently struts her
independence as she declares war against her roving, good-
timing husband.

In *One's On The Way* (written by Shel Silverstein, a *Playboy*
cartoonist and short-story writer–turned country songscribe),
Lynn takes only a slightly more passive stance as she cheerfully
depicts the harried everyday life of a Topeka housewife saddled
with a house full of kids and a typical (at least in Lynn's songs)
barfly husband. The protagonist of the song wistfully day-
dreams about a jet-set existence, and the song – which emotes
goodnatured but resigned optimism rather than grimness –
ends with a humorous, disjointed phone conversation with her
husband, who informs her that he's bringing a passel of his
drunken army buddies home for dinner. It's typical Loretta
Lynn all the way: sassy, good-hearted, hilariously insightful,
and deeply empathetic towards the lot of the everyday housewife and her dreams and disappointments.

Fist City, more vintage defiance from Lynn, expresses the
furious threats of a woman who's ready to duke it out with the
floozy who is trying to steal her husband's affections. The lyrics
are, at once, comic and impassioned: ("I'll take you by the head
of your hair and lift you off the ground," she warns her rival).
You Ain't Woman Enough (To Take My Man) (also written by
Lynn) displays similar justified truculence towards a potential
competitor for her husband's affections.

The Pill (written by Lorene Allen, Don McHan, and T.D.
Bayless) is in many ways the flip-side perspective of *One's On
The Way*. The woman in this song is mired in a similarly
dreary domestic predicament; only she's jubilantly found lib-
eration through the wonders of modern birth control. In its
day, *The Pill* was an extremely controversial song – though by

today's standards it seems tame. It vividly reminds us of the narrower lifestyle choices available to rural American women of two or three decades ago.

Loretta Lynn: Country Music Hall Of Fame is also highlighted by a pair of worthy duets. *Mr And Mrs Used To Be* (written by Joe Deaton and recorded in 1964), features revered 1950s honky-tonk king Ernest Tubb. It's the anguished confessional of a man and woman who alternately berate and console each other over their failed marriage. *After The Fire Is Gone*, with Conway Twitty, deals with the pain and discomfiture of a couple who are stuck in a troubled relationship long after the passion and infatuation has faded to disillusionment. Lynn and Twitty (see the "Basic Recordings" entry in this chapter) recorded dozens and dozens of duets (many of them major chart hits, quite a few of them maudlin and trifling chart fodder) during the 1970s, but *After The Fire Is Gone* is one of their all-time best.

Dolly Parton, by dint of her high profile as a film star and TV host, and on account of her flamboyant self-styled persona (as a sort of warm-hearted, bubbly, latterday Mae West), has become almost synonymous with modern country music in the minds of the general public. Ironically, much of her music of the late 1970s and the 1980s has drawn far more heavily from pop stylings than from her own *bona fide* down-home Appalachian roots.

Those who only know Parton from her more modern-day musical and media incarnations and are only familiar with her more popular crossover hits (*Here You Come Again*, *Nine To Five*, and *Islands In The Stream* – a duet with Kenny Rogers) may be shocked to hear her late 1960s and early 1970s recordings. They remind us how thoroughly homespun, countrified, and *un*cosmopolitan Parton once was, and just how far she has evolved – image-wise and music-wise – in the years since, as time and fame have put ever greater distance between herself and her Smoky Mountain roots.

My Tennessee Mountain Home (1973) was recorded at a point when Parton was on the cusp of national stardom. It is her heartfelt tribute to the mountain heritage and the humble family circumstances into which she was born in East Tennessee's Smoky Mountains in 1946. Other country singers may sing of backwoods hard times with varying degrees of candor and credibility; but Parton, one of 11 children to grow up in the ramshackle little house (just a shack, really) pictured on the cover of this LP, certainly knew hard times firsthand.

Parton left her mountain home, near Sevierville, Tennessee, for Nashville in 1964, fresh out of high school. Remarkably, within two weeks of her arrival in Music City, she landed a recording contract with Monument Records. (Ironically, her uniquely high-pitched vocal style was, at first, considered a bit too strident for country music of the sixties.) In 1967, however, Parton had her very first country hit with a Curly Putman composition called *Dumb Blonde* (which, in actuality railed against the stereotypes suggested by the title). This first early chart exposure landed her a spot as a singer in the band of Porter Wagoner, a leading recording artist and Grand Ole Opry star of the day.

By the time she recorded **My Tennessee Mountain Home**, Parton was already well on the way to establishing herself as a country star in her own right. And arguably, making an LP as personal and autobiographical as this at such an early and crucial stage in her solo career, was a bit of a risk. One also senses in these extremely personal songs (all of which Parton composed) that she was already looking back with a certain painful longing: looking back – as she puts it in one of the songs – to "the good old days when times were bad."

My Tennessee Mountain Home opens with *The Letter*, a moving recitation of an actual epistle that Parton wrote home to her parents shortly after her arrival in Nashville. *The Letter* expresses not only her hopefulness for the future, but her homesickness, and her acute sense of appreciation of her uprising. Each of the songs that follow – *Old Black Kettle*, *Daddy's Working Hands*, *The Better Part Of Life*, *The Good Old Days When Times Were Bad*, and others – use various perspectives to explore her heritage, strong family bonds, and the profound effect they've had in guiding her through her adult life. *Dr Robert F. Thomas* is a loving tribute to the country physician who delivered Parton and many of her brothers and sisters. The LP's title song, with its dobro trills and vivid natural imagery, celebrates the natural beauty of Tennessee's Smoky Mountains.

In most of the songs on side 2 of **My Tennessee Mountain Home** Parton uses her past to measure the triumphs, disappointments, and complexities of her adult life and burgeoning fame. *The Wrong Direction Home* – much like the entire LP, really – is one of the most eloquent and sustained odes to homesickness ever written. These aforementioned songs, and others, like *Back Home* (about a woman who decides to abandon the misery and hassles of big city life and return to the mountains) and *The Better Part Of Life* (which conveys an almost painful nostalgia for the past), highlight Parton as a startling vocalist whose unmistakable style would only lose a modicum of its soulfulness as it grew more polished and refined in later years.

The solid line-up of veteran Nashville studio stars of the day – Pete Drake, steel guitar; Buck Trent, electric banjo; Johnny Gimble, fiddle; Jerry Carrigan, drums; Charlie McCoy, harmonica – provide austere arrangements that never intrude or draw undue attention to themselves at the expense of Parton's thoroughly sincere and inspired lyrics and performances.

Also highly recommenced is Parton's **Greatest Hits** (Vol. 1 – RCA 8505–2–R), a solid CD collection of Parton's biggest chart records from the 1970s and very early 1980s. For those wishing to delve even deeper into her extensive catalogue, there is also the 2-CD collection, **Dolly Parton: The RCA Years: 1967–86** (RCA 66127–2). **Coat Of Many Colors** is another landmark early Parton LP.

Discographical Details

64 Loretta Lynn: Country Music Hall Of Fame

Loretta Lynn
MCA MCAD-10083

Success/Mr And Mrs Used To Be (with Ernest Tubb)/*Blue Kentucky Girl/You Ain't Woman Enough/Don't Come Home A-Drinkin' (With Lovin' On Your Mind)/Fist City/I'm A Honky Tonk Girl/Your Squaw Is On The Warpath/Wings Upon Your Horns/Coal Miner's Daughter/After The Fire Is Gone* (with Conway Twitty)/*You're Looking At Country/One's On The Way/The Pill/When The Tingle Becomes A Chill/Out Of My Head And Back In My Bed*

65 My Tennessee Mountain Home

Dolly Parton
RCA AYL1-3764 (LP)

The Letter/I Remember/Old Black Kettle/Daddy's Workin Boots/Dr Robert F. Thomas/In The Good Old Days (When Times Were Bad)/My Tennessee Mountain Home/The Wrong Direction Home/Back Home/The Better Part Of Life/Down On Music Row

(v) Neo-Rockabilly and "Honky-Tonk Rock"

Gary Stewart's 1975 album, **Out Of Hand**, heralded the arrival of an important new talent on the country scene. In his sadly brief musical heyday, this Kentucky-born, Florida-raised honky-tonker sang like a young Jerry Lee Lewis wired on amphetamines and cheap wine. His voice had a frenzied tremolo and a manic intensity that, at times, sounds as eerie as it is thrilling. He could also wail like George Jones and bend a tearful note like Lefty Frizzell. "I'm just a country boy from Kentucky that grew up on rock n' roll," Stewart explained to *Rolling Stone Magazine* in 1976 when asked about his roots and inspirations. "Both of them together – progressive country, rockabilly, whatever you wanta call it – is what you get."

Stewart's performances on **Out Of Hand** are among his best ever. (Some of the music on his subsequent RCA albums, like **Steppin' Out** and **Your Place Or Mine** show glimpses of this same fire.) Stewart's music is indeed a frenzied mixed bag of rockabilly, honky-tonk, and Southern rock sensibilities; as such, it earned him praise in the rock press which heralded him as the long-missing link between country and rock-and-roll. "Except for Jerry Lee Lewis," opined *The Village Voice*, "there has never been a 'billy' singer like him." Added *Rolling Stone*: "Stewart . . . epitomizes rockabilly in the vintage country-boy-gone-crazy mold."

Admittedly, nearly all the songs on **Out Of Hand** deal in one way or another with the wild side of life. Archetypal honky-tonk themes like hard living, faithless or fallen women, wild days, wilder nights, and the ever-present demon of drink, are recurrent. Many of the songs deal with temptation . . . and yielding to it. In the title song (written by Tom Jans and J. Barry), Stewart wails out the lament of a frightened and confused man who is torn between his fear and desire as the casual extramarital affair he's dabbled in suddenly lurches out of control. *She's Actin' Single (I'm Drinkin' Doubles)*, written by Wayne Carson, is one of country music's all-time classic drinking songs as well as Stewart's only number 1 single. Once again, as in the title tune, his voice seems to tremble and resonate with a panoply of twisted, half-hidden emotions: rage, fright, sorrow, despair, and self-pity. He sings the chorus with such teeth-clenching anguish, it's as if he's about to implode with pain. *Sweet Country Red* is a gentle, empathetic tribute to a fallen woman, while *Williamson County* (co-written by Stewart himself) is a haunting Appalachian-flavored tale of jealousy, murder, and retribution. In *Back-Slider's Wine* (by M. Murphey), a ruined man, about to pass out amidst the spilled beer and peanut shells on a filthy barroom floor, laments his own alcoholic ruination and warns others away from a similar fate. Even *I See The Want To In Your Eyes*, the closest thing to a love song here, has intimations of lust on the sly.

Producer Roy Dea (who has produced all of Stewart's records to date) obviously knew what he had on his hands with Stewart, even if some of the veteran Nashville session pickers on **Out Of Hand** seemed not to. The fact that Stewart sometimes had to rise above the plodding arrangements seemed to inspire him to sing and play (guitar, piano) with even more reckless abandon.

Ultimately, the brilliant music on **Out Of Hand** is like the first installment of a glorious promise that was never paid in full. Stewart has continued to record sporadically in the years since, but he has never really held a candle to these early performances. This long-out-of-print album was only recently given new life when it was reissued on CD.

Gary's Greatest (Hightone HCD 8030) is a highly recommended collection of Stewart's vintage 1970s and early 1980s RCA recordings.

Discographical Details

66 Out Of Hand

Gary Stewart

Hightone HCD 8026 (originally released by RCA)

Drinkin' Thing/Honky Tonkin'/I See The Want To In Your Eyes/This Old Heart Won't Let Go/Draggin' Shackles/She's Actin' Single (I'm Drinkin' Doubles)/Back-Sliders Wine/Sweet Country Red/Out of Hand/Williamson County

Basic Recordings

67 Will The Circle Be Unbroken

The Nitty Gritty Dirt Band (and Various Guest Artists)

EMI E22V-46589

Grand Ole Opry Song/Keep On The Sunnyside/Nashville Blues/You Were My Flower/The Precious Jewel/Dark As A Dungeon/Tennessee Stud/Black Mountain Rag/Wreck On The Highway/The End Of The World/I Saw The Light/Sunny Side Of The Mountain/Nine-Pound Hammer/Lovin' You (Might Be The Best Thing Yet)/Honky Tonkin'/You Don't Know My Mind/My Walkin' Shoes/Lonesome Fiddle Blues/Cannonball Rag/Avalanche/Flint Hill Special/Tagary Mountain/Earl's Breakdown/Orange Blossom Special/Wabash Cannonball/Lost Highway/Way Down Town/Down Yonder/Pins And Needles (In My Heart)/Honky Tony Blues/Sailin' Along To Hawaii/I'm Thinkin' Tonight Of My Blue Eyes/I Am A Pilgrim/Wildwood Flower/Soldier's Joy/Will The Circle Be Unbroken/Both Sides Now

This popular California-based country-rock band journeyed to Nashville in 1972 to record this heartfelt 3-LP collection with some of the leading veteran luminaries of traditional country and bluegrass music, including Roy Acuff, Flatt and Scruggs, Mother Maybelle Carter, Doc Watson, Merle Travis, Jimmy Martin, and Vassar Clements. **Will The Circle Be Unbroken** did much to reawaken the interest in old-time country music among younger, more urbane, and more rock-oriented listeners.

68 As Is

Bobby Bare

Columbia FC 37157 (LP)

New Cut Road/She Is Gone/Dropping Out Of Sight/Summer Wages/White Freight Liner Blues/Dollar Pool Fool/Learning To Live Again/Call Me The Breeze/Take Me As I Am (Or Let Me Go)/Let Him Roll

A laconic but moving singer, Bare first gained attention in the early 1960s with folk-pop hits like *Detroit City* and *Four Strong Winds*. He was also on the fringes of the Outlaw movement. His contributions to country music of the 1970s go beyond his singing abilities; he also had a rare gift for spotting great new songs and new songwriters. This collection, which was produced by Rodney Crowell (see "Essential Recordings," in the chapter on the 1980s) features original songs by Guy Clark, Tom T. Hall, Townes Van Zandt, Willie Nelson, Ian Tyson, Boudleaux Bryant, and others.

269 Old Five And Dimers Like Me

Billy Joe Shaver

CBS KZ 32293 (LP) (originally released on Monument)

Black Rose/Old Five And Dimers Like Me/LA Turnaround/Jesus Christ, What A Man/Played The Game Too Long/I Been To Georgia On A Fast Train/ Willy, The Wandering Gypsy And Me/Low Down Freedom/Jesus Was Our Savior And Cotton Was Our King/Serious Souls/Bottom Dollar

Next to Kris Kristofferson, Tom T. Hall, and Mickey Newbury, Billy Joe Shaver is probably the most vividly original songwriter to have surfaced in Nashville in the early 1970s. Shaver's songs have also been recorded by Willie Nelson, Kristofferson, and nearly all the other major artists involved in the Outlaw scene, as well as by non-Outlaws like Bobby Bare and Tom T. Hall. In fact, versions of quite a few of these selections can also be heard on the Waylon Jennings album, **Honky Tonk Heroes** (see "Essential Recordings," this chapter). At his best, Shaver imbued his introspective lyrics and musical tales of wanderlust, hard times, and low-down dirt farming with the authentic rusticity and world-weariness of someone who's lived it all himself – which Shaver certainly has. His brand of musical Americana conjures up traditions that go all the way back to formative American songwriters like Woody Guthrie, Jimmie Rodgers, and even Stephen Foster, and beyond. This 1973 LP was produced by fellow songwriter Kris Kristofferson.

270 Behind Closed Doors

Charlie Rich

Epic EK 32247

Sunday Kind Of Woman/Till I Can't Take It Anymore/We Love Each Other/ You Never Really Wanted Me/I Take It On Home/I'm Not Going Hungry Anymore/If You Wouldn't Be My Lady/The Most Beautiful Girl/Nothing In The World/Behind Closed Doors/Peace On You

Rich, a versatile Arkansas-born white blues singer and former Sun Records rockabilly neophyte found a new incarnation working in the early 1970s with Nashville producer Billy Sherrill as one of country music's most popular country-to-pop crossover crooners. Though this selection showcases only one side of a brilliantly multi-dimensional singer, the music on this multi-million-selling album is one of the quintessential distillations of the early 1970s country-to-pop "Nashville sound."

271 Greatest Hits (Vol. 1)

Ronnie Milsap

RCA 8504-2-R

(I'd Be) A Legend In My Time/(I'm A) Stand By My Woman Man/Pure Love/Daydreams About Night Things/It Was Almost Like A Song/Smoky

Mountain Rain/Please Don't Tell Me How The Story Ends/Back On My Mind Again/What A Difference You've Made In My Life

This blind former white R & B singer made some of the snappiest country music of the early 1970s before he discovered a fondness for Barry Manilow songs and found even greater commercial success in the easy listening pop-crossover mode later in the decade. This album constitutes some of his best, earliest, and most country recordings

72 20 Greatest Hits

Loretta Lynn and Conway Twitty
MCA MCAD-5972

After The Fire Is Gone/It's Only Make-Believe/Pickin' Wild Mountain Berries/ Lead Me On/Louisiana Woman, Mississippi Man/As Soon As I Hang Up The Phone/Spiders And Snakes/Feelins'/The Letter/God Bless America Again/I Can't Love You Enough/From Seven Till Ten/I've Already Loved You In My Mind/You're The Reason Our Kids Are Ugly/The Sadness Of It All/That's All That Matters To Me/It's True Love/You Know Just What I'd Do/Lovin' What Your Lovin' Does To Me/I Still Believe In Waltzes

These two artists (each of whom also had immense solo success during the 1970s) were one of the most celebrated and popular male-female duet teams of the 1970s. (Unlike Tammy Wynette and George Jones their alliance was purely a musical one.) Their duets, as this comprehensive collection attests, encompassed humor as well as pathos.

73 20 Greatest Hits

John Conlee
MCA MCAD-5925

Rose-Colored Glasses/Lady, Lay Down/Backside Of Thirty/Before My Time/ Friday Night Blues/She Can't Say That Anymore/What I Had With You/Miss Emily's Picture/Busted/Nothing Behind You, Nothing In Sight/I Don't Remember Loving You/Common Man/I'm Only In It For The Love/In My Eyes/As Long As I'm Rockin' With You/Way Back/Years After You/Working Man/Blue Highway/Old School/

John Conlee, who worked as a mortician before venturing into country music, was responsible for some of the most wry and intelligent commentaries on the loneliness and economic hard times of blue collar life heard in the late 1970s and very early 1980s. Some of these tracks, with their syrupy background vocals and lush strings, are admittedly a touch over-produced by today's standards. Nonetheless, they stand the test of time well. Even though some of these selections were originally released in the early and mid-1980s, this is still the most comprehensive and worthwhile compilation of Conlee's relatively slender but impressive body of work.

74 The Best Of Don Williams, Vol. 2

Don Williams
MCA MCAD-31172

(Turn Out The Light And) Love Me Tonight/'Till All The Rivers Run Dry/ Rake And Ramblin' Man/I'm Just A Country Boy/Some Broken Hearts Never

Mend/Tulsa Time/She Never Knew Me/Falling In Love/I've Got A Winner In You/You're My Best Friend/Say It Again

A former member of the Pozo Seco Singers, a pop/folk trio that enjoyed brief chart success in the 1960s, this tall Texan turned his hand to country music and, in the 1970s and early 1980s, sustained a huge following with his soulful, introspective style. The best of Williams's music often suggests cautious strength, serenity and hopefulness amidst the madness of the modern world.

275 Greatest Hits

Moe Bandy

Columbia CK 38315

Rodeo Romeo/Following The Feeling/My Woman Loves The Devil Out Of Me/ It Was Always So Easy (To Find An Unhappy Woman/I Cheated Me Right Out Of You/Barstool Mountain/In The Middle Of Losing You/Hank Williams/ You Wrote My Life/It's A Cheatin' Situation/Someday Soon

Though he does not possess the remarkable honky-tonk vocal skills of a George Jones or a Merle Haggard, Moe Bandy nonetheless deserves much credit for keeping the subgenre of honky-tonk "cheatin' and drinkin' " songs alive during the 1970s and early 1980s, until he was eclipsed in the charts by younger, more telegenic contenders like George Strait and John Anderson.

This compilation also contains material from the 1970s as well as the early 1980s. Yet, for the money, it's one of the best Bandy hits packages currently on the market.

276 20 Greatest Hits

Conway Twitty

MCA MCAD-5976

Hello Darlin'/Fifteen Years Ago/I Can't See Me Without You/Last Date (Lost Your Love On Our Last Date)/Baby's Gone/You've Never Been This Far Before/I'm Not Through Loving You Yet/Linda On My Mind/There's A Honky Tonk Angel (Who'll Take Me Back In)/I Can't Believe She Gives It All To Me/I See The Want-To In Your Eyes/Don't Cry, Joni/Georgia Keeps Pulling On My Ring/I've Already Loved You In My Mind/Don't Take It Away/I May Never Get To Heaven/I'd Love To Lay You Down/Rest Your Love On Me/Tight-Fittin' Jeans/Redneckin' Love-Makin' Night

This former 1950s rock-and-roller (*It's Only Make Believe*) from Friars Point, Mississippi, turned to country music in the 1960s, and enjoyed immense popularity (more than 40 number 1 singles) – though in recent years his approach to hit-making became somewhat formulaic. Twitty, who died unexpectedly in mid-1993 while still energetically touring and pursuing his long, successful career, can be heard at his zenith on this and other mid-1970s recordings. This excellent CD compilation gathers many of Twitty's classic hits from his vintage years with MCA.

277 Greatest Hits, 1973–76

Tanya Tucker

Columbia CK 33355

Delta Dawn/Blood Red And Goin' Down/The Jamestown Ferry/What's Your Mama's Name/I Believe The South Is Gonna Rise Again/Would You Lay With

Me (In A Field Of Stone)/Love's The Answer/Rainy Girl/No Man's Land/The Man That Turned My Mama On

Tanya Tucker first made her mark during the 1970s as a child singer (actually a young teenager) who sang sultry, provocative songs of adult love and lust. Some of Tucker's biggest and best hits from this era (she has since re-kindled her career as an *adult* singer singing sultry, provacative songs of adult love and lust) are collected here.

78 Stardust

Willie Nelson
Columbia CK 35305
Stardust/Georgia On My Mind/Blue Skies/All Of Me/Unchained Melody/September Song/On The Sunny Side Of The Street/Moonlight In Vermont/Don't Get Around Much Anymore/Someone To Watch Over Me

An artist without Willie Nelson's sterling credentials and immense across-the-board appeal (see "Essential Recording," this chapter) would have had trouble pulling off a project like this: a collection of sterling 1930s and 1940s pop standards. Yet it's a testimonial to Nelson's immense versatility that he succeeded brilliantly on this 1978 collection, which was produced by Booker T. Jones and has sold millions of copies. (In typical Nelson fashion, he'd preceded this release with **From Willie To Lefty**, (1977), a fine, ultra-stripped-down honky-tonk tribute to his hard country idol, the late Lefty Frizzell.)

79 Anniversary: Twenty Years Of Hits

Tammy Wynette
Epic EGK 40625
Apartment No. 9/Your Good Girl's Gonna Go Bad/I Don't Wanna Play House/ D-I-V-O-R-C-E/Stand By Your Man/Singing My Song/Run, Woman, Run/ We Sure Can Love Each Other/Good Lovin' (Makes It Right)/Bedtime Story/ Till I Get It Right/Kids Say The Darndest Things/Another Lonely Song/We're Gonna Hold On (with George Jones)/*Golden Ring/*(with George Jones)/*You And Me/One Of A Kind/Two Story House* (with George Jones)

With her massive late 1960s hit *Stand By Your Man*, Tammy Wynette (See "Essential Recordings," this chapter: George Jones and Tammy Wynette) became a sort of unofficial spokeswoman for the unliberated rural American woman. Though occasionally given to musical bathos and melodrama, as well as crass over-production at the hands of producer Billy Sherrill, Wynette was nonetheless one of the most important women singers of the 1970s, and early 1980s.

80 Whiskey Bent And Hellbound

Hank Williams, Jr
Warner/Curb 237–2
Whiskey Bent And Hellbound/Tired Of Being Johnny B. Good/Outlaw Women/ (I Don't Have) Anymore Love Songs/White Lighning'/Women I've Never Had/ OD'd In Denver/Come And Go Blues/Old Nashville Cowboys/The Conversation

Hank Williams, Jr, son of country music avatar Hank Williams, Sr, started out as a child star and slavish imitator of his father's honky-tonk hard country style. But, by the mid-1970s the younger Williams found his own voice and proceeded to carve out a massive following with music that owed much to the rowdy sound and spirit of the Outlaws and the Southern rockers. This is one of a half-dozen or so vintage LPs that Williams made during the mid- and late 1970s, some of which are considered some of the best-ever fusions of country and Southern rock.

281   17 Greatest Hits

David Allan Coe

Columbia (CD) 40185

She Used To Love Me A Lot/Mona Lisa Lost Her Smile/The Ride/Now I Lay Me Down To Cheat/Tennessee Whiskey/If That Ain't Country/Longhaired Redneck/Jody Like A Melody/Please Come To Boston/You Never Even Called Me By My Name/This Bottle (In My Hand)/Would You Lay With Me (In A Field Of Stone)/Jack Daniels, If You Please/Take This Job And Shove It/ Willie, Waylon, And Me/Pledging My Love/Hank Wiliams Junior – Junior (with Dicky Betts and Kris Kristofferson)

David Allan Coe, an ex-convict and motorcycle gangmember from Ohio, was one of the most talented and outrageous figures to emerge in the back-draft of the Outlaw movement. His songs could be, by turns, tender and intro-spective, bitter and belligerent. This is the strongest of several compilations that span Coe's recording career, which straddled the 1970s and 1980s.

282   The Freddy Fender Collection

Freddy Fender

Reprise: 9 26638–2

Tell It Like It Is/Vaya Con Dios/Wasted Days And Wasted Nights/You'll Lose A Good Thing/I Can't Stop Loving You/It's All In The Game/Before The Next Teardrop Falls/Pledging My Love/Secret Love/Since I Met You, Baby

This brilliant Mexican-American singer and occasional actor (he appeared in Robert Redford's *Millagro Beanfield Wars*) from Texas's Rio Grande Valley, was formerly billed as the "Chicano Elvis" and had been recording for nearly two decades when, in 1975, legendary Texas producer Huey Meaux broke him into the country market. This collection of his vintage country recordings vividly showcases his bold, inimitable style and his rich, teary alto.

283   20 Favorites

The Kendalls

Epic EGK 45249

Thank God For The Radio/If You Let Him Drive You Crazy (He Will)/Love Is A Long, Hard Road/Sweet Desire/I'm Already Blue/Bye Bye Love/Pitts-burgh Steelers/I'd Dance Every Dance With You/You'd Make An Angel Want To Cheat/Blue, Blue Day/Just Like Real People/I Had A Lovely Time/Curtain In The Window/It Don't Feel Like Sinnin' To Me/Temporarily Out Of Order/ Cryin' Time/Pick Me Up On Your Way Down/Heartaches By The Number/ Heaven's Just A Sin Away/Once More

This father-and-daughter duet team (who, ironically specialized in "cheatin' " songs) swept the charts and the awards (winning both a Grammy and a Country Music Association Award) for their massive 1977 duet hit, *Heaven's Just A Sin Away*. The Kendalls never recaptured the magic of this initial burst of success and it's safe to say that all 20 of the cuts on here (some of which are competent re-recordings of some of their bigger hits) weren't all exactly "hits." Even so, the Kendalls' vibrant harmonies never fail to captivate, even in this slightly warmed-over re-make package, which is currently the closest facsimile of a genuine "hits" collection that is available on them.

84 The Best Of The Statler Brothers

The Statler Brothers
Mercury 822 524–2
Bed Of Rose's/Whatever Happened To Randolph Scott/Do You Remember These/Carry Me Back/Flowers On The Wall/The Class Of '57/I'll Go To My Grave Loving You/Pictures/Thank You, World/New York City/Susan When She Tried

This central Virginia-based gospel quartet got its start singing in the choir of the Mt Olivet Presbyterian Church in Staunton, Virginia. The Statlers, with the help of Johnny Cash, turned to country music in the early 1960s, and reigned in the country charts for years. (They are eight-time recipients of the Country Music Association's annual "Vocal Group Of The Year" award.) Their bold baritone harmonies hark nostalgically back to the turn-of-the-century era of the barbershop quartet. Their earliest work is, by far, their strongest, and is well represented here. (A handful of these songs, initially released on Columbia, were re-recorded by the Statlers when they moved over to Mercury, which released this package.)

85 Greatest Hits

Johnny Rodriguez
Mercury CS 826 271–4 (cassette)
That's The Way Love Goes/We're Over/You Always Come Back To Hurting Me/Dance With Me (Just One More Time)/Love Put A Song In My Heart/ Born To Lose/Faded Love/I Couldn't Be Me Without You/I Just Can't Get Her Out Of My Mind/Jealous Heart/Just Get Up And Close The Door/Love Promise/Pass Me By (If You're Only Passing Through)/Ridin' My Thumb To Mexico/Something

This immensely talented, handsome Tex-Mex singer had an impressive string of country hits before losing his creative focus during the later 1970s. Rodriguez's authoritative country vocal prowess is aptly captured on this compilation of his best 1970s hits.

86 All-Time Greatest Hits

Eddie Rabbitt
Warner Bros 26467–2
I Love A Rainy Night/Drivin' My Life Away/Gone Too Far/Suspicions/I Can't Help Myself (Here Comes The Feelin')/Rocky Mountain Music/Two Dollars In The Jukebox/Do You Right Tonight/Pour Me Another Tequila/Hearts On Fire

This New Jersey-born songwriter (he wrote the Elvis Presley hit, *Kentucky Rain*) turned country singer started out in the mid-1970s with an impressive series of smooth country hits like *Rocky Mountain Music* and *Drinkin' My Baby Off My Mind* that stylistically owed as much to country-popster John Denver as to George Jones. By the turn of the decade, however, Rabbitt was breaking new ground with a rhythmically compelling hybrid brand of neo-rockabilly. (Rabbit was at his musical best right at the turn of the decade; hence a few of these selections are drawn from the very early 1980s.)

287 Greatest Hits

Charley Pride

RCA CD 6917–2–R

You're My Jamaica/When I Stop Leaving (I'll Be Gone)/Honky Tonk Blues/ Where Do I Put Her Memory/Roll On Mississippi/A Whole Lotta Things To Sing About/(She's Just) An Old Love Turned Memory/Burgers And Fries

One of country music's precious few commercially successful black singers, Pride possesses a finely-honed, robust singing style molded heavily in the spirit and tradition of Hank Williams. Pride was also one of the biggest superstars of the late 1960s and early 1970s. (No one had had more consecutive number 1 records until the super country-rock quartet, Alabama, came along.) It's difficult to recommend this deplorably skimpy (only eight songs) CD collection, since it offers such a meager sampling of his vast body of work. Yet, sad to say, it's about the best compilation available at the moment.

288 Ann Murray's Country Hits

Ann Murray

Liberty C21K–46487

Time Don't Run Out On Me/Walk Right Back/Cotton Jenny/Nobody Loves Me Like You Do/He Thinks I Still Care/Another Sleepless Night/Hey, Baby/I Don't Think I'm Ready For You/It's All I Can Do/Just Another Woman In Love/A Little Good News/Lucky Me/Somebody's Always Saying Goodbye/Son Of A Rotten Gambler/Blessed Are The Believers

Canadian songstress Ann Murray, best known for her many pop hits, also enjoyed considerable reverse crossover (from pop *to* country) success. Of the considerable number of popsters who've invaded the country charts, Murray, with her warm, gorgeous, low-register singing style, has been one of the most consistently tasteful. This compilation gathers Murray's best country chart-toppers (some of which were released during the 1980s) in one package.

289 The Best Of Mickey Newbury

Mickey Newbury

Capitol/Curb D2–77455

Sunshine/Blue Sky Shining/Danny Boy/She Even Woke Me Up To Say Goodbye/An American Trilogy/Makes Me Wonder If I Ever Said Goodbye/ Shenandoah/Ain't No Blues Today/Hand Me Another Of Those/It Just Doesn't Matter Anymore/Gone To Alabama/Any Way You Want Me

Mickey Newbury, a friend and musical contemporary of Kris Kristofferson, was – like Kristofferson – generally considered one of the most innovative and cutting-edge country songwriters of the early 1970s – though Newbury had more or less retreated into obscurity by the late 1970s. This compilation offers a definitive glimpse of some of Newbury's most starkly original material as performed by him. (Many of these songs were popularized by Elvis Presley and other leading artists of the day.)

0 All-Time Greatest Hits

Crystal Gayle
Curb/Cema D21K–77360

Talkin' In Your Sleep/When I Dream/Why Have You Left The One You Left Me For/Wrong Road Again/You Never Miss A Real Good Thing (Till He Says Goodbye)/Don't It Make My Brown Eyes Blue/I've Cried (The Blues Right Out Of My Eyes/Everybody Oughta Cry/I Hope You're Havin' Better Luck Than Me/I'll Do It All Over Again/I'll Get Over You/Somebody Loves You

Crystal Gayle, Loretta Lynn's younger sister, infused the country charts with her warm pop sound. This collection highlights the commercial high water mark of her career, during both the 1970s and early 1980s.

1 17 Greatest Hits

Larry Gatlin
Columbia CK 40187

Sure Feels Like Love/Sweet Becky Walker/Take Me To Your Lovin' Place/ Taking Somebody With Me When I Fall/What Are We Doin' Lonesome/Broken Lady/Denver/All The Gold In California/She Used To Sing On Sunday/Almost Called Her Baby By Mistake/Houston (Means I'm One Day Closer To You)/I Don't Wanna Cry/I Just Wish You Were Someone I Love/Love Is Just A Game/Midnight Choir/Night Time Magic/Statues Without Hearts

Best known for his crystal clear alto, Larry Gatlin, often backed by his brothers Steve and Rudy, composed and sang some of the most lovely and ethereal country songs of the 1970s and early 1980s. This package is his most representative "hits" collection currently available, even though, inexplicably, it does not include benchmark songs like *Penny Annie* and *Runaway*.

2 To Lefty From Willie

Willie Nelson
Columbia CK 34695

Mom And Dad's Waltz/Look What Thoughts Will Do/I Love You A Thousand Ways/Always Late (With Your Kisses)/I Want To Be With You Always/She's Gone, Gone, Gone/A Little Unfair/That's The Way Love Goes/I Never Go Around Mirrors/Railroad Lady

In this sterling collection, Nelson salutes 1950s honky-tonk king Lefty Frizzell (see "Essential Recordings", Honky-Tonk chapter) and splendidly reprises a collection of Frizzell classics.

3 Willie Nelson Sings The Songs Of Kristofferson

Willie Nelson
Columbia CK 36188

Me And Bobby McGee/Help Me Make It Through The Night/The Pilgrim/ Chapter 33/Why Me/For The Good Times/You Show Me Yours (And I'll Show

You Mine)/Loving Her Was Easier (Than Anything I'll Ever Do Again)/ Sunday Mornin' Comin' Down/Please Don't Tell Me How The Story Ends

In reference to celebrated songwriter Kris Kristofferson's limited vocal abilities, a critic once joked that this is "the best album Kris Kristofferson ever recorded!" Indeed, Nelson does bring a special magic to these stunningly original songs – in fact, these are some of the best-ever renditions of these oft-recorded Kristofferson classics.

294 Dreamin' My Dreams

Waylon Jennings
RCA APL1–1062 (LP)
Are You Sure Hank Done It This Way/Waymore's Blues/I Recall A Gypsy Woman/High Time (You Quit Your Low Down Ways)/I've Been A Long Time Leaving (But I'll Be A Long Time Gone)/Let's All Help The Cowboys Sing The Blues/The Door Is Always Open/Let's Turn Back The Years/She's Looking Good/Dreaming My Dreams With You/Bob Wills Is Still The King

Co-produced by legendary Nashville producer Jack Clement, this, like **Honky Tonk Heroes** (see "Essential Recordings," this chapter) is vintage Waylon Jennings – Jennings in his most soulful and melodic incarnation.

295 The Outlaws

Various Artists
RCA APL1–1321 (LP)
Waylon Jennings: *My Heroes Have Always Been Cowboys/Honky Tonk Heroes*; Jessi Colter: *I'm Looking For Blue Eyes/You Mean To Say*; Waylon Jennings and Jessi Colter: *Suspicious Minds*; Waylon Jennings and Willie Nelson: *Good-Hearted Woman/Heaven Or Hell*; Willie Nelson: *Me And Paul/Yesterday's Wine*; Tompall Glaser: *T For Texas/Put Another Log On The Fire*

This cleverly packaged compilation really gave definition to the Outlaw movement in the public imagination and was a tremendous building block in both Waylon Jennings's and Willie Nelson's careers. It also features Jennings's wife, the gifted Jessi Colter, as well as artist/producer/songwriter Tompall Glaser, another important "first generation" Outlaw.

296 Songs I'll Always Sing

Merle Haggard
Capital SLB-8086 (2-LP set)
Okie From Muskogee/The Emptiest Arms In The World/Mama Tried/Swingin' Doors/Uncle Lem/Fightin' Side Of Me/Sing Me Back Home/Silver Wings/Sing A Sad Song/Honky Tonk Night Time Man/Kentucky Gambler/I'm A Lonesome Fugitive/Things Aren't Funny Anymore/Daddy Frank (The Guitar Man)/I Forget You Every Day/Workin' Man Blues/Love And Honor/Branded Man/Someday We'll Look Back/I Take A Lot Of Pride In What I Am

Towering figure that he is, Merle Haggard has cropped up repeatedly throughout this book. This set collects his vintage hits from his Capital years, the late 1960s and early 1970s, when he was one of the most vital and popular artists on the scene.

Alternative Country   8

Geoffrey Himes

Before the mid-1960s, the whole concept of "alternative-country music" would have been inconceivable. Can you imagine Jimmie Rodgers, Hank Williams or George Jones – all born dirt poor in the South, tired of manual labor and hungering for respect – seeking out an alternative to a best-selling record? Of course not: the promise of financial success was a crucial inspiration for their efforts. In fact, the very desperation of their quest for a little money in the pocket supplied the emotional edge that made their early recordings so special.

Franklin Delano Roosevelt, however, constructed a social safety net underneath Rodgers's fans to make sure they would never have to worry about starving again. And Lyndon Johnson allowed Williams's fans to send their kids to college. And when these kids from farms and small towns got to college, they had enough financial security to start worrying about things other than making ends meet. They enjoyed the middle-class luxury of contemplating the meaning of life, social injustice, literature and unmarried cohabitation in their dorm rooms and cheap apartments.

These backwater kids, who had probably been Jones fans in high school, were as embarrassed about their background as immigrants from Ireland or Italy might have been about theirs. Like those immigrants, though, the children of country music had no choice but to eventually come to terms with their origins. So they looked for an alternative-country music that could accommodate their new middle-class tastes in folk-music realism, rock-and-roll aggression and singer–songwriter irony. In other words, it was this new audience that created alternative-country artists and not the other way around. As soon as there was an audience eager to buy records and concert tickets for a different approach, artists rushed in to fill the void.

Prescient as always, Bob Dylan was the first to spot the

opening for this new music. Dylan had grown up in the north Minnesota town of Hibbing, far from country's Southern heartland but typical of the isolated, small towns that are country's natural constituency. His first musical hero was Hank Williams, supplanted by Elvis Presley in high school, and then by Woody Guthrie in college.

Guthrie is described today as a folk singer, but he was really the first alternative-country artist in a time when there was no room for such a concept. Guthrie grew up in the oil-field boomtowns of Oklahoma, and the songs he first learned (and later adapted to his own lyrics) were the same Appalachian ballads and cowboy songs adapted by Rodgers and the Carter Family. Guthrie, however, put these sources to different uses; he was more interested in making political and literary points than hits, and his peculiar brand of country music left listeners puzzled until it was explained away as folk music.

The strong country influence on Guthrie and Presley – and by extension on his own folk music and rock-and-roll – was not lost on Dylan, and as early as 1966 he traveled to Nashville to record much of **Blonde On Blonde** with country music's top studio musicians. **Blonde On Blonde** was not a country album, but **The Basement Tapes**, recorded in 1967 with the Band, arguably was, and **John Wesley Harding**, recorded in 1967 with Nashville A-Team players, definitely was. By the time of 1969's **Nashville Skyline** and 1970's **New Morning**, the country character of Dylan's new music was unmistakable.

This was not mainstream country music in the style of contemporaries like George Jones, Buck Owens, and Roger Miller; these were songs about a skeptic fed up with *Too Much Of Nothing*, the wind howling *All Along The Watchtower* and a bohemian joking about his *Country Pie*. Although **John Wesley Harding** hit number 2 on the pop album charts and **Nashville Skyline** produced the number 7 pop single *Lay, Lady, Lay*, neither album got much airplay on country radio. And yet these recordings were indisputably country music; you could hear it in the steel guitars, the two-beat bounce, the drawling vocals, the detached fatalism of the story-telling, the harmonica figures, the acoustic guitars, and the Appalachian melodies.

Between 1967 and 1973, Dylan released a steel-guitar arrangement of *All Along The Watchtower* (which Jimi Hendrix turned into an FM hard-rock classic), wrote *You Ain't Going Nowhere* (a centerpiece of the Byrds' **Sweetheart Of The Rodeo** album), recorded *Girl Of The North Country* as a duet with Johnny Cash, played *Nashville Skyline Rag* on an Earl Scruggs TV special, recorded *I'd Have You Anytime* as a country duet with George Harrison and had a hit with a classic cowboy song, *Knocking On Heaven's Door*.

This was clearly an alternative form of country music, and it had an electrifying effect on musicians all over the country: on the Haggard/Hendrix fans in Lynyrd Skynyrd; on the closet country fans in the Byrds; on Cash's daughter Rosanne and in-laws Rodney Crowell and Carlene Carter; on the Flatt and Scruggs fans who became the New Grass Revival; on Beatles fans like John Hiatt and Neil Young; and on cowboy bohemians like Joe Ely, Willie Nelson, Steve Earle, Jerry Jeff Walker, and Townes Van Zandt. These artists followed Dylan's lead and created the alternative-country music that a new audience was hungering for.

Often considered too understated for rock radio and too strange for country radio, many of these artists carved out a niche for themselves with alternative-radio airplay, enthusiastic press, loyal club followings and modestly but steadily selling albums. The influence of these alternative-country artists has been huge on the new generation of talent that took over Nashville at the end of the 1980s, but rarely have the alternative pioneers themselves been able to benefit. Nashville has finally come to terms with electric guitars and snare-drum backbeats, but the city that demands certitude from its platitudes still has a problem with irony, and until mainstream country can accept the ambiguities and injustices of real life, there will always be a need for an alternative.

Essential Recordings

(i) Country-Rock

The best of Dylan's alternative-country albums is **John Wesley Harding**, and it may well be his best album of any description. In 1965 and 1966, Dylan had released three of the most famous and precedent-shattering rock-and-roll albums of all time – **Bringing It All Back Home**, **Highway 61 Revisited** and **Blonde On Blonde**; had singlehandedly invented folk-rock and shocked his old fans during his electrified performance at the Newport Folk Festival, and had circled the world with the Band in one of most legendary rock tours ever.

Caught up in a swirl of prolific fertility, constant motion, surrealistic lyrics, loud stomping music, controversy, celebrity, drugs, and no sleep, Dylan's career seemed to prefigure the rush into exhilarating change and excruciating tension that the whole American society was heading for. And just as America's mad dash cracked up on a cluster of assassinations, drug deaths and violent demonstrations, so did Dylan himself literally come to a crashing halt in a motorcycle accident on July 29, 1966.

The songwriter and the culture as a whole needed a simple,

solid, comforting place to recuperate, and Dylan believed they both could find it in country music. To heal his spirit as well as his bones, the singer holed up with his wife and kids in the Catskill Mountains and spent many days with the Band and a home recorder in the basement of the Band's house called Big Pink. They fooled around with a new kind of bohemian country music that combined the sing-along melodicism and parable-like stories of the Carter Family and the honky-tonk bounce and confessionalism of Hank Williams with a quirky absurdism that threw everything off-kilter. The best of these experiments were released eight years later as **The Basement Tapes**.

After that fruitful summer, Dylan returned to Nashville in October with a dozen alternative-country songs that ranked with the finest writing he has ever done. He recorded them simply, with himself on acoustic guitar, harmonica and/or piano backed by drummer Kenny Buttrey and bassist Charlie McCoy and on the final two love songs by pedal steel guitarist Pete Drake. In sharp contrast to the fierce, accusatory voice of his rock-and-roll albums, Dylan now sang with the dignified stoicism of Johnny Cash, the understated story-telling of Merle Travis and the bluesy fluidity of his own harmonica.

This wasn't just country music, this was a stripped-down, ancient-sounding country music that might have been recorded by Ralph Peer in Bristol, Virginia, in 1927. Most of the lyrics take the form of biblical parables, and the music takes the form of white Southern hymns. There are references to St Augustine, Judas, the wicked messenger, heaven and divine bolts of lightning; there's even a sermon-like recitation, à la Luke the Drifter. In the context of 1967, this was a bold statement that the truth didn't necessarily lie in ever more complex and extravagant art forms, nor in a rejection of the American past, for here in the simple form of traditional country-gospel songs was the most incisive commentary of the era.

John Wesley Harding doesn't need an historical context, however, to exert its power on us today. Like the album's title character, Dylan never makes "a foolish move" in these economical tales. Although these songs sound very traditional, they each have a special twist that replaces the fatalism of mainstream country with the irony of alternative country.

There's a sly humor in the tale of a poor defendant who uses a lightning bolt to escape when everyone else kneels to pray, and in the story of the wicked messenger who is told to either bring good news or not bring any. There's heartbreaking tragedy in the confession of one who watched St Augustine put to death and felt powerless to intervene. There's an assertive independence in the warning to a landlord, "If you don't underestimate me, I won't underestimate you." That line is typical of the aphorisms sprinkled throughout the album, the kind of quotable one-liners that belong in a Farmer's Almanac.

The album's most powerful song is *I Pity The Poor Immigrant*, the ultimate hymn for a country whose citizens mostly came from somewhere else. Dylan indicts his character for falling in love with wealth itself and turning his back on his neighbor, but the singer's anger turns to sympathy when he recognizes how alone the immigrant is when his visions shatter like glass. After ten biblical parables like this, Dylan closes the album with two straightforward country love songs, *Down Along The Cove* and *I'll Be Your Baby Tonight*, which glowed with romantic tenderness and pointed the way to **Nashville Skyline**.

In the following year, 1968, the Byrds consolidated Dylan's experiments in country-rock with **Sweetheart Of The Rodeo**; just as they had once consolidated his folk-rock with **Mr Tambourine Man**. Only two of the five Byrds who made the **Mr Tambourine Man** album in 1965 were still around in 1968. As a former folkie banjo player and a former bluegrass mandolinist respectively, Roger McGuinn and Chris Hillman had solid roots in country music, and had used country performers like Vern Gosdin and Clarence White on their recordings as early as 1966. McGuinn, always eager to follow Dylan's lead, wanted to include country-rock as part of the next album, but when Hillman got his new friend Gram Parsons involved, everything changed.

Parsons was just 13 and living in Florida when his father, a country singer–songwriter, committed suicide. He thus had a special connection to country music, and he formed the International Submarine Band in 1966 to play country-rock in the face of the hippie explosion. Hillman, whose first love had always been country, was entranced and brought Parsons into the Byrds. The two new friends convinced McGuinn that it wasn't enough to make country part of the next album; it had to be the whole album. **Sweetheart Of The Rodeo** was full of gorgeous 3-part vocal harmonies and pretty steel guitar fills, but it had enough of a rock-and-roll sensibility, the drum fills and ironic vocals, to make it alternative-country.

The album opened and closed with a pair of songs from '**The Basement Tapes**: *You Ain't Going Nowhere* and *Nothing Was Delivered*. As they had so often in the past, the Byrds make the Dylan songs more musical with bouncier rhythms, lusher harmonies and smoother edges, but this time they do it with country ingredients. Between those two bookends is the full spectrum of country song types: a Louvin Brothers hymn, a Woody Guthrie outlaw tale, a Merle Haggard prison tune and a Cindy Walker heartbroken, homesick lament.

Each is done with the sustained, church-like vocal harmonies that were the Byrds' unchanging trademark; Parsons's lazy Florida drawl is set against McGuinn's nasal Chicago chirp and Hillman's broad California croon. The vocals never betray a hint of treating the lyrics with anything but respect, but a studied lack of melodrama give the lyrics the distance of alternative country – as if the singers are outsiders who envy the country certainties they can't quite share. Protruding through the deliberate, smooth vocals are the jabbing fills of Jaydee Maness's steel guitar, Clarence White's electric guitar and Jon Corneal's drums. No matter how closely the Byrds tried to imitate traditional country music, their rock-and-roll sensibility gave everything a subtle spin that made this something new.

The album sold weakly and generated much controversy. Many of the Byrds' former hippie fans reacted as if they'd been betrayed by the band's switch to country music, but when Columbia Records twisted some arms to get the Byrds a slot at the Grand Ole Opry, Nashville's reaction was quite chilly. Moreover, when the company discovered that Parsons was still under contract to LHI Records, Columbia made the Byrds erase Parsons's lead vocals on several tracks and record McGuinn's voice in its place. In the wake of that controversy, both Parsons and Hillman left the band. (Parsons's original vocals on three **Sweetheart** tracks plus two outtakes can be heard on the 4-CD boxed set, **The Byrds**.)

For all that, **Sweetheart Of The Rodeo** is perhaps the most influential alternative-country album ever made. One of Emmylou Harris's best-ever compositions is called *The Sweetheart Of The Rodeo* and the 1980s country vocal duo of Janis Gill and Kristine Arnold called itself Sweethearts of the Rodeo. McGuinn and Hillman joined the Nitty Gritty Dirt Band 21 years later to do another version of *You Ain't Going Nowhere* and finally got their overdue country hit with it. Parsons went on to form the Flying Burrito Brothers and then record two legendary solo albums before an untimely death at 26 in 1973. Hillman went on to play with the Flying Burrito Brothers, Mannasas, the Souther Hillman Furay Band, and his own country-hit-makers, the Desert Rose Band. McGuinn shuffled different personnel through the Byrds until 1973, when he closed down the band in favor of solo projects.

The country-rock sound soon proliferated exponentially with acts like the Eagles, Linda Ronstadt and Crosby, Stills and Nash having tremendous commercial success with it. Other country-rock bands that made a little noise include the Nitty Gritty Dirt Band, Poco, the Pure Prairie League, and Firefall, but all these acts were too willing to settle for the simple formula of country vocals and a rock-and-roll beat. The best country-rock was made by idiosyncratic personalities like Dylan, McGuinn, Parsons, Robbie Robertson, Neil Young, John Fogerty, and Lowell George, who could both love country music and doubt it at the same time.

Discographical Details

97   John Wesley Harding

Bob Dylan

Columbia CGK 09604

John Wesley Harding/As I Went Out One Morning/I Dreamed I Saw St Augustine/All Along The Watchtower/The Ballad Of Frankie Lee And Judas Priest/Drifter's Escape/Dear Landlord/I Am A Lonesome Hobo/I Pity The Poor Immigrant/The Wicked Messenger/Down Along The Cove/I'll Be Your Baby Tonight

98   Sweetheart Of The Rodeo

The Byrds

Columbia CK 09670

You Ain't Going Nowhere/I Am A Pilgrim/The Christian Life/You Don't Miss Your Water/You're Still On My Mind/Pretty Boy Floyd/Hickory Wind/One Hundred Years From Now/Blue Canadian Rockies/Life In Prison/Nothing Was Delivered

(ii) Southern Rock

If country-rock was made by intellectuals who discovered country through folk music, Southern rock was made by working-class kids who grew up breathing in country music with the air around them. If country-rock was a lot closer to the sound of traditional country, Southern rock was a lot closer to the spirit. There was nothing ironic about Southern rockers; they sang about whiskey, guns, hard work and cheating women with the same firsthand experience as Merle Haggard and George Jones. The biggest difference between these honky-tonk heroes and the young Southern rockers was that the latter sang with the guitar amps cranked and the drummers flailing away.

And why shouldn't they? Hank Williams sang for a largely rural audience, and his musicians played the kind of hands-on equipment farmers would feel comfortable with. The generation of Duane Allman and Ronnie Van Zant grew up driving super-charged cars through the streets of big towns and faced the prospect of working in a shipyard or steel mill. Why shouldn't they sing their honky-tonk blues with the technology appropriate for their experience?

If country music is defined as a sound – a combination of steel guitars, lonesome vocals and two-step beats that resembles

Ernest Tubb – then Southern-rock can't really be considered country. But if country music is defined as a constituency – Southern working-class whites – and as a spirit – an obsession with the dichotomies of marriage/cheating, home/rambling, church/drinking, and repentance/sinning – then Southern-rock is an integral part of country. The dominance of the country charts in the early 1990s by such Southern-rock heirs as Hank Williams Jr, Travis Tritt, and the Kentucky Headhunters indicates that the latter definitions are correct.

For Southern boys like Allman and Van Zant, the mid-1960s presented a dilemma: how could they reconcile the sound of their generation, the slashing guitars of the Rolling Stones, with the sound of their region, the twangy laments of George Jones? Both Allman and Van Zant instinctively realized that both Jones and Mick Jagger were white boys singing the blues, and that they could invent a new kind of rock-and-roll by locating that territory where Southern-country music overlapped Southern blues. More specifically, if they could take a Lester Flatt or Chet Atkins guitar run, replicate it on a loud, distorted electric amplifiers and put the whole thing over a Slim Harpo boogie groove or a Muddy Waters stomp, they really had something.

The Allman Brothers Band did it first. Florida's Duane Allman had already made a reputation as a session guitarist for Aretha Franklin, Wilson Pickett and Eric Clapton. He really wanted to lead his own band, however, and he formed a sextet with his kid brother Gregg (an adequate organist and terrific blues singer), country-rock guitar picker Dicky Betts, R & B drummer Jaimoe Johanson, rock drummer Butch Trucks and rock bassist Berry Oakley. The debut album, **The Allman Brothers Band**, was released in 1969; it wasn't a hit, but its mix of blues, rock, country, and jazz improvisation turned on a light in the head of every Southern rocker who heard it.

Among those listening were a bunch of working-class friends from Jacksonville, Florida, the kind of kids who would name their band after Leonard Skinner, the high school gym teacher who had hassled them for their long hair and bad attitudes. Lynyrd Skynyrd went one better than the Allmans by featuring three lead guitarists instead of two (Allen Collins, Gary Rossington, and Ed King), and honky-tonk pianist Billy Powell anchored a rhythm section that also included bassist Leon Wilkeson and drummer Bob Burns. The heart of the band, though, was lead singer/lyricist Ronnie Van Zant, who made the down-to-earth storytelling of country music count for something in Southern rock.

Never was that as obvious as on the band's 1973 debut album, **(pronounced leh-nerd skin-nerd)**. Duane Allman was already two years dead, and the album ends with *Free Bird*, the eulogy for Allman that became an rock-radio standard, thanks to the pretty country melody that Collins played on slide guitar. Van Zant's story-telling talents were better showcased on other tunes, however.

Perhaps the best example is *Gimme Three Steps*, which would be easier to recognize as a classic country cheating song if you removed the catchy guitar riff Rossington lifted from the Rolling Stones' *Tumbling Dice*. The singer is dancing down at the local roadhouse with Linda Lu when her husband bursts in with a Colt .44 ready for business. Van Zant doesn't pretend to be innocent and he doesn't pretend that he's not scared; all he asks for is a three-step headstart toward the door. This refreshing lack of self-pity and the economical detail of the narrative combine with the bouncy shuffle to turn this honky-tonk lament into a good laugh at a near-escape from death.

Guns pop up again in *Mississippi Kid*, a 12-bar blues about a man determined to fetch his cornbread-baking woman back from Alabama and ready to pistol-whip anyone who gets in his way. It gets its country feel from an acoustic arrangement that features a mandolin and harmonica. Another favorite country topic is tackled on *Poison Whiskey*, a graphic tale about a doctor cutting open a Louisiana Cajun and examining the effects of "20 years of rotgut whiskey." Van Zant does nothing to glamorize drinking on this hard-hitting song, and Powell's Moon Mullican-like piano solo cements the number's country links.

Tuesday's Gone features another country ballad melody by Collins much like *Free Bird*, but with a better lyric from Van Zant. He sings that women pass by like the days of the week, like the scenery outside his train, but there's something in his aching, lonesome vocal that belies the carefree tone of the narrative. Van Zant was a great singer, able to communicate the sense that he wasn't interested in the listener's sympathy or agreement, that he sang out of some irrepressible compulsion to tell what really happened. The guttural growl in his voice clearly came from the blues, but that quality of forlorn fatalism, the hint that we are all swimming against some giant tide, just as clearly comes from country music.

Van Zant never sounded as country as he does on *Simple Man*, a haunting ballad delivered over arpeggiated country chords. He sings of getting some front-porch advice from his mama to forego the North's temptations of the fast life and the easy dollar and to retain a Southern simplicity. Rossington's guitar slashes furiously across the patient country rhythm and Van Zant's vocal captures the same desperation, the contradiction between wanting to remain distinctively Southern and yet realizing that he will never be simple. Out of that contradiction bloomed the need for Southern rock as an alternative to Nashville country.

Lynyrd Skynyrd went on to make many more good albums, delivering a stinging rebuttal to Neil Young's *Southern Man* with *Sweet Home Alabama* and covering songs by Merle Haggard, J.J. Cale, and Jimmie Rodgers along the way. Their sound got harder and harder as they became arena-rock stars, but they continued to write such country-inflected material as *Swamp Music, The Ballad Of Curtis Lowe, Whiskey Rock-A-Roller*, and *Georgia Peaches*.

Eventually, they fell prey to the same death-curse that haunted the Allmans; on October 20, 1977, the band's single-engine Corvair plane crashed into a wooded Mississippi swamp, killing Van Zant, new guitarist Steve Gaines, backup singer Cassie Gaines and manager Dean Kilpatrick and seriously injuring Collins, Rossington, Powell, and Wilkeson. The survivors formed other bands and eventually reformed Lynyrd Skynyrd in 1987, but it was never the same without Van Zant.

Ironically, though, Lynyrd Skynyrd became a major influence in commercial country music in the late 1980s and early 1990s, as Hank Williams Jr, the Kentucky Headhunters, and Travis Tritt all scored hits with a Skynyrd-derived sound. So many Southern kids with Ronnie Van Zant's "Simple Man" dilemma had moved into the country audience that the Southern-rock alternative had become the country mainstream.

Discographical Details

299 (pronounced leh-nerd skin-nerd)

Lynyrd Skynyrd
Sounds of the South MCA-363
*I Ain't The One/Tuesday's Gone/Gimme Three Steps/Simple Man/Things Goin'
On/Mississippi Kid/Poison Whiskey/Free Bird*

(iii) Blues-Country

Jimmie Rodgers picked up music from black railroad workers; Hank Williams learned from a black street singer named Tee-Tot; Bob Wills tried to imitate the black swing bands like the Count Basie Orchestra; Elvis Presley's first single was a remake of an Arthur Crudup blues tune; Ray Charles enjoyed his biggest hits when he recorded two country albums; even today Reba McEntire sings Aretha Franklin hits in her live show.

African American music has always been a crucial ingredient in country music (and country music has been a big influence on black singers from Sonny Terry to Al Green), and as the above examples imply, the biggest innovations in country music have often come when the music reconnects to its alter ego, the blues. With their parallel emphasis on storytelling, steady rhythms, expressive vocals, marital problems, money troubles and hard drinking, country music and the blues are like half-brothers that the family has tried to hide.

Although the South has experienced the most virulent racism in the US, interaction between the races is much more common there than anywhere else. As a result, white and black Southern musicians influence one another greatly but are forced to disguise that fact as much as possible. Country audiences obviously enjoy the African American quality in singers from Hank Williams and Elvis Presley to Reba McEntire and Wynonna Judd, but if that bluesiness becomes too obvious that same audience will turn its back on the offender. As a result, most country singers attempt a balancing act of keeping enough blues in their music to keep it interesting but not so much that it alienates their listeners.

Some singers have been unwilling or unable to play this game, however, and in the post-Dylan era enough of an alternative audience exists that blues-country singers like J.J. Cale, Lucinda Williams, Bonnie Raitt, Delbert McClinton, John Hiatt, Charlie Rich, James Talley, Jesse Winchester, Marshall Chapman, and others have sustained careers on the fringes of the music industry. They haven't scored country hits with their blues-drenched vocals, but they have made some of the best country music of the past 30 years.

J.J. Cale, an Oklahoman who played in a Tulsa bar band with a teenaged Leon Russell and later followed his pal out to LA, is a notorious recluse. He very rarely performs in public, and when he does release the infrequent album he usually keeps his photo off the front cover. He spent years living in an Airstream trailer outside his 16-track studio in Anaheim, California, content to tinker with his guitars and recording equipment and record tracks until he had enough for an album. This enigmatic elusiveness is well in keeping with his music, which features both vocals and guitar licks as languid and drowsy as the blues-country swamp music he draws on.

Cale has never sold many records and has never dented country radio, but his influence on other musicians has been immense. His songs have been recorded by Eric Clapton (*After Midnight*, *Cocaine*), Lynyrd Skynyrd (*Call Me The Breeze, I Got The Same Old Blues*), Waylon Jennings (*Clyde*), and Santana (*The Sensitive Kind*). One can make the argument that Clapton and the Dire Straits' Mark Knopfler have built their whole careers atop Cale's lazy, minor-key blues-country feel on the guitar. And who can blame them, for it is one of the most seductive sounds in pop music.

The secret of Cale's sound is his ability to establish the angst and steady beat of a minor-chord blues and then makes it all flow effortlessly with the help of his legato melodies. Instead of the usual pop-music methodology of creating tension in the verse and releasing it in the chorus, Cale is continually creating and releasing tension at the same time, as if he were a stoic old man who shrugs off life's hardships in the very act of recognizing them. He anchors his frustrations in the bluesy rhythmic chords even as he's letting them go in the legato lead phrases and in the subtle Appalachian melody fills.

Cale's best album is still his first, 1972's **Naturally**, which he made only because Clapton's 1970 Top 20 pop success with *After Midnight* had put pressure on Cale to record himself. Taped in Nashville with the city's top session pickers as well as Cale's old Okie cronies, the album features a dozen songs that the singer had been saving up after as many years in the business. He even scored a Top 25 pop hit with *Crazy Mama*, a very lazy love song informed not so much by the anxiousness of lustful anticipation as the relaxed feeling of sexual satisfaction, expressed in stretched-out slide guitar phrases. Similar slide guitar marks his own version of *After Midnight*, whose lyrics anticipate a romantic rendezvous but whose performance seems to be already experiencing the tryst.

Call Me The Breeze is a 12-bar blues about a rambler who blows into town with the wind and blows out the same way. Traditional blues seldom sound so fluid and easy, but Cale sails through the song on an airy country melody and lots of arpeggiated picking. *Clyde* is a bouncy number about a barefoot, front-porch bass player, and is filled with infectious country touches: twin fiddles, dobro, and bluegrass guitar.

The album's most powerful songs, though, are a pair of slow ballads. *Call The Doctor* is a plea from someone sinking into sickness, but it is delivered with so little self-pity and such acceptance of fate that it is far eerier than the most anguished lament. *Magnolia* is quite simply one of the prettiest country love songs ever written. Cale relates how the scent of a magnolia tree reminds him of a woman he left behind in New Orleans, and the minor-to-major chord changes evoke both the longing for lost love and the sweetness of a magnolia blossom. The patient melody seems to hover between heartbreak and fond memories, and only grows more intense in the striking bridge, and more intense still on the tender guitar solo.

Much like Bonnie Raitt, Marshall Chapman, James Talley, and hundreds of others, Lucinda Williams went to a middle-class college in the 1960s, when rural blues were considered the purest of the folk art forms. For a generation hungering for authenticity in a culture of artifice, there were few things as appealing as a Robert Johnson song. Like the others, Williams worked hard to play the blues well, then noticed the close relationship between those blues and country, and learned to play that genre just as well. Again like the others, she learned there wasn't a big market for such traditional musics, and scrambled to find alternative audiences for the music she loved so much.

Williams released two albums for the Old Left label, Folkways Records: **Ramblin'**, a 1979 collection of traditional blues and country tunes by Johnson, Hank Williams, the Carter Family, Memphis Minnie and others, and **Happy Woman Blues**, a 1980 gathering of 11 original folk-blues songs. The releases made barely a ripple and she disappeared for eight years of bouncing around between Louisiana, Texas and California, playing hippie coffeehouses, working as a waitress and recording demos for that elusive big record contract. All the while she worked on her songwriting and mastered the common qualities of blues, country, and folk: the economical narrative, the telling visual detail, the unsentimental honesty, the melodic seduction and the rhythmic hammer.

So when she gave up on the big record deal in the sky and released **Lucinda Williams** on the New Left label, Rough Trade Records, in 1988, she seemed to have come out of nowhere. It was hailed by critics as one of the best country albums of the decade, and while country radio ignored it, the critics were vindicated when two songs from the album were later turned into Top 10 country hits by Patty Loveless (*The Night's Too Long*) and Mary Chapin Carpenter (*Passionate Kisses*). Neither the Loveless nor the Carpenter versions had the dramatic power of the originals by Williams, whose studied lack of melodrama gave her stories a conversational "realness", and thus sharpened the edge of their ironic twists.

When she sings on *The Night's Too Long* about Sylvia, a waitress from Beaumont, Texas, who's tired of small tips, "small town boys", and all "these silly dresses and nylon hose," you can tell from the accuracy of the details that Williams has been in those shoes. Without any fancy metaphors, Williams describes how Sylvia "bought an old rusty car," moved to Houston and landed a job as a secretary – thus summing up in one verse the massive demographic shifts in the country audience. Even in "all new clothes," though, Sylvia hasn't lost her taste for a country band, a cold beer and a sweaty cowboy. The way she delivers the depressing details of day jobs with a blues singer's weariness on the verses and then shifts into the hopeful yearning of rodeo sweetheart on the choruses illustrates the benefits of mixing these two genres.

On the dobro-laced and "Tex-Mex"-flavored *Big Red Sun Blues*, she evokes the image of a broken-hearted young wife standing on her front-porch. Looking down at her small diamond ring and out at the wide, open road, she ponders whether to stay or go. The bouncy, catchy melody keeps us right beside her until she makes her decision in the song's final line. On *Changed The Locks*, a ferocious blues stomp, Williams emphasizes that she's so fed up with an ex-lover that not only is she going to change the locks on her front door and her phone number, but she's also going to rip up the railroad tracks coming into her town and, if that's not enough, change the name of the town itself.

On the album's best song, *Side Of The Road*, Doug Atwell's lonesome Texas fiddle sets up Williams's explanation to a lover that she likes having him in the car, but that she also needs to pull off every once in a while and spend some time by herself. Such a double message requires a convincing confidence, and Williams's vocal is brimming with just that. Such implacable self-assurance is the ultimate feminism, and it radiates through the final verse as Williams describes walking off through the tall grass along the interstate to feel her own skin and think her own thoughts.

A similar double message fires *Passionate Kisses*. Williams isn't afraid to admit she needs love, but she's not willing to put up with less than the love she needs. "Is it too much to ask?" she sings with a country plaint and a bluesy insistence, a combination that puts the double message across. "I want a comfortable bed that won't hurt my back, food to fill me up . . . Shouldn't I have all this and passionate kisses?" Leading her lean country-rock quartet on acoustic guitar, Williams bears down on the questions as if she won't quit until she gets an answer.

Discographical Details

300 Naturally

J.J. Cale
Shelter SHL/18010
Call Me The Breeze/Call The Doctor/Don't Go To Strangers/Woman I Love/ Magnolia/Clyde/Crazy Mama/Nowhere To Run/After Midnight/River Runs Deep/Bringing It Back/Crying Eyes

301 Lucinda Williams

Lucinda Williams
Rough Trade US 47CD
I Just Wanted To See You So Bad/The Night's Too Long/Abandoned/Big Red Sun Blues/Like A Rose/Changed The Locks/Passionate Kisses/Am I Too Blue/ Crescent City/Side Of The Road/Price To Pay/I Asked For Water (He Gave Me Gasoline)

(iv) Folk-Country

In the 1920s, there was no real difference between folk and country music. It was all rural acoustic string music played by Anglo-Irish-Americans, and *Billboard* lumped it together under the rubric, "Hillbilly." When the Carter Family showed up for an open audition in Bristol, Virginia, in 1927, the songs they sang for Victor engineer Ralph Peer were folk songs their family had been singing for generations. Peer turned the tunes into country hits.

By the 1960s, though, the terms "folk music" and "country music" had come to mean very different things. Country music was a commercial enterprise, delivering to its faithful audience morality tales about cheating, drinking, family, home and hard work with a lively two-step beat and sense of humor or a sense of bathos, but never a hint of irony. Folk music, on the other hand, had been usurped by urban intellectuals who were first entranced by the untainted purity of the music but who eventually twisted it around to their concerns: social injustice, alienation, ambiguous relationships, and the ironic tension between the way things are and the way they should be.

Urban intellectuals deserve a music they can call their own, and some of these bohemian folkies (Bob Dylan, Paul Simon, Pete Seeger) were spectacularly good songwriters. This so-called "folk music," though, had grown quite a distance apart from its southern Appalachian origins and from its close cousin, country music. And yet not so far apart that members of each camp couldn't recognize the lingering similarities and yearn for the advantages of their counterparts.

Folk singers like John Prine, Steve Goodman, Mary Chapin Carpenter, Greg Brown, T-Bone Burnett, Guy Clark, and Nanci Griffith envied the ability of country singers to connect with a broad audience via two-step rhythms and uninhibited emotionalism. On the other hand, country singers like Rosanne Cash, John Anderson, Kathy Mattea, and Emmylou Harris, who had gotten their start in folk coffeehouses before moving to Nashville, still longed for the freedom of "folk" artists to wrestle with social injustice and intimate confessions.

Putting the two branches of hillbilly music back together was a fairly simple manner. The folkies just had to loosen up a little, add a little honky-tonk kick behind their guitar-strumming and acknowledge that some of the world's dirtiest wars go on inside people's bedrooms. The country performers had to grow up a bit and admit that the world is not so easily summed up in platitudes about flag, family, and home; they had to make room for doubt, ambiguity, and the humor that comes with irony.

No one personifies this process better than John Prine, a Chicago mailman whose three biggest heroes were Hank Williams, Bob Dylan, and Roger Miller. He made up songs while he delivered letters, and Dylan's influence was obvious in his subject matter: Vietnam (*Sam Stone*), jingoism (*Your Flag Decal Won't Get You Into Heaven Anymore*), and strip mining (*Paradise*). The songs ended up sounding a lot more like Miller, however, with their short lines, plain language, comic twists and two-step bounce. While Dylan was apt to describe the chimes of freedom ringing "through the mad mystic hammering of the wild ripping hail," Prine was more likely to advise you to "blow up your TV . . . throw away your paper . . . eat a lot of peaches, try to find Jesus on your own."

Prine sang these songs on the Chicago folk-club circuit, because there was no call in the local honky-tonks for songs about Vietnam veterans with heroin habits. It was on that circuit that Kris Kristofferson, himself a new country star, first heard Prine. When Kristofferson invited his new friend on stage during a 1971 show at New York's Bitter End, Jerry Wexler of Atlantic Records was in the audience and offered Prine a contract the next day. The debut album, **John Prine**, came out later that year, and it remains the best possible example of how country and folk can make each other better.

All of Prine's albums (except maybe **Pink Cadillac**) are good, but his first one, which had ten years of songwriting to choose from, is the best. Most of the 13 songs have since become standards, still performed by country and folk singers alike in every club that favors an acoustic guitar. Though the album was recorded in Memphis with Elvis Presley's R & B band, the emphasis was kept squarely on Prine's voice and lyrics. On the front cover, a denim-clad, 24-year-old Prine sat on a haystack, and on the back, Kristofferson compared his discovery to "stumbling onto Dylan when he first busted onto the Village scene."

With its fiddle part and list of Appalachian place names, *Paradise* harkens back to the Carter Family songs where folk and country were synonymous. His description of idyllic summers in Western Kentucky is rich in details ("The air smelled like snakes and we'd shoot with our pistols, but empty pop bottles was all we would kill"), but like most Prine songs this one takes a surprising twist. He relates the true story of how the Peabody Coal Company bought up the whole town of Paradise and turned it into an open-pit mine. He tells this story, not with the polemical anger of a leftist folk singer but with the deadpan observations of a Kentucky fatalist who can appreciate even the bitterest joke.

In 1971, songs about Vietnam were still pretty rare outside

the folk community, so it was pretty daring for Prine to give *Sam Stone* a Johnny Cash arrangement (years later Cash recorded Prine's *Unwed Fathers*). Even years later, after dozens of songwriters have taken their shot at Vietnam, no one has come up with an approach as original as Prine's. The verses are delivered by a detached narrator who describes how the morphine used to treat a shrapnel-shattered knee and battle-shattered nerves in an army hospital bloomed into a heroin habit, but the choruses come from the veteran's young son who sings, "There's a hole in daddy's arm where all the money goes/And Jesus Christ died for nothing I suppose."

Other songs tackle unusual subjects for such a country-sounding album: the despair of the elderly (*Hello In There*), the pleasures of marijuana (*Illegal Smile*), and the futility of suicide (*Six O'Clock News*). Some of the best numbers, though, dealt with the mainstream country subjects of romance that can't get started and romance that has gone on too long. *Far From Me* is a just-right portrait of a couple breaking up in a parking lot without ever saying the actual words. *Donald And Lydia* describes another couple, obviously in love with each other but too shy to do anything about it. *Angel From Montgomery*, which boasts the album's catchiest melody (and was recorded in a famous version by Bonnie Raitt), is sung from the perspective of an elderly woman trapped in a stale marriage, who wonders, "How can a person go to work in the morning/And come home in the evening with nothing to say?"

Prine has gone on to enjoy a long career of glowing reviews, modest sales and a reputation that allows him to play mid-sized theaters. He moved to Nashville and wrote some country hits for Don Williams and Tammy Wynette, but his own albums (now on his own label, Oh Boy Records) maintain that delicate balance of folk and country that has inspired a generation of songwriters.

If Prine moved from Chicago's folk coffeehouses to a place on a Tammy Wynette album, then Rosanne Cash made the opposite journey, from the inner sanctum of Nashville to the commercial fringes where country confessions meet literary folk. Cash – daughter of Johnny Cash, step-daughter of June Carter, step-granddaughter of Mother Maybelle Carter, step-sister of Carlene Carter and ex-wife of Rodney Crowell – was well connected to country music's royalty, and she started out as a progressive country singer, not unlike Emmylou Harris. Cash even had her fair share of number 1 country hits like *Seven-Year Ache*, *If You Change Your Mind* and *Tennessee Flat Top Box* (originally a hit for her father, Johnny, in the 1950s).

Even though 1988's **King's Record Shop** album yielded

three hit singles, it marked a sharp move toward an alternative-country emphasis on questions rather than answers. That shift was completed with her 1990 album, **Interiors**, which was hailed by critics as her career best, but which failed to dent country radio at all. For the first time, she wrote or co-wrote all the songs and produced the album herself. The result was a harrowing portrait of a marriage in trouble, an example of what country music can do when it shrugs off old assumptions and approaches adult romance with a new honesty. The auto-biographical source of the album was confirmed when Cash and Crowell separated a year later.

The songwriting on **Interiors** is uneven, but the vocals are so raw and open that they transcend the description of "confessional" for a far riskier degree of self-exposure. The music, recorded in Nashville with Crowell's road band, brings a chamber-music feel to country motifs, using drums sparingly and emphasizing instead closely bunched harmonies on acoustic pianos and guitars. There's a hushed, folk-like feeling to the performances that only reinforces the intimacy of the confidences Cash provides.

The album's title refers to the private doubts and agonies that often underlie our public facades, and this theme crops up in many of the songs. The album's first song describes the romantic battles that occur *On The Inside* where casual observers never notice them, but even more eloquent than Cash's lyrics is her bruised, reluctant vocal. She describes a similar relationship with the same quiet, aching vocal over acoustic guitars on *Land Of Nightmares* ("The ocean's calm outside my door/The storm rages inside my head") and *Mirror Image* ("A cold heart here but no one knows it").

Old folkie John Stewart helped her with the lyrics to *Dance With The Tiger*, which restates the album theme in the opening line, "In every woman and man lies the seed of fear/Of just how alone are all who live here." That sense of loneliness is reinforced by the very sparse arrangement that frames Cash's forlorn, whispery voice with little more than Stewart's spare guitar lines and a hand drum. Crowell joins her for an affecting duet vocal on her slow lament for a dying relationship that's still okay *On The Surface*.

Rather than simply surrender to her own bleak descriptions, though, Cash demands a better alternative. She sings *I Want A Cure* in a weary, weakened voice that's desperate enough to accept a chemical cure as well as a mental one. Cash sings that *What We Really Want* is love, and the buoyant pop melody fills with the optimism of Steuart Smith's guitars. More defiant is the feminist anthem, *Real Woman*, which Cash co-wrote with Crowell. Cash argues with steely determination that she doesn't "want to fake my smile," that she doesn't "want to be a man"; she wants to let the real woman inside her come out.

Cash followed up **Interiors** with a 1993 post-divorce album, **The Wheel**, which employed a similar sound and a similar approach to relationships, and which was nearly as good. Some observers, even Cash herself, have questioned if these albums are country music. They certainly fall far outside the Nashville mainstream, but country music is marriage music. If rock and pop are about falling in love the first time, country music (and the blues) is about falling in love for the tenth or twelfth time. Cash is using country materials (the acoustic guitar, the mandolin, the conversational tone, the wife's lament) to tackle country subject matter. Perhaps she hasn't deserted the country tradition so much as she has shown us where it reunites with folk music in the road ahead.

Discographical Details

02 John Prine

John Prine
Atlantic 191–56–2
Illegal Smile/Spanish Pipedream/Hello In There/Sam Stone/Paradise/Pretty Good/Your Flag Decal Won't Get You Into Heaven Anymore/Far From Me/ Angel From Montgomery/Quiet Man/Donald And Lydia/Six O'Clock News/ Flashback Blues

03 Interiors

Rosanne Cash
Columbia CK 46079
On The Inside/Dance With The Tiger/On The Surface/Real Woman/This World/What We Really Want/Mirror Image/Land Of Nightmares/I Want A Cure/Paralyzed

(v) Texas's Cosmic Cowboys

Texans have always prided themselves on their ornery independence, and since the late 1960s a community of hippie–cowboy poet–singers has flourished in Texas, demonstrating its couldn't-care-less autonomy from the Nashville way of doing things with every recording. The "Outlaw" successes of Willie and Waylon are just the tip of an iceberg that gets progressively weirder as it plunges below the surface into the shadowy waters of alternative-country.

Texas has a lot of different musical traditions, from the honky-tonk of George Jones and the western swing of Bob Wills to the electric blues of T-Bone Walker and the "Tex-Mex" of Flaco Jimenez. All these exerted their influence on the

"Cosmic Cowboys," as they were dubbed, but the most crucial
influence was the story-telling tradition of the old cowboy
songs (such as *Buffalo Skinners*, also sung by neighboring Okie
Woody Guthrie) and of the old acoustic Texas blues singers
like Blind Lemon Jefferson. Texas songwriters were already
used to long narratives with lots of clever word-play when Bob
Dylan came along and introduced the notion of alternative-
country music.

If Dylan was blowing minds elsewhere in the country, his
songs seemed like the most natural thing in the world to guitar-
strummers like Townes Van Zandt, Jerry Jeff Walker, and Guy
Clark who'd been listening to Lightnin' Hopkins and Ramblin'
Jack Elliott all along. What Dylan provided was the hope that
you could make a living doing these songs. Van Zandt, Walker,
and Clark figured if Dylan could do it New York-style, they
could do it Texas-style. If Dylan were going to blend his
country and folk sources with rock, blues, and art songs, the
Texans were going to blend theirs with honky-tonk, western
swing and "Tex-Mex." The result was some of the quirkiest
and best country music of the past 30 years.

Walker went off to New York to try to become a Northern
folkie before coming to his senses and returning home to Texas
and alternative-country music. Van Zandt and Clark haunted
the Gulf Coast around Houston and Galveston, and an inexplicable scene developed around Lubbock (more on that later).
But the whole "Cosmic Cowboy" scene didn't coalesce until
the Amarillo World Headquarters opened in an abandoned
National Guard armory outside of Austin in 1972. Willie
Nelson kicked it off, and before long every Texan songwriter
with one foot in the honky-tonk and the other in Woodstock
was gathering there, singing each other's songs and providing a
friendly competitiveness that inspired better and better writing.

The broadest definition of Texas's "Cosmic Cowboys"
would include Nelson, Walker, Clark, Waylon Jennings, Joe
Ely, Jimmie Dale Gilmore, Butch Hancock, Terry Allen, Ray
Wylie Hubbard, Willis Alan Ramsey, Bill and Bonnie Hearne,
Steve Young, Darden Smith, Gary P. Nunn, Steve Fromholz,
B.W. Stevenson, Champ Hood, Jo Carol Pierce, Nanci Griffith,
Steve Earle, Lyle Lovett, and Robert Earl Keen Jr. One thing
they have in common is that most of them credit Townes Van
Zandt as a primary influence. "Townes Van Zandt is the best
songwriter in the whole world," Earle once declared, "and I'll
stand on Bob Dylan's coffee table in my cowboy boots and say
that."

The best overview of Van Zandt's career is **Live At The
Old Quarter, Houston, Texas,** a solo acoustic live album
recorded in 1973 and released in 1977. The Old Quarter, home

to both Hopkins and Walker, was an 18' × 32' room with bare brick walls and an open-air "smoking" deck on the roof. The intimacy of the occasion allowed Van Zandt to sing in the weary, off-handed tone that suits his songs best. It's the aged voice of someone who has witnessed every disappointment and betrayal and no longer cares about anything but the story. And the stories that travel across that thin, wavering but oh-so-telling voice are too austere for sentimentality to squeeze in.

The album begins with Van Zandt's best-known song, *Pancho And Lefty*, which Nelson and Merle Haggard turned into a number 1 country hit ten years later. Van Zandt picks his acoustic guitar arpeggios; in a matter-of-fact voice, he raises the romantic notion that living on the road will make you "free and clean," and immediately dashes it by pointing out that years on the road actually leaves you with skin like iron.

Then he tells of Pancho, a legendary outlaw with a fast horse and a faster gun, only to blow away that myth with a tuneful, sing-along chorus that claims that the police merely toyed with Pancho and could have picked him up any time. Pancho's betrayal by his old pal Lefty is never stated, merely implied by Van Zandt's masterful presentation of circumstantial evidence. Just when he seems to be directing our sympathies to Pancho, Van Zandt points out that Pancho at least got a hero's death in a Mexican desert, while Lefty wound up cold and guilty in a Cleveland hotel.

This push-and-pull of romantic notions and sobering reality is typical of Van Zandt's writing. In *Don't You Take It Too Bad*, he advises a lover not to worry about feeling unloving; that's just the way life goes. He sings valentines to *Loretta*, who "tells me lies I love to believe," and to *Kathleen*, whom he likes to visit when the sun doesn't shine. On the unusually honest love song, *No Place To Fall*, he confesses his own inconstancy as a lover, but asks a woman to hold his hand as long as time and space allow.

White Freight Liner Blues is a lively truck song, but if you listen closely, you realize that the singer isn't riding the trucks but only listening to the whine of their wheels as they whiz past Houston while he imagines what it must be like to drive to New Mexico. He sings two Woody Guthrie-style "talking blues" about college fraternities and cheap wine. Even his prettiest love song, *If I Needed You*, later a big duet hit for Emmylou Harris and Don Williams, is thrown into the subjunctive.

Perhaps his attitude is best summarized by *For The Sake Of The Song*. In the verses, he takes comfort in the thought that an ex-lover is singing sad songs about him, but in the typically deflating chorus he realizes she's singing just "for the sake of the song." There's something about Van Zandt's writing and singing that lets us know he doesn't care if we sympathize with his perspective – or even agree with it. He's simply singing "for the sake of the song," because it wells up inside him and has to come out. That shrug-of-the-shoulder, take-it-or-leave-it approach liberates us as listeners and, paradoxically, makes Van Zandt more compelling than he would be otherwise.

There must be something in the water in Lubbock, for this nondescript, mid-sized West Texas city has produced musical talent all out of proportion to its population. The Lubbock area is most famous for its favorite son, Buddy Holly, but it also yielded such notable Crickets as Sonny Curtis (who wrote *I Fought The Law*), guitarist Tommy Allsup (who played with Bob Wills), and Waylon Jennings (who was displaced on the fatal plane when Ritchie Valens claimed a seat). A generation later, Lubbock also produced Joe Ely, Jimmie Dale Gilmore, Butch Hancock, Tommy Hancock, Terry Allen, Jo Carol Pierce, and the Texana Dames.

If Hancock is the best songwriter of this bunch and Gilmore the best pure singer, Ely offers the best total package of singing, writing, rocking and honky-tonking. With his dark, wavy hair and road-creased face, Ely looks like a bantamweight fighter in a black cowboy suit, and he attacks every song with the fury of a boxer looking for an early knockout. That intensity captured the imagination of the British punk band, the Clash, who saw in Ely their dream of the uncompromised American cowboy troubador. They took Ely back to England in 1980 to open a series of their shows, and Ely brought along the best band of his career (guitarist Jesse Taylor, accordionist Ponty Bone, steel guitarist Lloyd Maines, pianist Reese Wynans, etc.). The resulting tapes, released as **Live Shots**, captured Ely's inspired blend of honky-tonk, rockabilly, "Tex-Mex," blues, and "cosmic cowboy" at its best.

The album opens with an extravagantly frivolous boast, "I keep my fingernails long so they click when I play the piano," and the unmistakably country melody is rocked so hard by Wynans's piano and Ely's guitar that one fears the instruments and performers will fly apart before the song is done. Ely's own composition, *Honky Tonk Masquerade*, the title of an earlier studio album and an achingly melodic tale of romantic betrayals in Texas barrooms, leads naturally into a stomping version of Hank Williams's *Honky Tonkin'*, a duet with Carlene Carter. *Long Snake Moan* is a medley of Carl Perkins's *Matchbox*, John Lee Hooker's *Crawling King Snake*, and other songs that illustrates perfectly how rockabilly is the result of country musicians playing the blues; it climaxes with Ely howling at the moon like Jerry Lee Lewis.

The album concludes with three songs by Hancock, whose Dylanesque verbal flourishes are given a muscular solidity by Ely's no-nonsense approach. "Spanish is the loving tongue," Hancock wrote, "but she never spoke Spanish to me." With the Mexican embellishment of Ponty Bone's accordion, Ely's heartbroken stoicism transforms those lines from irony to tragedy. Hancock's *Fools Fall In Love* runs one clever variation after another on the metaphor of tumbling into romance, but the sheer terror of that free fall is captured in Ely's vocal and guitar fills. In *Boxcars*, one of Hancock's best songs, a man caught between bank debts and a dry farm watches a train roll by, contemplating escape inside an empty boxcar or beneath the lethal wheels. If the metallic edge of Ely's guitar suggests the desperation that might choose one of those alternatives, the weariness of his vocal suggests the fatalism that will let the train pull away as the farmer returns home.

When the 10-song, 12-inch album version of **Live Shots** was released in 1980, it came with a 4-song, 7-inch bonus EP recorded live in Texas and produced by Dylan keyboardist and Lynyrd Skynyrd producer Al Kooper. The EP included a song apiece by Ely, Hancock, and Gilmore as well as *Not Fade Away*, a tribute to the most famous Lubbockite of all, Buddy Holly. When MCA reissued the album on CD in 1993, it included all 14 songs. This is perhaps the best alternative-country album of all, for it has all the ingredients: the Dylan-esque songwriting, the Southern-rock muscle, the bluesy gritti-ness, the personal confessions, the boisterous swagger, the Texan eccentricity and the hot picking.

Discographical Details

04 Live At The Old Quarter, Houston, Texas

Townes Van Zandt
Tomato TOM-2-7001
Pancho And Lefty/Mr Mudd And Mr Gold/Don't You Take It Too Bad/Two Girls/Fraternity Blues/If I Needed You/Brand New Companion/White Freight Liner Blues/To Live Is To Fly/She Came And She Touched Me/Talking Thunderbird Blues/Rex's Blues/Nine-Pound Hammer/For The Sake Of The Song/Chauffeur's Blues/No Place To Fall/Loretta/Kathleen/Why She's Acting This Way/Cocaine Blues/Who Do You Love/Tower Song/Waiting 'Round To Die/Tecumseh Valley/Lungs/Only Him Or Me

05 Live Shots

Joe Ely
MCA MCAD-10816
Fingernails/Midnight Shift/Honky Tonk Masquerade/Honky Tonkin'/Long Snake Moan/I Had My Hopes Up High/She Never Spoke Spanish To Me/

*Johnny's Blues/Fools Fall In Love/Boxcars/Crazy Lemon/Not Fade Away/
Treat Me Like A Saturday Night/Wishin' For You*

(vi) Hot Pickers

For years, Nashville was saddled with the unfair reputation that the local musicians couldn't play anything difficult or fancy. In fact, the town was loaded with talented players just champing at the bit to show what they could do. The mainstream country formula pulled the reins in tightly, however, asking the top session pickers to play the simple harmonies and rhythms with absolute perfection rather than attempt something more ambitious. Even the town's instrumental stars, like Boots Randolph and Floyd Cramer, played it safe. Chet Atkins, whose technical mastery of the guitar was unparalleled, recorded his own instrumental albums as one-take afterthoughts squeezed into his schedule as a busy producer and executive at RCA.

Farther from Nashville, especially in the western swing and Bakersfield bands, adventurous picking was more highly prized, and players in the Bob Wills, Buck Owens, and Merle Haggard bands recorded some hot instrumentals. For the most part, though, the possibilities of the country instrumental slumbered until finally awakened by alternative-country forces in the 1970s.

Oddly enough, this stimulus came from the direction of bluegrass, the most conservative of country subgenres. Bluegrass had always placed a high premium on instrumental dexterity, however, and the younger generation of acoustic pickers who grew up under Dylan's spell saw no reason to limit themselves. If they could play Bill Monroe's *Uncle Pen*, why couldn't they play John Coltrane's *Naima*? After all, one tune was as challenging as the other, and they'd obviously be better players if they could do both.

Leading the way with this new thinking was David Grisman, a New Jersey kid who fell in love with bluegrass, learned all of Bill Monroe's mandolin parts, and soon found himself winning the Best Bluegrass Band award at the 1964 Union Grove Fiddle Contest when he was only 18. It didn't take long for him to get restless, though, and in 1967 he formed the folk-rock group Earth Opera with fellow bluegrass dropout Peter Rowan, a Monroe alumnus. Grisman and Rowan then took their experiment one step further with Muleskinner, a 1972 band that included fiddler Richard Greene (formerly with Monroe), guitarist Clarence White (formerly with the Byrds), and banjoist Bill Keith. In 1973, Grisman and Rowan recorded the **Old And In The Way** album with the Grateful Dead's Jerry Garcia and bluegrass fiddler Vassar Clements.

Through all these incarnations, Grisman was constantly working with the raw materials of bluegrass (the instrumentation and melodic motifs) in an effort to expand the harmonic scope of both the ensemble and solo playing. He insisted that the music had to be instrumental so the musicians wouldn't be obscured by a singer. He eventually split with Greene and Rowan over this issue and formed the first David Grisman Quintet with guitarist Tony Rice, fiddler Darol Anger, mandolinist Todd Phillips, and bassist Joe Carroll. With Bill Amatneek replacing Carroll, this was the line-up that made **The David Grisman Quintet** in 1976 and revolutionized the whole concept of country picking.

Changes had already been brewing. Rice had been exploring similar territory with Ricky Skaggs as members of J.D. Crowe and the New South; Skaggs then hooked up with dobroist *extraordinaire* Jerry Douglas in Boone Creek. Other bluegrass bands, such as the Seldom Scene (featuring John Starling and Mike Auldridge) and the New Grass Revival (featuring Sam Bush and John Cowan), were experimenting along the same lines. As the 1970s turned into the 1980s, these handful of "newgrass" bands, as they were dubbed, became the vehicles for the hottest young country pickers to prove themselves. Grisman hired fiddler Mark O'Connor, guitarist Mike Marshall, bassist Rob Wasserman, and Douglas. Crowe used Douglas and singers Doyle Lawson and Keith Whitley. The New Grass Revival hired banjoist Bela Fleck and guitarist Pat Flynn.

For a while, the "newgrass" movement had a negligible effect on mainstream country. As the 1980s began, however, there was a call in Nashville for a more "traditional" country sound, and when producers went looking for the top acoustic pickers, they turned inevitably to the "new-grass" crowd. Almost overnight, musicians who had been sleeping in cheap motels near summer bluegrass festivals were living in Nashville and playing on sessions for Dolly Parton, Randy Travis, Don Williams, Reba McEntire, George Strait, and many more.

When Skaggs crossed over to commercial country radio (see the chapter on "The 1980s and Beyond"), he brought along many of his old "newgrass" pals, but no one made these pickers more welcome in Nashville than Emmylou Harris (again, see "The 1980s and Beyond"). Over the years, the neo-traditional singer recorded with the likes of Skaggs, Rice, Douglas, Greene, O'Connor, Bush, Auldridge, Starling, Carl Jackson, Byron Berline, Herb Pederson, Hank DeVito, Steve Fishell, Bryan Bowers, Albert Lee, Ray Flacke, and Buddy Spicher.

While they played on many of the biggest albums in country music, these players never abandoned their "newgrass" origins and continued to make adventurous instrumental albums. No recording better demonstrates this marvelous music than **The Telluride Sessions** by Strength in Numbers, the all-star quintet of Bush, Fleck, Douglas, O'Connor, and bassist Edgar Meyer. The five had played on each other's solo albums and live dates in various combinations for years, but they didn't adopt this lineup with this name until the 1987 Telluride Bluegrass Festival in Colorado. "In a way we've grown up with each other," Fleck said. "We've listened to each other grow and played on each other's records. I feel cosmically it's been a band all along."

Most all-star get-togethers either degenerate into formless jam sessions or get overwhelmed by one strong personality. Strength in Numbers avoided both dangers by having each member write one tune with each other member. After carefully arranging the resulting ten instrumentals, the band recorded them in January, 1989. The meticulous preparation lent a chamber-music precision to the proceedings, and allowed each picker to display his prowess without obscuring the emotional identity of each piece.

One Winter's Night, for example, boasts a gorgeous ballad melody that evokes the peaceful snowscape of the title. It opens with the rich harmonies of the tune's composers, O'Connor and Meyer, bowing their fiddle and bass respectively. Douglas then steps forward to restate the melody on his dobro like a woman bemoaning the miles of snow and ice that separate her from her lover. By contrast, *Texas Red* is a joyful piece that finds Bush's mandolin and O'Connor's fiddle leaning into the up-tempo rhythm impatiently while Fleck scatters banjo notes here and there like a sparkler going off in the night.

The brisk pace of *Duke And Cookie* gives all five players a chance to show how quickly they can think on their feet as they rip off sudden flurries of notes. *Pink Flamingos* boasts an unmistakable sense of humor in the way Bush sets up our harmonic expectations and then pulls away the payoff just before we reach it. *The Lochs Of The Dread* combines the Celtic and reggae influences implied by its title, while the mandolin duet between Bush and O'Connor on *Macedonia* alludes to the East European roots of the instrument. Every influence and allusion, however, is incorporated into the sound of Appalachia, and when the band digs into a melodic line as full of feeling as Douglas's ballad lament on *No Apologies*, the effect is not unlike Hank Williams wailing about being lonesome and blue.

While the others each mastered the existing possibilities of their instruments, Fleck completely reinvented the banjo by slowing down his phrasing so each individual note could be heard. This enabled him to play single-note melody lines and variations, each with its own percussive accent, like no other banjoist before him. He pushed even further in this direction with his inspired country-jazz-funk band of the 1990s, Bela Fleck and the Flecktones.

The "newgrass" pickers weren't the only instrumentalists pushing the boundaries of country music in the 1970s and beyond. There were western swing players like Lucky Oceans, Floyd Domino, Paul Glasse and Gene Elders; western guitar hot-shots like Pete Anderson, Bill Kirchen, and Junior Brown, and a whole pack of dazzling rockabilly guitarists from the DC area (Danny Gatton, Roy Buchanan, Evan Johns, Steuart Smith, and Pete Kennedy) who combined breathtaking speed and a healthy contempt for genre limitations. Together they proved that alternative-country needn't apologize for its chops when compared to blues, rock, or even jazz.

Discographical Details

06 The Telluride Sessions

Strength in Numbers
MCAD MCAD-6293
Future Man/Texas Red/Pink Flamingos/Duke And Cookie/One Winter's Night/ Macedonia/The Lochs Of The Dread/No Apologies/Slopes/Blue Men of Sahara

Basic Recordings

(i) Country-Rock

07 Nashville Skyline

Bob Dylan
Columbia CK 09825
Girl Of The North Country/Nashville Skyline Rag/To Be Alone With You/I Threw It All Away/Peggy Day/Lay, Lady, Lay/One More Night/Tell Me That It Isn't True/Country Pie/Tonight I'll Be Staying Here With You

As his follow-up to **John Wesley Harding**, Dylan went even deeper into country with a whole album of straightforward love songs backed by Nashville's finest. One was a duet with Johnny Cash (*Girl Of The North Country*); one was a Top 10 pop hit (*Lay, Lady, Lay*); and one was one of the most harrowing heartbroken laments ever sung (*I Threw It All Away*).

08 Farther Along: The Best Of The Flying Burrito Brothers

The Flying Burrito Brothers
A & M CD 5216
Christine's Tune (Devil in Disguise)/Sin City/Do Right Woman/Dark End Of The Street/Wheels/Juanita/Hot Burrito No. 1/Hot Burrito No. 2/Do You Know

How It Feels/Break My Mind/Farther Along/Cody Cody/God's Own Singer/ Wild Horses/Dim Lights/Just Because/Six Days on the Road/To Love Somebody/Close Up The Honky Tonks/Sing Me Back Home/I Shall Be Released

After Gram Parsons and Chris Hillman quit the Byrds in the wake of **Sweetheart Of The Rodeo**, they formed the Flying Burrito Brothers and recorded three albums before Parsons split again for a solo career. This anthology collects the best of those three albums plus a handful of outtakes. As opposed to the Appalachian sound of **Sweetheart Of The Rodeo**, these songs have more of a Buck Owens/Bakersfield sound and are thus Parsons's most commercial-sounding work.

309 The Band

The Band
Capitol C2-46493

Across The Great Divide/Rag Mama Rag/The Night They Drove Old Dixie Down/When You Awake/Up On Cripple Creek/Whispering Pines/Jemima Surrender/Rockin' Chair/Look Out, Cleveland/Jawbone/The Unfaithful Servant/ King Harvest (Has Surely Come)

Four Canadians and an Arkansas Razorback, this quintet backed rockabilly pioneer Ronnie Hawkins, played on their own as the Hawks, and backed up Bob Dylan before releasing their 1968 debut album, **Music From Big Pink** (which included two songs from **The Basement Tapes**, plus a Lefty Frizzell hit). Even better is this, their 1969 second album, which included one of the greatest Civil War songs (*The Night They Drove Old Dixie Down*), one of the greatest union songs (*King Harvest*), one of the greatest old-folks songs (*Rockin' Chair*), and one of the greatest racetrack songs (*Up On Cripple Creek*). Garth Hudson was the best honky-tonk pianist of his generation; songwriter Robbie Robertson was another James Burton on the guitar, and Levon Helm and Richard Manuel were amazing country singers.

310 Green River

Creedence Clearwater Revival
Fantasy FCD-4514–2 (F-8393)

Green River/Commotion/Tombstone Shadow/Wrote A Song for Everyone/Bad Moon Rising/Lodi/Cross-Tie Walker/Sinister Purpose/The Night Time Is The Right Time

John Fogerty, the leader of this northern California quartet, drew the inspiration for both his lyrics and music from the American South and from the blues and honky-tonk that epitomized that region for him. The country influence is most obvious in the four brilliant songs at the center of this album: *Wrote A Song For Everyone*, the twangy lament of a young draftee in a rural welfare office; *Bad Moon Rising*, a hillbilly two-step filled with biblical omens; *Lodi*, the confession of a weary honky-tonk singer; and *Cross-Tie Walker*, a Johnny Cash-like railroad song. Fogerty's songs have since been recorded by such country figures as Cash, Emmylou Harris, Jerry Lee Lewis, Carlene Carter, and Rick Nelson.

11 GP/Grievous Angel

Gram Parsons
Reprise 9 26108–2

Still Feeling Blue/We'll Sweep Out The Ashes In The Morning/A Song For You/Streets Of Baltimore/She/That's All It Took/The New Soft Shoe/Kiss The Children/Cry One More Time/How Much I've Lied/Big Mouth Blues/Return Of The Grievous Angel/Hearts On Fire/I Can't Dance/Brass Buttons/$1000 Wedding/Cash On The Barrelhead/Hickory Wind/Love Hurts/Ooh Las Vegas/ In My Hour Of Darkness

Parsons's two legendary solo albums have been combined on one CD by Reprise. With Emmylou Harris singing harmonies, Elvis Presley's T.C.B. Band (James Burton, Glen D. Hardin, and Ron Tutt) playing rhythm, and Merle Haggard's engineer producing, the albums sound great, but it is Parsons's songwriting that made them so memorable. He had a way of combining country's enduring multi-generational values and rock's impatience that created a terrific dramatic tension. Plus, he was a hell of a singer.

12 Harvest

Neil Young
Reprise CD 2277–2

Out On The Weekend/Harvest/A Man Needs A Maid/Heart Of Gold/Are You Ready For The Country/Old Man/There's A World/Alabama/The Needle And The Damage Done/Words (Between The Lines Of Age)

Young's fourth solo album, released in 1972, was mostly recorded in Nashville with the likes of drummer Kenny Buttrey and steel guitarist Ben Keith. It's not necessarily Young's best album, but it's his best country effort and certainly his best-selling recording – both the album and the *Heart Of Gold* single went to number 1 in the pop-charts. Young's pinched, nasal voice takes some getting used to, but he's a terrific songwriter, matching catchy melodies to arresting stories, and he has a way of putting them across in the most personal manner.

(ii) Southern Rock

13 Brothers And Sisters

The Allman Brothers Band
Polygram 825 092–2

Wasted Words/Ramblin' Man/Come And Go Blues/Jelly Jelly/Southbound/ Jessica/Pony Boy

This isn't the Allman Brothers' best album (that would be the blues-drenched **At Fillmore East**), but it best exemplifies the country side of the band's musical personality. Dicky Betts had more room to explore his lifelong love for country music after the 1971 death of bandleader Duane Allman, and Betts wrote and sang the hit single, *Ramblin' Man*, typical of many of Allman's songs that married country lyrics and country melodies to the band's trademark shuffle/swing rhythms and jazzy guitar fills and solos. Betts also wrote the instrumental, *Jessica*, which elaborates a catchy country guitar lick into dizzying variations.

314 Gold and Platinum

Lynyrd Skynyrd

MCA MCAD2–6898

Down South Jukin'/Saturday Night Special/Gimme Three Steps/What's Your Name/You Got That Right/Gimme Back My Bullets/Sweet Home Alabama/ Free Bird/That Smell/On The Hunt/I Ain't The One/Whiskey Rock-A-Roller/ Simple Man/I Know A Little/Tuesday's Gone/Comin' Home

This greatest-hits collection collects most – but not all – of Skynyrd's other important songs. If you want even more, avoid the 3-CD box set, **Lynyrd Skynyrd**, and start collecting the individual albums, especially **Second Helping** and **Street Survivors**.

315 Rebel Rousers: Southern-Rock Classics

Various Artists

Rhino R2 70586

The Allman Brothers Band: *Statesboro Blues*; Black Oak Arkansas: *Jim Dandy*; Travis Wammack: *Funk No. 49*; Wet Willie: *Keep On Smilin'*; Elvin Bishop: *Fooled Around And Fell In Love*; The Marshall Tucker Band: *Heard It In A Love Song*; The Ozark Mountain Daredevils: *Jackie Blue*; The Outlaws: *Freeborn Man* (live version); Johnny Van Zant Band: *Coming Home*; .38 Special: *Caught Up In You*; Rossington Collins Band: *Don't Misunderstand Me*; Lynyrd Skynyrd: *Free Bird* (live version)

This anthology gives a good overview of the other Southern-rock bands. South Carolina's Marshall Tucker Band, led by brothers Toy and Tommy Caldwell, brought more countrified melodicism to Southern rock than anyone else. Elvin Bishop was an alumnus of Chicago's Paul Butterfield Blues Band, Johnny Van Zant and .38 Special's Donnie Van Zant were the younger brothers of Skynyrd's Ronnie, and the Rossington Collins Band was named after the surviving guitarists from the Skynyrd plane crash.

(iii) Blues-Country

316 Fully Realized

Charlie Rich

Mercury SRM-2-7505

Mohair Sam/I Can't Go On/Dance Of Love/A Field Of Yellow Daisies/I Washed My Hands In Muddy Water/Everything I Do Is Wrong/She's A Yum Yum/It Ain't Gonna Be That Way/Just A Little Bit Of You/Moonshine Minnie/Down and Out/Lonely Weekends/No Home/So Long/The Best Years/ Party Girl/You Can Have Her/Have I Stayed Away Too Long/Hawg Jaw/ Something Just Came Over Me/Double Dog Dare Me/Just A Little Bit Of Time/Blowin' Town/Tears A-Go-Go

Before he became a mainstream "countrypolitan" star with hits like *Behind Closed Doors* and *The Most Beautiful Girl*, Rich was a rockabilly singer– pianist at the end of the Sun Records era and then a blues-country singer in the Ray Charles mode. This anthology collects his two great albums for Smash Records, 1965's **The Many New Sides Of Charlie Rich** and 1966's **Fast Talkin', Slow Walkin', Good Lookin' Charlie Rich**, when producer

Jerry Kennedy allowed Rich to combine country songwriting, blues vocals, jazzy piano and rockabilly arrangements with exhilarating results. Also worth finding is Rich's 1992 **Pictures And Paintings**.

17   The Best Of Delbert McClinton

Delbert McClinton
MCA MCA-5917
Let Love Come Between Us/It's Love, Baby (Twenty-Four Hours a Day)/ Victim Of Life's Circumstances/Love Rustler/Pledging My Love/Turn On Your Love Light/Ruby Louise/Two More Bottles Of Wine/Hold On To Your Honey/ Before You Accuse Me

Texas's McClinton (who taught John Lennon how to play harmonica on an early British tour) was part of the progressive-country movement of the early 1970s, but his albums for ABC were much bluesier than those by counterparts like Willie and Waylon. McClinton wasn't afraid to use R & B horn charts and funky rhythms, but he was also capable of writing classic honky-tonk numbers like *Two More Bottles Of Wine* (later a hit for Emmylou Harris) and *Victim Of Life's Circumstances*, and his Otis Redding/George Jones vocals were perfect for the material.

18   Nick Of Time

Bonnie Raitt
Capitol CDP 7 91268 2
Nick Of Time/Thing Called Love/Love Letter/Cry On My Shoulder/Real Man/ Nobody's Girl/Have A Heart/Too Soon To Tell/I Will Not Be Denied/I Ain't Gonna Let You Break My Heart Again/The Road's My Middle Name

This 1989 album was not only the long overdue commercial breakthrough for Raitt and the catalyst for her dominance of the 1990 Grammy Awards, but it's also the best showcase for the country side of her music. Drawing on Nashville songwriters like John Hiatt, Mike Reid, and Larry John McNally, the album took up the honky-tonk subjects of searching for romance and excitement in middle age. The four best songs were written by Raitt herself and by her LA alter ego, Bonnie Hayes. Best of all, it featured Raitt's gloriously robust voice, sliding through notes and timbres with expressive fullness.

19   Slow Turning

John Hiatt
A & M CD 5206 DX 003682
Drive South/Trudy And Dave/Tennessee Plates/Icy Blue Heart/Sometime Other Than Now/Georgia Rae/Ride Along/Slow Turning/It'll Come To You/Is Anybody There/Paper Thin/Feels Like Rain

Indiana's Hiatt – who has written songs for such country stars as Willie Nelson, Freddy Fender, Rosanne Cash, Rodney Crowell, Emmylou Harris, Gail Davies, Ronnie Milsap, Suzy Bogguss, Asleep at the Wheel, and the Nitty Gritty Dirt Band – has had equal success with such blues singers as Aaron Neville, Johnny Adams, Buddy Guy, and Jeff Healey. He can work both sides of the street because he writes new songs that sound like lost gems from 1950s radio with their clever use of working-class vernacular and their compact tunefulness. This 1988 album captures Hiatt singing a dozen of his best tunes with his usual reckless abandon, backed by a great Louisiana swamp band.

320　Got No Bread/Tryin' Like The Devil

James Talley

Bear Family BCD 15433 AH

W. Lee O'Daniel And The Light Crust Doughboys/Got No Bread, No Milk, No Money, But We Sure Got A Lot Of Love/Red River Memory/Give Him Another Bottle/Calico Gypsy/To Get Back Home/Big Taters In Sandy Land/ Intro/No Opener Needed/Blue-Eyed Ruth And My Sunday Suit/Mehan, Oklahoma/Daddy's Song/Take Me To The Country/Red River Reprise/Forty Hours/Deep Country Blues/Give My Love To Marie/Are They Gonna Make Us Outlaws Again/She Tries Not To Cry/Tryin' Like The Devil/She's The One/ Sometimes I Think About Suzanne/Nothin' But The Blues/You Can't Ever Tell

Like his hero and fellow Okie Woody Guthrie, Talley had political motivations for combining blues and country music as a way to bring together black and white working-class audiences. His motivations wouldn't have mattered very much if he hadn't proven so gifted at capturing the mundane details and daily trials of blue-collar life in such charmingly naturalistic songs. Talley became the darling of the Jimmy Carter administration and of critics like Peter Guralnick, but he never sold many records and at last report was working as a realtor in Nashville. His songs still stand up, though, and Germany's Bear Family combined Talley's 1975 and 1976 Capitol albums into this single CD.

321　The Best Of Jesse Winchester

Jesse Winchester

Rhino/Bearsville R2 70085

Tell Me Why You Like Roosevelt/Mississippi, You're On My Mind/Yankee Lady/The Brand New Tennessee Waltz/Biloxi/Talk Memphis/Bowling Green/ Do It/Defying Gravity/Say What/I'm Looking For A Miracle/Do La Lay/Skip Rope Song/Everybody Knows But Me/Rhumba Man/A Showman's Life/Dangerous Fun/All Of Your Stories

Winchester grew up in Memphis and wound up in Canada as a draft evader during the Vietnam War. Those two experiences define his music, for his songs are fished up from the deep currents of the Mississippi River where country and blues swirl together, but he also has an outsider's perspective on things. Though he later became a successful Nashville songwriter for the likes of Wynonna Judd, Winchester's first seven solo albums were dominated by quiet storytelling in the country/blues manner but with a knowing distance. Eighteen songs from those albums are on this anthology.

(iv) Folk-Country

322　The Essential Steve Goodman

Steve Goodman

Buddah 0698

The I Don't Know Where I'm Goin', But I'm Goin' Nowhere In A Hurry Blues/Donald And Lydia/You Never Even Call Me By My Name/Election

*Year Rag/Eight Ball Blues/City Of New Orleans/Turnpike Tom/Yellow Coat/
Jazzman/Would You Like To Learn To Dance/The Dutchman/Six Hours
Ahead Of The Sun/Song For David/Chicken Cordon Blues/Somebody Else's
Troubles/The Loving Of The Game/I Ain't Heard You Play No Blues/Don't
Do Me Any Favors Anymore/Lincoln Park Pirates/The Ballad of Penny Evans*

Goodman, John Prine's buddy from the Chicago folk scene, is best known for
writing the best train song of the space age, *City Of New Orleans*, but he had
a deep well of memorable songs, some of them recorded by David Allan Coe
(who had a country hit with *You Never Even Called Me By My Name*),
Johnny Cash, John Denver, Jimmy Buffett, Joan Baez and, of course, Arlo
Guthrie. Goodman shared Prine's gift for simple storytelling and sneaky
humor, and this anthology collects the best of his early work.

3 All On A Rising Day

Peter Rowan
Sugar Hill SH-CD-3791

*Midnight Highway/Last Train/Howlin' At The Moon/Mr Time Clock/Behind
These Prison Walls Of Love/Deal With The Devil/Undying Love/The Wheel Of
Fortune/All On A Rising Day/Freedom Walkabout/Prayer Of A Homeless
Wanderer/John O'Dreams*

Rowan, a former member of Bill Monroe and the Blue Grass Boys, co-
founded Earth Opera with David Grisman, and joined his brothers in the
Rowans. Splitting his time between Texas and Nashville, Rowan developed
into a fine songwriter who combined the freedom of bohemian folk music
with the craftmanship of mainstream country. He always made a point of
playing with the hottest bluegrass players around, and this 1991 album
(which features Sam Bush, Jerry Douglas and Stuart Duncan) is no exception. The songs range from ghost stories and road tales to populist visions,
and the contrast between Rowan's calm vocals and the band's excited picking
works splendidly.

4 Lone Star State Of Mind

Nanci Griffith
MCA MCAD-31300

*Lone Star State Of Mind/Cold Hearts, Closed Minds/From A Distance/Beacon
Street/Nickel Dreams/Sing One For Sister/Ford Econoline/Trouble In The
Fields/Love In A Memory/Let It Shine On Me/There's A Light Beyond These
Woods (Mary Margaret)*

Griffith is the Joni Mitchell of Texas, a literary bohemian with a small but
achingly pure voice and a drawer full of folk songs with the kind of melodic
hooks that country and pop singers love. When Kathy Mattea turned Griffith's *Love At The Five And Dime* into a country hit, the Texas folkie moved
to Nashville in search of her own hit. The first result was this 1987 album, a
superb example of the folk-country hybrid, but one that didn't crack country
radio. Included is the first (and best) recorded version of *From A Distance*, a
tribute to Kate Wolf and Rosalie Sorrels (*Ford Econoline*), and a reworking of
Griffith's best song (*Mary Margaret*).

325   One More Goodnight Kiss

Greg Brown

Red House RHR 23

One More Goodnight Kiss/Say A Little Prayer/Mississippi Moon/Cheapest Kind/Canned Goods/I Can't Get Used To It/Rooty Toot Toot For The Moon/ Walking Down To Casey's/Speed Trap Boogie/Our Little Town/Wash My Eyes

Iowa's Brown is a fixture on the folk coffeehouse circuit, but his vocals have a deep, honky-tonk flavor and his songs have been recorded by Willie Nelson and Michael Johnson. His lyrics capture small-town Mid-Western life with accurate, telling details, and his narratives contrast the strength of family and community with the encroachment of external economic and cultural forces. This 1988 album is his best, a guide to surviving hard times with *Canned Goods*, *A Little Prayer* and *One More Goodnight Kiss*.

326   T-Bone Burnett

T-Bone Burnett

Dot MCA-5809

River of Love/Poison Love/Shake Yourself Loose/No Love At All/Annabelle Lee/I Remember/Little Daughter/Oh No, Darling/Time/The Bird That I Held In My Hand

In 1986, T-Bone Burnett, fellow traveler of both Bob Dylan and Elvis Costello, was invited to make a one-off country album for the resurrected Dot label, and he came up with an album so spare in its acoustic arrangements, so ancient in its themes of children, marriage and grief, and so true in its vocals that it could only seem like an alternative to mid-1980s Nashville. The picking by Jerry Douglas, David Hidalgo, and Byron Berline was exquisite, and when Burnett sings of a "river of love" and a "grief that floods," he gives them both the inevitability of gravity.

(v) Texas's Cosmic Cowboys

327   Old No. 1

Guy Clark

RCA APL1-1303 (reissued on CD as Sugar Hill SH-CD-1030)

Rita Ballou/LA Freeway/She Ain't Goin' Nowhere/A Nickel For The Fiddler/ That Old-Time Feeling/Texas – 1947/Desperados Waiting For The Train/Like A Coat From The Cold/Instant Coffee Blues/Let Him Roll

With his cragged features and swept-back thick hair, Clark looks like a nineteenth century Southern senator, and he has the deep, resonant voice of an old-fashioned orator. His themes are anything but patrician, however, and his songs about carpenters, gardeners, barmaids, grandfathers, cooks, winos, and lovers sum up modern Texas as well as the collected novels of Larry McMurtry. A selfless advocate of his fellow Texan singer–songwriters, Clark takes his time writing songs and recording them. All his albums are good, but this 1975 outing contains his best and best-known songs.

28   Contrary To Ordinary

Jerry Jeff Walker

MCA MCA-3041

Tryin' To Hold The Wind Up With A Sail/Saturday Night Special/Suckin' A Big Bottle Of Gin/What Are We Doing?/Till We Gain Control Again/Contrary To Ordinary/We Were Kinda Crazy Then/Deeper Than Love/I Spent All My Money Lovin' You/Carry Me Away

Walker is best known for composing one classic song, *Mr Bojangles*, but he has spent the bulk of his career as a skillful interpreter of other people's songs. His ability to sound like a raucous drunk on the up-tempo party songs and like a wistful philosopher on the ballads served as a blueprint for Jimmy Buffett's career and made Walker a favorite of live audiences. This album illustrates both sides of Walker's musical personality on songs by Butch Hancock, Lee Clayton, Bobby Charles, and Guy Clark's wife Susanna.

29   Tougher Than Leather

Willie Nelson

Columbia CK 38248

My Love For The Rose/Changing Skies/Tougher Than Leather/Little Old-Fashioned Karma/Somewhere In Texas (Pt 1)/Beer Barrel Polka/Summer of Roses/Somewhere In Texas (Pt 2)/My Love For The Rose/The Convict And The Rose/Changing Skies/I Am The Forest/Nobody Slides, My Friend

It's a tribute to Nelson's genius that he can top the country charts with a mainstream Nashville single, and then turn around and release an anachronistic tribute to bygone styles, and then another album at the furthest fringes of alternative-country – often all in the same year. Nelson had a near brush with death when his lungs collapsed in 1982, and he used the time in the hospital to compose this story-suite of songs about an Old West gunslinger's confrontation with death. The 1983 release was too dark and weird for country radio, but it may well be Nelson's best album.

30   Willis Alan Ramsey

Willis Alan Ramsey

Shelter SRZ-8008

Ballad Of Spider John/Muskrat Love/Geraldine And The Honeybee/Wishbone/ Satin Sheets/Goodbye Old Missoula/Painted Lady/Watermelon Man/Boy From Oklahoma/Angel Eyes/Northeast Texas Women

When the Austin singer–songwriter scene was just gathering steam in 1972, a 21-year-old Willis Alan Ramsey released a debut album that was an almost perfect distillation of the era. His leisurely swamp rhythms and understated but sophisticated guitar lines recalled J.J. Cale, while his sweet melodies and off-handed vocals recalled Townes Van Zandt. Songs from this one album were recorded by Jimmy Buffett, Waylon Jennings, America, David Bromberg, and Captain and Tenille (who took *Muskrat Love* to number 4 on the pop charts), but Ramsey dropped out of sight. As of this writing, he hasn't released a follow-up album and remains one of the most perplexing mysteries in Texas.

331 Guitar Town

Steve Earle

MCA MCAD-31305

Guitar Town/Goodbye's All We've Got/Hillbilly Highway/Good Ol' Boy (Gettin' Tough)/My Old Friend The Blues/Someday/Think It Over/Fearless Heart/Little Rock 'N' Roller/Down The Road

If Bruce Springsteen had grown up in Texas, listening to Lefty Frizzell on the radio in a beat-up pick-up truck, he might have sounded a lot like Steve Earle. Earle has "The Boss's" ability to tell blue-collar stories with just the right details and just the right guitar licks, but Earle sets his tales in small Texas towns and gives his riffs a tell-tale twang. Earle, who once played bass for Guy Clark, cut some singles for Epic that went nowhere, but 1986's **Guitar Town** was his debut album, and he never topped this country-rock evocation of the forgotten kids too small for a football scholarship, too restless to stay home, and too tough to give up.

332 Lyle Lovett

Lyle Lovett

MCA/Curb MCAD-31307

Cowboy Man/God Will/Farther Down the Road/This Old Porch/Why I Don't Know/If I Were The Man You Wanted/You Can't Resist It/The Waltzing Fool/An Acceptable Level Of Ecstasy (The Wedding Song)/Closing Time

The same year Earle's debut appeared, so did this equally astonishing debut, complete with effusive liner notes by Guy Clark. Also produced by Tony Brown, **Lyle Lovett** has a bit of a western swing feel to go with its deliciously wry lyrics and dry vocals. "If I were the man you wanted," he sang, "I would not be the man that I am;" and a refusal to meet other people's expectations fills these songs with a sharp, literate intelligence that confused country radio but excited the alternative-country audience. With his gravity-defying hair and his insistence on fleshing out his Townes Van Zandt-like tunes with cello and gospel vocals, Lovett is one of a kind, even among Texas's eccentrics.

333 One Road More

The Flatlanders

Charly CRM 2038

You've Never Seen Me Cry/Dallas/Tonight I Think I'm Gonna Go Downtown/ She Had Everything/Bhagavan Decreed/Rose From The Mountain/Down In My Hometown/One Road More/Waitin' For A Train/Hello Stranger/One Day At A Time/Stars In My Life/Not So Long Ago/I Know You/The Heart You Left Behind/Jole Blon/Keeper Of The Mountain

The Flatlanders' one and only album is such a resonant, timeless piece of country music that it could have been recorded at the Bristol field recordings in 1927, on the Louisiana Hayride Radio show in 1948, at the Sun Studios in Memphis in 1955, or on Austin City Limits last week. In fact, it was recorded in 1972, released only on 8-track, promptly shelved, and finally released in 1980 when members Joe Ely, Butch Hancock, and Jimmie Dale Gilmore won solo renown. Featuring four songs apiece by Hancock and Gilmore, plus numbers from such heroes as Jimmie Rodgers and Willie

Nelson, the all-acoustic album didn't feature a drummer, but it did have Ely's dobro, Tommy Hancock's fiddle, and Steve Wesson's musical saw. The saw's eerie, quivering sound matched Gilmore's pure, high voice perfectly. The British release contains four more songs than the US release.

4 Fair And Square

Jimmie Dale Gilmore

Hightone HCD 8011

White Freight Liner Blues/Honky Tonk Masquerade/Fair And Square/Don't Look For A Heartache/Trying To Get To You/Singing The Blues/Just A Wave, Not The Water/All Grown Up/Ninety-Nine Holes/Rain Just Falls

Gilmore's best solo album is this 1988 release which marries his pure country tenor to consistently marvelous songs written by Ely, Hancock, Van Zandt, Gilmore himself and the underrated David Halley. Produced by Ely, the album is a near-perfect showcase for the best singing, songwriting, and picking Texas has to offer.

5 Own And Own

Butch Hancock

Sugar Hill SH-CD-1036

Dry Land Farm/Wind's Dominion/Diamond Hill/1981: A Spare Odyssey/Firewater (Seeks Its Own Level)/West Texas Waltz/Horseflies/If You Were A Bluebird/Own And Own/Fools Fall In Love/Yella Rose/Like A Kiss On The Mouth/The Ghost Of Give-and-Take Avenue/Tell Me What You Want To Know/Just A Storm/Just Tell Me That/When Will You Hold Me Again

Hancock has not only written many of the best songs recorded by Ely and Gilmore, but he has also contributed material to Jerry Jeff Walker and Emmylou Harris. His own versions of the songs emphasize his strumming acoustic guitar, harmonica solos, and gravelly voice. Hancock can get away with sounding so much like Bob Dylan, because he's one of the few anywhere who can match Dylan's flamboyant imagery and playful humor – all with a distinctly Texan spin. Hancock is so prolific that he was able to play 140 original songs in seven consecutive nights in Austin, never repeat a single title and release the results on a "No 2 Alike" cassette series. His own recordings have been issued on his own, impossible-to-find, Rainlight Records label, but in 1991 Sugar Hill released 13 of the best numbers from the Rainlight releases on this CD, and added four new songs produced by Ely.

(vi) Hot Pickers

6 The David Grisman Quintet

The David Grisman Quintet

Kaleidoscope F-5 (LP)

E.M.D./Swing 51/Opus 57/Blue Midnite/Pneumonia/Fish Scale/Richochet/Dawg's Rag

Recorded in 1976 and released the following year, this was the album that opened the doors for every long-haired picker looking for a way out of the bluegrass trap. Using the familiar Appalachian instruments (Grisman and

Todd Phillips on mandolin, Tony Rice on guitar, Darol Anger on fiddle, and Bill Amatneek on string bass), the quintet took bluegrass and made it swing crisply, moan bluely, and digress endlessly. This all-instrumental album, dominated by Grisman's own compositions, featured both intricate chamber arrangements and free-wheeling solos, all expanding the possibilities of what hollow wooden instruments could do.

337 UFO Tofu

Bela Fleck and the Flecktones

Warner Bros 9 45016–2

The West Country/Sex In A Pan/Nemo's Dream/Bonnie And Slyde/Scuttlebutt/ UFO Tofu/Magic Fingers/True North/Life Without Elvis/Saresta/The Yee-Haw Factor/After The Storm

When the New Grass Revival disbanded at the end of 1989, Bela Fleck formed this quartet with Howard Levy on piano and harmonica, Victor Wooten on electric bass, and Roy "Futureman" Wooten on "drumitar," a hand-operated drum machine in the shape of a guitar. By understating his attack on the banjo, Fleck created a harp-like quality on the instrument, and by encouraging democratic improvisation by all members of the group, he built on his bluegrass, country, Celtic, blues and jazz sources into an unparalleled all-instrumental music. This album, the band's third and its last with Levy, is the best.

338 Cruisin' Deuces

Danny Gatton

Elektra 9 61465–2

Funhouse/Sun Medley (Mystery Train – My Baby Left Me – That's All Right)/Harlem Nocturne/Thirteen Women/Sky King/Beat Of The Night/So Good/It Doesn't Matter Anymore/Puddin' And Pie/Tragedy/Cruisin' Deuce/ Satisfied Mind

Although there's some singing (by Rodney Crowell, Delbert McClinton, and others) on this album, it's not done by Gatton, who dominates the proceedings with his blistering Telecaster picking. For years an underground legend among guitarists while he played in obscure rockabilly bands around DC, Gatton finally graduated to a major label in 1991 and played a straightahead bebop session with top jazz stars in 1992. Drawing on sources like Elvis Presley, the Everly Brothers, and the Byrds, this 1993 album brings him back to his country and rockabilly roots (his heroes include Hank Garland, Jimmy Bryant, James Burton, and Cliff Gallup). Gatton is lightning fast, harmonically ingenious, and capable of dozens of guitar sounds within the same song. What really distinguishes him, however, is his ability to make the guitar sound as anguished or joyful as the best hillbilly singer.

Irish Country: 1963-1993

Tom Gilmore

It has often been claimed that the origins of country music emanated from the British Isles, when the traditional fiddle tunes of Ireland and Scotland were taken by emigrants to the "New World" and fused with other musical influences to become the bluegrass or mountain folk music of the Southern States of America. Paddy Moloney, of the internationally famous Irish folk group the Chieftains, who took their traditional sounds to Nashville in 1992 for a more modern fusion of "new" country and the old folk tunes of Ireland on the CD **Another Country**, is a strong believer in the theory that the music may have first emerged in Ireland. While he admits that *Cotton-Eyed Joe* may well be the "national anthem of Texas," Paddy says that in reality it is an old Irish traditional reel called *The Mountain Top*, which he first heard his grandmother perform in her home in Ireland during his childhood days. "Did you wash your father's shirt, and did you wash it clean?" are, according to the leader of the Chieftains, really some of the words in the original old Irish tune that was to deviate to become *Cotton-Eyed Joe* in the USA. Like many other performers, Paddy says it was the musical exodus from the Ireland of the past and the emigrants who took their music with them as they went to seek a new life in the "New World" that helped form the bluegrass and early country sounds of America.

Irrespective of when this musical exodus occurred, it was not until the late 1950s or early 1960s that Irish singers started to take it all back home in a far more sophisticated, if somewhat sanitized form known in the Ireland of that era as country and western or sometimes country and Irish music. From the late 1950s Irish music fans witnessed a phenomenon known as the "showbands", with hundreds of them strutting their stuff, mainly a mixture of rock-and-roll and country, in big barn-like dancehalls which were erected in almost every town and medium-sized village in Ireland. In tandem, and in summer-time, the teenagers would sometimes dance to their favorites in huge canvas tents or "marquees", where once again they were entertained mainly on a diet of "country" music. It was "bas-tardized" country music in the eyes of many music critics, but it did introduce generations of Irish teenagers to "covers" of country songs, while the originals were successful in America for the likes of Jim Reeves, Marty Robbins, Hank Williams, and Bobby Bare.

In late 1961 Tom Dunphy, who was the country singer with the predominantly rock-and-roll band the Royal, recorded *Come Down The Mountain, Katie Daly*. It was a bluegrass tinged traditional tune on a 45 rpm record and, early in 1962, this officially became the first "showband" country single in Ireland. (In October of 1962 the first Irish Top 10 singles chart was broadcast on Irish national radio, RTE. It was compiled by sports journalist Jimmy McGee and the presenter was Harry Thuillier. Many country records were to top this chart in the years after 1962.) Dunphy's lead singer was Brendan Bowyer from Waterford City, who was later to gain a measure of inter-national acclaim for his Elvis Presley impersonations and the rock-and-roll song *The Hucklebuck*, a number 1 in the Irish Top 10 in 1965.

Many "purists" would claim that *Katie Daly* by Dunphy and the Royal was not "country," and that a cover version of a Bobby Bare song recorded by another Irish group was "unof-ficially" in their eyes the first "showband" country single, though the record books would dispute this claim. This was *Detroit City (I Wanna Go Home)* recorded in America early in 1963 by the Johnny Flynn Showband from Tuam, County Galway, with Dublin-born singer Gerry Cronin as the vocalist. But when the records were pressed and delivered to Ireland it could not be released because of the size of the hole in the centre! The record players on sale in Ireland had all got the small spindle centre, so a single made in America by an Irish band was useless in their homeland where it could not be played.

Neither Cronin nor Dunphy are alive today to continue the disputed claim to Ireland's first "showband" country single, as both died tragically young, the latter in a horrific car crash in 1976. Both were to have their share of success with country records later in their respective careers. Dunphy made number 1 in the Irish Top 10 in March of 1965 with *If I Didn't Have A Dime*, and Cronin with a new band, the Ohio, became known as Ireland's Johnny Cash for his recording of *Ring Of Fire*. The Johnny Flynn Band, with whom Gerry recorded that first country single, were to remain a top attraction for many years and had a number 1 with an Irish ballad, *Black And Tan Gun*, early in 1966.

However, prior to the formative years of the "showband" era, some Irish solo singers could be credited as having touched on the genre known as "country and Irish" music with some of their 78 rpm recordings. The most notable of these would be Bridie Gallagher from Donegal, who recorded for the Beltona label in 1957. One of her most memorable recordings from that year was *The Hills Of Donegal*, with *Mother's Last Goodbye* (Beltona BE 2698) on the B-side. Other female singers of that era to introduce country sounds to Irish audiences included Rose Tynan in Dublin, Nita Norry, Eileen Donaghy in Northern Ireland, Eileen Reid and her band the Cadets from Dublin, and Sligo songstress Maisie McDaniel, the latter being the first female country singer to have her own network TV show.

In 1963 McDaniel had a fan club of over 5,000 in Ireland and she had toured with such stars as Jim Reeves, Cliff Richard, and Johnny Mathis. At the peak of her popularity she owned homes both in Ireland and England. But when she made a comeback attempt in 1985 she had gone through the rigors of a broken marriage and two serious car accidents, and was reduced to living in a mobile home at the bottom of a hillside in her native Sligo – sadly, her comeback attempt failed to gain her star status again. But 22 years earlier, in June 1963, the Fontana label released one of her best country records, *Something Special*, coupled with *This Song Is Just For You*. In August of the same year Fontana was to go one step further by releasing an EP featuring Maisie, which contained her versions of country standards *Jambalaya*, *I Fall To Pieces*, *Pick Me Up On Your Way Down*, and *Someday* (Fontana TE 17397).

While some modern "new" country enthusiasts in Ireland may ridicule the contribution by the "showbands" in popularizing this type of music among Irish fans, nobody can deny that they were there in abundance recording "covers" of American country songs especially in the 1960s and 1970s. The first ever LP recorded by an Irish "showband" was titled **Presenting The Capitol Showband** recorded by this eight-piece band in Dublin's Eamonn Andrews Studios for the London-based Delyse label in 1962. It contained mostly Irish ballads performed to a "showband" beat but one of the most popular tracks was an old country standard, *Silver Threads And Golden Needles*.

It was the more pop-sounding *Foolin' Time*, featuring singer Butch Moore from Dublin, that was to give the Capitol their first hit in February 1964. Their country singer Des Kelly, from County Galway, had to wait until February 1967 for his first chart hit, a number 3 with his cover version of the Bobby Bare classic *Streets Of Baltimore*. Des's brother, the late Johnny Kelly, was to score a number 1 that same year with folk-country number *The Black Velvet Band*. But in 1964, Eileen Reid and the Cadets were to hit the high spots with *Fallen Star*, giving her a number 1 in April of that year followed by a number 4 with a beautiful country song *I Gave My Wedding Dress Away*. This became her best-known hit even though it only reached number 4 in the Irish singles charts in October 1964. Across the Irish Sea in the UK a Waterford-born lad who was not a product of the "showband" era in his homeland, Val Doonican, was hitting the high spots in the UK pop charts with a country song *Walk Tall*. That same song released on the Decca label was also to be a number 2 for him in Ireland, in November 1964.

That year was also to be momentous, if tragic, in the history of country music, with the death of Jim Reeves in a plane crash in July. He had earlier toured some of the major ballrooms in Ireland and created a lasting impression with the young music fans who flocked in their thousands to see him. (On the negative side it has been said that he was disgusted at the lack of proper dressing rooms and of properly tuned pianos at most of these venues.) But he made his mark with the Irish fans, and it was the local "showbands" who were to cash in on this in a big way in the years following his death.

One of the most successful of all of these Jim Reeves "clones" was a young Longford carpenter-turned-singer named Larry Cunningham and his band, the Mighty Avons, who were to even achieve British chart status with their *Tribute To Jim Reeves* early in 1965. This song by Cunningham was written by Sligo-born solicitor, the late Eddie Masterson, and was released on the King label. Apart from taking Cunningham and the Mighty Avons into the British Top 30, it was also to reach number 9 in the Irish charts. Larry Cunningham and the Mighty Avons were to become one of the biggest box-office attractions in Ireland and among Irish exiles in concert halls and ballrooms in the UK and the USA as well. He departed to front a different band in 1968 and was later to become one of the first Irish singers to record in Nashville (see later in this chapter).

Another Irish country singer to make the British pop charts in the mid-1960s was Frankie McBride, from Tyrone, in Northern Ireland, who was to take the melancholy American country song *Five Little Fingers* to number 19 in the UK charts in the summer of 1967, with the same song giving him a number 2 record in Ireland. Apart from another Irish chart hit in that same year with *Burning Bridges*, it was to be 1980 and

the "Urban Cowboy" movement before he was to make the
lower regions of both the Irish and British charts again. This
time it was with a cover version of a song from that film titled
Could I Have This Dance For The Rest Of My Life, released on
the Northern Ireland based Mint label.

Back in the mid-1960s, however, for a brief period, the
popularity of country music in Ireland was to take a back seat
with the Irish ballad boom of 1966 and 1967. The reason for
this renaissance of old Irish ballads with a younger generation
who were also listening to the Beatles and the Monkeys, among
other beat groups, is unclear. But the rebellious nature of many
of these songs might suggest that it was activated by the
nationwide celebrations to mark the 50th anniversary of the
1916 Irish War of Independence. The ballad groups were to
make a brief take-over in the charts and on the live music scene
from the showbands and the fledgling country scene which had
been spluttering at the starting blocks since the early 1960s.
Tommy Drennan and the Monarchs, a showband from
Limerick, managed to cross over the chasm between Irish
ballads and country music very successfully. On the Irish side
an old ballad like *Boolavogue* could take him into the Top 5 as
far back as 1974, while almost a decade later his guitar player
Dennis Allen was writing almost all of his hit records, like the
country-flavoured *Love And The Country* single.

Another of the early showbands to flirt with country music
was the Royal Blues from Mayo, but their lead singer Doc
Carroll had his biggest hit in the mid-1960s with a rock-and-
roll song, *Old Man Trouble*. The Dixies from Cork were
viewed more as a pop band than a country group, even though
they recorded many country songs as far back as 1965, when
they went in to the studios to perform their version of the
classic *He's Got You*, followed by *Ebony Eyes* in 1966.

While the Irish ballad boom years of the mid-1960s almost
killed off the embryonic country music recording business,
which was taking its still somewhat tentative steps towards
being the dominant music force, many of the ballad singers
themselves were later to make the transition to country music.

A young fellow named Johnny McEvoy was to the fore in
this field. It was as a ballad singer that McEvoy, who was
something of a Bob Dylan look-alike, rocketed to the number 1
spot in the Irish pop charts just prior to Christmas of 1966
with the Irish song *Muirsheen Durkin*. But after a few other
chart hits with old Irish ballads Johnny fronted his own
country band with much success. He later also gained acclaim
as a writer of original songs. His band was to be the spawning
ground for Gloria Sherry who was to have Ireland's biggest-
selling country single of all time many years later with *One Day*

At A Time. While all this was happening and other ballad singers, especially Danny Doyle from Dublin, were following McEvoy towards the country scene, similar efforts by some outsiders to popularize American-style country music in Ireland was a failure. Today those names are almost totally forgotten, but two that spring to mind instantly include the American-born Casey and his band, the High Chaperell, who tried and failed with the single *Skip-A-Rope*, and British boy Johnny Regan, who fronted a band called the Tumbleweeds, gaining a tiny measure of success in the early 1970s. But one could honestly say that it was as the ballad boom era came to a sudden halt in about 1968 that the golden era for country music of the ilk performed by Big Tom, Johnny McEvoy, Brendan Shine, and of course Margo O'Donnell was to take the Irish recording scene by storm.

More than most, Margo was responsible for the popularity of this new form of music known as "country and Irish" during this period which the purists might say was a downturn for what they termed "pure" country. After she hit the charts with *The Road By The River* in February of 1968 Margo, still a teenager, became a local superstar, but it was 1970 before she had her first number 1 on the Ruby label with *I'll Forgive And I'll Try To Forget*. Margo remains until this day as the queen of "country and Irish" music. Again, like her male counterpart of that time, Big Tom, many critics would say that their type of "country and Irish" music was terrible and damaged the image of "pure" country, but that is a matter of opinion. As the old adage states, "doctors differ and patients die."

Essential Recordings

(i) International Influences

Other sections of this book deal in detail with the international country music scene but briefly one has to make passing references to a few international names who influenced the Irish stars of the 1950s, 1960s, and 1970s. In the 1950s Jim Reeves songs had started to filter through to the Irish public; *Hang Down Your Head, Tom Dooley*, by Doc and Merle Watson, made some impression too with the youngsters of that era, as did Hank Locklin with Irish-flavoured songs such as *Irish Eyes*, and of course Johnny Cash's *Forty Shades Of Green*, written after he was on holiday here in 1959. But it has to be said that the records of Jim Reeves, especially after his death, were possibly the biggest international influence of all on Irish country singers. Sean Fagan who was lead singer with The Pacific Showband had his biggest hit of all with his cover version of the Jim Reeves classic *Distant Drums*, which was a Top 5 song for him late in 1964, and he was just one of countless Irish singers to record covers of Reeves's songs down through the years.

With the advent of TV it must also be said that the international ambassador of country music, George Hamilton IV, was a huge influence too, especially in the early 1970s as some of his British and Canadian TV shows were also screened in Ireland.

He also gave the music a certain degree of respectability among those who hated cowboy hats, boots and gun-slinging singers. George was different; his was a more folksy (almost pop) sophisticated style of presentation, and with his pin-striped suit many Irish TV viewers called him "the Singing Bankmanager". His singing of songs by writers such as Gorden Lightfoot and even Bob Dylan influenced many local artists to do likewise. Charley Pride and some of his records such as *The Snakes Crawl At Night* and *Crystal Chandeliers* were covered by Irish acts as well.

Of the international women singers, the late Patsy Cline was not the force one would have expected with the Irish record buyers of the 1960s. Earlier still in the mid-1950s a young lady of Irish origins named Ruby Murray had taken the British charts by storm and some of her songs had some country connotations too. But it was Dolly Parton and Tammy Wynette and their songs that were among the most popular models for local Irish women singers in the 1970s.

In Ireland, the "purists" had their own local stars back in the late 1960s playing Irish interpretations of authentic American country music to the thousands that flocked to see them in the dancehalls and carnivals – groups such as the Smokey Mountain Ramblers, Brian Coll, Tommy Fee, or Ray Lynam, a man to later gain something of an international reputation.

The Smokey Mountain Ramblers gained the attention of many of the teenagers of the late 1960s with their infectious blend of bluegrass and country music, even though most of the kids of that era hadn't got a clue what bluegrass music was, let alone realize that it might have originated in Ireland generations earlier as traditional fiddle tunes! The Ramblers had an exciting fiddle player who had his origins in Poland and whose name was George Kaye. He could play the fiddle over his head, behind his back and really inject life into their music. Later on in the 1970s his style was to be emulated and perhaps at times even bettered (from a showmanship point of view) by "the Dancing Fiddler," Mick McManus, and later still by his replacement in another of the "pure" Irish country bands, the Cotton Mill Boys. The Smokey Mountain Ramblers hit the

Irish charts first in February 1969 with *The Little Folk*, followed by *But You Love Me Daddy* in 1970 and *Just Beyond The Moon* which went to number 8 in early 1971. On the Ruby record label they released one excellent album but it had only limited sales success. The album **The Best of The Smokey Mountain Ramblers** was also released on the Dolphin label (DOLB 7004) but again with less than hectic sales. Their earlier hit singles featured the smooth vocals of Pat Ely, who was to have a few other hits in the 1970s as lead singer with the Rocky Tops.

The Cotton Mill Boys were also pioneers of "pure" country music in Ireland in the late 1960s and early 1970s. Their 1969 single *Goodbye My Darling/Little Lisa Jane* (Target 17857) was a classic example of good "pure" Irish country sounds. They were based in Dublin City, which was more of a base for rock music, but the "Cottons", as they were often called, were a city born and bred bunch of country pickers and singers. In 1969 their album titled **The Cotton Mill Boys** was released on the Marble Arch label (MAL 1345) with the emphasis strongly on the bluegrass side of the band. The spring of 1970 saw them make their chart debut with *Silver-Haired Daddy Of Mine*, but it was six years later and following seven other chart hits before they finally made the number 1 spot with vocalist Tony Hughes singing *The Wedding Song* in September 1976.

In the meantime the "Cottons" released some excellent quality country albums and some others, such as the **25 Country Hits** series, with the emphasis as much on quantity as on the quality and aimed at exploiting the commercial possibilities of the market to the full. They did this by reaching number 1 in the LP charts with one of their **25 Country Classics** (Halp 137) albums. But another of far greater artistic excellence, **Country Boy Gerry Madigan**, released in the mid-1970s, failed to make any similar impact on the Irish charts. This latter album was made in association with folk-rock duo Terry and Gay Woods and consisted mostly of bluegrass tunes and songs.

The Cotton Mill Boys were now recording for the Hawk label in Dublin and English TV audiences will still remember them for their huge success on the top-rated Thames TV show "Opportunity Knocks" during the 1975/6 period. They won this TV talent competition on a number of occasions but the most memorable of all was probably for their version of the old bluegrass tune *Orange Blossom Special*. By this time the Cotton Mill Boys had made some changes in their line-up. Some of the lads including musicians "Buddy" Boland and Tommy Kinsella had long since departed to help form another reasonably successful country band named Bill Ryan and Buckshot, while their original "dancing" fiddle player Mick McManus had danced on to different pastures as well. But their latest fiddle player Charlie Arkins amazed the TV audiences with his ability to play *Orange Blossom Special* on the fiddle while holding it over his head, behind his back, between his legs and in many other unusual positions. Their lead singer was Tony Hughes and another showman/musician and vocalist with the band was keyboards player, the late Des Wilson from Dundalk, County Louth.

After their British TV success they released an album titled **Orange Blossom Special** on the Hawk label (Halp 158) which included another song from their wins on the "Opportunity Knocks" TV show, their interpretation of the old Buddy Holly classic *Raining In My Heart*, which also went to number 2 for them in the Irish singles charts prior to Christmas 1976. Other chart singles were to follow in Ireland including a number 2 with their cover version of the Kenny Rogers song *Lucille* in the summer of 1977 featuring the late Des Wilson on vocals, but as Gerry Madigan and others departed, the band faded from the scene and failed to ever achieve the international potential that they once seemed capable of attaining.

As we refer to international potential we must turn our attention to another man who started out his country music career not too long after the launch of the Cotton Mill Boys and that is Ray Lynam with his band the Hillbillies. Without a doubt, Lynam has been one of the most important figures in the development of country music in Ireland. And his involvement spans from the late 1960s right through to the 1990s, with his recordings getting more diverse, and much more rock-oriented, along the way.

To this day many fans feel that if Lynam had been born in Nashville, USA, instead of Moate, Ireland, he would be an international star. But in the late 1960s and early 1970s when Lynam and his Hillbillies started to record for the fledgling Release label they found it difficult enough to gain any great chart success until February 1972 when *The Selfishness Of Man* spent two weeks in the Irish Top 20, reaching a high of number 14. His debut album was titled **Meet Ray Lynam** on the Release label (BRL 4017) and this hit the shops in 1971.

Lynam was one of the first Irish country singers to record in Nashville along with people like Larry Cunningham, Brian Coll, and Philomena Begley, followed by countless others later on in the 1970s. But to many, Lynam was Ireland's answer to George Jones, and his band the Hillbillies were almost all brilliant country musicians. He was always the "respectable" sound of Irish country to those who would deride music of this genre. In the early 1990s, as the teenagers went wild for the sounds of Garth Brooks, Billy Ray Cyrus, Travis Tritt and other "young fellows", Lynam always remained respected by even pop and rock critics in Ireland as a purveyor of "new" country as well as being acclaimed by the older fans too. He is now seen as something of a father figure to a fledgling "new" country scene in Ireland but in the opinion of some of the fans who loved his music in the early 1970s he has sold his soul to modern rock-and-roll.

Lynam and his Hillbillies had a string of Irish chart hits for a decade starting in 1972 including *Brand New Mister Me*, *I Can't Believe That You've Stopped Lovin' Me*, *Borrowed Angel*, *Second Hand Flowers*, *The Door Is Always Open*, *I've Loved You All Over The World*, *You're The One I Sing My Love Songs To*, and *Sweet Music Man* between 1972 and 1979. In the latter year he had what was perhaps his most memorable song of all, titled *I Don't Want To See Another Town*. This song was an original from the pen of his steel and lead guitarist Kevin Sheerin but this Eagles-style country-rocker still only managed to peak at number 13 in the Irish pop charts. To many it is still regarded as "the" Irish country-rock classic song of the 1970s. It was included on the album **Music Man** which also featured a fine rendition of the Eagles' *Lyin' Eyes*. This was on Release (BRL 4104). Kevin Sheerin, who is still involved in songwriting and performing with his present band the New Hillbillies, was to leave Lynam's band in the mid-1980s along with keyboards player/producer John Ryan, fiddler Billy Conden, and drummer Billy Bourgoyne, to join the Daniel O'Donnell band.

It was also during the early 1970s that Lynam and Philomena Begley were to have such duet hit singles as *You're The One I Can't Live Without*, and *My Elusive Dreams*, which was a number 3 in the Irish charts. They became known as Ireland's answer to George Jones and Tammy Wynette; they were also voted Top European Country Duo at the International Festival in Wembley, London, and Begley, who was later to hit the high spots with *Blanket On The Ground*, was to become known as "Ireland's Queen of Country Music," a title that she has never since lost.

Lynam was one of the first of the Irish singers to record in Nashville but while he and Begley were very successful on record they seldom toured together and both worked independently on the live scene with their respective backing bands. In the early 1990s, Lynam remained contracted to the Ritz label in London for most of his recorded work, while Begley is in the same recording stable as well.

He is, and always was, the acceptable voice of country music in Ireland even among the rock fraternity. And while many of the purists might feel that he has strayed too far from his country roots, the CD released on the Ritz label in 1991 is a representative cross-section of Lynam's work. Indeed the CD **The Very Best Of Ray Lynam** is a fine example of modern country-rock sounds performed by an Irish artist and one album that can stand shoulder to shoulder with some of the best modern sounds emanating out of Nashville in the 1990s.

Begley's road to stardom was very different to that of Lynam as she came into the Irish country scene from being a lead singer with a traditional Irish Ceili band vocalizing on the odd country song from about 1963 onwards. When the Old Cross Ceili Band were to change their name and image to become Philomena Begley and the Country Flavour in 1971, they were to hit the charts first with *Here Today, Gone Tomorrow* which peaked at number 7, and *Never Again Will I Knock On Your Door*, which reached a much lower number 15 and only remained in the Irish singles charts for about four weeks in early 1972. However, her album titled **Truck-Driving Woman** was a huge success, but the former Old Cross Ceili Band, now the Country Flavour, parted company with Begley by the summer of 1972, and she was to have the first of many chart hits with her new band, the Ramblin' Men, which was titled *Ramblin Man*, in September of that year. Her old band the Country Flavour struggled on for a while, firstly with a new singer named Marlena and later still with some minor success with her replacement Eileen King, who had a small-time hit with *Knock On My Window Tonight, Love*.

Meanwhile Begley was going from strength to strength under her new manager Tony Loughman, who was later to be associated with concert tours by such international stars as Porter Wagoner, Tom T. Hall, and Hank Locklin. *Light In The Window* and *Wait A Little Longer Please, Jesus* gave her Top 10 hits in 1973–4, but the best and biggest was yet to come. In the summer of 1975 Billie Jo Spears was to "crack" the pop and country charts with *Blanket On The Ground* in many countries around the world. But in Ireland it spent a mere three weeks in the Top 30, reaching a high of number 11, while Begley's version spent three months in the same charts going as high as number 5. Ever since, Begley has become identified with that song in Ireland and even in many parts of England as well, and has been voted Top British Female Country Singer on many occasions. In the singles charts in Ireland she followed up the success of *Blanket On The Ground* with *Once Around The Dancefloor* in 1976, *For The First Time In A Long Time*, which also made number 5 in the summer of 1977, *Cottage On The Hill* and *Whiskey-Drinking You* in the early 1980s, and later on that decade she had another hit with her cover version of the ABBA song *The Way Old Friends Do*.

In Scotland she has amassed a large following too and her most successful disc there was the album **Country, Scotch And Irish** on the Scotch Disc label. Back home in more recent times her 25th anniversary duet album, **In Harmony** (Ritz 0061) with a new recording partner, Mick Flavin, and her **30 Years A Country Queen** CD (1993) have all been steady sellers alongside much of her earlier work. The latter CD (Ritz 552), featuring everything from her rendition of the country-rock CD hit *Bing Bang Boom* to oldies such as Bill Anderson's *Bright Lights And Country Music*, is a good indication of Philomena Begley's current musical preoccupations. Her 1990 album **Reflections** on the K-tel label (KCD 310), featured former singing partner Ray Lynam in the role of production co-ordinator and backing vocalist on one track, *I'm So Afraid Of Losing You Again*. Though she is quite used to recording in Nashville and touring with such stars as Don Williams and Hank Locklin, she performs more frequently now in the concert halls of England and Scotland than in her native country.

During the "showband boom" of the 1960s a somewhat strange combination of rock, jazz and country musicians emerged to form the Plattermen, but it was only in later years and after he had left the band that their lead singer Brian Coll became a country star. Indeed, he was doing country material while a member of the Plattermen but not with any great degree of chart success. His first single with this band was *Kathleen* in 1965. On stage he was Ireland's answer to Slim Whitman because of his ability to yodel songs such as *China Doll*, and *Rose Marie*.

Brian also recorded some original material by Irish songwriters during his stint with the Plattermen; perhaps his most memorable song was *The Blazing Star of Athenry*, which was a track on their mid-1960s album titled **The Rose Of Tralee**. The song tells the sad tale of a young Irish emigrant who joined the American army and died fighting for the land of the "Stars and Stripes" far away in Vietnam and far from his lover, a young lady from the Irish town of Athenry. This memorable number was written by Johnny McCauley, who later achieved far greater songwriting success as the man who composed most of Big Tom McBride's massive hits during the 1970s and 1980s.

Coll was an early pioneer for the country cause. Like a lot of other country singers he came from Northern Ireland, Tyrone to be exact, and many of his 1960s band, the Plattermen, were from the same area. (Indeed, their rock singer Rob Strong is today better known as the father of one of the stars in the early 1990s film, "The Commitments." That son of a former Irish showband star is Andrew Strong.) Without much chart success

Coll decided to break away from the Plattermen and form his own band in 1969. Fronting the new group, named the Buckarooes, he was one of the first to record for the fledgling Release label, going as high as number 7 in the Irish charts in late 1970 with the "country and Irish" song *Give An Irish Girl To Me*. This was a follow-up to an earlier record which failed to chart, titled *Astoreen Bawn, When Are You Coming Home*. It was all a far cry from the more "pure" country Slim Whitman-style sounds he had been making earlier, but he was to return to his earlier style with success, even recording in Nashville early in the 1970s. In 1971 Coll had his biggest hit of all with *These Are My Mountains* reaching number 3 in the Irish pop charts: it remained in the Top 30 for almost four months.

Like his Release Records stablemate Ray Lynam, Coll also boasted a top-quality backing band. Outstanding musicians among these were Arty McGlynn, on steel and lead guitar, who is today a much respected trad-rock musician, while his piano player Jim Bradley, from Derry, was also in much demand for session work on many recordings by other artists, especially Big Tom.

The high, lonesome sounds of McGlynn's steel guitar were much in evidence on Coll's hits, such as *When My Blue Moon Turns To Gold* (which peaked at number 8 in 1972), *The Moon Behind the Hill, She's Mine, Cover Mama's Flower*, and another Johnny McCauley composition *Hometown On The Foyle*, during the 1972–5 period when Coll also went to Music City, USA to record the best-selling album **Brian Coll In Nashville**. But his star was to start fading in the mid- to late 1970s and his last major chart hit single was a cover version of Porter Wagoner's *The Farmer* in the summer of 1976.

At one stage Coll was considered alongside Lynam as a possible Irish singer to make the breakthrough in the Nashville scene in the mid-1970s, but this was not to be. He continued to tour with many changes in his backing band and then a brain haemorrhage in the early 1990s almost claimed his life. On his return to health Coll made a comeback but his records failed to make any impression on the pop charts and a new generation of live music fans seemed to be no longer interested in what they might consider his "dated" Slim Whitman style of country.

Of course, during the period when artists like Coll, Lynam, and Begley were becoming household names in Ireland in the early 1970s, they did not achieve a comparable success in America. International success on the scale later achieved by acts such as Daniel O'Donnell in the UK was not on the cards either for these Irish stars, and indeed one man who came to the UK from India in search of this sort of success, Roly Daniels, ended up as a country singer in Ireland.

In the embryonic stages of the Release label in Dublin the name of Roly Daniels was among those being bandied about as one who might also be destined for international stardom. He had been making chart singles with a reasonable degree of success since 1966, when, as lead vocalist with pop bands such as Big Jim Farley's band and the Nevada, he first charted with *Throw A Little Lovin' My Way* on the Belfast-based Emerald label. He then had three minor chart hits on the international CBS label, the best known being *Angel She Was Love*, which went to number 10 in the summer of 1969, before he seemed to change from being a big ballad pop singer to a country artist. In May of 1971 his beautiful rendition of the American country song *Sunny Tennessee* peaked at number 11 in the Irish charts for Daniels on the Release label. *My Wild Mountain Rose* was less successful for him a few months later, but in 1992 his country career was to really reach its zenith with his cover version of Conway Twitty's *Hello Darlin'*. Under normal circumstances this song was so popular that it probably could, would, and perhaps should have reached the number 1 spot, but this was not to be. It was to end up stuck at number 2 mainly because of the political unrest in the country which saw a civil rights song, *The Men Behind The Wire*, by Belfast ballad group the Barleycorn holding down the number 1 spot in the early part of 1972. It was to remain almost 10 months among the bestsellers, while Daniels's country number 2 was gone from the charts within three months of its entry in January 1972.

But even a number 2 against such stiff opposition was enough to establish Daniels and his band Green County as a major force on the Irish country scene for almost a decade. He remained one of those tipped by some observers as a contender for stardom in the States too, but visits to Nashville were not to result in any deal with a major American label. In Ireland he continued to chalk up the hits, with another cover version of an American song, Charlie Rich's *The Most Beautiful Girl*, also taking him back to the number 2 slot in the spring of 1974.

By the early 1980s he was back with a subsidiary of his earlier Emerald label, Mint Records. A duet with female vocalist Ann Williamson, *Like Strangers*, was to be a minor hit for them early in 1983. But after that Daniels seemed to fade from the scene somewhat, and started to concentrate more on the breeding of race-horses, such as the very successful Hazy Dawn.

Daniels made a comeback CD titled **Ol' What's His Name** 1992 but while it was of excellent quality the sales were not very significant. This time, he was recording on the Star label owned by steel guitarist/producer/arranger Basil Hendricks who, many years earlier, was a backing musician for Daniels in one of his bands. Indeed, British-born Hendricks has over the years made a major contribution to the Irish country music scene as one of the finest steel guitar players in Britain and Ireland. He has worked the live scene with most of the big names, such as Daniels, Begley, and T.R. Dallas, and proved his worth as a session musician/producer for countless others as well.

Another Irish star who was tipped for international stardom in the 1970s and early 1980s was Brendan Quinn, from Magaherafelt, in County Derry. His success started with a cover version of the Faron Young hit *Four In The Morning* which went to number 5 for him on the Velvet label in 1972. His greatest chart achievement was having a number 1 with the sentimental *Daddy's Little Girl* in the summer of 1977. In between all this he was tipped for the British charts with his version of another Charlie Rich hit, *Behind Closed Doors*, released on the Dublin-based Hawk label in the spring of 1974.

But Rich's original was to win the chart war in England and, like Daniels, he was also to turn to duet recordings for a time during the 1980s. His single *Rest Your Love On Me Awhile*, recorded along with Gloria Sherry, had a short shelf-life in the Irish Top 20, reaching number 15 in February 1981. Later on in the 1980s he was to team up with another Irish female star, Susan McCann, for an album on the North of Ireland-based Top Spin label, but international hits eluded him.

He released an album, **Melodies And Memories**, on the Ritz label in 1992. In more recent times has also been involved in the heavier country-rock scene with the group Kickin' Mule, which also features trad-folk player Arty McGlynn in its line-up.

Another "pure" country band similar in many ways to the Cotton Mill Boys or the Smokey Mountain Ramblers was Frankie Carroll and the Ranchers, formed in late 1969. Their lead singer Frankie Carroll from Tuam, Country Galway, was a thin giant of a man, well over six feet tall with a voice not unlike that of Johnny Cash, who became known as "Mr Bassman" after his first single, titled *Daddy Sang Bass*, was released on the Dolphin label shortly after the formation of the band. But in spite of releasing other good country singles, including their best-known one, *Mr Bassman*, Frankie and the Ranchers did not have a lot of success in the Irish pop charts.

However, an album, **The Best Of Frankie Carroll And The Ranchers**, also on Dolphin, released in late 1971, was a steady seller among country fans in Ireland, with Sean Dunphy, another star from the pop Eurovision Song Contest and the showband era, who also touched on the country scene (albeit slightly), predicting great things for Frankie and The Ranchers in the album's liner notes. But the band was later split up and Frankie Carroll went on to work as a bass player/ country vocalist with Brendan Shine's band, followed by a stint with Frank McCaffrey and the Country Folk, where he recorded a duet EP on the IRL label, **Maggie**, with McCaffrey singing the high notes. Later still, he was to move to Brendan Bowyer's band, the Big 8, following the tragic death of Tom Dunphy in a car crash in 1976. He worked on the club scene in Las Vegas, where this group was known as the Irish Show-band, before retiring from the music scene to live in Chicago in 1990. His earlier singing partner Frank McCaffrey has continued to work the live scene, and some of his more recent recordings on the Ritz label have gained a measure of commercial success in parts of England, most notably the CD **A Place In My Heart** (Ritz 110), which contains the track *It's Our Anniversary*.

This song was written by the late Des Wilson, who was himself a fine country singer, first with his own band and later with the Cotton Mill Boys during the halcyon days when they were winning the talent show "Opportunity Knocks" on British TV. During this time with the Cottons, Wilson himself had gone to number 2 in the Irish charts with his version of the Kenny Rogers hit *Lucille*, but he died shortly before Frank McCaffrey's 1990 success with his song *It's Our Anniversary*.

Donegal singer John Kerr straddled the borders of the Irish ballads and country scene with many of his recordings. His biggest success was *Three Leaf Shamrock*, which went to number 1 in 1972. Another man to cross the same musical divide was Dermot O'Brien, from County Louth, who had his first hit with a cover version of the Johnny Cash song *I Walk The Line* as far back as 1966. However, he was to have far greater success with Irish songs and went to number 1 that same year with the ballad *The Merry Ploughboy*, after which all of his other ten hit singles before his departure from the Irish scene in the 1970s were Irish ballads. O'Brien was to find success in the late 1980s and 1990s on the Irish club/pub circuit in the United States. Apart from those names, only a few of the Irish country acts having aspirations to international stardom achieved success, and then only in the 1980s and early 1990s.

Discographical Details

339 The Very Best Of Ray Lynam

Ray Lynam

Ritz CD 513

If We're Not Back In Love By Monday/What A Lie/He Stopped Loving Her Today/You Put The Blue In Me/You Win Again/The Gambler/The Moon Is

*Still Over Her Shoulder/Beautiful Woman/To Be Lovers/Mona Lisa Lost Her
Smile/Girls, Women And Ladies/Hold Her In Your Hand/Speak Softly (You're
Talking To My Heart)/I'll Never Get Over You/Rainy Days, Stormy Nights/I
Don't Want To See Another Town*

(ii) The Era of Big Tom, Big Brendan, Big Chiefs

1967 was to herald the start of a country music explosion on
both the live and recording scenes in Ireland. And leading this
country music revival was a six-foot-plus, gangling giant of a
man from Monaghan named Big Tom McBride, and his band,
the Mainliners.

When he was spearheading the country music boom in
Ireland it was Big Tom's sentimental songs about mothers who
had died and couples living in *The Sunset Years Of Life* that
were taking him to the high spots in the charts. His first hit was
with a Country "weepie" titled *Gentle Mother* (Emerald MD
1060) in January of 1967, followed by his rendition of a Porter
Wagoner classic, *Old Log Cabin For Sale*, later that year. To
many country "purists" in Ireland Big Tom represented Irish
country music at its worst – they loathed his records and his
live shows. But he was the country "King," to thousands of
fans who packed every ballroom and marquee in Ireland to see
him perform, especially in the late 1960s and throughout the
1970s and early 1980s as well. At the peak of his popularity, he
owned his own recording studio.

Irrespective of the critics' views on his music, and they were
sharply divided in this on radio, TV, and in the press, one still
has to admit that he introduced the songs of country
"Outlaws" such as Waylon Jennings, Willie Nelson and Kris
Kristofferson to a whole generation of Irish people. These were
in his own inimitable style and far removed from the sound of
the originals, but one has to give him some credit for not
setting out to record "straight" copies of the original songs.

Big Tom's earlier recordings from 1967 to 1970 were mostly
country-and-Irish material or the more dated songs of Porter
Wagoner. He must have been a big fan of Porter as he recorded
"covers" of countless Wagoner songs during this period.
However, it was his 1972 album **Ashes Of Love** (Denver DNV
3) that was to become the first Irish country LP to sell in
excess of 50,000 copies, even though it was ridiculed by
reviewers on its release. Songs like Kristofferson's *Sunday
Morning Christian* and the Waylon and Willie standard *Good-
Hearted Woman* were to prove the most successful from this LP
which saw Big Tom reach the very pinnacle of superstardom in
Ireland. He had three consecutive number 1 singles in the Irish
pop charts, first with *Broken Marriage Vows* in 1972, *I Love*

You Still in early 1973, and *Old Love Letters* in the summer of 1974.

Many people have said that some of Big Tom's success is also due in some way to the unique sound of his backing band, the Mainliners, especially the organ sounds of John Beattie and lead guitarist Seamus McMahon. However, in the mid-1970s he was to split from the Mainliners, to front a new group named the Travellers, and it was with them that he had what was possibly his biggest hit of all, *Four Country Roads*, in August, 1981. This was an original by his friend and regular songwriter Johnny McCauley and apart from becoming a best-selling Irish single, the album of the same name (Denver DNV 11) was also to top the Irish charts.

By this time Big Tom was recording mostly original material from the pen of Johnny McCauley, who lived in London, and West of Ireland journalist Michael Commins, and, later still, by a member of his first backing group, Henry McMahon. He even went to Nashville to record a full album of originals with some of America's top session musicians but this one, titled **Blue Wings**, was not to be a great success at all, and Big Tom retired for a short period in the late 1980s before returning in more recent times to play selected live dates with his original backing band, the Mainliners. Since they have come back together Big Tom and the Mainliners have released a CD, **Big Tom And The Mainliners Today** (MCM CD 001), recorded in Northsound Studios, Dungannon, County Tyrone (a recording house founded by another country star from yesteryear, Gene Stuart). He continues to make some recordings on the small independent label MCM. The most memorable to date is *The GNR Steam Train*, but in spite of its popularity it failed to make the charts.

Big Tom McBride was responsible for attracting thousands of Irish teenagers in the late 1960s to the sounds of "country and Irish" music and **20 Golden Greats**, a CD of some of his earlier material, re-released in 1992, is the best example of the sound that made the big man from Monaghan famous in his homeland. He attracted lots of criticism along the way, especially from those who dislike the sad country songs about dead mothers, dead dogs, broken marriage vows, lost love, and loneliness.

But Big Tom became one of the most successful country artists ever in Ireland singing his "heart" songs in his own inimitable style; and while this album is not for the country/rock fraternity, it is a good example of what "country and Irish" music sounded like at a time when the Beatles were all the rage with the rest of the world.

Back in the mid-1970s, his replacement in the Mainliners,

John Glenn, was to have several chart hits, most notably *Sunnyside Of The Mountain*, which reached number 5 in the singles charts in the summer of 1975. His debut album released soon afterwards also became a bestseller. A number of other hit singles followed, the best-remembered of which would be *Little Country Town In Ireland*, on the Misty label, which went to number 6 in the singles charts in 1977. And even though he has been unable to sustain the same chart success as Big Tom, Glenn has still survived on the Irish and Scottish live country music circuit up to the 1990s. In late 1992 he joined forces with Margo O'Donnell on the live circuit, but this partnership yielded no duet recordings, and they went their separate ways early in 1993.

Margo departed to front the Travellers who were for many years Big Tom's band. On his departure they first had Joe Murray as lead vocalist; he scored only one major chart hit, *Tender Years*, in the late 1980s. However, with Margo fronting the band, Murray was to depart, and they were to change their name from the Travellers to Margo and her Band early in 1993.

Big Derek Davis, a broad-shouldered journalist from Belfast, adopted the stage name of Mean Tom and joined the Cork-based band Pat Lynch and the Treetops for a period in the late 1960s and early 1970s. Because he looked so similar to Big Tom he became very popular for a time, but it was to be the late 1980s and long after he had gone on to a different career as a top TV chat show host, that he got to realize his lifelong ambition by recording an album **On The Road** in Nashville, released on the Harmac label.

Scottish singer Pat Roper came to Ireland and fronted a country band called the Spotlights in 1970 and the following year he became a one-hit wonder, reaching number 3 in the charts with *The Ring Your Mother Wore*. He later emigrated to America and in the 1990s Pat remains a popular attraction on the Irish pub/club scene around New York.

From 1970 until 1993 another big fellow, Brendan Shine, was to have almost 40 hit singles in Ireland, but most of his were of the "country and Irish" genre so much hated by some pop fans and by many of the purists on the country-rock scene as well.

Big Brendan Shine, from Athlone, in the Irish midlands, was a former Ceili band singer and accordion player who had his first "country and Irish" hit in 1970, when *Bunch Of Violets Blue* reached number 6 in the Irish pop charts. He was to strike the number 1 spot in the summer of 1971 with *O'Brien Has No Place to Go*, and twice more, with *Where The Three Counties Meet* and *Abbeyshrule*, in 1973 and 1974 respectively. He was to take a far greater country stance for a few years after this charting with his version of Don William's *Turn Out The Lights And Love Me Tonight*, the Crystal Gayle classic *Down The Wrong Road Again*, and a cover version of *Sally G*, written and originally recorded by Paul McCartney. These were all on the album **New Roads** (Play 1012) and were possibly his most memorable country recordings.

However, his biggest chart single of all came in 1979 when, with the launch of the national pop music radio station, 2FM, Shine had the first number 1 in their charts with the humorous "country and Irish" song *Do You Want Your Old Lobby Washed Down*. This was to remain a staggering 37 weeks in the Irish charts for Shine and while he has had many hit singles since then, none of them was ever to emulate the success of this one. He started to turn his attention to the British scene and has made both the singles and LP hot 100s there (albeit the lower regions) with a number of records in recent years. In fact Brendan Shine spends more of his time working on the live circuit in the UK than in his native Ireland today.

Several years prior to Brendan Shine's massive 37-week stint in the Irish singles chart, another singer from the Irish midlands named Dermot Hegarty had fared even better with his "country and Irish" song *Twenty-One Years*, which spent a full 39 weeks in the Irish bestsellers. Hegarty was one of the first artists to join the fledgling Release label in 1968, and was to become a director of the company for some time. (Before its demise in the early 1980s Release was one local record label which did a lot for home grown Irish country artists.) However, Hegarty, like Shine, was never to emulate the phenomenal success of his biggest hit in spite of releasing many other singles in the years following 1970. Though his band, the Plainsmen, was a country outfit most of Hegarty's hits were in the "country and Irish" idiom, and he even reached number 9 with another song, *After Twenty-One Years*, in 1972 followed by a rebel ballad about a jailbreak, *Nineteen Men*, which went to number 1 in 1974. Like so many of the country stars from that era Hegarty now spends most of his time working as a cabaret artist in the Irish clubs around England.

Hegarty's replacement in the Plainsmen was a young country singer from Derry, Brian Harkin. His style was very different from Hegarty's, and for his records and live shows, he adopted an American country style. Harkin did not have a great deal of chart success. He is probably best remembered for his version of the Tom Paxton folk-country song *Ramblin' Boy*, which had a very brief chart life for Brian in Ireland in the spring of 1976. Later on he was to leave the live scene and go back to his day job while only making occasional cabaret appearances. Harkin died very suddenly in the early 1990s.

While Hegarty was selling records by the thousands in the early 1970s for the Release label, the rival Dublin-based company Ruby Records were having similar success with another Dermot – a young fellow from Sligo named Dermot Henry. His biggest seller was the "country and Irish" flavored *If Those Lips Could Only Speak*, which spent over 20 weeks in the bestsellers and reached number 1 early in 1971. Henry was a velvet-voiced country singer backed by a very competent country band named the Virginians. Their other biggest seller was a folk-country song *The Gypsy* which reached number 1 in the fall of 1972. He emigrated to the USA and is still working very successfully as a cabaret artist among the Irish in their clubs and pubs, especially around New York.

In the late 1960s Larry Cunningham was to leave his band the Mighty Avons and form a new backing band, the Country Blue Boys. After reaching number 1 with (yet another!) "country and Irish" song, *Slaney Valley*, in 1972 he was to chart regularly until his retirement in 1985. The LP **Country My Way** (Release SRL 3004) was one of the first of many best-selling albums for Cunningham on the Release label, and he also teamed up with Margo O'Donnell for one big-selling single *Yes, Mr Peters* in early 1976. He was one of the first to record for Release in Nashville and to be voted Europe's Top Country Singer at one of the Wembley International Festivals in the early 1970s, Ray Lynam and Philomena Begley being voted Top European Duo around the same time. Cunningham was a star on the Irish country scene for almost two decades, and today he is a successful businessman in his native Granard, County Longford.

Gene Stuart, who replaced Larry Cunningham in the Mighty Avons, was more of a Charley Pride sound-alike who was to go as high as number 3 with his first single, *Before The Next Teardrop Falls*, early in 1970. His version of the Pride hit *Kiss An Angel Good Morning* also took Stuart into the Top 10 in 1972; after parting company with the Mighty Avons he was to have several other Top 10 hits with his new band, the Homesteaders, in the mid-1970s. He opened his own recording studio and set up his own record label (see above), and though he continues to record and perform, he would now no longer be a major attraction on either the live or the recording scenes. (Another member of the Mighty Avons, Ronnie Griffiths, was to have some success as lead singer with his country band, American Pie, in the early 1970s.)

Speaking of Irish "sound-alikes" of American singers, Jim Tobin from County Westmeath, who fronted a band named the Firehouse in 1969, was uncannily similar in style to Jim Reeves. His first album, **Jim Tobin Remembers Jim Reeves**

(Release BRL 4012), and his first single, which was also a cover of a Reeves song, *This Is It* (Honey COMB.15), reached number 5 in the Irish singles charts early in 1970.

A number of other hits were to follow during this decade, but strangely enough it was a very different style of song that was to give him his only number 1, *Welcome John Paul 2*, in 1979. This was far removed from Jim Reeves-style country; in fact it was a tribute song to the Roman Catholic Pope who was visiting Ireland that year. Tobin had most of his hits on the Hawk label but this last one was on the CMR label owned by his manager, Senator Donie Cassidy, who was at one time a member of the brass section of his backing band. Senator Cassidy had his measure of international success, later managing the folk duo Foster and Allen, but his first "charge," Jim Tobin, was to retire from the Irish recording scene in the mid-1980s.

While most of the country stars of the Irish scene fronted large backing bands, Mary D'Arcy and Eamonn McRory were to hit the high spots for a time as the duo Two's Company on the cabaret scene and with their recordings of mostly country or Irish songs. They first hit the Irish Top 10 in 1969 on the Honey label with an Irish-flavored song *Eileen McManus* followed four years later by their version of the old Jean Shepard/Ferlin Husky classic *Dear John*. Their biggest chart success was with a cover version of the Don Williams hit *You're My Best Friend* in 1975. Early in the 1990s Two's Company added three backing musicians and became Two's Company 5: a good sampler of some of their best-known hits is the CD **Two's Company Live** on the Apollo label (APCD 32).

Big Chief Flaming Star and The Indians were one of the most colorful and exciting country-pop groups to emerge on the Irish scene in the early 1970s. They were formerly members of the Casino Country band but changed image and came on stage as a bunch of fully feathered Indians with a high energy blend of country and pop songs at their live concerts and dance dates. The lead singer with the Casino, Ian Corrigan, from County Cavan did not move on with the Indians, but fronted his own new band, Country Style, whose biggest success in the singles charts came in 1973 with the country song *House Of Pride*.

In spite of having a huge following and a spate of best-selling albums the Indians did not make any impact at all in the Irish singles charts. Not that this ever seemed to bother them, as the crowds at their gigs continued to get bigger and bigger through the 1970s (so also did Big Chief Flaming Star's Indian regalia!) They were launched with the single *Tobacco* and their most successful LP was **Travellin' Indian Band**. But as the 1980s dawned and their popularity in Southern Ireland dipped and even died in some parts, the Indians started to concentrate more on the lucrative Northern Ireland and UK live scene. Here, they continued to work successfully right up to the early 1990s.

Discographical Details

0 20 Golden Greats

Big Tom and the Mainliners
Ainm ARCD 003
B.J. The D.J/Old Rustic Bridge/I'll Settle For Old Ireland/The Country Hall Of Fame/Sunset Years Of Life/Be Careful Of Stones That You Throw/Wedding Bells/The Kentucky Waltz/A Bunch Of Violets Blue/The Carroll County Accident/Gentle Mother/The Cold Hard Facts Of Life/Blue Eyes Crying In The Rain/Old Log Cabin For Sale/Flowers Foe Mama/Give My Love To Rose/Isle Of Inishfree/Tears On A Bridal Bouquet/Sing Me Back Home/My Own Washings

(iii) Winds of Change for Irish Country

As the 1970s progressed the number of new country singers emerging in Ireland seemed to rapidly slow down and this was largely owing to the demise of the dancehalls and the carnivals, which were rapidly being replaced by the disco scene.

Hugo Duncan and his band the Tallmen were among the new country bands to emerge as an attraction on the live music circuit in the early 1970s, with his debut single *Dear God* reaching number 3 in the pop charts early in 1971. Duncan had several other hits in this period and even in the 1990s he continued to record such albums as the CD **Ireland's Favourite Singer** on the Homespun label, but his live work is now mostly on the cabaret/club/hotel scene.

When the hotels and the cabaret lounges with their more plush surroundings, carpets, seating and late-night drink licenses discovered that they could compete with the dancehalls by having late-night discos, work on the live scene for both pop and country bands started to decline rapidly in the 1970s. However, before this happened a few new country stars emerged on the Irish recording scene, but though they had some big hits, they were successful on the live music circuit for a far shorter time than many of their predecessors.

The biggest-selling Irish country single of all time was to emerge in the 1977–8 period when Gloria Sherry, from County Monaghan, spent a staggering 86 weeks in the Irish Top 30 with her number 1 single *One Day At A Time* on the Release label. This was a fine rendition of the Marijohn Wilkin/Kris

Kristofferson song which for a time looked as if it might also take Sherry into the British charts. But another version was rush-released by UK singer Lena Martell and it went to the top of the pop charts over there. But in Ireland it was Sherry's golden era and an album titled **When I Sing For Him** (RRL 8004) was also a bestseller for her, but in spite of releasing other excellent singles, including the original *Liffey Tinker*, she was never again to scale the same heights in the Irish charts. She and her husband Don retired from the scene in the mid-1980s to concentrate on raising their two children, and an attempted comeback in the early 1990s met with limited success.

Gerry Reynolds, lead singer with the Hi-Lows, was another "one hit wonder" when he went to number 8 in the Irish charts in 1972 with his version of the Tom T. Hall composition *One Hundred Children*.

Another Irish country star from the late 1970s who shone briefly in the charts was T.R. Dallas (real name Tom Allen), who came to prominence during the time when the TV soap "Dallas," starring "J.R. Ewing" (Larry Hagman), was one of the most popular programmes with viewers on either side of the Atlantic. T.R. Dallas even made the lower regions of the British pop Top 100 with his single *Who Shot J.R. Ewing* on the Youngblood label (which also had a minor hit in the UK with Hoyt Axton's single *Della And The Dealer*). In Ireland T.R. Dallas was to have even greater chart success in the fall of 1980 with his version of the Mac Davis song *It's Hard To Be Humble* going to number 6 and remaining in the charts for almost five months. A best-selling album of the same name was to follow on the CMR label, but in spite of releasing many other singles in the 1980s and early 1990s, he was never again to have much chart success. In recent times he was a founder of the Foam label and has toured extensively abroad, sometimes as support act for international folk stars Foster and Allen – "T.R." is a brother of Tony Allen of this duo.

While they are viewed more as a folk act, Foster and Allen, who have sold almost twelve million albums world-wide, have almost always included some country material in their records since they first made the British Top 20 with *A Bunch Of Thyme* in 1981. Their more recent releases, especially the 1992 album **Heartstrings** (Telstar 2608) feature a "smattering" of country songs, including a very fine version of the American country song *Love Me*, and their CDs are frequently in the British and Australian pop charts.

Tony Stevens, from Cork, was another new name to make his mark on the Irish country scene in the late 1970s and early 1980s, especially with his debut release on the Hawk label,

Send Me No Roses. But while Stevens would also flirt with the pop/big ballad scene, his biggest hit in Ireland was a cover version of the Willie Nelson/Julio Iglesias classic *To All The Girls I've Loved Before*. He even made the lower regions of the British charts with his single *Ladies Love* on the CMR label but then after a barren period both on the live and recording scene he seemed poised for a comeback in November 1992 when a bad road accident resulted in his being seriously injured. However, Stevens recovered, and his abiding ambition is to continue to make successful country records in the 1990s.

Denis Allen, a former member of Tommy Drennan's band, started to record many of his own originals and had his biggest hit of all in the late 1970s with his own composition *Limerick, You're A Lady*; but though he recorded some other fine originals in the 1980s he was never to emulate the chart success of his biggest hit single. Likewise Ann Breen, from Downpatrick, Northern Ireland, was to spend almost two years in the lower regions of the British Top 100 pop charts with her single *Pal Of My Cradle Days* in 1980–1 but while still working extensively in England she was never to repeat this success.

Susan McCann, from Newry, County Down, suddenly emerged on the Irish country music scene in the spring of 1977 and went straight to number 1 with her record *Big Tom Is Still The King*, a tribute song to Irish singer Big Tom and based on the American song *Bob Wills Is Still The King*, by Waylon Jennings. For the Northern Ireland housewife it was to be the start of a career that has given her a significant measure of international stardom in recent years. In 1982 she won the European Gold Star Award, Europe's premier TV country music talent contest show at the time, and her winning song *While I Was Making Love to You*, on the Top Spin label, was also a Top 20 hit in Ireland. The following year she was to have an even bigger hit with the single *When The Sun Says Goodbye To The Mountains* going to number 3 in the Irish pop charts.

By this time McCann had started to tour in Europe and had gained a loyal following, especially in Switzerland and Norway where she still tours frequently. She had string of best-selling albums in Ireland for the Top Spin and K-tel labels before joining up with British label Prism Leisure in 1990 and making her first entry into the British country charts with the albums **Country Love Affair**, followed the next year by a higher chart placing for her **Diamonds And Dreams** album and this chart success was surpassed in the UK country charts in late 1992 and early 1993 with her Prism Leisure CD **Memories**. She has also also appeared in concerts all over the US, playing the Florida Strawberry Fair in 1991 and 1992 alongside such American greats as Garth Brooks and Travis Tritt. Like

Philomena Begley and several other Irish stars McCann has recorded many times in Nashville and appeared on the Grand Ole Opry as well.

But when some other acts started out in the late 1970s and early 1980s, country music was on the decline in Ireland and other local artists had only brief chart success with country songs. Glen Curtin, from Cork, had a number 1 with his revival of the old classic *Red Sails In The Sunset*. Other Top 10 entries followed with his versions of American country hits *Me And The Elephant* and *Tears On The Telephone* on the Crashed label, but after a few more minor hits Glen Curtin emigrated to the USA in the mid-1980s to work on the Irish pubs/clubs circuit in New York. Similarly shortlived were the records of Jesse and the James Boys from County Kerry who are best remembered for their 1982 Top 20 entry with the country song *Diane*. By this time the disco boom had hit Ireland, and apart from a few of the olders stars such as Big Tom, none of the new country names seemed to be able to attract the large attendances to live shows.

The live country scene in Ireland was almost dead when a good-looking young fellow in his twenties named Daniel O'Donnell emerged on the scene in 1986. He is the younger brother of country star Margo, but in spite of having steady sales for one of his early releases, *The Two Sides Of Daniel O'Donnell*, only in the late 1980s did he achieve superstar status both in Ireland and the UK. By the early 1990s O'Donnell had sold over two million albums, mostly in England, where he appeared on the leading TV show "Top of the Pops" in 1992, performing his British Top 20 single *I Just Wanna Dance With You*. Written by American singer–songwriter John Prine, this also made the number 2 spot in the Irish pop charts. His album **Follow Your Dream** (Ritz 701), written by Shay Healy, was also a Top 20 hit in England and the video of the same went to number 1 in the British pop music video charts. Since the late 1980s his albums have dominated the British country music charts and it was not at all unusual for O'Donnell to occupy half of the places in the UK Top 10 country albums charts with his releases. The rock group U2 are possibly Ireland's biggest record-sellers worldwide, followed by folk acts such as Foster and Allen or the Chieftains, but Daniel O'Donnell is fast catching up on them especially with a Top 10 best-selling compilation album in the Australian charts in 1993. He is the most commercially successful country artist to emerge from either Ireland or the UK. While many of his songs are cover versions of old country and Irish classics, he has more recently recorded many originals.

Strange as it may seem, O'Donnell has achieved greater success abroad than in his homeland where many sections of the media who did not like, or indeed understand, his style of music have often been scathing in their reviews of his records and shows. But O'Donnell was voted Ireland's Top Entertainment Personality for 1992 and his success in the British pop charts in particular has done a lot to silence his critics in his homeland in the early 1990s. While his music might lack the "gravel and guts" appeal of many of the new country stars in the US, it has to be admitted that he has a massive following, especially among women, all over the UK and Ireland.

Attempts at breaking into the American country scene have been less successful even though he recorded an album under top producer Allen Reynolds in Nashville in 1990. This CD, titled **The Last Waltz**, was said to "represent a pioneering transatlantic, crossover set of recordings" according to O'Donnell's British publicist Tony Byworth but it failed to gain the desired deal with any major American label. Even so, it probably contains the best of his earlier material.

The rise and rise of O'Donnell resulted in a rebirth for the country music scene in Ireland with a host of other local singers making the charts, all of which may have been helped along by regional "pirate" radio stations operating for some time all over the country in the late 1980s. A former ballad singer from County Tipperary, Louise Morrissey, made a smooth transition from the traditional Irish music scene to country, and one of her biggest hit singles was *The Night Daniel O'Donnell Came To Town*. She was one of several Irish singers to win the European Gold Star Award and her album **When I Was Yours** (CMR 1042) is a good example of her fine singing style. Some other major stars to emerge include Mick Flavin, from Longford, who is rated by many to have the finest country voice ever to come out of Ireland. He had a lot of success on the Dublin-based Harmac label with some of his earlier releases before getting a contract with Ritz in London who had been instrumental in much of Daniel O'Donnell's international success. Flavin has been making inroads in to the UK concert scene, especially on his tours with Philomena Begley; and his albums, especially **Sweet Memory**, released in 1992, have all been steady sellers, with British sales on the increase all the time.

Michael O'Brien, from County Clare, had a hit single with *The Veil Of White Lace* even prior to O'Donnell's emergence on the Irish scene but despite having a few best-selling albums for both the Failte and K-tel record labels he has curtailed his touring and recordings in recent years. John Hogan, from

Offaly, also in the Irish midlands, emerged on the Irish scene around the same time as Mick Flavin, with some best-selling albums for K-tel, before changing labels to Ritz of London in 1990. Early in 1993 he went to Nashville to record an album under producer Ronnie Light, who has also worked with Charley Pride. (Irish producer John Ryan was also working on this session in Nashville's Reflection's Studio.) This CD, for release in 1993, features revivals of such country classics as *Back Home Again*, *Blue Moon On Kentucky* and *That's All Right, Mama* as well as some originals written by Hogan himself. A singer with a sob in his voice, not unlike that of the late great Hank Williams, John Hogan has in recent times started to develop his career on the UK club and concert scene as well as touring in his native Ireland.

Sandy Kelly, from Sligo, is another Irish singer gaining some international attention in the 1990s, especially for her unique style in interpreting the songs of the late Patsy Cline. This resulted in a great friendship developing between Kelly, top Nashville producer Harold Bradley, and Cline's husband, Charlie Dick, leading to a recording session in Bradley's Barn studio in Nashville in 1989 just after Kelly had come to the attention of Johnny Cash. This was to be one of Kelly's biggest breaks of all, as she and Johnny Cash recorded the duet single *Woodcarver* together in Nashville and it became a Top 10 hit for them in Ireland. It was also included on the best-selling K-tel album **I Need To Be In Love**. Since then she has toured with Johnny Cash in Europe and worked in the USA with Willie Nelson while also touring the top venues in the UK early in 1993 with Slim Whitman and George Hamilton IV. She starred in her own top-rated 24-programme TV series in Ireland in 1992–3, and has made the transition from being a former pop singer to the country fold very well indeed. In 1993 she was selected to play the lead role as Patsy Cline in a major theatrical production on the singer's life and music, touring all over the UK and finishing up in London's West End in 1994.

Declan Nerney, from Drumlish, in Country Longford, has also emerged as a major attraction on the country circuit, both at live concerts and dances, and on the recording scene as well. A former backing musician for people such as Brian Coll and Gene Stuart, Nerney then became a producer arranger before starting to record himself and his unusual falsetto voice proved to be an instant success with the Irish country fans. Recording for the CMR label, he scored in the charts with his single *The Marquee In Drumlish*, which was a nostalgic look at the country stars of yesteryear, written by one of Big Tom's backing musicians Henry McMahon.

His album **Three Way Love Affair** (CMR 1047) was one of the few local country albums to make the Irish Top 30 pop charts in 1992 and, like a lot of the newer Irish country stars, Nerney is now also looking towards the British scene for further success.

Sally O'Brien, from Country Derry, has also emerged in the 1990s as another new Irish name to make an impact on the international country scene. She was discovered at a talent contest by impresario Tony Loughman, who was also very involved in the career of Susan McCann and, later on, in the launch of country duo Logue and McCool. O'Brien has recorded an album of duets with Porter Wagoner in Nashville, where she has also appeared on the Grand Ole Opry, and in the short space of the first three years of the 1990s she has released a staggering seven CDs and an equal number of music videos. Her first CD for the Music Box label was **The World Of Country** recorded under producer Porter Wagoner in Nashville. She has also followed in the footsteps of Susan McCann by appearing at Dolly Parton's theme park in Tennessee, and has worked on the club and concert circuit in the UK too.

For a time in the early 1990s Logue and McCool seemed set to become one of the most sensational success stories on the Irish and British country scene. Chris Logue is blind and Pat McCool confined to a wheelchair, but their first record, which was an excellent cover version of George Strait's hit *The Cowboy Rides Away*, became a hit and resulted in a recording contract with Harmac and a best-selling CD recorded in Nashville in 1990. However, after a few other critically acclaimed albums Logue and McCool split up in early 1993.

Kathy Durkin, from Country Cavan, had one of the biggest hit singles in Ireland, either pop or country, of the early 1990s with her version of the Rita McNeill composition **Working Man**, which reached number 2 in the Irish pop charts in 1990, although it was the original by the Canadian singer–songwriter that was to be the hit in the UK. Durkin recorded several great albums for the Harmac label, and her CD **Kathy's Favourites** (Harmac 77) features her hit single *Working Man*. She was not to emulate the success of that song in the singles charts in spite of some other fine releases, especially the Dr Hook song *The Ballad Of Lucy Jordan* in 1992, and for health reasons was forced to take a break from live touring in early 1993.

Sean O'Farrell is another young Irish singer in his twenties to emerge in the early 1990s as a force to be reckoned with on the Irish country scene. From County Meath, he has the same clean-cut image as Daniel O'Donnell but like a lot of the new crop of country singers he is probably unfortunate that the more bland type of country songs are no longer in fashion with the younger audiences and the number of live venues in Ireland is fast diminishing. However, O'Farrell can mix his programme with the more modern sounds of Garth Brooks, and he has had favourable reaction in England on the concert scene, and for his album **Songs Just For You** (K-tel 354).

Another Irish singer having major success on the British country albums charts is Sean Wilson, from Derry, who has released over a dozen albums but with far greater success in the UK than in his homeland. Recording for both the T.C. label and, in more recent times, Prism Leisure, Wilson mixes country tracks alongside old Irish classics and has had a huge commercial success in the UK.

Eamonn McCann has been dubbed as Ireland's Randy Travis for his 1992 CD **Gold In The Mountains** (Harmac 78). While most of his recorded work features good cover versions of country classics, he has also been writing and recording some excellent songs of his own.

Shunie Crampsey, from Donegal, emerged on the Irish scene in the 1990s as a writer of hits for Daniel O'Donnell and Mick Flavin, to name but two. This was to later lead to a brief recording contract for Crampsey with Ritz of London, but after a few singles which failed to set the charts alight he was dropped from the label, and an excellent album containing many of his own compositions was to end up released on the small independent Doon label.

Dominic Kirwan, from Tyrone, seems to have been more successful for the Ritz label especially in the UK, where he is following in the footsteps of Daniel O'Donnell as a major concert attraction. His first three CDs have also been steady sellers in England and Scotland, as have his two music videos, and he has emerged as a popular attraction on TV in the UK too. His long-playing CD, **Don't Let Me Cry Again**, featured an original song from the pen of British pop-country entertainer and songwriter Raymond Froggett; indeed, Kirwan's style is closer to the pop-country or even big ballad scene than that of Daniel O'Donnell.

Mary Duff, from County Meath, has toured extensively with O'Donnell, and has released several CDs for Ritz of London, but like Kirwan and many others she has enjoyed greater success in the UK than in Ireland. She now spends most of her time touring with her band in England and Scotland where her Ritz album **Silver And Gold**, released in 1992, became a steady seller. From Waterford, Paddy O'Brien has enjoyed some success outside his homeland with regular tours of Austria and Switzerland as a result of his appearance on the

European Gold Star Awards show in Holland in the late 1980s. Some of his earlier recordings were with the Failte and Harmac labels and his **Keep On The Sunnyside** album for the latter company has been one of his most successful. Kevin Prendergast, from Mayo, is also a Failte Records recording artist, even though much of his material veers more towards the Irish than the American country sounds.

Sharon Turley, from Athlone, County Westmeath, who was only 20 when she toured in the UK as support act for Foster and Allen, is another emerging young country singer who had her debut single released by the London based I & B label. She has been recording in Roseland Studio in Moate, County Westmeath, under the guidance of Tony Allen (of Foster and Allen) and her manager and top musician Frank Scorr. Turley shows promise of being successful more in the country-rock vein like American singers such as Kathy Mattea or Reba McEntire, both of whom she greatly admires.

Other names to emerge on the Irish country scene in the late 1980s and 1990s include Chuck and June, Seamus McGee, Finbar Harte and Noel Cassidy. However, most of these new Irish stars have been badly hit by the ever-decreasing number of live venues in their homeland with young people far more interested in the discos or else in the emerging Irish rock scene. This has spawned some very successful new groups such as the Saw Doctors, the Hot House Flowers and the Stunning, who occasionally include some original country-rock songs in their releases.

Discographical Details

1   The Last Waltz

Daniel O'Donnell

Ritz CD 0058

Here I Am In Love Again/We Could/Last Waltz/When Only The Sky Was Blue/Heaven With You/You Know I Still Love You/Talk Back Trembling Lips/The Shelter Of Your Eyes/When We Get Together/Ring Of Gold/A Fool Such As I/Memory No. 1/Look Both Ways/Little Patch Of Blue/Marianne

2   I Need To Be In Love

Sandy Kelly

K-tel CD 303

Crazy/Always/All Alone Am I/It's Not Over 'Till It's Over/When I Need You/Sweet Dreams/Woodcarver (with Johnny Cash)/*Just Out Of Reach/I Fall To Pieces/He Is Beautiful To Me/I Will Always Love You/Faded Love/I Need To Be In Love/The Wind Beneath My Wings*

(vi) Original Irish Country Music

One of the biggest criticisms of the Irish country music scene down through the years has been the lack of original material – too many artists were satisfied to merely copy American country hits, and sometimes (though not always) the Irish version might be of inferior quality. This lack of originality may have stifled any interest the younger generation in Ireland in the 1990s might have in this type of music, and they turned instead to the emerging rock scene for original material. How-ever, as people like Garth Brooks, Mary Chapin Carpenter, Vince Gill captured the imagination of the young people of America with their more aggressive style of country, this has resulted in a small number of new Irish acts emerging on the local scene and reaching out to pop audiences, mostly in Dublin city.

Chris Meehan's Rednecks, and Hank Halfhead and the Ramblin' Turkeys are pioneers of this scene, playing their brand of country-rock long before the likes of Garth Brooks made it internationally popular. Hank Halfhead is the stage name of broadcaster Neil Toner, and his first record with the Ramblin' Turkeys, *Walkin' Boss*, made the Irish pop charts. He has concentrated on writing a lot of the group's material and established a very loyal following at live venues in his native Dublin as in some of the other major cities. The tape **Dublin Two-Step** is a good example of what "new" country in Ireland really sounds like and also includes some other good songs, such as *Fallen Angel*, and *Strange Train*.

But when it comes to commercial success outside Ireland for the newer generation of country or country-rock singers/song-writers, Mick Hanly has made the biggest impact of all in the US. His success has been as the songwriter of the Hal Ketchum American Top 10 hit of 1992, *Past The Point Of Rescue*. Since this song charted in America, Hanly has made several visits to Nashville, working in collaboration with some other song-writers in Music City. He has continued to record and perform in Ireland too, and has gained critical acclaim for his original songs. One of his earlier albums recorded in 1987, **Still Not Cured** (WEA RH LP 1) is one of the finest examples of what good "new" Irish country should sound like.

Charlie McGettigan, from County Leitrim, has also been writing great country songs since the mid-1980s. Other artists in the folk scene, such as Maura O'Connell (who now lives in Nashville), had a hit with McGettingan's song *Feet Of A Dancer*, and he has been recording his own songs for several different labels. In 1993 he released his first CD for ANEW Records of Dublin, **Charlie McGettigan**, which contains ten of his own fine songs.

Johnny McEvoy is a survivor from the ballad boom years of the mid-1960s who has regularly been writing his own songs, but many would say that they are more in the folk idiom. He veered much closer to country with his 1991 CD **The Original Johnny McEvoy** (Play Records 1028). It contained 13 originals from the pen of McEvoy, including *The Band Played Red River Valley* and one fine Irish/American country ballad, *Lincoln's Army*.

The Whole Chicken Band are a zany country-rock band who have been gaining some popularity with younger audiences in the 1990s, and who write much of their own material. They recorded some of their earlier singles for Harmac but without very much commercial success. In 1993 they changed to the CMR label with a fine original single CD by their lead singer Mark Oliver. Another act in the same vein is Cajun Paddy, from Donegal, who commenced their recording career in the early 1990s with two CD singles for the Play label. *Ireland In The '90s* is a hard-hitting original song which is less than complimentary to the Irish politicians of this era. It has gained extensive airplays especially on regional radio stations.

The Chieftains were known internationally for well over two decades as a folk group, but they introduced Irish country music to a huge world-wide audience with their Grammy Award-winning CD **Another Country**, recorded with some of the biggest names in Nashville. The group teamed up with Emmylou Harris, Willie Nelson, Ricky Skaggs, Jeff Hanna, Don Williams, Chet Atkins, and the Nitty Gritty Dirt Band, and demonstrated how Irish folk music can be fused with country, bluegrass and rock-and-roll to reveal a "new" international country style of the 1990s, which also takes the music back to its earthy roots. The success of this CD (RCA 09026 60939 2) has resulted in another recording session in Nashville early in 1993 for the Chieftains, this time alongside such diverse acts as Tom Jones and Carlene Carter.

According to Paddy Moloney of the Chieftains, he may have waited 33 years to take their style of country-trad music to America, but the Irish emigrants have been taking their fiddle tunes across the Atlantic for three generations prior to the formation of the Chieftains. Even modern American country music owes much to the amalgamation of the old fiddle tunes of the emigrants from the British Isles to the mountain music of native Americans. The Chieftains are at the forefront in the 1990s with another, and perhaps more modern fusion of the two music styles from either side of the Atlantic Ocean.

Discographical Details

343 Still Not Cured

Mick Hanly

WEA RH LP 1 (LP)

*Back Again (Without The Fairfare/The Silence/Sorry I Said/Where It's At/
Neighbour/Still Not Cured/Search For The Light*

344 Another Country: The Chieftains In Nashville

The Chieftains

RCA Victor 09026 60939 2

*Happy To Meet/I Can't Stop Lovin' You/Wabash Cannonball/Heartbreak
Hotel/Goodnight Irene/Cunla/Nobody's Darling But Mine/Cotton-Eyed Joe/
Tahitian Skies/Killybegs/Paddy's Green Shamrock Shore/Did You Ever Go A-
Courtin' Uncle Joe/Will The Circle Be Unbroken.*

Basic Recordings

Discographical Details

345 The Very Best Of Tom Dunphy

Tom Dunphy

EMI Talisman STAL (1) 1049

*Katie Daly/What Will Mary Say/Liverpool Lou/Goodbye And God Bless You/
Marta/Bless Your Heart, My Darling/Leaving Loving You/If I Didn't Have A
Dime/Listen To Me/Count Me In/I Heard The Bluebirds Sing/She Was You/
Kevin Barry/Smell The Flowers*

346 Dolphin Country

Various Artists

DOLB 7006 (LP)

Johnny Kelly: *I'll Be All Smiles Tonight*; Philomena Begley: *Wild Side Of Life*;
Gene Stuart: *Come On Home And Sing The Blues For Daddy*; Sean Dunphy:
Old Tighe; Smokey Mountain Ramblers: *Little Folk*; The Ventures: *Patches*;
Gene Stuart: *Before The Next Teardrop Falls*; Des Kelly: *Southern Dixie
Flyer*; Frankie Carroll: *Daddy Sang Bass*; The Virginians: *Absence Makes The
Heart Grow Fonder*; Casey: *Skip-A-Rope*; The Annalees: *Little Pedro*

347 Country Calling

Brian Coll

Homespun 412 (LP)

*Hometown On The Foyle/Picture On The Wall/She's Mine/Tonight I'll Throw
A Party/China Doll/These Are My Mountains/The Farmer/Time Changes
Everything/Little Bit Slow To Catch On/Fool's Castle/Second Fiddle/Mail Call*

48   Songs Fresh From Nashville

Larry Cunningham

Release BRL 4023 (LP)

There's Been A Change In You/Night Coach To Dallas/Evening/Yes It's True/ Seems Like I'm Always Leaving/Color Of Love/Missing You Was All I Did Today/It's Not The Miles You Travel/All The Difference In The World/I Guess I Had Too Much To Dream Last Night/The Clown With The Tears On His Face/The Mission

49   Irish Hit Parade '71

Various Artists

EMI Talisman STAL (1) 1014

Pat Lynch: *When We Were Young*; Margo: *Gradh Mo Chroi*; Tommy Drennan: *Love Is A Beautiful Song*; Gene Stuart: *I'd Rather Love You And Lose You*; Michael Landers: *If I Could Be A Sailor Man*; Ian Corrigan: *Gallant John Joe*; Dermot Henry: *If Those Lips Could Only Speak*; Margo: *I'll Forgive And I'll Try To Forget*; Gene Stuart: *Don't Go*; Tommy Drennan: *Taxes By The Score*; Mick Roche: *My Woman, My Woman, My Wife*; Tim Pat: *Poor, Poor Farmer*

50   Irish Country Flavour

Various Artists

Harmac HM 54

Big Tom: *Old Log Cabin*; Foster and Allen: *I Love You Because*; Kathy Durkin: *Kentucky Girl*: Brian Coll: *Sea Of Heartbreak*; Mick Flavin: *Love's Gonna Live Here*; Joe Flynn: *My Thanks To You*; Noel Cassidy: *We'll Sweep Out The Ashes*; Paddy O'Brien: *Devil Woman*; Frankie McBride: *Five Little Fingers*; Susan McCann: *I Fall To Pieces*; Tony Allen: *He'll Have To Go*; Louise Morrissey: *Tennessee Waltz*; Brian Coll: *The Hanging Tree*; Noel Cassidy: *Food On The Table*; Joe Flynn: *New Moon Over My Shoulder*; Sandy Kelly and Mick Flavin: *I Heard The Bluebirds Sing*

51   Thoughts Of Country

Various Artists

Ritz CD 518

Daniel O'Donnell: *Stand Beside Me*; Dominic Kirwan: *Almost Persuaded*; Mick Flavin: *Jennifer Johnson And Me*; Mary Duff: *Dear God*; Charley Pride: *Four In The Morning*; Philomena Begley: *The Way Old Friends Do*; Ray Lynam: *Back In Love By Monday*; John Hogan: *Still Got A Crush On You*; Mick Flavin and Philomena Begley: *Daisy Chain*; Billie Jo Spears: *Apologizing Roses*; Philomena Begley: *Queen Of The Silver Dollar*; Mick Flavin: *Travellin' Light*; Charley Pride: *Amy's Eyes*; Mary Duff: *Forever And Ever, Amen*; Philomena Begley and Mick Flavin: *Just Between You And Me*; Sonny Curtis: *No Stranger To The Rain*; Daniel O'Donnell: *Take Good Care Of Her*; John Hogan: *Don't Fight The Feelings*; Margo: *Sweethearts In Heaven*; Dominic Kirwan: *Sea Of Heartbreak*

352   Diamonds And Dreams

Susan McCann

Prism Leisure CD 591

Love Me One More Time/When I Hear The Music/Have You Ever Been Lonely/String Of Diamonds Medley/Always/You're Never Too Old To Love/He Never will Be Mine/Lovin' You/I Vow To Thee, My Country/Yellow Roses/ Sonny's Dream/Broken Speed Of The Sound of Loneliness/Rose of My Heart/ Hillbilly Girl With The Blues/Everything Is Beautiful/Give Me More Time

353   In Harmony

Philomena Begley and Mick Flavin

Ritz CD 0061

No Love Left/Just Between You And Me/I'm Wasting Your Time And You're Wasting Mine/'Til A Tear Becomes A Rose/Always Always/We're Strangers Again/We'll Get Ahead Someday/All You've Got To Do Is Dream/Daisy Chain/Don't Believe Me I'm Lying/You Can't Break The Chains Of Love/Let's Pretend We're Not Married Tonight/How Can I Help You Forgive Me/Somewhere Between

354   Charlie McGettigan

Charlie McGettigan

Anew NEWD 401

Let Me Know About It/Our Love Is Real/I Fell Out Of Love/I Can't Quite Believe That You Don't Care/The Guy Who Lives Next Door/A Bed For The Night/You're On My Mind Again/The Longest Day/Feet Of A Dancer/Light A Penny Candle

355   The Original

Johnny McEvoy

Play 1028

Runaround Angel/As Soon As I Can/Play The Game/No Other Love I'll Know/Leaves In The Wind/I Can't Believe/The Band Played Red River Valley/Lincoln's Army/Rich Man's Garden/The Wheels Go Around/Tonight You're With Another/Michael/Long Way From The Sun

356   Tonight

The Whole Chicken Band

CMR 116 (single)

Tonight/Sweet, Sweet Love

357   Ireland In The '90s

Cajun Paddy

Ireland In The '90s/Codename, The Dial/Ireland In The '90s (extended vocal version)

58 Dublin Two-Step

Hank Halfhead and the Rambling Turkeys

HH 001

Dublin Two-Step/Safest Place/Crazy Fool/Strange Train/Nightlife/Nowhere Road/All Over Again/Fallen Angel

The 1980s and Beyond 10

Bob Allen

The very early 1980s were, at least from a creative standpoint, a period of relative bleakness in country music. The Outlaw movement, which had pumped renewed vitality and experimentation into Nashville music of the mid- and late 1970s, had pretty much run its course. Willie Nelson and Waylon Jennings were superstars now and were still making decent enough records; but their original fire of innovation and rebellion had cooled, and now they were merely part of the music establishment.

At the same time, many of hard country's dependable mainstays – artists who, throughout the 1970s, had kept the spirit of founding fathers Jimmie Rodgers, Hank Williams, and Lefty Frizzell alive, and preserved country music's sometimes fragile link with its own past – were also beginning to pass their musical peaks. Many of these figures – like George Jones, Conway Twitty, Dolly Parton (whose music had taken a gradual shift toward pop music as she charted broader commercial horizons), Tammy Wynette, and Charley Pride (one of country music's only black superstars) – still showed commercial vitality; but their music had, in some cases, lapsed into predictability and redundancy.

Thus, it was clearly time for new blood, for a changing of the guard. The problem was that Nashville's record industry, by the early 1980s, had once again slipped into a conservative posture, and was largely resistant to new talent. The record labels tended to merely keep milking their dependable cash cows – i.e. established artists – rather than invest capital and energy in developing new ones.

It was a sign of the times that one of the commercially dominant figures of the early 1980s was Kenny Rogers, a country-pop warbler who'd earned fleeting success in the 1970s heading a pop/rock group called Kenny Rogers and the First

Edition. Rogers shrewdly revived his recording career, using the country charts as a vehicle (as any number of failed rockers and popsters have attempted to do in the years since) to cross over and lever his way back to pop stardom. In the early country phase of this calculated transmogrification, Rogers made some quite acceptable country records (*Lucille, Coward Of The County*); but the drift of his music thereafter made it clear that his involvement in country music was skin-deep and pragmatic.

An even more disturbing barometer of how dismal and directionless country's commercial mainstream had become by the early 1980s was the LA-to-Nashville "bimbo" invasion. During these years, any number of modestly talented but nubile Southern California pop songstresses recorded half-baked "country" records which, remarkably, made minor dents in the country record charts. (A California singer named Carole Chase even had evanescent success with an Los Angeles-produced LP of "country-disco" dubiously entitled **Sexy Songs**.)

In thrashing about for new formulas for boosting the music's demographic appeal the Nashville industry once again showed a willingness to make whatever compromises necessary in order to appeal to a more urban, and suburban, audience – even if this new audience's interest proved merely a mile wide and an inch deep.

The impetus for much of this pandering was an immensely popular 1980 Hollywood feature film called "Urban Cowboy," starring John Travolta (who'd recently risen to stardom playing a flashy disco dancer in the film, "Stayin' Alive") and Debra Winger. "Urban Cowboy," which glorified the lifestyle of a mechanical bull-riding nightclub cowboy, did exceptionally well at the box office. The accompanying soundtrack album – which actually contained nearly as much music from rock-and-roll artists like the Eagles and Linda Ronstadt as it did genuine country music – was a similarly huge success. Suddenly, it seemed that all of America had adopted country music (or at least the watered-down notion of country music purveyed by "Urban Cowboy") as its newest national fad. People who didn't know Roy Acuff from Mario Lanza began setting their car radio push-buttons to country stations. And, predictably, country radio stations began watering down their playlists to ensure that these Johnny-come-lately, fair-weather fans heard the sort of country-pop pablum they were looking for.

But the bottom fell out of the "Urban Cowboy" boom quicker than anyone could have imagined, as America left its newly-purchased Tony Llama cowboy boots and Merle Haggard LPs to gather dust in the closet and went off chasing some new fad. Country record sales, which had attained a 16

percent market share of overall domestic record sales in the
very early 1980s, had plummetted to a rather unrespectable 9
percent by 1984. Even *The New York Times* ran a front-page
story on the Nashville music industry's fiscal crisis which
almost sounded like an obituary for country music.

But already change, renewal, experimentation, and innovation were bubbling under and would soon burst forth in the
form of a dramatic grassroots resurgence – one which had been
quietly building momentum behind the scenes since the beginning of the decade. The impetus for this revival came from a
new generation of artists at the street, club, and grassroots level
who shared a sincere reverence for country music's raw, sometimes raunchy, fiddle/steel-guitar/guitar roots. These artists,
many alienated and disillusioned by the drab musical piffle of
the "Urban Cowboy" craze, were intent upon restoring some
degree of integrity to country's mainstream. They were dedicated to not just reviving but reinventing the spirit of the 1950s
and 1960s honky-tonk, rockabilly, and bluegrass fervor. They
brought to this musical renewal a vivid fire and energy such as
only youth can bring.

In the process, this new wave of tradition-conscious artists –
Emmylou Harris, Ricky Skaggs, John Anderson, George Strait,
Reba McEntire were among the first of many – proved that the
audience for unadulterated country music – expertly and
lovingly performed music with genuine, heartfelt links to its
own past – had never really gone away even during those years
when the country record industry had seriously devalued it.

But, of course, the overall musical ebbs and flows of the
1980s and early 1990s were, like those of the 1970s, far more
complex and overlapping than a cursory examination might
suggest. Despite the surge toward neo-traditionalism, any
number of "Lite-Country" or "country-to-rock/pop-crossover"
singers still flourished throughout the decade, and often made
worthy music within their own aesthetic parameters. One of the
biggest record sellers of the entire 1980s was, in fact, Alabama,
a talented but often formulaic band that carved out a huge
youthful following with its tame, clean-cut, but frequently
inspired brand of Southern country-rock.

And as the neo-traditionalist boom gathered momentum, it
inspired mini-trends and fads of its own – the most noteworthy
being the deluge of the so-called "Hat Acts" of the late 1980s
and early 1990s: photogenic male "hunksters" who not only
looked good in white cowboy hats and tight jeans, but also
could sing a good honky-tonk song. (Garth Brooks, Clint Black,
and Alan Jackson are three of many contenders in this industry-
driven subgenre who went on to particular prominence.)

It's important to note that by the early 1980s, the country

music industry had fallen under the leadership of a younger, more adventurous generation of producers, publishers, and executives (most notably, Tony Brown, MCA staff producer and president of Nashville operations who signed many of the most important new artists of the 1980s). Much as a result of this changing of the guard, the industry opened its floodgates wider than ever before to stylistic diversity – everything from the unfettered Hank Williams-style hard country sounds of singers like Kentuckian Marty Brown and South Carolinian Aaron Tippin, to pop-, folk-, and even jazz-inflected artists like Mary Chapin Carpenter, Lyle Lovett, K.T. Oslin, k.d. lang, and Steve Earle. This ultimately expanded – and diluted – both the definition and identity of country music even further. The only common thread unifying these new artists was utter originality and formidable talent.

Sitting high astride the country music boom of the early 1990s is, of course, Garth Brooks, a young Oklahoma singer whose eminently accessible mainstream style (which has subtle inflections of pop, rock, and even folk music) and energetic live show, as well as his outspokenness about various social issues, have earned him vast record sales that easily outdistance any previous country artist, and put him on equal commercial footing with the likes of Michael Jackson, U2, and Madonna.

During the 1980s and early 1990s, technology – for better or worse – has also continued to shape country music. Digital recording has become pro forma, and the compact disc has all but phased out vinyl (the LP). Yet, despite the many technological leaps, some of the best albums of the decade (like Dwight Yoakam's **Guitars, Cadillacs, Etc., Etc.** – see "Essential Recordings," this chapter; the O'Kanes' first LP, and the Kentucky Headhunters' 1988 debut album – see "Basic Recordings," this chapter) were made in small, out-of-the-way studios and/or produced on shoestring budgets – proving once again, that more often than not, *spirit* will prevail over technology almost every time.

Essential Recordings

(i) Country-Rockers and "Newgrass" Country

Emmylou Harris came of age in the distant northern Virginia satellite suburbs of Washington, DC. She cut her musical teeth as a folk singer and as a fringe figure on the early 1970s California country-rock scene. (She was a protégé of pioneer country-rocker, the late Gram Parsons.) Thus it's somewhat ironic that she should become a key player in country music's early 1980s roots-conscious revival.

Harris, the daughter of a career military man, was born in Alabama. She was valedictorian of her high school graduating class and later attended the University of North Carolina before briefly taking acting classes at Boston University.

Harris's recording career as a country artist really began to flourish in the mid-1970s; but it was on her 1980 album, **Roses In The Snow** (a companion piece of sorts to her 1979 **Blue Kentucky Girl** – also an outstanding record) that she achieved one of the true milestones of her career and set the tone for much of what was to come.

Roses In The Snow was, in many respects, a bluegrass album and an exercise in purism that flew brashly in the face of prevailing commercial wisdom. Except for its more sophisticated recording techniques (it was recorded in Harris's home in Los Angeles area utilizing her then-husband/producer Brian Ahern's "Enactron Truck" mobile studio), **Roses In The Snow** might have easily passed as a sublime relic of an earlier and more innocent age. The arrangements are gentle and all-acoustic – banjos, dobros, mandolins, archtop guitars, auto-harps, and other old-timey instrumentation – and hark back to the long-gone era of the Carter Family. The majority of the songs on the album are either public domain numbers or songs originally recorded years ago by celebrated bluegrass, gospel, and country artists like Ralph Stanley (*The Darkest Hour Is Just Before Dawn*), Ira and Charlie Louvin (*You're Learning*), and A.P. Carter (*Gold Watch And Chain*). Surprisingly, Harris also saw fit to include a very rootsy acoustic version of Paul Simon's *The Boxer*, which she so vividly reworks as a folk tune that it blends almost seamlessly with the other, older selections.

Though *I'll Go Stepping Too* (Tom James and Jerry Organ) has a bit of a honky-tonk theme, most of the music on **Roses In The Snow** has an almost hushed, reverential intensity – as if Harris and the other musicians realized the importance of what they were doing and were determined to recapture the simple, wholesome, melancholy beauty of old-timey Appalachian music.

Harris assembled a splendid cast of musicians for this project: eminently talented neophytes like guitarists Albert Lee, Tony Rice, bassist Emory Gordy, Jr, dobro wizard Jerry Douglas, piano player Buck White, autoharpist Bryan Bowers, and Brian Ahern on 12-string guitar. Willie Nelson plays gut string guitar on one track. Harmony vocals and duets are supplied on various cuts by Dolly Parton, Johnny Cash, Ricky Skaggs, and the Whites, a revered country-gospel family ensemble.

Ricky Skaggs (see "Essential Recordings," this chapter) was more than just another picker on **Roses In The Snow**; he was a guiding force. Besides his lovely hand-in-glove harmonies with Harris and his impeccable contributions on fiddle, mandolin, acoustic guitar, and banjo, Skaggs (at the time, a member of Harris's Hot Band – as were quite a few of the above-mentioned instrumentalists) also functioned as a sort of unofficial associate producer on this project, bringing a lifetime's worth of credence, authority, and intimate involvement with eastern Kentucky gospel/bluegrass musical traditions.

Though **Roses In The Snow** did not immediately set loose a back-to-the-basics revolt in country music, its surprising commercial success and its heartfelt intensity – which came in the midst of an era of considerable artistic bankruptcy and musical contrivance – served as an important counter-balance to the shortlived, faddish "Urban Cowboy" bandwagon, on which way many artists had jumped at the expense of their musical integrity.

Eastern Kentuckian Ricky Skaggs is, like Emmylou Harris, often credited with being one of the true forerunners of country music's 1980s renaissance of traditionalism. **Waitin' For The Sun To Shine**, his 1981 major label debut, was like a flash of pure white lightning bolting across the overcast landscape of mainstream country music in the early 1980s. Skaggs's inspired blend of traditional (bluegrass, gospel, rockabilly) and contemporary influences (electrified instruments, a heavy bottom beat, and his own gentle, lilting, highly accessible vocal style) quickly captured listeners' imaginations.

"I set out to create a more traditional, back-to-the-basics kind of sound – to bring back the mandolin, fiddle, banjo, and steel guitars that had really been lost by the wayside," explained Skaggs, who clearly envisioned himself in his earlier days as a man with a musical mission. "It was something I felt the fans wanted, and it was certainly something I wanted . . . To me, traditional music has a value in it, a wholesomeness and warmth that some other kinds of music don't have. It's our heritage. It's our roots. It's everything we're about."

Skaggs was born in Cordell, Kentucky in 1954; the region he hails from has produced countless other country and bluegrass greats – the Judds and Loretta Lynn, to name but two. Skaggs was immersed in bluegrass music from an early age and was more or less a child prodigy. (He plays a half dozen or so different instruments and, aside from his own numerous self-produced albums, has produced records on everyone from obscure bluegrass artists to Dolly Parton.)

By age seven, Skaggs was appearing on a local television show hosted by bluegrass masters Flatt and Scruggs. And he was still in his teens when he and fellow Kentuckian Keith Whitley (see "Basic Recordings," this chapter) joined bluegrass legend Ralph Stanley's band. (Skaggs and Whitley, in 1971, also made a memorable duet album called **Second Generation Bluegrass** which has since been re-released on CD by Rebel Records.) Later, Skaggs became a member of the celebrated Washington, DC-based bluegrass band, the Country Gentlemen.

Skaggs began his transition from bluegrass to mainstream country when he joined Emmylou Harris's Hot Band (which has been a springboard for other 1980s notables – Rodney Crowell, producer Tony Brown, guitarist Albert Lee, producer Emory Gordy, Jr, among them). He assisted Harris tremendously on her ground-breaking 1980 **Roses In The Snow**, (see "Essential Recordings," above).

By the time Skaggs made **Waitin' For The Sun To Shine**, he was already a studio veteran and had recorded and/or produced numerous independent label projects for himself and others. Functioning as his own producer, Skaggs brought to **Waitin' For The Sun To Shine** and his other noteworthy early Columbia LPs a disarmingly simple but magical formula – one which would have doubtlessly eluded an artist not so completely immersed in bluegrass and gospel traditions as Skaggs, or who lacked such a lucid, headstrong musical vision.

Essentially what Skaggs did on **Waitin' For The Sun To Shine** (and on his other early Columbia LPs) was to draw material from greats of earlier generations like Bill Monroe, Flatt and Scruggs, and the Stanley Brothers, and overlay it with an aggressive, at times almost rocking electric guitar, bass, and drum beat. Yet Skaggs – here and on later albums – never shies away from contemporary material when it fits the framework of his own wholesome purist musical vision. (Skaggs is an outspoken Christian fundamentalist and steadfastly avoids songs fraught with drinking, infidelity, or other recurrent honky-tonk themes; even on a song of lost love like the swingy *Low And Lonely* on **Waitin' For The Sun To Shine**, his tone is more wistful than bitter.) The title tune, for instance, which was one of Skaggs's first number 1 hits, was written by Sonny Throckmorton, one of the most prolific mainstream Nashville songwriters of the early 1980s.

Besides the updated rhythm and electrification, Skaggs's smooth, wistful vocal style (a far cry indeed from the strident bluegrass warbling and yelping of old-timers like Monroe and Stanley!) also serves to update the old-timey material on **Waitin' For The Sun To Shine** and make it more accessible to mainstream listeners. Graceful vocal and instrumental accompaniment also comes from the Whites, a superbly talented gospel-country family group whose members include Skaggs's wife Sharon and his piano-playing father-in-law, Buck White.

For quite a few years previous to his belated late 1980s success as a recording artist, Rodney Crowell was a formidable behind-the-scenes influence in the Nashville music industry, as a songwriter and producer.

Born in Houston, Texas, Crowell is the son of a construction worker (by day)/honky-tonk bandleader (by night). (Crowell takes special pride in the fact that his Kentucky-born father and his mother met at a Roy Acuff concert in Tennessee.) By the time the boy was 11, Crowell's father had put his son to work in his band as a drummer and occasional singer. "My father played Hank Williams, Lefty Frizzell, and all that great old Ray Price twin fiddle stuff, as well as quite a few Appalachian 'dead baby' songs," Crowell recalled in a late 1980s interview with *Country Music Magazine*.

After briefly studying English literature and political science in college, Crowell left Texas for Nashville in 1972, in search of a different kind of higher education "I was 21, didn't have a penny, didn't know a soul. I slept out at the lake in my car."

Within a few years, Crowell had become the lead guitarist in Emmylou Harris's highly esteemed Hot Band (see above), and had fallen in with a coterie of progressive (and mostly Texas-to-Nashville-transplanted) songwriters like Guy Clark ("the Picasso of country writers," says Crowell), Townes Van Zandt, Billy Joe Shaver, and Steve Earle. Soon, he was turning out classic compositions which have since been recorded by a multitude of country and rock artists – everyone from Willie Nelson (*Angel Eyes*), Waylon Jennings (*I Ain't Livin' Long Like This*), George Jones (*Here We Are*), and Emmylou Harris (*Amarillo, Bluebird Wine*), to rockers Bob Seeger (*Shame On The Moon*), and the Grateful Dead (*California Earthquake*).

Crowell's own early albums – obscure masterpieces like **Ain't Livin' Long Like This** (1978), **But What Will The Neighbors Think** (1980), and **Rodney Crowell** (1981) – did little, sales- or chart-wise, but earned him a cult following and made him a hero with music critics. In the late 1970s, he also made a mark producing records for other artists, most notably Rosanne Cash, the talented daughter of singer Johnny Cash, whom Crowell married in 1979. Crowell produced practically all of Cash's critically acclaimed hit albums (see "Basic Recordings," this chapter), as well as LPs by Guy Clark, Bobby Bare, (see also "Basic Recordings" listings, 1970s chapter), guitarist Albert Lee, and actress Sissy Spacek.

With **Diamonds And Dirt**, his own fifth album, Crowell finally found success in his own right as a recording artist – something which, despite his best efforts, had eluded him his first 15 or so years in Nashville. For the first time, his rather immense and diverse talent seemed to come into sharp focus.

The critical accolades that greeted **Diamonds And Dirt** were echoed eloquently by veteran music journalist Chet Flippo, for many years a contributing editor to *Rolling Stone*. Flippo called Crowell: ". . . the closest we'll ever get to the real missing link between Hank Williams and the vacuum left by Elvis, between the arch-sober almost-Victorian country realism of Hank and the raucous-yet-romantic industrial age of rock and roll as best posited by Elvis or Rodney's fellow Texan Buddy Holly."

If Crowell's influences, musical proclivities, and technical prowess (as producer) often tended to be far-ranging, **Diamonds And Dirt** (which he co-produced with noted producer Tony Brown, a former member of Crowell's road band, the Cherry Bombs) focused his talents into a more accessible package "When I made **Street Language** [the hard-hitting Southern country-rock LP that preceded **Diamonds And Dirt**], I was very keen on production and very influenced by some of the leading rock producers," Crowell explained to *Country Music Magazine*:

> But I got so caught up in the production I think I blinded myself to the human aspects with **Diamonds And Dirt**, I just shifted my focus from the technical aspect to the human aspect . . . [And] I finally realized that as a singer, I'm definitely coming from that early era of my life when I listened to Merle Haggard and Hank Williams, along with Chuck Berry and the Beatles.

Crowell wrote or co-wrote all the songs on **Diamonds And Dirt**, except for the Harlan Howard classic, *Above And Beyond*. He and co-producer Brown infused the up-tempo tracks with a pulsating neo-rockabilly gusto and a compelling rhythmic intensity. Instrumentals are supplied by a top-notch assortment of blue chip session players: Mark O'Connor and Glen Duncan on fiddle, Barry Beckett (a noted producer in his own right) on piano and organ, Michael Rhodes on bass, Eddie Bayers and Russ Kunkle on drums, and the amazing electric lead guitarist Steuart Smith. (A member of Crowell's road band, the Dixie Pearls, Smith also played guitar with distinction on many of Rosanne Cash's best recordings from the 1980s.) Guest vocals are also heard from Rosanne Cash, Vince Gill, and others.

Crowell, who is an outstanding singer and showman as well as producer and songwriter, has indeed never sounded more confident and poised than he does on **Diamonds And Dirt**. In fact, on the more introspective ballads he, at times, brings to mind a young Roy Orbison as he ruminates on the tribulations or vicissitudes of adult love and loss – themes that were no doubt heavy on his mind, since his lengthy marriage to Cash was, at the time of this recording, in its final months.

But a more lighthearted side of Crowell is no less in evidence. You can hear it on the opening cut – the neo-rock-abillyish *Crazy Baby, I Couldn't Leave You If I Tried* (a song that wryly charts the murky waters between devotion and co-dependency, and which features a sassy echo-plexed vocal from Crowell and a latterday Ray Price-style instrumental rhythmic shuffle). *She's Crazy For Leavin'*, in a similar spirit, offers a wacky take on another out-of-control romance, and was co-written by Crowell and Guy Clark. Both of these aforementioned songs, each in its own way, expresses or implies our ability to survive the emotional extremes and excesses that we put each other through in the name of love. *I Know You're Married*, on the other hand, is the roguish, impassioned confession of a reckless man who is determined to pursue a dangerous love. (Or perhaps it's merely a whimsical *passion* – we're never sure, since Crowell's vocal is so fraught with tantalizing ambiguity.) Steuart Smith displays his technocratic and pyrotechnical guitar wizardry with some outstanding rhythm/lead figures which frame the song nearly as much as Crowell's fervent lead singing does. *Brand New Rag* is a cool, riffy love song featuring a pulsating organ and more sizzling guitar from Steuart. This song once again demonstrates Crowell's fine attention to rhythm, groove, and attitude, and his genius for exquisitely understated production.

On other songs – like *After All This Time*, a lovely ballad about the sadness and regret of a man under the spell of a troubled love – Crowell movingly conveys all the weight, complexity, and ambivalence of adult love. *I Didn't Know I Could Lose You* is the quietly incredulous admission of a stunned man who ponders how a love so intense and all-consuming could have slipped away so quietly when he wasn't even looking. *It's Such A Small World*, a duet with Rosanne Cash, is the tale of an estranged couple who accidentally run into each other in a strange city and, with a mixture of caution and hopefulness, explore the possibility of rekindling their relationship.

The Last Waltz, the closing cut on **Diamonds And Dirt**, is similarly steeped in the travail of a tumultuous relationship. In the song, even as he confronts his own painfully mixed feelings and acknowledges that there is indeed "no easy way out," Crowell cautiously envisions a brighter day when both his and his lover's feelings toward each other will be clearer, and love will be back on more solid ground. He turns in a beautiful lead vocal here, which is double-tracked in the chorus to great effect.

Discographical Details

359   Roses In The Snow

Emmylou Harris

Warner Bros 3422–2

Roses In The Snow/Wayfaring Stranger/Green Pastures/The Boxer/Darkest Hour Is Just Before The Dawn/I'll Go Stepping Too/You're Learning/Jordan/ Miss The Mississippi/Gold Watch And Chain

360   Waitin' For The Sun To Shine

Ricky Skaggs

Epic EK 37193 D698

If That's The Way You Feel/Don't Get Above Your Raising/Your Old Love Letters/Low And Lonely/Waitin' For The Sun To Shine/You May See Me Walkin'/Crying My Heart Out Over You/Lost To A Stranger/I Don't Care/So Round, So Firm, So Fully Packed

361   Diamonds And Dirt

Rodney Crowell

Columbia CK 44076

Crazy Baby/I Couldn't Leave You If I Tried/She's Crazy For Leavin/After All This Time/I Know You're Married/Above And Beyond/It's Such A Small World (with Rosanne Cash)/*I Didn't Know I Could Lose You/Brand New Rag/The Last Waltz*

(ii) Women of the 1980s and 1990s

In many ways, Reba McEntire, a former rodeo rider from rural southeastern Oklahoma, has become for the 1980s and early 1990s what a figure like Loretta Lynn was for the 1960s and 1970s: a musical spokesperson for rural American women and their everyday fears, concerns, and preoccupations. "Any comparisons with Loretta Lynn sure don't hurt my feelings," McEntire noted in a 1986 interview with *Country Music Magazine*. "It's particularly flattering, because Loretta sings for the woman and says things for the women that they couldn't say to their husbands, but wanted to. And that's what I'm trying to do now . . . sing for the women of the 1980s and '90s," added McEntire, who was, herself, divorced and remarried around the turn of the decade "The only difference is, back then, Loretta would sing a song like *Don't Come Home A-Drinkin' With Lovin' On Your Mind*. But nowadays, I'll sing a song that says, 'Don't even consider coming home, because we're not gonna put up with it no longer.' That's the '80s and '90s woman."

McEntire, who was "discovered" when she sang the national anthem at an Oklahoma rodeo and caught the attention of a Nashville songwriter who happened to be in the audience, made her major-label debut with Mercury in 1976. For the next eight years, she turned out decent enough albums that managed to gloss over her exceptional vocal power and persuasiveness.

By 1984, however, McEntire, who was then in her late twenties, had moved on to a new label (MCA) and a new producer: Harold Shedd, who'd had immense success producing the country-rock supergroup Alabama's early albums and hit singles. Working with Shedd, McEntire at last found the creative freedom to set her own stylistic course and delve into her own musical heritage, which was rooted heavily in the western swing and hard country music she'd grown up with in her native Oklahoma. The resulting album, **My Kind Of Country** (1984), was a far more back-to-the-basics musical collection than anything McEntire has put out either before or since. Many consider it her all-time best.

"Western swing, that's my roots, that's my heritage," McEntire later explained. "The old Ray Price songs are something I'll never get away from . . . [But] it seemed like when I did **My Kind Of Country**, nobody was doing that kind of thing, and it really did feel like country music was slipping away."

My Kind Of Country was another shining example (as were the debut LPs of Kentuckian Ricky Skaggs, Floridian John Anderson and Texan George Strait, all of whom were beginning to make their presences felt in the country charts by the time McEntire released this album) of a new generation of country artists coming of age and laying claim to their grassroots musical heritage. Though McEntire would begin drifting toward a wider, more pop-based approach on subsequent albums, **My Kind Of Country** is an almost willful exercise in rootsiness. Reprising songs that had been popularized in earlier decades by faded but not-forgotten stars like Ray Price, Faron Young, Connie Smith, and Carl Smith, McEntire fervently captured the swingy and honky-tonk twin fiddle/guitar hard country sound that was popularized by these aforementioned 1950s and 1960s heroes. Yet, with her powerhouse vocal style – remarkable for its range, as well as its emotional subtlety – McEntire does more than just pay tribute to the past; she breathes renewed vitality into it and makes its best traditions her own as she revamps them for the 1980s. From her lovely double-tracked lead vocal on *How Blue*, right on through to the soaring anguish of *You've Got Me (Right Where You Want Me)* (an oldie written by Connie Smith and George Richie), McEntire sings with authority and pathos. On her lovely rendition of *I Want To Hear It From You* (written by Fred Carter, Jr) she sounds uncannily like Patsy Cline revisited. McEntire breathes similarly vast emotional dimension and anguish into Harlan Howard's *Somebody Should Leave*, a heart-rending, guilt-ridden song about a crumbling marriage.

My Kind Of Country's inspired retro-1950s and 1960s charm and fervor is given almost perfect instrumental symmetry by a consummate line-up of veteran session players, including Sonny Garrish (steel guitar), Brent Rowan (lead guitar), Ray Edenton (acoustic guitar), Johnny Gimble and Mark O'Connor (fiddles), Eddie Bayers (drums), and Jerry Douglas (dobro)

This album (as well as her subsequent **Have I Got A Deal For You**) served to raise McEntire's profile considerably, and proved a major building block in her gradual ascendance from obscure Oklahoma singer to one of the most influential and popular stars of the 1980s and 1990s.

When Naomi and Wynonna Judd, a mother-and-daughter duet team from Ashland, Kentucky (Naomi was born there in 1946, Wynonna in 1964) made their recording debut in 1983, Nashville was still recovering from an "Urban Cowboy" hangover haze. From 1983 until they disbanded in late 1991, the Judds distinguished themselves with a solid run of chart-topping singles, including *Mama, He's Crazy, Grandpa, Give A Little Love, Change Of Heart, Born To Be Blue*, and *Love Can Build A Bridge*

In 1983, the notion of an Appalachian-bred, southeastern Kentucky-born, acoustic-based mother and daughter team like the Judds making a serious dent in the country charts seemed novel at best, improbable at worst. But their sparkling, precise, spontaneous harmonies and their sure-footed sense of Appalachian tradition (which suggested – as did the music of fellow Kentuckian Ricky Skaggs, another eastern Kentuckian – an earlier, more intimate era of American life), along with their strong familial bonds, infused their music with a precision and integrity far beyond mere vocal and technical prowess. And the Judds quickly became the darlings of Nashville's jaded record industry and the public alike.

The intimacy and robust vitality of the Judds' back-porch harmonies were certainly a welcome contrast to the slick, urbane, over-produced treacle of early 1980s superstars like Kenny Rogers, and Dolly Parton. Daughter Wynonna Judd was just a precocious 17-year-old when she and her mother made their debut on RCA; yet she quickly made an impression as possibly the gutsiest and most talented female vocalist to come down the country pike since Patsy Cline. Like Cline, Wynonna's style and sensibilities would prove to be as heavily anchored in pop music as in country.

The Judds also drew strongly from the longstanding tradition of earlier Appalachian and eastern Kentucky family musical ensembles – a tradition fostered through the decades by everyone from the Carter Family, the Delmore Brothers, the Wilburn Brothers, the Stanley Brothers, and the Everly Brothers. Naomi Judd was specifically steeped in the musical legacy of homespun harmony teams like Hazel and Alice, and the Boswell Sisters.

Yet there was more than just tradition at work. The Judds (who, in reality, came to Nashville from Kentucky by way of Hollywood) also had a savvy, at times almost urbane, sophistication of image and sound, and a no less sure-footed appreciation of contemporary musical influences.

Wynonna, in particular, was strongly steeped in the folk, pop, blues, and rock music which she'd grown up listening to in southern California. Emmylou Harris, jazz-folk singer Joni Mitchell, white blues-rock maven Bonnie Raitt, and white country-soul-R & B master Delbert McClinton were particularly strong influences. So was blues legend Muddy Waters. (Wynonna never played down the fact that she – unlike her mother, who'd came of age a generation earlier in rural eastern Kentucky – had not been a country music fan as a teenager.)

When Wynonna and her mother gave their first (nonpaying) public performance – at a garden party in northern California in the late 1970s, where they billed themselves as "the Kentucky Sweethearts" – their eclectic repertoire gave a hint of the far-ranging influences that would later coalesce in their distinctive duet sound: The Andrews Sisters' *Bei Mir Bist Du Schon*, Ella Fitzgeralds's *Cow Cow Boogie*, and the Delmore Brothers' *Hillbilly Boogie*.

The Judds' hand-in-glove, preternaturally smooth, precise harmonies were the result of years of informal yet intense practice. Naomi Judd, for her part, realized when her daughter was still a small child, that Wynonna possessed remarkable potential as a singer. And, early on, Naomi learned to superbly shade Wynonna's much stronger lead vocals with her own lower-range harmonies and shadow leads.

"Our music just evolved naturally from the very beginning," Naomi recalled of the many years of front-porch and back yard musical woodshedding which preceded the Judds' recording debut:

> We never did make a conscious effort to sit down and start singing together. It just happened. As the years went by, I'd teach Wynonna the words to songs. Because my voice is a shade lower than hers, I'd naturally go into a harmony instead of singing with her . . . And we just kept doing it

> more and more and getting better and better . . . It finally got
> to where all I had to do was raise my eyebrows and Wynonna
> knew to go up. We're almost telepathic in that regard.

As they embarked upon their professional recording career,
the Judds had the good fortune to fall in with two men who
would play a crucial role in capturing Naomi's and Wynonna's
spontaneous live harmonies on record: producer Brent Maher
and guitarist/session leader Don Potter (who Naomi has often
affectionately referred to as "the Third Judd)." Maher and
Potter wisely adorned the Judds' earliest records with an
exceedingly tasteful, intriguing, and hook-laden acoustic instrumental tapestry that perfectly enhanced the intimacy and clarity
of their seamless vocal blend. "We never had an electric guitar
on their records until about the third album," Maher later
recalled.

Though Naomi Judd would later come into her own as a
songwriter, in the early stages of the Judds' career, Maher contributed heavily towards helping Naomi and Wynonna choose
material that best lent itself to their harmonies. He also assisted
the two of them (who were, at the outset, complete studio neophytes) in perfecting their intricate harmony arrangements
through extensive pre-production and "work tape" recording
sessions.

Working with Maher and Potter, the Judds made consistently excellent records in the course of their eight years
together. (Naomi was sidelined by illness in 1991; Wynonna has
since gone on to an illustrious solo career (see "Essential
Recordings," below). **Why Not Me** (1984), their second album
(which eventually became their first of several million-selling
albums), captures the Judds in all their unaffected vitality. In
some ways, it sounds slightly more spontaneous and less
stylized than some of their later albums, as they gradually
drifted toward somewhat more sophisticated and adventurous
electrified instrumental arrangements, and as Wynonna's lead
vocals gradually became more prominent in the overall vocal
mix.

The ten selections on **Why Not Me** are rife with subtle but
irresistible rhythmic twists and tasteful flourishes of acoustic
guitar, steel guitar, and dobro that convey the Judds' subtle
blend of rustic charm and contemporary panache. While the
music here captures the adroit fluency of their harmonies as
vividly as any of their later albums, **Why Not Me** also hints at
their stylistic range, which would widen as time went on and
they continued to draw from sources as diverse as bluegrass,
fifties pop, rockabilly, and even show music.

In addition to the great harmonies and intimate acoustic

arrangements, the charm of **Why Not Me** also resides in the intelligently chosen material. (Naomi Judd did write one worthy selection, *Mr Pain*.) The title tune was co-written by Harlan Howard and Sonny Throckmorton – two of Nashville's most revered and prolific veteran songwriters – along with Brent Maher. *Why Not Me*, the title tune, which has endured as one of the signature hits of the Judds' extensive repertoire, is a song of yearning and romantic desire. It's propelled by an understated but relentlessly insinuating acoustic guitar hook that underpins and gives urgency to the lyrics. *Bye Bye Baby Blues*, with its seductive melody, proves a perfect vehicle for Wynonna's formidable lead, while *Drops Of Water* showcases the sultry, earthy folk-pop-blues edge that Wynonna also contributed to the Judds' sound. All in all, the music on **Why Not Me** accomplishes the rather incredible feat of being folksy, down-home, and slightly urbane, all at the same time.

Veteran music critic Joe Sasty of *The Washington Post* echoed the overall critical approval that greeted **Why Not Me**. Sasty praised the album for its "seamless flowing tapestries of acoustic instrumentation." Added Sasty: "The rich liquid vocals of daughter Wynonna are marvelously unaffected, her sultry stylings casually touching on bluegrass, jazz-rock . . . lusciously melodic and indivisibly pop in the most natural way."

As a tribute to the Judds' brilliant eight-year run, RCA Records compiled **The Judds Collection, 1983–1990** (RCACD-66045–2), a tasteful 3-CD sampler of the band's musical high water marks, along with some of the aforementioned work tapes that preceded their early master sessions. This collection also comes highly recommended to anyone eager to hear more of this Kentucky-born mother and daughter's enticing harmonies.

Long before the Judds (see previous 1980s "Essential Recordings" entry) were forced to retire in 1991, at the height of their popularity, owing to Naomi Judd's illness, there'd already been much speculation about daughter Wynonna Judd's eventual solo career. Her vocal talents were so immense and undeniable and such an overwhelming ingredient in the Judds' vocal formula that it seemed merely a matter of time before she stepped out on her own.

Wynonna, the younger Judd's self-named 1992 solo debut album, certainly lived up to all these expectations. With sales in excess of two million (and still counting), it proved a real *tour de force* in terms of launching her solo career. *Rolling Stone* hailed it as the best album out of Nashville in a decade.

Part of the success of **Wynonna** is attributable to the supporting cast that the younger Judd assembled for the making of this album. First and foremost of these is producer Tony Brown, who is himself worth a few words here. Probably the most influential and commercially successful Nashville producer of the late 1980s and early 1990s, Brown is a former keyboard player for Elvis Presley and an alumnus of Emmylou Harris's legendary Cherry Bombs (see also Emmylou Harris "Essential Recordings" entry, this chapter) and Rodney Crowell's Hot Band (see Crowell, "Essential Recordings," this chapter). Brown, in his more recent incarnation as executive producer/president of MCA Records/Nashville, also signed and produced numerous noteworthy 1980s artists like Rodney Crowell, Reba McEntire, Lyle Lovett, Joe Ely, Patty Loveless, Marty Stuart, Marty Brown, Vince Gill, and Kelly Willis – an incredibly diverse roster of talent.

Brown, Wynonna Judd, and the rest of the musical cast on **Wynonna** went to great lengths to ensure that Wynonna's cutting of the musical umbilical cord from the Judds was a smooth, natural, yet definitive musical transition. There are a few selections here that do hew closely to the Judds' trademark sound, and thus imbue **Wynonna** with a warm familiarity. *When I Reach The Place I'm Goin'*, for instance (on which Wynonna's mother Naomi makes her only guest vocal appearance), is the sort of quasi-inspirational, acoustic-flavoured, Appalachian-style ballad that would have been right at home on an early Judds album. So is *My Strongest Weakness*, a love lament co-written by Naomi and celebrated Nashville songwriter/artist Mike Reid. *All Of That Love From Here*, which is Wynonna's heartfelt tribute to Naomi ("My Mama taught me how to stand alone/She let me go but she still holds on"), is a heartfelt ballad, much like *Grandpa (Tell Me 'Bout The Good Old Days)*, one of the most popular hits from the Judds' extensive catalogue.

But the majority of the songs on here are birds of a somewhat different feather. *It's Never Easy To Say Goodbye* was co-written by Allen Shamblin, who also co-wrote several hits for blues-rocker Bonnie Raitt, one of Wynonna's all-time music heroes; it's also Wynonna's artistic tip of the hat to Raitt and the immense influence she's had on Wynonna's style. Naturally, the song invites comparisons between Judd and Raitt, and Wynonna more than lives up to them.

What It Takes, the opening cut, was written by talented British songwriter/recording artist Brendan Croker, whose highest profile thus far has been as a member of rock guitarist Mark Knopfler's "Brit country" band, the Notting Hillbillies. *What It Takes* is propelled by Wynonna's swaggering, sassy vocal bravado and the taut electric guitar lines of George Marinelli (a member of pop singer Bruce Hornsby's band) and

Steuart Smith, a brilliant young guitarist who was a force as a member of Rodney Crowell's band and as a player on Crowell's critically acclaimed LPs. The intense lead fills, riffs, and flourishes of Smith and Marinelli are an essential ingredient in the compelling electrified edge of so many of the cuts on **Wynonna**.

She Is His Only Need, the first single release from **Wynonna**, is a lovely ballad penned by leading Nashville song scribe Dave Loggins (who also contributes background vocals on the track). The song's intricate phrasing, rhythmic shifts, and subtle emotional colorings prove a perfect showcase for Wynonna as she soulfully runs the gamut of the octaves – from growling breathy alto to trembling falsetto. *No One Else On Earth*, with its deftly layered and textured instrumental tracks, subtle horn flourishes, and vocal backing from country-R & B-blues belter John Cowan (former lead singer of the New Grass Revival) is another vocal *tour de force*. *Live With Jesus* is a gutsy gospel number which was written by the distinguished British country songwriter, Paul Kennerley (husband of Emmylou Harris), who also plays all instruments on the track and produced it in his home studio.

Wynonna Judd's follow-up album, **Tell Me Why** (1993), also produced by Tony Brown, was no less vocally impressive. However, in the wake of her newfound solo popularity, Wynonna (after the massive success of **Wynonna**, she dropped her last name) moved closer to her rock-and-roll and torchy R & B pop roots, and in the process some of the intimate country flavor that so ennobled her debut LP, was perhaps lost.

Discographical Details

2 My Kind Of Country

Reba McEntire

MCA MCAD-31108 D848

How Blue/That's What He Said/I Want To Hear It From You/It's Not Over (If I'm Not Over You)/Somebody Should Leave/Everything But My Heart/ Don't You Believe Him/Before I Met You/He's Only Everything/You've Got Me (Right Where You Want Me)

3 Why Not Me

The Judds

RCA PCD1-5319-RE

Why Not Me/Mr Pain/Drops Of Water/Sleeping Heart/My Baby's Gone/Bye Bye Baby Blues/Girls Night Out/Love Is Alive/Endless Sleep/Mama, He's Crazy

364 Wynonna

Wynonna Judd

Curb/MCA MCAD-10529

What It Takes/She Is His Only Need/I Saw The Light/My Strongest Weakness/When I Reach The Place I'm Goin'/No One Else On Earth/It's Never Easy To Say Goodbye/A Little Bit Of Love (Goes A Long, Long Way)/All Of That Love From Here/Live With Jesus

(iii) Neo-Honky-Tonkers

It's telling that one of the freshest, exciting, and most influential albums of the mid-1980s came like a lightning bolt out of southern California and had minimal connections to Nashville (another indication that the Nashville music industry has often tended to follow trends rather than create them). Dwight Yoakam's **Guitars, Cadillacs, Etc., Etc.** (1986) was recorded in Studio City, and Hollywood, California and sent an incredible buzz of excitement through the Nashville industry when it began receiving national airplay from country radio.

Yoakam's sound on **Guitars, Cadillacs, Etc., Etc.** (and to a lesser extent on his more recent albums) is a compelling, and inspired throw-back to the twangy, swaggering hard country/honky-tonk traditions of the 1950s and 1960s. And resonating just under the surface of lead guitarist/producer Pete Anderson's heavily reverbed and tremoloed Telecaster licks, and the crashing drums, bold fiddle lines, basic five-piece honky-tonk arrangements are also vestiges of the rockabillyish frenzy of Buck Owens's early Bakersfield (California) sound. (Yoakam would later coax Buck Owens out of retirement and the two men would briefly record together, enjoying particular success with their duet revival of the Owens chestnut, *The Streets Of Bakersfield*.)

Yoakam's voice is not remarkable; at times he can sound shrill and strident in the higher registers, and he lacks the rich bottom end resonance of a George Jones or a Randy Travis. Yet the intensity of his musical vision, his sincere roots-consciousness, and his scowling James-Dean-in-a-cowboy hat, punk-country attitude more than compensated for these limitations on **Guitars, Cadillacs, Etc., Etc.**, his major label debut. (Six of these tracks first appeared in 1984 on an independent AK Records EP of the same title.) Yoakam, better than practically anyone else of his generation, re-captured the charming swagger, sneer, and bravado of many of the early rockabilly greats.

Seven of the ten songs on **Guitars, Cadillacs** are Yoakam originals, and they brilliantly reinvoke the spirit of earlier epochs in country music. *It Won't Hurt*, for instance, is a forlorn, "face-down-in-your-beer" barstool weeper. The title song is the mournful confession of a jilted dimestore cowboy who finds himself alone in LA's neon jungle searching for solace in the crowded barrooms and loud hillbilly music – convincing stuff, particularly coming from Yoakam who is, himself, a Kentucky-born, Ohio-raised, college-educated teetotaler. *Bury Me (Along The Big Sandy)* and *Miner's Prayer* are Yoakam's superb Appalachian-style odes to his own Kentucky origins. (*Bury Me* also features stirring vocal accompaniment from Maria McKee, former lead singer of the West Coast country ensemble, Lone Justice.)

Significantly, Yoakam also reprises three well-known and aptly chosen country classics: a bold rendition of Johnny Horton's 1950s hit, *Honky Tonk Man*, which does ample justice to the original; a wistful rendition of Harlan Howard's oft-recorded *Heartaches By The Number*; and a revved-up version of Johnny Cash's familiar *Ring Of Fire*, which he reinvents as a quasi-country-rocker.

Yoakam's hard-edged musical approach (which he himself has called "austere, raw-edged, rockin' country . . . pure stripped-down hillbilly music") was both spontaneous and studied. His rural roots are genuine enough; but Yoakam, who majored in history and drama at Ohio State University, never sounded on his later albums quite as unposed, unaffected, and unselfconscious as he does here. **Guitars, Cadillacs, Etc., Etc.** was also Yoakam's conscious effort to fill the serious void he sensed in early 1980s country music. "We're tragically close to eliminating pure country music entirely," the always articulate, history-conscious singer observed in a late 1980s interview with *Country Music Magazine*. "Hillbilly music, white American hillbilly music, is real close to extinction because of various cultural movements and the distancing of youths from country in the 1960s . . . But there's a segment of the country audience, I don't have to tell them what I do – they know."

North Carolina-born Randy Travis had already been hanging around the fringes of Nashville's music scene (as a club singer and short order cook) for several years when **Storms Of Life**, his 1986 major label debut, thrust him into the front ranks of country artists. Texas superstar George Strait (see "Basic Recordings," this chapter), who debuted in the early 1980s, had already paved the way for Travis's style of hard country balladry. But Travis, with his marvelously rich baritone, added fresh new dimension to the genre.

Storms Of Life quickly established Travis as a once- or twice-in-a-generation vocal talent – a restrained but powerful singer anchored heavily in the George Jones/Merle Haggard tradition. His first album sold a million copies within a few months of its release and resulted in several number 1 singles. Travis was soon a major force in country music's "new traditionalist" movement, which was now in full swing.

Travis – unlike other mid-1980s young turks (Dwight Yoakam, Marty Stuart, and Steve Earle, for instance) – shies away from the more frenzied neo-rockabilly influences on **Storms Of Life**, and operates more comfortably in the somewhat subdued but emotionally complex territory of slow-to-medium-tempo balladry. Though he was only in his late twenties at the time he recorded **Storms Of Life**, Travis, on his two original songs included here, also proves to be songwriter of insight and empathy beyond his years.

Send My Body, one of these Travis originals, is a jaunty novelty song about a wrongly condemned man who not only stoically accepts his fate, but seems downright wistful about it. *Reasons I Cheat*, the other Travis original, is the confession of a forlorn middle-aged man who is trapped in a job, a marriage, and a life, that grind him down, and who finds his only solace in the arms of a younger woman. It's a sad, knowing song made all the more powerful by the fact that Travis himself was single, childless, and still a young man when he wrote and sang it.

Diggin' Up Bones (by Paul Overstreet and Al Gore) is a sardonic, slightly macabre lament in a similar vein, about a man who is haunted by a long-dead love affair.

Drawing on other songs by well-known Nashville songwriters like Paul Overstreet, Joe Allen, Johnny MacCrae, and Troy Seals, Travis mines refreshingly familiar honky-tonk themes. The title song, as well as the tongue-in-cheek *There'll Always Be A Honky Tonk Somewhere*, lament the gradual fading of the rural landscape in favor of a modern high-tech, suburban world. Whereas *The Storms Of Life* (the title song) is the lament of a well-meaning good ole boy who's been bypassed by a changing world, *There'll Always Be A Honky Tonk Somewhere* is the flip side of the coin. The song makes the reassuring point that even after such artifacts and totems of modern consumerism like the Super Bowl and video games have gone the way of the Edsel and the hula hoop, there will still be a hardcore group of true country believers somewhere, huddled around a jukebox, drinking beer, listening to country oldies, and keeping the honky-tonk spirit alive – much as Travis does on this, his first major-label album.

After Randy Travis, no another singer set country music so resoundingly on its collective ear until Alan Jackson made his immensely impressive debut three years later with **Here In The Real World** (1989). Jackson, in fact, seemed at first almost too good to be true – truly a record company publicist's dream, with his blond, blue-eyed, six-foot-four good looks, his robust, expressive country baritone, and his sure-footed hard country instincts. The nine original songs on **Here In The Real World** also distinguished Jackson as a songwriter of facility, insight, and empathy. All in all, he set some awfully high standards with this, his first album – standards he has seldom, if ever, faltered from in the years, and albums, since.

Jackson hails from the small city of Noonan, Georgia, where he was born in 1958. Before coming to Nashville in the mid-1980s to try his hand in the music business, he worked at numerous jobs, including car salesman, store clerk, mechanic, and fork lift operator. It took him nearly four years of toiling as a contract songwriter, singing on the club circuit, and being turned down by every major label (he was passed on more than once by some of them) before he finally made his mark with **Here In The Real World**.

On this album – and, really, to no less extent on **Don't Rock The Jukebox, A Lot About Livin'**, and other fine albums he's since recorded – Jackson proves a worthy pretender to the longstanding Merle Haggard/George Jones/Randy Travis hard country vocal tradition. His smooth, effortless-sounding, yet deeply affecting style also conjures up memories of other, less celebrated but hardly less gifted balladeers of an earlier generation, like Vern Gosdin and Cal Smith.

Jackson's sterling original material on **Here In The Real World** is bolstered with basic, on-target fiddle/guitar/steel guitar arrangements by co-producers Scott Hendricks and Keith Stegall – the latter being a songwriter and former recording artist of considerable repute who also produced some of Randy Travis's (see "Essential Recordings," above) earliest independent label releases. (Remarkably, Jackson and his producers completed the sessions for this outstanding album in a mere four days.)

The title tune, which was Jackson's first Top 5 single, is a sad, regretful appraisal of the way life, despite our best wishes and most sincere efforts, does not always adhere to the happy-ending scenarios of B-movies, where the good guys win and the hero gets the girl. *She Don't Get The Blues (She Gives 'Em)* is a fervent honky-tonker with a strong dancehall lyric hook. *Wanted (One Good-Hearted Woman)*, which became one of the first of Jackson's numerous number 1 hits, is the earnest and moving testimonial of a man who searches for always-elusive true love by placing an advertisement in the lonely hearts "personal" columns – a potentially corny subject which Jackson makes to sound devastatingly earnest. In the rousingly auto-biographical *Chasin' That Neon Rainbow*, Jackson recalls his

346 The 1980s and Beyond

own early struggles as a musician. *Dog River Blues* is a cleverly written, compelling slice of nostalgia about growing up in small-town Georgia. *Home* is the singer's moving salute to his mother and father and the love and inspiration they gave him as a child; *I'd Love You All Over Again* is an eye-watering tribute to his wife, Denise.

There's not a weak song or the slightest lapse of inspiration on **Here In The Real World**. Taken as a whole, it's an understated (simply because Jackson makes it all sound so effortless!) and nearly flawless debut, which, not surprisingly, sold over a million copies and quickly thrust him to the forefront of the new generation of talented hard country singers. "When I came (to Nashville), I wanted to carry on the tradition of real country music," Jackson observed around the time that **Here In The Real World** was released. "And I'd like to stay that way . . . You know that country song, *Who's Gonna Fill Their Shoes?*," Jackson added, referring to a hit single by George Jones that laments the passing of country greats like Hank Williams and Lefty Frizzell and ponders whether or not their legacy will be carried on. "Well, I don't know whether I can fill their shoes," Jackson offered. "But I'd sure like to try."

Four or five LPs later, Jackson still seems to be sticking to his guns, and the "fit" still seems to be a damned fine one.

John Anderson (born in the central Florida town of Apopka in 1954) is one of those rare artists who has ridden in both the locomotive and the caboose in terms of country's gradual 1980s swing back toward musical conservatism. In the very late 1970s and very early 1980s, Anderson first made an impact with inspired hard country hits like *The Girl At The End Of The Bar*, *Lyin' Blue Eyes*, *She Just Started Likin' Cheatin' Songs*, *Wild And Blue*, and *Would You Catch A Falling Star* (many of which he wrote or co-wrote himself). At the time, he was one of the few hard country practitioners able to dent the country charts (Moe Bandy was another). His critically acclaimed albums from this era – **John Anderson** (1980), **John Anderson 2** (1981), **I Just Came Home To Count The Memories** (1981), and **Wild And Blue** (1983) – have often been included as various critics' "picks" as the best country LPs of the last 20 years (ironically, they're not currently available on CD), and come highly recommended.

"John Anderson . . . is probably the best country singer-songwriter Nashville has produced in the last decade," *The Nashville Gazette* noted in an early 1980s review that mirrored the initial critical response to Anderson: "He is the George Jones/Buck Owens/Lefty Frizzell/Webb Pierce of the 80s, and is far and away the most exciting honky tonk stylist in recent memory."

As the 1980s progressed, however, Anderson's musical output became increasingly erratic. His growing penchant for novelty songs (like *Swingin'*, a lighthearted ditty that is the all-time biggest hit of his career, and one of the most popular and heavily-played jukebox hits of the last 20 years) and his fondness for quasi-rockers seemed to undermine his credibility with country radio – a relentless, all-powerful, yet often capricious force that can make or break careers in country music.

But in 1992, at age 37, after a nearly decade-long slump, Anderson signed with a new record label (BNA, a subsidiary of RCA), went to work with a new co-producer (James Stroud), and bounced back heartily with **Seminole Wind**, his strongest album in more than a decade, and one which recaptured all the honky-tonk fervor and inspiration of his earliest work in the late 1970s and early 1980s.

Seminole Wind is a totally natural synthesis of the essential ingredients that made Anderson's earliest records so irresistible: a thoroughly down-home musical disposition seasoned with sly humor, and a dash of (what Anderson himself calls) "rockabilly outlaw" attitude. (Despite his thoroughly hard country vocal style, which is hauntingly reminiscent of George Jones, Merle Haggard, and the like, Anderson's first real musical exposure as a young teenager was in a junior high school rock band that specialized in pre-metal hard rock of Jimmi Hendrix, the Doors, and Steppenwolf.)

Seminole Wind opens with *Who Got Our Love*, a drawling, low-moaning, tongue-in-cheek love lament that is vintage Anderson. This radio-friendly tune was written by Anderson and longtime co-writer Lionel Delmore, who collaborated with Anderson on some of his fine hits of the late 1970s and early 1980s (*Girl At The End Of The Bar* and *Swingin'*). *Who Got Our Love* is balanced with a pair of stirring honky-tonk ballads on which Anderson spryly struts his vocal chops: *Last Night I Laid Your Memory To Rest*, co-written by Anderson's sister, Donna Kay, along with Frankia W. Treat, and *Let Go Of The Stone*, by the redoubtable country songwriting team of Max D. Barnes and Max Troy Barnes. *Look Away* is a wry ironic commentary on the "yuppy-ization" of the New South, written by Bobby Braddock, the celebrated Nashville songwriter responsible for numerous George Jones and Tammy Wynette hits of the 1970s and 1980s (such as *Golden Ring*, and *He Stopped Loving Her Today*).

On side 2 of **Seminole Wind** Anderson strays a little further out of the mainstream with fine effect. He infuses *Steamy Windows*, Tony Joe White's, funky white-soul ode to lust and body heat with a smoldering, lurid R & B intensity, which is accompanied by some equally steamy lead guitar work by session man Dan Huff. On *When It Comes To You*, a haunting tale of love gone sour and the ensuing bitter contest of wills, Anderson is joined by composer Mark Knopfler (best known as the leader of Dire Straits, the British rock supergroup). Knopfler underlines Anderson's compelling vocal with some equally stark lead guitar fills.

Seminole Wind is closed out by the title song, which was a number 1 single in late 1992, and also has a strong pro-ecology message. (Anderson later explained that he was inspired to compose the song after listening to his 94-year-old grandmother's tales of growing up in central Florida, and after riding around his home state and observing the many environmental changes that had transpired since he was a child.) His stirring lyrics – which lament the destruction of the natural environment in personal, at times almost mystical, terms – are framed by the lovely instrumental interplay of Gary Smith's piano and Joe Spivey's evocative fiddle-playing.

Seminole Wind, which ultimately sold in excess of a million copies, quickly re-established Anderson as a force to be reckoned with on the early 1990s country scene – fitting justice for a man who had stalwartly plied his own hard-headedly determined brand of hard country music in the late 1970s and early 1980s and did much to keep that musical tradition alive during a time when Nashville's preoccupation was with slick country-popsters like Kenny Rogers, Barbara Mandrell, and latterday Dolly Parton. As *US* Magazine noted in 1981: "In the fading hardcore country tradition of George Jones, Merle Haggard, and Lefty Frizzell he [Anderson] has brought renewed beauty and elegance to the twin-fiddle, steel guitar tradition of the old-time honky tonk balladeer."

Discographical Details

365   Guitars, Cadillacs Etc., Etc.

Dwight Yoakam
Reprise 25372–2
Honky Tonk Man/It Won't Hurt/I'll Be Gone/South Of Cincinnati/Bury Me (with Maria McKee)/Guitars, Cadillacs/Twenty Years/Ring Of Fire/Miner's Prayer/Heartaches By The Number

366   Storms Of Life

Randy Travis
Warner Bros 25435–2
On The Other Hand/The Storms Of Life/My Heart Cracked (But It Did Not Break)/Diggin' Up Bones/No Place Like Home/1982/Send My Body/Messin'

With My Mind/Reasons I Cheat/There'll Always Be A Honky Tonk Somewhere

Here In The Real World

Alan Jackson

Arista ARCD 8623

Ace Of Hearts/Here In The Real World/Blue-Blooded Woman/Wanted/Chasin' That Neon Rainbow/She Don't Get The Blues/I'd Love You All Over Again/ Dog River Blues/Home/Short Sweet Ride

67 Seminole Wind

John Anderson

BNA 61029-2

Who Got Our Love/Straight Tequila Night/Last Night I Laid Your Memory To Rest/Let Go Of The Stone/Look Away/Steamy Windows/Hillbilly Hollywood/Cold Day In Hell/When It Comes To You/Seminole Wind

Basic Recordings

(i) The Men: Neo-Honky-Tonkers and Latterday Country Crooners

68 Greatest Hits

George Strait

MCA MCAD-5567

Unwound/Down And Out/If You're Thinkin' You Want A Stranger (There's One Coming Home)/Fool-Hearted Memory/Marina Del Ray/Amarillo By Morning/A Fire I Can't Put Out/You Look So Good In Love/Right Or Wrong/ Let's Fall To Pieces Together

This vastly popular and immensely talented Texas singer would be right at the top of many people's "Essential Recordings" list for the 1980s; it's a razor's edge call that he's not included in that section of this chapter.

Strait, as a singer, is certainly the equal to anyone who came along during the 1980s; he's resolutely grounded in the Merle Haggard tradition. Ironically, Strait recalls that his own moment of stylistic epiphany came some years before his recording debut when he first heard Merle Haggard's 1970 LP salute to Bob Wills, **The Best Damn Fiddle Player In The World**. Which is to say he's also something of a latterday Bob Wills western swing disciple. His Ace in the Hole Band is one of the most accomplished ensembles in the business – almost like the 1980s successors to Merle Haggard's Strangers. Strait's irresistible brand of swingy, big-band Texas dancehall music (heard in his live shows, as well as on quite a few of his records) has often been referred to as "Texas swing."

Yet Strait has never shied away from mainstream contemporary love ballads either. In fact, they have become his forte. Hits like *Marina Del Ray*, and *You Look So Good In Love*, *Amarillo By Morning*, and his many other chart-topping ballads are really the basis of his massive, multi-platinum appeal.

This early "hits" collection is as good a sampling as any of Strait's rich talents. Yet the fact is, he's one of most consistent artists in country music;

he's made more than a dozen studio albums since the early 1980s, and has yet to make a bad one. Truthfully it's hard to go wrong with just about any Strait album you might choose to acquire.

369   Chiseled In Stone

Vern Gosdin

Columbia CK 40982

Who You Gonna Blame It On This Time/It's Not Over, Yet/Nobody Calls From Vegas Just To Say Hello/I Guess I Had Your Leavin' Coming/Chiseled In Stone/Do You Believe Me Now/Tight As Twin Fiddles/Is It Raining At Your House/Set 'Em Up, Joe/There Ain't Nothing Wrong (Just Ain't Nothing Right/

Some have called Vern Gosdin a poor man's George Jones. And indeed, his rustic hard country vocal style does often bring to mind the Jones influence. Yet Gosdin, as evidenced by this, perhaps the strongest album of his long career, demonstrates a homespun power, style, and rustic pathos all his own. Particularly moving is the lovely powerful title tune.

370   I Wonder Do You Think Of Me

Keith Whitley

RCA 9809-2-R

Talk To Me, Texas/Between An Old Memory And Me/It Ain't Nothin'/I'm Over You/Turn This Thing Around/Lady's Choice/Brother Jukebox/Tennessee Courage/Heartbreak Highway/I Wonder Do You Think Of Me

Keith Whitley began his career as a bluegrass prodigy. He and Ricky Skaggs played together in the legendary Ralph Stanley's band as teenagers. Later, he was lead singer and front man for the premier "newgrass" ensemble, J.D. Crowe and the New South, with whom he recorded several critically acclaimed albums, including **Somewhere Between**. But all through his early years as a bluegrass star Whitley was a devoted Lefty Frizzell honky-tonk disciple at heart. And after finally making an uneasy transition from bluegrass to mainstream country, it took him four albums to really come into his own, which he did gloriously on **I Wonder Do You Think Of Me**.

This exquisite CD suggests that Whitley may well have gone on to be one of country's leading male vocalists of the 1990s, were it not for the fact that he died tragically (of an alcohol/drug overdose) in 1989, while still in his early thirties, and just a few weeks before the release of **I Wonder Do You Think Of Me**.

371   A Thousand Winding Roads

Joe Diffie

Epic EK 46047

Home/If The Devil Danced (In Empty Pockets)/If You Want Me To/New Way (To Light Up An Old Flame)/There Goes The Neighborhood/Almost Home/I Ain't Leavin' Til She's Gone/Coolest Fool In Town/Liquid Heartache/Stranger In Your Eyes

A solid journeyman honky-tonk singer in the George Jones tradition and a deft songwriter as well, Oklahoma-born Diffie decided to try his hand in Nashville after losing his job in a Oklahoma foundry. Beginning his career as a Music Row demo singer, he graduated up to the majors with this solid debut album, which resulted in a string of hard country hits.

72 It's All About To Change

Travis Tritt
Warner Bros 26589-2
The Whiskey Ain't Workin' (with Marty Stuart)/*Don't Give Your Heart To A Rambler/Anymore/Here's A Quarter (Call Someone Who Cares)/Bible Belt/It's All About To Change/Nothing Short Of Dying/If Hell Had A Jukebox/Someone For Me/Homesick*

When Travis Tritt, from Marietta, Georgia, arrived on the scene in the late 1980s with a hokey novelty song called *Country Club*, nobody seemed to take him very seriously. Yet with subsequent releases since (most of which have sold in excess of a million copies) he's proven to be a formidable latterday successor to the 1970s Outlaws with his good-natured rebel image and his infectious, sometimes irreverent brand of Southern country-rock. He's also carved out a huge following much like that enjoyed by rough and rowdy 1970s and early 1980s musical antiheroes like Waylon Jennings and Hank Williams, Jr, to whom, stylistically, he owes a lot.

73 High And Dry

Marty Brown
MCA MCAD-10330
High And Dry/Your Sugar Daddy's Long Gone/Indian Summer Blues/Every Now And Then/I'll Climb Any Mountain/Don't Worry Baby/Honky Tonk Special/Wildest Dreams/Ole King Kong/Nobody Knows

Kentuckian Marty Brown, when he emerged with this debut album, sounded fresh off the farm – like he had a musical pipeline straight back to the glory days of Hank Williams and Jimmie Rodgers. His voice is rustic and unadorned, in the purest tradition of the aforementioned country music greats to whom his original songs often pay implicit homage. Brown's second album, **Wild Kentucky Skies** (1993, MCA MCAD-10672) is no less highly recommended.

74 Yours Truly

Earl Thomas Conley
RCA 3116-2-R D1110
You Got Me Now/Brotherly Love (with Keith Whitley)/*One Of Those Days/Hard Days And Honky Tonk Nights/Keep My Heart In Line/If Only Your Eyes Could Lie/The Perfect Picture (To Fit My Frame Of Mind)/Borrowed Money/Shadow Of A Doubt/I Wanna Be Loved Back*

Earl Thomas Conley is one of those enigmatic figures who was more or less ignored by the critics while scoring a slew of number 1 country hits. Though he has been consistently overshadowed by more charismatic singers (like his former RCA labelmates, Clint Black and Keith Whitley), Conley deserves much credit for writing a number of minor country classics and bringing consistent good taste and conservatism to country music's mainstream. **Yours**

Truly is one of his later and best RCA albums. A highlight is *Brotherly Love,* a moving duet with his friend, the late Keith Whitley.

375   This One's Gonna Hurt You

Marty Stuart

MCA MCAD-10596

Me And Hank And Jumpin' Jack Flash/High On A Mountain Top/This One's Gonna Hurt You (For A Long, Long Time) (with Travis Tritt)/*Down Home/ Just Between You And Me/Hey, Baby/Doin' My Time* (with Johnny Cash)/ *Now That's Country/The King Of Dixie/Honky Tonk Crowd*

This Mississippi-born former bluegrass prodigy is an alumnus of both Lester Flatt's (of Flatt and Scruggs) and Johnny Cash's road bands. Stuart made several critically acclaimed independent label recordings, and had a brief fling as a neo-rockabillyist before finally coming into his own as a country artist in the late 1980s with his own high-energy brand of country, which he himself has referred to as "hillbilly rock." Like many of the best of his generation, Stuart has a deep appreciation of country music's past that borders on reverence, and echoes though nearly every track of this CD. "What I have a passion to do," Stuart once explained, "is to take what I've learned and been a part of in the past with all the masters and then bridge it into the future. I'm crusading for hillbilly music."

376   Put Yourself In My Shoes

Clint Black

RCA 2372-2-R

Put Yourself In My Shoes/The Gulf Of Mexico/One More Payment/Where Are You Now/The Old Man/This Nightlife/Loving Blind/Muddy Water/A Heart Like Mine/The Goodnight-Loving

This Texas-born singer emerged as part of the late 1980s "Hat Pack" of young, photogenic country singers who also happened to sing pretty well. With this, his second album, Black achieved immense popularity and resolutely proved that, underneath the hat and behind his Marlboro Man good looks, he is a formidable songwriter and a vocalist of power and persuasion.

377   Haunted Heart

Sammy Kershaw

Mercury 314 514 332-2

A Memory That Just Won't Quit/Queen Of My Double Wide Trailer/Still Lovin' You/She Don't Know She's Beautiful/I Can't Reach Her Anymore/ Haunted Heart/Neon Leon/What Might Have Been/You've Got A Lock On My Love/Cry, Cry, Darlin'

Louisiana-born Sammy Kershaw made a strong impression with his 1991 debut album, **Don't Go Near The Water**, as a gifted vocalist steeped uncannily in the George Jones mode. On this, his second album, Kershaw broadens his stylistic range as a country balladeer and lets a little more of his innate flair for comedy and extroversion come to the fore on winning novelty songs like *Neon Leon* and *Queen Of My Double Wide Trailer.*

'8 Longnecks And Short Stories

Mark Chestnutt

MCA MCAD–10530

Old Country/Old Flames Have New Names/I'll Think Of Something/It's Not Over (If I'm Not Over You)/Uptown, Downtown (Misery's All The Same)/ Bubba Shot The Jukebox/Postpone The Pain/Talking To Hank (with George Jones)/*I'm Not Getting Any Better At Goodbyes/Who Will The Next Fool Be*

This solid journeyman honky-tonk singer hails from the same east Texas region as country great George Jones. Though he has been consistently eclipsed in the charts by more charismatic country "Hat Pack hunks" like Clint Black, Garth Brooks, and George Strait, Chestnutt demonstrates on this, his second album (released in 1992), that he's second to none when turned loose on no-frills honky-tonk weepers and barroom anthems.

'9 When I Call Your Name

Vince Gill

MCA MCAD–42321 D 912

Never Alone/Sight For Sore Eyes/Oh, Girl (You Know Where To Find Me)/ Oklahoma Swing (with Reba McEntire)/*When I Call Your Name/Ridin' In The Rodeo/Never Knew Lonely/We Won't Dance/We Could Have Been/Rita Ballou*

Vince Gill is an exquisitely talented Oklahoma-born singer/songwriter/guitarist, former lead singer of the country-pop group Pure Prairie League, and also an alumnus of the Cherry Bombs, Rodney Crowell's esteemed 1970s road band. Gill has (like his friend, Crowell) long been revered as a behind-the-scenes force in Nashville's record industry. He arrived in Nashville in 1984 and struggled through quite a few years and quite a few albums before finally coming into his own as a country vocalist. He broke through in spades with **When I Call Your Name** (1989), which was produced by Tony Brown (a former bandmate from Gill's woodshedding years in Crowell's Cherry Bombs).

Amidst country music's sea of deep baritones, Gill possesses a achingly pure tenor that lends itself beautifully to ballads and country-rockers alike. Gill's subsequent MCA albums are also highly recommended; and his early solo albums on RCA are not far off the mark, either, even though fewer people got to hear them.

30 No Fences

Garth Brooks

Liberty C21S-93866

The Thunder Rolls/New Way To Fly/Two Of A Kind, Workin' On A Full House/Victim Of The Game/Friends In Low Places/Wild Horses/Unanswered Prayers/Same Old Story/Mr Blue/Wolves

When he emerged in the late 1980s, Brooks was just another faceless contender in "the Hat Pack." But Brooks quickly broke out of the pack and has since gone on to achieve an astounding level of superstardom and a mass popularity never previously enjoyed by a country artist. His record sales (after less than a half-dozen albums) have far outpaced those of any previous country artist. Brooks's recent albums have become slightly more ponderous and introspective (though they've continued to sell astronomically). Yet here, on his second album, recorded when he was still on the cusp of becoming a cultural phenomenon, Brooks still sounds delightfully fresh and unselfconscious.

381   You've Got To Stand For Something

Aaron Tippin

RCA 2374–2-R

In My Wildest Dreams/I've Got A Good Memory/You've Got To Stand For Something/I Wonder How Far Is Over You/Ain't That A Hell Of A Note/The Man That Came Between Us (Was Me)/She Made A Memory Out Of Me/Up Against You/The Sky's Got The Blues/Many, Many, Many Beers Ago

Aaron Tippin, a South Carolina-born airplane pilot and semi-professional body builder, turned Nashville songwriter, delved deeply and resolutely into the hard country Hank Williams/Jimmy Rodgers mode, on this, his solid first album, on which he co-wrote all ten songs. Says Tippin of his musical intent: "Jimmie Rodgers, Hank Sr, Ernest Tubb, Hank Snow, Hank Thompson, Lefty (Frizzell) . . . I love those guys; they are my influences . . . I hope that what I'm doing is bringing some of their greatness back into my music."

382   Lee Roy Parnell

Lee Roy Parnell

Arista ARCD 8625

Oughta Be A Law/Fifty-Fifty Love/Where Is My Baby Tonight/Crocodile Tears/Family Tree/Let's Pretend/You're Taking Too Long/Mexican Money/ Down Deep/Red Hot

Not since Delbert McClinton (see Chapter on 1970s, "Basic Recordings") has anyone rocked up country with a fiery white R & B/blues twist the way Parnell has. This young Texan's vocal fire and impressive songwriting skills are vividly captured on this 1990 debut CD.

383   Turning For Home

Mike Reid

Columbia CK 46141

Walk On Faith/Till You Were Gone/I'll Stop Loving You/I Got A Life/ Turning For Home/As Simple As That/Everything To Me/Constant Companion/This Road/Even A Strong Man/Your Love Stays With Me

This former professional football star, turned preeminent Nashville songwriter (his songs have been recorded by numerous leading artists of the day) has also distinguished himself as an arresting vocal stylist whose vivid original songs manage to be inspirational without being preachy. This, his first major-label effort, showcases him at his best, as both a writer and singer.

(ii) Women of the 1980s and 1990s

384 80's Ladies

K.T. Oslin
RCA CD 2193-2-R
Wall Of Tears/I'll Always Come Back/Younger Men/Eighties Ladies/Do Ya/
Two Hearts/Doctor, Doctor/Lonely But Only For You/Old Pictures

This middle-aged former New York actress looked like a long shot to become
a country star when RCA Records Nashville division first signed her in the
mid-1980s. But Oslin quickly struck gold with her "Plain Jane" image and
her provocative, sometimes corrosive commentaries, many of which dealt with
the travails and anguish of being single (or divorced), over thirty, and female
in the modern world. With this album, and her subsequent releases, Oslin
became a heroine to every American woman whose phone never rings on
Friday nights and who's spent too many dateless Saturdays alone.

385 State Of The Heart

Mary Chapin Carpenter
Columbia CK 44228 D619
How Do/Something Of A Dreamer/Never Had It So Good/Read My Lips/This
Shirt/Quittin' Time/Down In Mary's Land/Goodbye Again/Too Tired/Slow
Country Dance/It Don't Bring You

A former Washington, DC, area club folk singer, Mary Chapin Carpenter
has, in recent years, taken country music by storm with her folky, ruminative
ballads and articulate pop-tinged ruminations on life and lost love. Carpenter,
who has become one of the hottest artists of the early 1990s, has demonstrated that – surprisingly enough – literacy and even – God forbid! – a touch
of urbanity are not necessarily mutually exclusive with fine country music.

386 Put Yourself In My Place

Pam Tillis
Arista ARCD 8642 D378
Put Yourself In My Place/Melancholy Child/Maybe It Was Memphis/Blue
Rose Is/Don't Tell Me What To Do/One Of Those Things/Draggin' My Chains/
Ancient History/I've Seen Enough To Know/Already Fallen

The daugher of 1960s and 1970s country star Mel Tillis, Pam Tillis has, in
the 1990s, won a reputation of her own with her torchy, sultry singing style
and her penchant for offbeat romantic commentaries. This 1991 album is one
of her strongest efforts to date.

387 Only What I Feel

Patty Loveless
Epic AEC 53236
You Will/How About You/Nothin' But The Wheel/Love Builds The Bridges
(Pride Builds The Walls)/Mr Man In The Moon/Blame It On Your Heart/
You Don't Know How Lucky You Are/All I Need (Is Not To Need You)/
What's A Broken Heart/How Can I Help You Say Goodbye

Kentucky-born Patty Loveless (actually a distant cousin of 1960s and 1970s country queen Loretta Lynn) established herself as one of the leading neo-honky-tonk women singers in the mid-1980s "neo-traditionalist" movement. Loveless's edgy style of hard country bears a palpable mark from her years singing in North Carolina rock bands before she turned to Nashville and country music. Though Loveless recorded a string of memorable albums for MCA, all her previous work pales against this, her 1993 Epic debut (which was produced by her husband, celebrated producer Emory Gordy, Jr). This is a classic, buoyed by an outstanding and utterly moving collection of songs and some of the very best vocal performances Loveless has ever rendered. With it, she has reclaimed her place as one of country music's most important singers.

388   Willow In The Wind

Kathy Mattea

Mercury 836 950-2

Come From The Heart/Here's Hopin'/Burnin' Old Memories/She Came From Fort Worth/True North/Hills Of Alabam'/Willow In The Wind/Love Chooses You/I'll Take Care Of You/Where've You Been

This West Virginia-born singer, after shaking off her initial musical image as a latterday middle-of-the-road Ann Murray, has enlivened country's mainstream with her ulta-tasteful folk and pop sensibilities. In terms of her eclecticism and the high level of artistry and musicianship consistently heard on this and her other late 1980s and early 1990s albums, Mattea seems on her way to winning a reputation as a sort of latterday Emmylou Harris – that is, an artist whose name is almost synonymous with impeccable musical taste, credibility, and the courage to continually evolve and stylistically redefine herself.

389   Shadowland

k. d. lang and the Reclines

Sire 25724-2

Western Stars/Lock, Stock And Teardrops/Sugar Moon/I Wish I Didn't Love You So/(Waltz Me) Once Again Around The Dance Floor/Black Coffee/Shadowland/Don't Let The Stars Get In Your Eyes/Tears Don't Care Who Cries Them/I'm Down To My Last Cigarette/Busy Being Blue/Honky Tonk Angels Medley

Canadian singer k. d. lang has since moved on to pop music after about a half-decade fling as a country artist. Yet – whether she's charting pop or country waters – she's a technically remarkable singer cast heavily in the Patsy Cline tradition. Lang's abiding flair for high camp and her androgynous image have sometimes suggested there was an element of parody in her work; but, more often than not, her sheer vocal artistry puts to rest any doubts about her sincerity.

390   Trisha Yearwood

Trisha Yearwood

MCA MCAD-1029

She's In Love With The Boy/The Woman Before Me/That's What I Like About You/Like We Never Had A Broken Heart (with Garth Brooks)*/Fools*

Like Me/Victim Of The Game/When Goodbye Was A Word/The Whisper Of Your Heart/You Done Me Wrong (And That Ain't Right)/Lonesome Dove

This banker's daughter from Monticello, Georgia, made her dramatic debut in 1991 with this debut album that sold a million copies within eight months of its release. The very first single *She's In Love With The Boy*, hit the number 1 spot. Yearwood's strong assertive vocal style ("a voice that marries rock n'roll power with down-home feeling," said Paul Kingsbury, editor of the *Journal Of Country Music*) and penchant for assertive songs quickly made her something of a role model for women of the 1990s. Her talents are also well represented on her second album, **Hearts In Armor.**

91 Somewhere Between

Suzy Bogguss
Capitol CDP 7 96247 2 D 586
Somewhere Between/Guilty As They Come/I'm At Home On The Range/My Sweet Love Ain't Around/Handyman's Dream/I Want To Be A Cowboy's Sweetheart/Cross My Broken Heart/Take It Like A Man/Hopeless Romantic/ Night Rider's Lament

With this fine album, Suzy Bogguss got off to a promising start as one of the late 1980s leading "back-to-the-basics" female contenders. The fact that the title song is an old Merle Haggard tune tells you where her heart was, even if her more recent albums have tended to be a bit slicker.

92 Infamous Angel

Iris DeMent
Warner Bros 9 45238–2 (originally released on Rounder)
Let The Mystery Be/These Hills/Hotter Than Majave In My Heart/When Love Was Young/Our Town/Miles Of Elbow Room/Infamous Angel/Sweet Forgiveness/After You're Gone/Mama's Opry/Higher Ground

This brilliant Arkansas-born, California-raised singer has a traditional (gospel, bluegrass, folk) bent – sort of like the best of Emmylou Harris and Nanci Griffith rolled into one. This immensely impressive debut collection of all-original songs was produced by Jim Rooney, one of Nashville's most talented and under-appreciated producers.

93 Bang Bang

Kelly Willis
MCA MCAD 10141
I'll Try Again/Too Much To Ask/The Heart That Love Forgot/Sincerely (Too Late To Turn Back Now)/Baby, Take A Piece Of My Heart/Bang Bang/ Hidden Things/Not Afraid Of The Dark/Standing By The River/Settle For Love

This northern Virginia-born singer cut her musical teeth in the thriving Austin, Texas, "alternative country" scene and wowed listeners with her booming, yet soulfully country-blues voice. This, her second album, is her best effort to date.

394 Temptation

Shelby Lynne

Morgan Creek/Mercury 2959–20018–2

Temptation/Feelin' Kind Of Lonely Tonight/Tell Me I'm Crazy/Little Unlucky At Love/Some Of That True Love/The Rain Might Wash Your Love Away/ Don't Cry For Me/I Need A Heart To Come Home To/Come A Little Closer/ Where We Go From Here

Shelby Lynne made three straight-ahead country albums in the late 1980s and early 1990s, all three of which somehow failed to properly capture her powerful, dusky vocal charms. With the help of producer Brent Maher (the Judds' longtime producer), Lynne re-casts herself here in a big band/western swing mode and sounds not only magnificent, but utterly convincing.

395 Bobbie Cryner

Bobbie Cryner

Epic AEC 53238

He Feels Guilty/Too Many Tears Too Late/Daddy Laid The Blues On Me/I Think It's Over Now/Leavin' Houston Blues/I Don't Care (duet with Dwight Yoakam)/*You Could Steal Me/I'm Through Waitin' On You/The One I Love The Most/This Heart Speaks For Itself*

On this, her major-label debut, this California-born, Kansas-raised singer re-enlivens the George Jones/Loretta Lynn honky-tonk tradition with great pathos and conviction. Cryner can bend and twist her notes almost like she took a Ph.D. in latterday George Jones balladry. She shines as a songwriter, as well.

396 Past The Point Of Rescue

Hal Ketchum

Curb D2–77450

Small Town Saturday Night/I Know Where True Love Lives/Old Soldiers/ Somebody's Love/Past The Point Of Rescue/Five O'Clock World/I Miss My Mary/Don't Strike A Match (To The Book Of Love)/Long Day Comin'/She Found The Place

This New York-born, Texas-to-Nashville songwriter brings a romantically intense and compelling sound to country music that is fused with folk and pop elements, as well.

397 A Bigger Piece Of The Sky

Robert Earl Keen, Jr

Sugar Hill SH-CD-1037

So I Can Take My Rest/Whenever Kindness Fails/Amarillo Highway/Night Right For Love/Jesse With The Long Hair/Blow You Away/Here in Arkansas/ Daddy Had A Buick/Corpus Christi Bay/Crazy Cowboy Dream/Paint The Town Beige

This Texas born country-folkie is another second-generation "graduate" of the Guy Clark/Townes Van Zandt "Lone Star" school of songwriting. The best of his galvanizing, sometimes eerie original songs subtly portray a society being consumed by its own penchant for violence.

98 This Town

Dave Mallet
Vanguard VCD 79566
This Town/The Road Goes On Forever/Main Street/Somewhere In Time/Rock-and-Roll Heart/Autumn/How Much More/Long Distance Lover/Pray For Rain/ Take Time/Old Soldiers/Change Of The Seasons

Best known for the hits he's written for everyone from John Denver to Nanci Griffith, Mallet is originally from New England, and his insightful songs personify the best of that murky area where folk meets country.

99 Ready For Love

Barry and Holly Tashian
Rounder CD 0302
Ready For Love/Let Me See The Light/Heaven With You/Heart Full Of Memories/Hearts That Break/Highway 86/The Price Of Pride/The Diamond/ Ring Of Gold/The Memories Remain/If I Knew Then/This Old Road

These country-folkies are perhaps best known as former members of Emmylou Harris's esteemed Hot Band, and played and sang on some of Harris's vintage recordings from the late 1970s and early 1980s. Their impressive singing and songwriting talents are in abundance on this 1993 album.

00 Culture Swing

Tish Hinojosa
Rounder CD 3122
By The Rio Grande/Something In The Rain/Bandera Del Sol (Flag Of The Sun)/Every Word/Louisiana Road Song/Corazon Viajero (Wandering Heart)/ Drifter's Wind/The Window/In The Real West/Chanate, El Vaquero (Chanate, The Cowboy)/San Antonio Romeo/Closer Still

This lovely and gifted Anglo-Hispanic ("Tex-Mex") singer shines here on her soulful interpretations of her fine original songs that bear the influence of everyone from Merle Haggard to Hazel Dickens.

01 Box Of Visions

Tom Russell
Philo CD PH 1158
Angel Of Lyon/Annette/Heart of Hearts/Purgatory Road/Manzanar/Waterloo/ Coney Island Moon/Hong Kong Boy/Wedding Dress Mary/Blood Oranges/The Extra Mile/Box Of Visions

This immensely gifted writer and singer has had a colorful, if somewhat obscure career grounded in anomoly. He's a country singer/songwriter living in New York City who, despite having songs recorded from everyone from Canadian cowboy Ian Tyson to Johnny Cash, has found most of his chart success in Europe. His eclectic music burns with an intensity that infuses the best of urban and rural sensibilities.

402 Walkin' On The Moon

Katy Moffatt

Philo PH 1128 (LP)

Carnival Man/Walkin' On The Moon/I'm Sorry, Darlin'/If Anything Comes To Mind/Papacita (Mama Rita)/Mr Banker/Borderline/Fire In Your Eyes/I'll Take The Blame/Hard Times On Easy Street/I Know The Difference Now

Another obscure country music vocal genius, Moffatt (whose brother Hugh is also a noted Nashville singer songwriter) made fine major-label recordings in the late 1970s that went unnoticed. She has since found her niche with a series of noteworthy independent label outings, such as this 1989 album.

(iii) Groups, Bands, and Duos

403 The Desert Rose Band

Desert Rose Band

MCA MCAD-5991

One Step Forward/Love Reunited/He's Back And I'm Blue/Leave This Town/ Time Between/Ashes Of Love/One That Got Away/Once More/Glass Hearts/ Hard Time

This outstanding California-based band, led by Chris Hillman, formerly of the Byrds and Flying Burrito Brothers, made a string of fine albums in the late 1980s and early 1990s. This is their first, and arguably their best.

404 Southern Star

Alabama

RCA 8587–2–R D1146

Song Of The South/Down On The River/High Cotton/Ole Baugh Road/The Borderline/I'm Still Dreamin'/Pete's Music City/Southern Star/If I Had You/ She Can/I Showed Her/Barefootin'/Dixie Fire

This ensemble maintained immense popularity throughout the 1980s (more than 25 number 1 records – a precedent-setting 21 of them consecutive) with their predictable music paeans to their Southern heritage. But on this album, the four-man Fort Payne, Alabama-based superband did an admirable job of shaking free of their tried and true formulas and injecting their unmistakable style with a brand-new level of energy and artistry.

405 Pickin' On Nashville

Kentucky Headhunters

Mercury 838 744–2 D1025

Walk Softly On This Heart Of Mine/Dumas Walker/Rag Top/Rock 'N' Roll Angel/Smooth/High-Steppin' Daddy/Skip A Rope/Some Folks Like To Steal/ Oh Lonesome Me/My Daddy Was A Milkman

This rowdy, good-timey Kentucky-based Southern country-rock band brought renewed vigor, irreverence, humor, and vitality to the country scene with this, its debut 1988 album. The Headhunters also deserve much credit for putting an honest, spontaneous, country-rock fire back into mainstream country.

Recommended Reading

The following list of books, magazines, and periodicals brings together the recommendations of contributors to this volume for further reading. (Note: Some of these titles may be out of print.)

Background, Reference, and General Histories

Ancelet, Barry Jean. *The Makers of Cajun Music*. Austin, Texas: University of Texas Press, 1984.

Artis, Bob. *Bluegrass*. New York: Hawthorne Books, 1975.

Broven, John. *South to Louisiana: the music of the Cajun Bayous*. Gretna, Louisiana: Pelican Publishing, 1987.

Cantwell, Robert. *Bluegrass Breakdown: the making of the old Southern sound*. Urbana: University of Illinois Press, 1984.

Carr, Patrick (ed.). *The Illustrated History of Country Music*. New York: Doubleday/Dolphin, 1988.

Country Music Foundation. *Country: the music and the musicians*. New York: Abbeville Press, 1988.

Daigle, Pierre V. *Tears, Love and Laughter: the story of the Cajuns and their music*. Ville Platte, Louisiana: Swallow, 1972.

Escott, Colin (with Martin Hawkins). *Good Rockin' Tonight*. New York: St Martin's Press, 1991.

Gentry, Linnell. *A History and Encyclopedia of Country, Western and Gospel Music*. Nashville: Clairmont Corp., 1969.

Gilmore, Mikal, and Parsons, Russ. *Honky Tonk Visions on West Texas Music: 1936–1986*. Lubbock, Texas: The Texas Tech University Museum, 1986.

Green, Douglas B. *Country Roots: the origins of country music*. New York: Hawthorn Books, 1976.

Grissom, John. *Country Music: white man's blues*. New York: Paperback Library, 1970.

Guralnick, Peter. *Lost Highway: journeys and arrivals of American musicians*. Boston: David R. Godine, 1979.

Hagan, Chet. *Grand Ole Opry.* New York: Henry Holt and Company, 1989.

Hannush, Jeff. *I Hear You Knockin': the sound of New Orleans rhythm and blues.* Ville Platte, Louisiana: Swallow, 1985.

Hemphill, Paul. *The Nashville Sound: bright lights and country music.* New York: Simon & Schuster, 1970.

Malone, Bill C. *Country Music USA: a fifty year history.* Austin: University of Texas Press, 1985.

Malone, Bill C. and McCulloh, Judith (eds). *The Stars of Country Music.* Urbana: University of Illinois Press, 1975.

Morthland, John. *The Best of Country Music: a critical and historical guide to the 750 greatest albums.* New York: Doubleday & Company, Inc. 1984.

Oermann, Robert K., and Green, Douglas B. *The Listener's Guide to Country Music.* New York: Facts On File, 1983.

Rosenberg, Neil. *Bluegrass: a history.* Chicago: University of Illinois Press, 1985.

Rosenberg, Neil. "Blue Moon of Kentucky: Bill Monroe, Flatt & Scruggs, and the Birth of Bluegrass". In *Country: the music and the musicians.* Pub. for The Country Music Foundation. New York: Abbeville Press, 1988.

Rothel, David. *The Singing Cowboys.* San Diego: A S. Barnes & Co., 1978.

Scruggs, Earl. *Earl Scruggs and the 5-String Banjo.* New York: Peer International Corporation, 1968.

Stambler & Landon. *The Encyclopedia of Folk, Country, and Western Music.* New York: St Martin's Press, 1982.

Tosches, Nick. *Country: the biggest music in America.* New York: Stein and Day, 1977.

Trischka, Tony and Wernick, Pete. *Masters of the 5-String Banjo, in Their Own Words and Music.* New York: Oak Publications, 1988.

Wolfe, Charles K. *Kentucky Country: folk and country music of Kentucky.* Lexington: University Press of Kentucky, 1982.

Wolfe, Charles K. *Tennessee Strings: the story of country music in Tennessee.* Knoxville: The University of Tennessee, 1977.

Country Biographies

Allen, Bob. *Waylon and Willie.* New York: Quick Fox, 1979.

Allen, Bob. *George Jones: the saga of an American singer.* New York: Doubleday, 1984.

Griffis, Ken. *Hear My Song – the story of the celebrated Sons of the Pioneers.* Los Angeles: John Edwards Memorial Foundation, 1974.

Haggard, Merle, with Russell, Peggy. *Sing Me Back Home.* New York: Times Books, 1981.

Pugh, Ronnie. *Ernest Tubb: let's say goodbye like we said hello.* Vollersode, Germany: Bear Family, 1991. Booklet included with Bear Family boxed CD set of the same name (BCD 15498).

Rooney, James. *Bossmen: Bill Monroe and Muddy Waters.* New York: Da Capo Press, 1971.

Rosenberg, Neil V. *Bill Monroe and His Blue Grass Boys: an illu-*

strated discography. Nashville: Country Music Foundation Press, 1974.

Tosches, Nick. *Hellfire: the Jerry Lee Lewis story*. New York: Delta, 1982; London: Plexus, 1982.

Townsend, Charles R. *San Antonio Rose: the life and music of Bob Wills*. Urbana, Illinois: University of Illinois Press, 1976.

Wolfe, Charles. *Lefty Frizzell: life's like poetry*. Vollersode, Germany: Bear Family, 1992. 152-page booklet included with Bear Family boxed CD set of the same name (BCD 15550).

Journals and Periodicals

Bluegrass Unlimited (monthly). Editor: Peter V. Kuykendall, Bluegrass Unlimited, Inc., Box 111, Broad Run, Virginia, 22014.

Country Music Magazine. Editor: Russell Barnard, 329 Riverside Drive, Bridgeport, Connecticut, 06880 (bi-monthly).

The Hillbilly Researcher. Editors: Al Turner and Phillip J. Tucker, 20 Silkstream Road, Burnt Oak, Edgware, Middlesex HA8 0DA, England (bi-monthly).

The Journal Of Country Music. Editor: Paul Kingsbury, The Country Music Foundation, 4 Music Square East, Nashville, Tennessee, 37203 (published three times a year).

The Journal Of The American Academy For The Preservation of Old-Time Country Music. Editor: Rick Kienzle, 329 Riverside Drive, Bridgeport, Connecticut, 06880 (bi-monthly).

Discographies

Ginell, Gary, (comp.). *The Decca Hillbilly Discography, 1927-1945*. Westport, Connecticut: Greenwood Press, 1989.

Whitburn, Joel. *Top Country Singles 1944-1988*. Menomonee Falls, Wisconsin: Record Research, 1989.

Glossary

Words in **bold type** within an entry refer readers to other entries.

Alternative country, synonymous with **progressive country**, refers to country music that is somewhat out of the mainstream, and to music, or artists, who tend to be a little more experimental and less subject to the commercial restraints faced by more conventional country artists, and who are thus more willing to sacrifice commercial success for purer artistic aims. Thus they're often apt to incorporate elements of other musical forms, be it rock, **blues, folk**, or even jazz. The term is often used to refer to various Texas musicians who were involved in or influenced by the **"Outlaw"** movement of the 1970s, or whose roots are embedded in Texas's fertile, cross-pollinated indigenous musical scene, which has created strains of country music quite different from Nashville's usual fare.

Appalachian, originating in or relating to a relatively isolated and remote multi-state region of the southeastern US.

Artist and repertoire (A & R), as in "A & R man," a term that refers to a record label staff person whose duties include finding and procuring songs for a recording session (usually from his or her connections in the country songwriting community and close associations with music publishers) and coordinating the logistics of the recording session itself: scheduling, hiring the session musicians, etc.

Back beat, an emphasis on the second and fourth beats in a meaure in addition to or instead of the usual emphasis on the first and third beats.

Back-yard, adjectivally refers to music that is informal, spontaneous, **down-home**, and unpolished. Synonymous with **"front-porch,"** or "back porch."

Bakersfield sound, a substyle of country music that emerged from Bakersfield, California in the 1960s, and which was personified by the music of Buck Owens and early Merle Haggard (both of whom lived and worked out of Bakersfield for years). The Bakersfield sound was typified by a more aggressive instrumental approach to country music, which borrowed somewhat from rock-and-roll – particularly in using the electric **Telecaster** guitar as an oft-featured lead instrument. As such, the Bakersfield sound was a welcome alternative to the blander **country-pop** music which was then in great favor in Nashville, and in turn had a significant influence on rock musicians of the day. The Bakersfield sound influenced everyone from the Beatles (who, like many rock musicians, were enamored of the guitar playing of the late Don Rich, Buck Owens's talented backup guitarist of many years) to 1970 California country-rockers like the Byrds, the Burrito Brothers, and the Eagles.

Bebop, a revolutionary form of jazz that arose in the 1940s and emphasized small combos and solos based on chord changes rather than melody.

Big-band (swing), the style of **swing** associated with the jazz orchestras and large ballroom dance ensembles of the 1930s and 1940s.

Blues, an African-derived American musical form distinguished by the flattening of thirds and sevenths and often by a 12-measure structure.

Blues-country, a fusion or amalgam of **blues** music and country music.

Bop, a nickname for **bebop**.

Boogie-woogie, an American musical style popular in the 1940s and 1950s and distinguished by syncopated, aggressive left-hand piano figures.

Break, a passage, usually near the middle of a song, where the lead singer stops singing and one or more instruments are featured, often playing elaborate lead passages.

Breakdown, a spirited song, or passage in a song, that contains lively, and often intricate interplay ("hot licks") between various instruments; most often used in reference to bluegrass music.

Brush-style, playing drums with brushes instead of drumsticks, in order to achieve a softer, subtler and more diffuse rhythmic and percussive effect.

Cajun, a word used to describe the French-speaking European American residents of Louisiana as well as their culture and music.

Cajun-jazz-rock, Cajun music played with elements of **jazz** and **rock-and-roll.**

Cajun-country, a fusion of **Cajun** music and **honky-tonk.**

Chanky-chank, a slang term for the two-step beat of **Cajun** music.

Chart, a written musical arrangement.

Chops, a high level of technical ability on a musical instrument.

Clawhammer, a very early down-stroke style of banjo-playing – also sometimes referred to as "fisting" – in which the bare hand (without picks) is held in a claw shape.

Cosmic cowboys, a slang term for Texas singer–songwriters who combine country and western music with bohemian lyrics.

Country picking; an ill-defined term that often refers to distinctly country instrumental performances featuring flashy solo performances on distinctly country instruments like banjo, fiddle, and steel guitar.

Country-cajun, a fusion or amalgam of country music and **Cajun** music.

Country-jazz, a fusion or amalgam of jazz and country music, usually through the common element of **swing.**

Country-pop, a fusion or admixture of country and pop music influences.

Country-rock, a fusion or admixture of country music and rock music.

Countrypolitan, a term often used to refer to the "Nashville sound" of "crossover country" style of fifties, sixties, and seventies country music which featured such pop-influenced refinements as lush orchestral strings (as opposed to steel guitars and fiddles) and which was often sung in a smooth manner totally devoid of any traces of twang or Southern accent. In recent years, as country has made a swing back towards more traditional styles, the term has taken on a somewhat derogatory ring among music critics.

Cover (version), a recording of a song that has previously been recorded by another artist. More specifically, it often refers to the recording of a song that has not only been previously recorded by another artist, but which has also already been released as a hit single, and is thus already well known to the listening audience.

Creole, a word used to describe African American residents of Louisiana, particularly those with a pronounced Caribbean and/ or European ancestry and influence. Also used to describe their cooking and music.

Crossover, refers to a record which is a hit in the country charts, and which "crosses over" and becomes a hit in the pop or rock charts, or (in some cases) the other way around.

Cut, a single song or selection off an LP or CD; also synonymous with a "track" or a "song."

Delta blues, **blues** that originated in the Delta area of northwest Mississippi, distinguished by the 12-bar form, driving rhythms, acoustic and slide guitar, and intensely emotional singing.

Dixieland, the earliest style of jazz as it appeared in **New Orleans** at the beginning of the century, distinguished by its instrumentation (clarinet, cornet, trombone, banjo, piano, tuba and drums) and its emphasis on collective improvisation.

Dobro, a stringed instrument very similar to a lap-style steel guitar, and which creates a sound somewhat similar to a steel guitar or a **blues** slide guitar. The dobro is often used in more traditional forms of country music, and is often featured in bluegrass music. In recent years, it has also come back into vogue in contemporary music, usually for the purpose of imbuing a modern song with hints of a "traditional" flavor.

Down-home, adjectivally refers to music (most often acoustic), an artist, or anything with a distinctly rural, Southern, informal feel or flavor and lighthearted attitude.

Easy listening, synonymous with "**countrypolitan**," "country-crossover," or "**country-pop**," this refers to country music with smooth, understated arrangements, which is relatively devoid of twang or Southern accent, and which is more noted for its smoothness than for the (modest) emotional demands it makes on the listener. Country music in this manner is intended to achieve greater sales by appealing to the larger pop-oriented or "**crossover**" audience.

Electric blues, **blues** played with amplified instruments and a full rhythm section.

Fill, a brief instrumental pattern or passage in a song that accentuates or embellishes the melody and/or lead vocal, and which may recur throughout the song.

Flat-picking, a style of guitar-playing in which (as opposed to finger-picking) the instrument is played with a single pick held between the thumb and forefinger.

Flip (side), the opposite side of a (vinyl) "single" record, which customarily contains one song on each side. The term comes from the days when a song would be released as a single (the "A" side of the record), with another song on the "B" or flip side. Disc jockeys, in addition to playing the designated single release on the A-side, would often "flip" the record and play the B-side as well.

Folk music, any music played for the entertainment and education of a self-contained community without any regard for wider recognition or commercial gain. Alternatively, a specific form of music adapted from Appalachian folk music and **delta blues** performed on acoustic instruments and expressing progressive politics or personal relationships, and favored by well-educated European Americans of the 1950s and onward.

Folk-blues, blues music informed or inflected with **folk music** attitudes, styles, or sensibilities, or vice versa: a fusion of folk music and blues music.

Folk-country, a fusion or amalgam of country music and **folk music** styles and attitudes.

Folk-pop, music that contains stylistic elements of both folk and pop music.

Folk-rock, music that is a fusion of, or which contains stylistic elements of, both **folk music** and **rock-and-roll**.

Folkie, a musician whose influences, attitudes, and orientations are anchored in or influenced by **folk music**, as defined in the alternative (second) definition under "folk music" above.

Freight train sound, a percussive and or rhythmic instrumental pattern that emulates or resembles the sound of a train chugging down the tracks. Can also refer to a harmonica, fiddle, or other instrumental passage that emulates the sound of a train whistle – a popular motif in country music.

Front-porch, synonymous with "informal." Usually refers to a recording or piece of music that has the loose, spontaneous, relaxed feeling of early rural music, which was often performed on a front-porch, on in a back yard (hence the phrases, "front-porch" or "**back-yard**" harmonies).

Gig, in musicians' jargon, a job, or an engagement, at a club, auditorium, fair, concert, etc.

Gospel, a form of African American religious music that blended the **blues** with European American religious music, with an emphasis on ecstatic vocal improvisation.

Grand Ole Opry, a live country radio show broadcast on WSM-AM, out of Nashville, Tennessee, which has the distinction of being the longest continuous running live radio show in the world. Founded in 1925, the Grand Ole Opry has often been called "the Cradle of Country Music," since all throughout the 1930s, until the early 1960s the Opry's influence was such that to be a star in country music one almost had to be a star on the Opry, as well. Its clear-channel AM broadcast was heard throughout much of the US, as well as part of Canada, and was central to the growing popularity of country music from the time of its inception, until recently. In more recent years, the Opry's influence on mainstream country music has diminished somewhat; and membership in the Opry is no longer essential to country stardom. (Even so, most performers consider it an honor, and present membership today includes everyone from veterans like Hank Snow to a modern superstar like Garth Brooks.)

Groove, a steady, syncopated rhythmic pattern.

Gumbo, a **Cajun** stew; thus, the term "gumbo" refers to a rich, flavorful musical mixture, be it of styles, voices and/or various instruments.

Hard country, traditional, old-style country music, often featuring bold steel guitar, fiddle, and other rural instrumentation, and vocals with bold Southern accents. Also often refers to **honky-tonk** music and other forms of early commercial country music that is heavy on steel guitars, fiddles, and twang, and thus unadulterated by more modern, urbanizing pop influences.

Hardscrabble, adjectival reference to a way of life that is meager, somewhat poor, with few amenities.

Hick, a derogatory term for a rural, Southern, presumably uncultured and uneducated, person. Synonymous with **hillbilly**, or rube.

High-lonesome, a term, most often used in describing bluegrass music, in which the vocalist sings in a mournful, plaintive, clear, and piercing high-register style. Even more specifically, it is often used to refer to this style of singing which was first attributed to bluegrass's founding father, Bill Monroe.

Hillbilly, a term (sometimes derogatory, sometimes not) for a Southern, rural, and presumably uneducated, person. In earlier decades, country music was often referred to – sometimes condescendingly – as "hillbilly" music. And almost in abreaction to this, country musicians and fans have since adopted the word as an emblem of pride to refer to each other, and to distinguish their music and musical tastes from that of more pop-influenced, and crossover-style "uptown" country music.

Hillbilly boogie, a white country variant of the sort of eight-to-the-bar **boogie-woogie** musical style which was a huge national musical trend in the late 1940s and early 1950s. Hillbilly boogie's growth paralleled that of **honky-tonk** music, and in many ways it was merely an up-tempo version of honky-tonk, and thus a precursor of sorts to rock-and-roll. By the 1950s, in fact, hillbilly boogie and honky-tonk had, at least in terms of definition, become inseparable. However, hillbilly boogie often tended toward novelty lyrics, while honky-tonk's themes tended to be sad.

Hillbilly-rock, a somewhat imprecise, slang term that can refer to rockabilly or any kind of old-style, hard, or **honky-tonk**-style country music with an aggressive beat.

Hokey, marked by hokum; artless, hickish, ridiculous in a foolish or low-comedy sort of way.

Hokum, in this context, music or musical comedy that is hokey, clumsily rural, humorous in a lowbrow manner, or has a blatant degree of disingenuousness, or false, insincere simplicity to it.

Hollow-body, an instrument – usually a guitar – with a hollow sounding board that amplifies and resonates the vibrations of the strings without the benefit of electrification. Despite the advent of electrification, many musicians continue to prefer non-electric, hollow-body stringed instruments for the unique and more intimate tones and timbres they create.

Honky-tonk, a term that is used loosely, but which usually refers to a brand of **hard country** music that originated in the barrooms and beerhalls of the South during the 1940s and 1950s – its leading progenitors being stars of that era like Hank Williams and Lefty Frizzell. The music these and other early hardcore brand of honky-tonk stars sang was, with its jukebox themes of alcoholism, adultery, and despair, a marked contrast to the often spiritually informed and somewhat more pristine **Appalachian**-style country music of someone like Roy Acuff or other popular stars of the **Grand Ole Opry**. Honky-tonk has endured over the years as one of the most influential and recurring substyles of country music, and is usually characterized by the heavy use of steel, fiddle, and electric guitars, and most often dwells on themes that tend to be very worldly. Often used generally in reference to drinking songs or barroom songs.

Honky-tonk rock, an imprecise term of vague definition which is often used to refer to **honky-tonk** music with a slightly more aggressive, **rock-and-roll**-style beat, or instrumental edge to it.

Hook, a recurring vocal or instrumental passage or figure in a song that tends to "hook" or tease the listener and capture and hold his or her attention.

Hopped-up, a slang term for speeding up a melody or rhythm. It can also refer to a loose, aggressive, somewhat flippant style of playing or singing that even, in some instances, implies a lack of inhibition similar to that achieved with drugs or alcohol.

Jazz-rock, music that represents a fusion of jazz and **rock-and-roll** music, or music that happens to contain stylistic elements of both.

Jitterbug, an exuberant dance form based on **swing** rhythms and popular in the 1940s.

Jive, African American slang for trickery and deceptive seduction, extended to refer to music that adopts an exaggerated posture for the entertainment of the audience.

Jug and washboard bands, bands that use home-made instruments, such as washboards, jugs, and saws. Such bands became popular during the Great Depression in the US when people wanted to make music, but could not afford instruments. Also sometimes referred to as skiffle bands or kazoo bands, these came into vogue again during the 1960s and 1970s, and their influence in country music persists today.

Jump-blues, a blues form that incorporated boogie and swing rhythms and became popular in the 1940s.

Lick, an instrumental (or vocal) passage in a song, usually in which one particular instrument (or voice) is emphasized.

Lite country, a derogatory term for pop-country music and its light, undemanding themes and arrangements. (Synonymous with "elevator music" or "wallpaper music.") Music which makes only limited demands on listeners' emotions. Music which is bland and overly-smooth.

Maven, a woman singer who is particularly well known, accomplished, and respected for her talents.

Medicine show, traveling shows that were popular in the early decades of this century. Sponsored by manufacturers of various patent medicines, these shows featured live music and other entertainment and were exploited by these companies as a means of promoting and advertising their "medicines" (which were generally useless, their main content being alcohol). Many early country stars and stars of the **Grand Ole Opry** got their starts performing in medicine shows, some even as late as the 1940s.

Memphis beat, an imprecise, ill-defined slang term and figurative expression sometimes used to refer to **rockabilly** and other Memphis-derived, rhythm-oriented forms of music.

Memphis rockabilly, the predominantly white Southern fusion of **rhythm and blues** and country music that flourished in Memphis during the mid-1950s. Although highly esteemed **rockabilly** was also recorded in other cities, the genre was largely defined by the work of Elvis Presley, Jerry Lee Lewis, Johnny Cash, and a few of their contemporaries who recorded for Sam Phillips's Memphis-based Sun label.

Minstrel show, musical stage shows which flourished, particularly in the Southern US in the mid- and late 1800s, and even survived into the 1950s, in which white performers in blackface make-up interpreted (usually for comic effect) and parodied black culture. Many legitimate early country artists got their starts as minstrel show performers.

Music City, an informal term for the city of Nashville, Tennessee, and its thriving country music recording industry, which is generally considered the country capital of the world.

Music Row, a rather small geographical area in South Nashville, about a mile or so from mid-town, which contains the vast bulk of Nashville's studios, music publishing companies, and management companies. 16th and 17th Avenues South (recently renamed Music Square East and Music Square West) are often considered the boundaries of the Music Row district; but in reality the industry has grown in recent years and gradually spread well beyond these streets. Today, various music business-related companies and organizations are actually spread all throughout Nashville, and around the country, for that matter.

Nashville country, a vague, imprecise term sometimes used to refer (occasionally with mildly derogatory implications) to country music written and recorded in Nashville (as opposed to southern California or other national hotbeds of country music).

National Barn Dance, a popular early live country music radio show, first broadcast by WLS in Chicago, in 1924, which played an important role in country music in earlier decades.

Neo-rockabilly, a modern adaptation or interpretation of the **rockabilly** sound, typically enhanced by additional instrumentation (such as drums and piano) and refinements in technology.

New Orleans, the state capital of Louisiana and one of the largest cities of America's deep South. Situated on the Mississippi River, New Orleans has long been a melting pot for various styles and amalgams of American popular and ethnic music, and, as such, has a rich musical heritage all its own which has heavily influenced country music.

New Orleans R & B, rhythm and blues created in Louisiana's largest city, with an emphasis on syncopated rhythms and counter-rhythms and a smooth, rolling vocal style.

Newgrass, progressive bluegrass music; more specifically, bluegrass-flavored music played by younger generations of artists, and which (unlike the traditional bluegrass of founding fathers like Bill Monroe or Ralph Stanley) often features electrified instrumentation, as well as arrangements and song choices from musical styles as far afield as **rhythm and blues** or even reggae and jazz.

Novelty number, a lighthearted, comical song, the main intent of which is to merely amuse or entertain listeners, as opposed to arousing deeper emotions.

Offbeat, another name for **backbeat**.

Okie, one of many thousands of people – mostly farmers and their families – who were uprooted and starved off their land in Oklahoma and other nearby Mid-Western states by the severe Dust Bowl drought and the Great Depression of the late 1920s and 1930s. The Okies, for the most part, settled in California, in search of new livelihood, and played a great part in the development of country music in that state. Merle Haggard and Buck Owens were merely two of many country artists whose families had originally come to California as part of this migration.

Oldie, a well-known song from earlier years, which has endured for its nostalgic value, and which, as such, has come to be associated with a specific era.

Outlaw, one of a rather tight-knit group of musicians who rose to the forefront and enjoyed great popularity in the mid-1970s through the early 1980s. The Outlaws emerged at a time when mainstream country music was mired heavily in the pop influence of artists like Ann Murray and John Denver. The music of the Outlaws, with its **rock-and-roll**-influenced vitality and counter-cultural insinuations, and its strong connections to the more basic, **hard country/honky-tonk/western swing** forms of previous decades, presented a fresh alternative to this. The term "Outlaws" refers to these artists' (Willie Nelson and Waylon Jennings prominent among them) somewhat counter-cultural image, as well as their "cowboyish" and "hippy-ish" personae, which contrasted with Nashville's then-prevailing clean-cut, sedate "leisure suit" image.

Pedal steel, a type of stationary steel guitar used extensively in country music on which the strings (and notes) are bent by pressing on foot pedals, creating a slide effect.

Picking, playing music – usually in an informal or "**front-porch**" setting: as in, "Do ya wanna do some pickin'?"

Pop-jazz, music that is a fusion of, or which contains elements of both, pop and jazz music.

Popster, an imprecise, derogatory term often used to refer disparagingly to a pop singer who attempts to sing a country song, or to achieve success in the country field, or who, in an insincere way, professes to be "country."

Progressive country, country music outside of the mainstream which tends to be more lyrically, thematically, and musically radical and adventurous than conventional "middle-of-the-road" country music such as is most often heard in the record charts. The term is synonymous with "**alternative country**."

Ragtime, a syncopated, notated piano style that was popular in America at the end of the nineteenth century and became the precursor to jazz.

Rapping, talking, reciting, or improvising a lyric or impromptu vocal presentation over music, usually with an insistent beat.

Retro-fitting, making music that is stylistically and emotionally true to an older form, style, or substyle of popular music (be it **honky-tonk, rockabilly,** or whatever), yet which also integrates themes, rhythms, and/or instrumentation of more contemporary music, as well.

Rhythm, the forward movement of a piece of music; the beat, the meter, and the flow of the music, usually established, in country music, by a combination of drums, bass guitar, and rhythm guitar, and sometimes supplemented by other percussive and rhythmic instruments.

Rhythm and blues, blues with a pronounced dance beat.

Riff, an instrumental passage in a song, usually one which is played or accentuated by a "lead" or dominant instrument in the arrangement – most often, but certainly not always, a guitar. An instrumental **hook**.

Rock-and-roll, a broad, generic term that refers to early or contemporary rock music, which is generally distinguished from country music by its rebellious attitude, its more aggressive beat, and its heavier emphasis on drums and more aggressive and louder guitars and instrumentation. (Though, in all fairness, the two forms of music exist in a non-exclusive continuum, and there is much music which transcends or straddles the two categories – that is, music that is both country *and* rock.)

Roots music, music played by contemporary musicians which is nonetheless rooted in specific styles and substyles of yesteryear; music with transparent origins in such indigenous American musics as **blues,** jazz, country, **folk,** and **gospel**.

Rubboard, a distinct percussive sound in old-time country, **Cajun,** and other ethnic and string band forms of music that is frequently achieved by rubbing a metal ice tray out of an old-fashioned refrigerator. Since the ridges are less pronounced than those of a washboard, the percussive sound that is achieved on a rubboard is often subtler and less specific than the sound of a washboard.

Sacred harp music, a form of *a cappella* religious singing distinguished by four-part harmonies and shape-note notation.

Side-man, a supporting musician – usually an instrumentalist – who backs up the leader, star, or featured musician in a band. The term can refer to a bandmember or backup musician in a live show, and can also mean a "session musician" – that is, a professional musician who is hired to play behind a featured artist on a studio recording. Synonymous with "session-man" or "session-picker."

Slap bass, a technique commonly employed in **rockabilly** recordings, the earliest of which were made without drums. The upright bass player would achieve a percussive effect by slapping the strings against the neck of the instrument.

Solid-body, an instrument, usually a guitar and, more specifically, usually an electric guitar, that has no hollow sounding box or resonator, but relies instead upon electrical amplification and sound reproduction to achieve its distinct and usually much crisper sound.

Soul music, rhythm and blues with the strong influence of pop music harmony and song form.

Southern rock, a generic term referring to musicians who make **rock-and-roll** that is particularly Southern in its inflections, attitudes, origins, and sensibilities. The term first came into wide usage in the 1970s when any number of rock-and-roll bands (the Allman Brothers, Lynyrd Skynyrd, the Marshall Tucker Band, Wet Willie, etc.) emerged from the South and achieved national prominence. Any number of prominent country artists of the 1970s – Hank Williams, Jr and Charlie Daniels being foremost among them – also had strong elements of Southern rock in their music. The terms is somewhat misleading, insofar as rock (or, if you will, rock-and-roll) had its first origins in the South, and was, at least in the beginning, very much a "Southern" sort of music.

Stomp, a rhythmic device that mimics the stomping of boots on a hardwood dance floor.

Swamp-pop, a form of music popular in the 1960s and 1970s, created by Cajuns who blended their own music with **New Orleans R & B**.

Swing, an American variation on rubato that creates a propulsive forward rhythm by lengthening some beats and shortening others.

Telecaster style, a distinctly sharp, bright electric guitar sound usually achieved on the Telecaster model of a Fender brand electric guitar. This sound was popular both in rock and country music. The "Telecaster country" style was personified by the exquisite guitar-playing of the late Don Rich, who played Telecaster in Buck Owens's band and was featured on many of Owens's classic records (which were themselves personifications of the "**Bakersfield sound**," the substyle which first brought use of the Telecaster to real prominence in country music in the 1960s and 1970s.

Tex-Mex, a form of music that blends the Norteno style of northern Mexico with the country and western and **rhythm and blues** sounds of South Texas.

Texas swing, a local variation of **western swing**.

Three-finger style, a specific style of banjo-**picking** or -strumming that is often referred to as "bluegrass style" picking, and which actually employs four fingers (all except the little finger).

Tin Pan Alley, a warren of music publishing companies on 28th Street in New York City, where staff songwriters turned out countless sentimental, easy-to-sing popular songs, many of which found their way into the repertoire of early country performers. Tin Pan Alley flourished from the early 1900s until the World War II years.

Two-step, music with a rhythm suited to a popular form of dance favored in the dancehalls of Texas and elsewhere.

Urban Cowboy, the title of a popular 1980 feature film starring John Travolta and Debra Winger, which depicted and romanticized a lifestyle built around country music and country dancing. The film was a box-office smash and unleashed a trendy, fleeting national fascination with country music. Today, the term has come to have a derogatory flavor, since much of the **crossover**-style country music that was made in Nashville and elsewhere in the early 1980s blatantly catered (or even pandered) to this trend, and – predicatably – was rather dismal: the result of country producers and artists attempting to capitalize on this trend and second-guess the somewhat more urbane tastes of this fickle new audience.

Walking bass, when the bass player plays a "walking" line, or broken arpeggios, instead of merely repeating notes.

Weeper, a slow country song with a very sad theme (most often romantic in nature) in which a mournful steel guitar is often used to emphasize the dolorous vocal.

Western swing, a European American form of swing that emphasizes country and western instrumentation (fiddle, steel guitar, mandolin, etc.) and repertoire.

Woodshedding, practicing or apprenticing. A musician's "woodshedding" years usually refers to the years that he or she learned the craft, either playing in woodsheds (or garages) or performing in small, insignificant venues for little or no pay.

Zydeco, an African American variation on **Cajun** that introduces many **rhythm and blues** elements.

Index

Note: Album titles are listed in **bold** type, song titles in *italic*. **Bold** page numbers indicate main references to artists.